EX MACHINA
BOOK FIVE

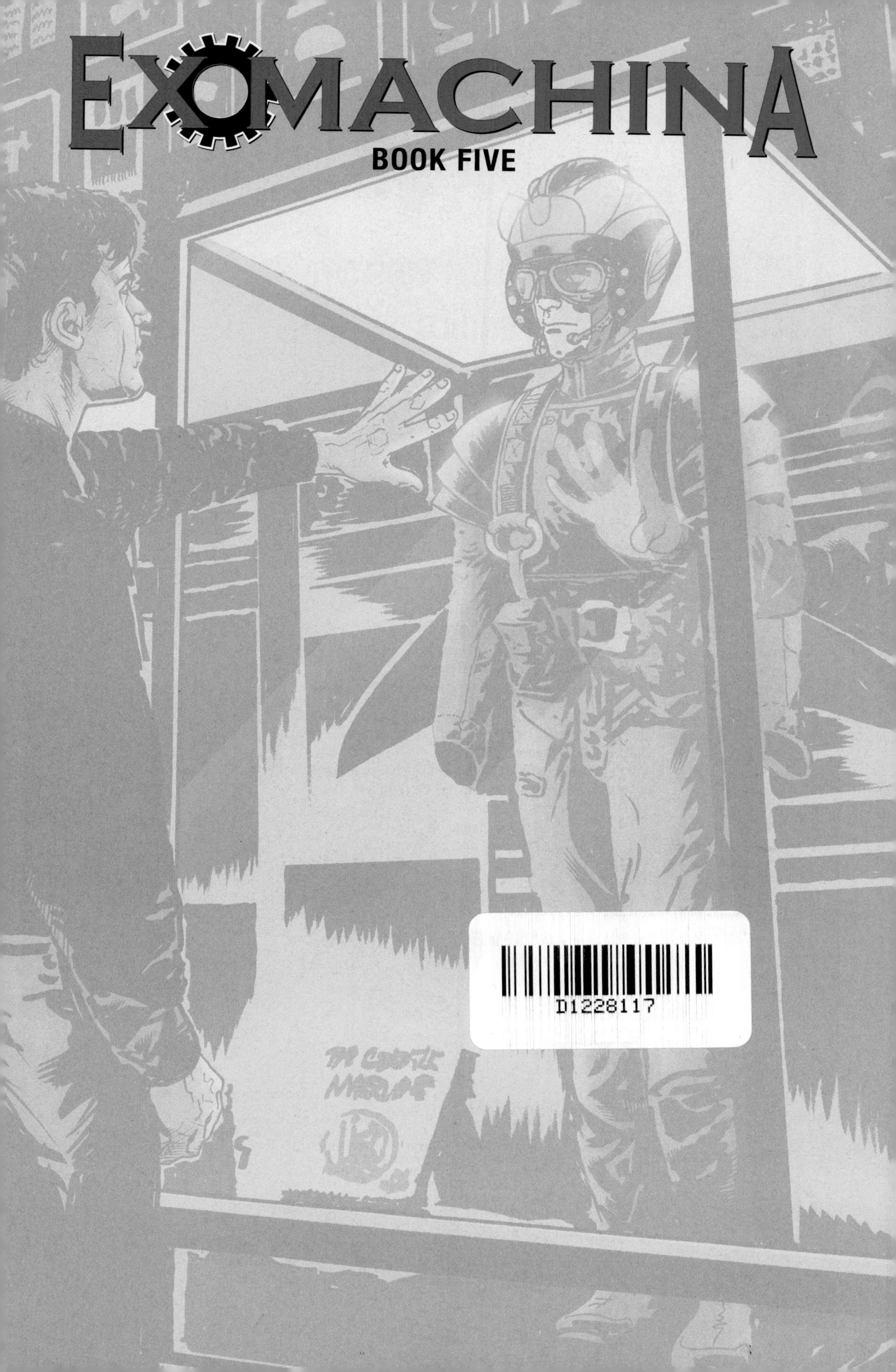

BRIAN K. VAUGHAN: WRITER

TONY HARRIS: PENCILS

JIM CLARK: INKS

JD METTLER: COLORS
JARED K. FLETCHER: LETTERS

JOHN PAUL LEON: *ARTIST ON GREEN*

EX MACHINA CREATED BY VAUGHAN & HARRIS

COLLECTED EDITION COVER BY TONY HARRIS

Ben Abernathy	Editor – Original Series
Kristy Quinn	Assistant Editor – Original Series
Robbin Brosterman	Design Director – Books
Shelly Bond	Executive Editor – Vertigo
Hank Kanalz	Senior VP – Vertigo and Integrated Publishing
Diane Nelson	President
Dan DiDio and Jim Lee	Co-Publishers
Geoff Johns	Chief Creative Officer
Amit Desai	Senior VP – Marketing and Franchise Management
Amy Genkins	Senior VP – Business and Legal Affairs
Nairi Gardiner	Senior VP – Finance
Jeff Boison	VP – Publishing Planning
Mark Chiarello	VP – Art Direction and Design
John Cunningham	VP – Marketing
Terri Cunningham	VP – Editorial Administration
Larry Ganem	VP – Talent Relations and Services
Alison Gill	Senior VP – Manufacturing and Operations
Jay Kogan	VP – Business and Legal Affairs, Publishing
Jack Mahan	VP – Business Affairs, Talent
Nick Napolitano	VP – Manufacturing Administration
Sue Pohja	VP – Book Sales
Fred Ruiz	VP – Manufacturing Operations
Courtney Simmons	Senior VP – Publicity
Bob Wayne	Senior VP – Sales

EX MACHINA BOOK FIVE
Published by DC Comics. Copyright © 2015 Brian K. Vaughan
and Tony Harris. All Rights Reserved.

Originally published in single magazine form by WildStorm
Productions as EX MACHINA #41-50, EX MACHINA SPECIAL #4
Copyright © 2009-2010 Brian K. Vaughan and Tony Harris.
All Rights Reserved. All characters, their distinctive likenesses
and related elements featured in this publication are trademarks
of DC Comics. The stories, characters and incidents featured in
this publication are entirely fictional. DC Comics does not read or
accept unsolicited ideas, stories or artwork.

DC Comics, 4000 Warner Blvd., Burbank, CA 91522
A Warner Bros. Entertainment Company.
Printed in the USA. 4/17/15. First Printing.

ISBN: 978-1-4012-5422-3

Library of Congress Cataloging-in-Publication Data

Vaughan, Brian K., author.
  Ex Machina. Book Five / Brian K. Vaughan ; illustrated by Tony
Harris.
   pages cm
  ISBN 978-1-4012-5422-3 (paperback)
  1. Graphic novels. I. Harris, Tony, 1969- illustrator. II. Title.
  728.E98 V389 2011
  741.5'973—dc23
                                    2011008631

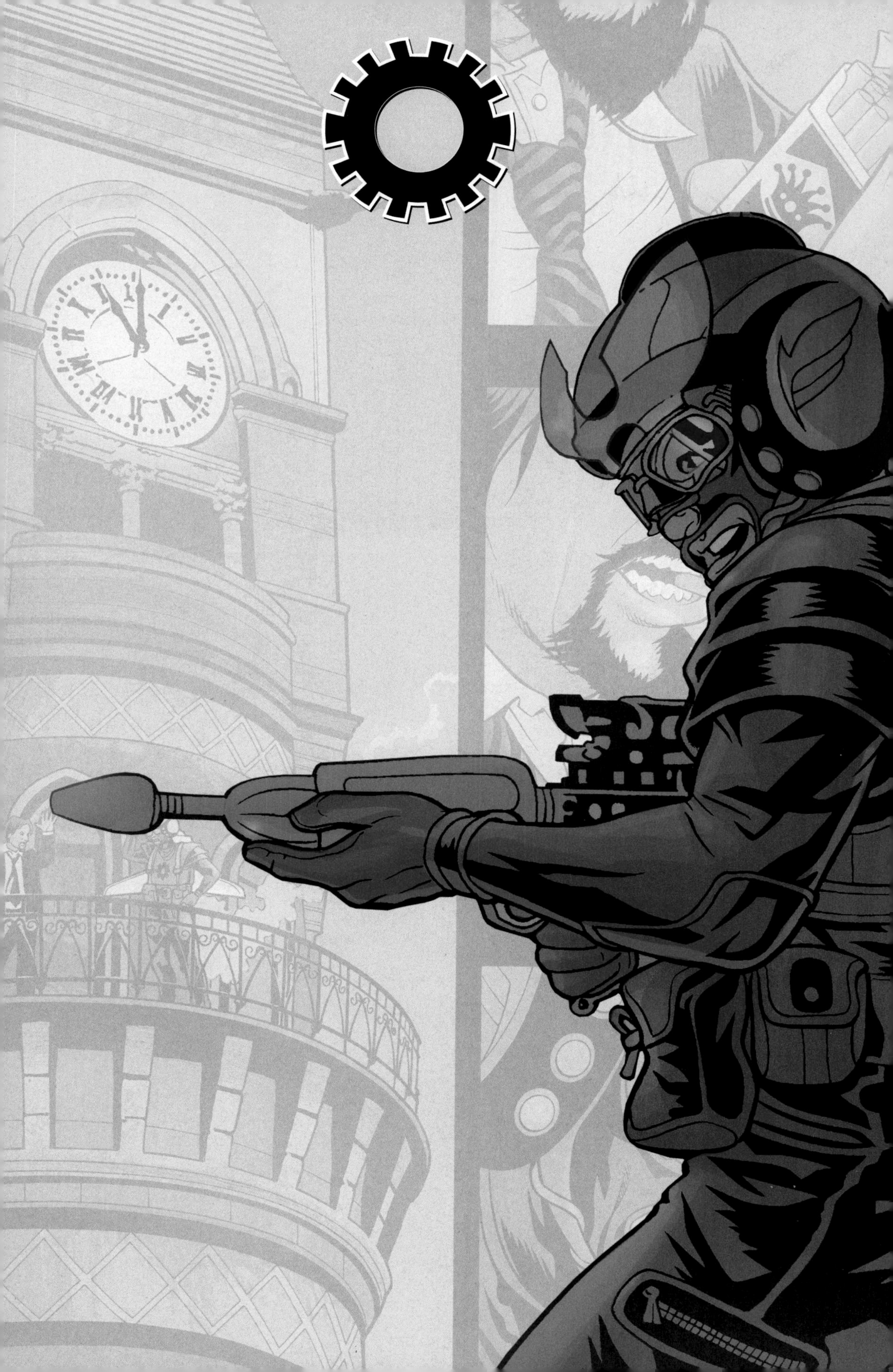

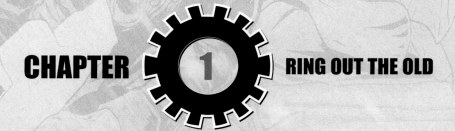

CHAPTER 1 RING OUT THE OLD

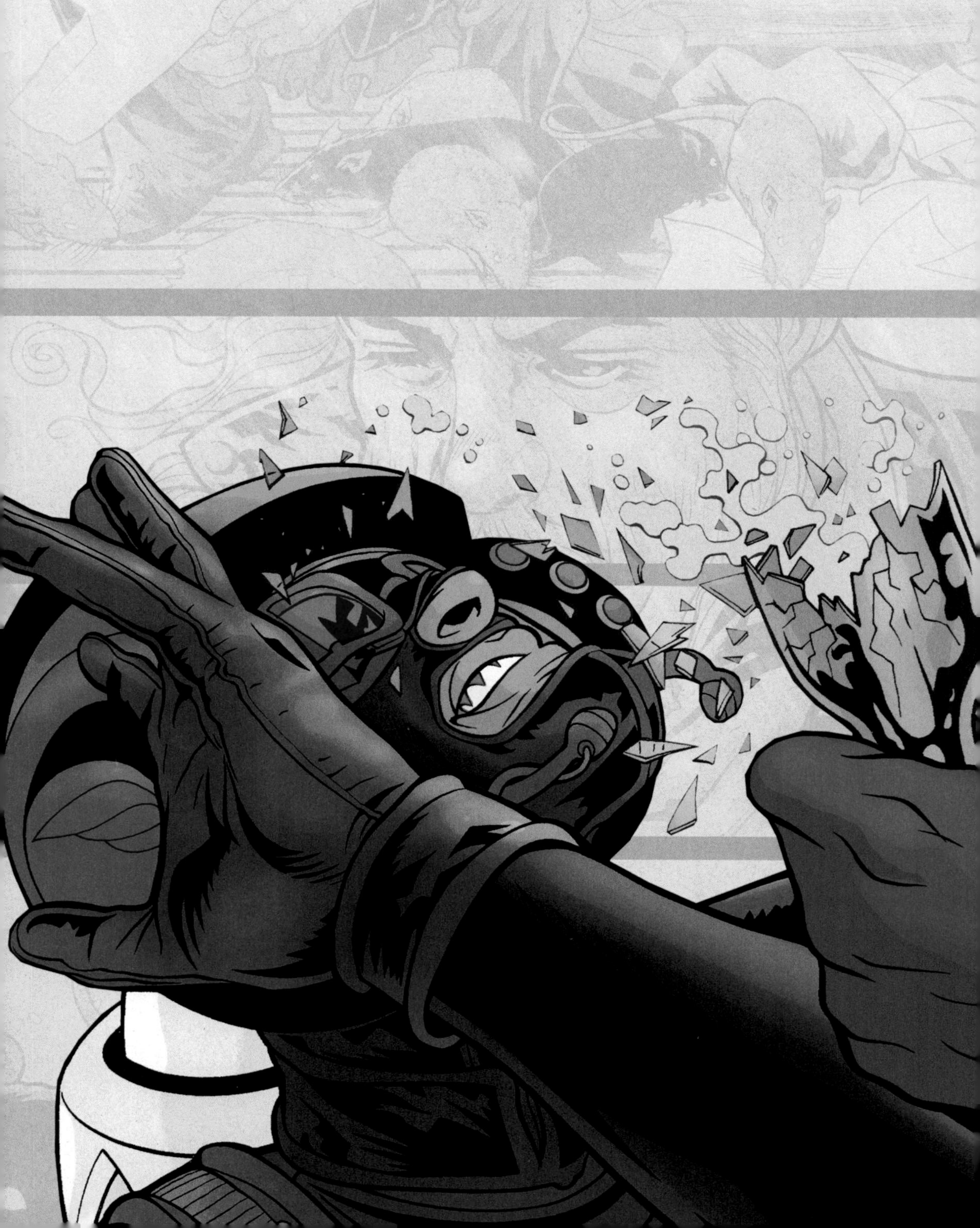

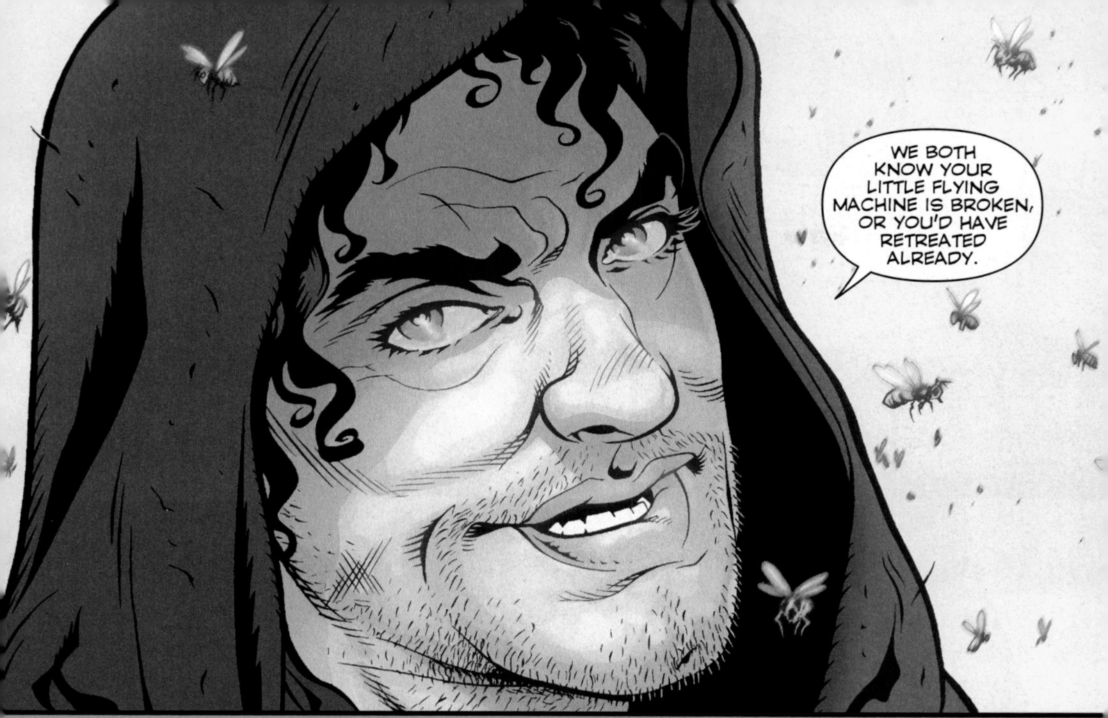
WE BOTH KNOW YOUR LITTLE FLYING MACHINE IS BROKEN, OR YOU'D HAVE RETREATED ALREADY.

TUESDAY, MARCH 27, 2001

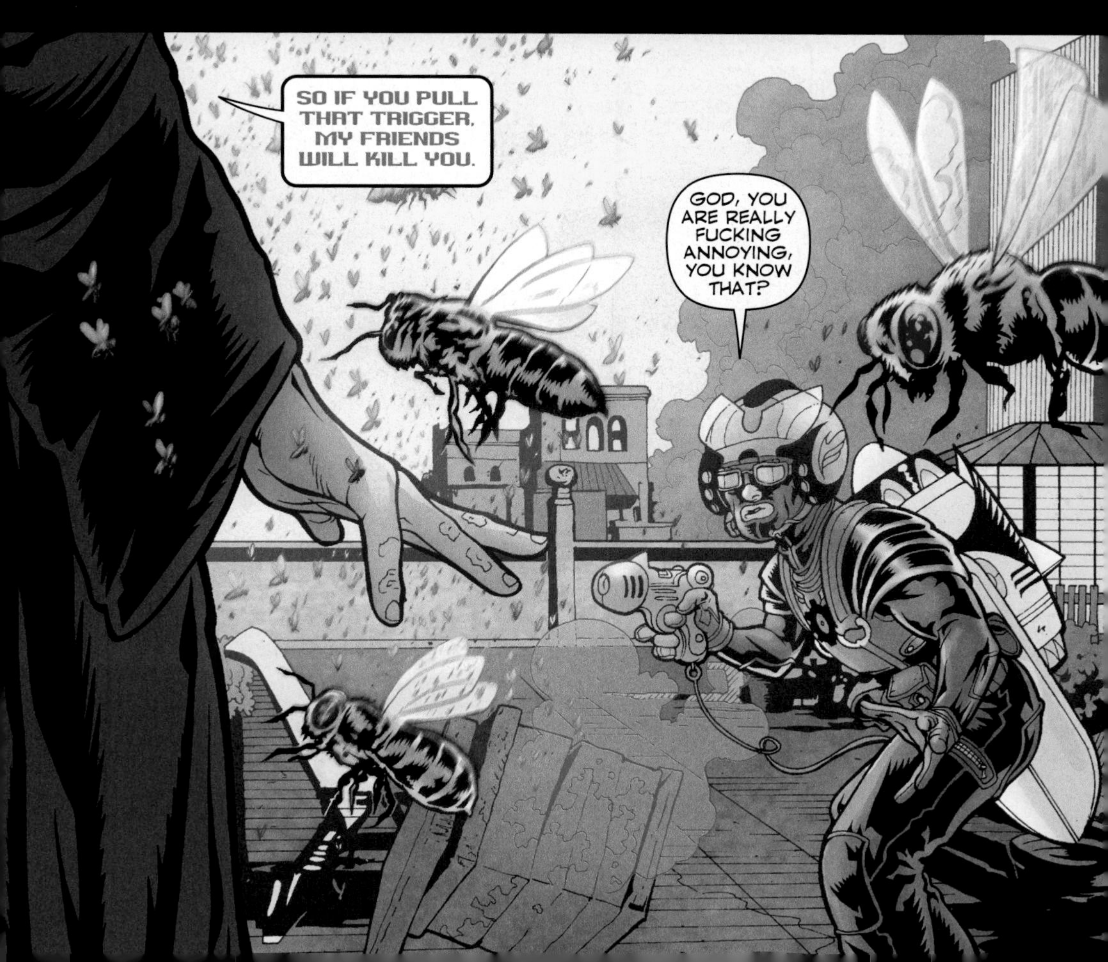
SO IF YOU PULL THAT TRIGGER, MY FRIENDS WILL KILL YOU.
GOD, YOU ARE REALLY FUCKING ANNOYING, YOU KNOW THAT?

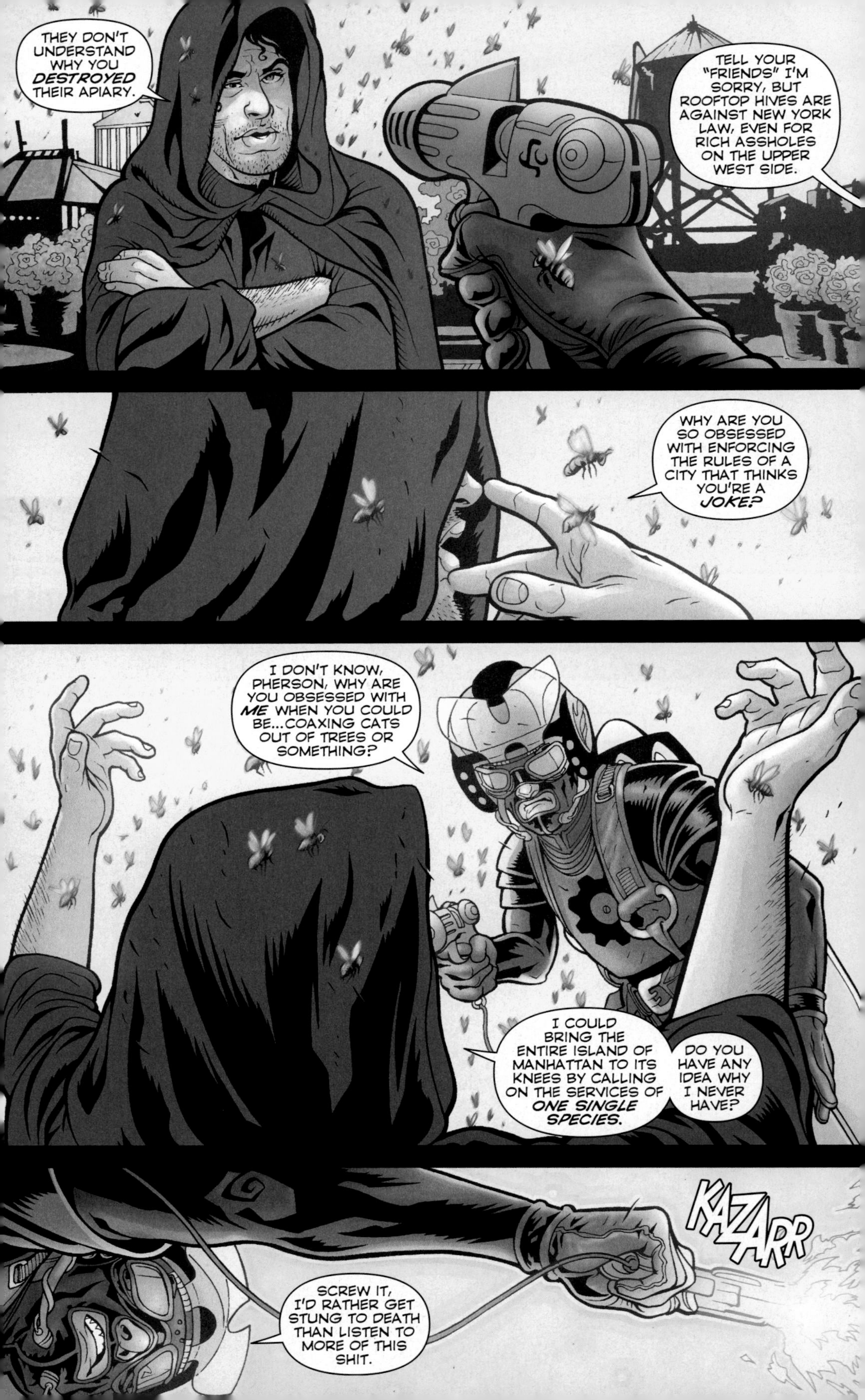
THEY DON'T UNDERSTAND WHY YOU DESTROYED THEIR APIARY.
TELL YOUR "FRIENDS" I'M SORRY, BUT ROOFTOP HIVES ARE AGAINST NEW YORK LAW, EVEN FOR RICH ASSHOLES ON THE UPPER WEST SIDE.
WHY ARE YOU SO OBSESSED WITH ENFORCING THE RULES OF A CITY THAT THINKS YOU'RE A JOKE?
I DON'T KNOW, PHERSON, WHY ARE YOU OBSESSED WITH ME WHEN YOU COULD BE...COAXING CATS OUT OF TREES OR SOMETHING?
I COULD BRING THE ENTIRE ISLAND OF MANHATTAN TO ITS KNEES BY CALLING ON THE SERVICES OF ONE SINGLE SPECIES.
DO YOU HAVE ANY IDEA WHY I NEVER HAVE?
KAZARRR
SCREW IT, I'D RATHER GET STUNG TO DEATH THAN LISTEN TO MORE OF THIS SHIT.

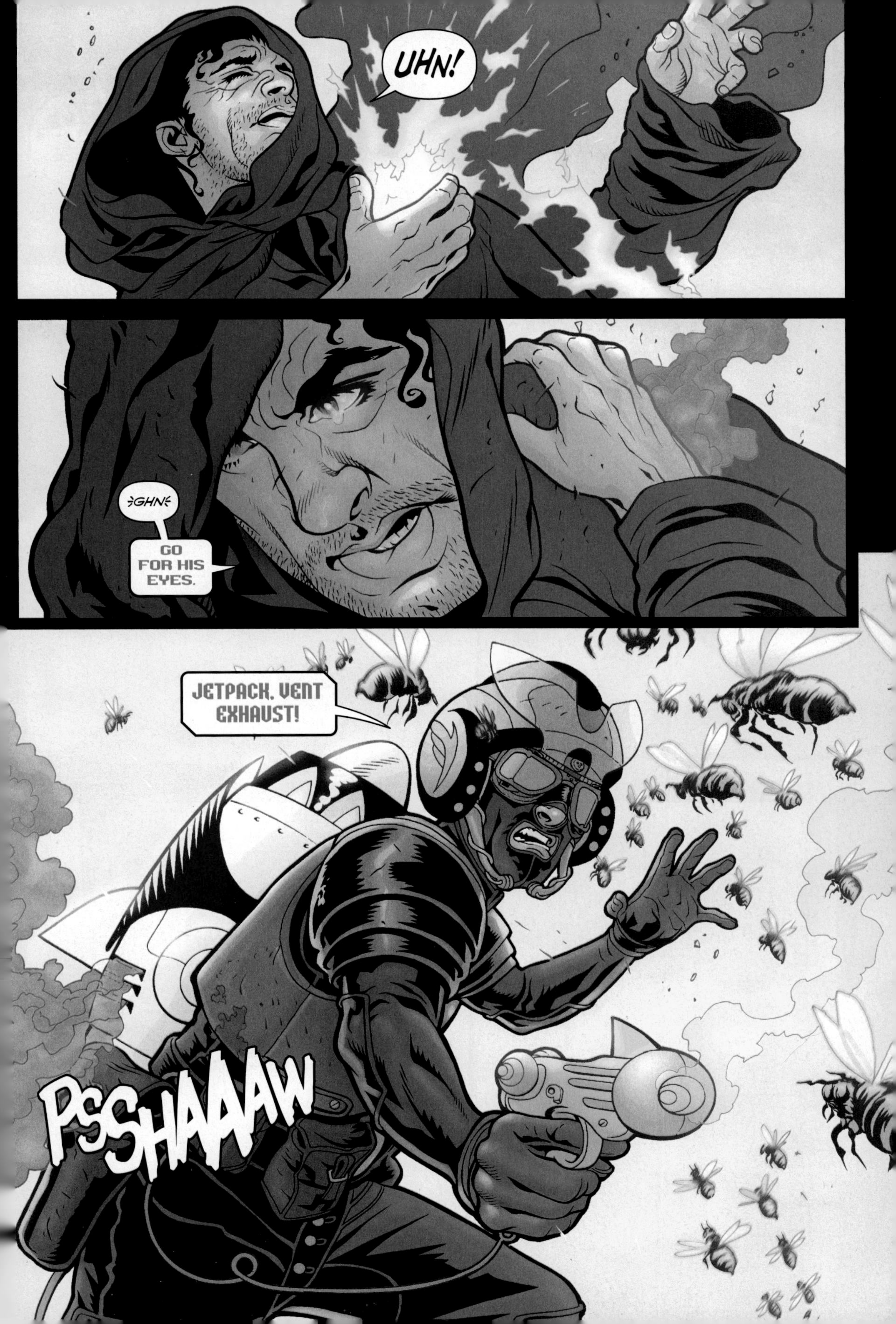
UHN!
GHN
GO FOR HIS EYES.
JETPACK, VENT EXHAUST!
PSSHAAAW

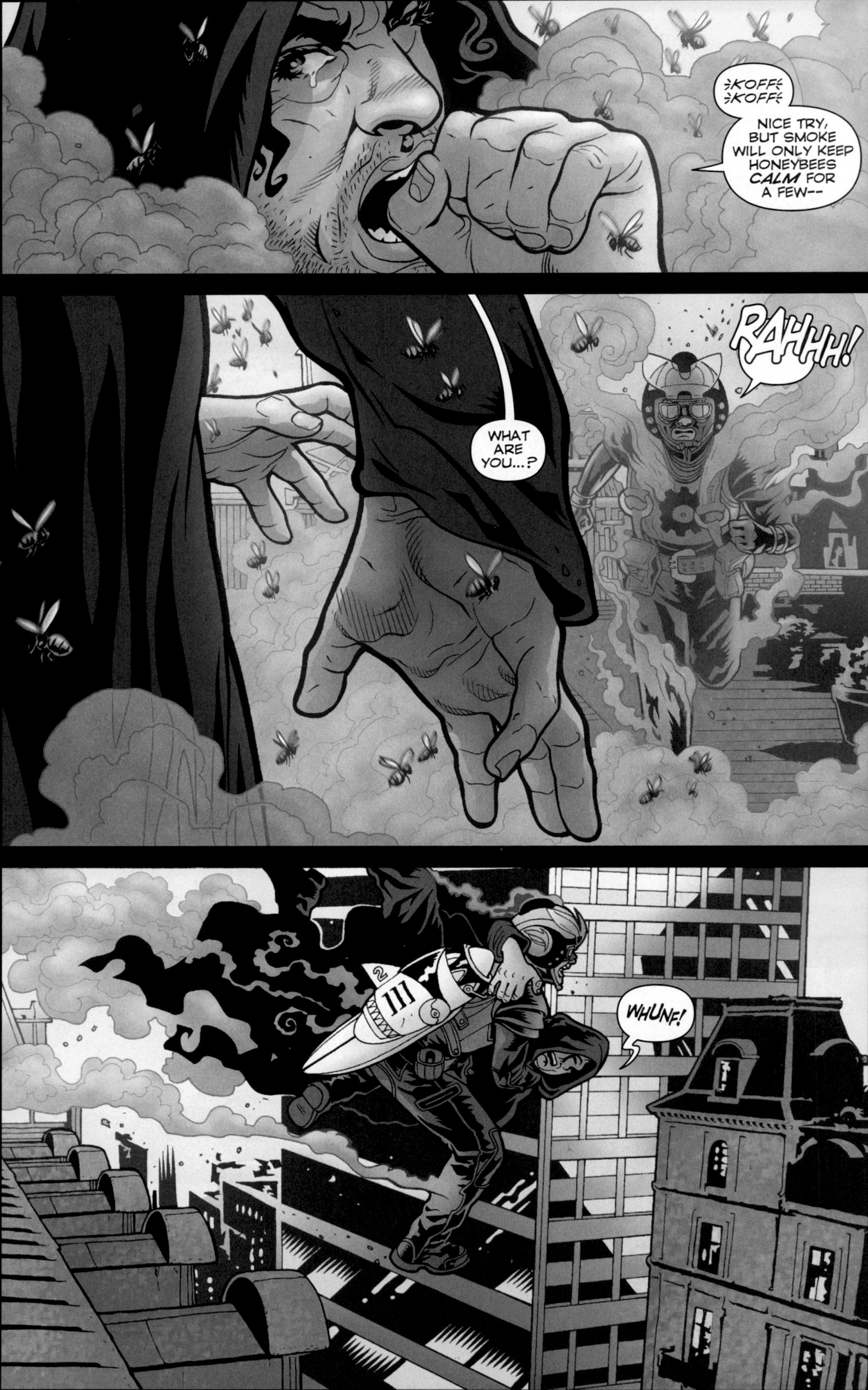
KOFF KOFF
NICE TRY, BUT SMOKE WILL ONLY KEEP HONEYBEES CALM FOR A FEW--
WHAT ARE YOU...?
RAHHH!
WHUNF!

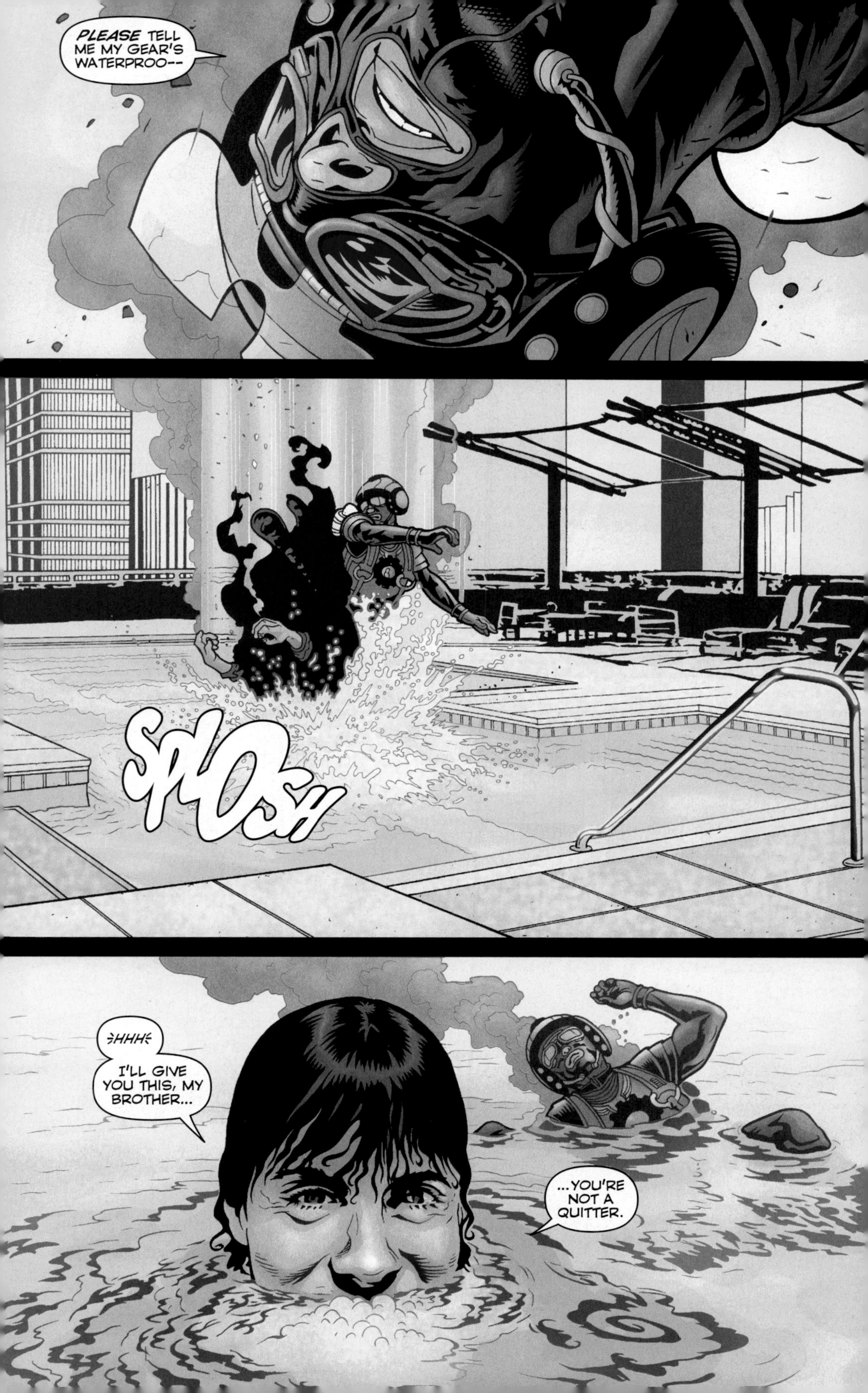
PLEASE TELL ME MY GEAR'S WATERPROO--
SPLOOSH
HHH
I'LL GIVE YOU THIS, MY BROTHER...
...YOU'RE NOT A QUITTER.

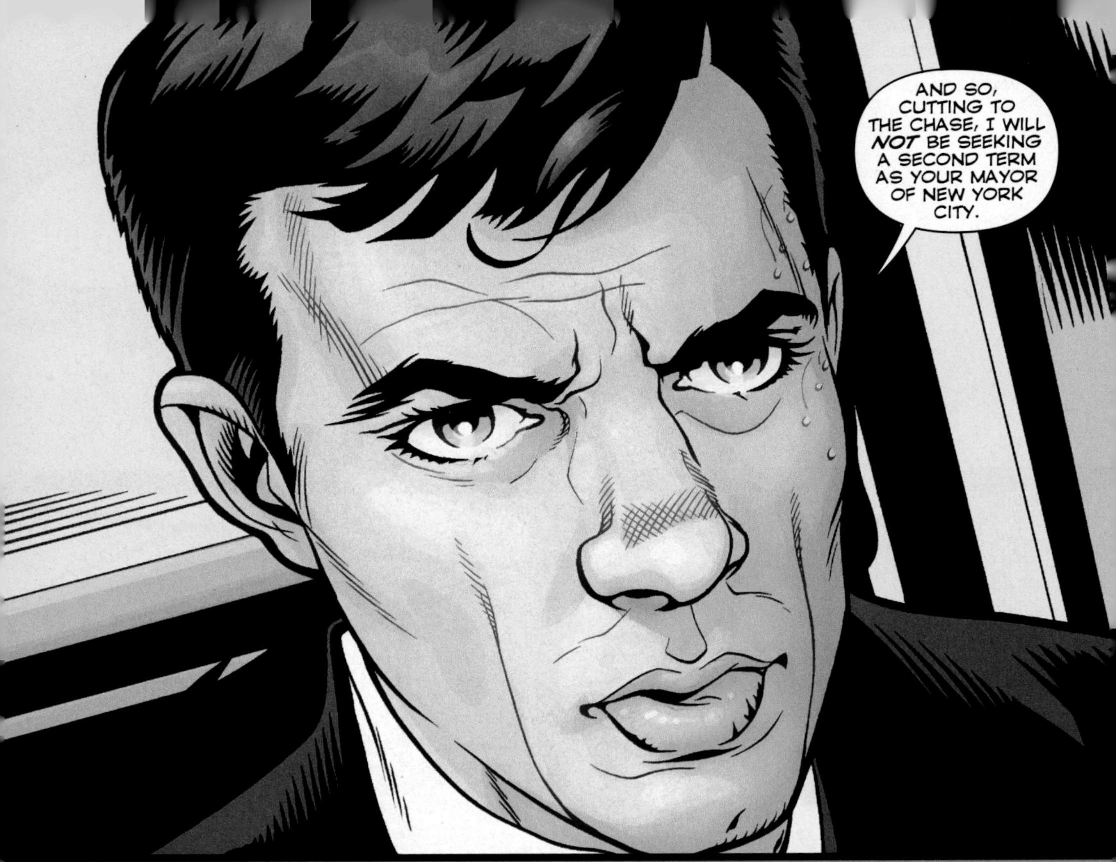
AND SO, CUTTING TO THE CHASE, I WILL *NOT* BE SEEKING A SECOND TERM AS YOUR MAYOR OF NEW YORK CITY.

WEDNESDAY, DECEMBER 29, 2004

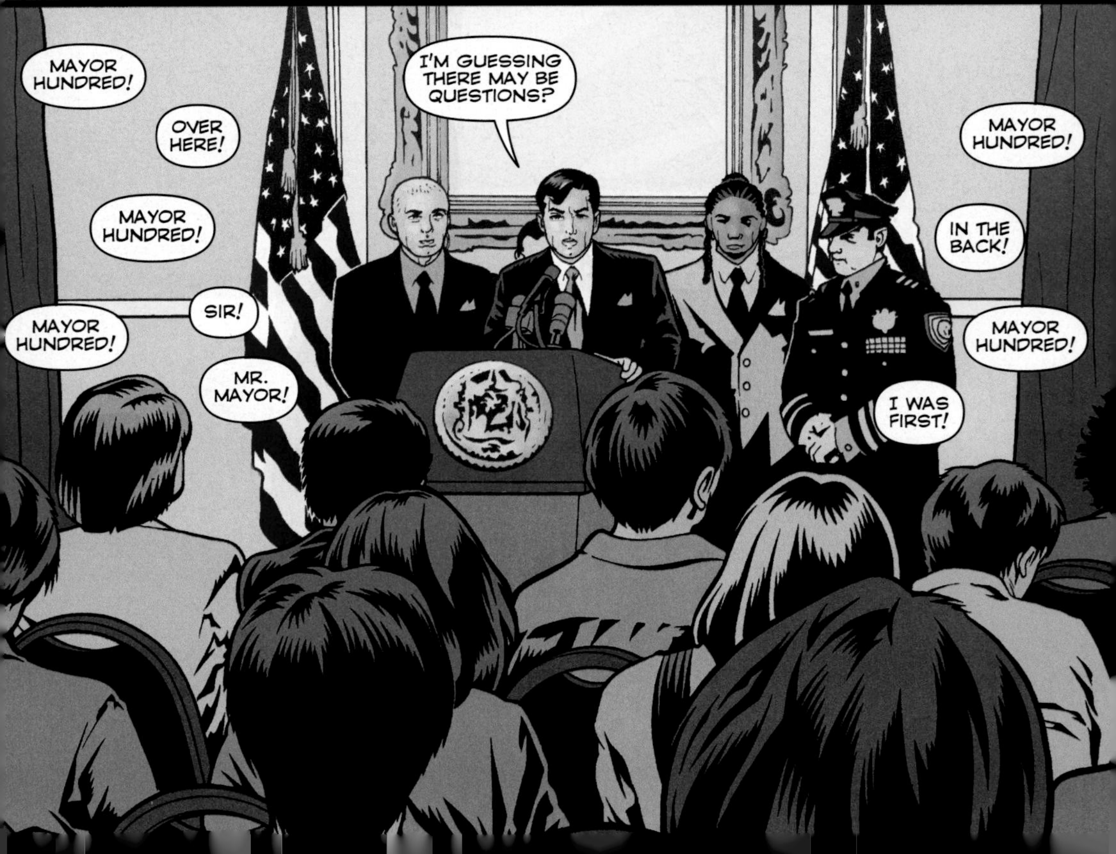
I'M GUESSING THERE MAY BE QUESTIONS?
MAYOR HUNDRED!
OVER HERE!
MAYOR HUNDRED!
SIR!
MAYOR HUNDRED!
MR. MAYOR!
MAYOR HUNDRED!
IN THE BACK!
MAYOR HUNDRED!
I WAS FIRST!

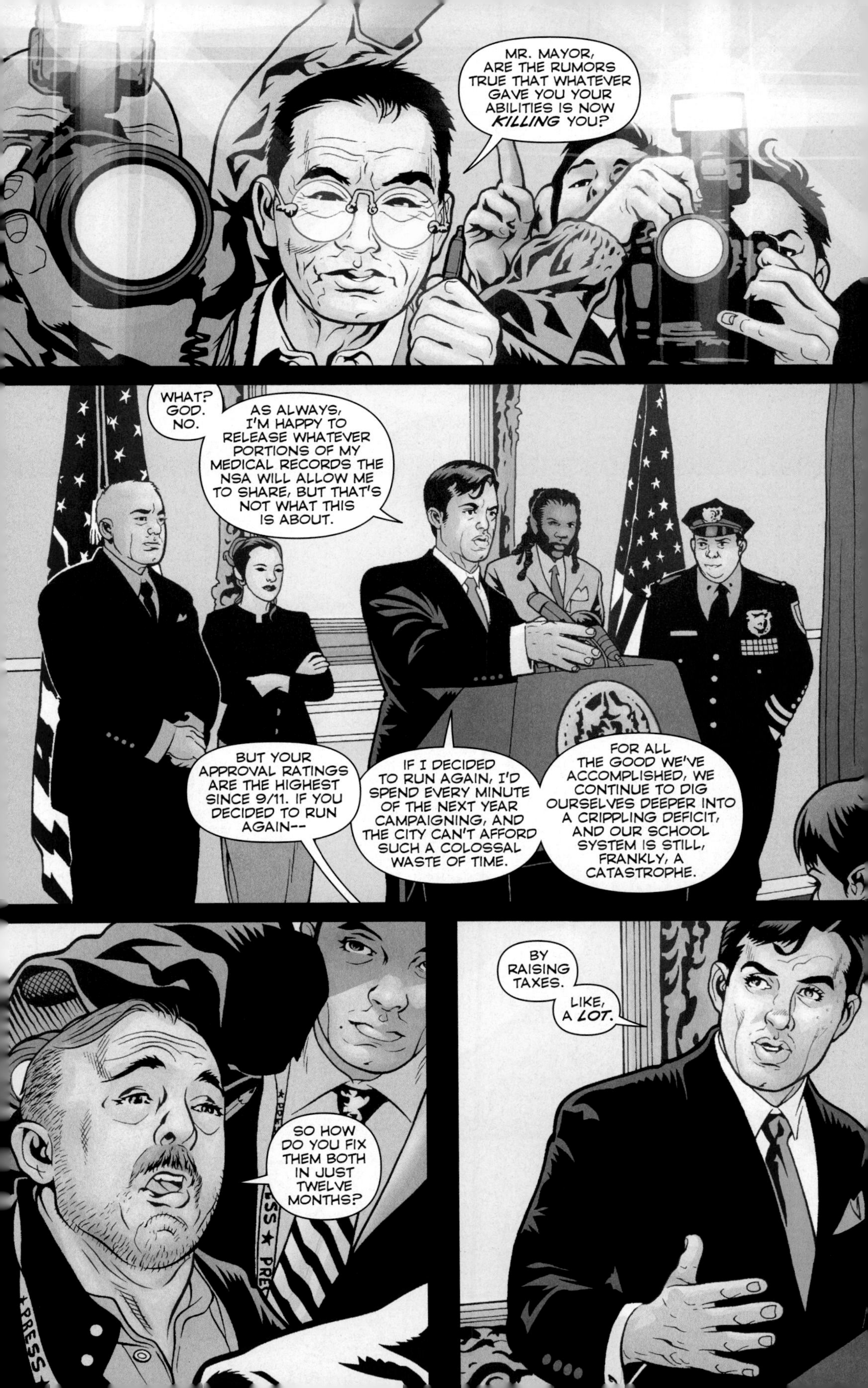
MR. MAYOR, ARE THE RUMORS TRUE THAT WHATEVER GAVE YOU YOUR ABILITIES IS NOW *KILLING* YOU?
WHAT? GOD. NO.
AS ALWAYS, I'M HAPPY TO RELEASE WHATEVER PORTIONS OF MY MEDICAL RECORDS THE NSA WILL ALLOW ME TO SHARE, BUT THAT'S NOT WHAT THIS IS ABOUT.
BUT YOUR APPROVAL RATINGS ARE THE HIGHEST SINCE 9/11. IF YOU DECIDED TO RUN AGAIN--
IF I DECIDED TO RUN AGAIN, I'D SPEND EVERY MINUTE OF THE NEXT YEAR CAMPAIGNING, AND THE CITY CAN'T AFFORD SUCH A COLOSSAL WASTE OF TIME.
FOR ALL THE GOOD WE'VE ACCOMPLISHED, WE CONTINUE TO DIG OURSELVES DEEPER INTO A CRIPPLING DEFICIT, AND OUR SCHOOL SYSTEM IS STILL, FRANKLY, A CATASTROPHE.
SO HOW DO YOU FIX THEM BOTH IN JUST TWELVE MONTHS?
BY RAISING TAXES.
LIKE, A *LOT*.
PRESS

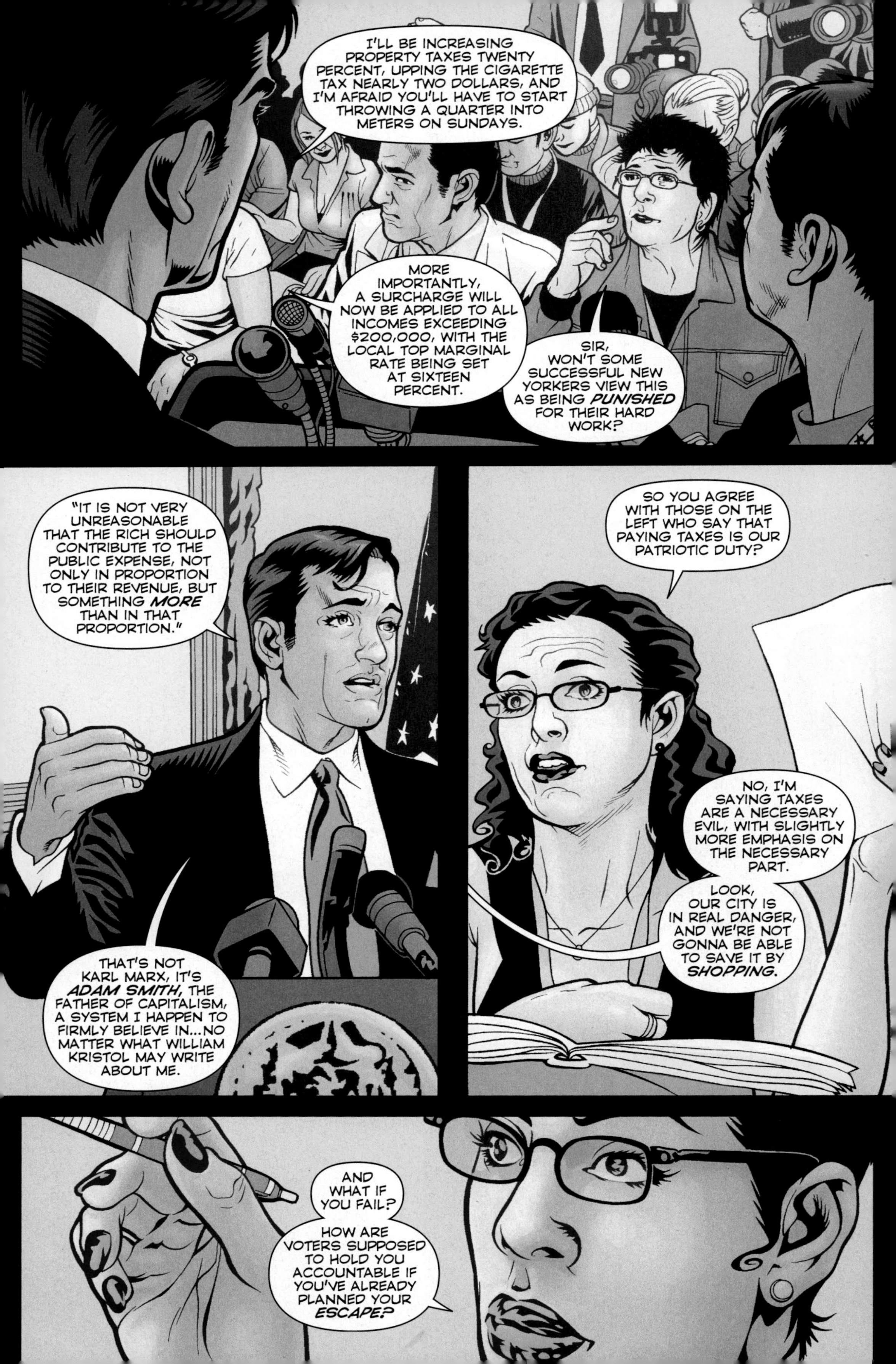
I'LL BE INCREASING PROPERTY TAXES TWENTY PERCENT, UPPING THE CIGARETTE TAX NEARLY TWO DOLLARS, AND I'M AFRAID YOU'LL HAVE TO START THROWING A QUARTER INTO METERS ON SUNDAYS.
MORE IMPORTANTLY, A SURCHARGE WILL NOW BE APPLIED TO ALL INCOMES EXCEEDING $200,000, WITH THE LOCAL TOP MARGINAL RATE BEING SET AT SIXTEEN PERCENT.
SIR, WON'T SOME SUCCESSFUL NEW YORKERS VIEW THIS AS BEING *PUNISHED* FOR THEIR HARD WORK?
"IT IS NOT VERY UNREASONABLE THAT THE RICH SHOULD CONTRIBUTE TO THE PUBLIC EXPENSE, NOT ONLY IN PROPORTION TO THEIR REVENUE, BUT SOMETHING *MORE* THAN IN THAT PROPORTION."
THAT'S NOT KARL MARX, IT'S *ADAM SMITH,* THE FATHER OF CAPITALISM, A SYSTEM I HAPPEN TO FIRMLY BELIEVE IN...NO MATTER WHAT WILLIAM KRISTOL MAY WRITE ABOUT ME.
SO YOU AGREE WITH THOSE ON THE LEFT WHO SAY THAT PAYING TAXES IS OUR PATRIOTIC DUTY?
NO, I'M SAYING TAXES ARE A NECESSARY EVIL, WITH SLIGHTLY MORE EMPHASIS ON THE NECESSARY PART.
LOOK, OUR CITY IS IN REAL DANGER, AND WE'RE NOT GONNA BE ABLE TO SAVE IT BY *SHOPPING.*
AND WHAT IF YOU FAIL?
HOW ARE VOTERS SUPPOSED TO HOLD YOU ACCOUNTABLE IF YOU'VE ALREADY PLANNED YOUR *ESCAPE?*

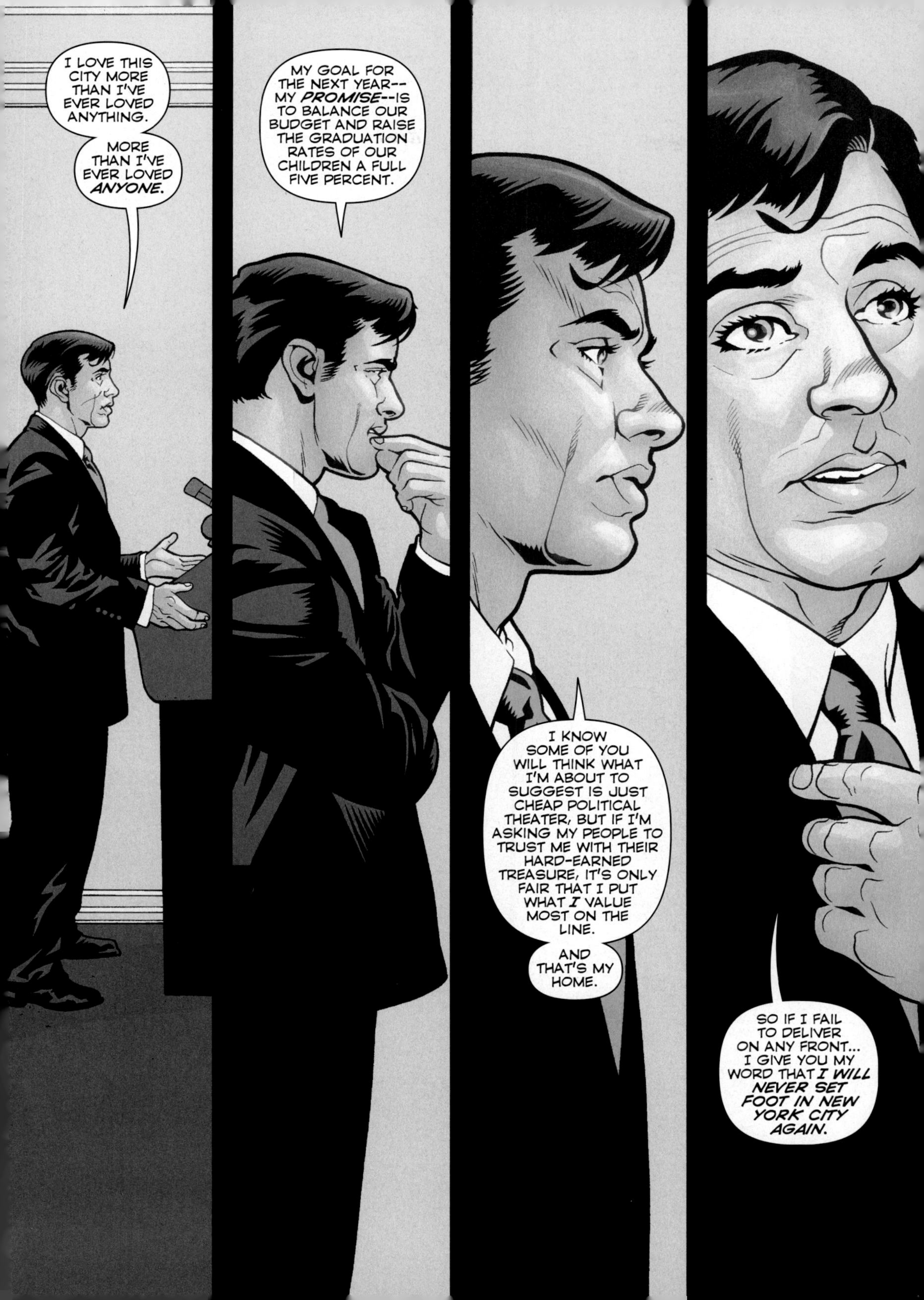
I LOVE THIS CITY MORE THAN I'VE EVER LOVED ANYTHING.
MORE THAN I'VE EVER LOVED *ANYONE.*
MY GOAL FOR THE NEXT YEAR-- MY *PROMISE*--IS TO BALANCE OUR BUDGET AND RAISE THE GRADUATION RATES OF OUR CHILDREN A FULL FIVE PERCENT.
I KNOW SOME OF YOU WILL THINK WHAT I'M ABOUT TO SUGGEST IS JUST CHEAP POLITICAL THEATER, BUT IF I'M ASKING MY PEOPLE TO TRUST ME WITH THEIR HARD-EARNED TREASURE, IT'S ONLY FAIR THAT I PUT WHAT *I* VALUE MOST ON THE LINE.
AND THAT'S MY HOME.
SO IF I FAIL TO DELIVER ON ANY FRONT... I GIVE YOU MY WORD THAT *I WILL NEVER SET FOOT IN NEW YORK CITY AGAIN.*

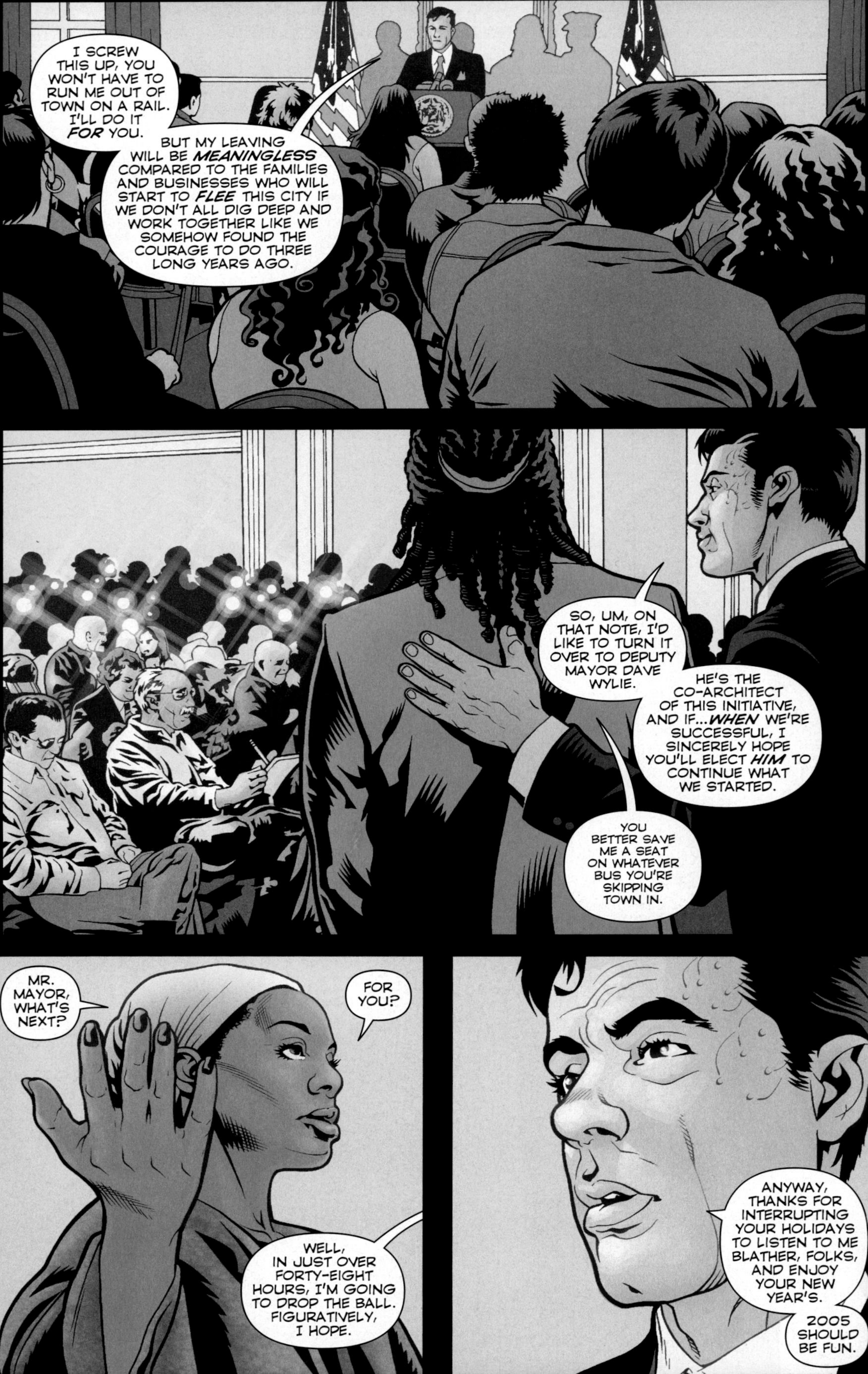
I SCREW THIS UP, YOU WON'T HAVE TO RUN ME OUT OF TOWN ON A RAIL. I'LL DO IT *FOR* YOU.
BUT MY LEAVING WILL BE *MEANINGLESS* COMPARED TO THE FAMILIES AND BUSINESSES WHO WILL START TO *FLEE* THIS CITY IF WE DON'T ALL DIG DEEP AND WORK TOGETHER LIKE WE SOMEHOW FOUND THE COURAGE TO DO THREE LONG YEARS AGO.
SO, UM, ON THAT NOTE, I'D LIKE TO TURN IT OVER TO DEPUTY MAYOR DAVE WYLIE.
HE'S THE CO-ARCHITECT OF THIS INITIATIVE, AND IF...*WHEN* WE'RE SUCCESSFUL, I SINCERELY HOPE YOU'LL ELECT *HIM* TO CONTINUE WHAT WE STARTED.
YOU BETTER SAVE ME A SEAT ON WHATEVER BUS YOU'RE SKIPPING TOWN IN.
MR. MAYOR, WHAT'S NEXT?
FOR YOU?
WELL, IN JUST OVER FORTY-EIGHT HOURS, I'M GOING TO DROP THE BALL. FIGURATIVELY, I HOPE.
ANYWAY, THANKS FOR INTERRUPTING YOUR HOLIDAYS TO LISTEN TO ME BLATHER, FOLKS, AND ENJOY YOUR NEW YEAR'S.
2005 SHOULD BE FUN.

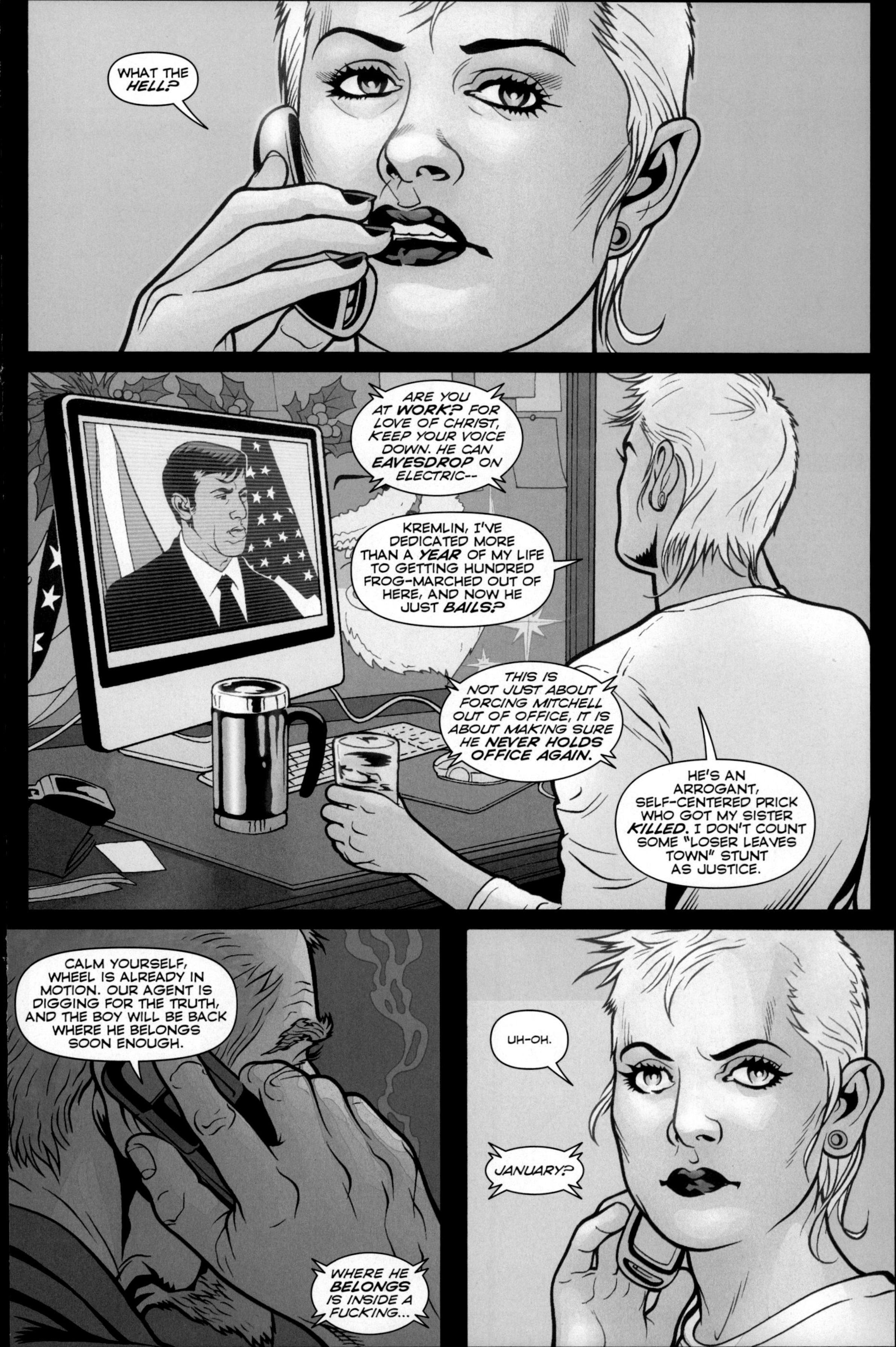
WHAT THE HELL?
ARE YOU AT WORK? FOR LOVE OF CHRIST, KEEP YOUR VOICE DOWN. HE CAN EAVESDROP ON ELECTRIC--
KREMLIN, I'VE DEDICATED MORE THAN A YEAR OF MY LIFE TO GETTING HUNDRED FROG-MARCHED OUT OF HERE, AND NOW HE JUST BAILS?
THIS IS NOT JUST ABOUT FORCING MITCHELL OUT OF OFFICE, IT IS ABOUT MAKING SURE HE NEVER HOLDS OFFICE AGAIN.
HE'S AN ARROGANT, SELF-CENTERED PRICK WHO GOT MY SISTER KILLED. I DON'T COUNT SOME "LOSER LEAVES TOWN" STUNT AS JUSTICE.
CALM YOURSELF, WHEEL IS ALREADY IN MOTION. OUR AGENT IS DIGGING FOR THE TRUTH, AND THE BOY WILL BE BACK WHERE HE BELONGS SOON ENOUGH.
WHERE HE BELONGS IS INSIDE A FUCKING...
UH-OH.
JANUARY?

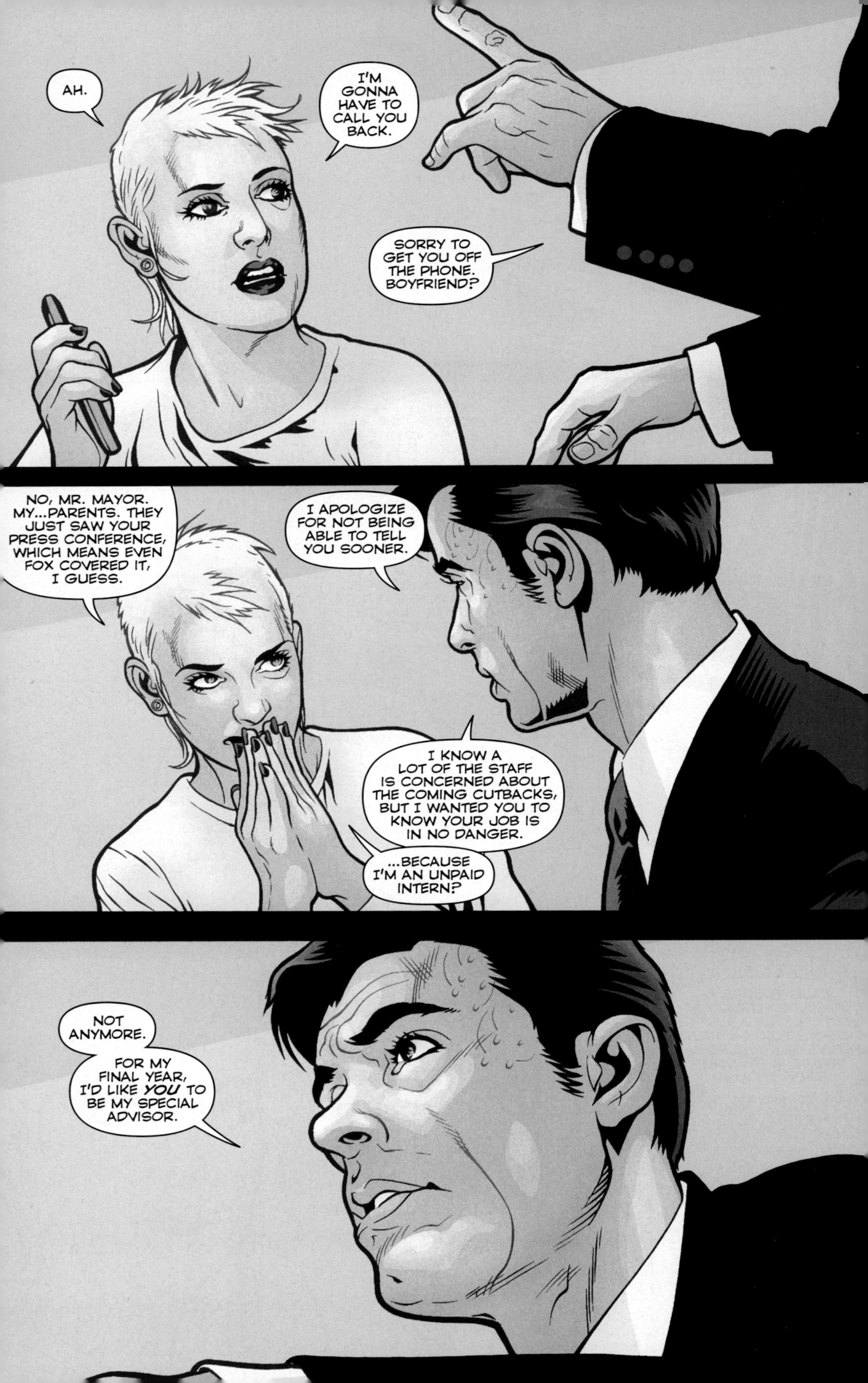
AH.
I'M GONNA HAVE TO CALL YOU BACK.
SORRY TO GET YOU OFF THE PHONE. BOYFRIEND?
NO, MR. MAYOR. MY...PARENTS. THEY JUST SAW YOUR PRESS CONFERENCE, WHICH MEANS EVEN FOX COVERED IT, I GUESS.
I APOLOGIZE FOR NOT BEING ABLE TO TELL YOU SOONER.
I KNOW A LOT OF THE STAFF IS CONCERNED ABOUT THE COMING CUTBACKS, BUT I WANTED YOU TO KNOW YOUR JOB IS IN NO DANGER.
...BECAUSE I'M AN UNPAID INTERN?
NOT ANYMORE.
FOR MY FINAL YEAR, I'D LIKE *YOU* TO BE MY SPECIAL ADVISOR.

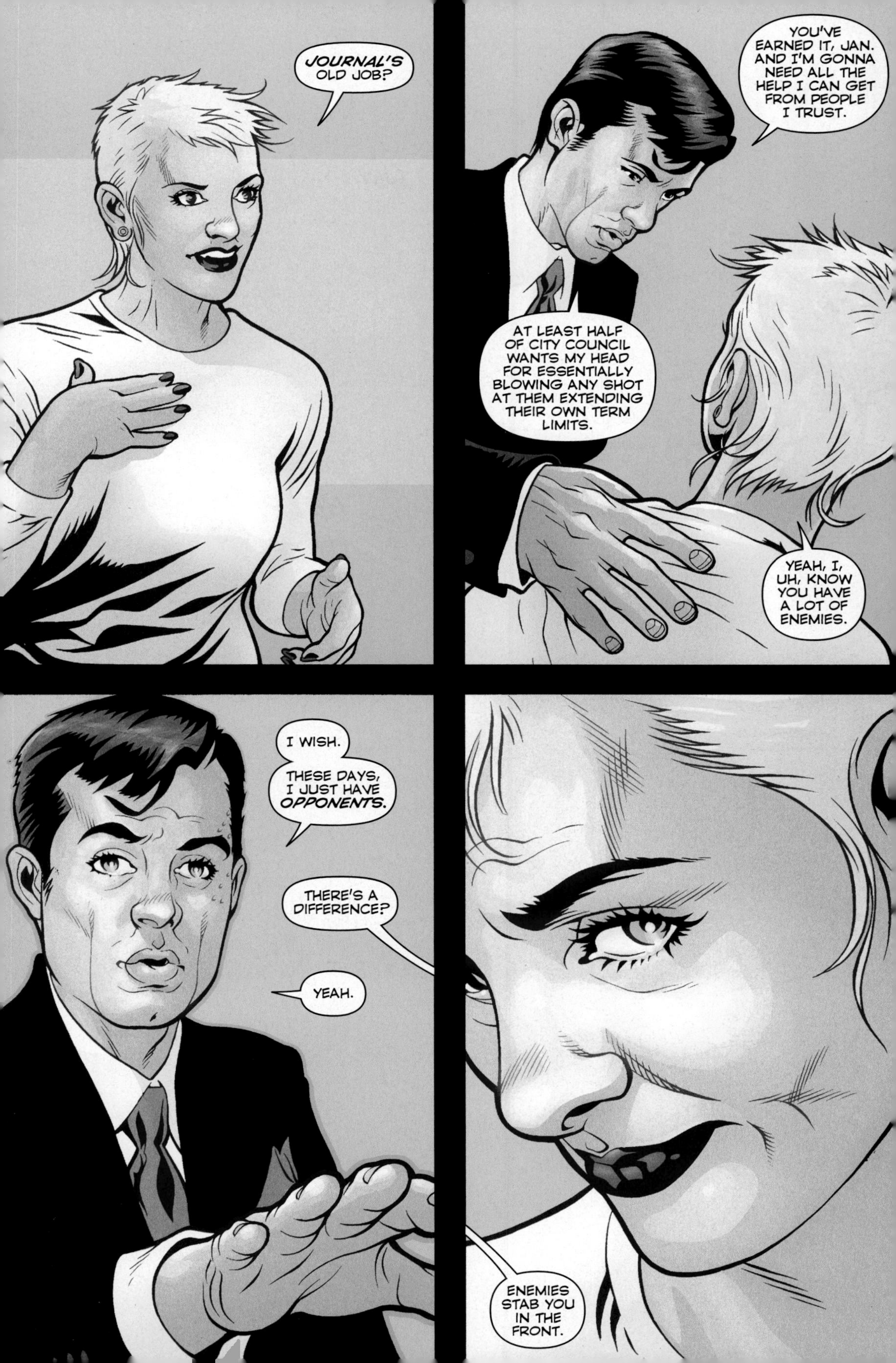

JOURNAL'S OLD JOB?
YOU'VE EARNED IT, JAN. AND I'M GONNA NEED ALL THE HELP I CAN GET FROM PEOPLE I TRUST.
AT LEAST HALF OF CITY COUNCIL WANTS MY HEAD FOR ESSENTIALLY BLOWING ANY SHOT AT THEM EXTENDING THEIR OWN TERM LIMITS.
YEAH, I, UH, KNOW YOU HAVE A LOT OF ENEMIES.
I WISH.
THESE DAYS, I JUST HAVE OPPONENTS.
THERE'S A DIFFERENCE?
YEAH.
ENEMIES STAB YOU IN THE FRONT.

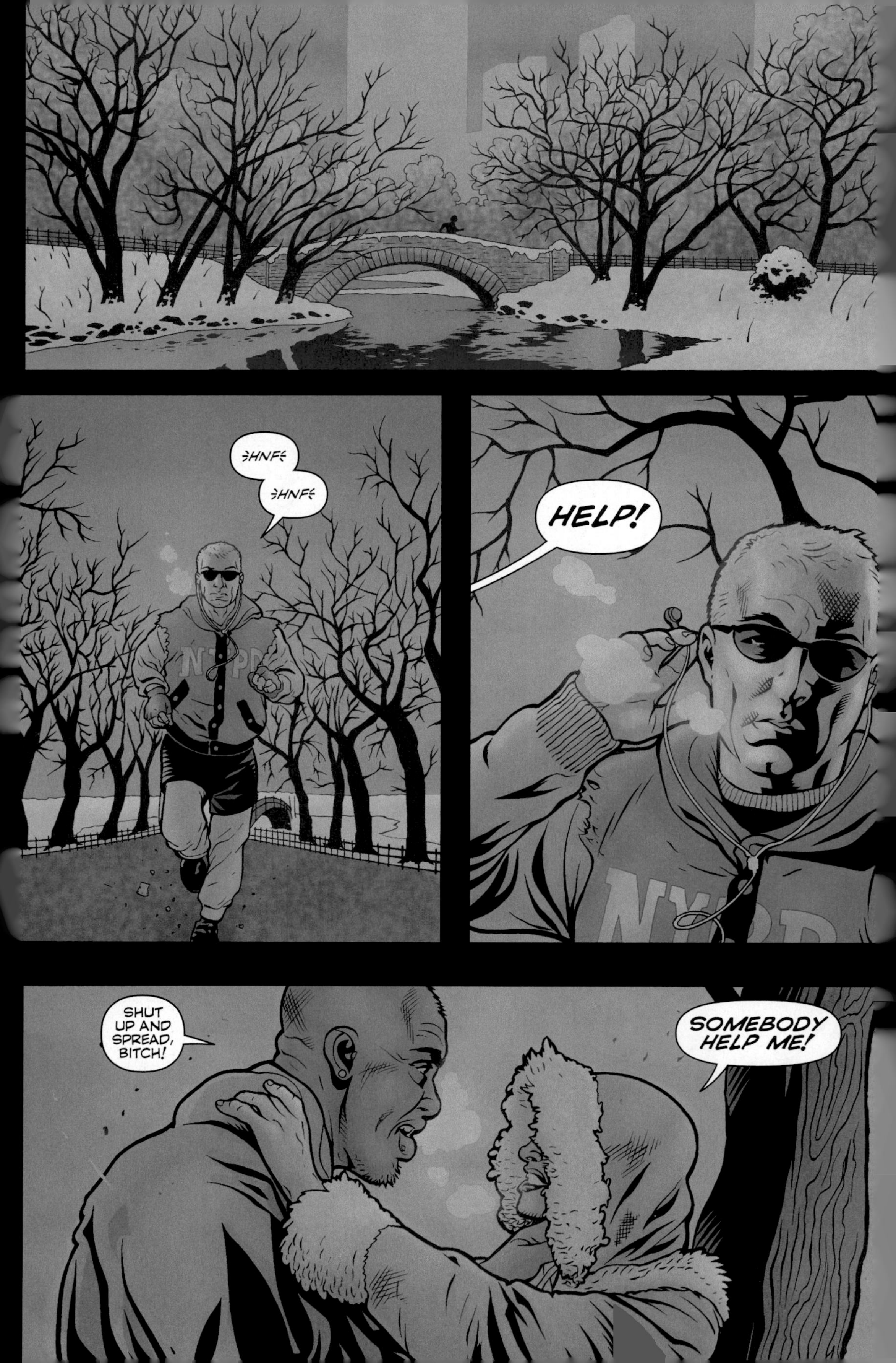
HNF
HNF
HELP!
SHUT UP AND SPREAD, BITCH!
SOMEBODY HELP ME!

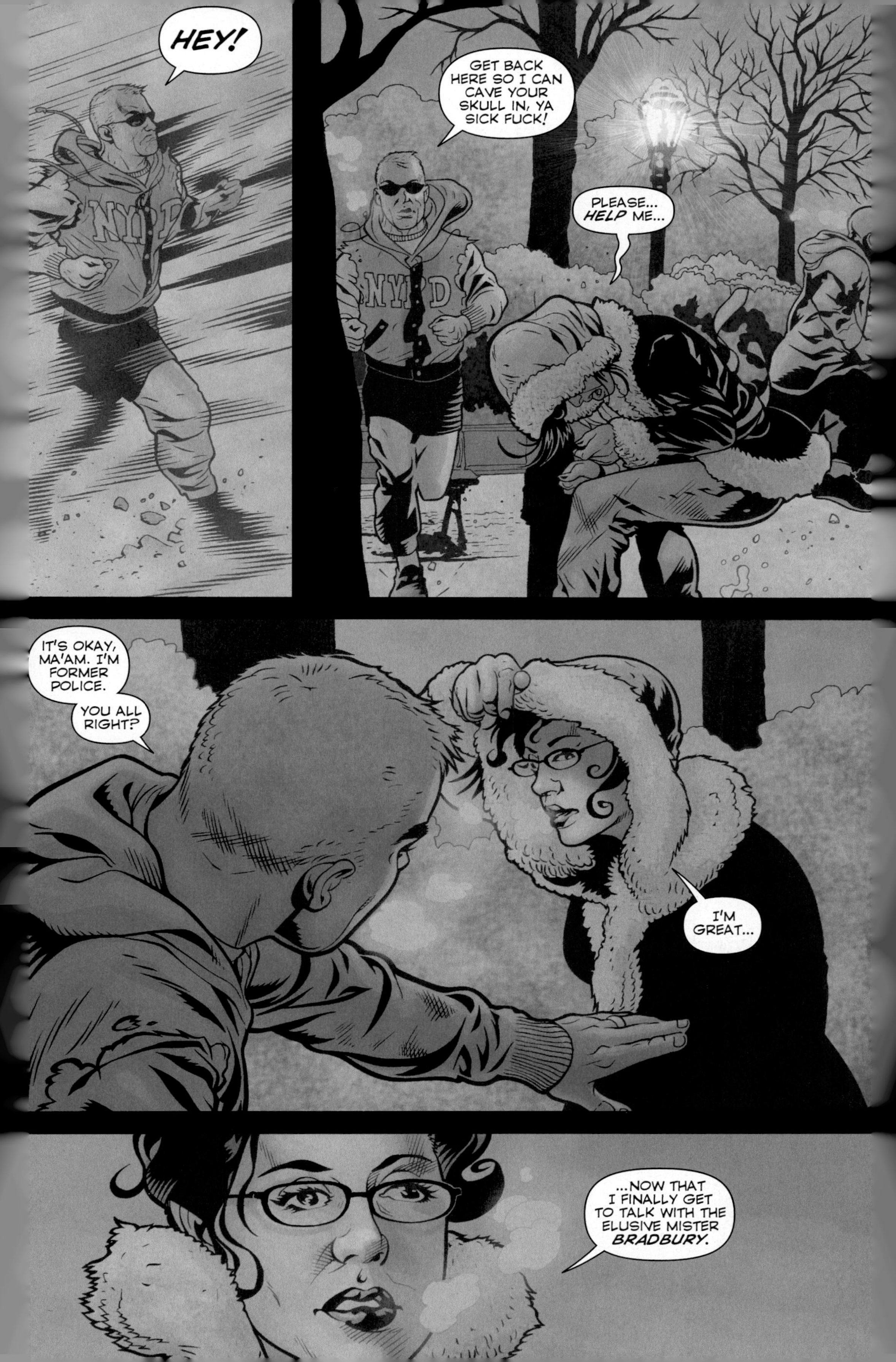
HEY!
GET BACK HERE SO I CAN CAVE YOUR SKULL IN, YA SICK FUCK!
PLEASE... HELP ME...
IT'S OKAY, MA'AM. I'M FORMER POLICE.
YOU ALL RIGHT?
I'M GREAT...
...NOW THAT I FINALLY GET TO TALK WITH THE ELUSIVE MISTER BRADBURY.

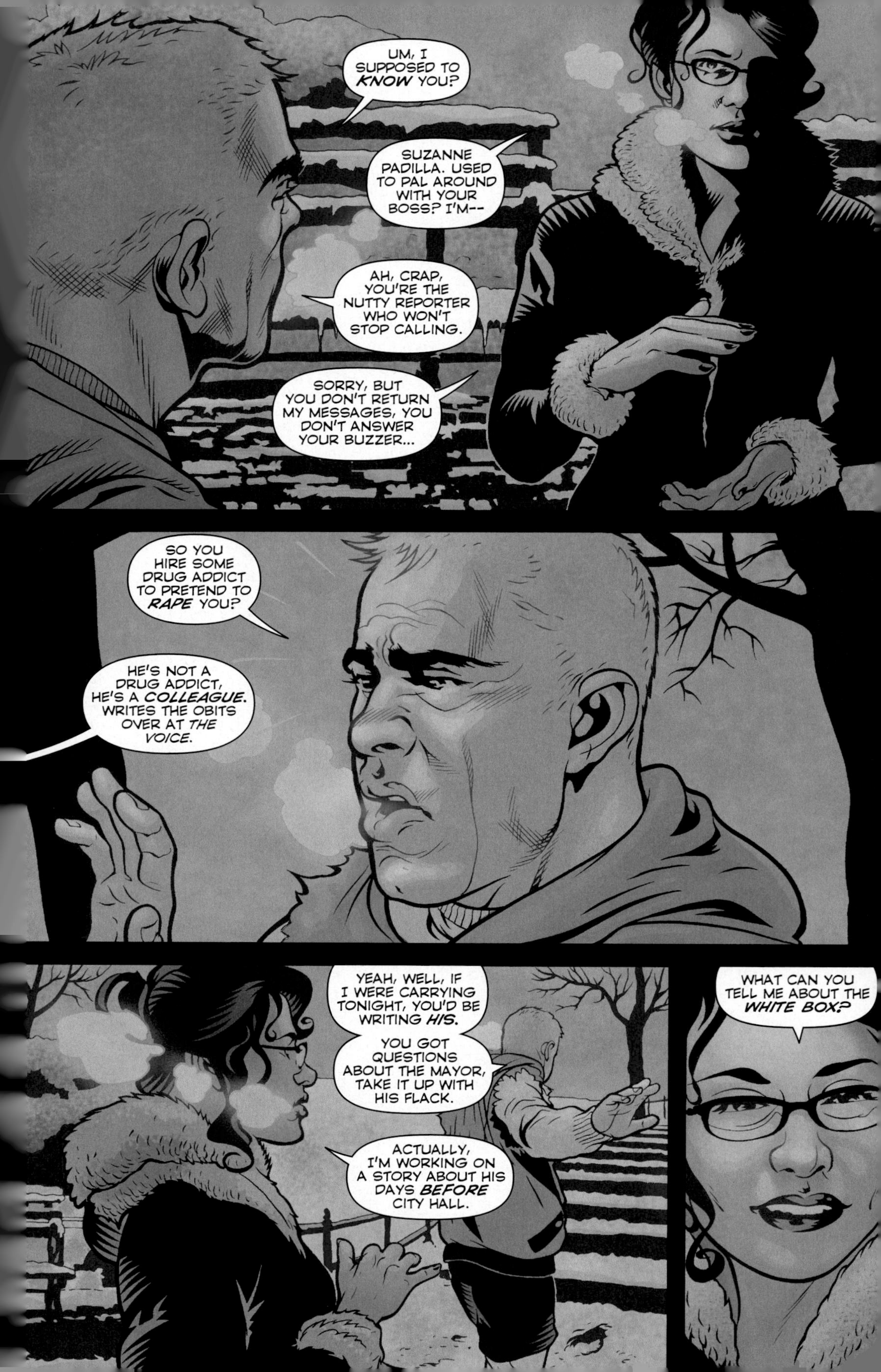
UM, I SUPPOSED TO *KNOW* YOU?
SUZANNE PADILLA. USED TO PAL AROUND WITH YOUR BOSS? I'M--
AH, CRAP, YOU'RE THE NUTTY REPORTER WHO WON'T STOP CALLING.
SORRY, BUT YOU DON'T RETURN MY MESSAGES, YOU DON'T ANSWER YOUR BUZZER...
SO YOU HIRE SOME DRUG ADDICT TO PRETEND TO *RAPE* YOU?
HE'S NOT A DRUG ADDICT, HE'S A *COLLEAGUE*. WRITES THE OBITS OVER AT *THE VOICE*.
YEAH, WELL, IF I WERE CARRYING TONIGHT, YOU'D BE WRITING *HIS*.
YOU GOT QUESTIONS ABOUT THE MAYOR, TAKE IT UP WITH HIS FLACK.
ACTUALLY, I'M WORKING ON A STORY ABOUT HIS DAYS *BEFORE* CITY HALL.
WHAT CAN YOU TELL ME ABOUT THE *WHITE BOX?*

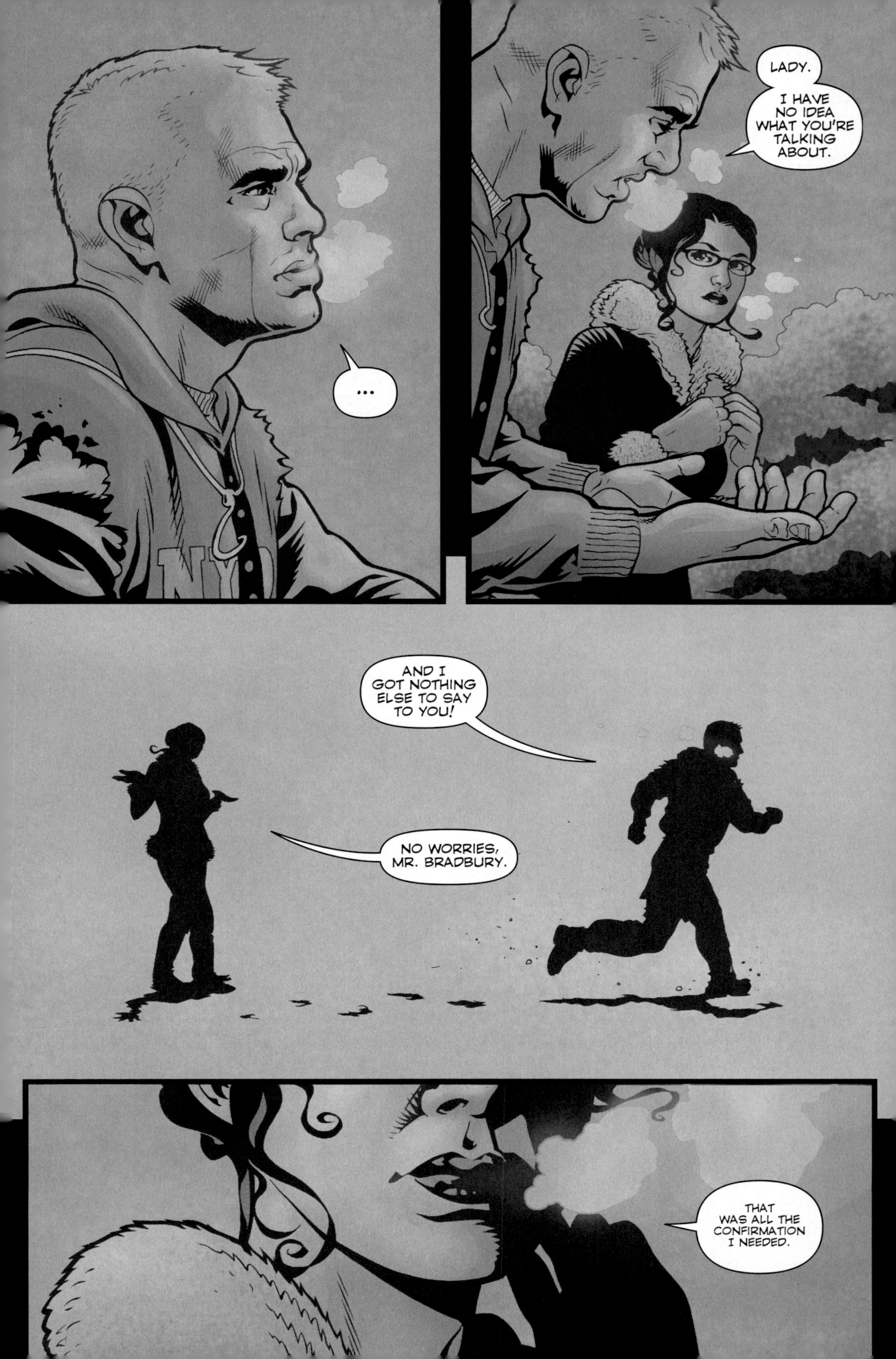
...
LADY.
I HAVE NO IDEA WHAT YOU'RE TALKING ABOUT.
AND I GOT NOTHING ELSE TO SAY TO YOU!
NO WORRIES, MR. BRADBURY.
THAT WAS ALL THE CONFIRMATION I NEEDED.

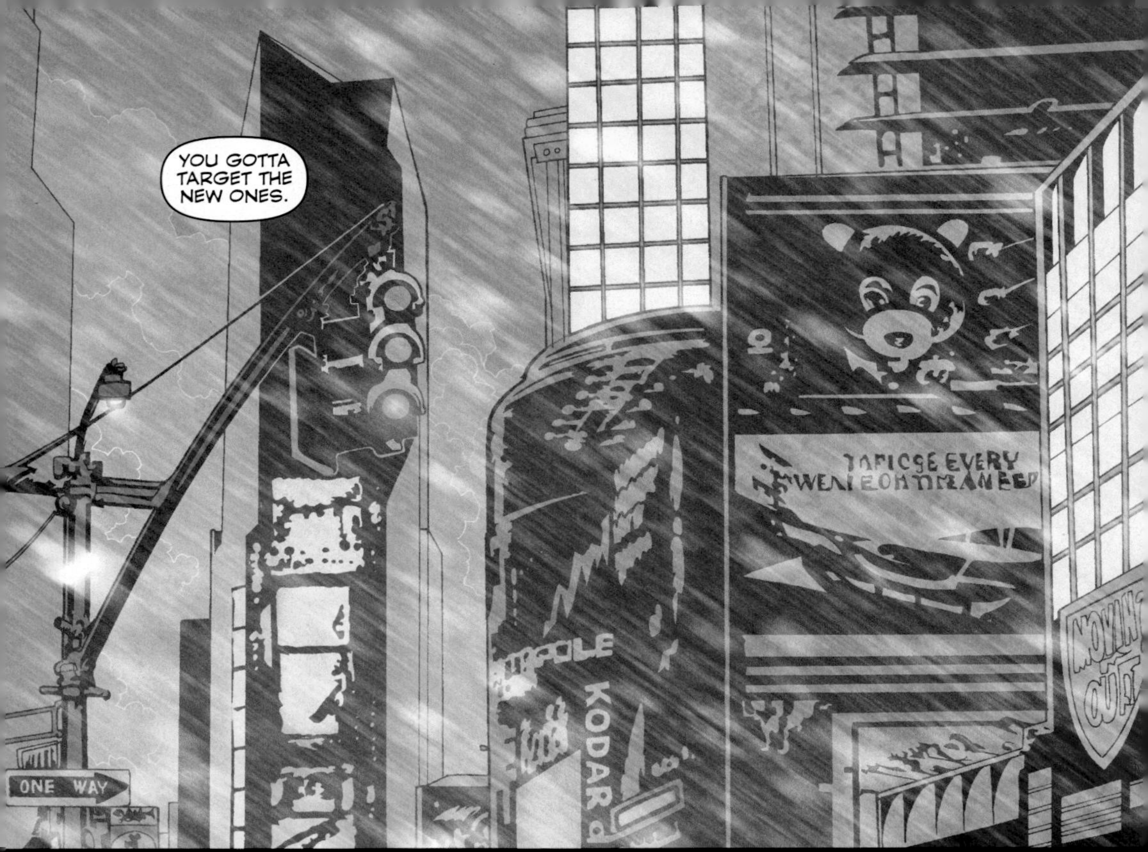
YOU GOTTA TARGET THE NEW ONES.
ONE WAY
KODAR

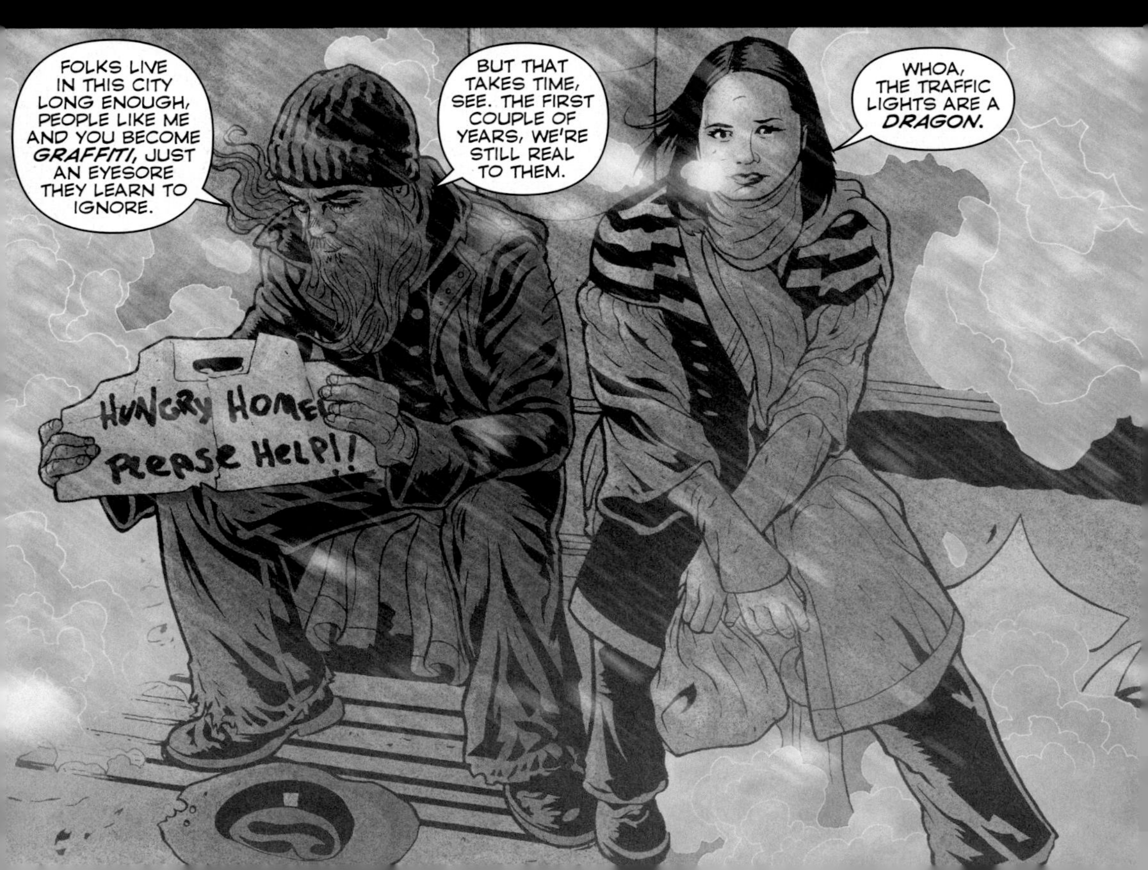
FOLKS LIVE IN THIS CITY LONG ENOUGH, PEOPLE LIKE ME AND YOU BECOME *GRAFFITI*, JUST AN EYESORE THEY LEARN TO IGNORE.
BUT THAT TAKES TIME, SEE. THE FIRST COUPLE OF YEARS, WE'RE STILL REAL TO THEM.
WHOA, THE TRAFFIC LIGHTS ARE A ***DRAGON.***
HUNGRY HOME
PLEASE HELP!!

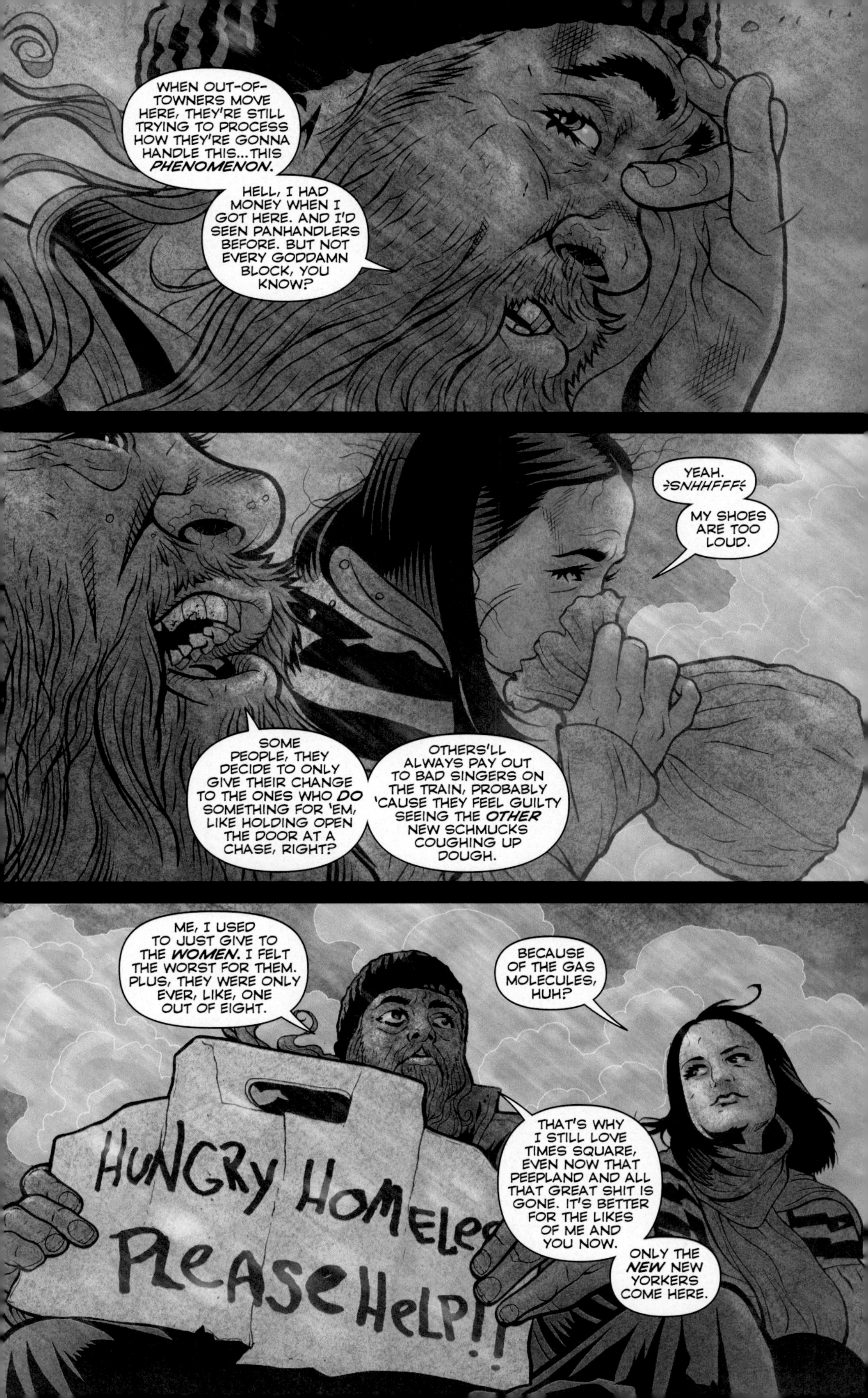
WHEN OUT-OF-TOWNERS MOVE HERE, THEY'RE STILL TRYING TO PROCESS HOW THEY'RE GONNA HANDLE THIS...THIS *PHENOMENON*.
HELL, I HAD MONEY WHEN I GOT HERE. AND I'D SEEN PANHANDLERS BEFORE. BUT NOT EVERY GODDAMN BLOCK, YOU KNOW?
YEAH. *SNHHFFF*
MY SHOES ARE TOO LOUD.
SOME PEOPLE, THEY DECIDE TO ONLY GIVE THEIR CHANGE TO THE ONES WHO *DO* SOMETHING FOR 'EM, LIKE HOLDING OPEN THE DOOR AT A CHASE, RIGHT?
OTHERS'LL ALWAYS PAY OUT TO BAD SINGERS ON THE TRAIN, PROBABLY 'CAUSE THEY FEEL GUILTY SEEING THE *OTHER* NEW SCHMUCKS COUGHING UP DOUGH.
ME, I USED TO JUST GIVE TO THE *WOMEN*. I FELT THE WORST FOR THEM. PLUS, THEY WERE ONLY EVER, LIKE, ONE OUT OF EIGHT.
BECAUSE OF THE GAS MOLECULES, HUH?
HUNGRY HOMELES PLEASE HELP!!
THAT'S WHY I STILL LOVE TIMES SQUARE, EVEN NOW THAT PEEPLAND AND ALL THAT GREAT SHIT IS GONE. IT'S BETTER FOR THE LIKES OF ME AND YOU NOW.
ONLY THE *NEW* NEW YORKERS COME HERE.

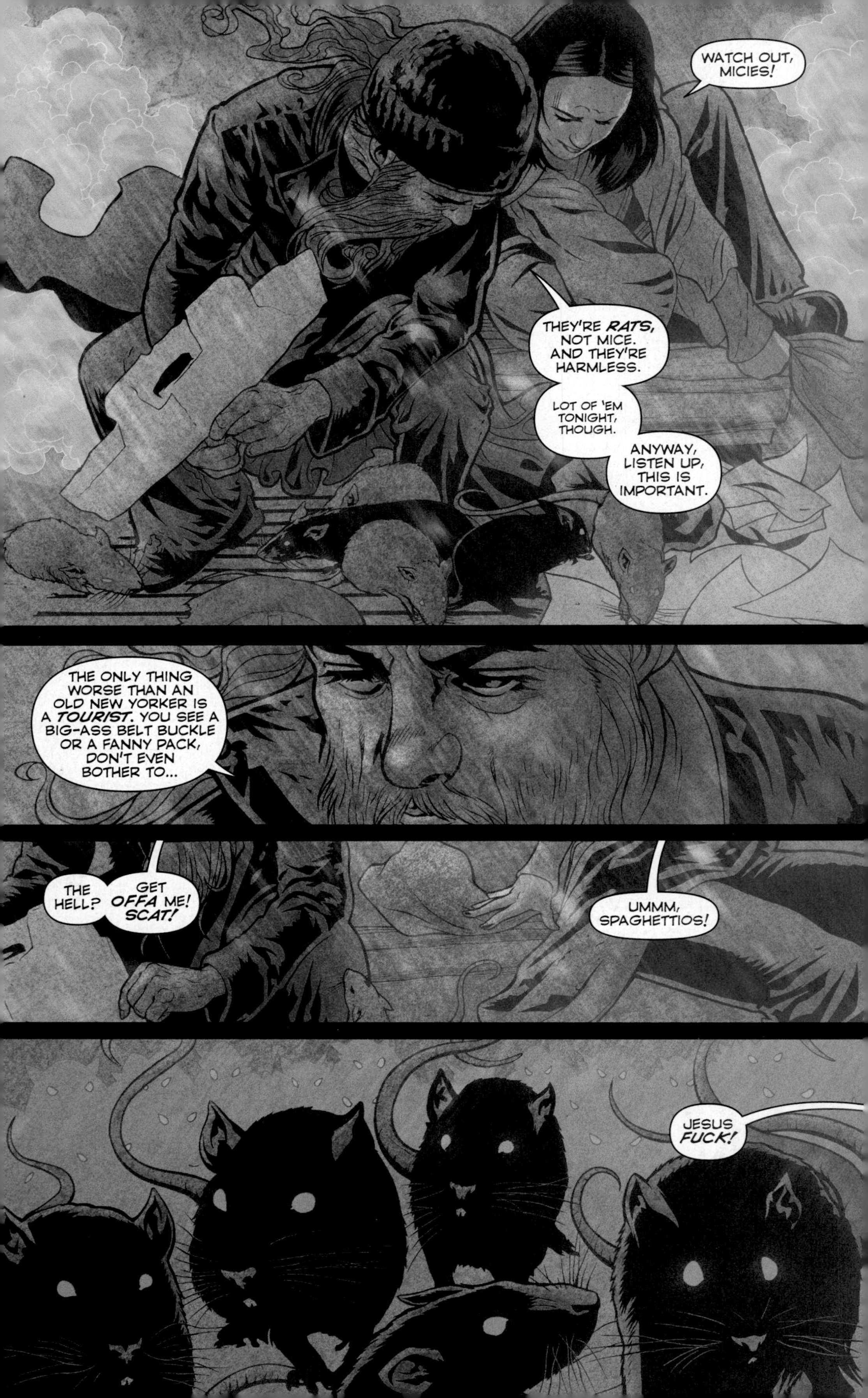
WATCH OUT, MICIES!
THEY'RE RATS, NOT MICE. AND THEY'RE HARMLESS.
LOT OF 'EM TONIGHT, THOUGH.
ANYWAY, LISTEN UP, THIS IS IMPORTANT.
THE ONLY THING WORSE THAN AN OLD NEW YORKER IS A TOURIST. YOU SEE A BIG-ASS BELT BUCKLE OR A FANNY PACK, DON'T EVEN BOTHER TO...
THE HELL?
GET OFFA ME! SCAT!
UMMM, SPAGHETTIOS!
JESUS FUCK!

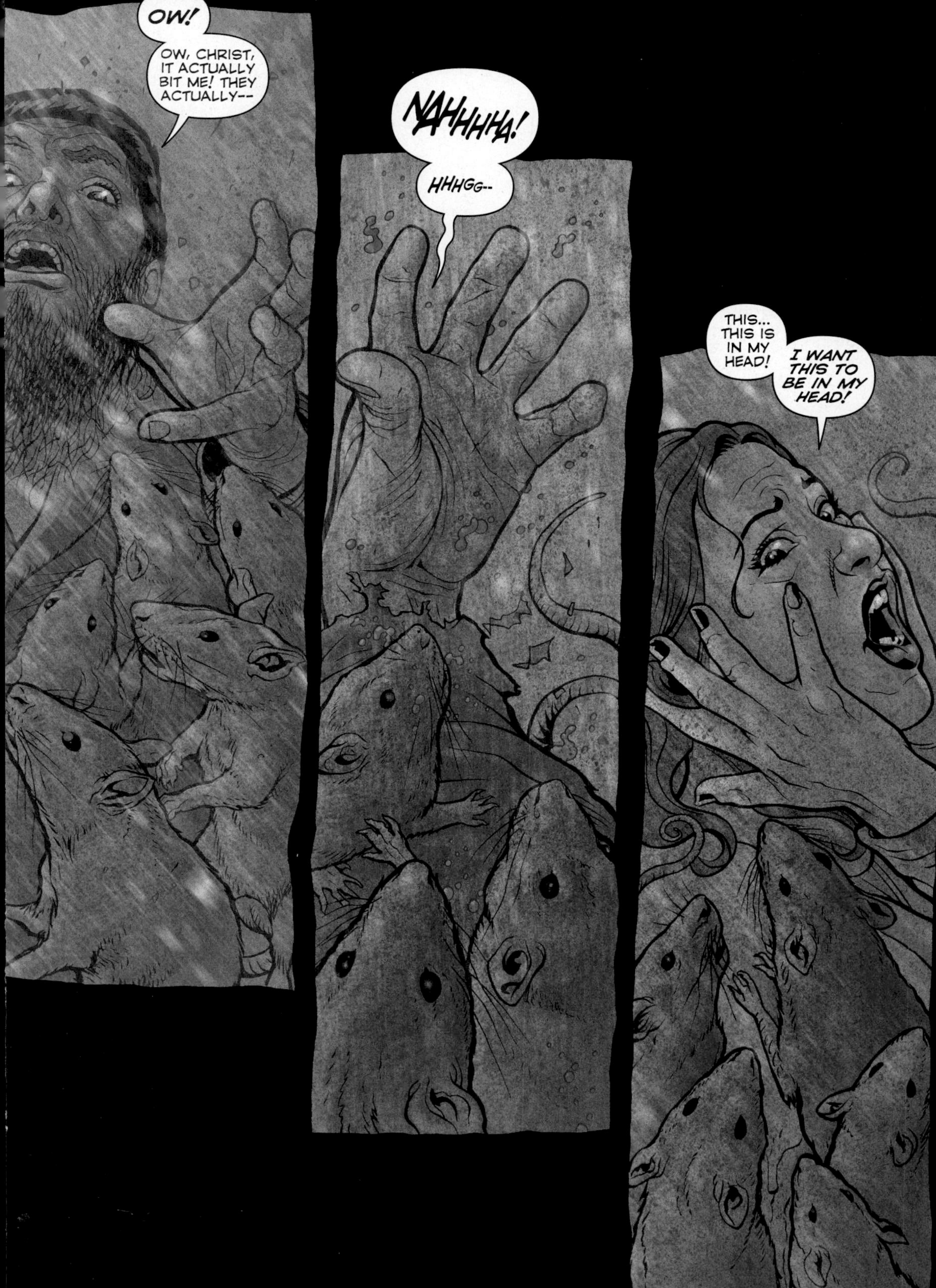
OW!
OW, CHRIST, IT ACTUALLY BIT ME! THEY ACTUALLY--
NAHHHHA!
HHHGG--
THIS... THIS IS IN MY HEAD!
I WANT THIS TO BE IN MY HEAD!

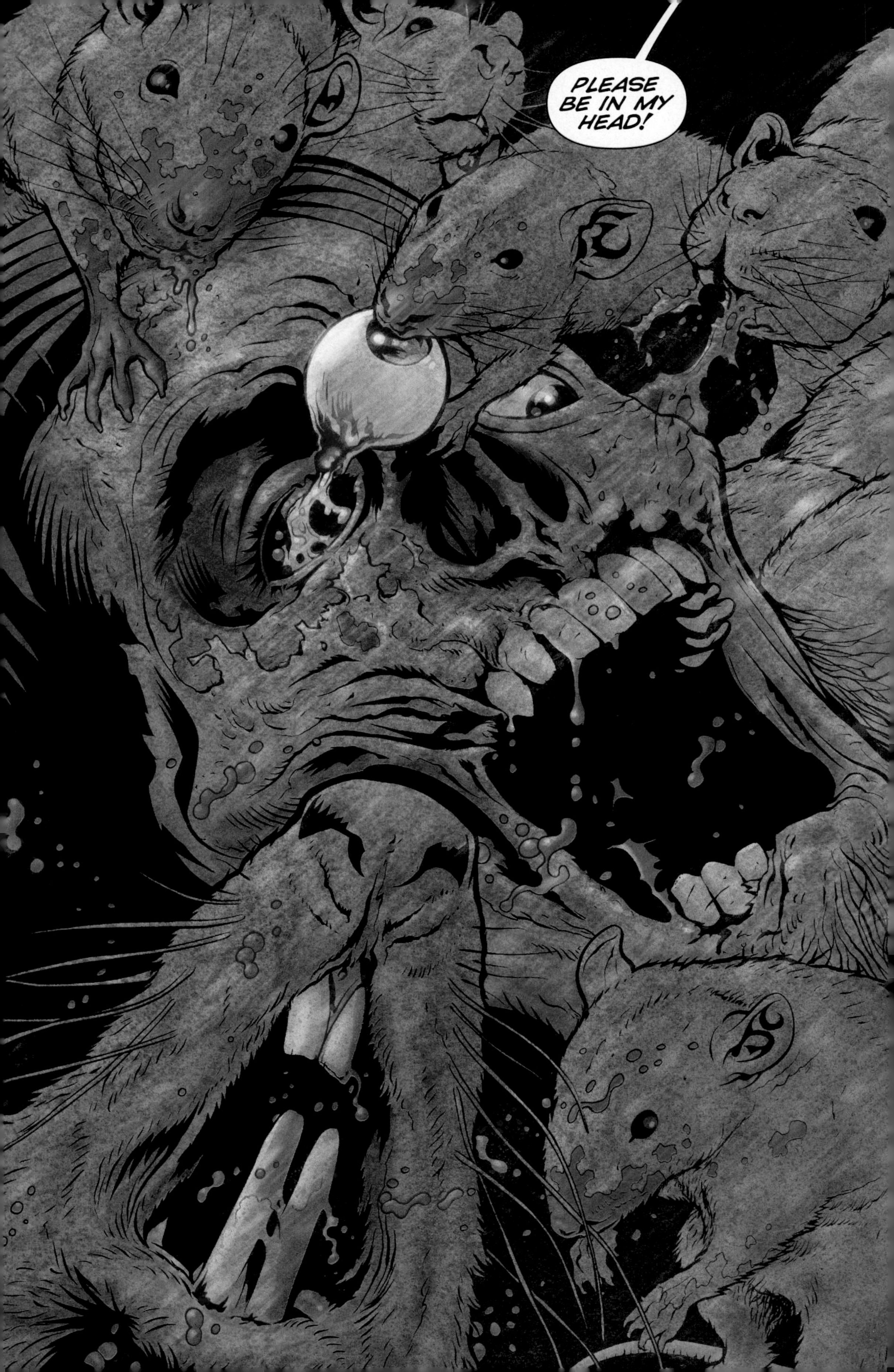
PLEASE BE IN MY HEAD!

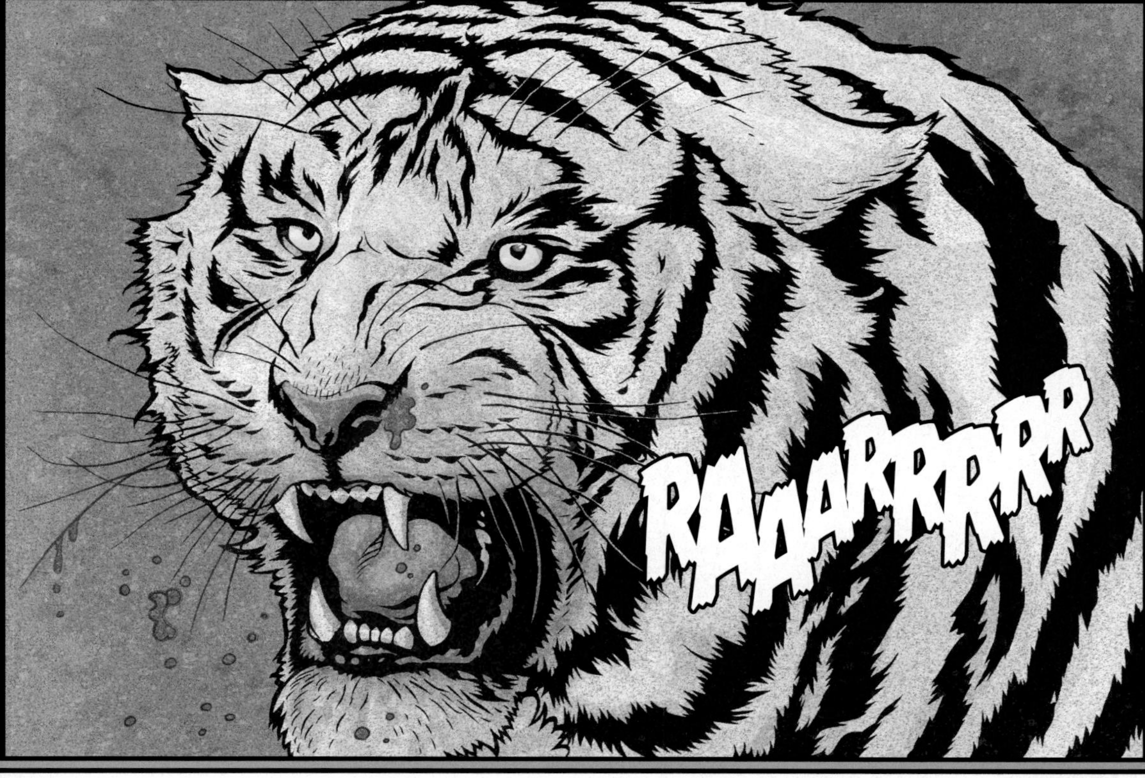
RAAARRRRR

FRIDAY, MARCH 29, 2001

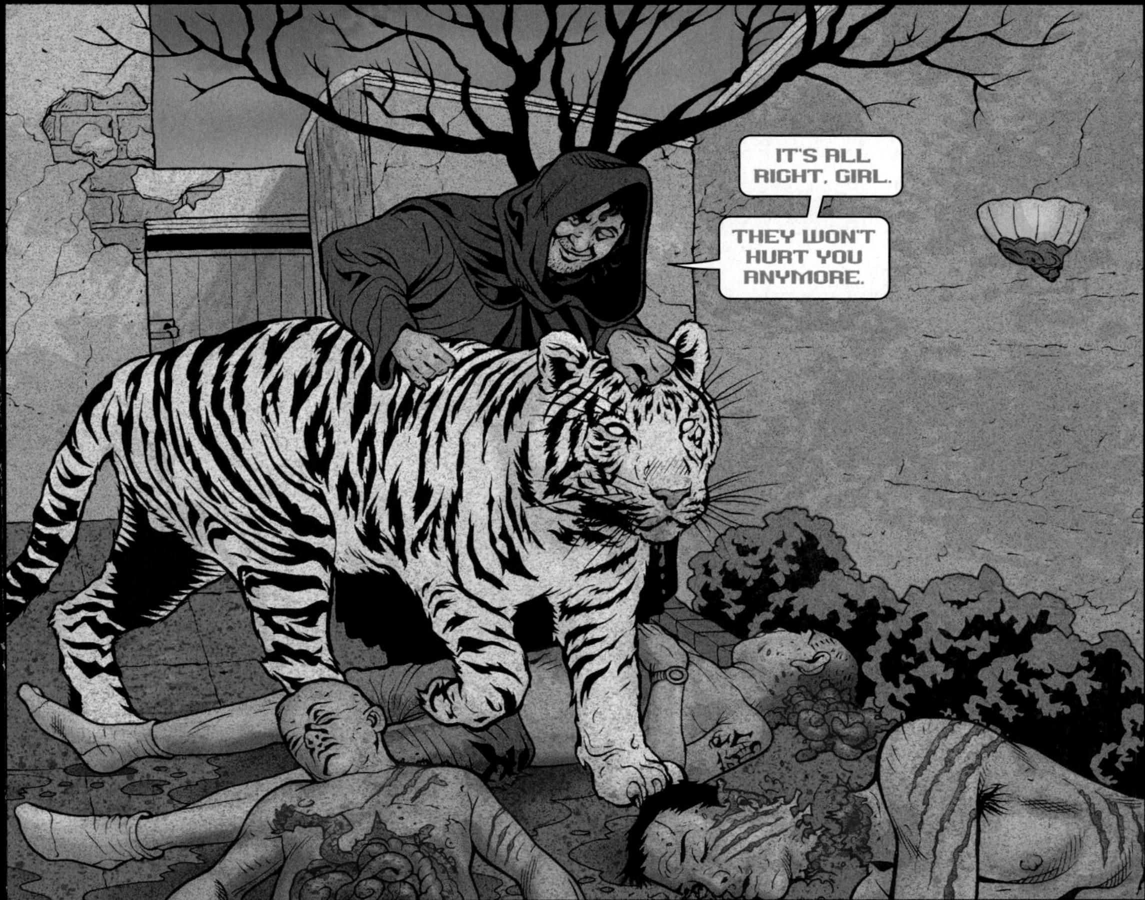
IT'S ALL RIGHT, GIRL.
THEY WON'T HURT YOU ANYMORE.

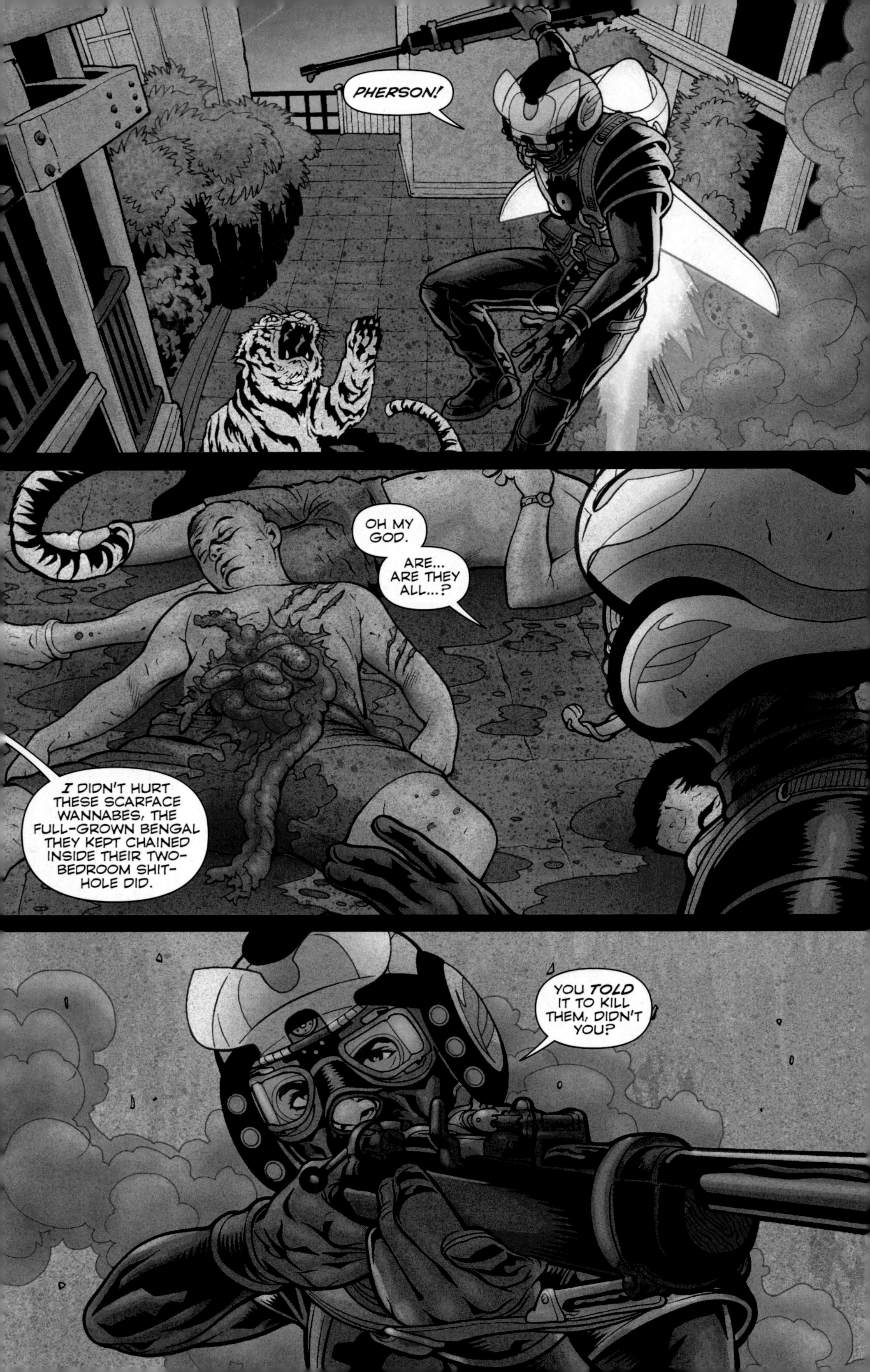
PHERSON!
OH MY GOD.
ARE... ARE THEY ALL...?
I DIDN'T HURT THESE SCARFACE WANNABES, THE FULL-GROWN BENGAL THEY KEPT CHAINED INSIDE THEIR TWO-BEDROOM SHIT-HOLE DID.
YOU TOLD IT TO KILL THEM, DIDN'T YOU?

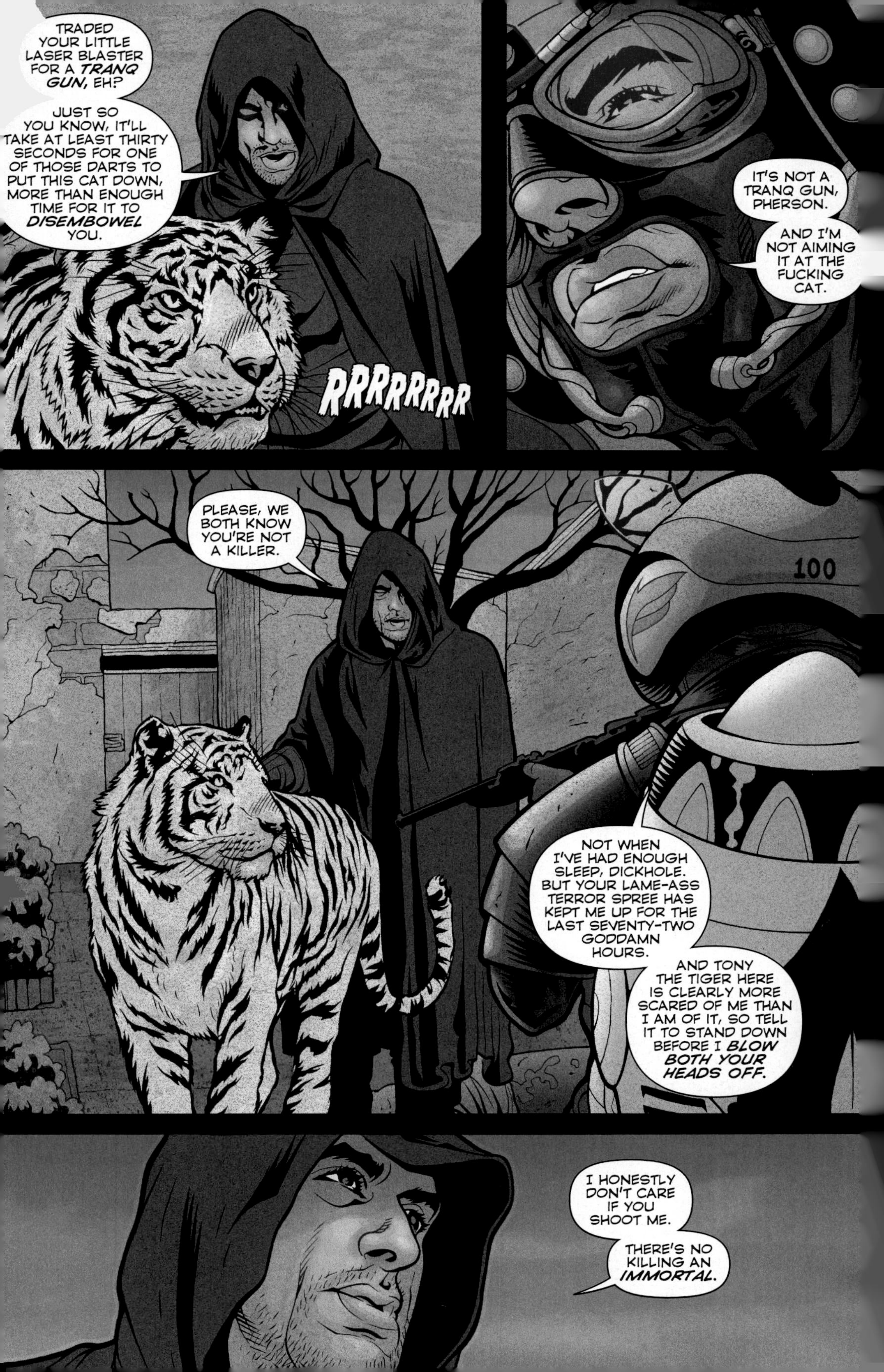

TRADED YOUR LITTLE LASER BLASTER FOR A *TRANQ GUN*, EH?
JUST SO YOU KNOW, IT'LL TAKE AT LEAST THIRTY SECONDS FOR ONE OF THOSE DARTS TO PUT THIS CAT DOWN, MORE THAN ENOUGH TIME FOR IT TO ***DISEMBOWEL*** YOU.
RRRRRRRR
IT'S NOT A TRANQ GUN, PHERSON.
AND I'M NOT AIMING IT AT THE FUCKING CAT.
PLEASE, WE BOTH KNOW YOU'RE NOT A KILLER.
100
NOT WHEN I'VE HAD ENOUGH SLEEP, DICKHOLE. BUT YOUR LAME-ASS TERROR SPREE HAS KEPT ME UP FOR THE LAST SEVENTY-TWO GODDAMN HOURS.
AND TONY THE TIGER HERE IS CLEARLY MORE SCARED OF ME THAN I AM OF IT, SO TELL IT TO STAND DOWN BEFORE I ***BLOW BOTH YOUR HEADS OFF***.
I HONESTLY DON'T CARE IF YOU SHOOT ME.
THERE'S NO KILLING AN ***IMMORTAL***.

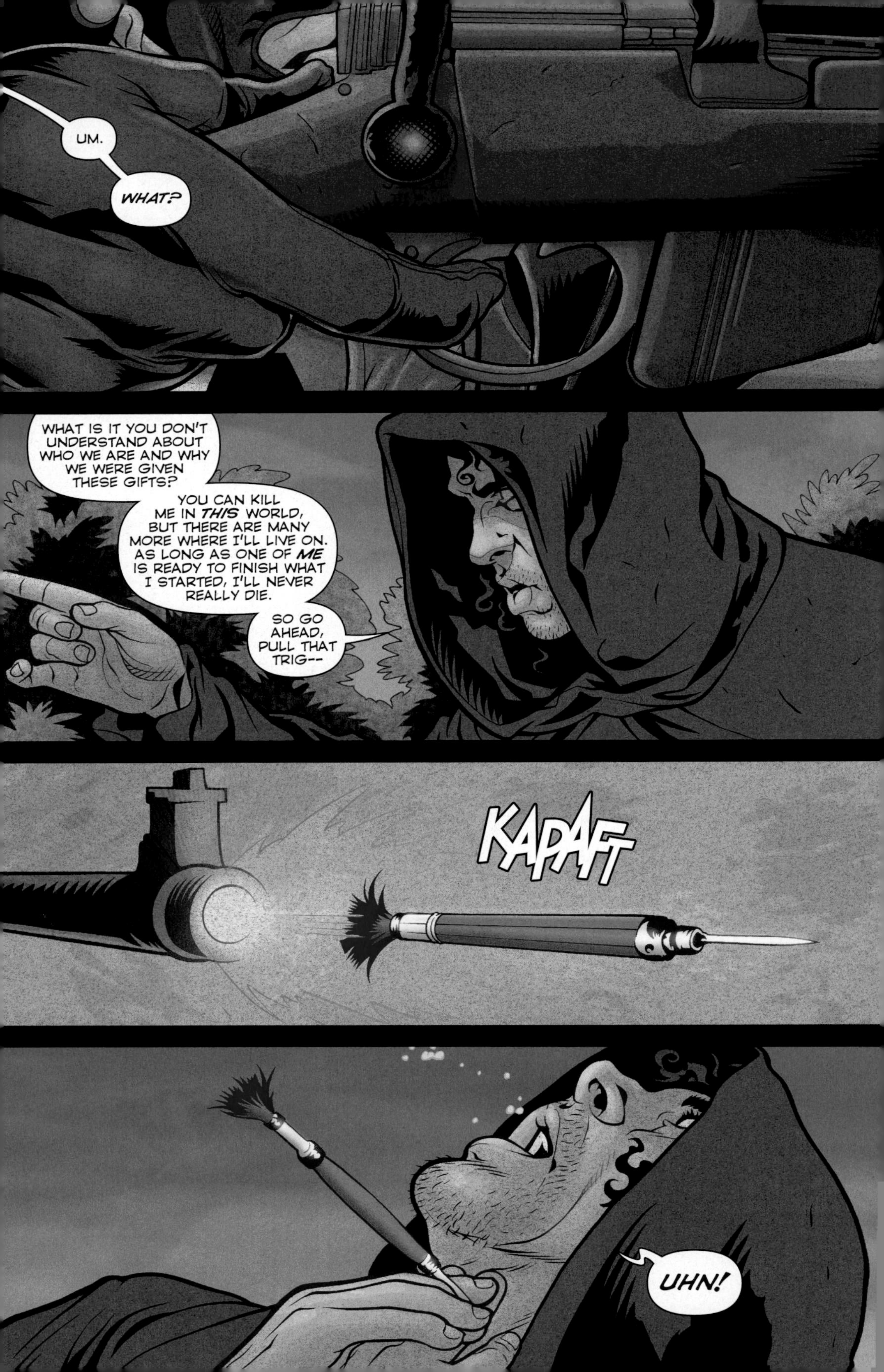
UM.
WHAT?
WHAT IS IT YOU DON'T UNDERSTAND ABOUT WHO WE ARE AND WHY WE WERE GIVEN THESE GIFTS?
YOU CAN KILL ME IN THIS WORLD, BUT THERE ARE MANY MORE WHERE I'LL LIVE ON. AS LONG AS ONE OF ME IS READY TO FINISH WHAT I STARTED, I'LL NEVER REALLY DIE.
SO GO AHEAD, PULL THAT TRIG--
KAPAFT
UHN!

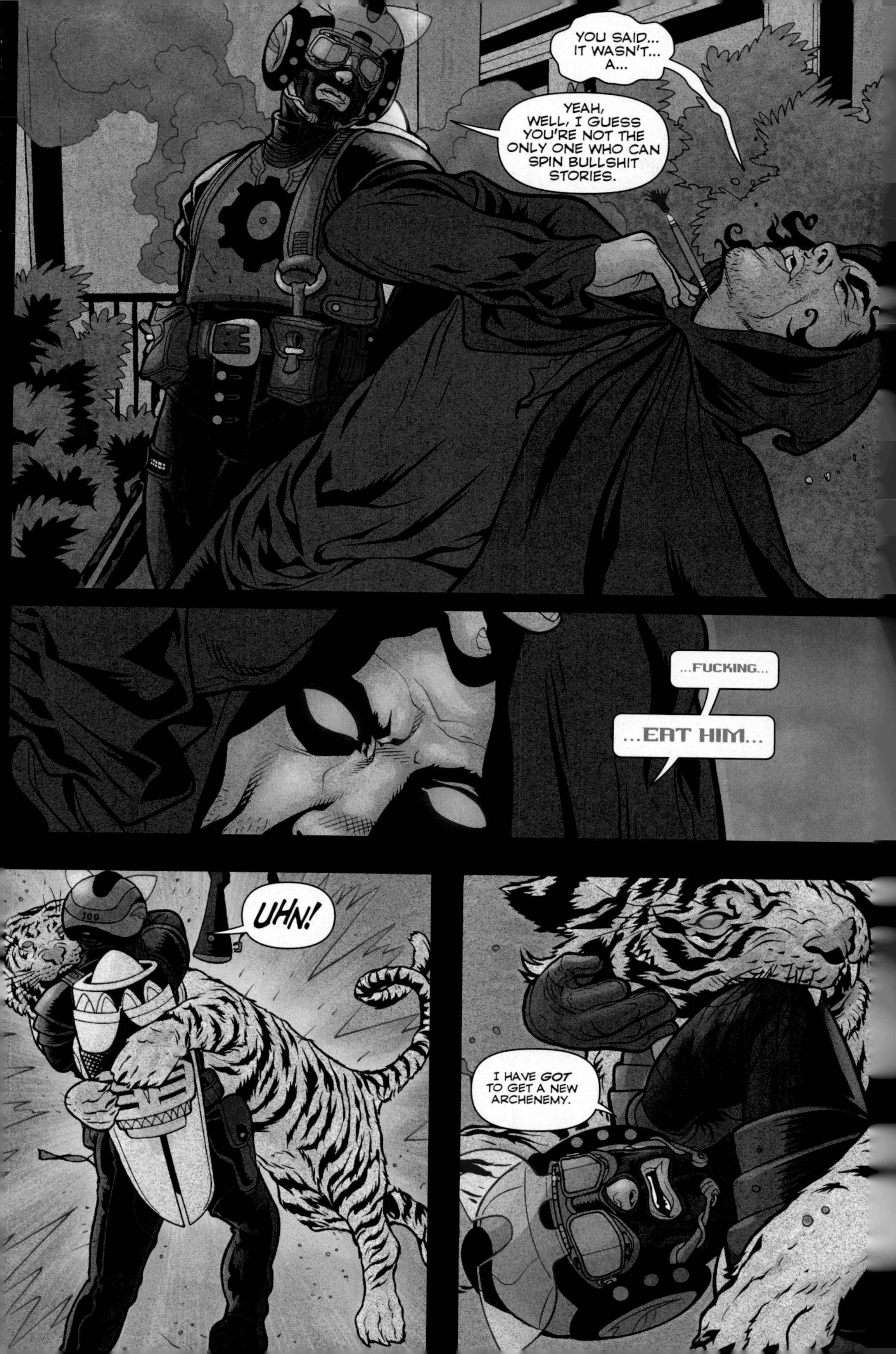
YOU SAID... IT WASN'T... A...
YEAH, WELL, I GUESS YOU'RE NOT THE ONLY ONE WHO CAN SPIN BULLSHIT STORIES.
...FUCKING...
...EAT HIM...
UHN!
I HAVE *GOT* TO GET A NEW ARCHENEMY.

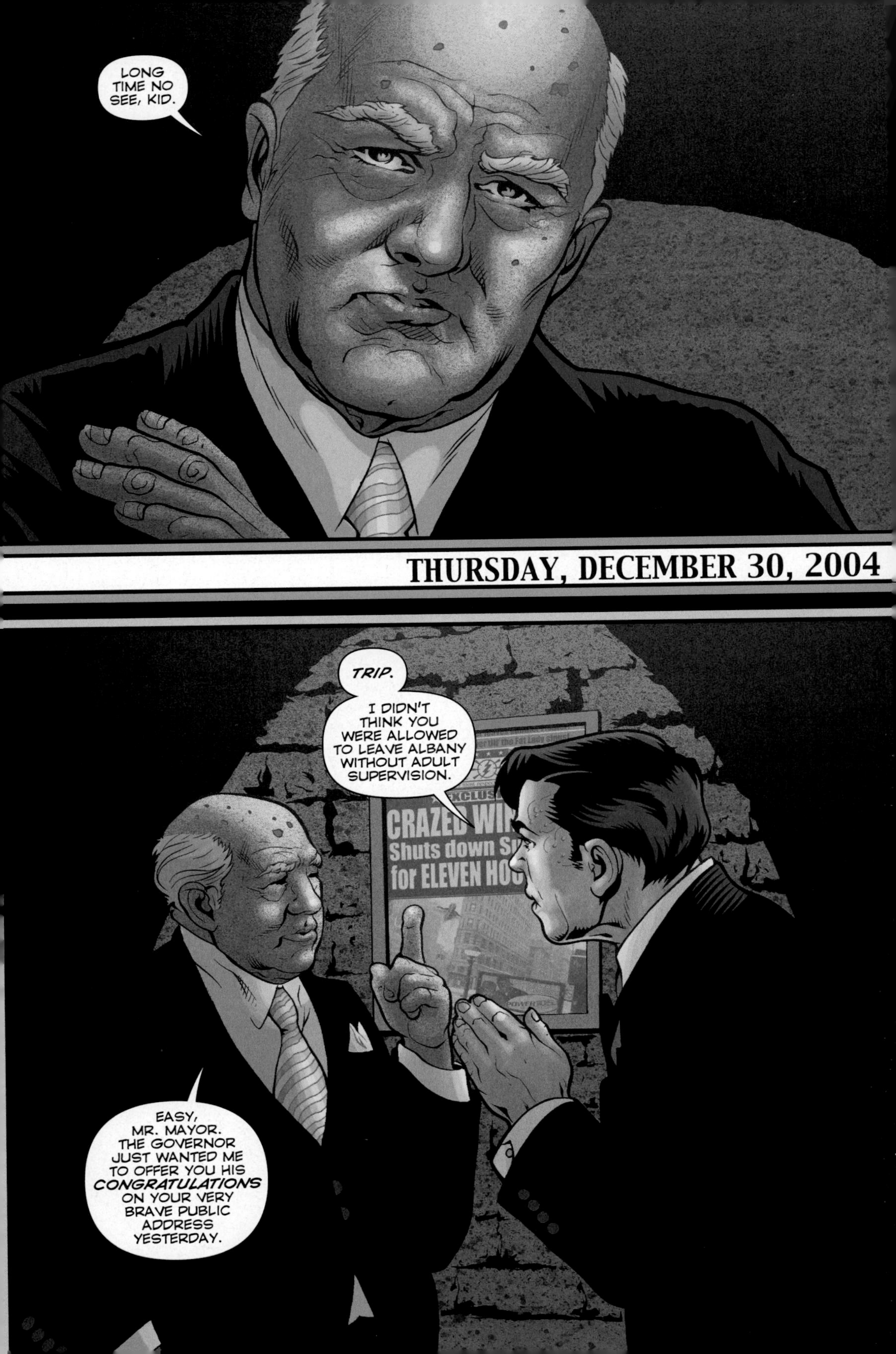

LONG TIME NO SEE, KID.
THURSDAY, DECEMBER 30, 2004
TRIP.
I DIDN'T THINK YOU WERE ALLOWED TO LEAVE ALBANY WITHOUT ADULT SUPERVISION.
EASY, MR. MAYOR. THE GOVERNOR JUST WANTED ME TO OFFER YOU HIS *CONGRATULATIONS* ON YOUR VERY BRAVE PUBLIC ADDRESS YESTERDAY.

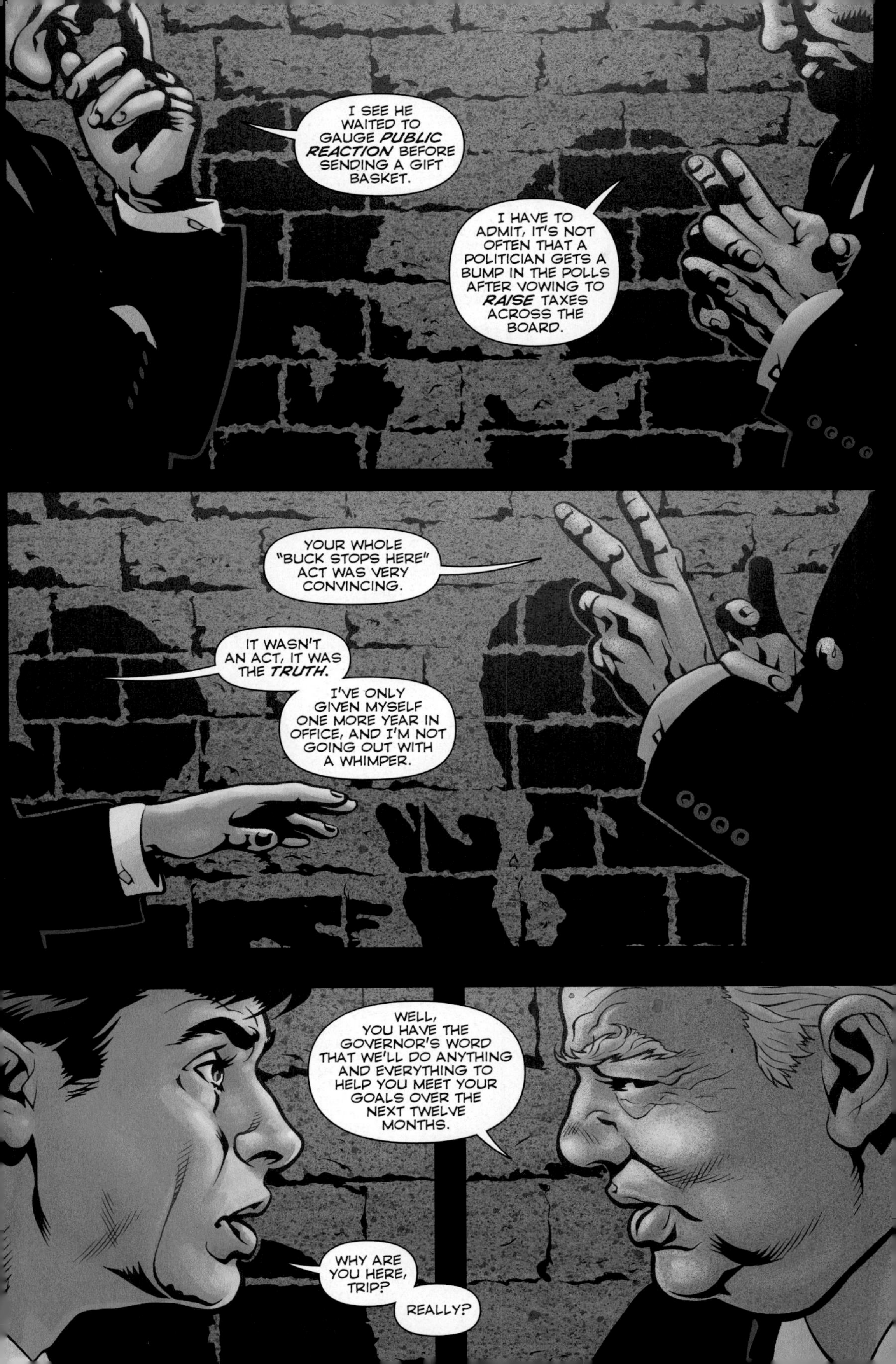
I SEE HE WAITED TO GAUGE PUBLIC REACTION BEFORE SENDING A GIFT BASKET.
I HAVE TO ADMIT, IT'S NOT OFTEN THAT A POLITICIAN GETS A BUMP IN THE POLLS AFTER VOWING TO RAISE TAXES ACROSS THE BOARD.
YOUR WHOLE "BUCK STOPS HERE" ACT WAS VERY CONVINCING.
IT WASN'T AN ACT, IT WAS THE TRUTH.
I'VE ONLY GIVEN MYSELF ONE MORE YEAR IN OFFICE, AND I'M NOT GOING OUT WITH A WHIMPER.
WELL, YOU HAVE THE GOVERNOR'S WORD THAT WE'LL DO ANYTHING AND EVERYTHING TO HELP YOU MEET YOUR GOALS OVER THE NEXT TWELVE MONTHS.
WHY ARE YOU HERE, TRIP?
REALLY?

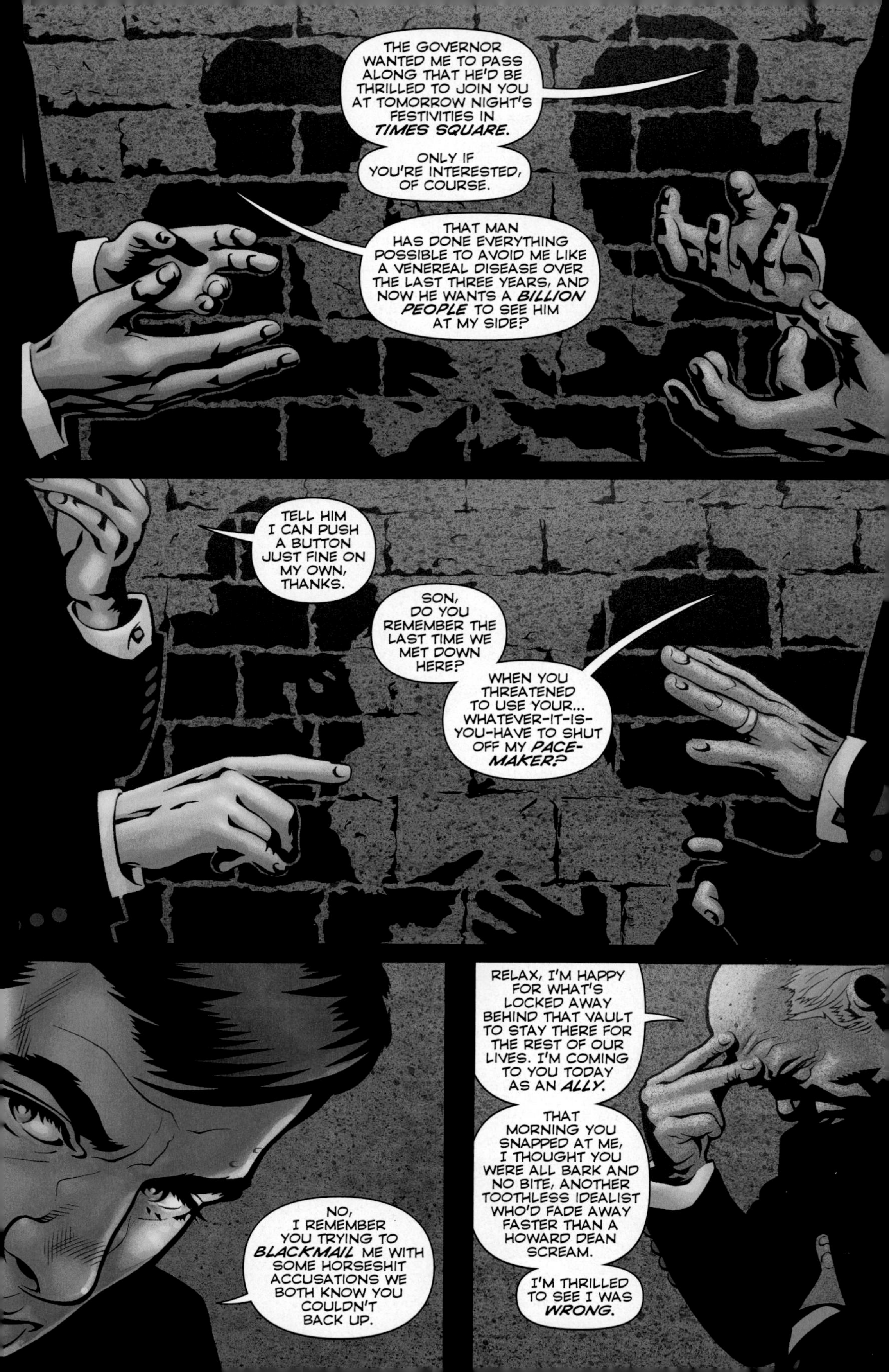
THE GOVERNOR WANTED ME TO PASS ALONG THAT HE'D BE THRILLED TO JOIN YOU AT TOMORROW NIGHT'S FESTIVITIES IN TIMES SQUARE.
ONLY IF YOU'RE INTERESTED, OF COURSE.
THAT MAN HAS DONE EVERYTHING POSSIBLE TO AVOID ME LIKE A VENEREAL DISEASE OVER THE LAST THREE YEARS, AND NOW HE WANTS A BILLION PEOPLE TO SEE HIM AT MY SIDE?
TELL HIM I CAN PUSH A BUTTON JUST FINE ON MY OWN, THANKS.
SON, DO YOU REMEMBER THE LAST TIME WE MET DOWN HERE?
WHEN YOU THREATENED TO USE YOUR... WHATEVER-IT-IS-YOU-HAVE TO SHUT OFF MY PACE-MAKER?
NO, I REMEMBER YOU TRYING TO BLACKMAIL ME WITH SOME HORSESHIT ACCUSATIONS WE BOTH KNOW YOU COULDN'T BACK UP.
RELAX, I'M HAPPY FOR WHAT'S LOCKED AWAY BEHIND THAT VAULT TO STAY THERE FOR THE REST OF OUR LIVES. I'M COMING TO YOU TODAY AS AN ALLY.
THAT MORNING YOU SNAPPED AT ME, I THOUGHT YOU WERE ALL BARK AND NO BITE, ANOTHER TOOTHLESS IDEALIST WHO'D FADE AWAY FASTER THAN A HOWARD DEAN SCREAM.
I'M THRILLED TO SEE I WAS WRONG.

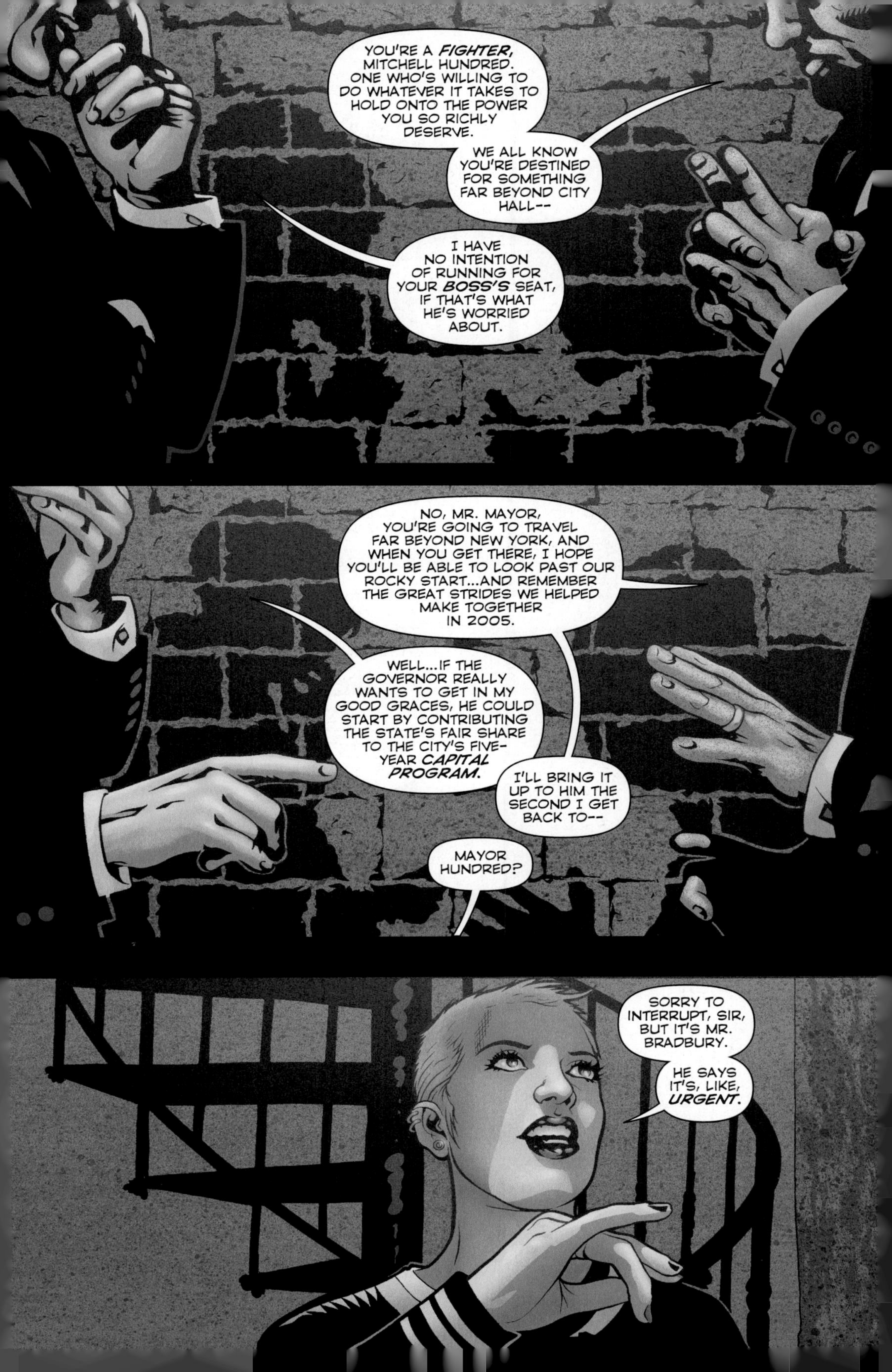
YOU'RE A FIGHTER, MITCHELL HUNDRED. ONE WHO'S WILLING TO DO WHATEVER IT TAKES TO HOLD ONTO THE POWER YOU SO RICHLY DESERVE.
WE ALL KNOW YOU'RE DESTINED FOR SOMETHING FAR BEYOND CITY HALL--
I HAVE NO INTENTION OF RUNNING FOR YOUR BOSS'S SEAT, IF THAT'S WHAT HE'S WORRIED ABOUT.
NO, MR. MAYOR, YOU'RE GOING TO TRAVEL FAR BEYOND NEW YORK, AND WHEN YOU GET THERE, I HOPE YOU'LL BE ABLE TO LOOK PAST OUR ROCKY START...AND REMEMBER THE GREAT STRIDES WE HELPED MAKE TOGETHER IN 2005.
WELL...IF THE GOVERNOR REALLY WANTS TO GET IN MY GOOD GRACES, HE COULD START BY CONTRIBUTING THE STATE'S FAIR SHARE TO THE CITY'S FIVE-YEAR CAPITAL PROGRAM.
I'LL BRING IT UP TO HIM THE SECOND I GET BACK TO--
MAYOR HUNDRED?
SORRY TO INTERRUPT, SIR, BUT IT'S MR. BRADBURY.
HE SAYS IT'S, LIKE, URGENT.

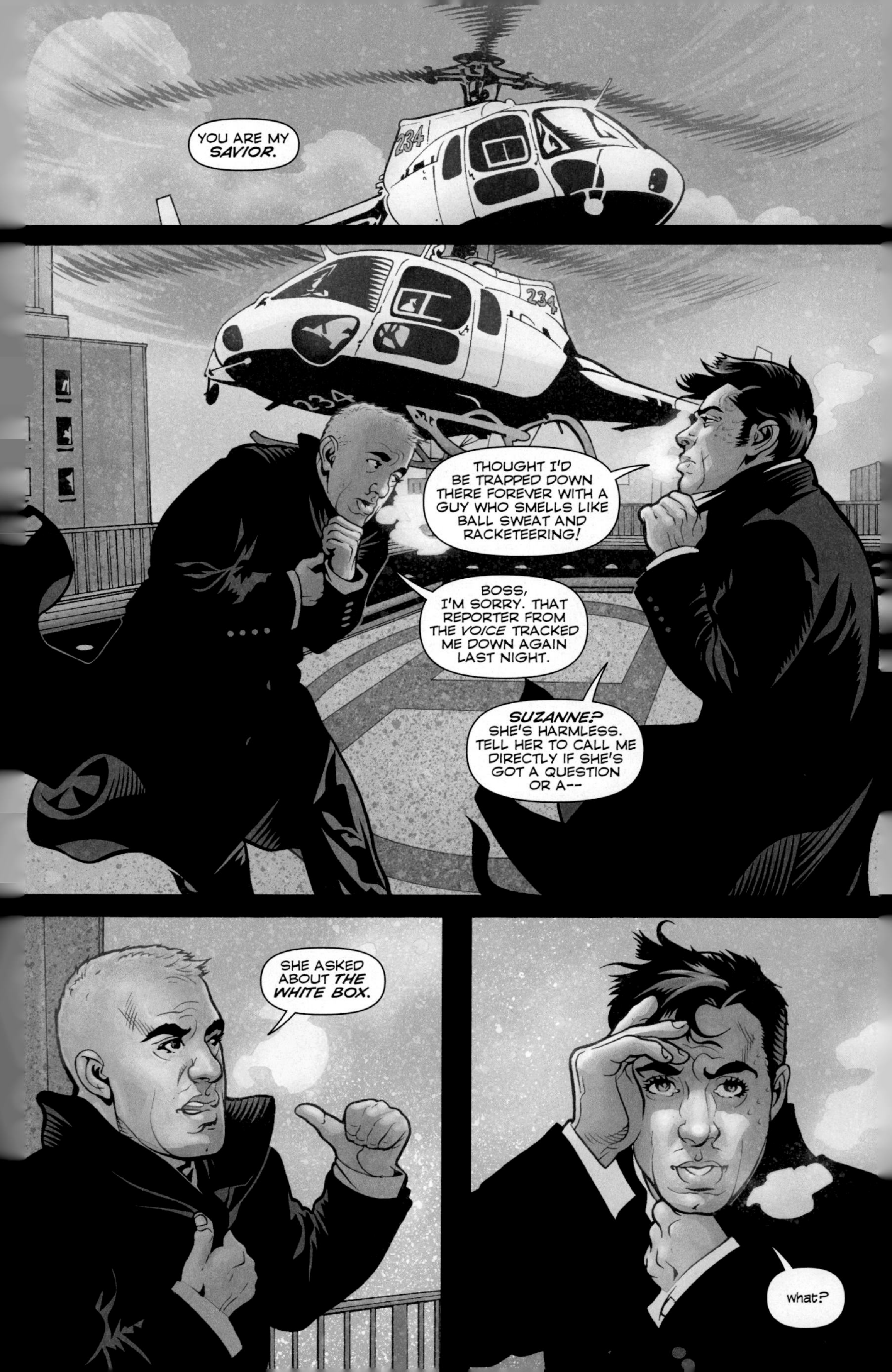
YOU ARE MY SAVIOR.
THOUGHT I'D BE TRAPPED DOWN THERE FOREVER WITH A GUY WHO SMELLS LIKE BALL SWEAT AND RACKETEERING!
BOSS, I'M SORRY. THAT REPORTER FROM THE VOICE TRACKED ME DOWN AGAIN LAST NIGHT.
SUZANNE? SHE'S HARMLESS. TELL HER TO CALL ME DIRECTLY IF SHE'S GOT A QUESTION OR A--
SHE ASKED ABOUT THE WHITE BOX.
what?

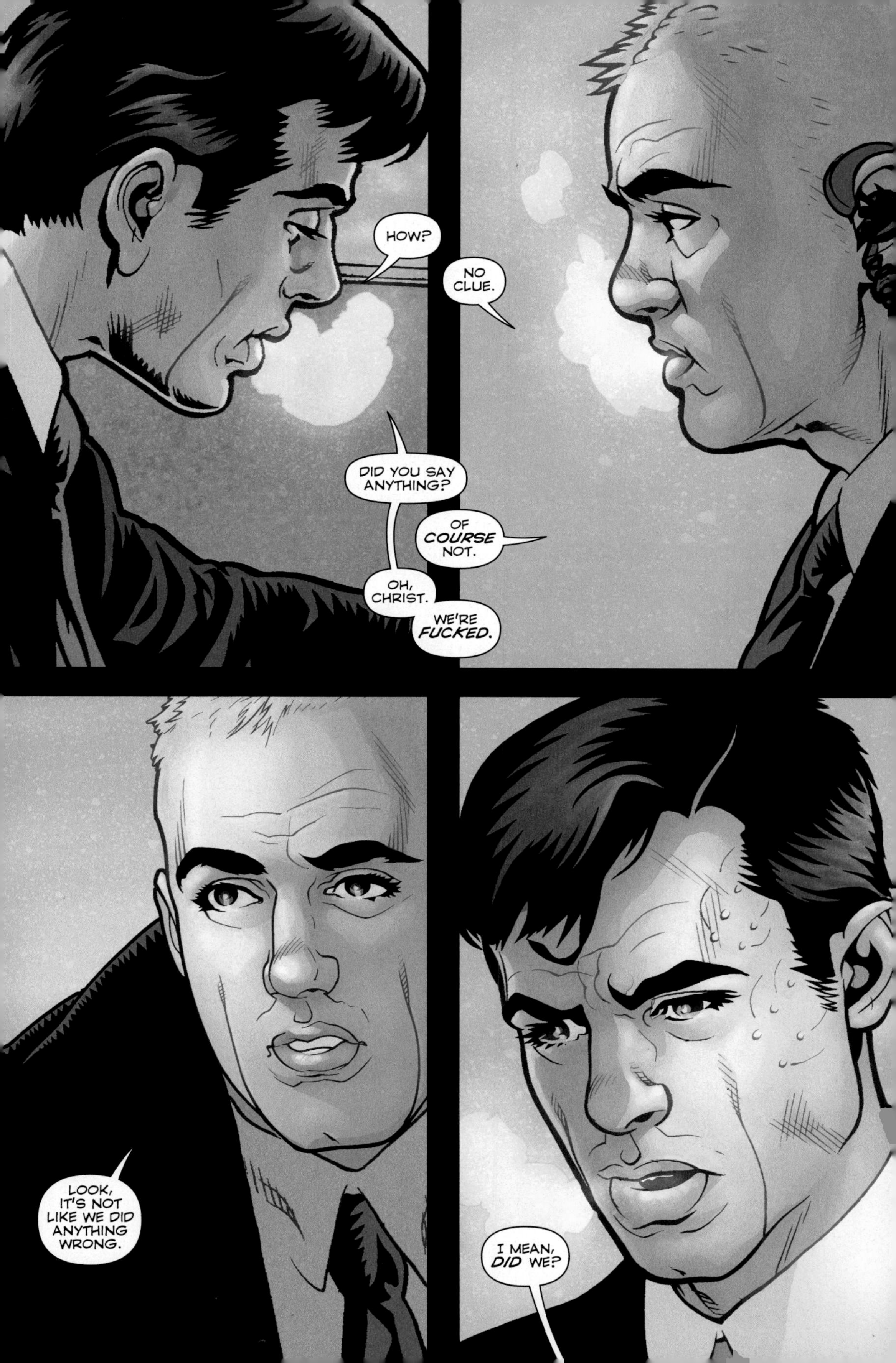
HOW?
NO CLUE.
DID YOU SAY ANYTHING?
OF *COURSE* NOT.
OH, CHRIST.
WE'RE *FUCKED*.
LOOK, IT'S NOT LIKE WE DID ANYTHING WRONG.
I MEAN, *DID* WE?

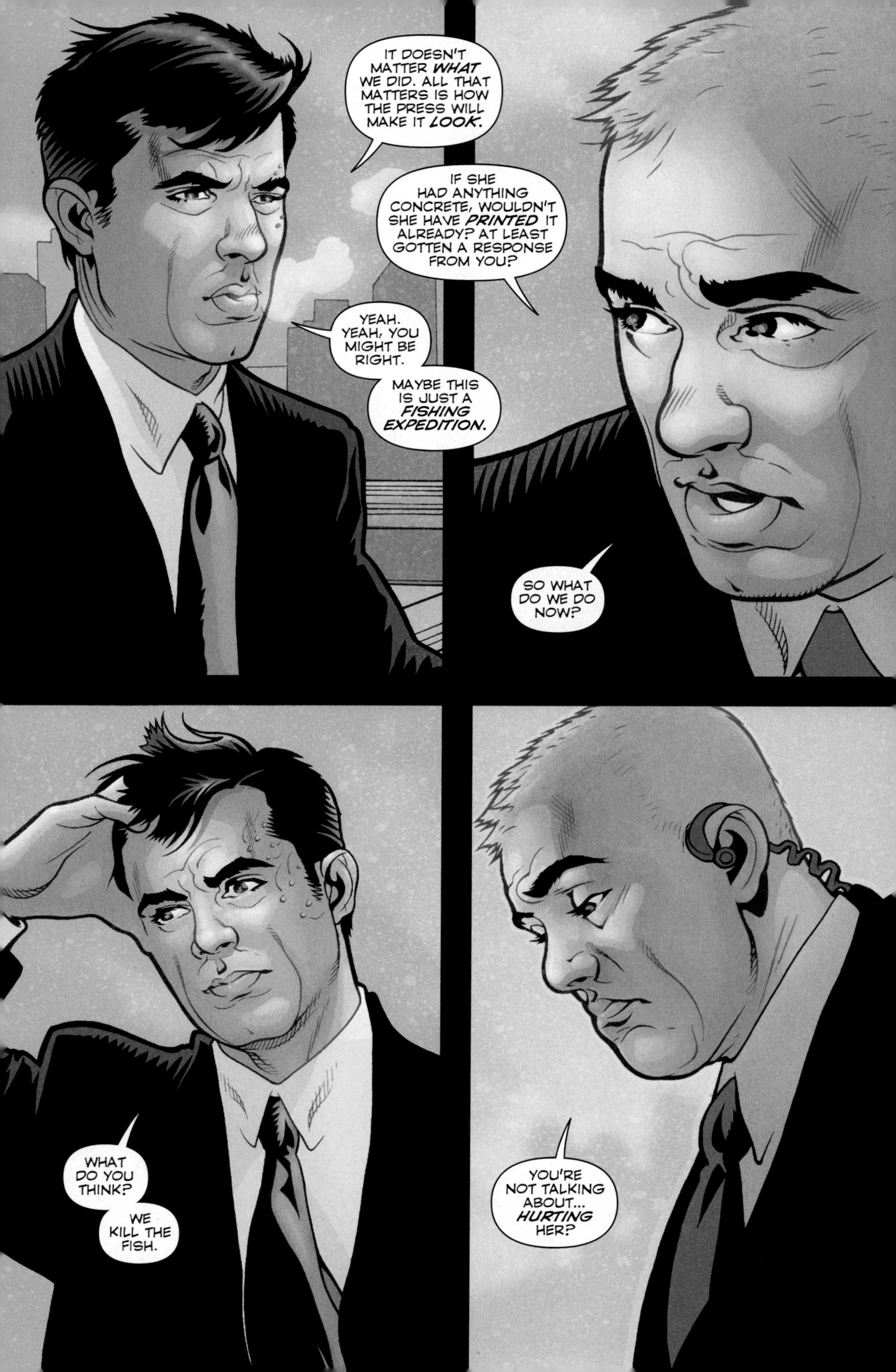
IT DOESN'T MATTER WHAT WE DID. ALL THAT MATTERS IS HOW THE PRESS WILL MAKE IT LOOK.
IF SHE HAD ANYTHING CONCRETE, WOULDN'T SHE HAVE PRINTED IT ALREADY? AT LEAST GOTTEN A RESPONSE FROM YOU?
YEAH. YEAH, YOU MIGHT BE RIGHT.
MAYBE THIS IS JUST A FISHING EXPEDITION.
SO WHAT DO WE DO NOW?
WHAT DO YOU THINK?
WE KILL THE FISH.
YOU'RE NOT TALKING ABOUT... HURTING HER?

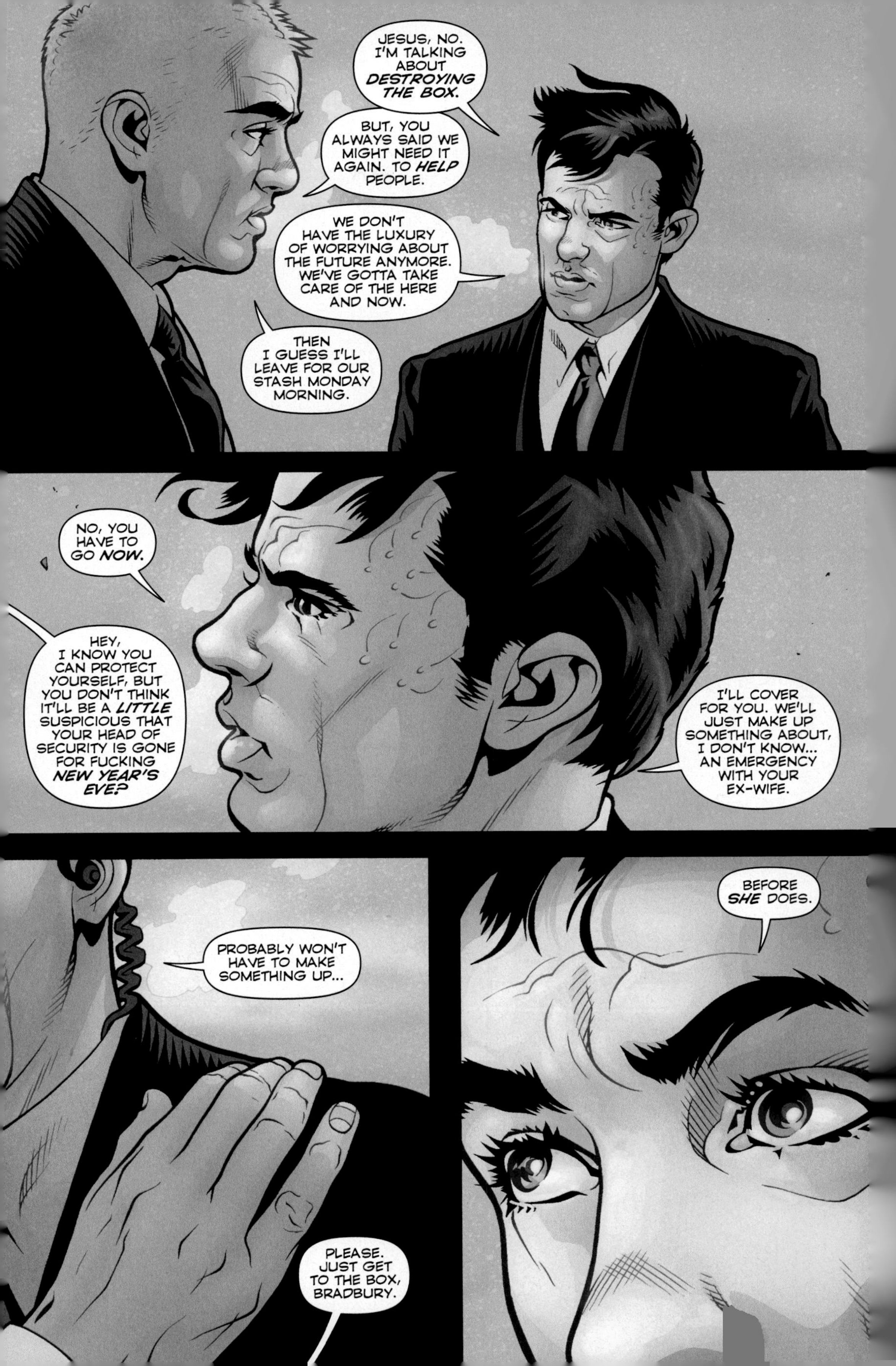
JESUS, NO. I'M TALKING ABOUT *DESTROYING THE BOX.*
BUT, YOU ALWAYS SAID WE MIGHT NEED IT AGAIN. TO *HELP* PEOPLE.
WE DON'T HAVE THE LUXURY OF WORRYING ABOUT THE FUTURE ANYMORE. WE'VE GOTTA TAKE CARE OF THE HERE AND NOW.
THEN I GUESS I'LL LEAVE FOR OUR STASH MONDAY MORNING.
NO, YOU HAVE TO GO *NOW.*
HEY, I KNOW YOU CAN PROTECT YOURSELF, BUT YOU DON'T THINK IT'LL BE A *LITTLE* SUSPICIOUS THAT YOUR HEAD OF SECURITY IS GONE FOR FUCKING *NEW YEAR'S EVE?*
I'LL COVER FOR YOU. WE'LL JUST MAKE UP SOMETHING ABOUT, I DON'T KNOW... AN EMERGENCY WITH YOUR EX-WIFE.
PROBABLY WON'T HAVE TO MAKE SOMETHING UP...
BEFORE *SHE* DOES.
PLEASE. JUST GET TO THE BOX, BRADBURY.

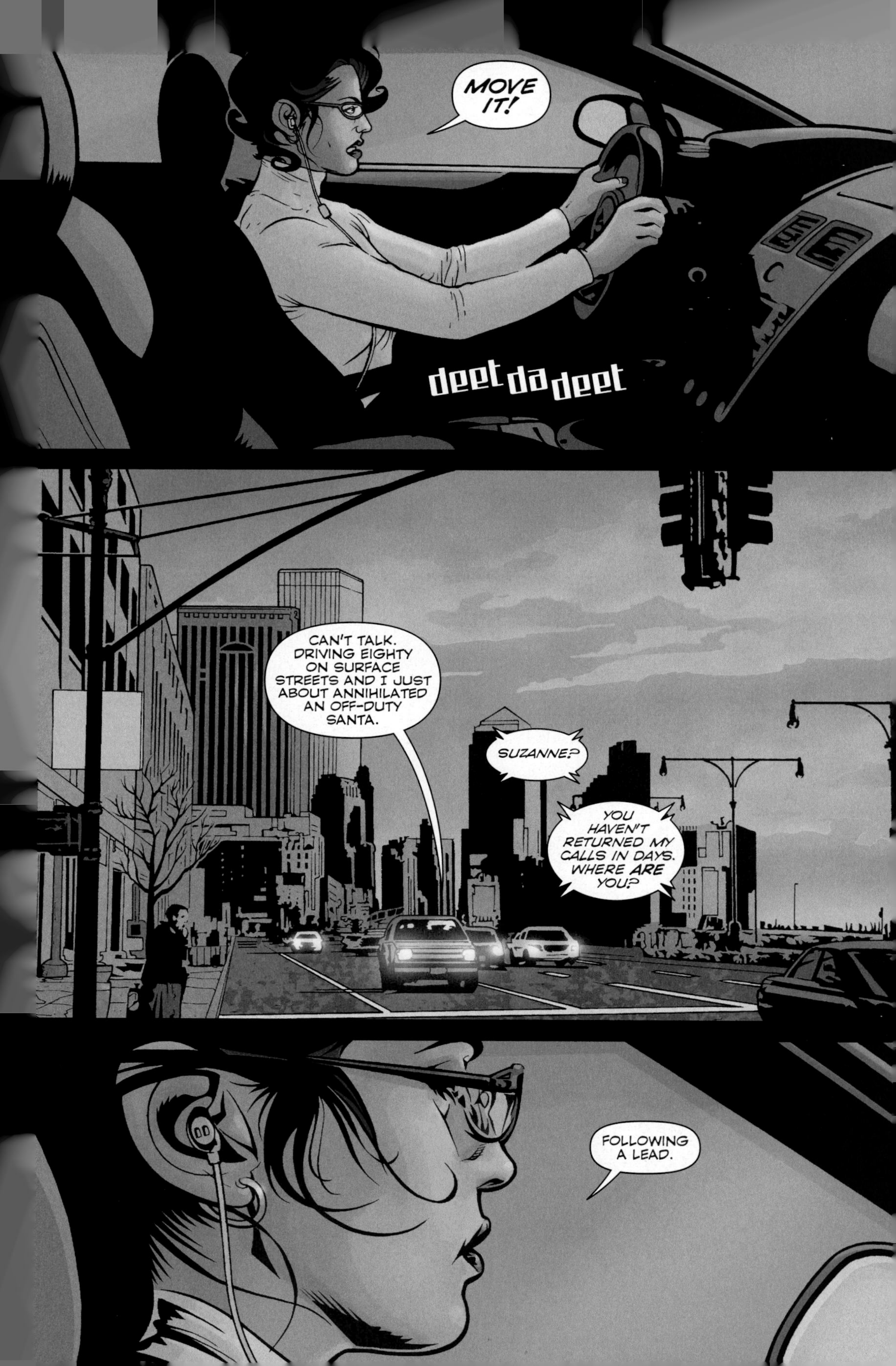
MOVE IT!
deet da deet
CAN'T TALK. DRIVING EIGHTY ON SURFACE STREETS AND I JUST ABOUT ANNIHILATED AN OFF-DUTY SANTA.
SUZANNE?
YOU HAVEN'T RETURNED MY CALLS IN DAYS. WHERE ARE YOU?
FOLLOWING A LEAD.

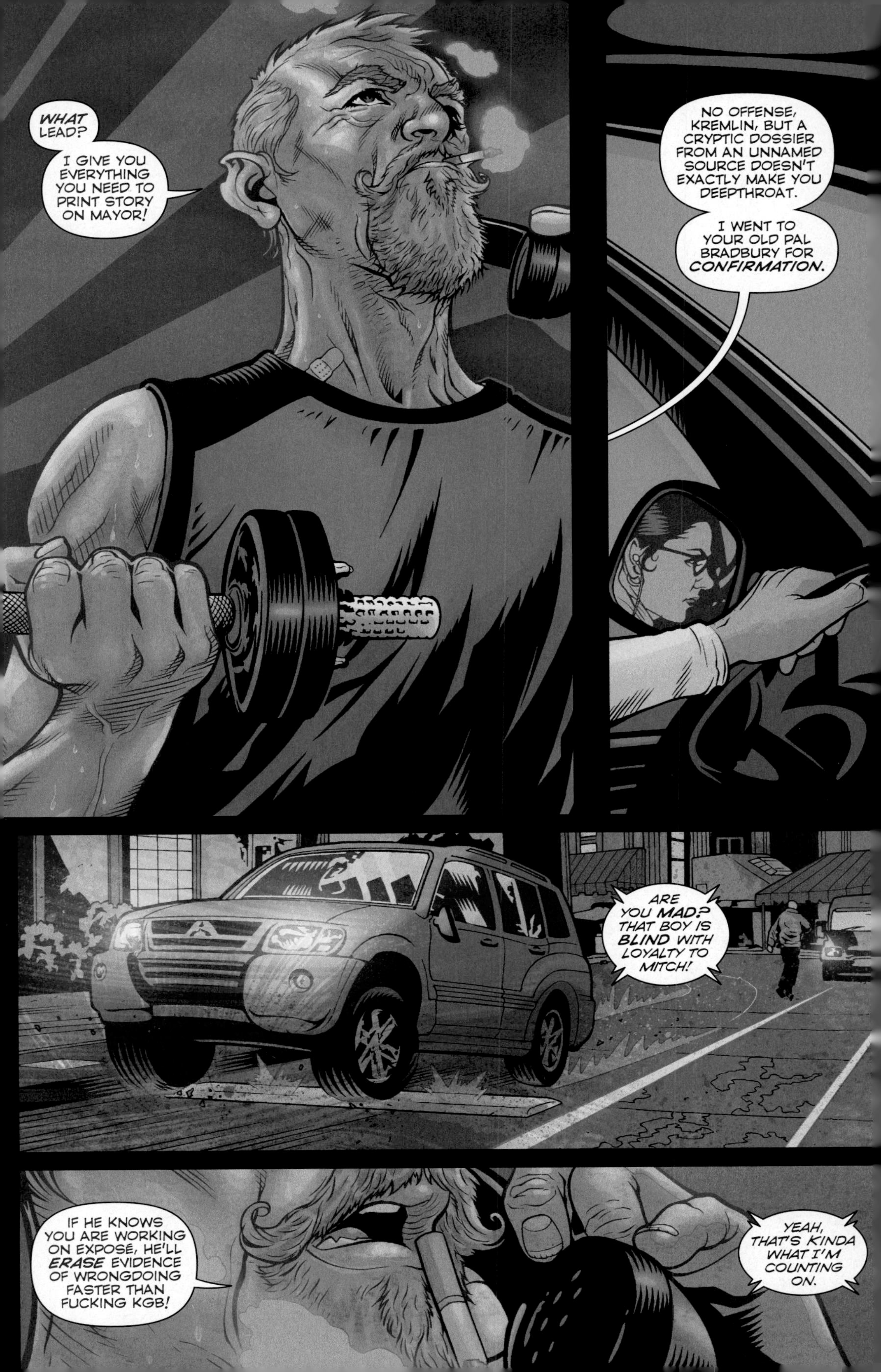
WHAT LEAD?
I GIVE YOU EVERYTHING YOU NEED TO PRINT STORY ON MAYOR!
NO OFFENSE, KREMLIN, BUT A CRYPTIC DOSSIER FROM AN UNNAMED SOURCE DOESN'T EXACTLY MAKE YOU DEEPTHROAT.
I WENT TO YOUR OLD PAL BRADBURY FOR CONFIRMATION.
ARE YOU MAD? THAT BOY IS BLIND WITH LOYALTY TO MITCH!
IF HE KNOWS YOU ARE WORKING ON EXPOSÉ, HE'LL ERASE EVIDENCE OF WRONGDOING FASTER THAN FUCKING KGB!
YEAH, THAT'S KINDA WHAT I'M COUNTING ON.

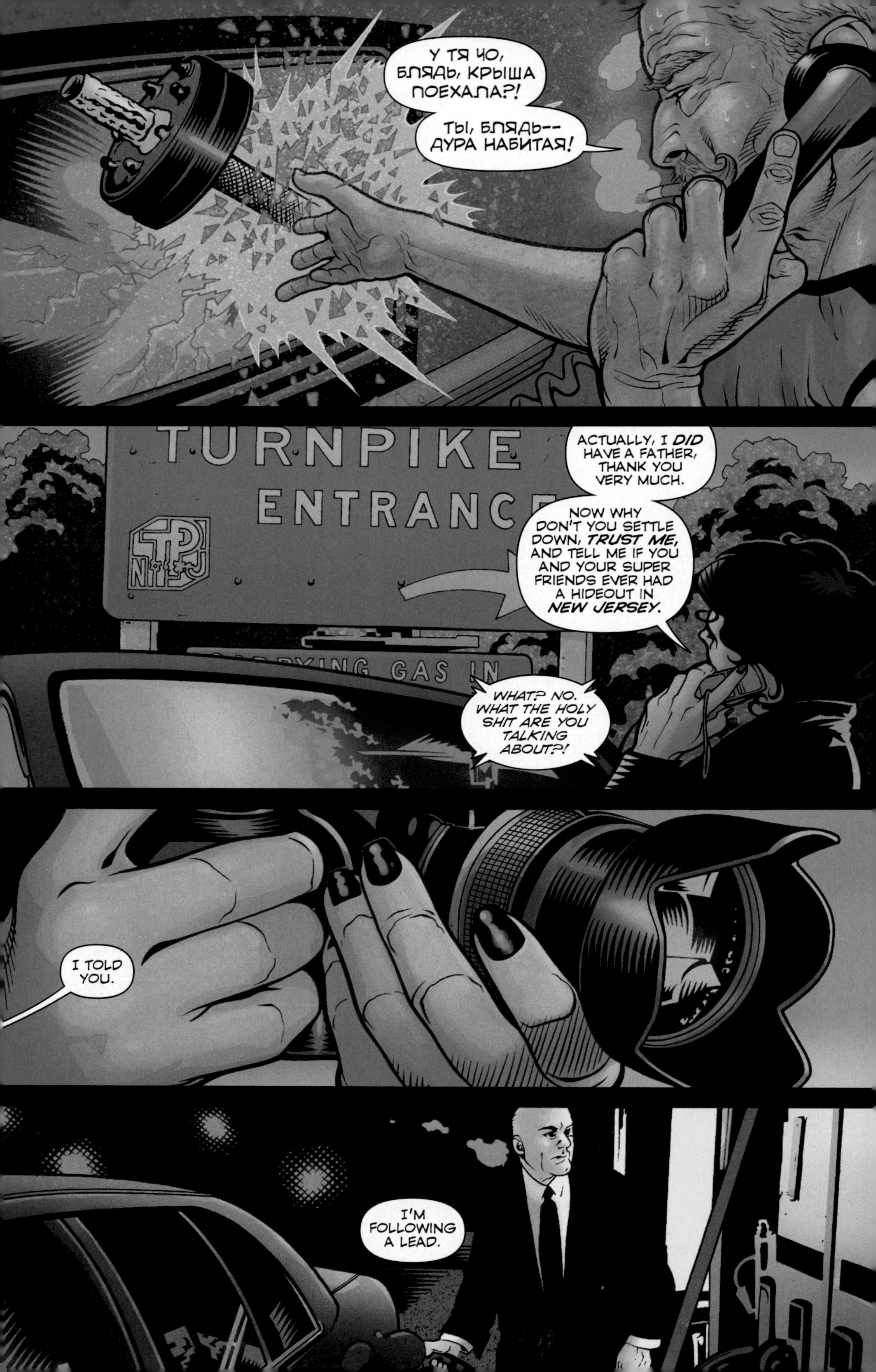
У ТЯ ЧО, БЛЯДЬ, КРЫША ПОЕХАЛА?!
ТЫ, БЛЯДЬ-- ДУРА НАБИТАЯ!
TURNPIKE ENTRANCE
ACTUALLY, I *DID* HAVE A FATHER, THANK YOU VERY MUCH.
NOW WHY DON'T YOU SETTLE DOWN, ***TRUST ME,*** AND TELL ME IF YOU AND YOUR SUPER FRIENDS EVER HAD A HIDEOUT IN ***NEW JERSEY.***
WHAT? NO. WHAT THE HOLY SHIT ARE YOU TALKING ABOUT?!
I TOLD YOU.
I'M FOLLOWING A LEAD.

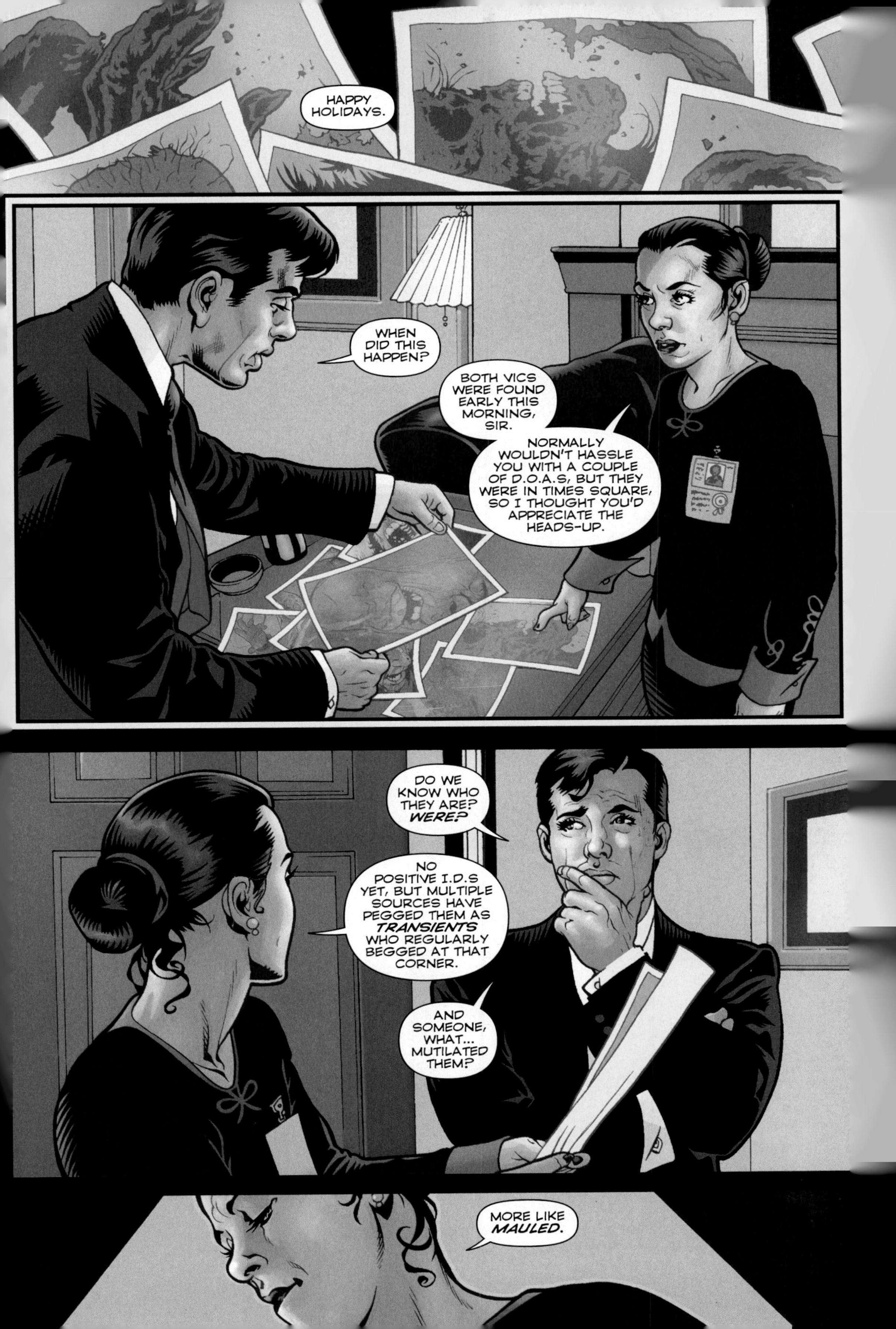
HAPPY HOLIDAYS.
WHEN DID THIS HAPPEN?
BOTH VICS WERE FOUND EARLY THIS MORNING, SIR.
NORMALLY WOULDN'T HASSLE YOU WITH A COUPLE OF D.O.A.S, BUT THEY WERE IN TIMES SQUARE, SO I THOUGHT YOU'D APPRECIATE THE HEADS-UP.
DO WE KNOW WHO THEY ARE? *WERE?*
NO POSITIVE I.D.S YET, BUT MULTIPLE SOURCES HAVE PEGGED THEM AS *TRANSIENTS* WHO REGULARLY BEGGED AT THAT CORNER.
AND SOMEONE, WHAT... MUTILATED THEM?
MORE LIKE *MAULED*.

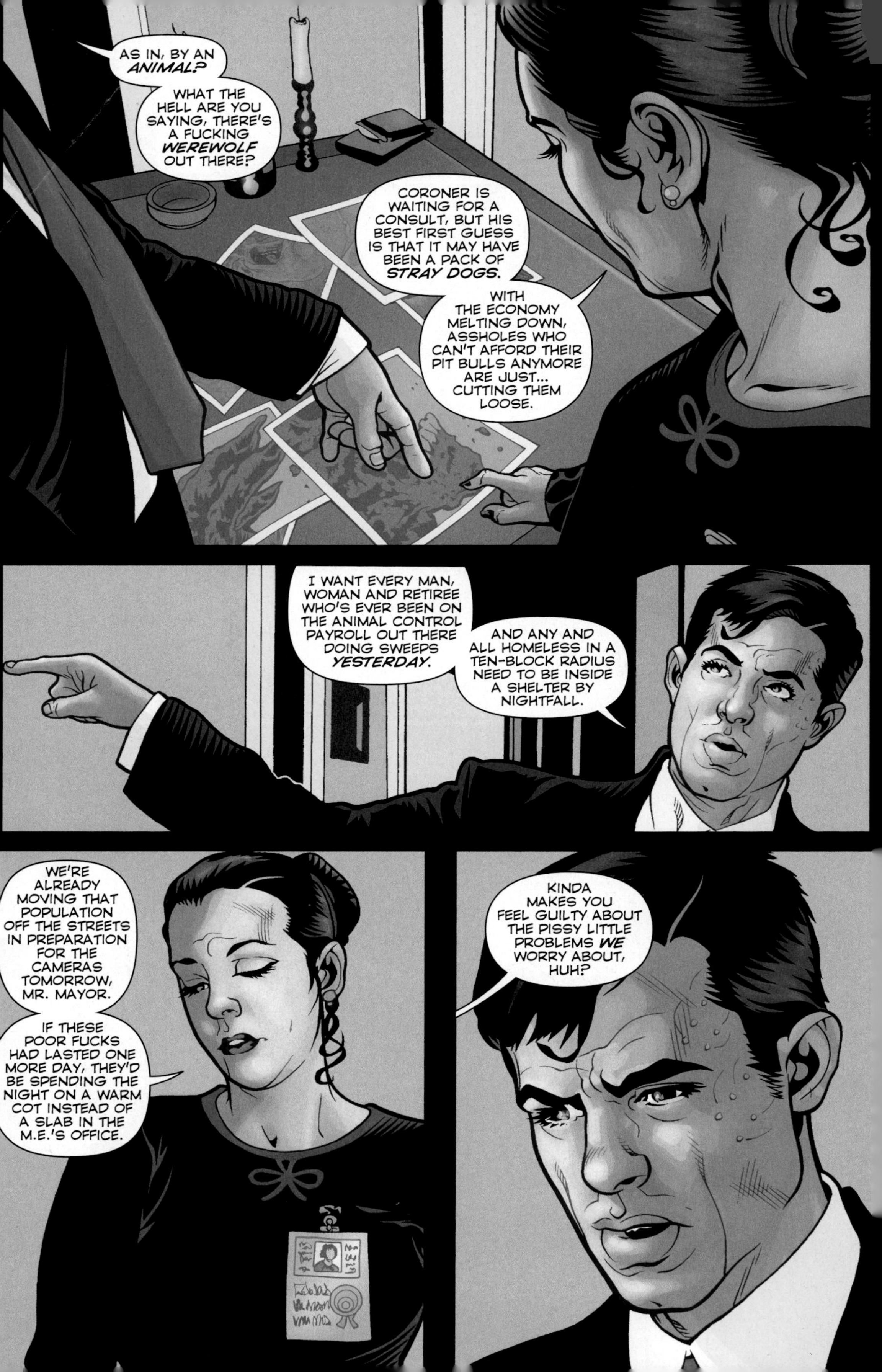
AS IN, BY AN *ANIMAL?*
WHAT THE HELL ARE YOU SAYING, THERE'S A FUCKING *WEREWOLF* OUT THERE?
CORONER IS WAITING FOR A CONSULT, BUT HIS BEST FIRST GUESS IS THAT IT MAY HAVE BEEN A PACK OF *STRAY DOGS.*
WITH THE ECONOMY MELTING DOWN, ASSHOLES WHO CAN'T AFFORD THEIR PIT BULLS ANYMORE ARE JUST... CUTTING THEM LOOSE.
I WANT EVERY MAN, WOMAN AND RETIREE WHO'S EVER BEEN ON THE ANIMAL CONTROL PAYROLL OUT THERE DOING SWEEPS *YESTERDAY.*
AND ANY AND ALL HOMELESS IN A TEN-BLOCK RADIUS NEED TO BE INSIDE A SHELTER BY NIGHTFALL.
WE'RE ALREADY MOVING THAT POPULATION OFF THE STREETS IN PREPARATION FOR THE CAMERAS TOMORROW, MR. MAYOR.
IF THESE POOR FUCKS HAD LASTED ONE MORE DAY, THEY'D BE SPENDING THE NIGHT ON A WARM COT INSTEAD OF A SLAB IN THE M.E.'S OFFICE.
KINDA MAKES YOU FEEL GUILTY ABOUT THE PISSY LITTLE PROBLEMS *WE* WORRY ABOUT, HUH?

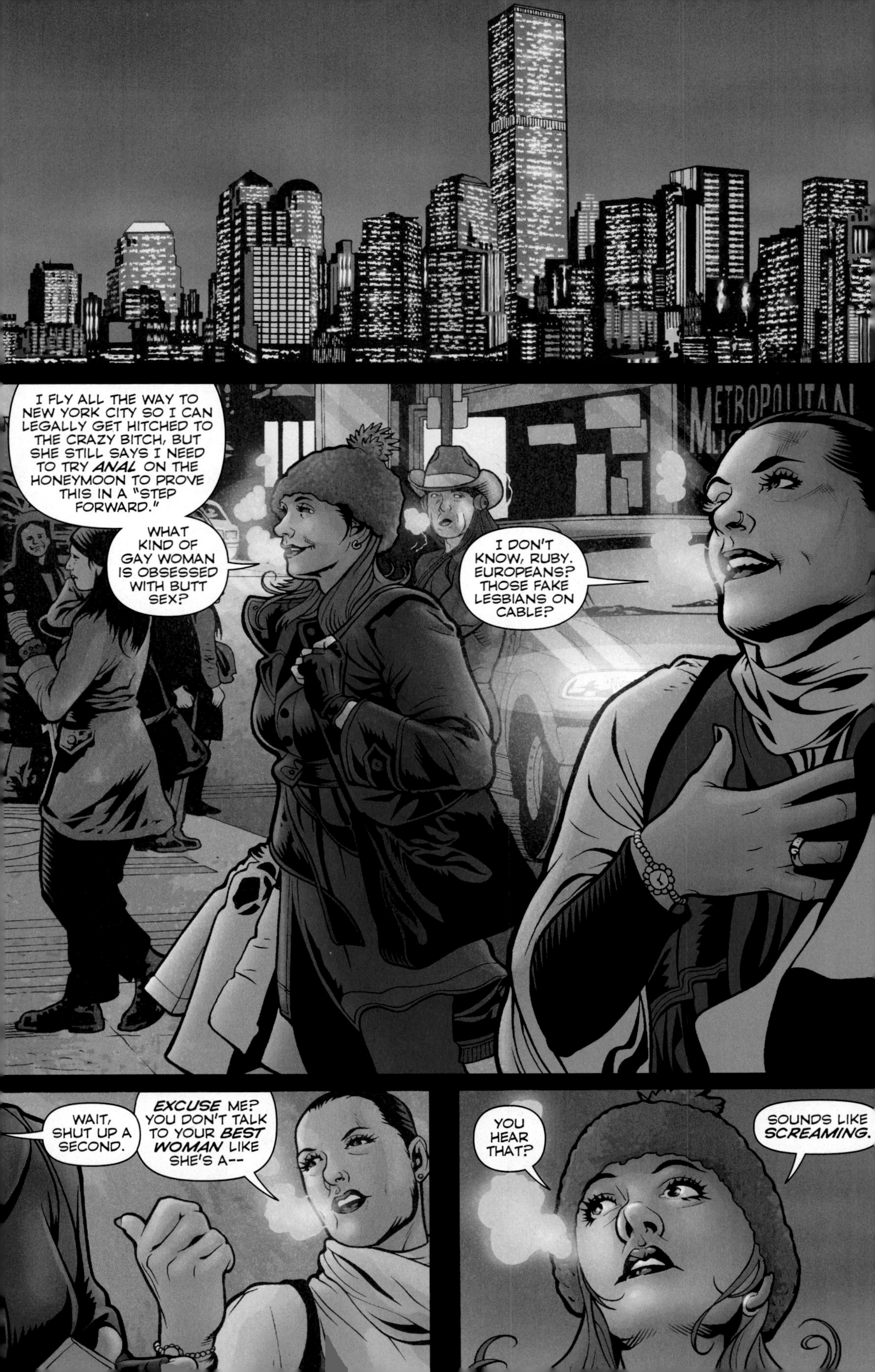
I FLY ALL THE WAY TO NEW YORK CITY SO I CAN LEGALLY GET HITCHED TO THE CRAZY BITCH, BUT SHE STILL SAYS I NEED TO TRY ANAL ON THE HONEYMOON TO PROVE THIS IN A "STEP FORWARD."
WHAT KIND OF GAY WOMAN IS OBSESSED WITH BUTT SEX?
I DON'T KNOW, RUBY. EUROPEANS? THOSE FAKE LESBIANS ON CABLE?
WAIT, SHUT UP A SECOND.
EXCUSE ME? YOU DON'T TALK TO YOUR BEST WOMAN LIKE SHE'S A--
YOU HEAR THAT?
SOUNDS LIKE SCREAMING.

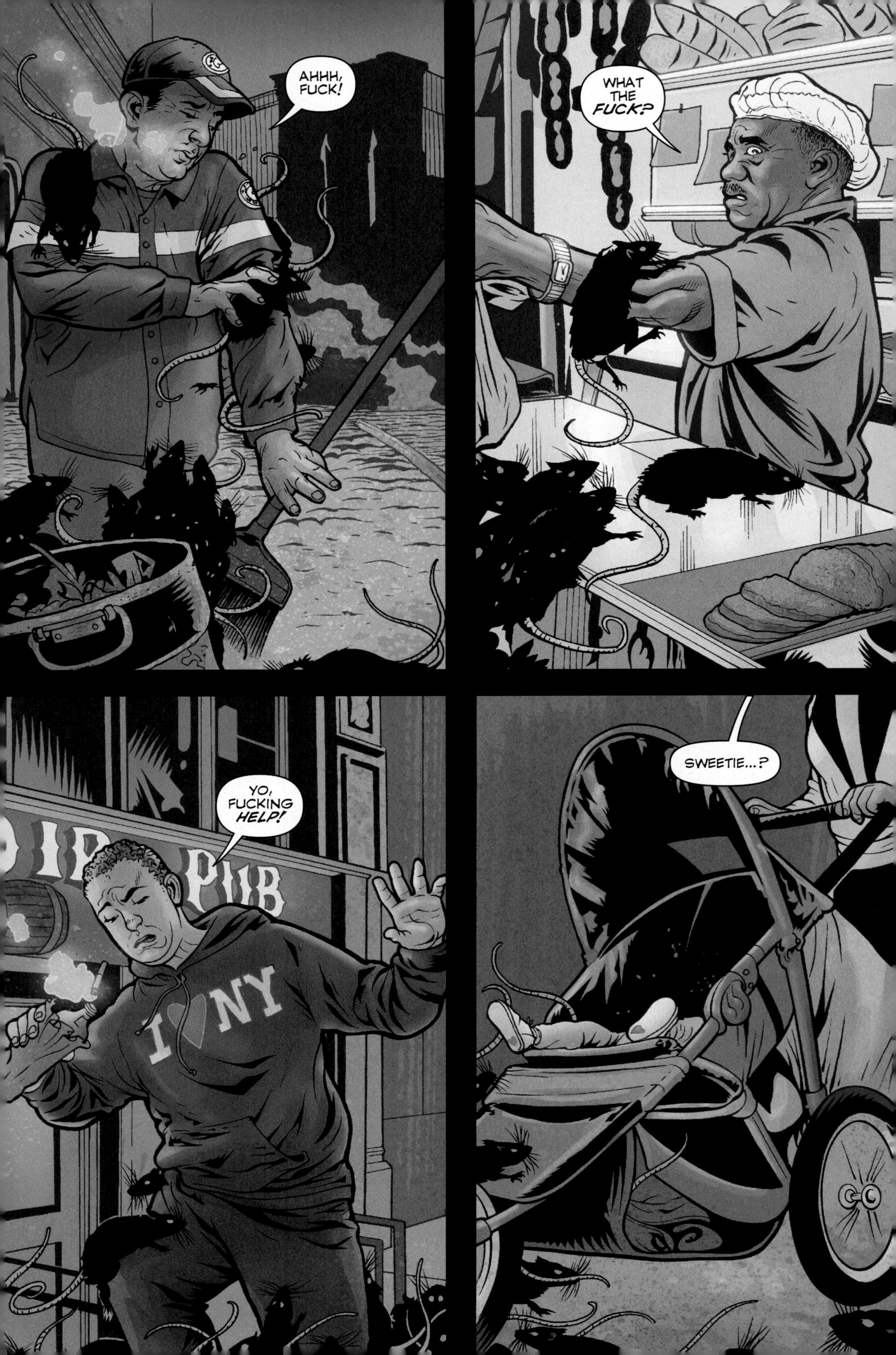
AHHH, FUCK!
WHAT THE *FUCK?*
YO, FUCKING *HELP!*
PUB
SWEETIE...?

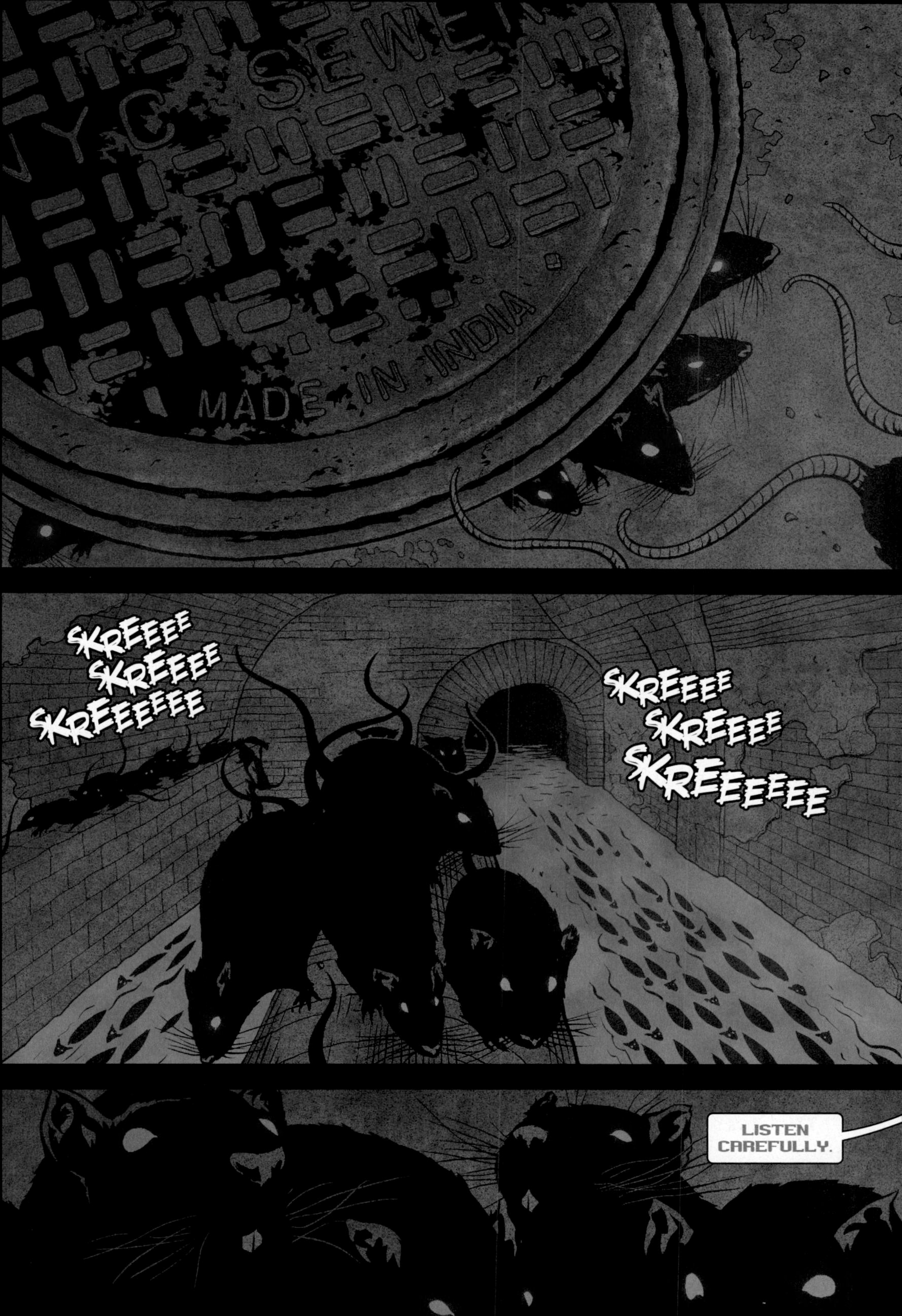
NYC SEWER
MADE IN INDIA
SKREEEE SKREEEEE SKREEEEEEE
SKREEEE SKREEEEE SKREEEEEEE
LISTEN CAREFULLY.

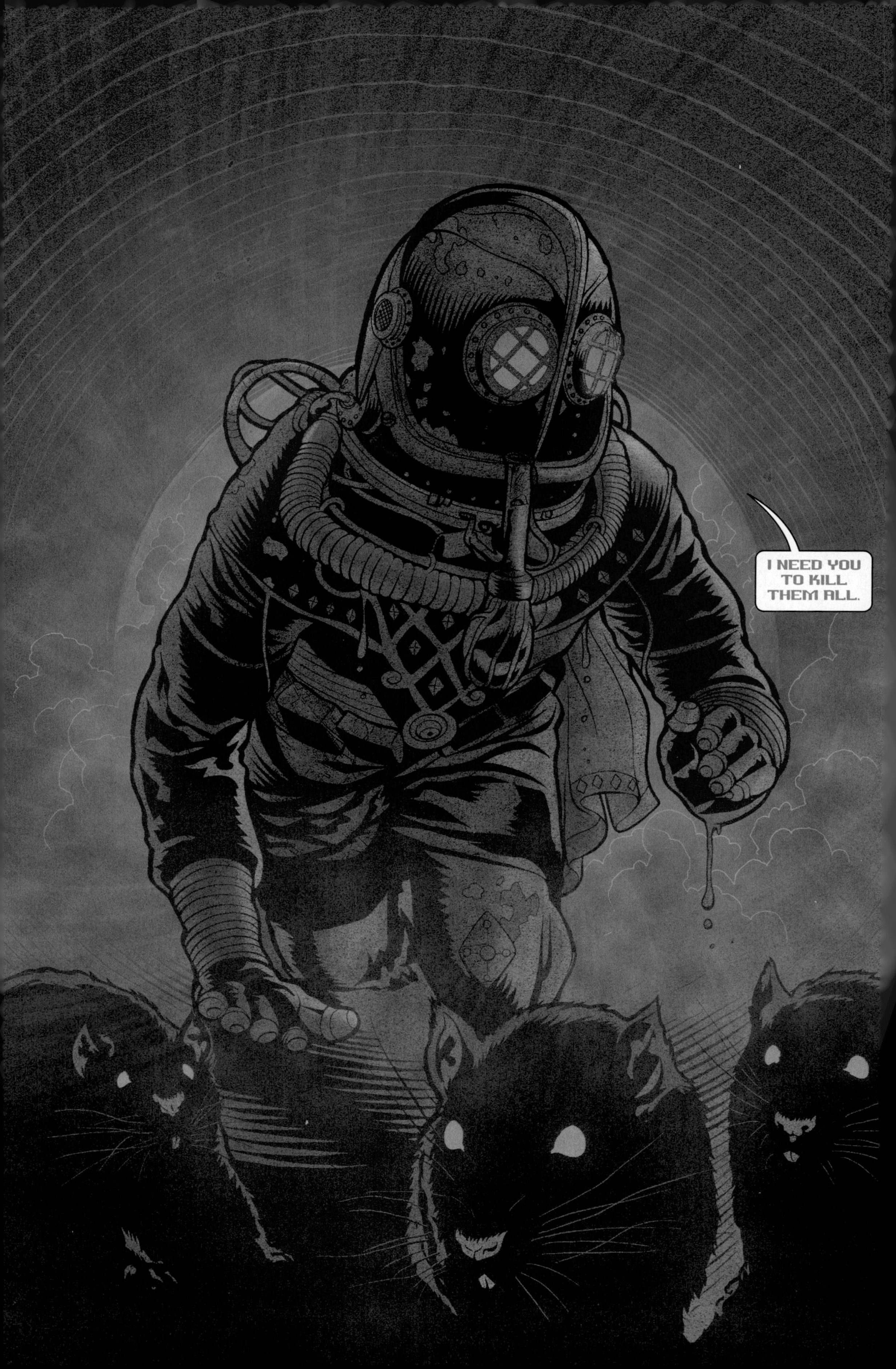
I NEED YOU TO KILL THEM ALL.

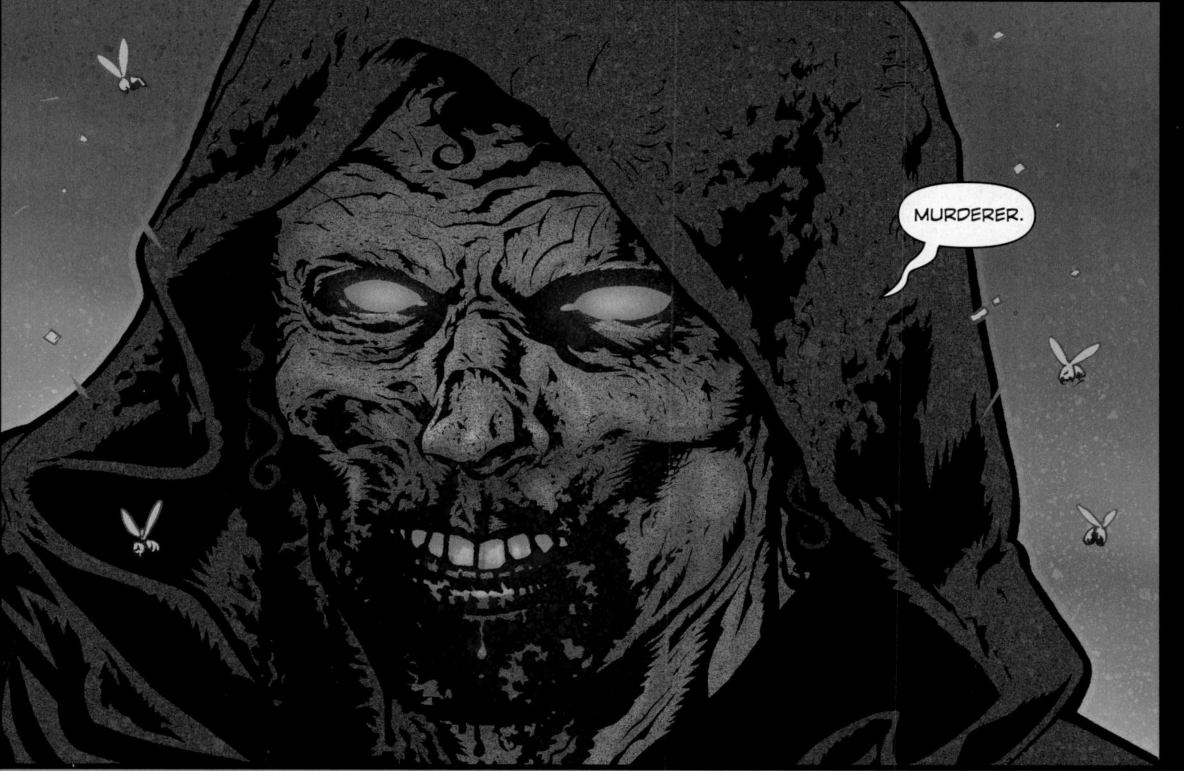
MURDERER.

FRIDAY, JUNE 1, 2001

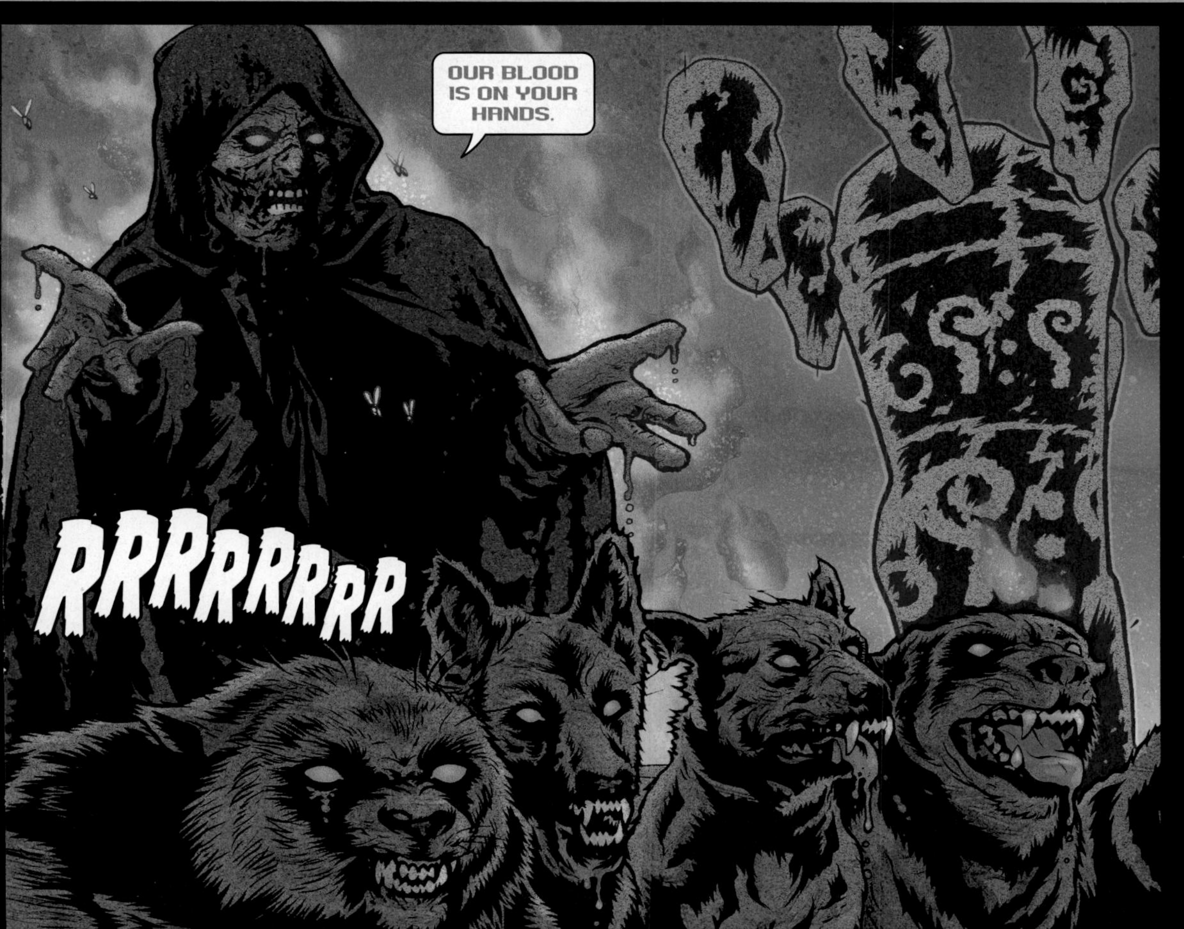
OUR BLOOD IS ON YOUR HANDS.
RRRRRRRR

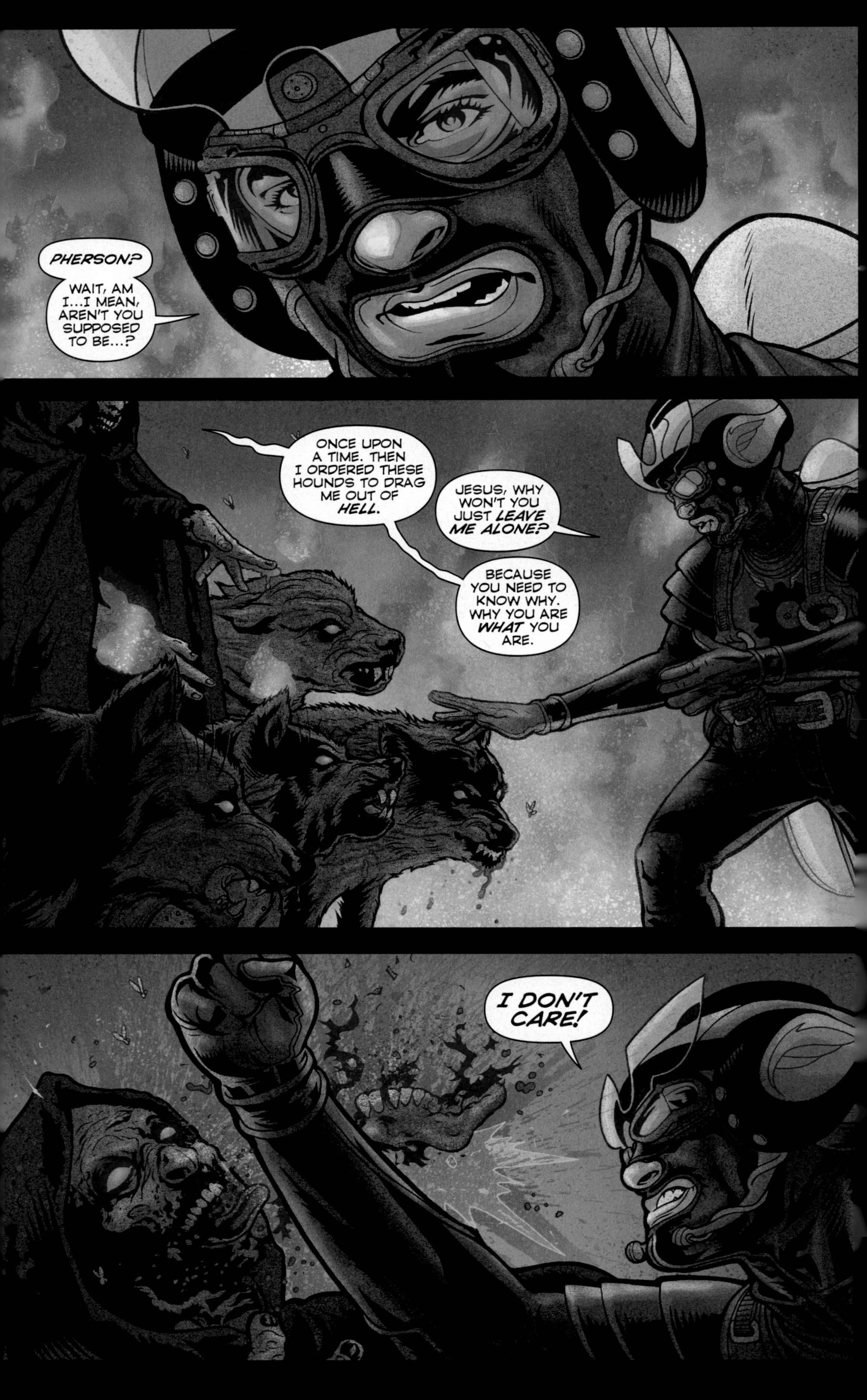
PHERSON?
WAIT, AM I...I MEAN, AREN'T YOU SUPPOSED TO BE...?
ONCE UPON A TIME. THEN I ORDERED THESE HOUNDS TO DRAG ME OUT OF HELL.
JESUS, WHY WON'T YOU JUST LEAVE ME ALONE?
BECAUSE YOU NEED TO KNOW WHY. WHY YOU ARE WHAT YOU ARE.
I DON'T CARE!

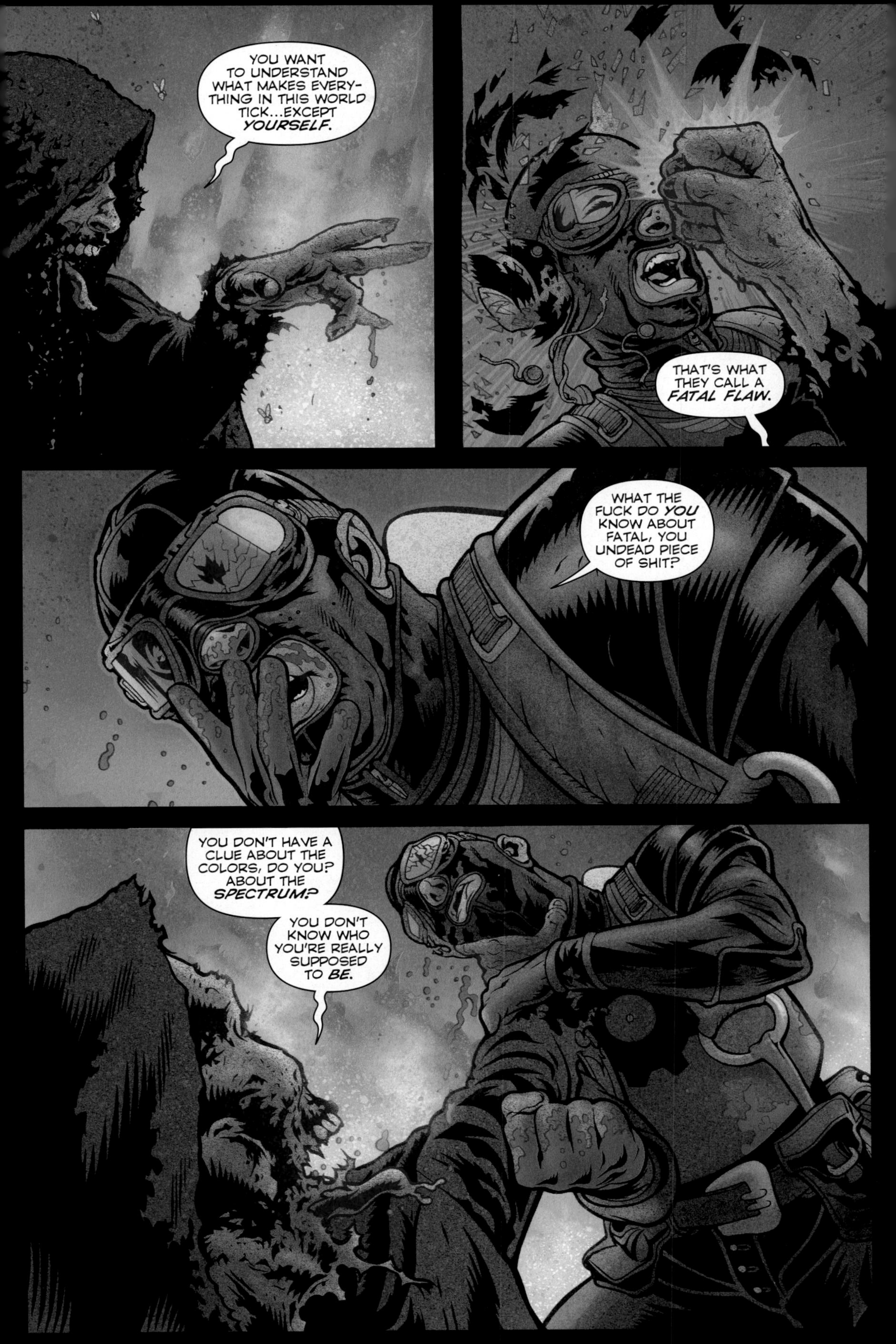
YOU WANT TO UNDERSTAND WHAT MAKES EVERY-THING IN THIS WORLD TICK...EXCEPT YOURSELF.
THAT'S WHAT THEY CALL A FATAL FLAW.
WHAT THE FUCK DO YOU KNOW ABOUT FATAL, YOU UNDEAD PIECE OF SHIT?
YOU DON'T HAVE A CLUE ABOUT THE COLORS, DO YOU? ABOUT THE SPECTRUM?
YOU DON'T KNOW WHO YOU'RE REALLY SUPPOSED TO BE.

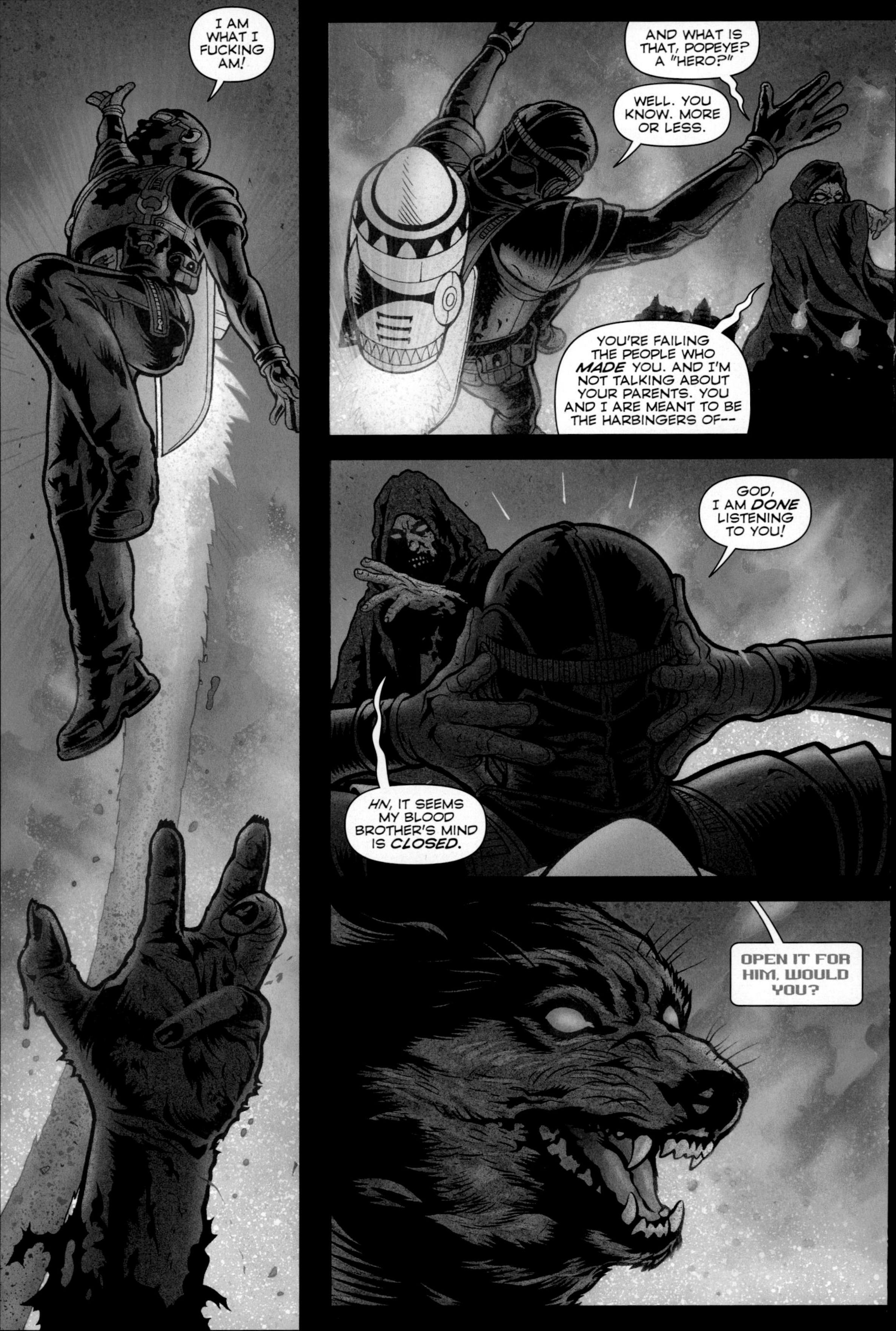
I AM WHAT I FUCKING AM!
AND WHAT IS THAT, POPEYE? A "HERO?"
WELL. YOU KNOW. MORE OR LESS.
YOU'RE FAILING THE PEOPLE WHO *MADE* YOU. AND I'M NOT TALKING ABOUT YOUR PARENTS. YOU AND I ARE MEANT TO BE THE HARBINGERS OF--
GOD, I AM *DONE* LISTENING TO YOU!
HN, IT SEEMS MY BLOOD BROTHER'S MIND IS *CLOSED*.
OPEN IT FOR HIM, WOULD YOU?

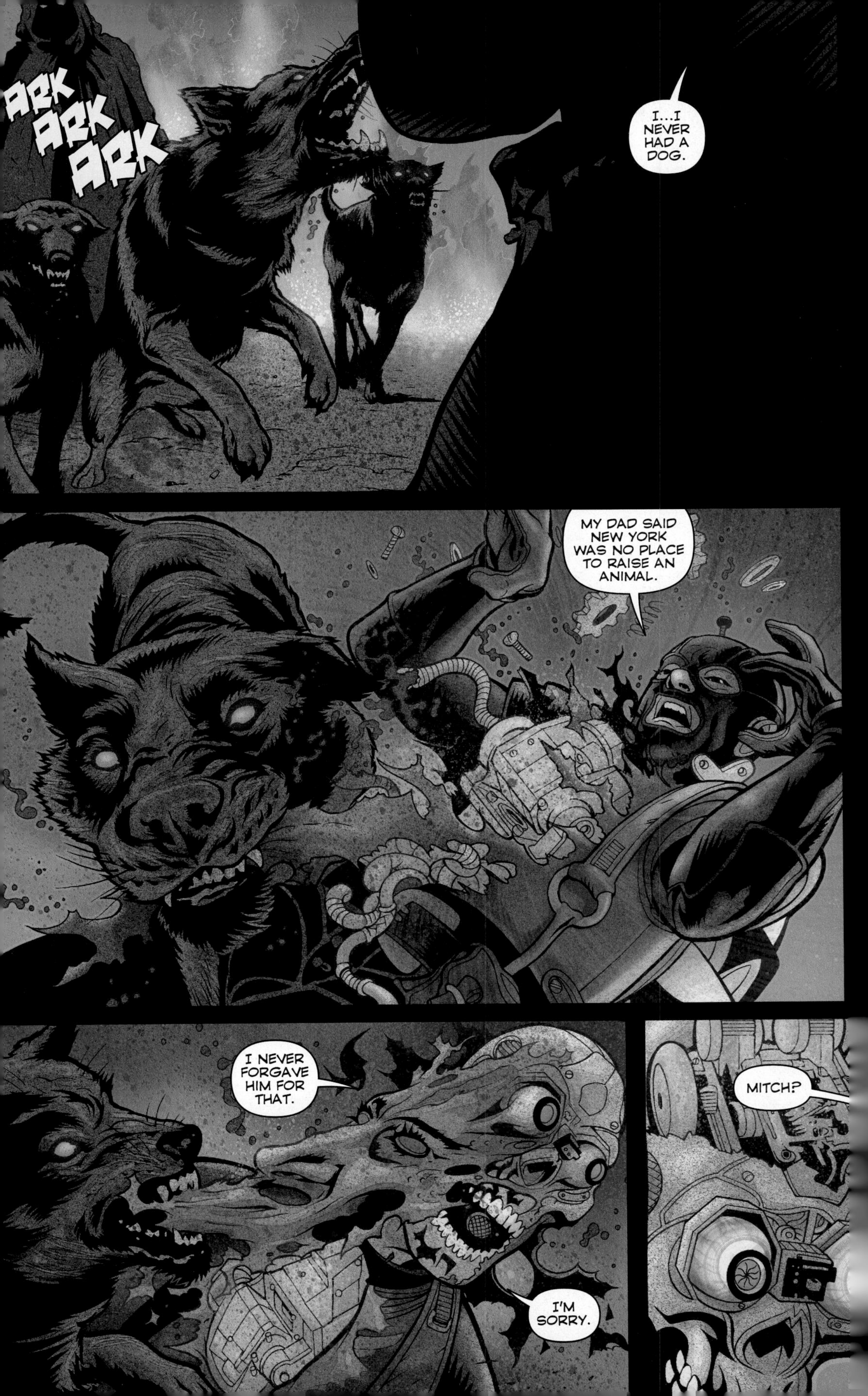
ARK ARK ARK
I...I NEVER HAD A DOG.
MY DAD SAID NEW YORK WAS NO PLACE TO RAISE AN ANIMAL.
I NEVER FORGAVE HIM FOR THAT.
I'M SORRY.
MITCH?

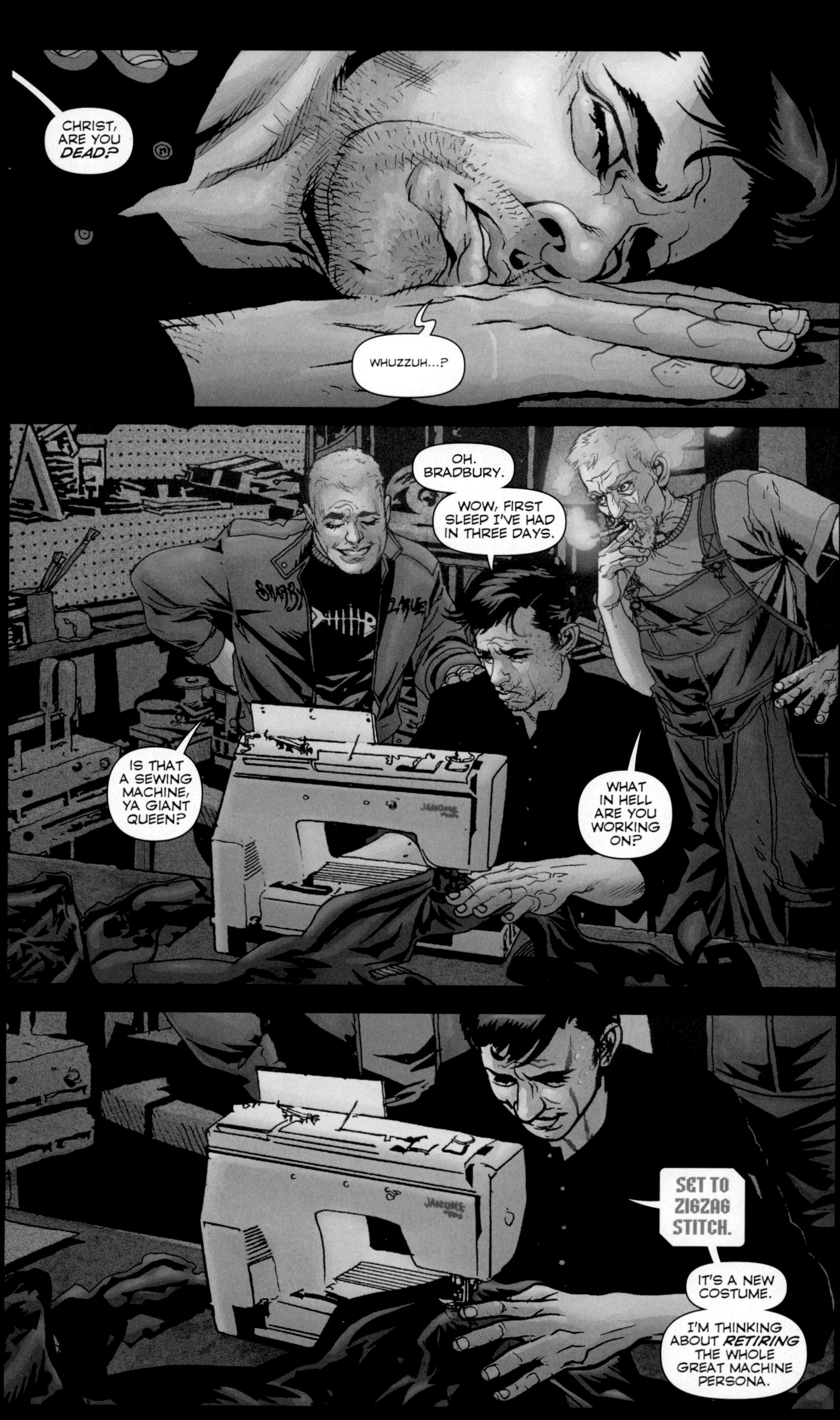
CHRIST, ARE YOU *DEAD?*
WHUZZUH...?
OH. BRADBURY.
WOW, FIRST SLEEP I'VE HAD IN THREE DAYS.
IS THAT A SEWING MACHINE, YA GIANT QUEEN?
WHAT IN HELL ARE YOU WORKING ON?
SET TO ZIGZAG STITCH.
IT'S A NEW COSTUME.
I'M THINKING ABOUT *RETIRING* THE WHOLE GREAT MACHINE PERSONA.

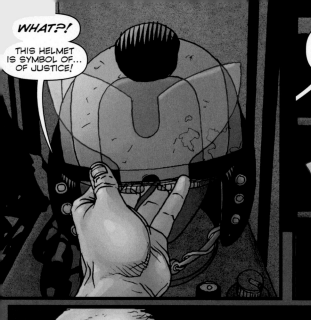

WHAT?!

THIS HELMET IS SYMBOL OF... OF JUSTICE!

YEAH, WELL, TELL THAT TO THE POOR BASTARD I SUMMARILY *EXECUTED.*

DON'T BE DENSE, MITCHELL.

PHERSON EXECUTED *HIMSELF.*

BESIDES, NO MATTER WHAT THIS ONE SAYS, WE DO NOT *KNOW* HE IS REALLY DEAD.

KREMLIN, YOU *SAW* THE PLACE THAT COCKLORD BLEW UP.

THERE WERE PARTS OF HIS BODY SCATTERED EVERYWHERE.

BUT NOT HIS *HEAD!*

GUYS, NONE OF THAT MATTERS ANYMORE.

ALL I KNOW IS... IT'S TIME FOR A CHANGE.

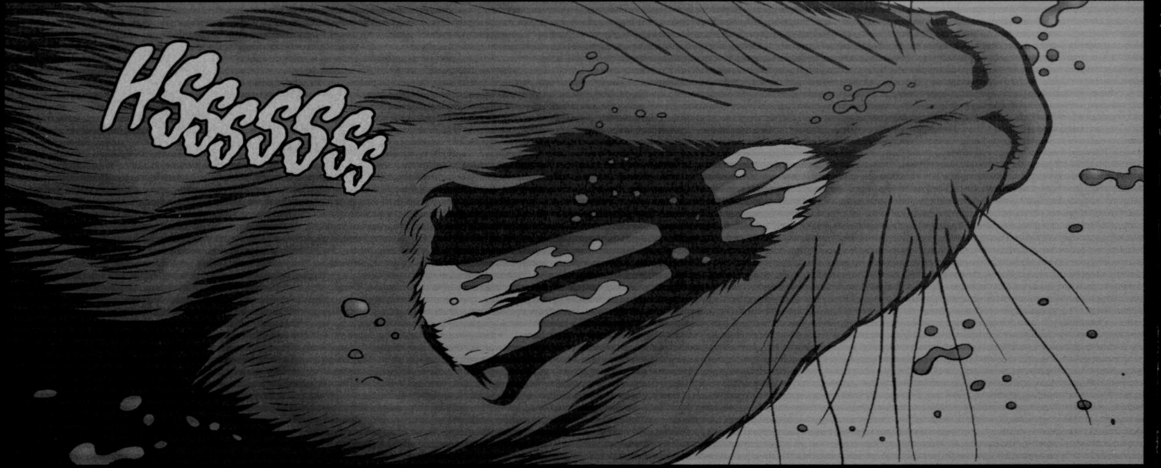
HSSSSSSS

THURSDAY, DECEMBER 30, 2004

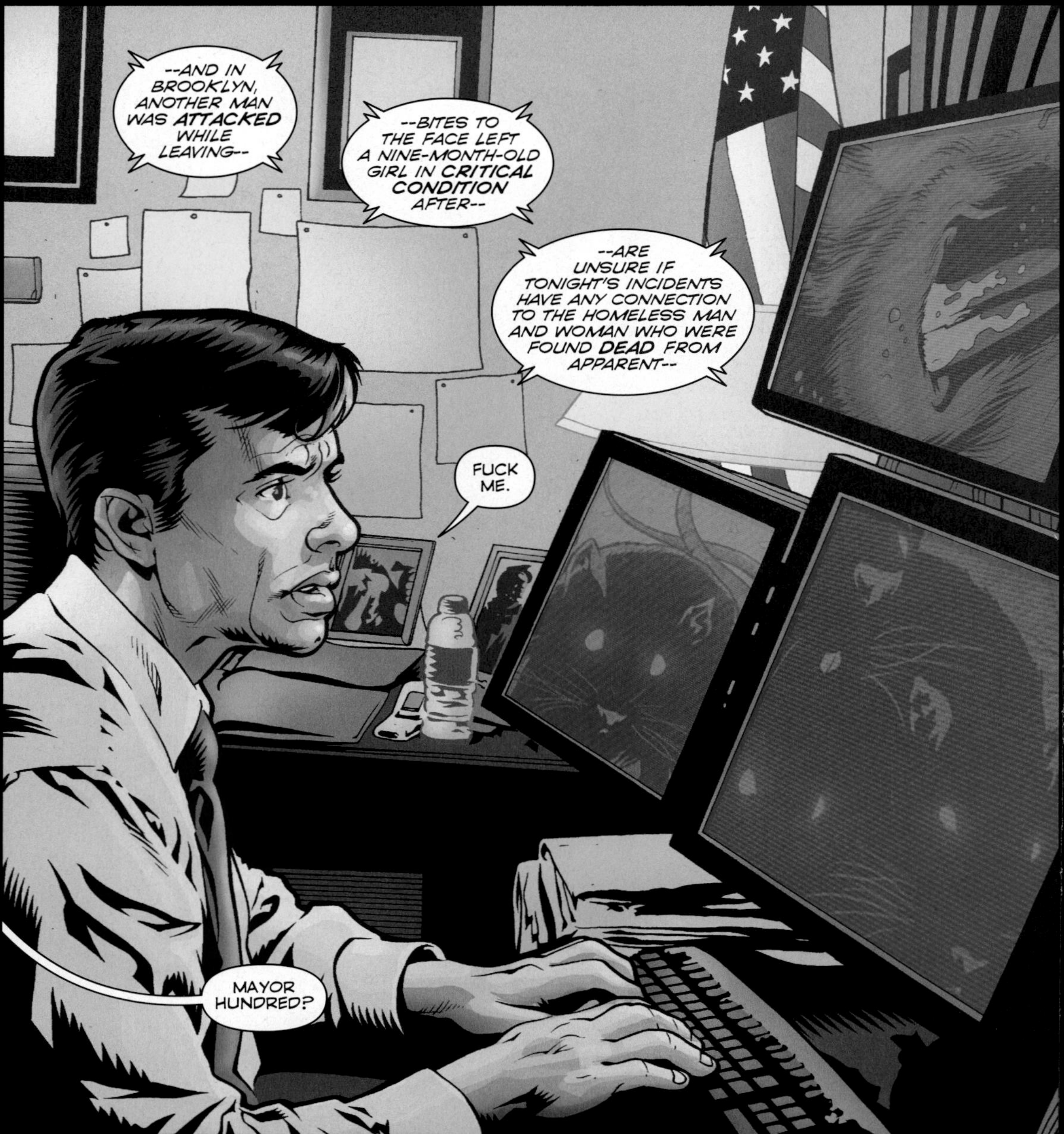
--AND IN BROOKLYN, ANOTHER MAN WAS ATTACKED WHILE LEAVING--
--BITES TO THE FACE LEFT A NINE-MONTH-OLD GIRL IN CRITICAL CONDITION AFTER--
--ARE UNSURE IF TONIGHT'S INCIDENTS HAVE ANY CONNECTION TO THE HOMELESS MAN AND WOMAN WHO WERE FOUND DEAD FROM APPARENT--
FUCK ME.
MAYOR HUNDRED?

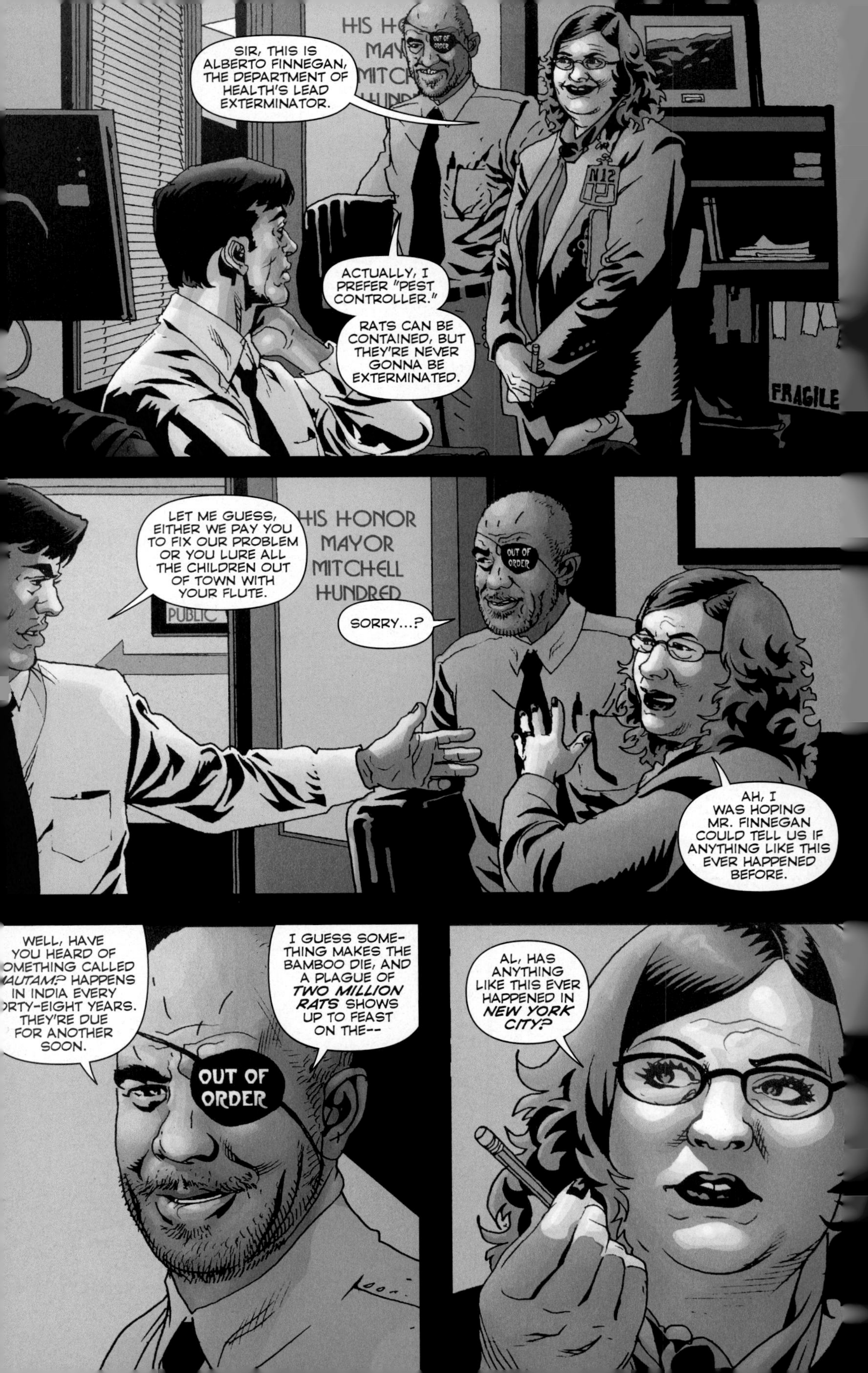
SIR, THIS IS ALBERTO FINNEGAN, THE DEPARTMENT OF HEALTH'S LEAD EXTERMINATOR.
ACTUALLY, I PREFER "PEST CONTROLLER."
RATS CAN BE CONTAINED, BUT THEY'RE NEVER GONNA BE EXTERMINATED.
FRAGILE
LET ME GUESS, EITHER WE PAY YOU TO FIX OUR PROBLEM OR YOU LURE ALL THE CHILDREN OUT OF TOWN WITH YOUR FLUTE.
HIS HONOR MAYOR MITCHELL HUNDRED
PUBLIC
OUT OF ORDER
SORRY...?
AH, I WAS HOPING MR. FINNEGAN COULD TELL US IF ANYTHING LIKE THIS EVER HAPPENED BEFORE.
WELL, HAVE YOU HEARD OF OMETHING CALLED *AUTAM?* HAPPENS IN INDIA EVERY ORTY-EIGHT YEARS. THEY'RE DUE FOR ANOTHER SOON.
I GUESS SOMETHING MAKES THE BAMBOO DIE, AND A PLAGUE OF ***TWO MILLION RATS*** SHOWS UP TO FEAST ON THE--
OUT OF ORDER
AL, HAS ANYTHING LIKE THIS EVER HAPPENED IN ***NEW YORK CITY?***

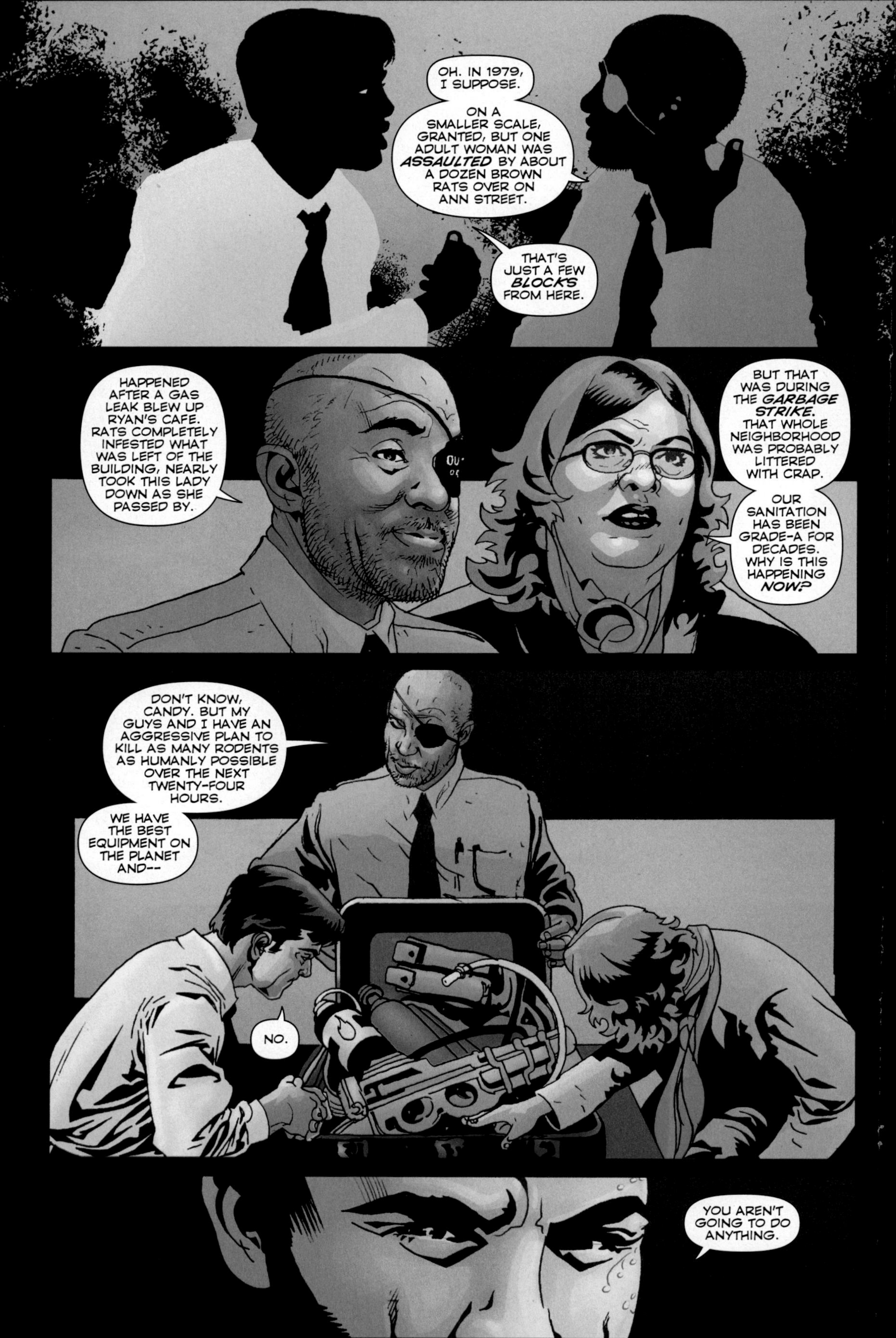
OH. IN 1979, I SUPPOSE.
ON A SMALLER SCALE, GRANTED, BUT ONE ADULT WOMAN WAS ASSAULTED BY ABOUT A DOZEN BROWN RATS OVER ON ANN STREET.
THAT'S JUST A FEW BLOCKS FROM HERE.
HAPPENED AFTER A GAS LEAK BLEW UP RYAN'S CAFE. RATS COMPLETELY INFESTED WHAT WAS LEFT OF THE BUILDING, NEARLY TOOK THIS LADY DOWN AS SHE PASSED BY.
BUT THAT WAS DURING THE GARBAGE STRIKE. THAT WHOLE NEIGHBORHOOD WAS PROBABLY LITTERED WITH CRAP.
OUR SANITATION HAS BEEN GRADE-A FOR DECADES. WHY IS THIS HAPPENING NOW?
DON'T KNOW, CANDY. BUT MY GUYS AND I HAVE AN AGGRESSIVE PLAN TO KILL AS MANY RODENTS AS HUMANLY POSSIBLE OVER THE NEXT TWENTY-FOUR HOURS.
WE HAVE THE BEST EQUIPMENT ON THE PLANET AND--
NO.
YOU AREN'T GOING TO DO ANYTHING.

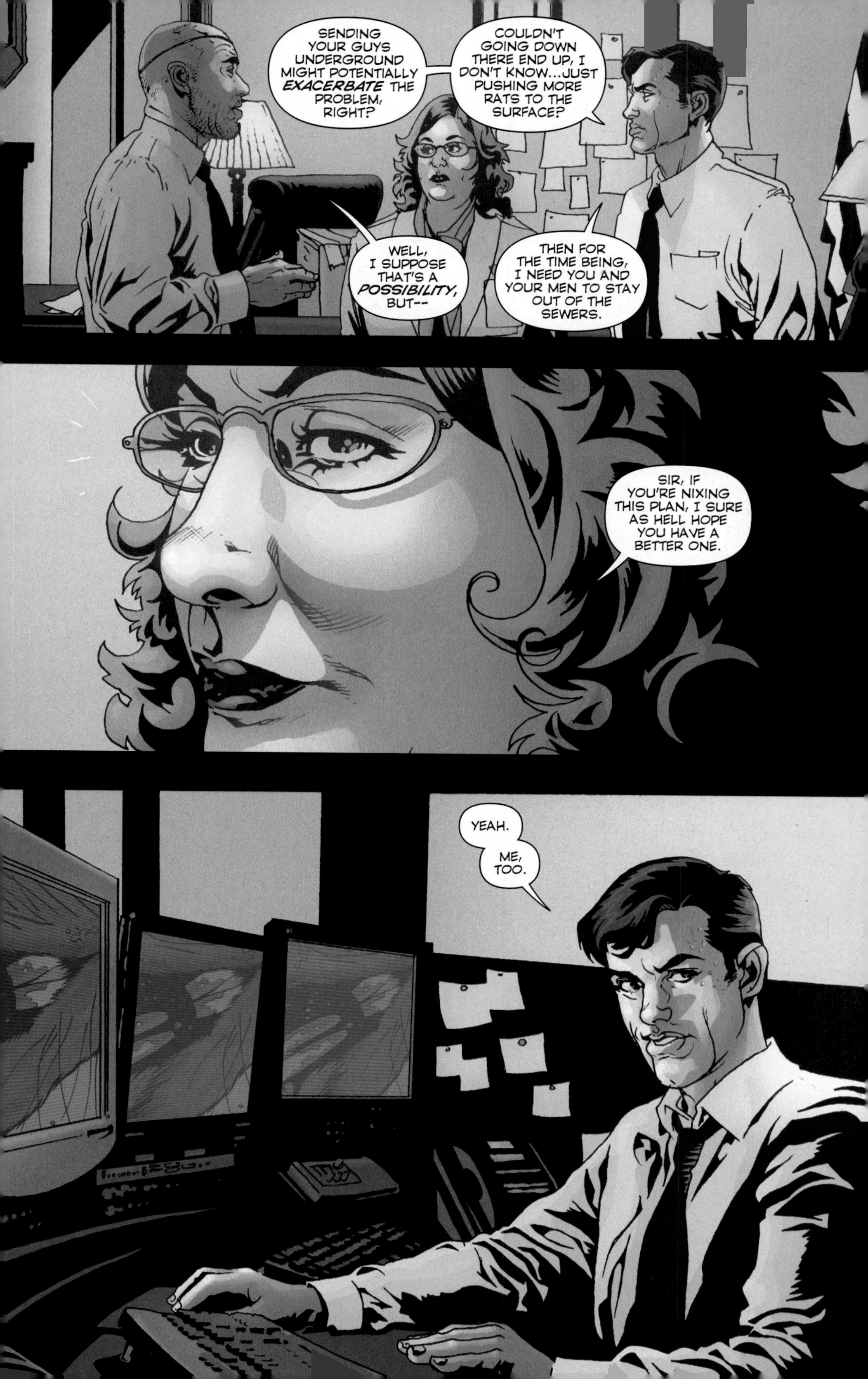
SENDING YOUR GUYS UNDERGROUND MIGHT POTENTIALLY EXACERBATE THE PROBLEM, RIGHT?
COULDN'T GOING DOWN THERE END UP, I DON'T KNOW...JUST PUSHING MORE RATS TO THE SURFACE?
WELL, I SUPPOSE THAT'S A POSSIBILITY, BUT--
THEN FOR THE TIME BEING, I NEED YOU AND YOUR MEN TO STAY OUT OF THE SEWERS.
SIR, IF YOU'RE NIXING THIS PLAN, I SURE AS HELL HOPE YOU HAVE A BETTER ONE.
YEAH.
ME, TOO.

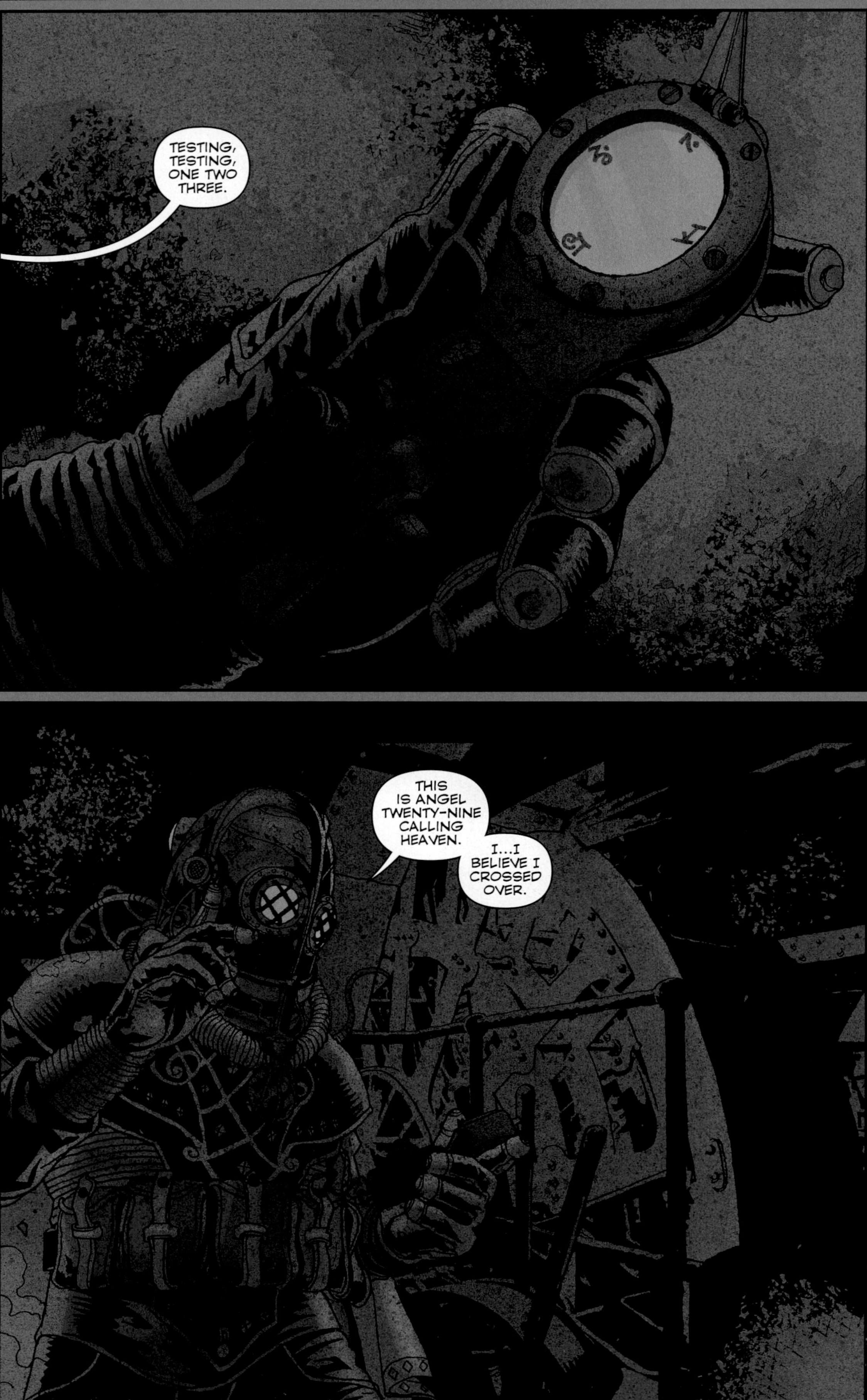
TESTING, TESTING, ONE TWO THREE.
THIS IS ANGEL TWENTY-NINE CALLING HEAVEN.
I...I BELIEVE I CROSSED OVER.

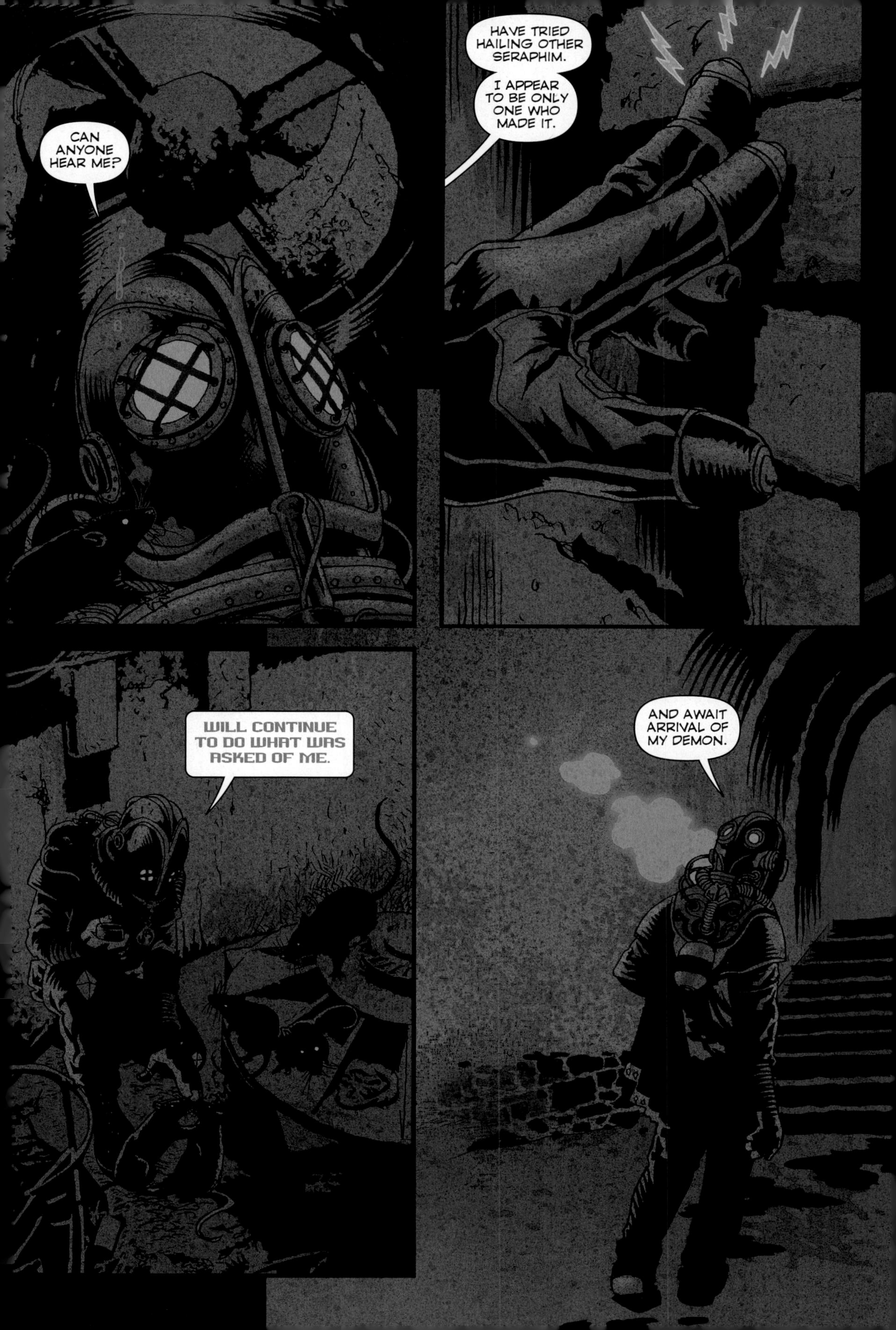

CAN ANYONE HEAR ME?
HAVE TRIED HAILING OTHER SERAPHIM.
I APPEAR TO BE ONLY ONE WHO MADE IT.
WILL CONTINUE TO DO WHAT WAS ASKED OF ME.
AND AWAIT ARRIVAL OF MY DEMON.

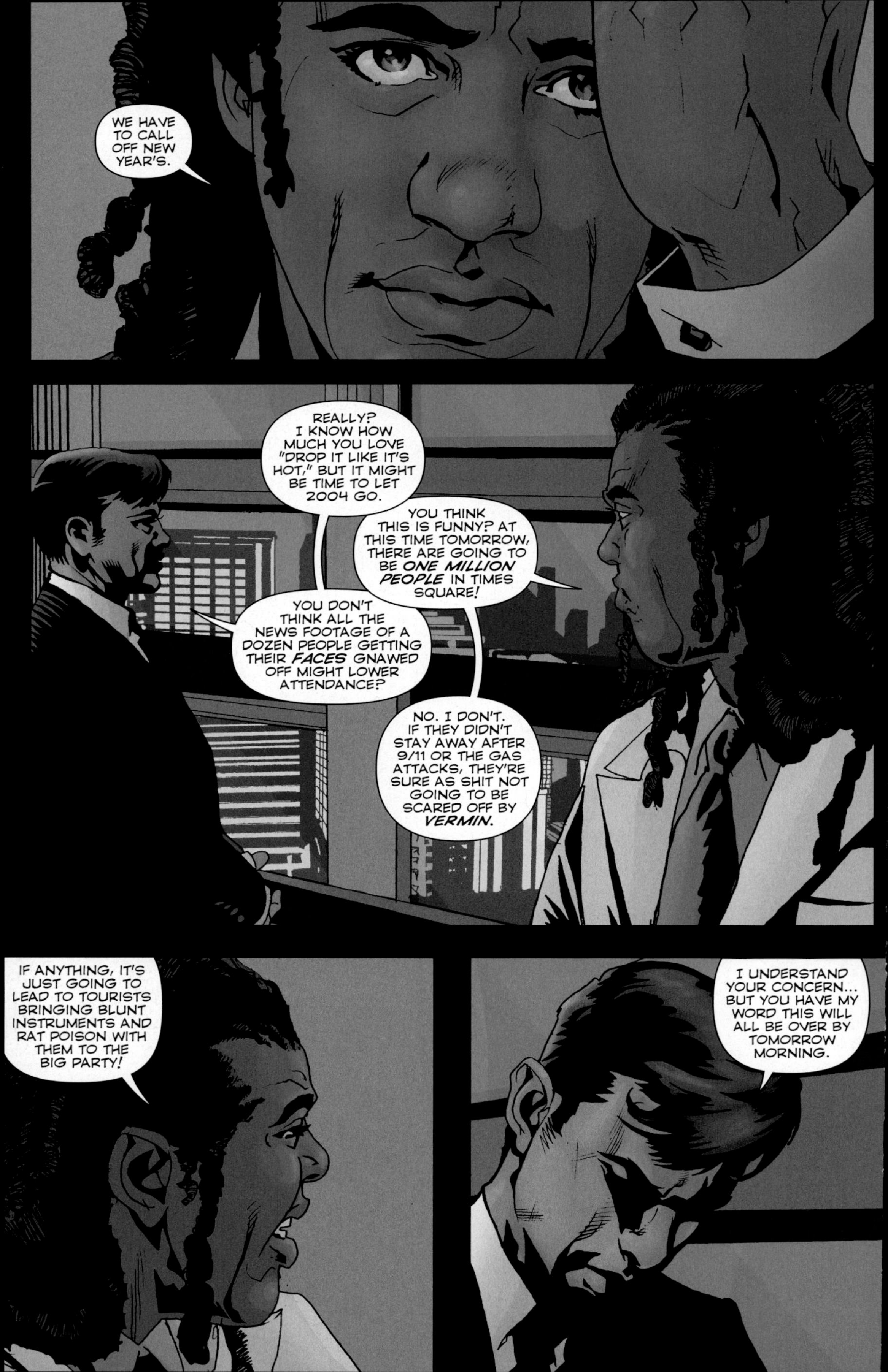
WE HAVE TO CALL OFF NEW YEAR'S.
REALLY? I KNOW HOW MUCH YOU LOVE "DROP IT LIKE IT'S HOT," BUT IT MIGHT BE TIME TO LET 2004 GO.
YOU THINK THIS IS FUNNY? AT THIS TIME TOMORROW, THERE ARE GOING TO BE ONE MILLION PEOPLE IN TIMES SQUARE!
YOU DON'T THINK ALL THE NEWS FOOTAGE OF A DOZEN PEOPLE GETTING THEIR FACES GNAWED OFF MIGHT LOWER ATTENDANCE?
NO. I DON'T. IF THEY DIDN'T STAY AWAY AFTER 9/11 OR THE GAS ATTACKS, THEY'RE SURE AS SHIT NOT GOING TO BE SCARED OFF BY VERMIN.
IF ANYTHING, IT'S JUST GOING TO LEAD TO TOURISTS BRINGING BLUNT INSTRUMENTS AND RAT POISON WITH THEM TO THE BIG PARTY!
I UNDERSTAND YOUR CONCERN... BUT YOU HAVE MY WORD THIS WILL ALL BE OVER BY TOMORROW MORNING.

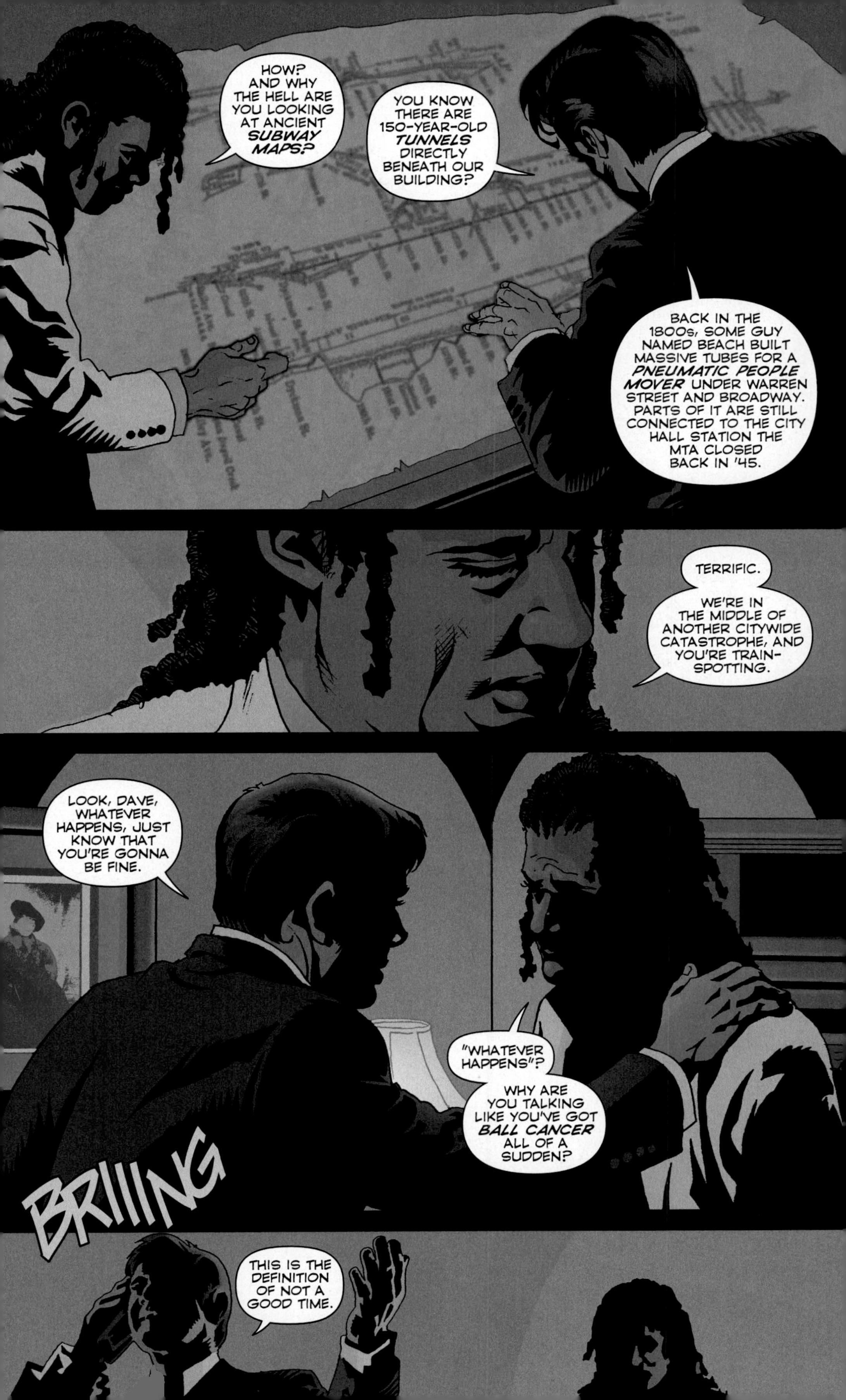
HOW? AND WHY THE HELL ARE YOU LOOKING AT ANCIENT *SUBWAY MAPS?*
YOU KNOW THERE ARE 150-YEAR-OLD *TUNNELS* DIRECTLY BENEATH OUR BUILDING?
BACK IN THE 1800s, SOME GUY NAMED BEACH BUILT MASSIVE TUBES FOR A *PNEUMATIC PEOPLE MOVER* UNDER WARREN STREET AND BROADWAY. PARTS OF IT ARE STILL CONNECTED TO THE CITY HALL STATION THE MTA CLOSED BACK IN '45.
TERRIFIC.
WE'RE IN THE MIDDLE OF ANOTHER CITYWIDE CATASTROPHE, AND YOU'RE TRAIN-SPOTTING.
LOOK, DAVE, WHATEVER HAPPENS, JUST KNOW THAT YOU'RE GONNA BE FINE.
"WHATEVER HAPPENS"?
WHY ARE YOU TALKING LIKE YOU'VE GOT *BALL CANCER* ALL OF A SUDDEN?
BRIIING
THIS IS THE DEFINITION OF NOT A GOOD TIME.

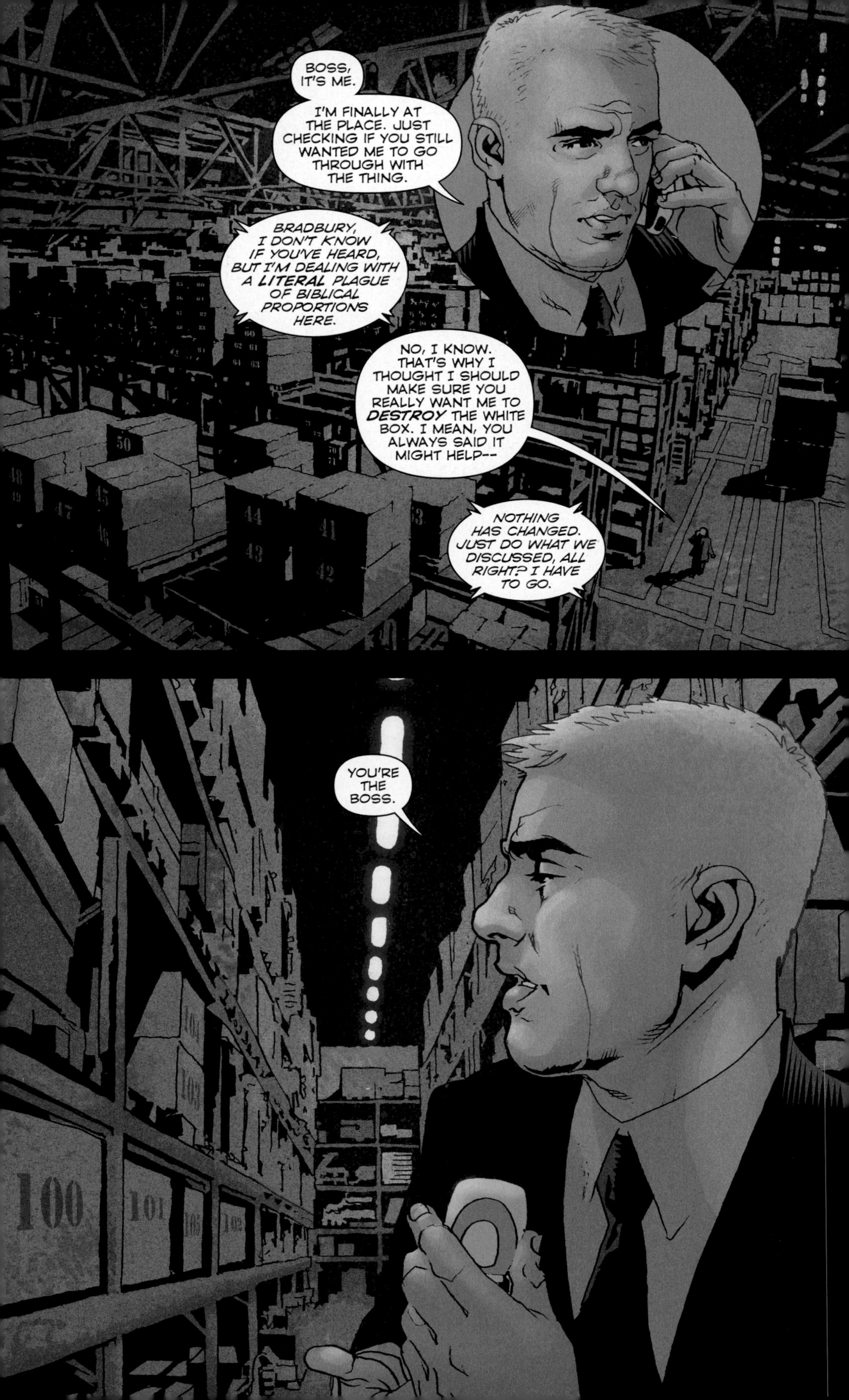
BOSS, IT'S ME.
I'M FINALLY AT THE PLACE. JUST CHECKING IF YOU STILL WANTED ME TO GO THROUGH WITH THE THING.
BRADBURY, I DON'T KNOW IF YOU'VE HEARD, BUT I'M DEALING WITH A LITERAL PLAGUE OF BIBLICAL PROPORTIONS HERE.
NO, I KNOW. THAT'S WHY I THOUGHT I SHOULD MAKE SURE YOU REALLY WANT ME TO DESTROY THE WHITE BOX. I MEAN, YOU ALWAYS SAID IT MIGHT HELP--
NOTHING HAS CHANGED. JUST DO WHAT WE DISCUSSED, ALL RIGHT? I HAVE TO GO.
YOU'RE THE BOSS.

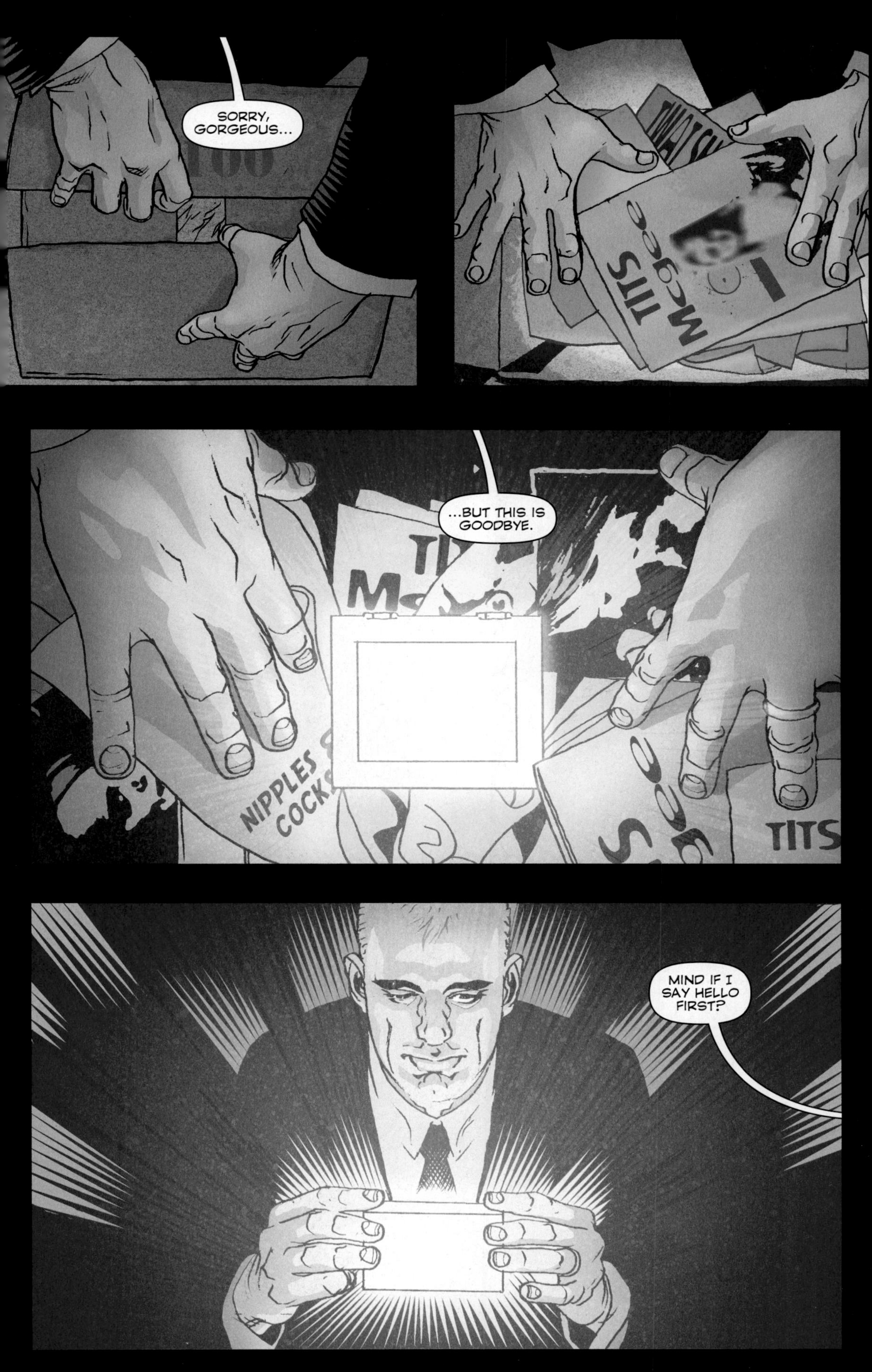
SORRY, GORGEOUS...
TITS
...BUT THIS IS GOODBYE.
TITS
MIND IF I SAY HELLO FIRST?

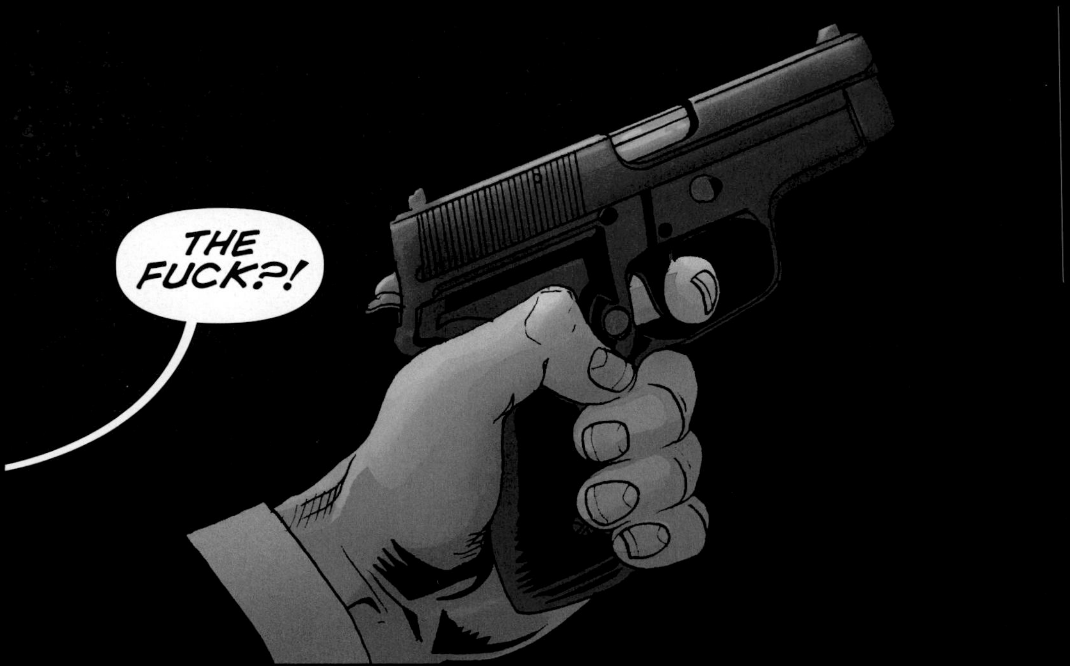
THE FUCK?!

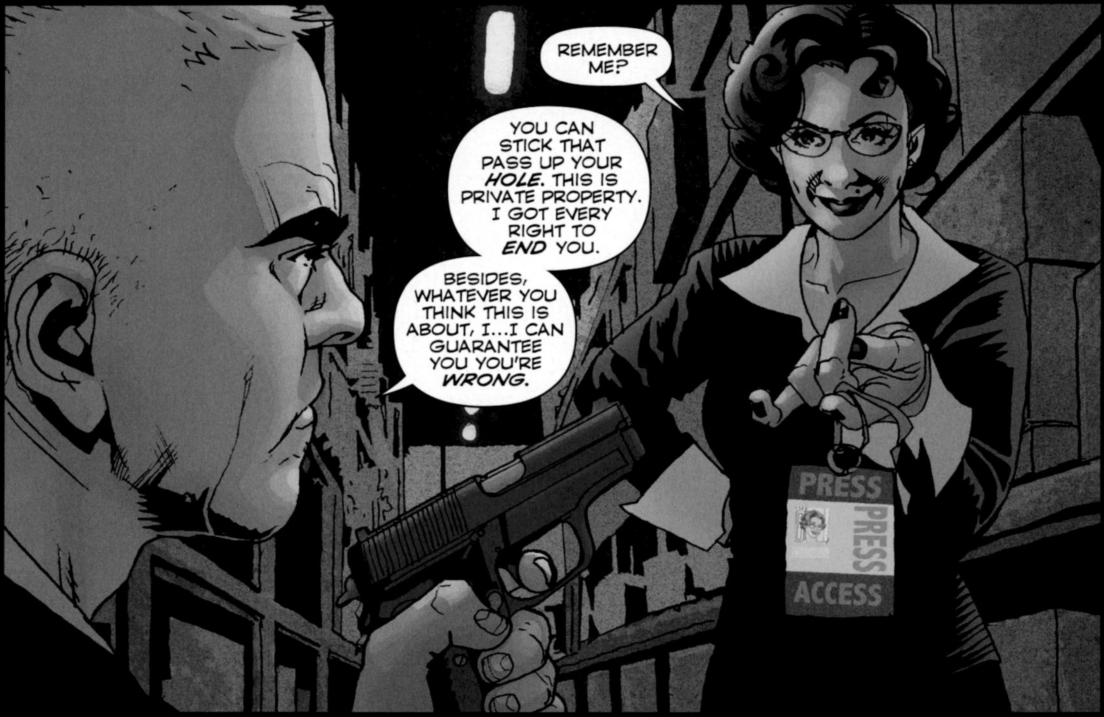
REMEMBER ME?
YOU CAN STICK THAT PASS UP YOUR ***HOLE***. THIS IS PRIVATE PROPERTY. I GOT EVERY RIGHT TO ***END*** YOU.
BESIDES, WHATEVER YOU THINK THIS IS ABOUT, I...I CAN GUARANTEE YOU YOU'RE ***WRONG***.
PRESS
PRESS
ACCESS

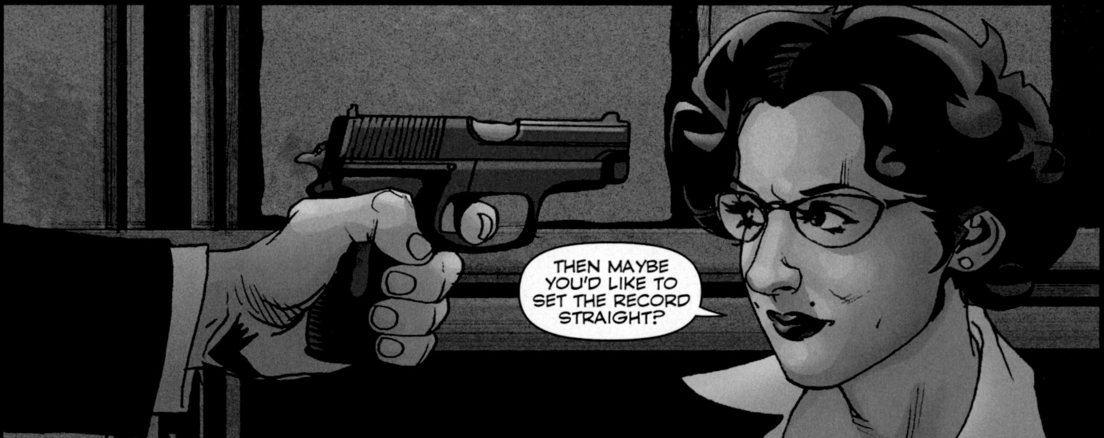
THEN MAYBE YOU'D LIKE TO SET THE RECORD STRAIGHT?

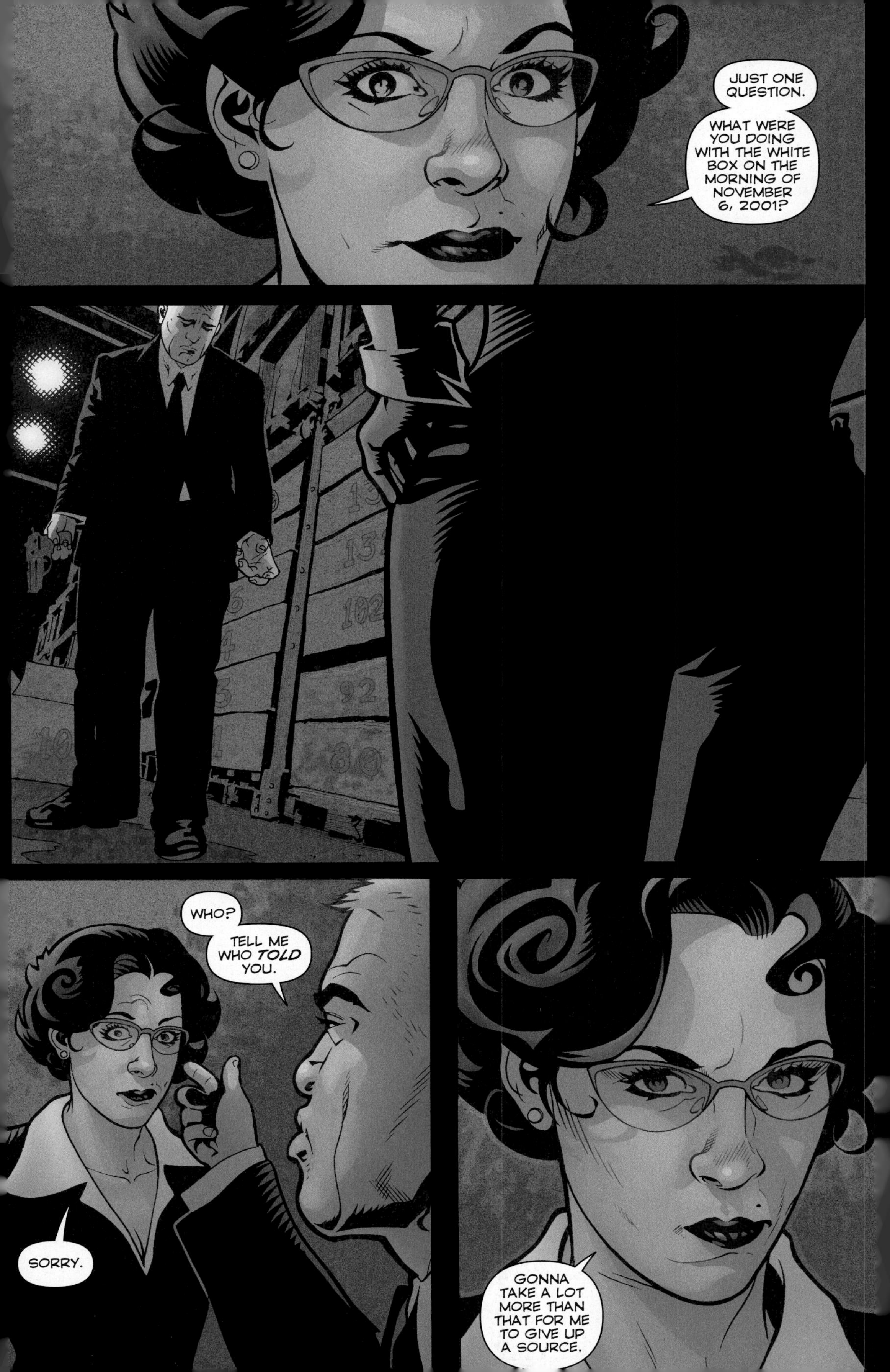
JUST ONE QUESTION.
WHAT WERE YOU DOING WITH THE WHITE BOX ON THE MORNING OF NOVEMBER 6, 2001?
WHO?
TELL ME WHO *TOLD* YOU.
SORRY.
GONNA TAKE A LOT MORE THAN THAT FOR ME TO GIVE UP A SOURCE.

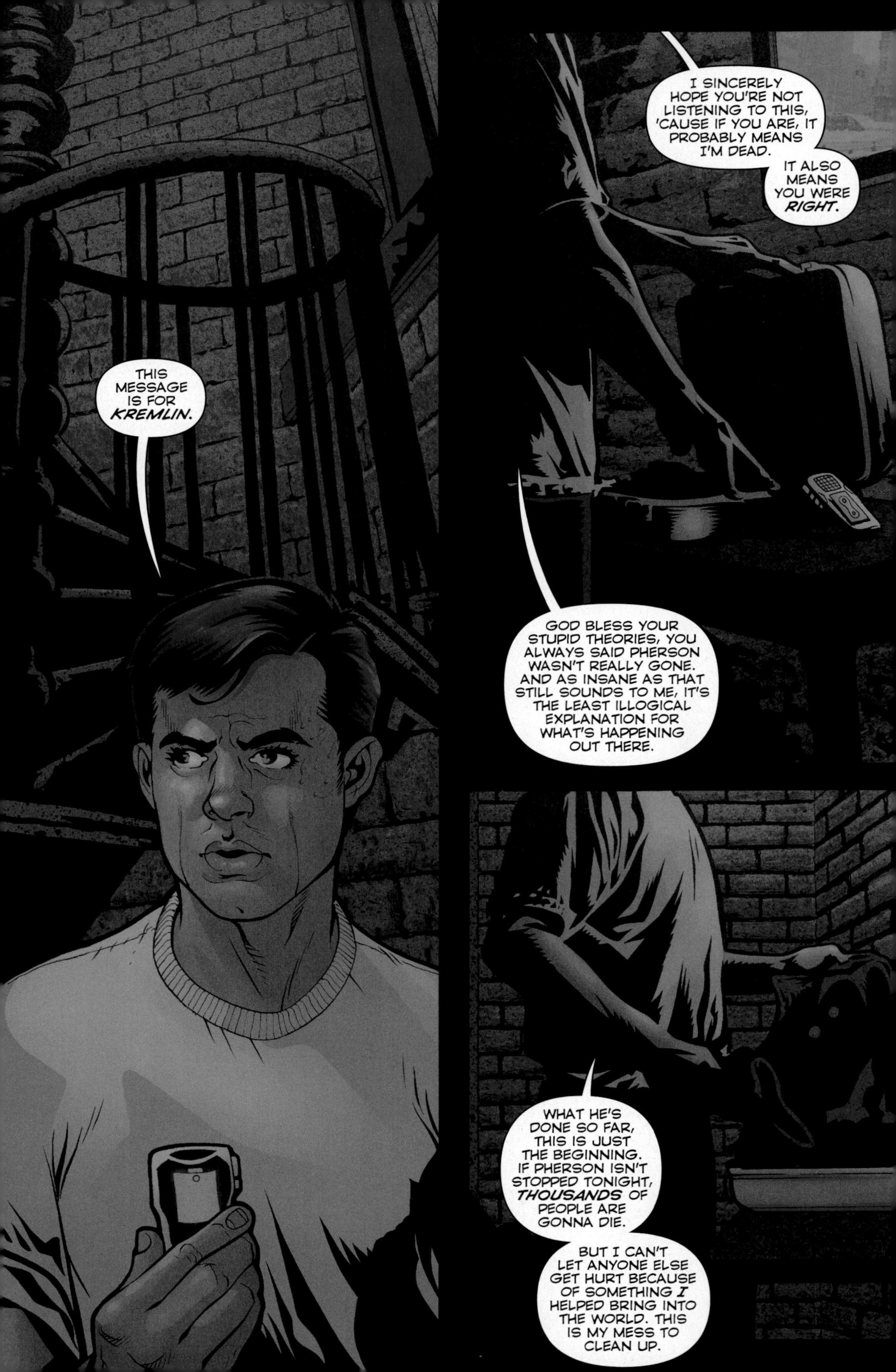
THIS MESSAGE IS FOR *KREMLIN*.
I SINCERELY HOPE YOU'RE NOT LISTENING TO THIS, 'CAUSE IF YOU ARE, IT PROBABLY MEANS I'M DEAD.
IT ALSO MEANS YOU WERE *RIGHT*.
GOD BLESS YOUR STUPID THEORIES, YOU ALWAYS SAID PHERSON WASN'T REALLY GONE. AND AS INSANE AS THAT STILL SOUNDS TO ME, IT'S THE LEAST ILLOGICAL EXPLANATION FOR WHAT'S HAPPENING OUT THERE.
WHAT HE'S DONE SO FAR, THIS IS JUST THE BEGINNING. IF PHERSON ISN'T STOPPED TONIGHT, *THOUSANDS* OF PEOPLE ARE GONNA DIE.
BUT I CAN'T LET ANYONE ELSE GET HURT BECAUSE OF SOMETHING *I* HELPED BRING INTO THE WORLD. THIS IS MY MESS TO CLEAN UP.

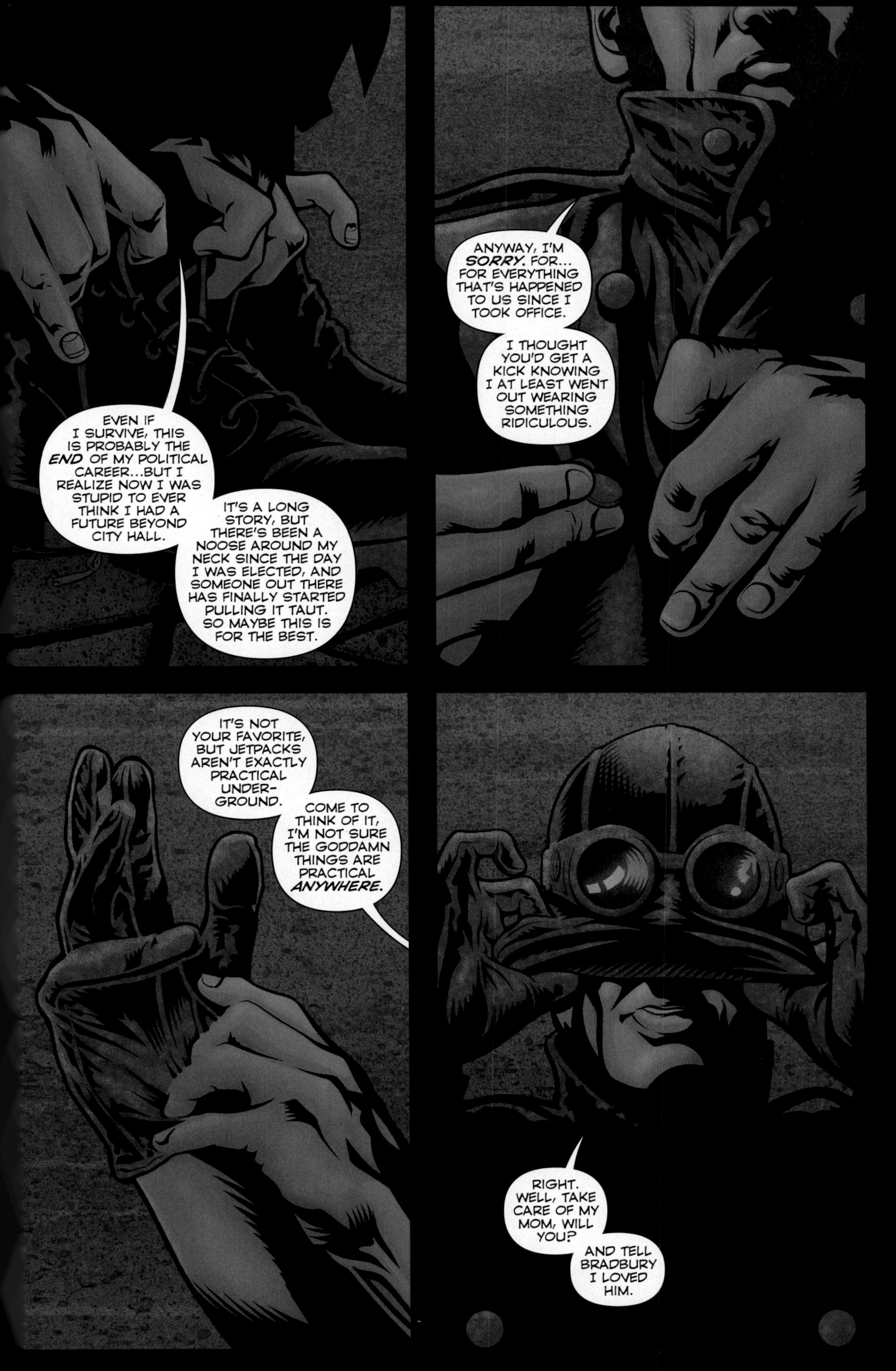
EVEN IF I SURVIVE, THIS IS PROBABLY THE END OF MY POLITICAL CAREER...BUT I REALIZE NOW I WAS STUPID TO EVER THINK I HAD A FUTURE BEYOND CITY HALL.
IT'S A LONG STORY, BUT THERE'S BEEN A NOOSE AROUND MY NECK SINCE THE DAY I WAS ELECTED, AND SOMEONE OUT THERE HAS FINALLY STARTED PULLING IT TAUT. SO MAYBE THIS IS FOR THE BEST.
ANYWAY, I'M SORRY. FOR... FOR EVERYTHING THAT'S HAPPENED TO US SINCE I TOOK OFFICE.
I THOUGHT YOU'D GET A KICK KNOWING I AT LEAST WENT OUT WEARING SOMETHING RIDICULOUS.
IT'S NOT YOUR FAVORITE, BUT JETPACKS AREN'T EXACTLY PRACTICAL UNDER-GROUND.
COME TO THINK OF IT, I'M NOT SURE THE GODDAMN THINGS ARE PRACTICAL ANYWHERE.
RIGHT. WELL, TAKE CARE OF MY MOM, WILL YOU?
AND TELL BRADBURY I LOVED HIM.

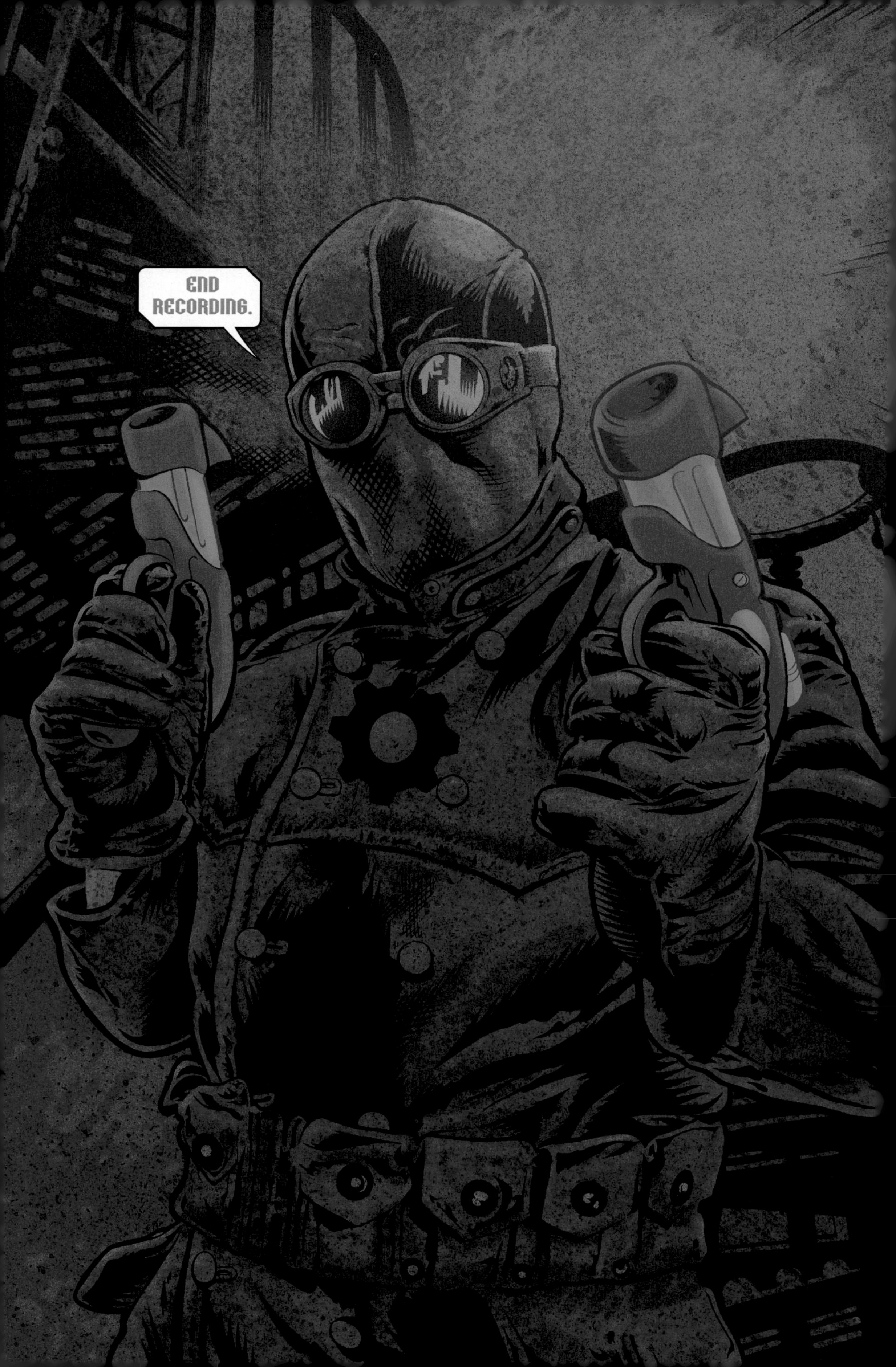
END RECORDING.

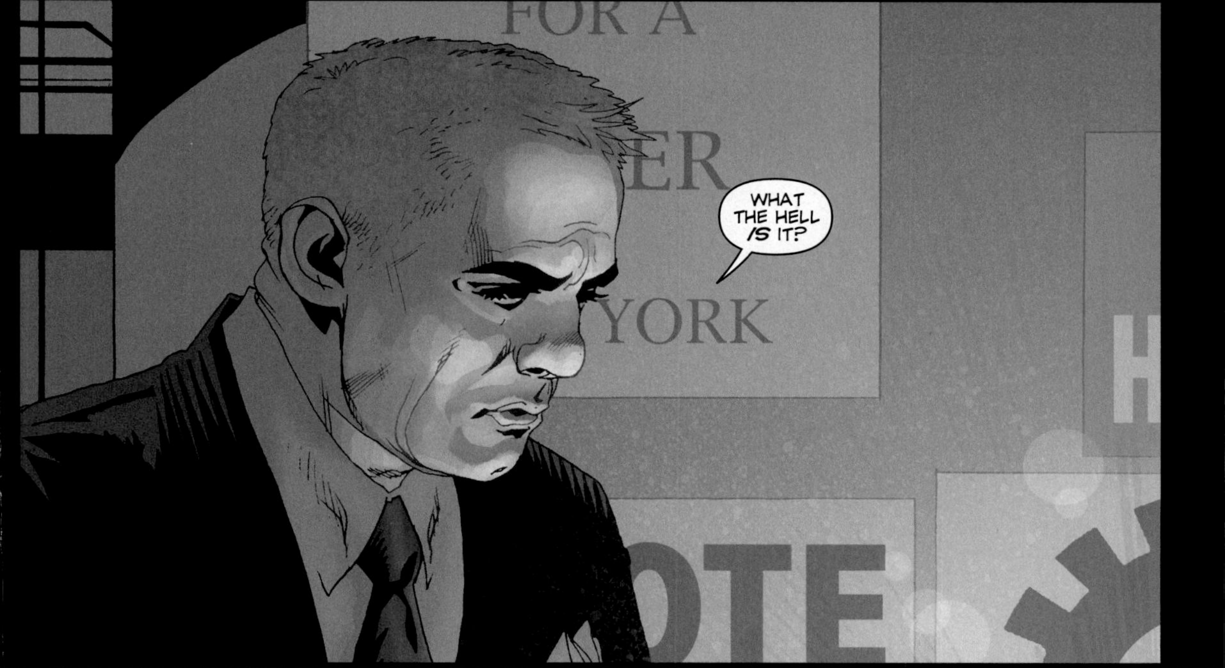
WHAT THE HELL *IS* IT?

MONDAY, NOVEMBER 5, 2001

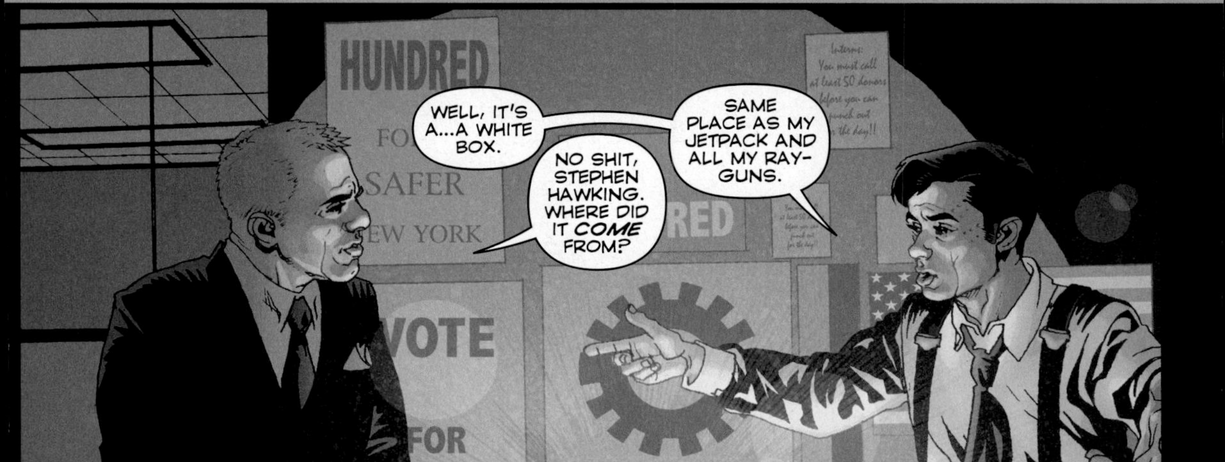
WELL, IT'S A...A WHITE BOX.
NO SHIT, STEPHEN HAWKING. WHERE DID IT *COME* FROM?
SAME PLACE AS MY JETPACK AND ALL MY RAY-GUNS.
HUNDRED
VOTE
FOR
HUNDRED

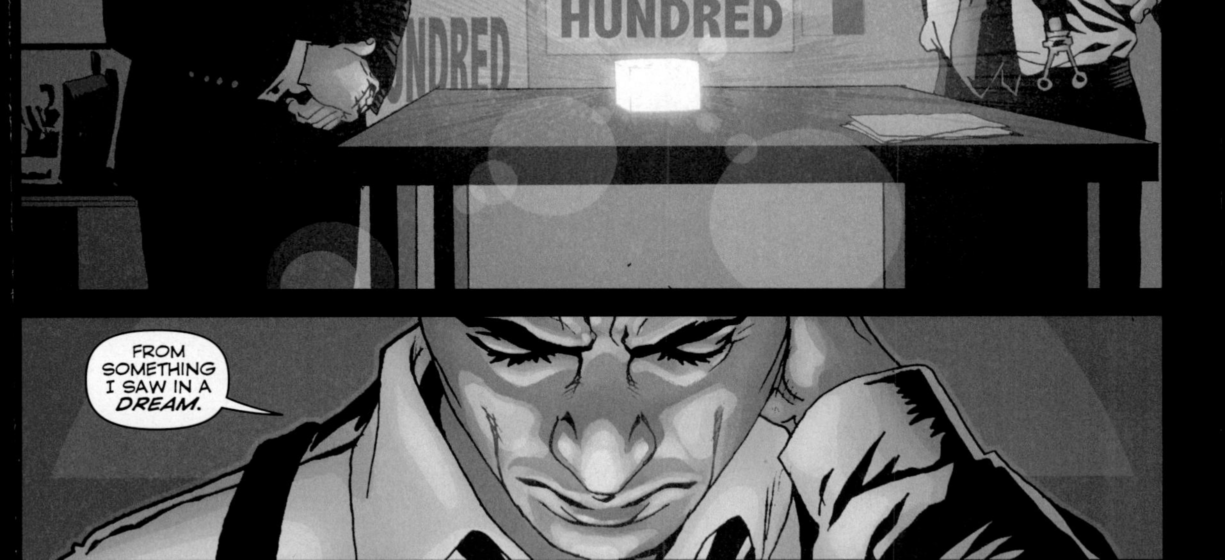
FROM SOMETHING I SAW IN A *DREAM*.

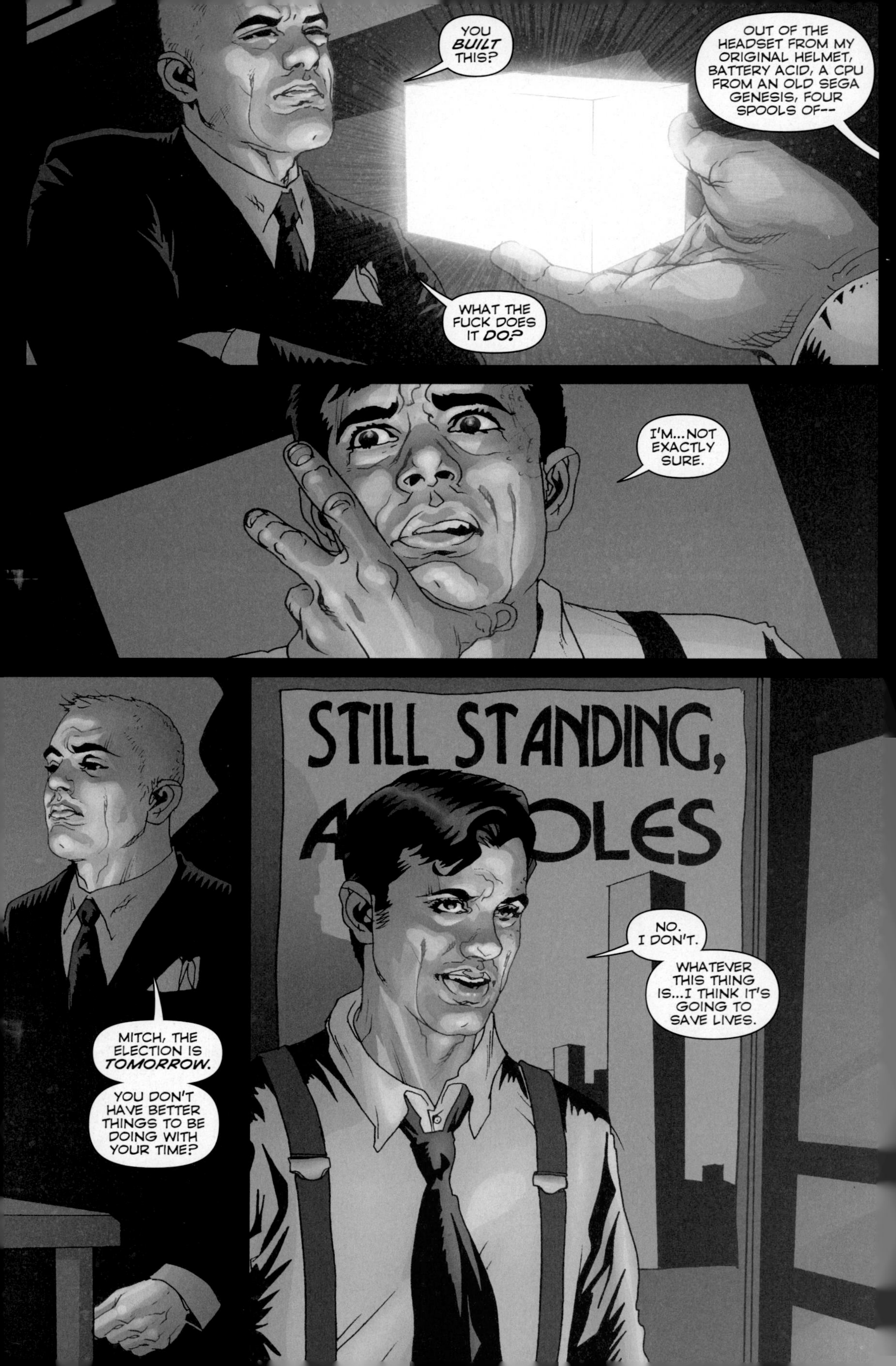
YOU *BUILT* THIS?
OUT OF THE HEADSET FROM MY ORIGINAL HELMET, BATTERY ACID, A CPU FROM AN OLD SEGA GENESIS, FOUR SPOOLS OF--
WHAT THE FUCK DOES IT *DO?*
I'M...NOT EXACTLY SURE.
STILL STANDING,
OLES
MITCH, THE ELECTION IS *TOMORROW*.
YOU DON'T HAVE BETTER THINGS TO BE DOING WITH YOUR TIME?
NO. I DON'T.
WHATEVER THIS THING IS...I THINK IT'S GOING TO SAVE LIVES.

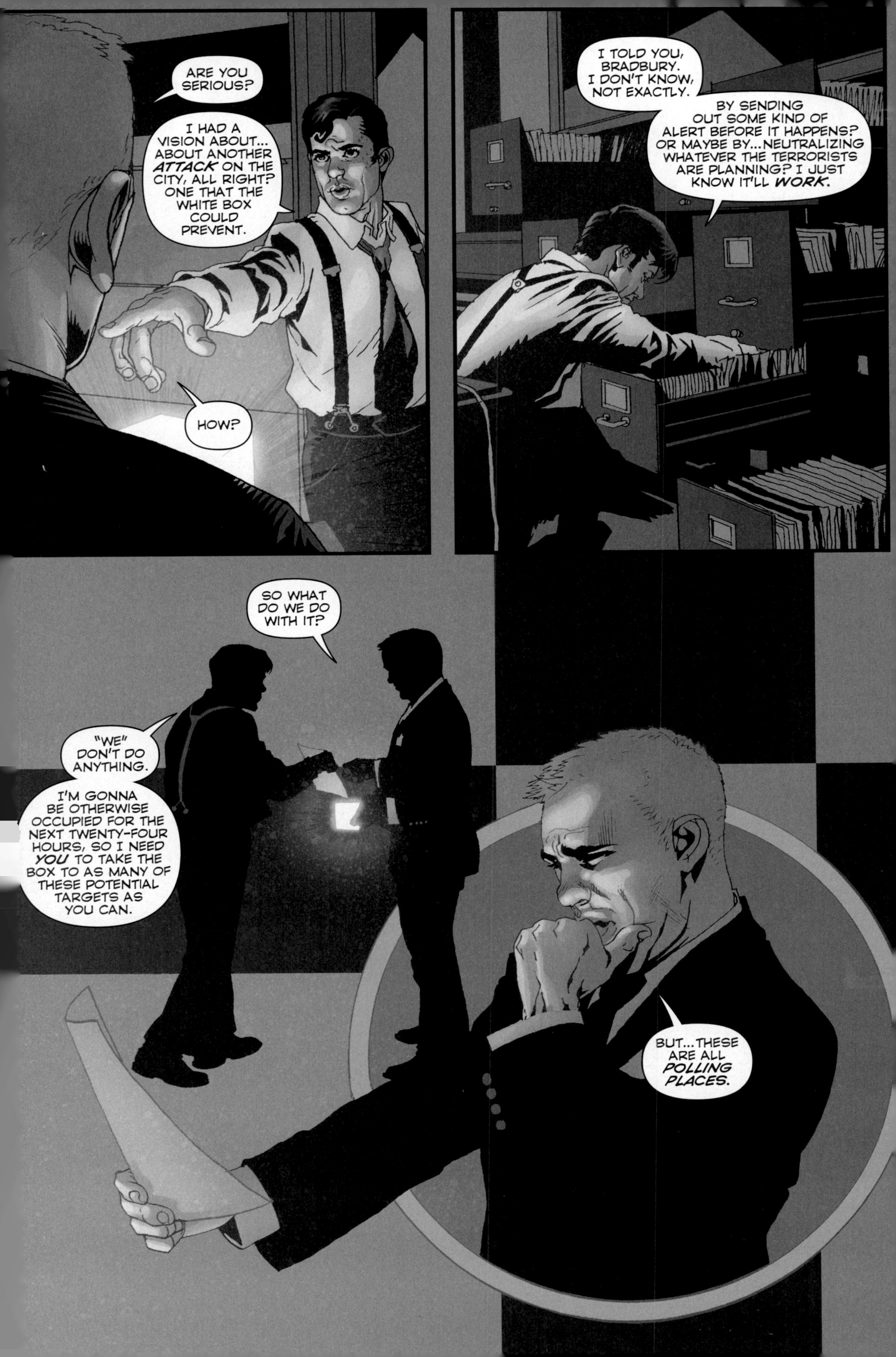
ARE YOU SERIOUS?
I HAD A VISION ABOUT... ABOUT ANOTHER ATTACK ON THE CITY, ALL RIGHT? ONE THAT THE WHITE BOX COULD PREVENT.
HOW?
I TOLD YOU, BRADBURY. I DON'T KNOW, NOT EXACTLY.
BY SENDING OUT SOME KIND OF ALERT BEFORE IT HAPPENS? OR MAYBE BY...NEUTRALIZING WHATEVER THE TERRORISTS ARE PLANNING? I JUST KNOW IT'LL WORK.
SO WHAT DO WE DO WITH IT?
"WE" DON'T DO ANYTHING.
I'M GONNA BE OTHERWISE OCCUPIED FOR THE NEXT TWENTY-FOUR HOURS, SO I NEED YOU TO TAKE THE BOX TO AS MANY OF THESE POTENTIAL TARGETS AS YOU CAN.
BUT...THESE ARE ALL POLLING PLACES.

I KNOW HOW IT LOOKS, BUT THE TERRORISTS HIT THE WORLD TRADE CENTER THE DAY OF THE *PRIMARIES,* REMEMBER?

IT MAKES SENSE THAT THEY MIGHT TRY TO STRIKE DURING ANOTHER...YOU KNOW, DEMONSTRATION OF DEMOCRACY IN ACTION.

STILL, IF ANYBODY *SEES* ME WITH THIS THING...

GREAT MACHINE CRAP!

THIS END UP

THEY WON'T. ALL EYES ARE GONNA BE ON *ME.*

AND STARTING TONIGHT, I'LL BE IN A DEPRIVATION TANK WITH MY OLD *NULLIFIER* AND A U.N. OBSERVER MAKING SURE I DON'T USE MY POWERS TO TAMPER WITH ANY VOTING MACHINES.

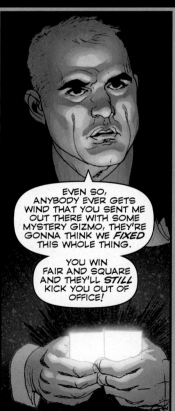

EVEN SO, ANYBODY EVER GETS WIND THAT YOU SENT ME OUT THERE WITH SOME MYSTERY GIZMO, THEY'RE GONNA THINK WE *FIXED* THIS WHOLE THING.

YOU WIN FAIR AND SQUARE AND THEY'LL *STILL* KICK YOU OUT OF OFFICE!

THAT'S A RISK I'M WILLING TO TAKE.

SOME THINGS ARE MORE IMPORTANT THAN WINNING.

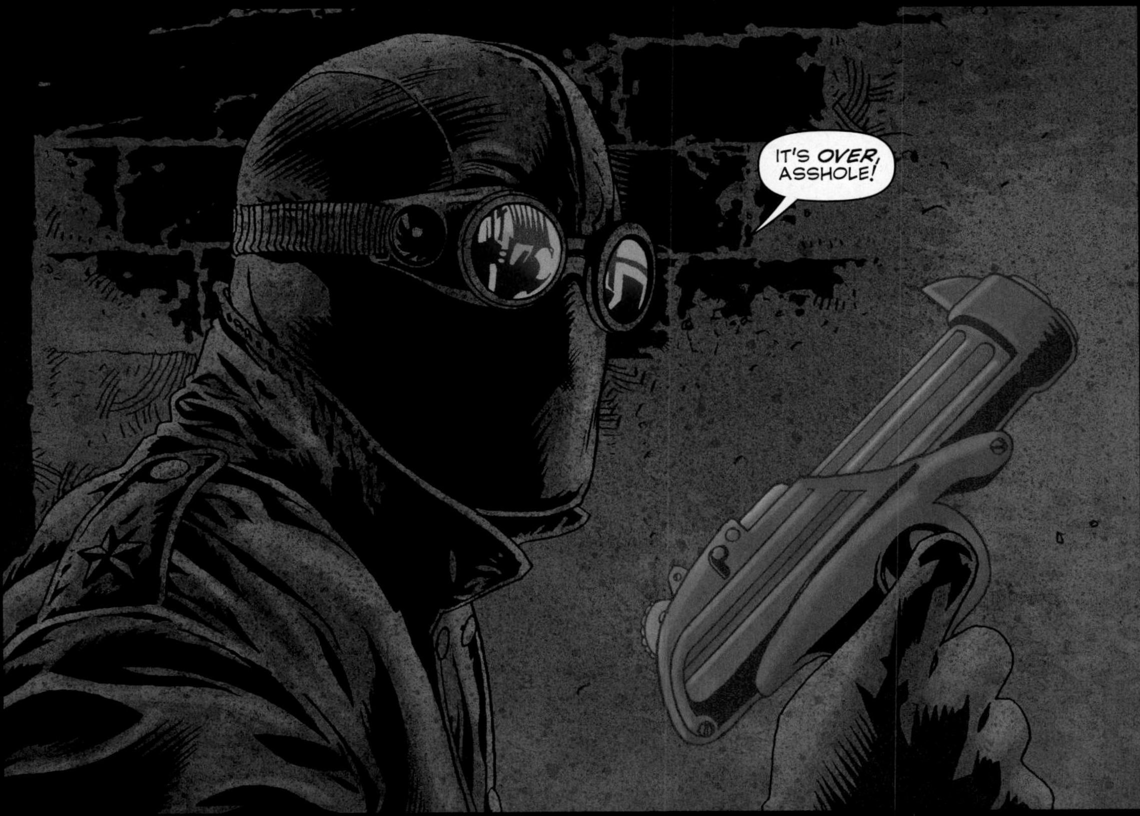
IT'S OVER, ASSHOLE!

THURSDAY, DECEMBER 30, 2004

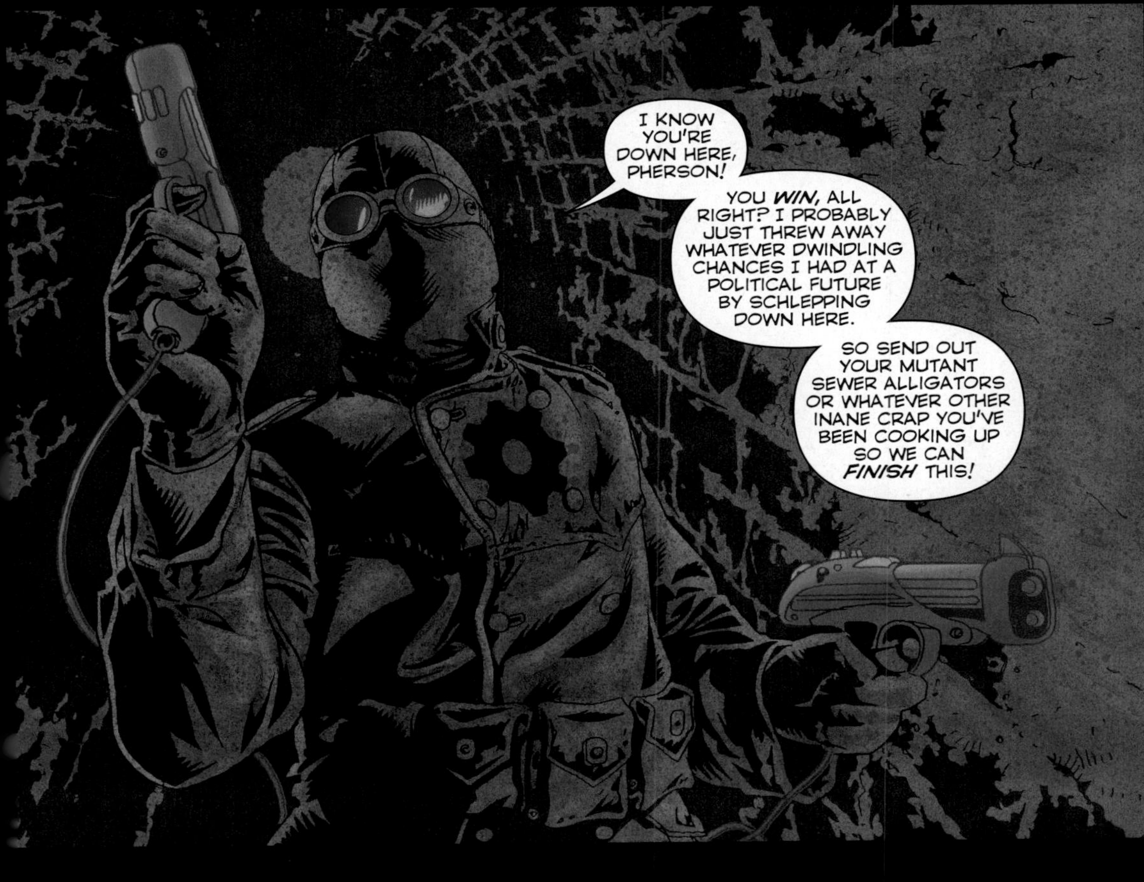
I KNOW YOU'RE DOWN HERE, PHERSON!
YOU WIN, ALL RIGHT? I PROBABLY JUST THREW AWAY WHATEVER DWINDLING CHANCES I HAD AT A POLITICAL FUTURE BY SCHLEPPING DOWN HERE.
SO SEND OUT YOUR MUTANT SEWER ALLIGATORS OR WHATEVER OTHER INANE CRAP YOU'VE BEEN COOKING UP SO WE CAN FINISH THIS!

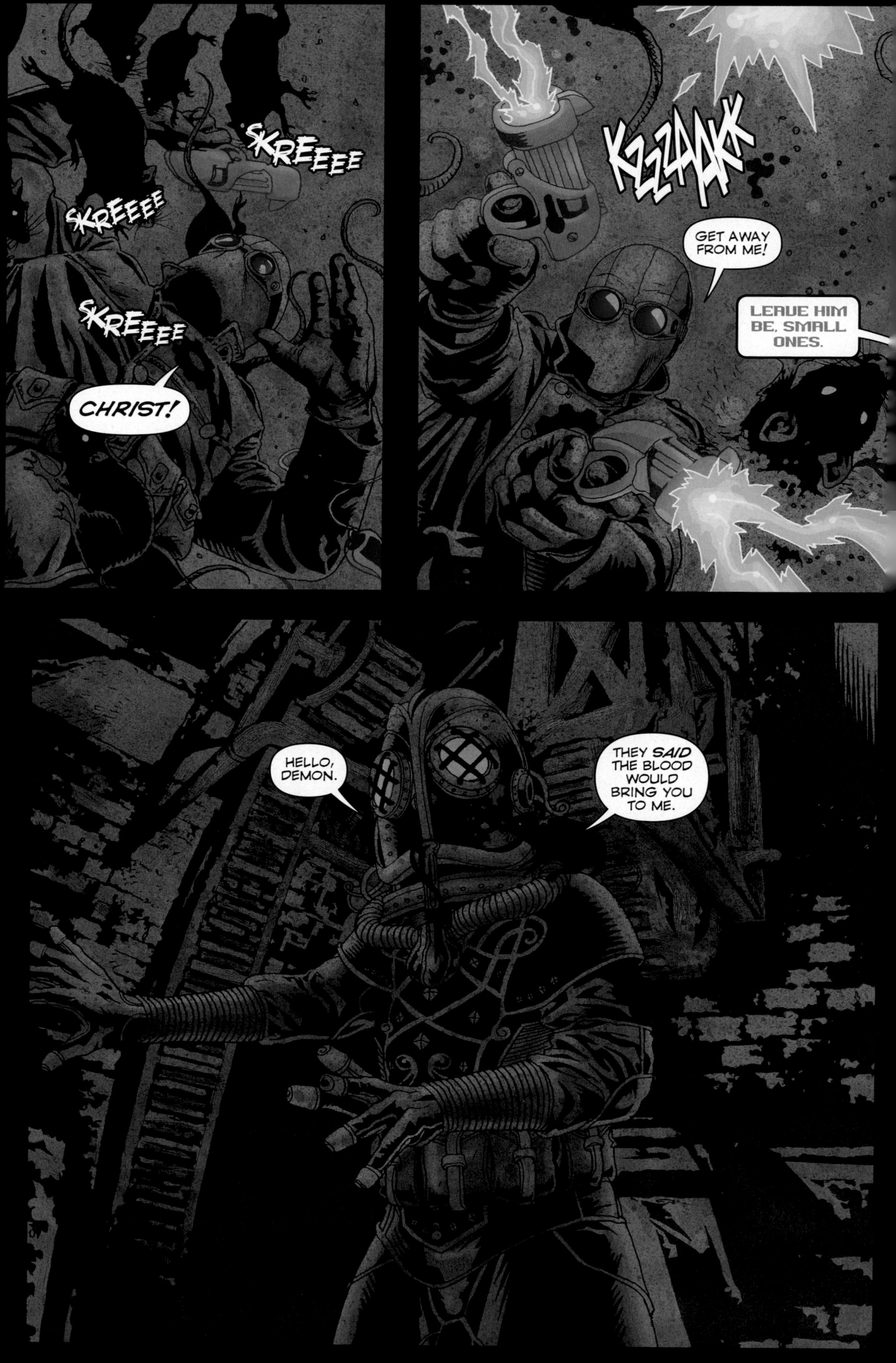
SKREEEE
SKREEEEE
SKREEEE
CHRIST!
KZZZAAKK
GET AWAY FROM ME!
LEAVE HIM BE, SMALL ONES.
HELLO, DEMON.
THEY SAID THE BLOOD WOULD BRING YOU TO ME.

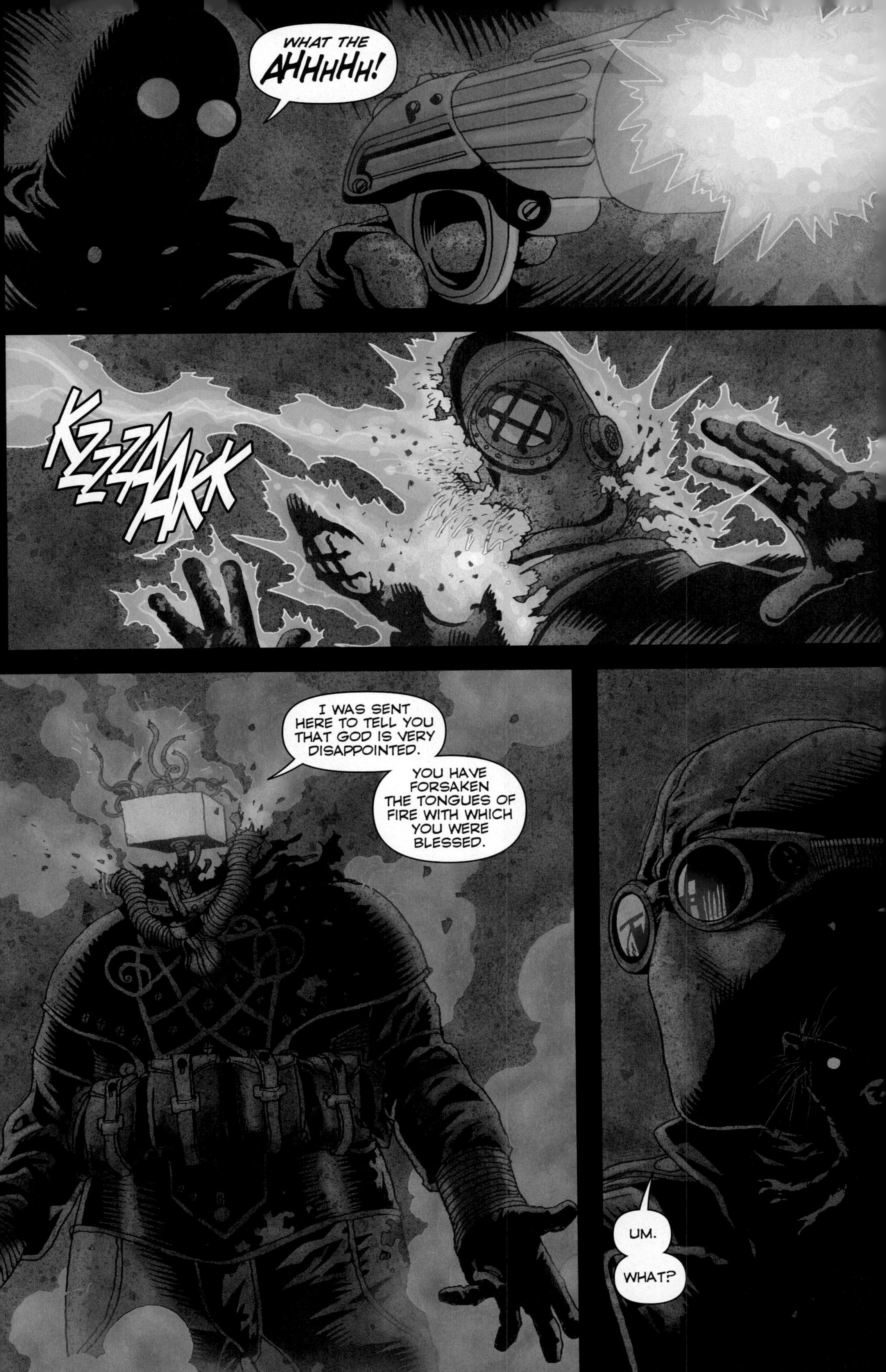
WHAT THE AHHHHH!
KZZZAAKK
I WAS SENT HERE TO TELL YOU THAT GOD IS VERY DISAPPOINTED.
YOU HAVE FORSAKEN THE TONGUES OF FIRE WITH WHICH YOU WERE BLESSED.
UM.
WHAT?

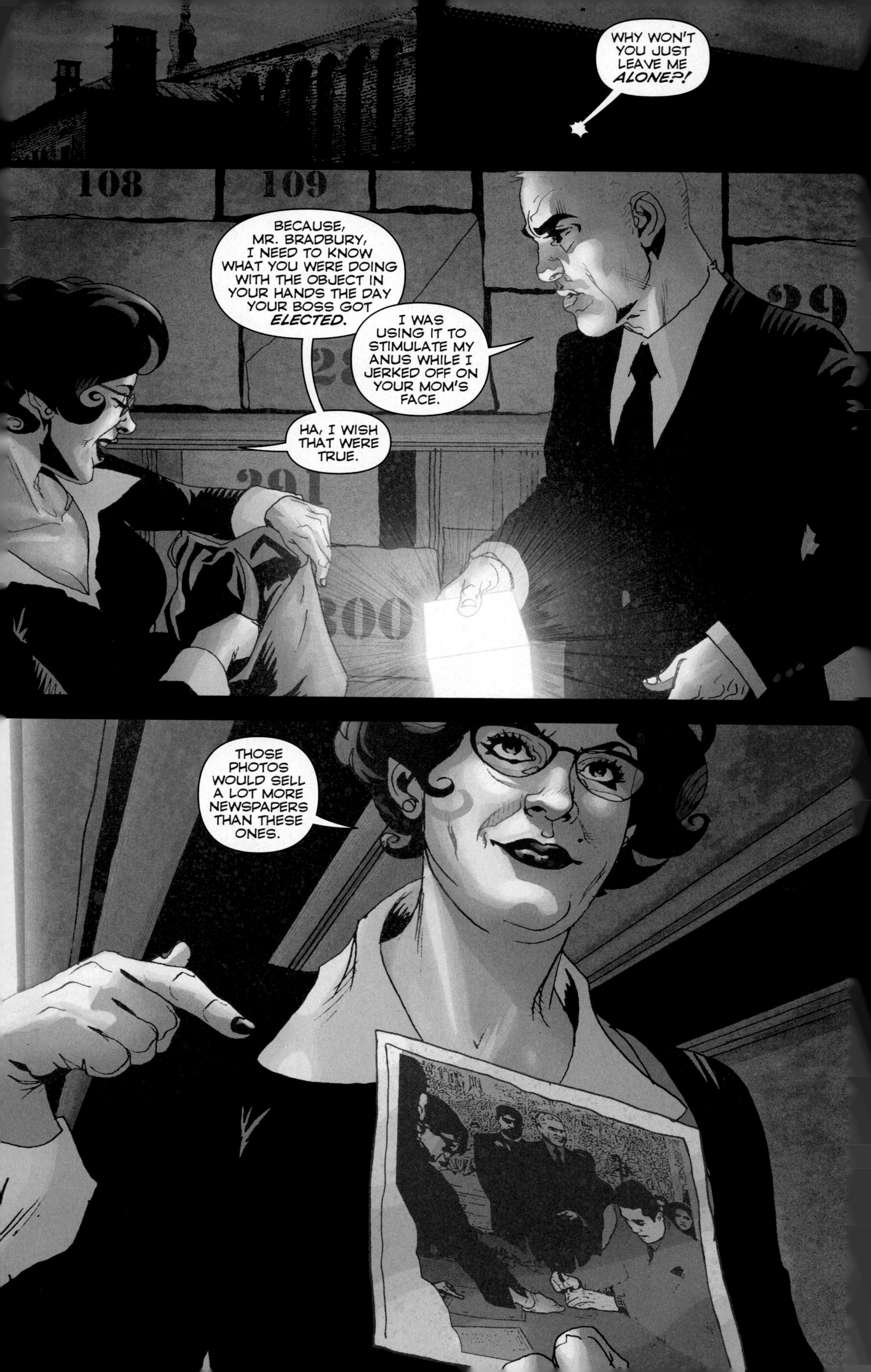
WHY WON'T YOU JUST LEAVE ME ALONE?!
BECAUSE, MR. BRADBURY, I NEED TO KNOW WHAT YOU WERE DOING WITH THE OBJECT IN YOUR HANDS THE DAY YOUR BOSS GOT ELECTED.
I WAS USING IT TO STIMULATE MY ANUS WHILE I JERKED OFF ON YOUR MOM'S FACE.
HA, I WISH THAT WERE TRUE.
THOSE PHOTOS WOULD SELL A LOT MORE NEWSPAPERS THAN THESE ONES.

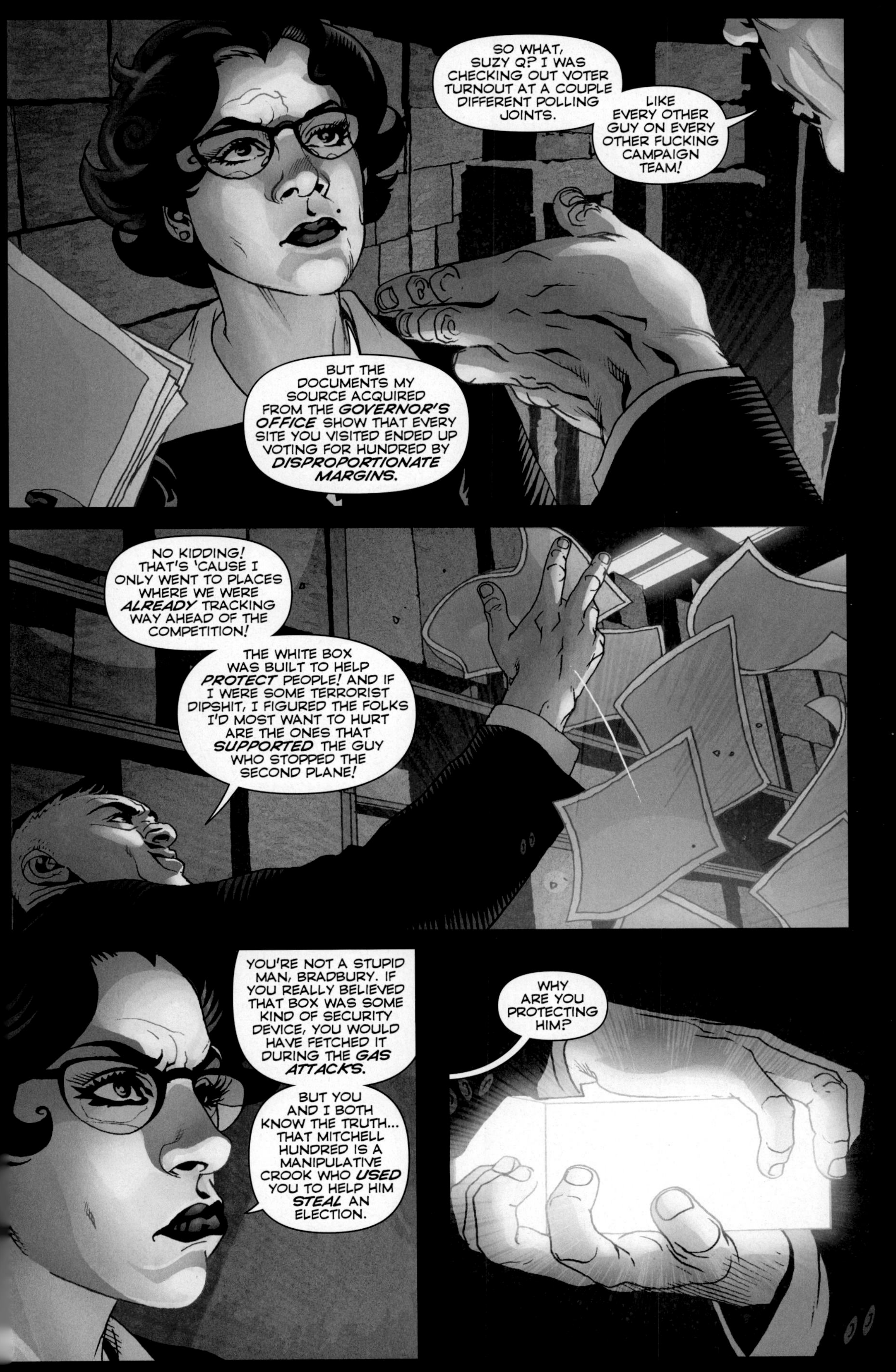
SO WHAT, SUZY Q? I WAS CHECKING OUT VOTER TURNOUT AT A COUPLE DIFFERENT POLLING JOINTS.
LIKE EVERY OTHER GUY ON EVERY OTHER FUCKING CAMPAIGN TEAM!
BUT THE DOCUMENTS MY SOURCE ACQUIRED FROM THE GOVERNOR'S OFFICE SHOW THAT EVERY SITE YOU VISITED ENDED UP VOTING FOR HUNDRED BY DISPROPORTIONATE MARGINS.
NO KIDDING! THAT'S 'CAUSE I ONLY WENT TO PLACES WHERE WE WERE ALREADY TRACKING WAY AHEAD OF THE COMPETITION!
THE WHITE BOX WAS BUILT TO HELP PROTECT PEOPLE! AND IF I WERE SOME TERRORIST DIPSHIT, I FIGURED THE FOLKS I'D MOST WANT TO HURT ARE THE ONES THAT SUPPORTED THE GUY WHO STOPPED THE SECOND PLANE!
YOU'RE NOT A STUPID MAN, BRADBURY. IF YOU REALLY BELIEVED THAT BOX WAS SOME KIND OF SECURITY DEVICE, YOU WOULD HAVE FETCHED IT DURING THE GAS ATTACKS.
BUT YOU AND I BOTH KNOW THE TRUTH... THAT MITCHELL HUNDRED IS A MANIPULATIVE CROOK WHO USED YOU TO HELP HIM STEAL AN ELECTION.
WHY ARE YOU PROTECTING HIM?

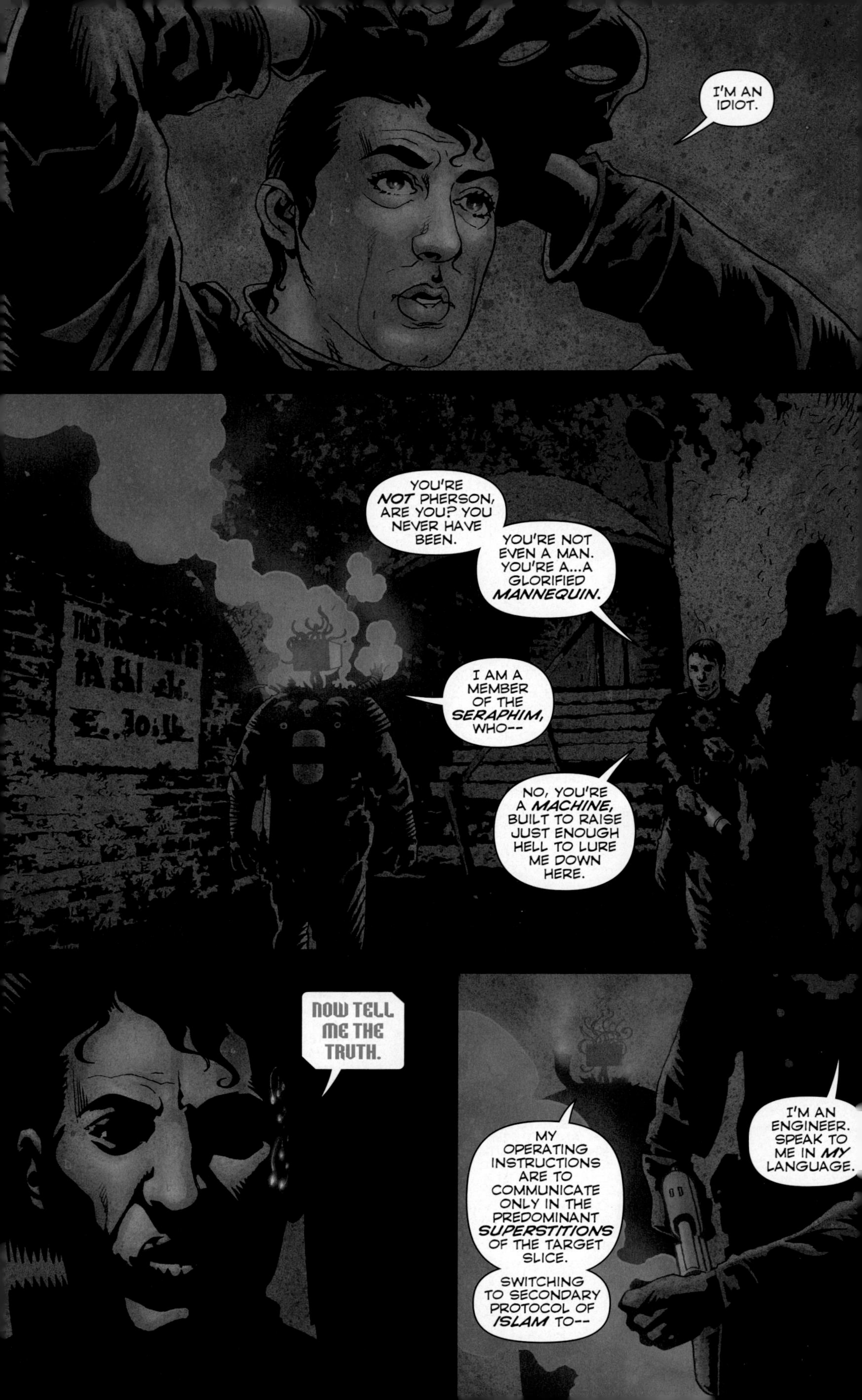
I'M AN IDIOT.
YOU'RE NOT PHERSON, ARE YOU? YOU NEVER HAVE BEEN.
YOU'RE NOT EVEN A MAN. YOU'RE A...A GLORIFIED MANNEQUIN.
I AM A MEMBER OF THE SERAPHIM, WHO--
NO, YOU'RE A MACHINE, BUILT TO RAISE JUST ENOUGH HELL TO LURE ME DOWN HERE.
NOW TELL ME THE TRUTH.
MY OPERATING INSTRUCTIONS ARE TO COMMUNICATE ONLY IN THE PREDOMINANT SUPERSTITIONS OF THE TARGET SLICE.
SWITCHING TO SECONDARY PROTOCOL OF ISLAM TO--
I'M AN ENGINEER. SPEAK TO ME IN MY LANGUAGE.

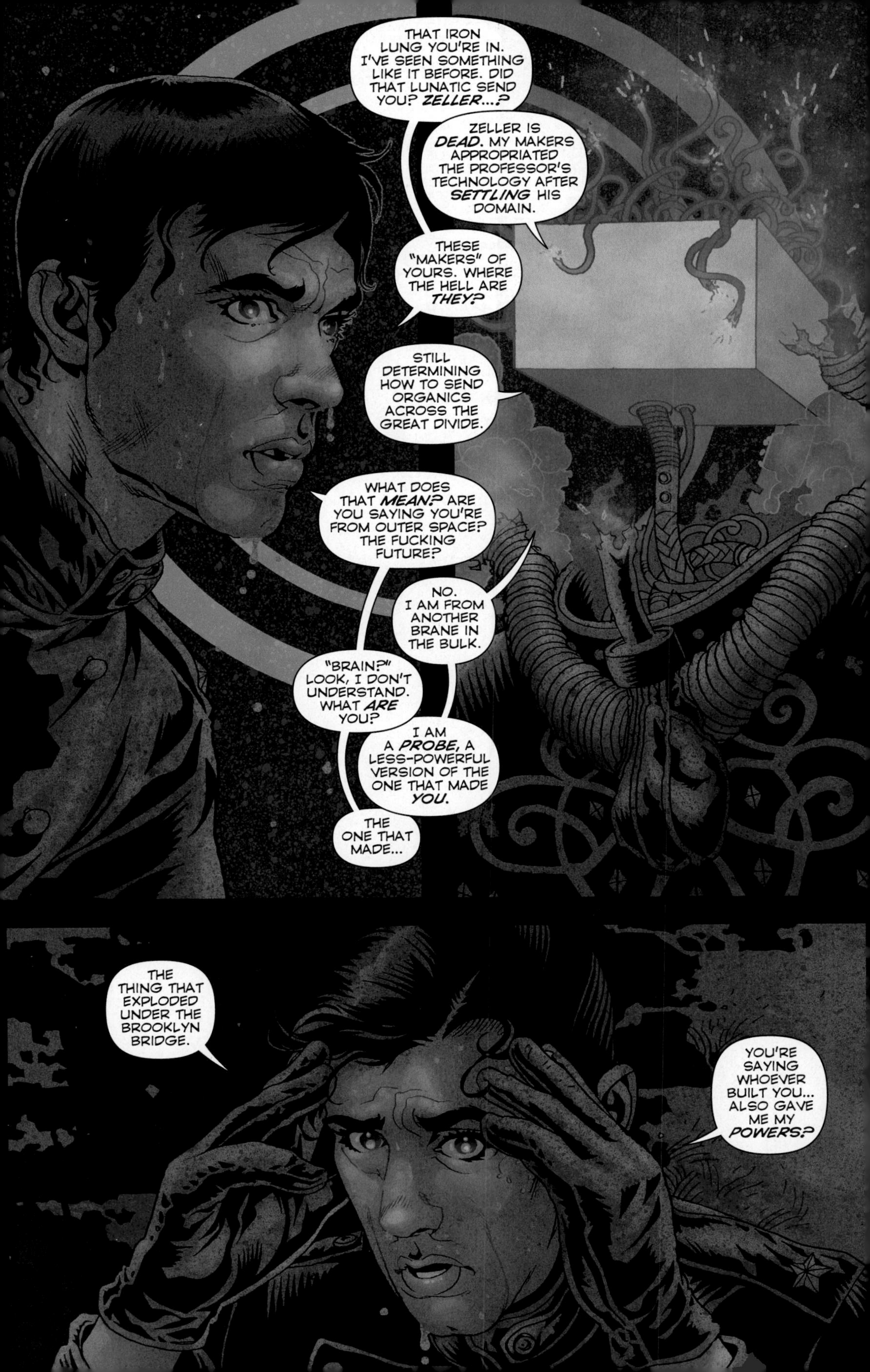
THAT IRON LUNG YOU'RE IN. I'VE SEEN SOMETHING LIKE IT BEFORE. DID THAT LUNATIC SEND YOU? ZELLER...?
ZELLER IS DEAD. MY MAKERS APPROPRIATED THE PROFESSOR'S TECHNOLOGY AFTER SETTLING HIS DOMAIN.
THESE "MAKERS" OF YOURS. WHERE THE HELL ARE THEY?
STILL DETERMINING HOW TO SEND ORGANICS ACROSS THE GREAT DIVIDE.
WHAT DOES THAT MEAN? ARE YOU SAYING YOU'RE FROM OUTER SPACE? THE FUCKING FUTURE?
NO. I AM FROM ANOTHER BRANE IN THE BULK.
"BRAIN?" LOOK, I DON'T UNDERSTAND. WHAT ARE YOU?
I AM A PROBE, A LESS-POWERFUL VERSION OF THE ONE THAT MADE YOU.
THE ONE THAT MADE...
THE THING THAT EXPLODED UNDER THE BROOKLYN BRIDGE.
YOU'RE SAYING WHOEVER BUILT YOU... ALSO GAVE ME MY POWERS?

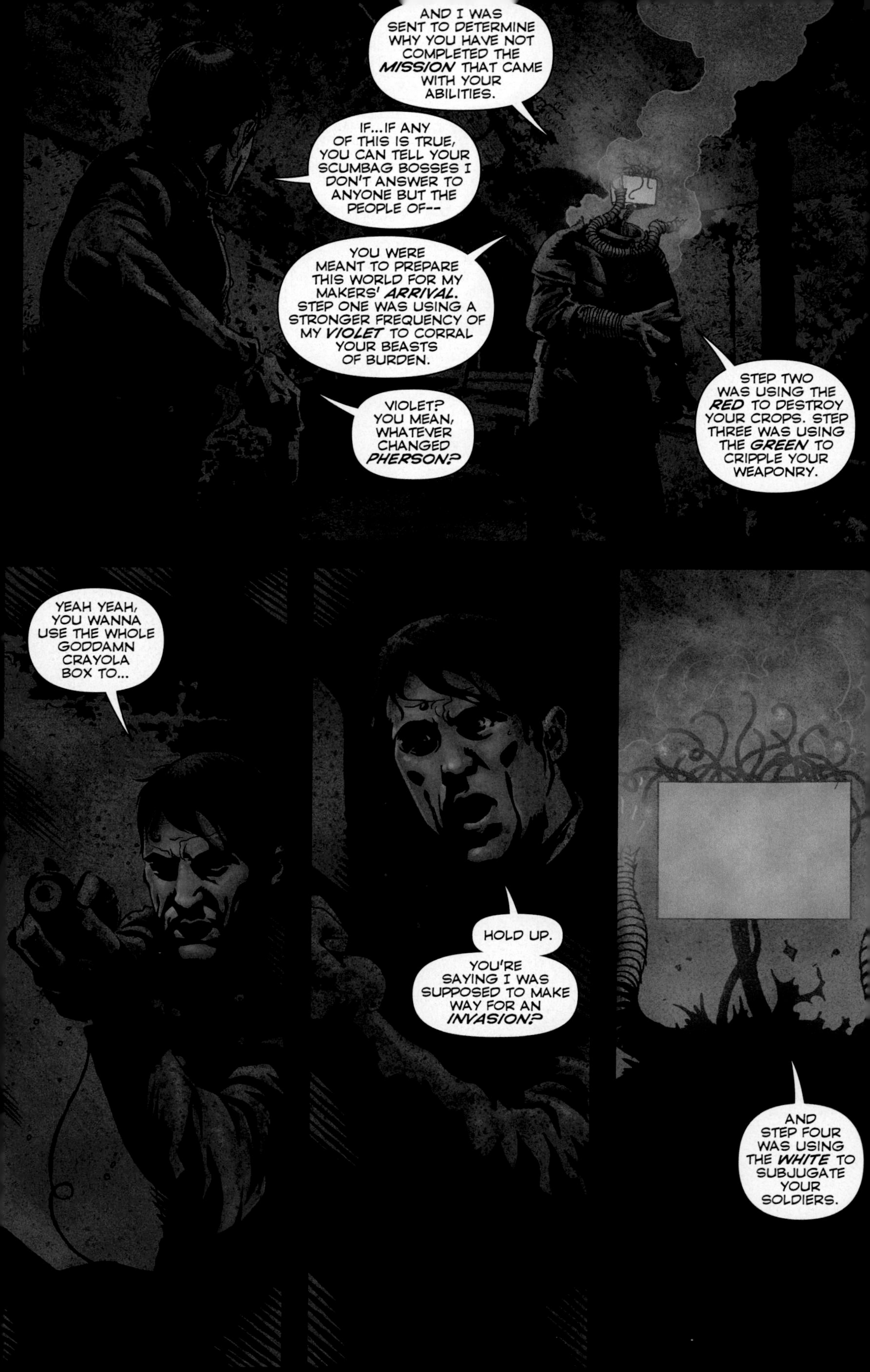
AND I WAS SENT TO DETERMINE WHY YOU HAVE NOT COMPLETED THE *MISSION* THAT CAME WITH YOUR ABILITIES.
IF...IF ANY OF THIS IS TRUE, YOU CAN TELL YOUR SCUMBAG BOSSES I DON'T ANSWER TO ANYONE BUT THE PEOPLE OF--
YOU WERE MEANT TO PREPARE THIS WORLD FOR MY MAKERS' *ARRIVAL.* STEP ONE WAS USING A STRONGER FREQUENCY OF MY *VIOLET* TO CORRAL YOUR BEASTS OF BURDEN.
VIOLET? YOU MEAN, WHATEVER CHANGED *PHERSON?*
STEP TWO WAS USING THE *RED* TO DESTROY YOUR CROPS. STEP THREE WAS USING THE *GREEN* TO CRIPPLE YOUR WEAPONRY.
YEAH YEAH, YOU WANNA USE THE WHOLE GODDAMN CRAYOLA BOX TO...
HOLD UP.
YOU'RE SAYING I WAS SUPPOSED TO MAKE WAY FOR AN *INVASION?*
AND STEP FOUR WAS USING THE *WHITE* TO SUBJUGATE YOUR SOLDIERS.

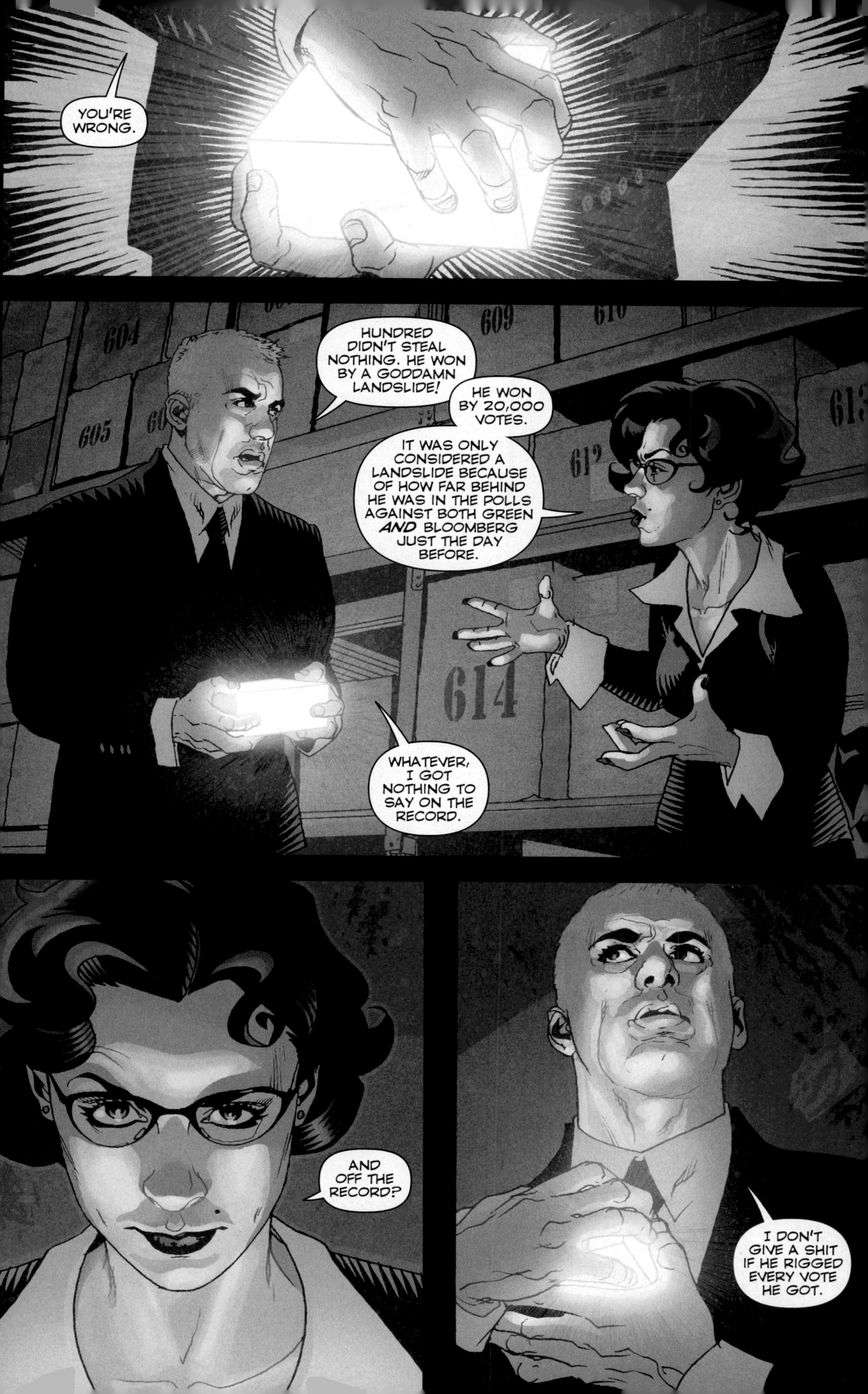
YOU'RE WRONG.
604
605
609
612
613
614
HUNDRED DIDN'T STEAL NOTHING. HE WON BY A GODDAMN LANDSLIDE!
HE WON BY 20,000 VOTES.
IT WAS ONLY CONSIDERED A LANDSLIDE BECAUSE OF HOW FAR BEHIND HE WAS IN THE POLLS AGAINST BOTH GREEN *AND* BLOOMBERG JUST THE DAY BEFORE.
WHATEVER, I GOT NOTHING TO SAY ON THE RECORD.
AND OFF THE RECORD?
I DON'T GIVE A SHIT IF HE RIGGED EVERY VOTE HE GOT.

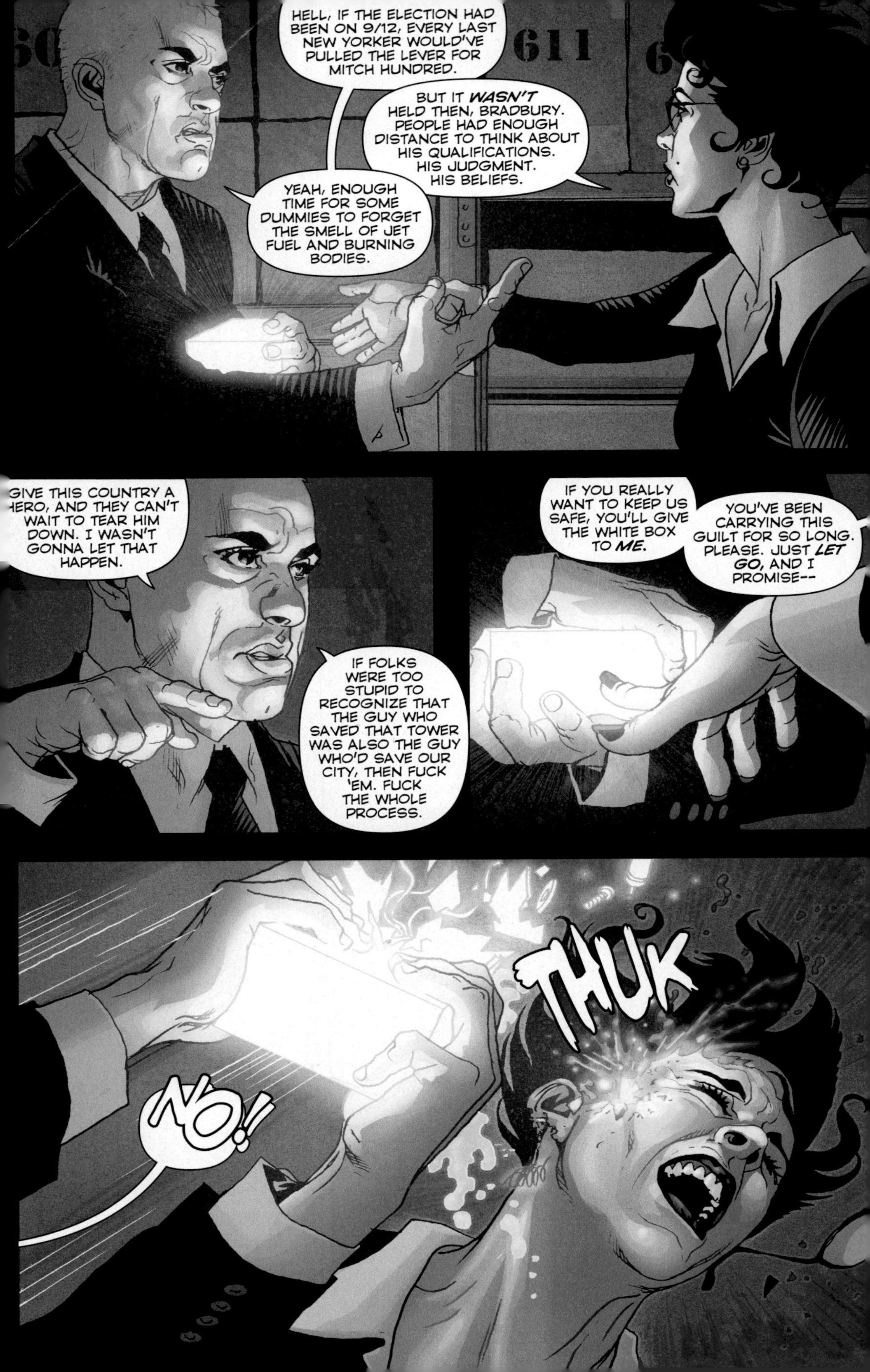
HELL, IF THE ELECTION HAD BEEN ON 9/12, EVERY LAST NEW YORKER WOULD'VE PULLED THE LEVER FOR MITCH HUNDRED.
BUT IT WASN'T HELD THEN, BRADBURY. PEOPLE HAD ENOUGH DISTANCE TO THINK ABOUT HIS QUALIFICATIONS. HIS JUDGMENT. HIS BELIEFS.
YEAH, ENOUGH TIME FOR SOME DUMMIES TO FORGET THE SMELL OF JET FUEL AND BURNING BODIES.
GIVE THIS COUNTRY A HERO, AND THEY CAN'T WAIT TO TEAR HIM DOWN. I WASN'T GONNA LET THAT HAPPEN.
IF FOLKS WERE TOO STUPID TO RECOGNIZE THAT THE GUY WHO SAVED THAT TOWER WAS ALSO THE GUY WHO'D SAVE OUR CITY, THEN FUCK 'EM. FUCK THE WHOLE PROCESS.
IF YOU REALLY WANT TO KEEP US SAFE, YOU'LL GIVE THE WHITE BOX TO ME.
YOU'VE BEEN CARRYING THIS GUILT FOR SO LONG. PLEASE. JUST LET GO, AND I PROMISE--
THUK
NO!!

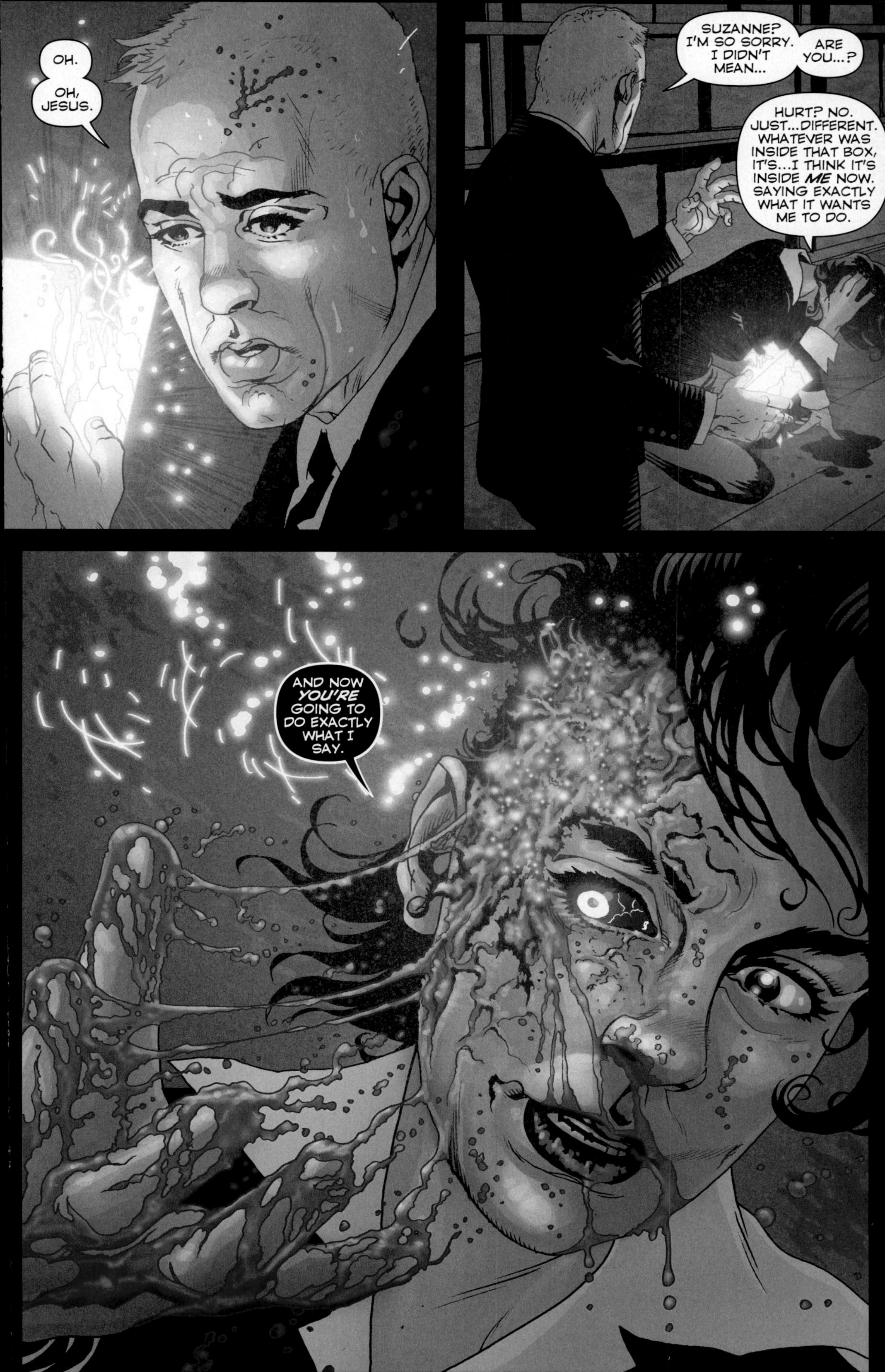

OH.
OH, JESUS.
SUZANNE? I'M SO SORRY. I DIDN'T MEAN...
ARE YOU...?
HURT? NO. JUST...DIFFERENT. WHATEVER WAS INSIDE THAT BOX, IT'S...I THINK IT'S INSIDE *ME* NOW. SAYING EXACTLY WHAT IT WANTS ME TO DO.
AND NOW *YOU'RE* GOING TO DO EXACTLY WHAT I SAY.

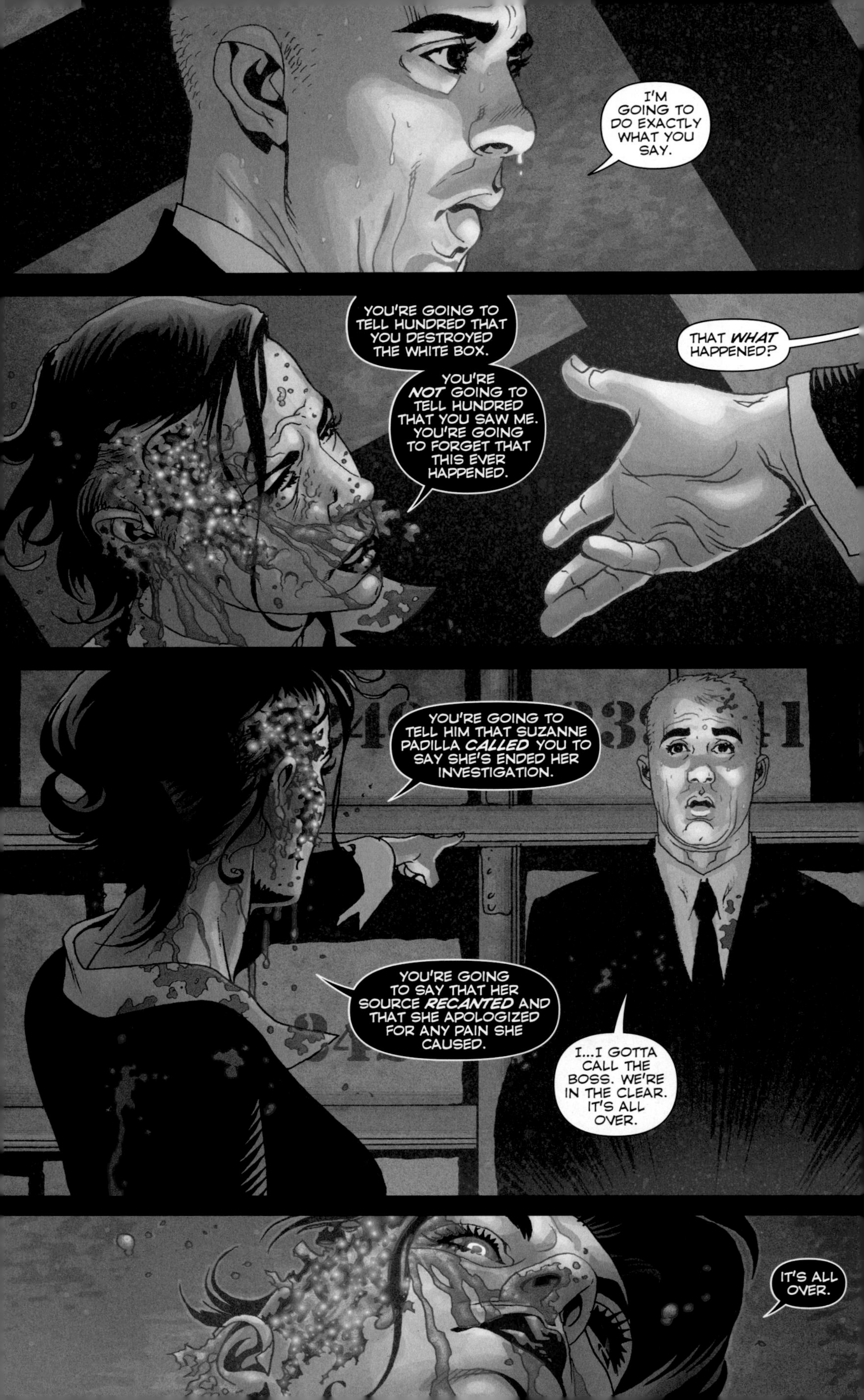
I'M GOING TO DO EXACTLY WHAT YOU SAY.
YOU'RE GOING TO TELL HUNDRED THAT YOU DESTROYED THE WHITE BOX.
YOU'RE NOT GOING TO TELL HUNDRED THAT YOU SAW ME. YOU'RE GOING TO FORGET THAT THIS EVER HAPPENED.
THAT WHAT HAPPENED?
YOU'RE GOING TO TELL HIM THAT SUZANNE PADILLA CALLED YOU TO SAY SHE'S ENDED HER INVESTIGATION.
YOU'RE GOING TO SAY THAT HER SOURCE RECANTED AND THAT SHE APOLOGIZED FOR ANY PAIN SHE CAUSED.
I...I GOTTA CALL THE BOSS. WE'RE IN THE CLEAR. IT'S ALL OVER.
IT'S ALL OVER.

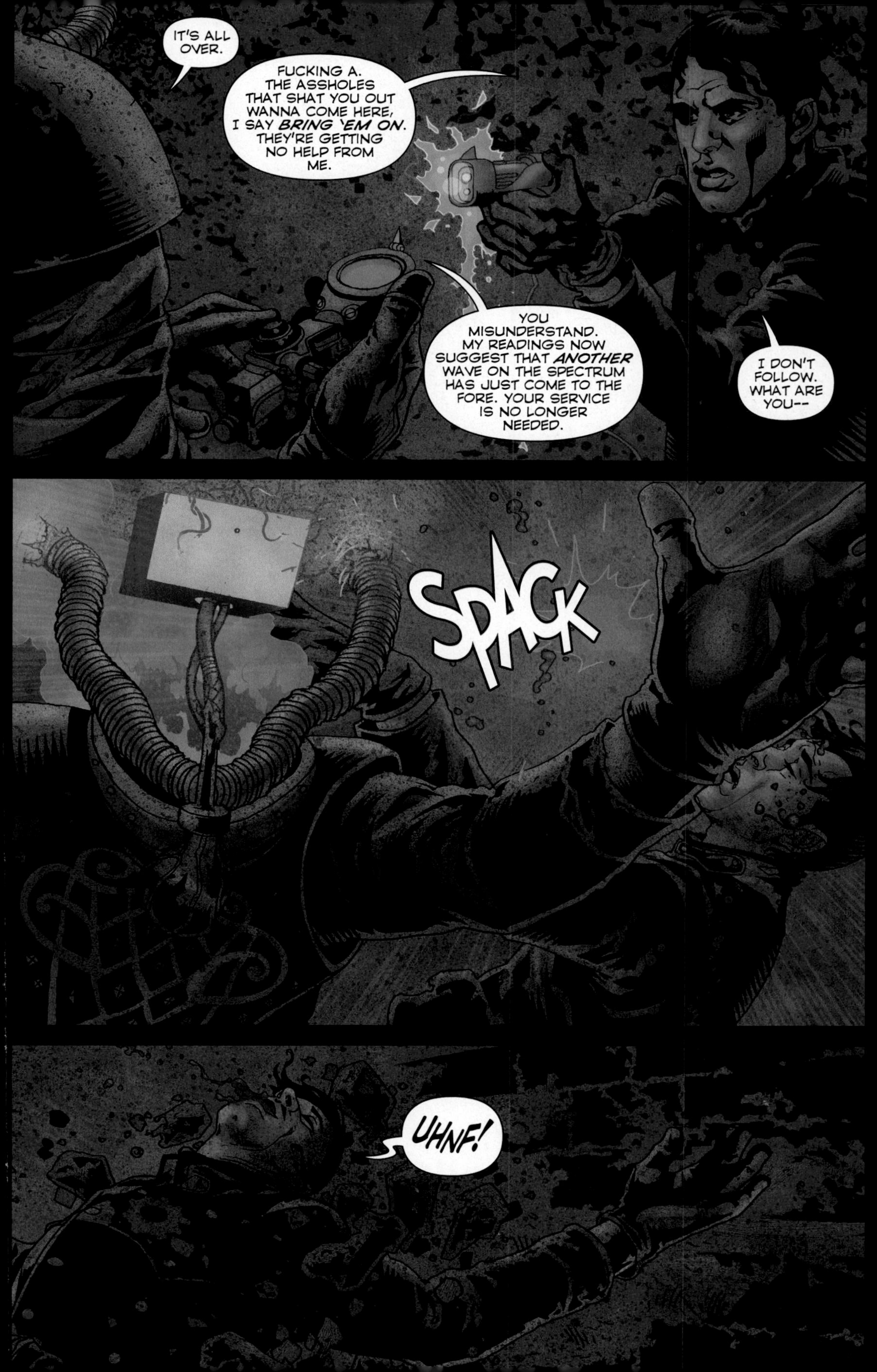
IT'S ALL OVER.
FUCKING A. THE ASSHOLES THAT SHAT YOU OUT WANNA COME HERE, I SAY *BRING 'EM ON*. THEY'RE GETTING NO HELP FROM ME.
YOU MISUNDERSTAND. MY READINGS NOW SUGGEST THAT *ANOTHER* WAVE ON THE SPECTRUM HAS JUST COME TO THE FORE. YOUR SERVICE IS NO LONGER NEEDED.
I DON'T FOLLOW. WHAT ARE YOU--
SPACK
UHNF!

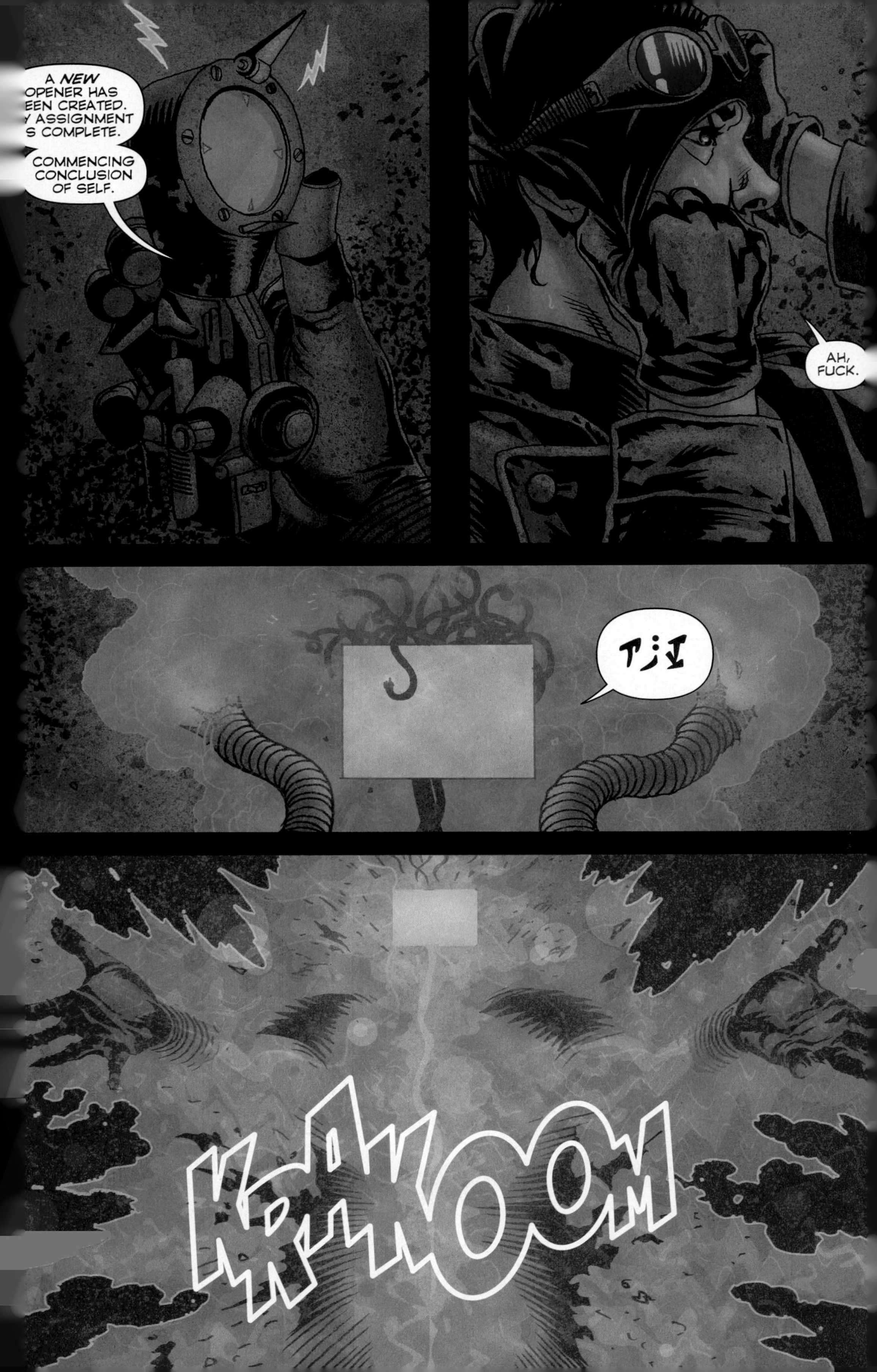
A NEW OPENER HAS EEN CREATED. Y ASSIGNMENT S COMPLETE.
COMMENCING CONCLUSION OF SELF.
AH, FUCK.
KRAKOOM

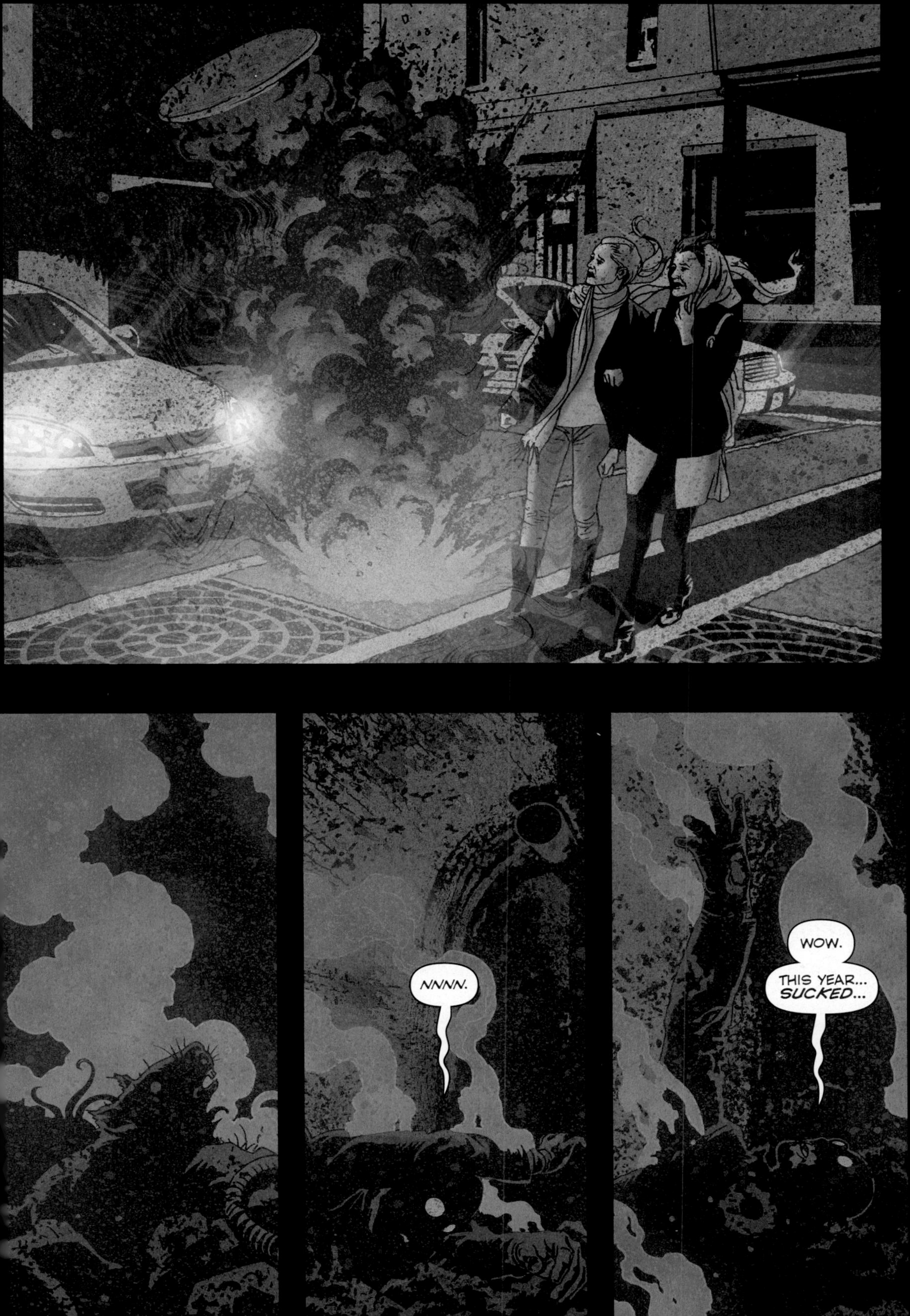
NNNN.
WOW.
THIS YEAR... SUCKED...

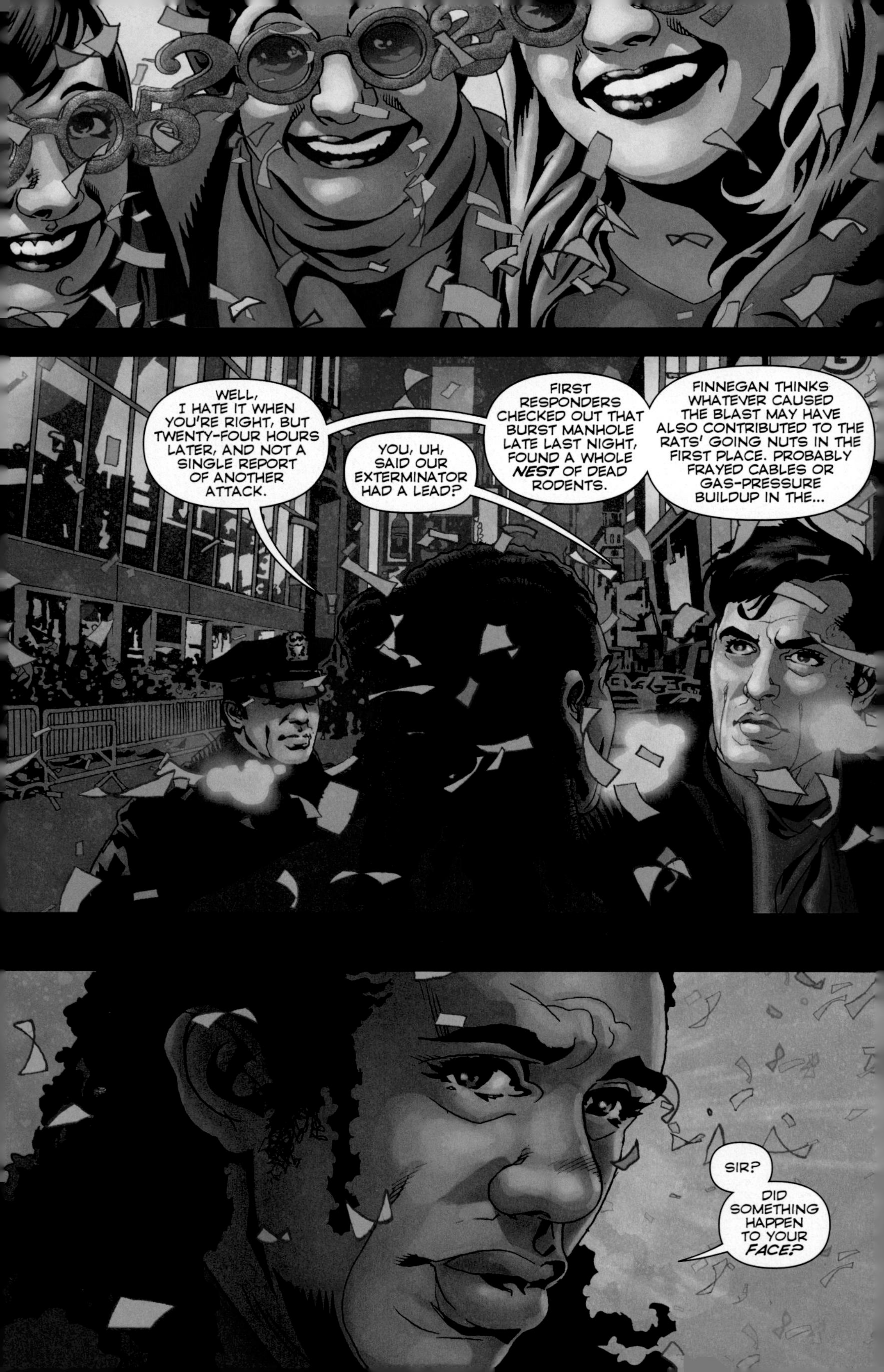
WELL, I HATE IT WHEN YOU'RE RIGHT, BUT TWENTY-FOUR HOURS LATER, AND NOT A SINGLE REPORT OF ANOTHER ATTACK.
YOU, UH, SAID OUR EXTERMINATOR HAD A LEAD?
FIRST RESPONDERS CHECKED OUT THAT BURST MANHOLE LATE LAST NIGHT, FOUND A WHOLE NEST OF DEAD RODENTS.
FINNEGAN THINKS WHATEVER CAUSED THE BLAST MAY HAVE ALSO CONTRIBUTED TO THE RATS' GOING NUTS IN THE FIRST PLACE. PROBABLY FRAYED CABLES OR GAS-PRESSURE BUILDUP IN THE...
SIR?
DID SOMETHING HAPPEN TO YOUR FACE?

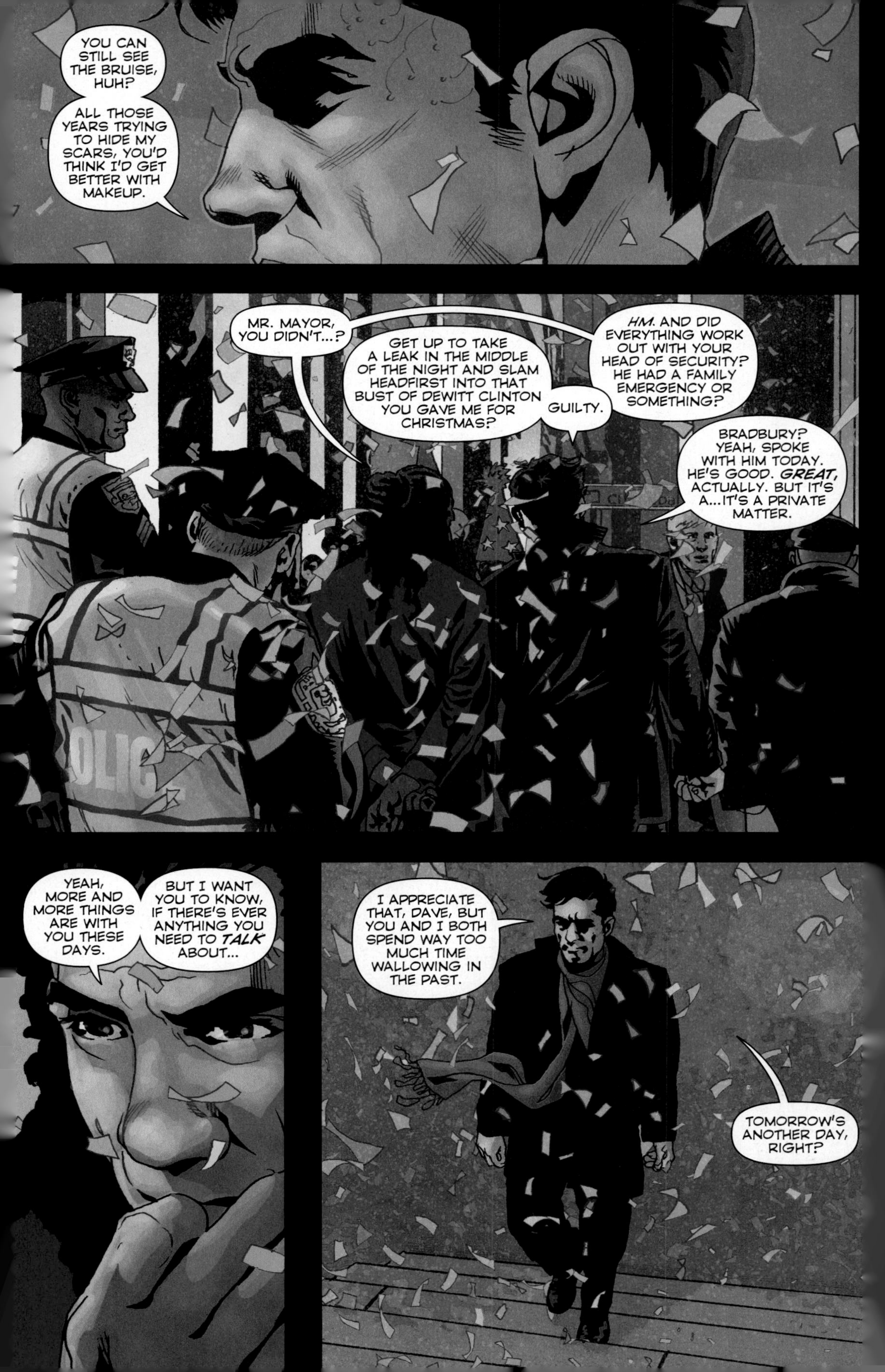
YOU CAN STILL SEE THE BRUISE, HUH?
ALL THOSE YEARS TRYING TO HIDE MY SCARS, YOU'D THINK I'D GET BETTER WITH MAKEUP.
MR. MAYOR, YOU DIDN'T...?
GET UP TO TAKE A LEAK IN THE MIDDLE OF THE NIGHT AND SLAM HEADFIRST INTO THAT BUST OF DEWITT CLINTON YOU GAVE ME FOR CHRISTMAS?
GUILTY.
HM. AND DID EVERYTHING WORK OUT WITH YOUR HEAD OF SECURITY? HE HAD A FAMILY EMERGENCY OR SOMETHING?
BRADBURY? YEAH, SPOKE WITH HIM TODAY. HE'S GOOD. ***GREAT,*** ACTUALLY. BUT IT'S A...IT'S A PRIVATE MATTER.
OLIC
YEAH, MORE AND MORE THINGS ARE WITH YOU THESE DAYS.
BUT I WANT YOU TO KNOW, IF THERE'S EVER ANYTHING YOU NEED TO ***TALK*** ABOUT...
I APPRECIATE THAT, DAVE, BUT YOU AND I BOTH SPEND WAY TOO MUCH TIME WALLOWING IN THE PAST.
TOMORROW'S ANOTHER DAY, RIGHT?

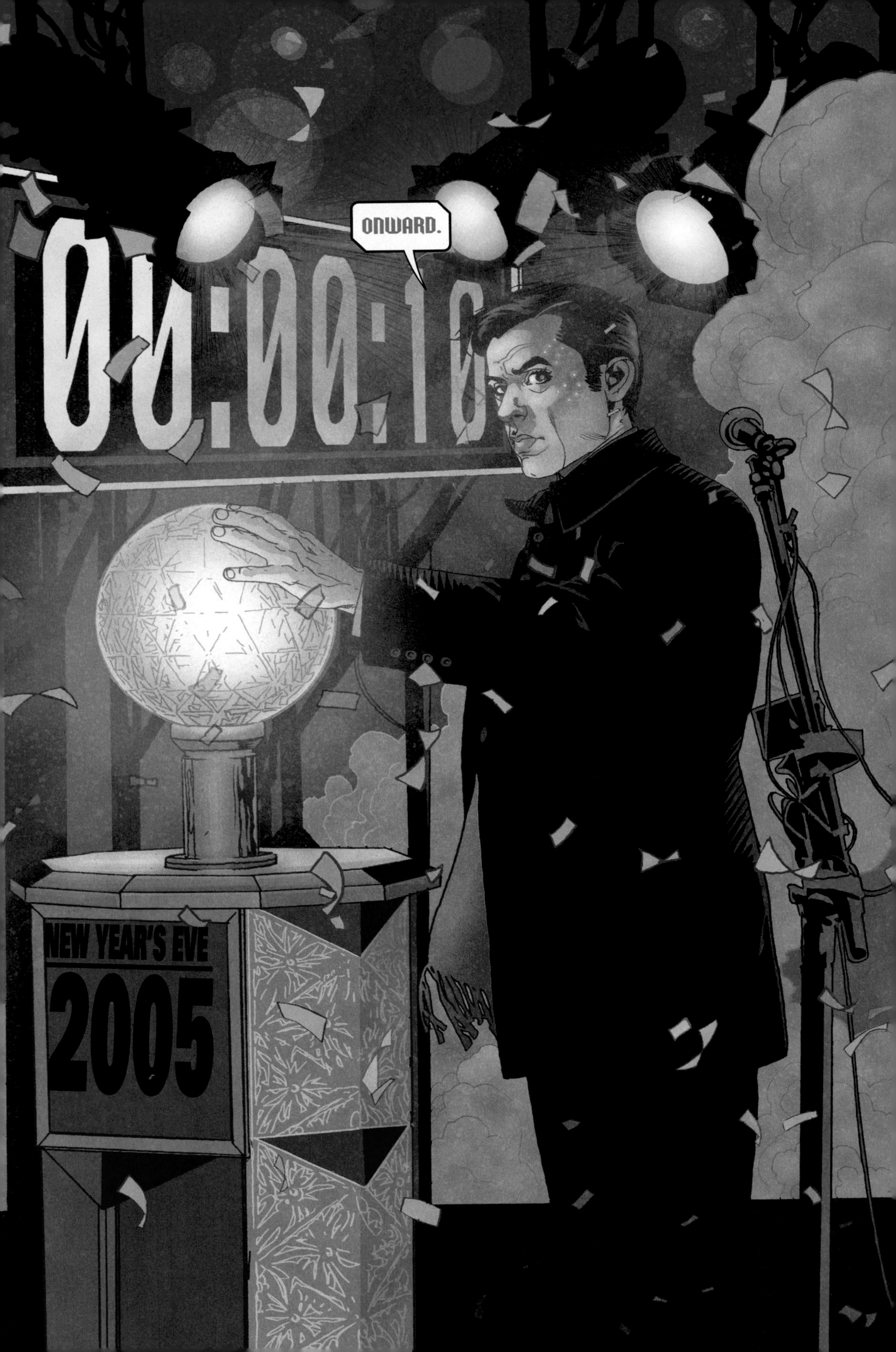

ONWARD.
00:00:10
NEW YEAR'S EVE
2005

CHAPTER 2 GREEN

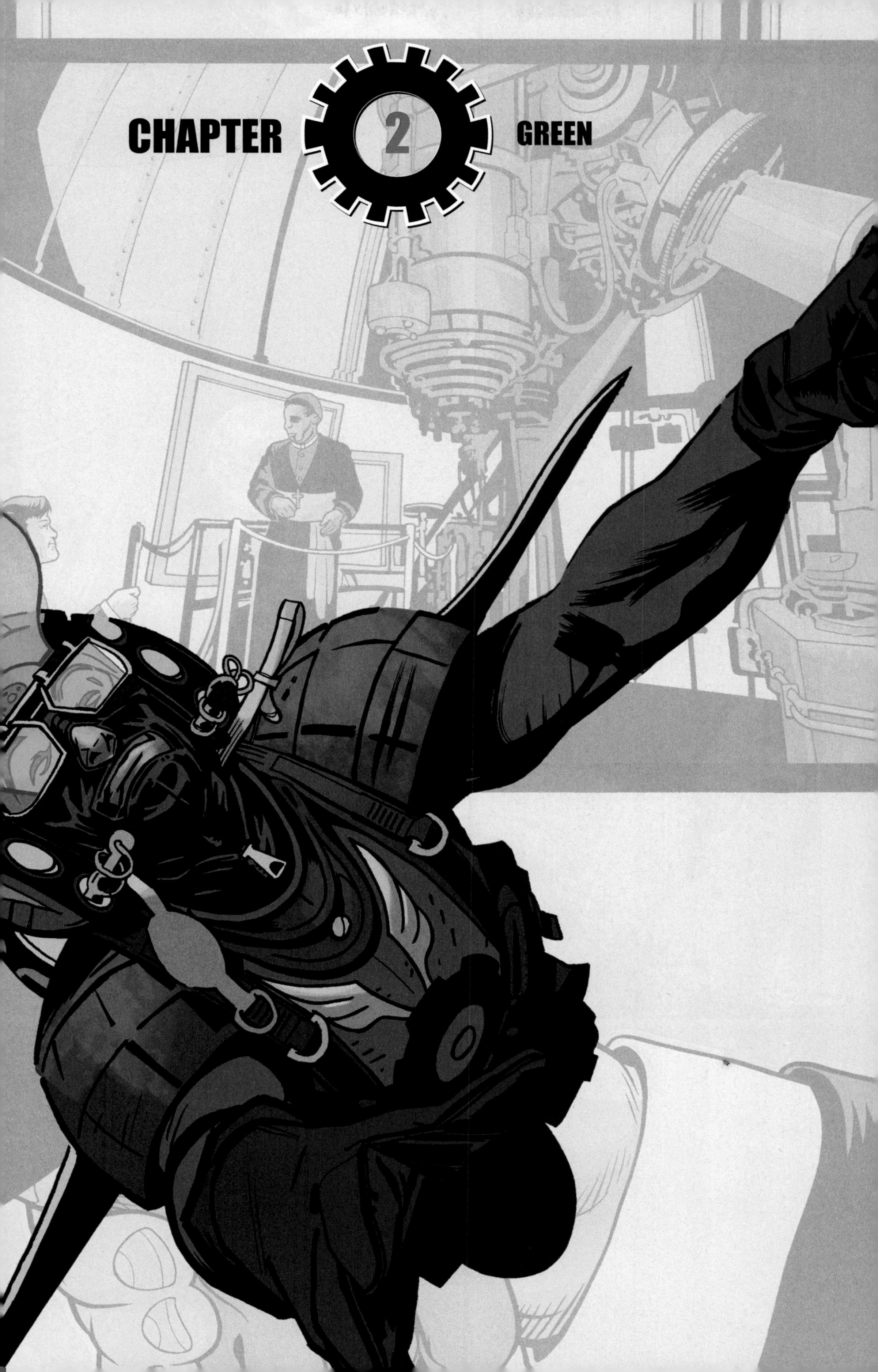

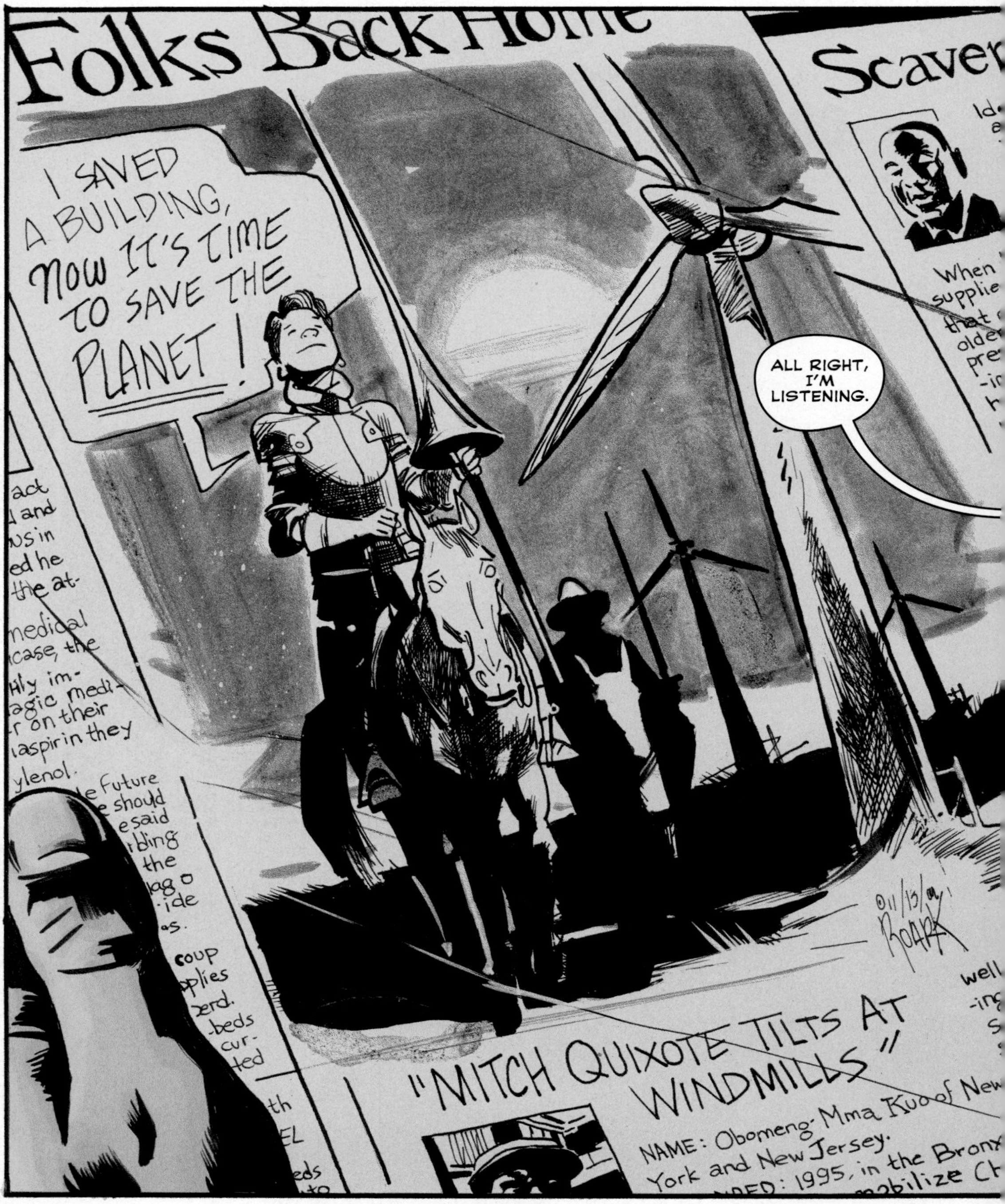

Folks Back Home
Scaver
I SAVED A BUILDING, NOW IT'S TIME TO SAVE THE PLANET!
ALL RIGHT, I'M LISTENING.
"MITCH QUIXOTE TILTS AT WINDMILLS"
NAME: Obomeng-Mma Kuo of New York and New Jersey.
©11/13/09 ROARK

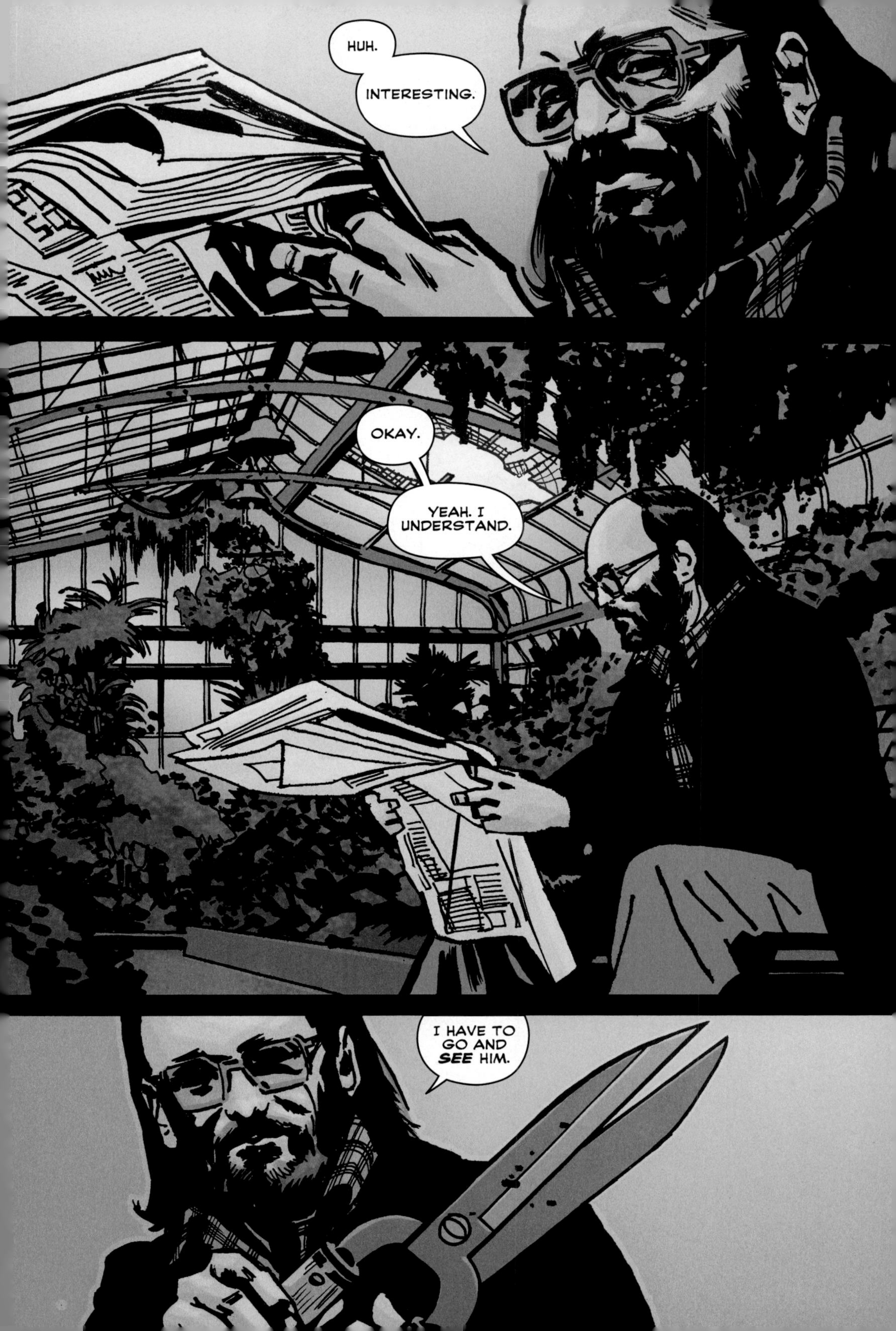
HUH.
INTERESTING.
OKAY.
YEAH. I UNDERSTAND.
I HAVE TO GO AND *SEE* HIM.

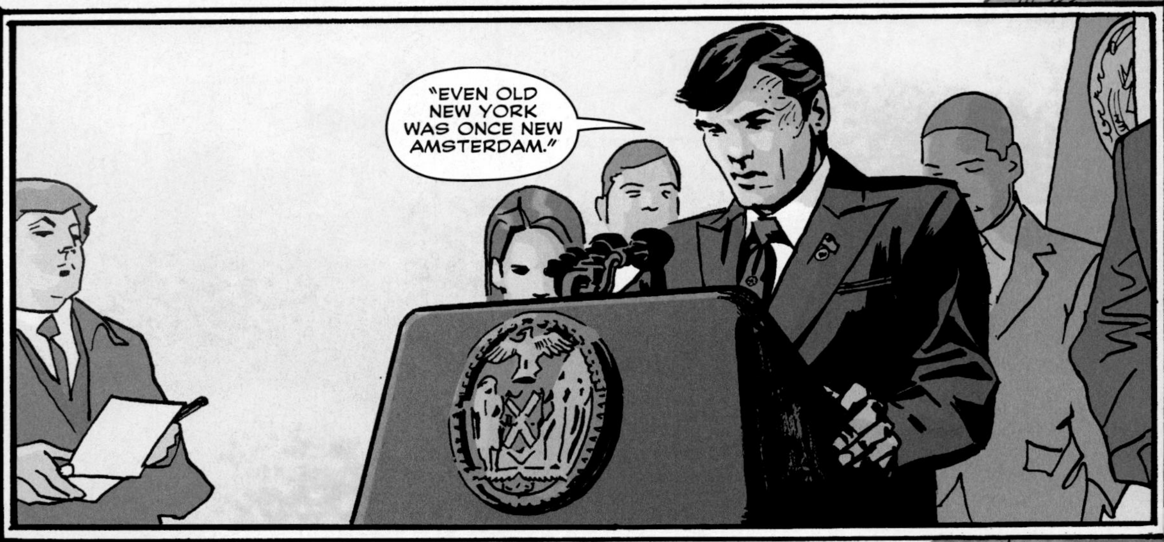
"EVEN OLD NEW YORK WAS ONCE NEW AMSTERDAM."

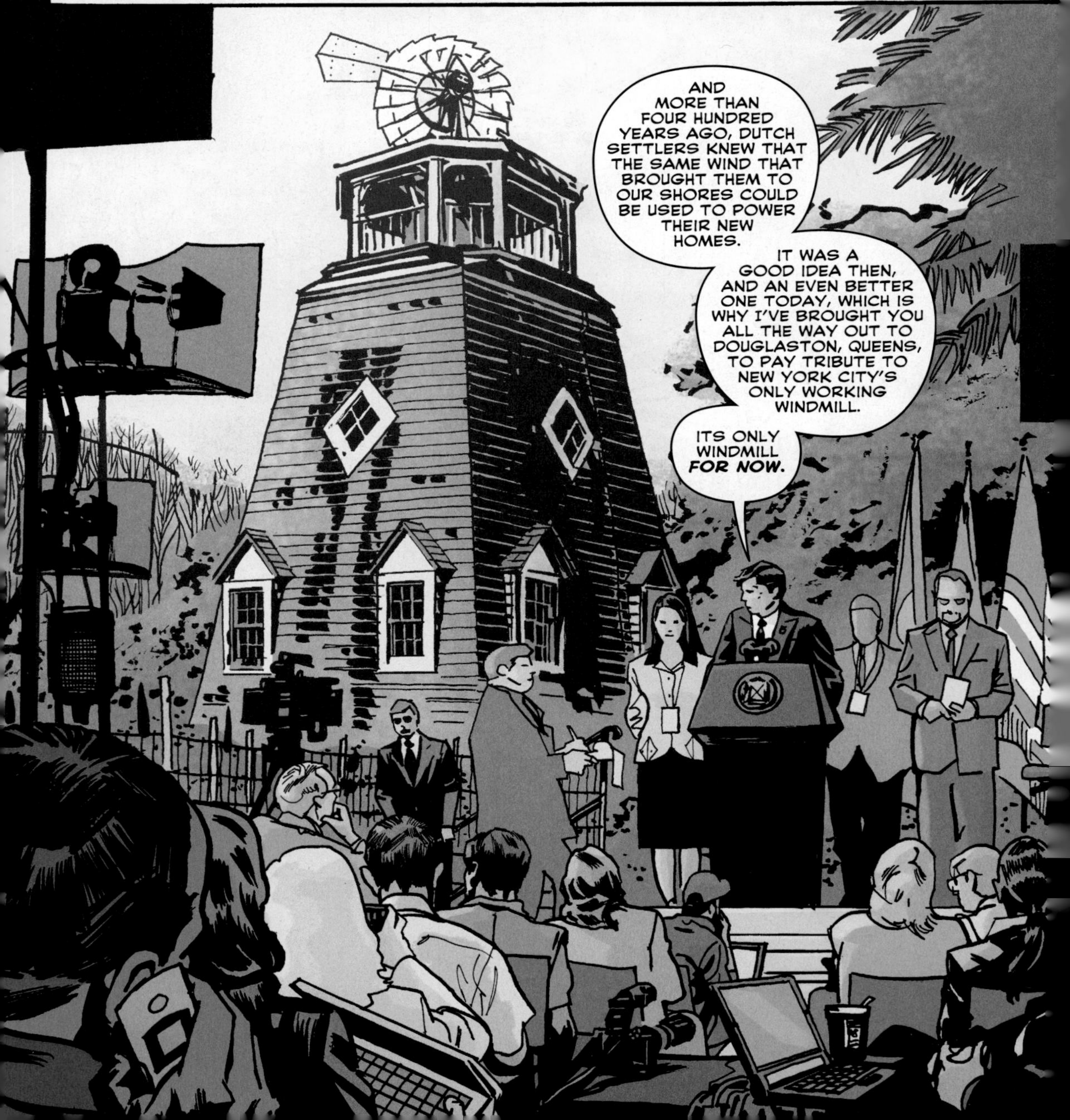
AND MORE THAN FOUR HUNDRED YEARS AGO, DUTCH SETTLERS KNEW THAT THE SAME WIND THAT BROUGHT THEM TO OUR SHORES COULD BE USED TO POWER THEIR NEW HOMES.
IT WAS A GOOD IDEA THEN, AND AN EVEN BETTER ONE TODAY, WHICH IS WHY I'VE BROUGHT YOU ALL THE WAY OUT TO DOUGLASTON, QUEENS, TO PAY TRIBUTE TO NEW YORK CITY'S ONLY WORKING WINDMILL.
ITS ONLY WINDMILL *FOR NOW.*

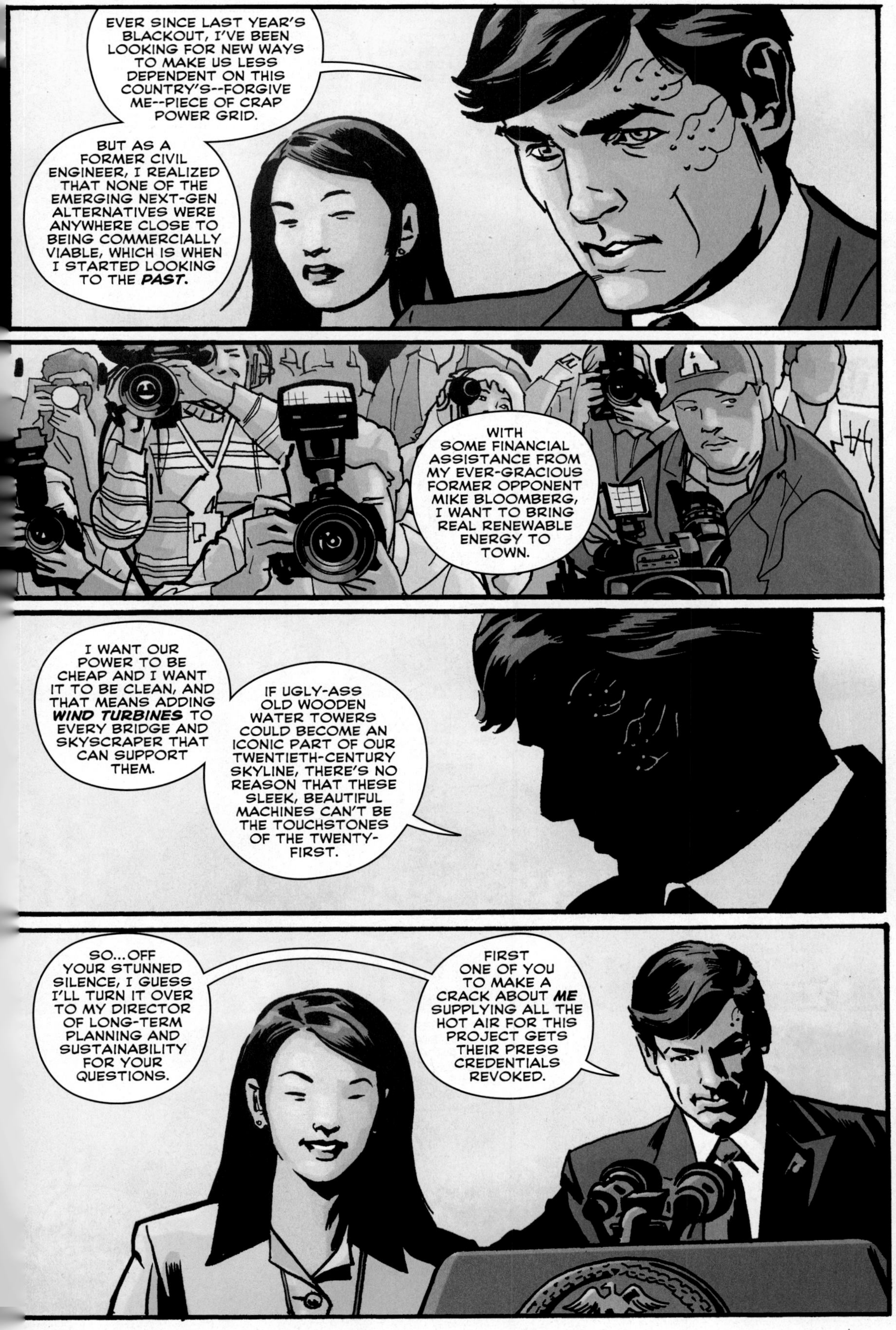
EVER SINCE LAST YEAR'S BLACKOUT, I'VE BEEN LOOKING FOR NEW WAYS TO MAKE US LESS DEPENDENT ON THIS COUNTRY'S--FORGIVE ME--PIECE OF CRAP POWER GRID.
BUT AS A FORMER CIVIL ENGINEER, I REALIZED THAT NONE OF THE EMERGING NEXT-GEN ALTERNATIVES WERE ANYWHERE CLOSE TO BEING COMMERCIALLY VIABLE, WHICH IS WHEN I STARTED LOOKING TO THE ***PAST***.
WITH SOME FINANCIAL ASSISTANCE FROM MY EVER-GRACIOUS FORMER OPPONENT MIKE BLOOMBERG, I WANT TO BRING REAL RENEWABLE ENERGY TO TOWN.
I WANT OUR POWER TO BE CHEAP AND I WANT IT TO BE CLEAN, AND THAT MEANS ADDING ***WIND TURBINES*** TO EVERY BRIDGE AND SKYSCRAPER THAT CAN SUPPORT THEM.
IF UGLY-ASS OLD WOODEN WATER TOWERS COULD BECOME AN ICONIC PART OF OUR TWENTIETH-CENTURY SKYLINE, THERE'S NO REASON THAT THESE SLEEK, BEAUTIFUL MACHINES CAN'T BE THE TOUCHSTONES OF THE TWENTY-FIRST.
SO...OFF YOUR STUNNED SILENCE, I GUESS I'LL TURN IT OVER TO MY DIRECTOR OF LONG-TERM PLANNING AND SUSTAINABILITY FOR YOUR QUESTIONS.
FIRST ONE OF YOU TO MAKE A CRACK ABOUT ***ME*** SUPPLYING ALL THE HOT AIR FOR THIS PROJECT GETS THEIR PRESS CREDENTIALS REVOKED.

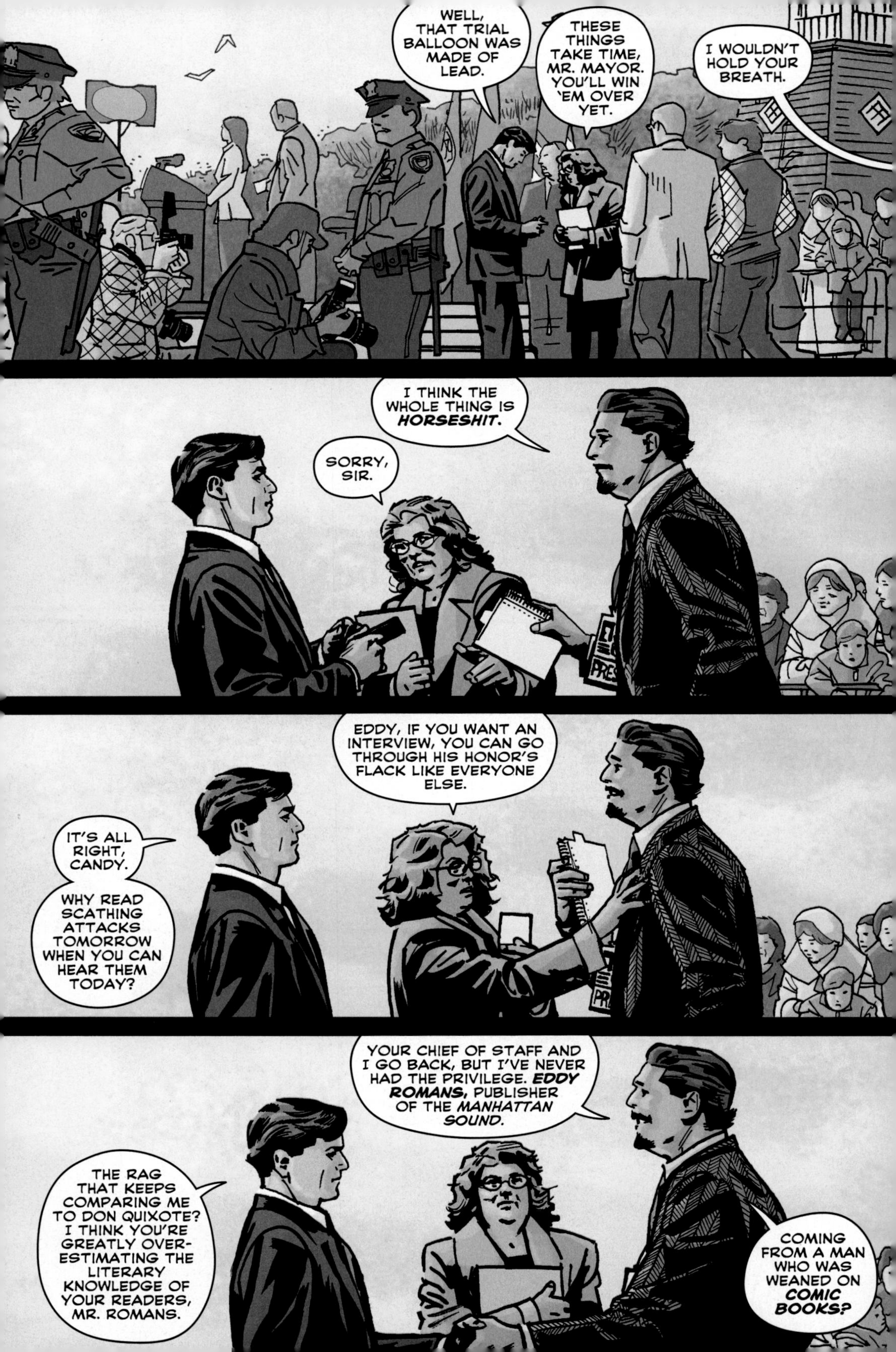

WELL, THAT TRIAL BALLOON WAS MADE OF LEAD.
THESE THINGS TAKE TIME, MR. MAYOR. YOU'LL WIN 'EM OVER YET.
I WOULDN'T HOLD YOUR BREATH.
I THINK THE WHOLE THING IS HORSESHIT.
SORRY, SIR.
PRESS
EDDY, IF YOU WANT AN INTERVIEW, YOU CAN GO THROUGH HIS HONOR'S FLACK LIKE EVERYONE ELSE.
IT'S ALL RIGHT, CANDY.
WHY READ SCATHING ATTACKS TOMORROW WHEN YOU CAN HEAR THEM TODAY?
YOUR CHIEF OF STAFF AND I GO BACK, BUT I'VE NEVER HAD THE PRIVILEGE. EDDY ROMANS, PUBLISHER OF THE MANHATTAN SOUND.
THE RAG THAT KEEPS COMPARING ME TO DON QUIXOTE? I THINK YOU'RE GREATLY OVER-ESTIMATING THE LITERARY KNOWLEDGE OF YOUR READERS, MR. ROMANS.
COMING FROM A MAN WHO WAS WEANED ON COMIC BOOKS?

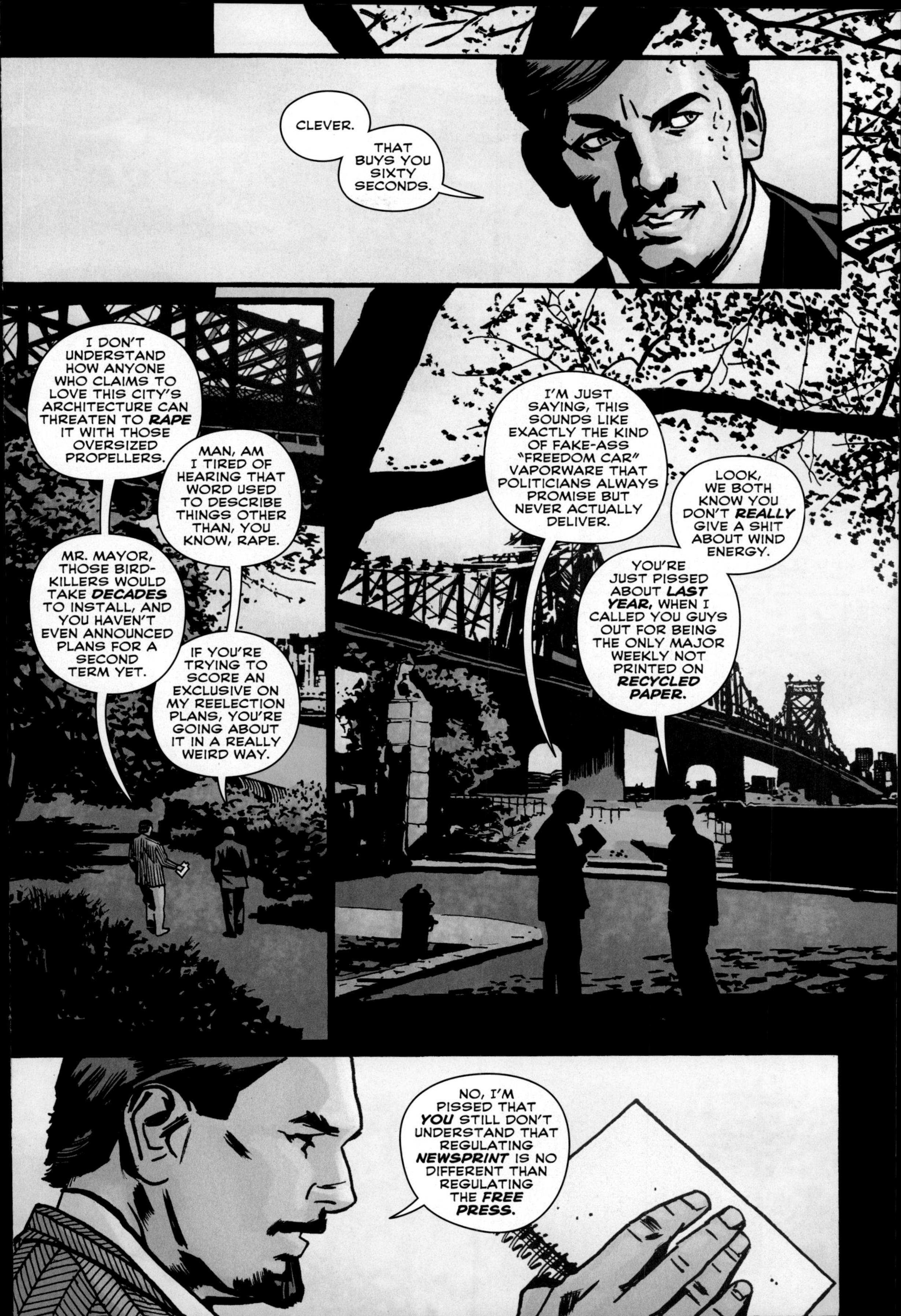
CLEVER.
THAT BUYS YOU SIXTY SECONDS.
I DON'T UNDERSTAND HOW ANYONE WHO CLAIMS TO LOVE THIS CITY'S ARCHITECTURE CAN THREATEN TO RAPE IT WITH THOSE OVERSIZED PROPELLERS.
MAN, AM I TIRED OF HEARING THAT WORD USED TO DESCRIBE THINGS OTHER THAN, YOU KNOW, RAPE.
MR. MAYOR, THOSE BIRD-KILLERS WOULD TAKE DECADES TO INSTALL, AND YOU HAVEN'T EVEN ANNOUNCED PLANS FOR A SECOND TERM YET.
IF YOU'RE TRYING TO SCORE AN EXCLUSIVE ON MY REELECTION PLANS, YOU'RE GOING ABOUT IT IN A REALLY WEIRD WAY.
I'M JUST SAYING, THIS SOUNDS LIKE EXACTLY THE KIND OF FAKE-ASS "FREEDOM CAR" VAPORWARE THAT POLITICIANS ALWAYS PROMISE BUT NEVER ACTUALLY DELIVER.
LOOK, WE BOTH KNOW YOU DON'T REALLY GIVE A SHIT ABOUT WIND ENERGY.
YOU'RE JUST PISSED ABOUT LAST YEAR, WHEN I CALLED YOU GUYS OUT FOR BEING THE ONLY MAJOR WEEKLY NOT PRINTED ON RECYCLED PAPER.
NO, I'M PISSED THAT YOU STILL DON'T UNDERSTAND THAT REGULATING NEWSPRINT IS NO DIFFERENT THAN REGULATING THE FREE PRESS.

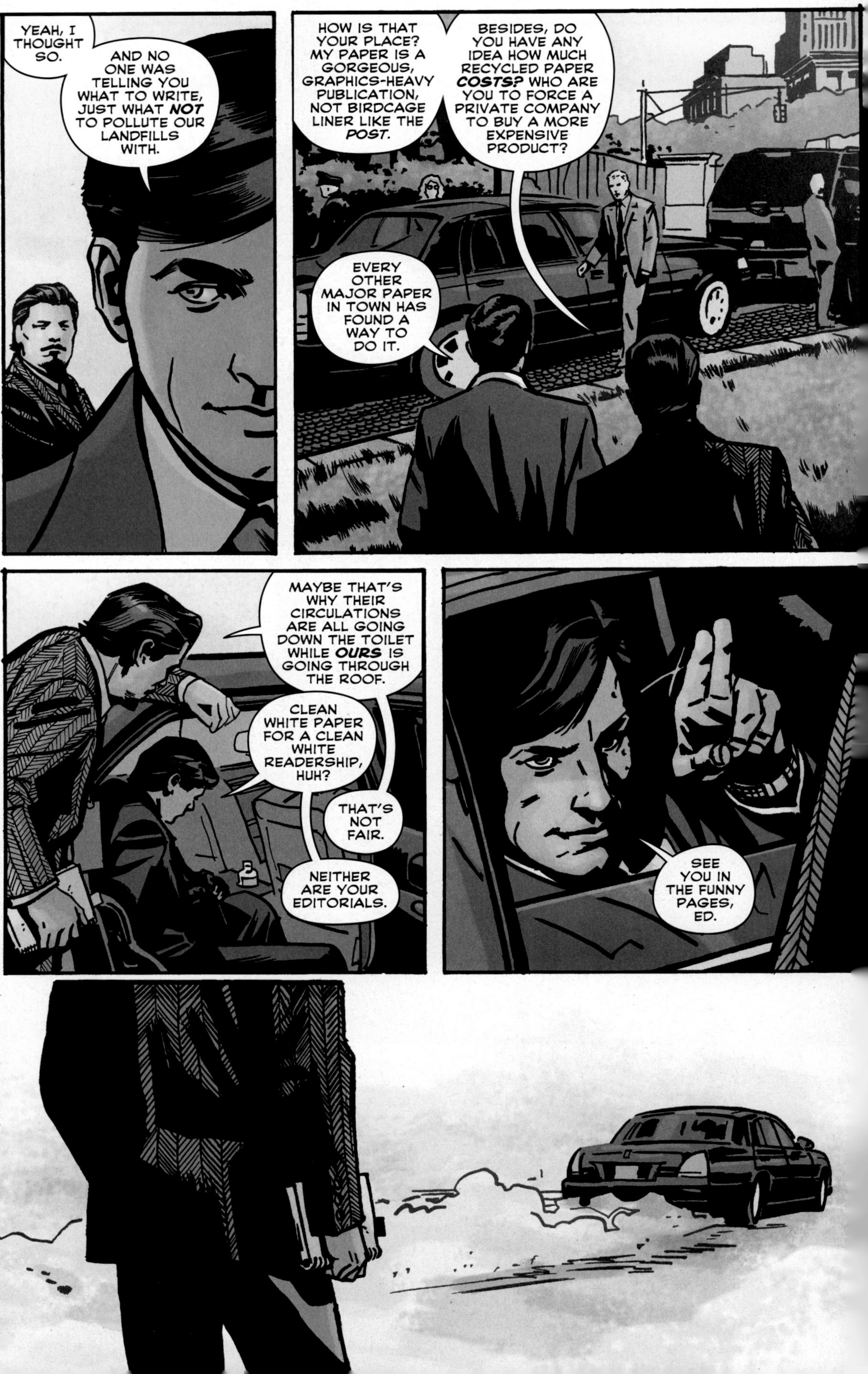
YEAH, I THOUGHT SO.
AND NO ONE WAS TELLING YOU WHAT TO WRITE, JUST WHAT NOT TO POLLUTE OUR LANDFILLS WITH.
HOW IS THAT YOUR PLACE? MY PAPER IS A GORGEOUS, GRAPHICS-HEAVY PUBLICATION, NOT BIRDCAGE LINER LIKE THE POST.
BESIDES, DO YOU HAVE ANY IDEA HOW MUCH RECYCLED PAPER COSTS? WHO ARE YOU TO FORCE A PRIVATE COMPANY TO BUY A MORE EXPENSIVE PRODUCT?
EVERY OTHER MAJOR PAPER IN TOWN HAS FOUND A WAY TO DO IT.
MAYBE THAT'S WHY THEIR CIRCULATIONS ARE ALL GOING DOWN THE TOILET WHILE OURS IS GOING THROUGH THE ROOF.
CLEAN WHITE PAPER FOR A CLEAN WHITE READERSHIP, HUH?
THAT'S NOT FAIR.
NEITHER ARE YOUR EDITORIALS.
SEE YOU IN THE FUNNY PAGES, ED.

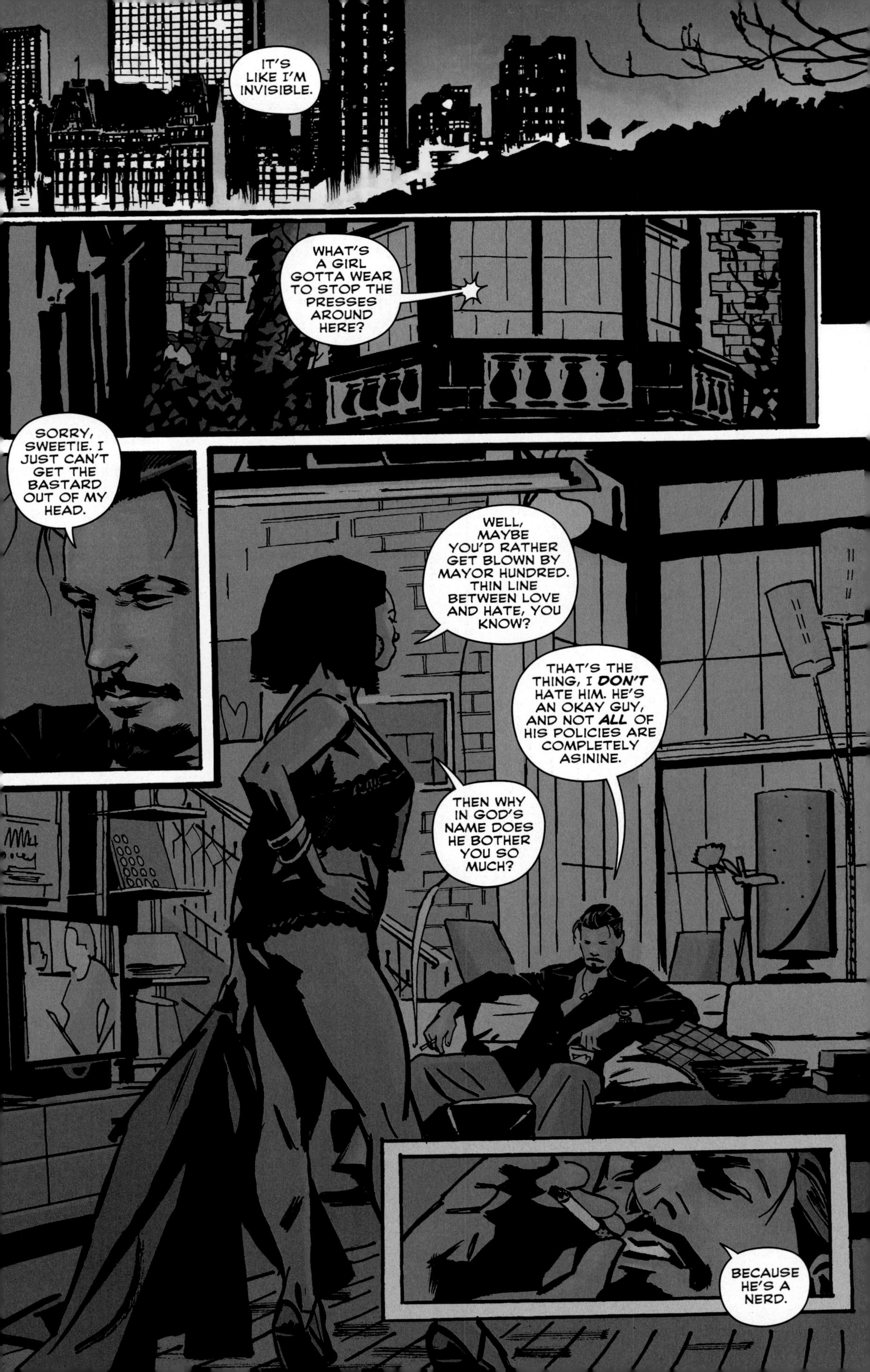
IT'S LIKE I'M INVISIBLE.
WHAT'S A GIRL GOTTA WEAR TO STOP THE PRESSES AROUND HERE?
SORRY, SWEETIE. I JUST CAN'T GET THE BASTARD OUT OF MY HEAD.
WELL, MAYBE YOU'D RATHER GET BLOWN BY MAYOR HUNDRED. THIN LINE BETWEEN LOVE AND HATE, YOU KNOW?
THAT'S THE THING, I DON'T HATE HIM. HE'S AN OKAY GUY, AND NOT ALL OF HIS POLICIES ARE COMPLETELY ASININE.
THEN WHY IN GOD'S NAME DOES HE BOTHER YOU SO MUCH?
BECAUSE HE'S A NERD.

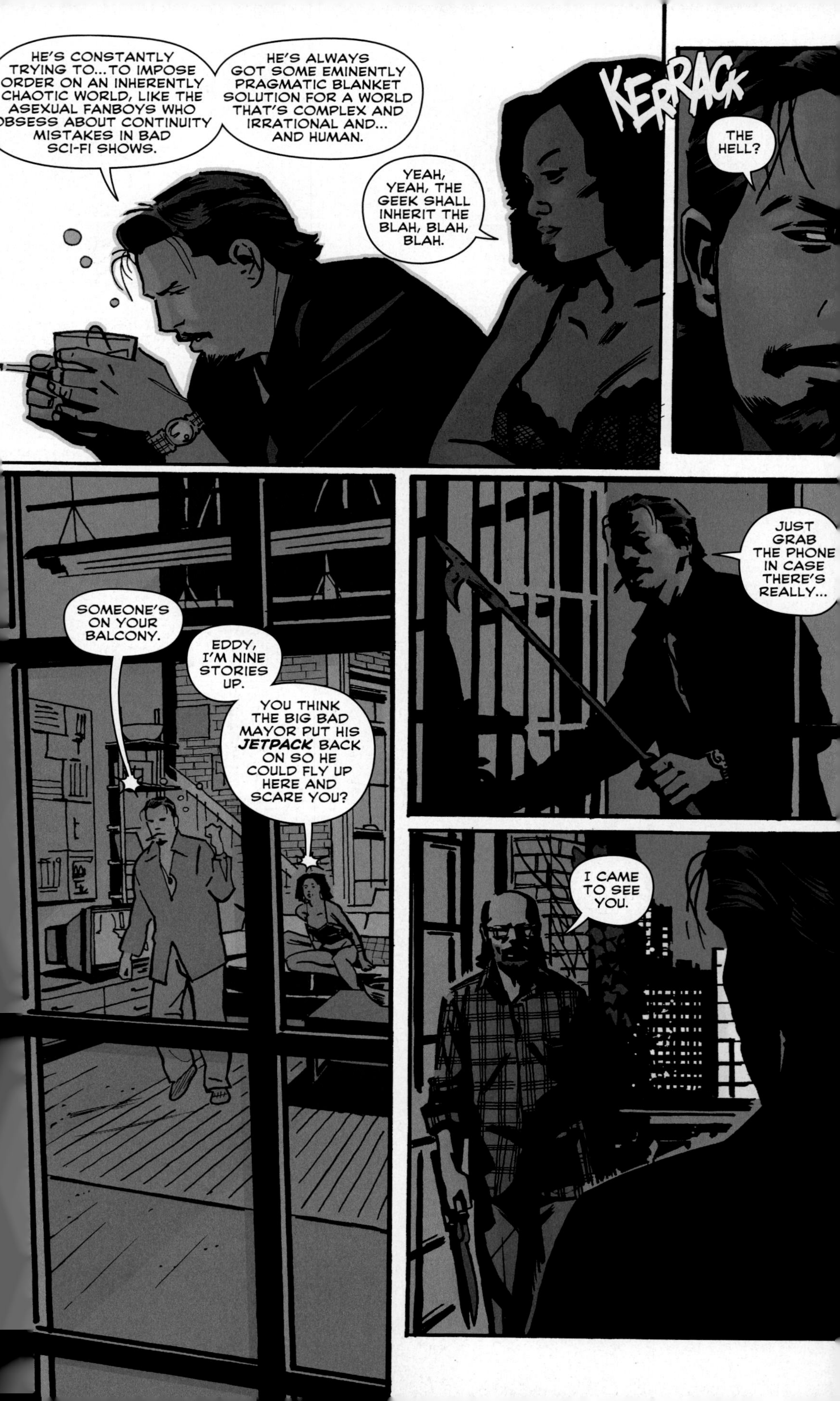
HE'S CONSTANTLY TRYING TO...TO IMPOSE ORDER ON AN INHERENTLY CHAOTIC WORLD, LIKE THE ASEXUAL FANBOYS WHO OBSESS ABOUT CONTINUITY MISTAKES IN BAD SCI-FI SHOWS.
HE'S ALWAYS GOT SOME EMINENTLY PRAGMATIC BLANKET SOLUTION FOR A WORLD THAT'S COMPLEX AND IRRATIONAL AND... AND HUMAN.
YEAH, YEAH, THE GEEK SHALL INHERIT THE BLAH, BLAH, BLAH.
KERRACK
THE HELL?
SOMEONE'S ON YOUR BALCONY.
EDDY, I'M NINE STORIES UP.
YOU THINK THE BIG BAD MAYOR PUT HIS *JETPACK* BACK ON SO HE COULD FLY UP HERE AND SCARE YOU?
JUST GRAB THE PHONE IN CASE THERE'S REALLY...
I CAME TO SEE YOU.

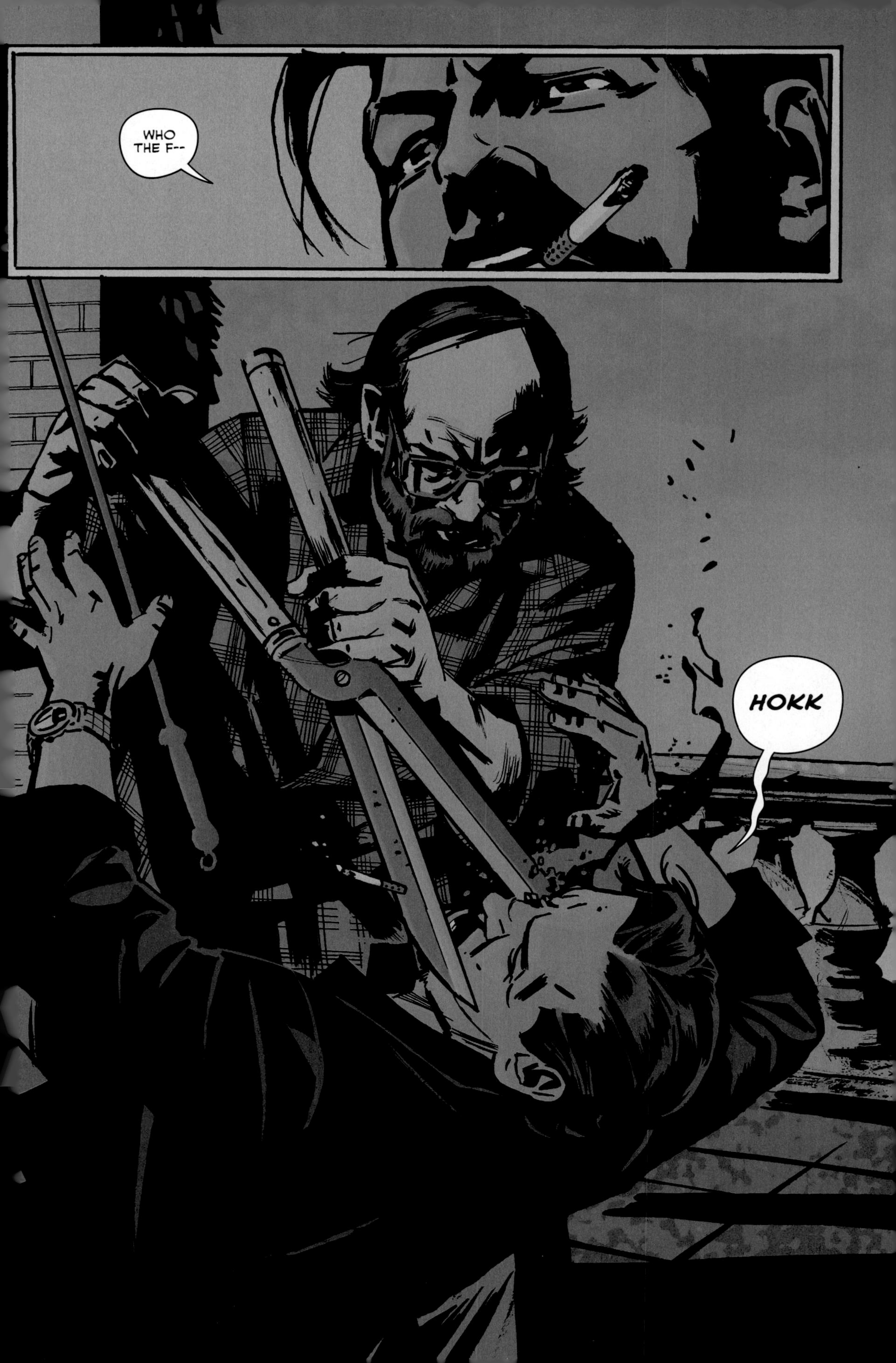
WHO THE F--
HOKK

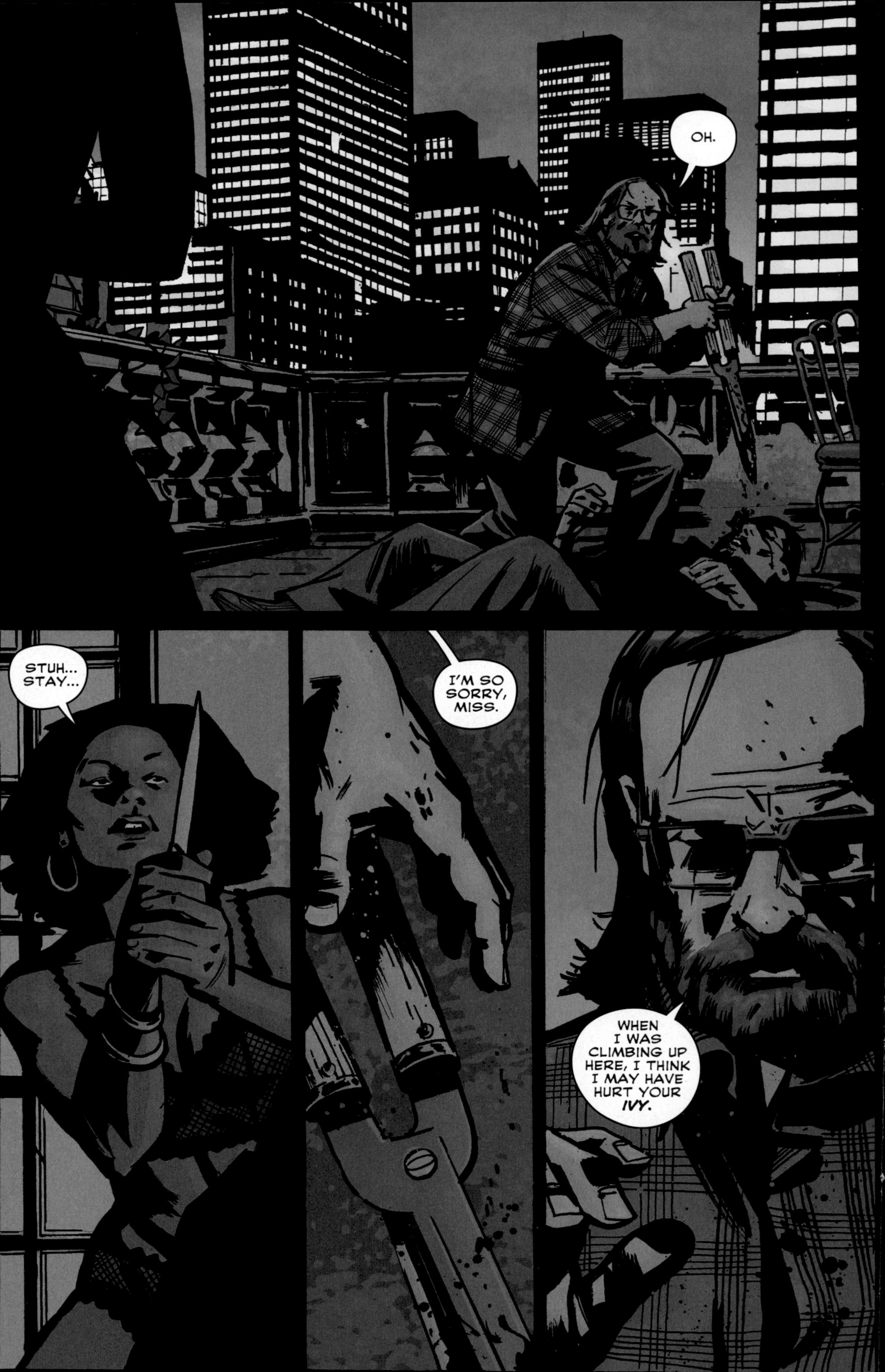
OH.
STUH... STAY...
I'M SO SORRY, MISS.
WHEN I WAS CLIMBING UP HERE, I THINK I MAY HAVE HURT YOUR *IVY*.

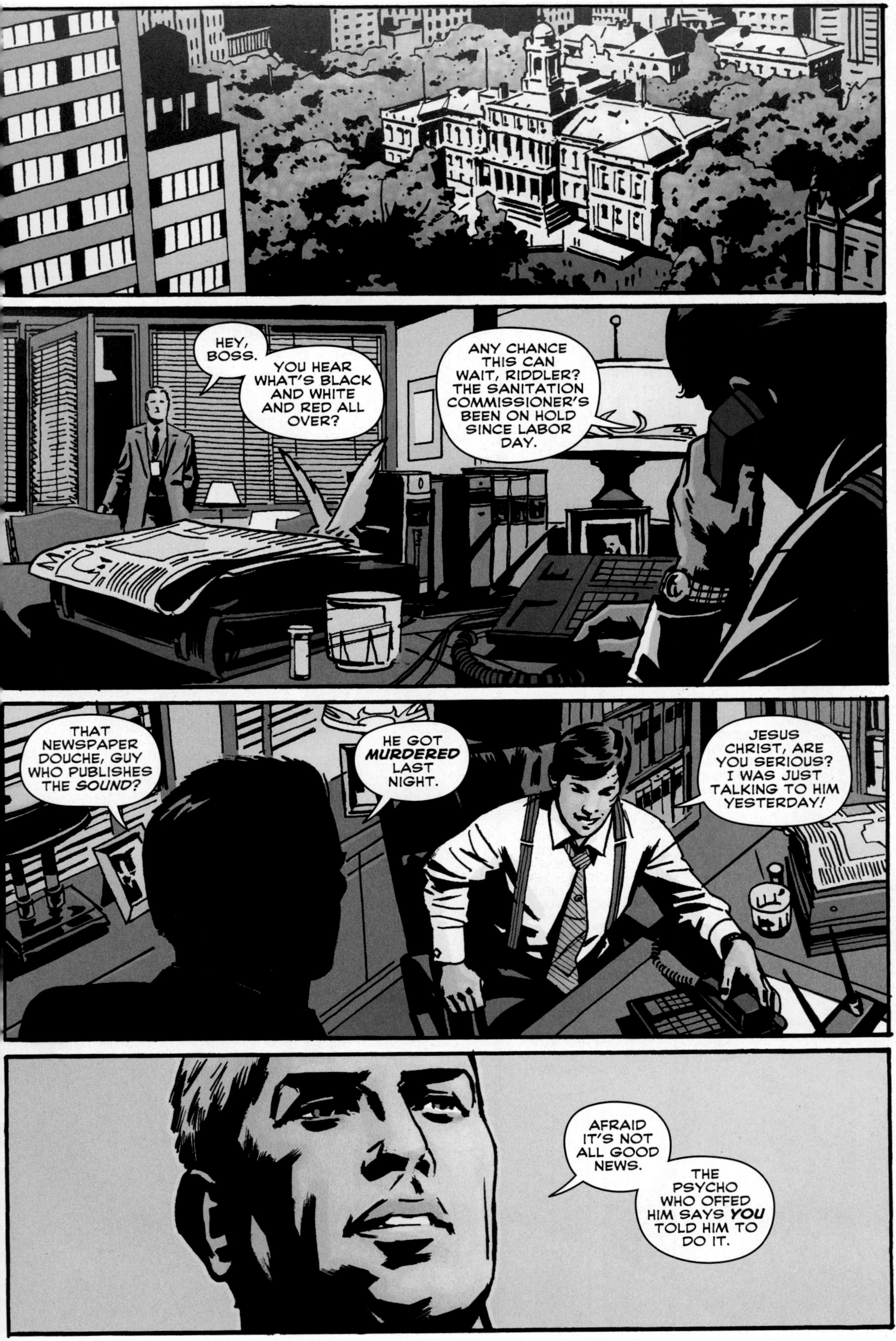
HEY, BOSS.
YOU HEAR WHAT'S BLACK AND WHITE AND RED ALL OVER?
ANY CHANCE THIS CAN WAIT, RIDDLER? THE SANITATION COMMISSIONER'S BEEN ON HOLD SINCE LABOR DAY.
THAT NEWSPAPER DOUCHE, GUY WHO PUBLISHES THE *SOUND*?
HE GOT ***MURDERED*** LAST NIGHT.
JESUS CHRIST, ARE YOU SERIOUS? I WAS JUST TALKING TO HIM YESTERDAY!
AFRAID IT'S NOT ALL GOOD NEWS.
THE PSYCHO WHO OFFED HIM SAYS ***YOU*** TOLD HIM TO DO IT.

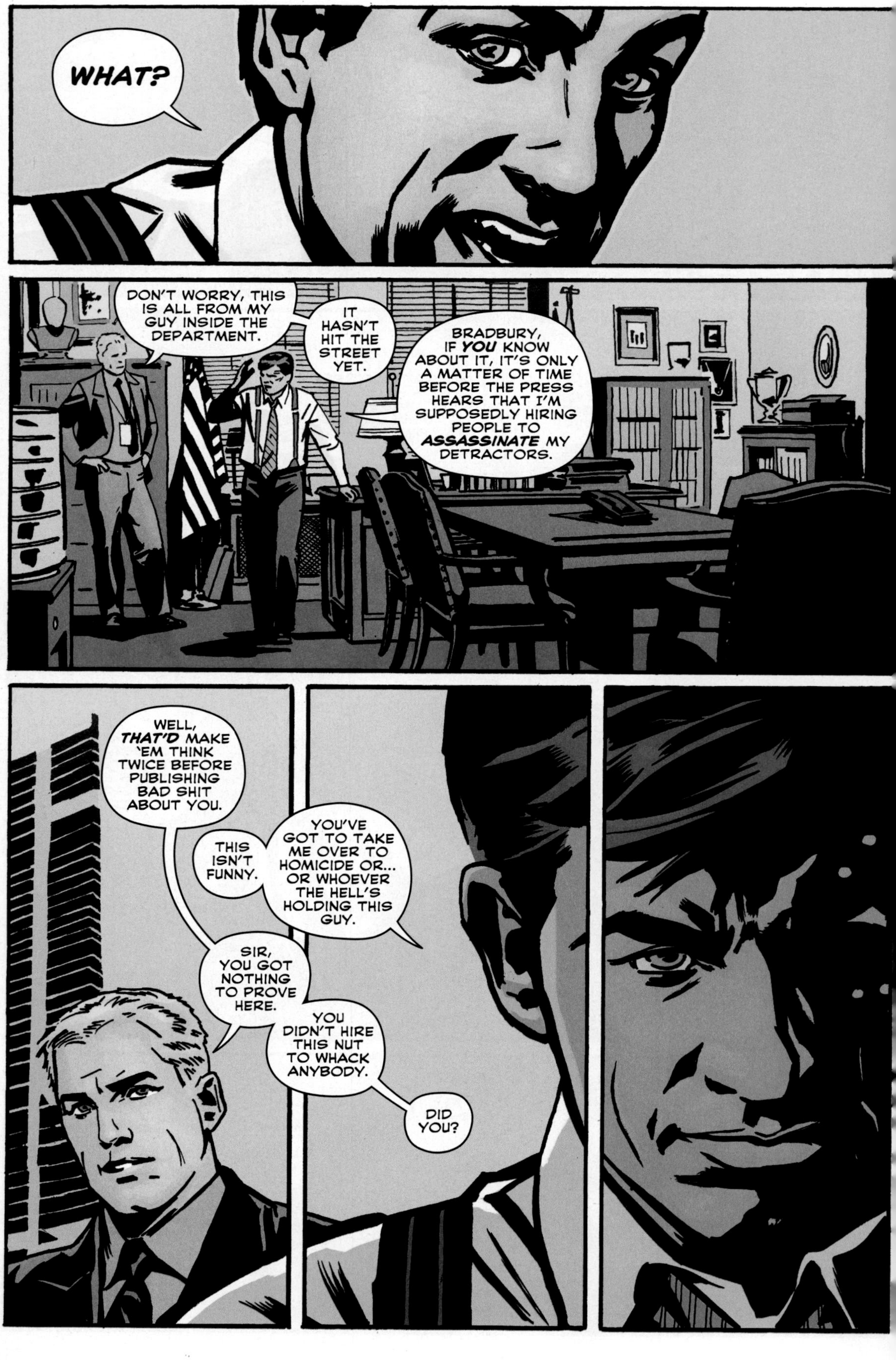
WHAT?
DON'T WORRY, THIS IS ALL FROM MY GUY INSIDE THE DEPARTMENT.
IT HASN'T HIT THE STREET YET.
BRADBURY, IF YOU KNOW ABOUT IT, IT'S ONLY A MATTER OF TIME BEFORE THE PRESS HEARS THAT I'M SUPPOSEDLY HIRING PEOPLE TO ASSASSINATE MY DETRACTORS.
WELL, THAT'D MAKE 'EM THINK TWICE BEFORE PUBLISHING BAD SHIT ABOUT YOU.
THIS ISN'T FUNNY.
YOU'VE GOT TO TAKE ME OVER TO HOMICIDE OR... OR WHOEVER THE HELL'S HOLDING THIS GUY.
SIR, YOU GOT NOTHING TO PROVE HERE.
YOU DIDN'T HIRE THIS NUT TO WHACK ANYBODY.
DID YOU?

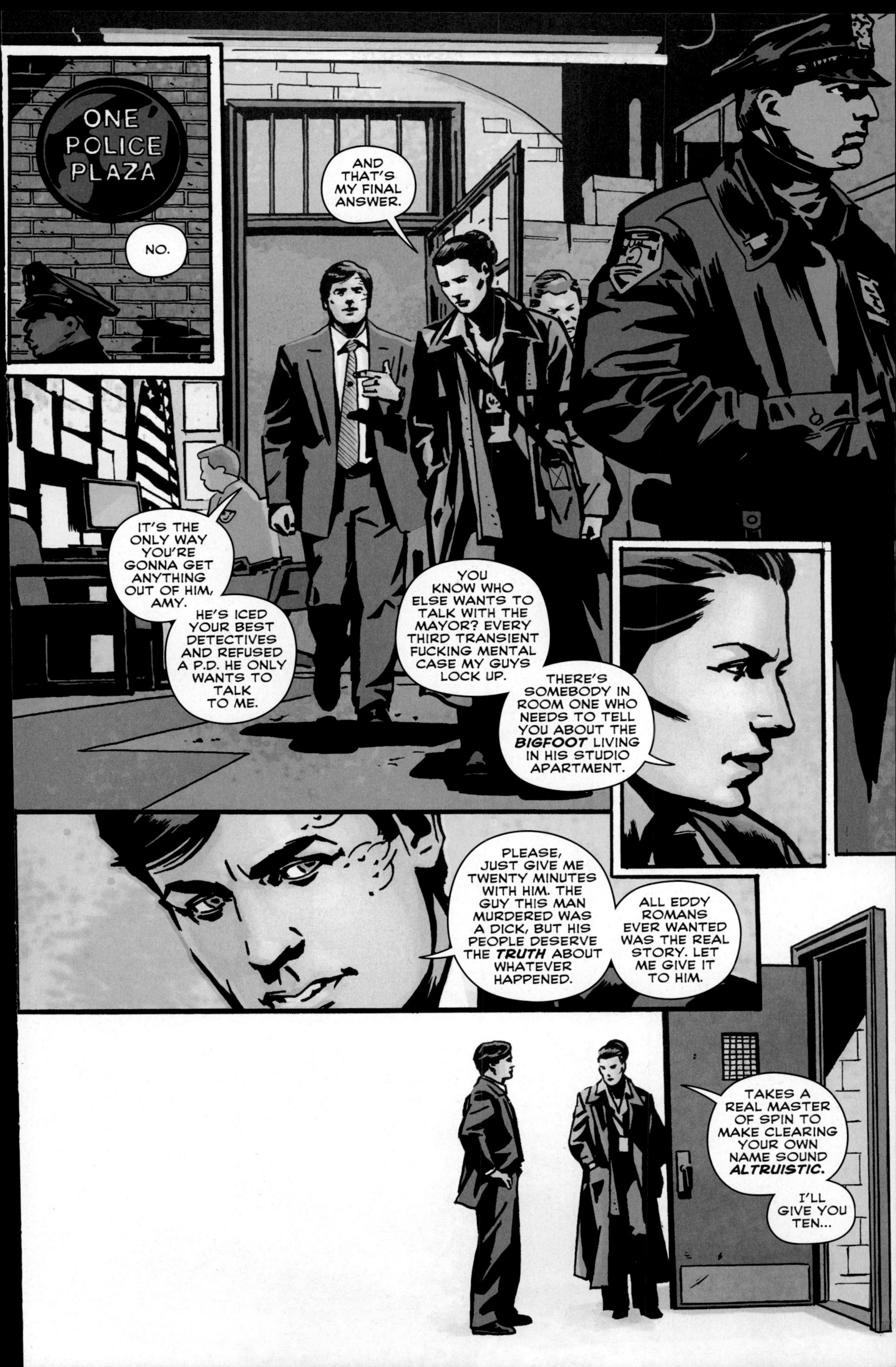
ONE POLICE PLAZA
NO.
AND THAT'S MY FINAL ANSWER.
IT'S THE ONLY WAY YOU'RE GONNA GET ANYTHING OUT OF HIM, AMY.
HE'S ICED YOUR BEST DETECTIVES AND REFUSED A P.D. HE ONLY WANTS TO TALK TO ME.
YOU KNOW WHO ELSE WANTS TO TALK WITH THE MAYOR? EVERY THIRD TRANSIENT FUCKING MENTAL CASE MY GUYS LOCK UP.
THERE'S SOMEBODY IN ROOM ONE WHO NEEDS TO TELL YOU ABOUT THE BIGFOOT LIVING IN HIS STUDIO APARTMENT.
PLEASE, JUST GIVE ME TWENTY MINUTES WITH HIM. THE GUY THIS MAN MURDERED WAS A DICK, BUT HIS PEOPLE DESERVE THE TRUTH ABOUT WHATEVER HAPPENED.
ALL EDDY ROMANS EVER WANTED WAS THE REAL STORY. LET ME GIVE IT TO HIM.
TAKES A REAL MASTER OF SPIN TO MAKE CLEARING YOUR OWN NAME SOUND ALTRUISTIC.
I'LL GIVE YOU TEN...

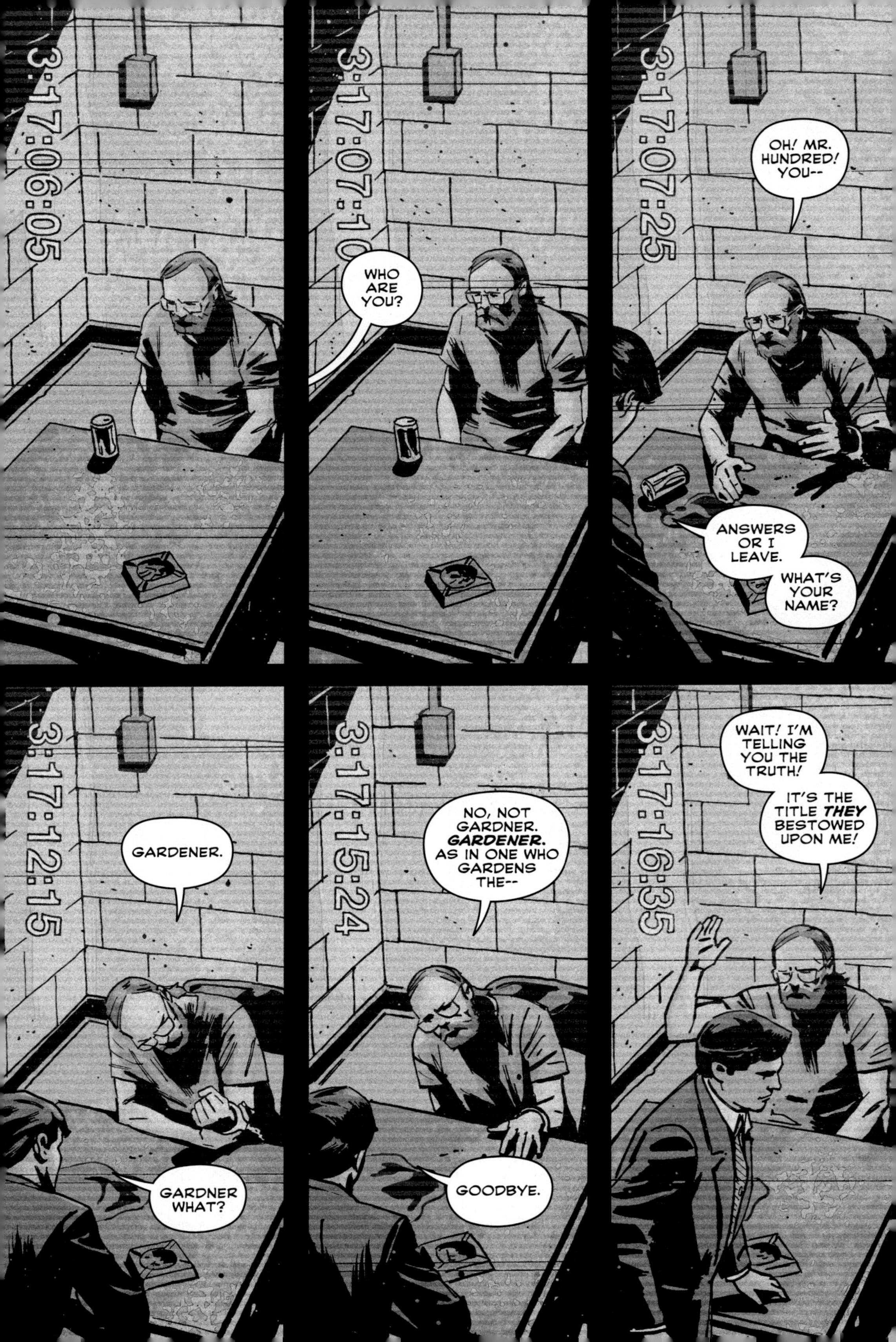
3:17:06:05
3:17:07:10
WHO ARE YOU?
3:17:07:25
OH! MR. HUNDRED! YOU--
ANSWERS OR I LEAVE.
WHAT'S YOUR NAME?
3:17:12:15
GARDENER.
GARDNER WHAT?
3:17:15:24
NO, NOT GARDNER. ***GARDENER.*** AS IN ONE WHO GARDENS THE--
GOODBYE.
3:17:16:35
WAIT! I'M TELLING YOU THE TRUTH!
IT'S THE TITLE ***THEY*** BESTOWED UPON ME!

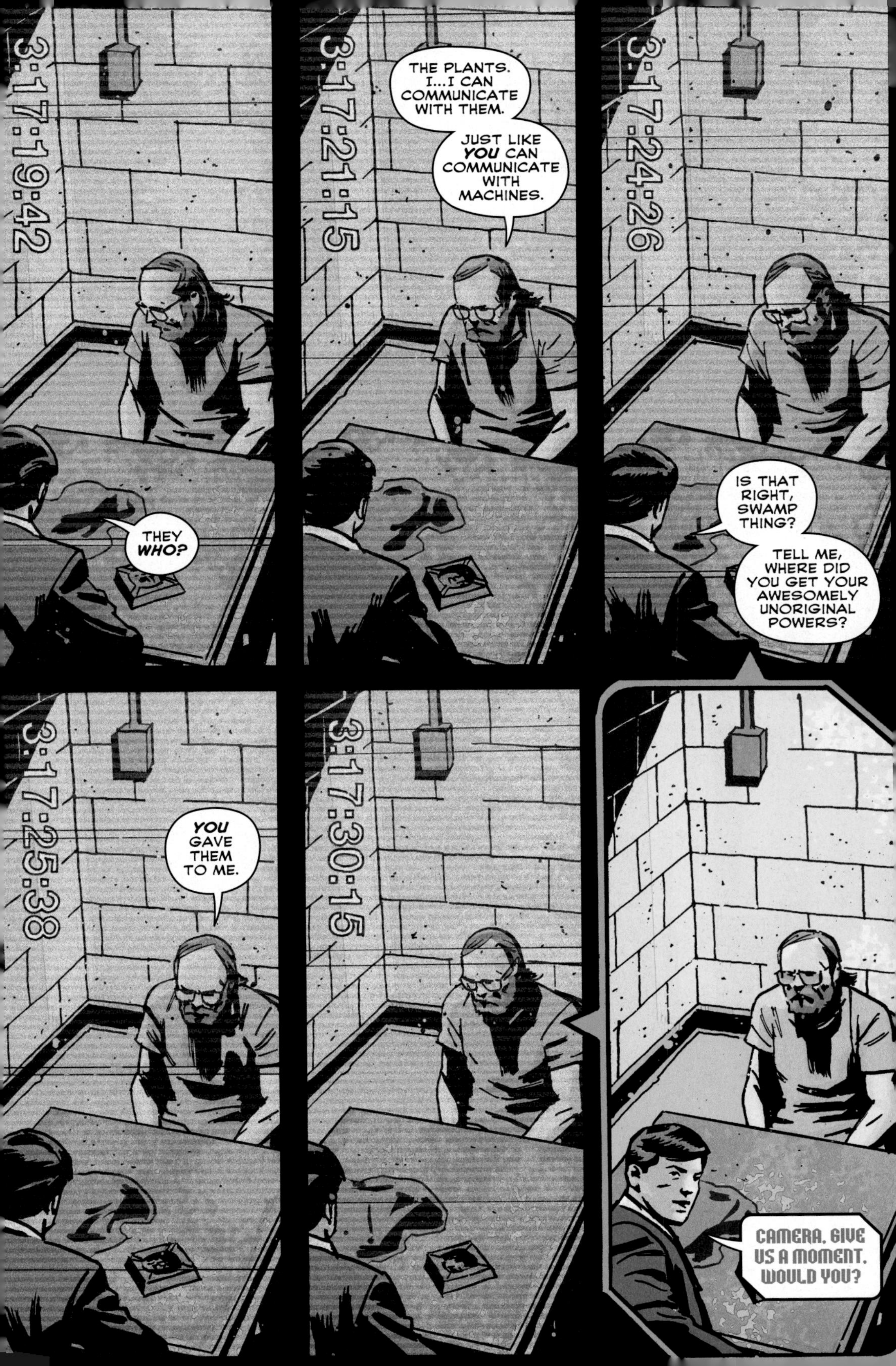
3:17:19:42
THEY WHO?
3:17:21:15
THE PLANTS. I...I CAN COMMUNICATE WITH THEM.
JUST LIKE YOU CAN COMMUNICATE WITH MACHINES.
3:17:24:26
IS THAT RIGHT, SWAMP THING?
TELL ME, WHERE DID YOU GET YOUR AWESOMELY UNORIGINAL POWERS?
3:17:25:38
YOU GAVE THEM TO ME.
3:17:30:15
CAMERA, GIVE US A MOMENT, WOULD YOU?

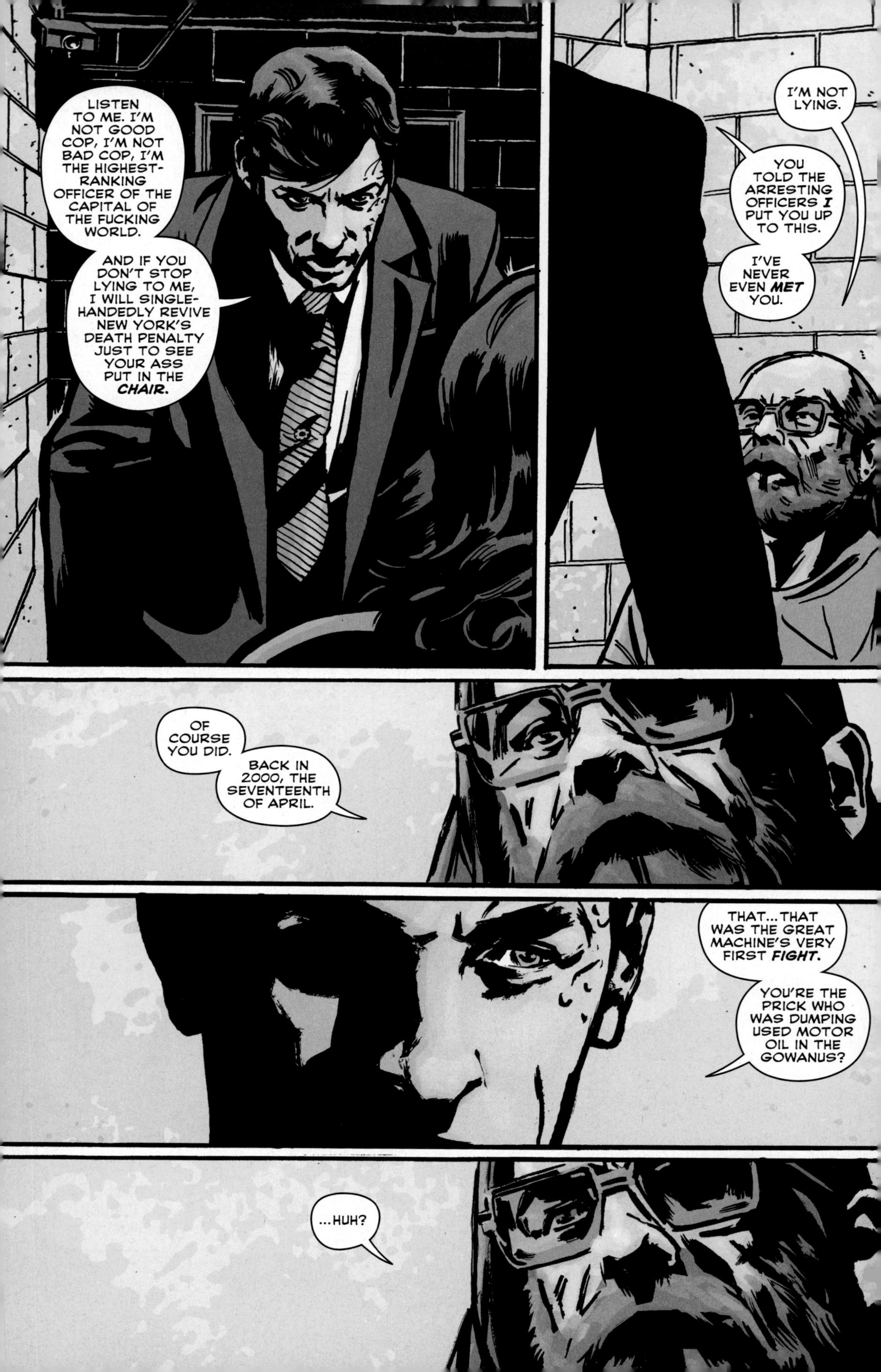

LISTEN TO ME. I'M NOT GOOD COP, I'M NOT BAD COP, I'M THE HIGHEST-RANKING OFFICER OF THE CAPITAL OF THE FUCKING WORLD.
AND IF YOU DON'T STOP LYING TO ME, I WILL SINGLE-HANDEDLY REVIVE NEW YORK'S DEATH PENALTY JUST TO SEE YOUR ASS PUT IN THE **CHAIR.**
I'M NOT LYING.
YOU TOLD THE ARRESTING OFFICERS ***I*** PUT YOU UP TO THIS.
I'VE NEVER EVEN ***MET*** YOU.
OF COURSE YOU DID.
BACK IN 2000, THE SEVENTEENTH OF APRIL.
THAT... THAT WAS THE GREAT MACHINE'S VERY FIRST ***FIGHT***.
YOU'RE THE PRICK WHO WAS DUMPING USED MOTOR OIL IN THE GOWANUS?
...HUH?

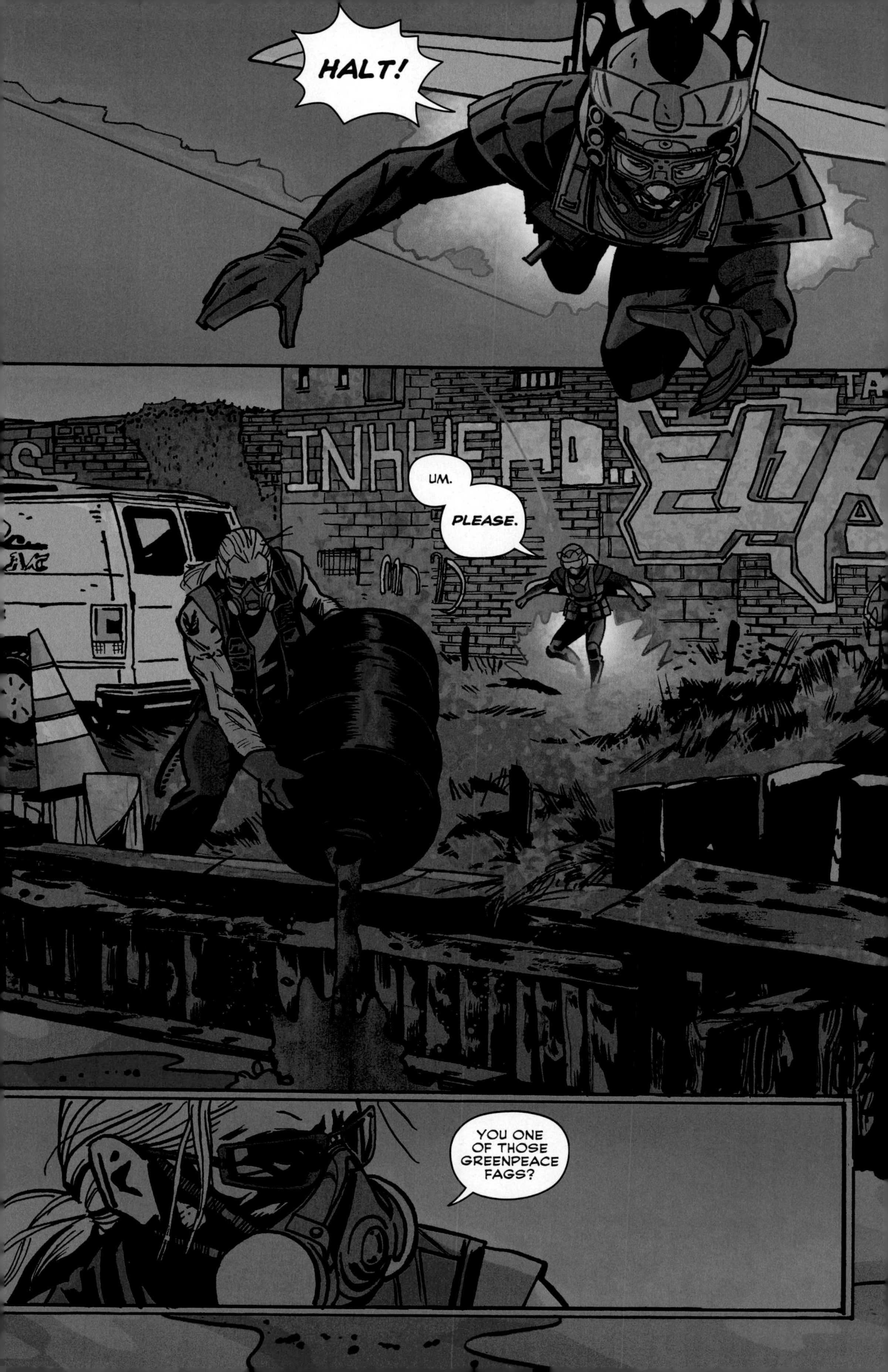
HALT!
UM.
PLEASE.
YOU ONE OF THOSE GREENPEACE FAGS?

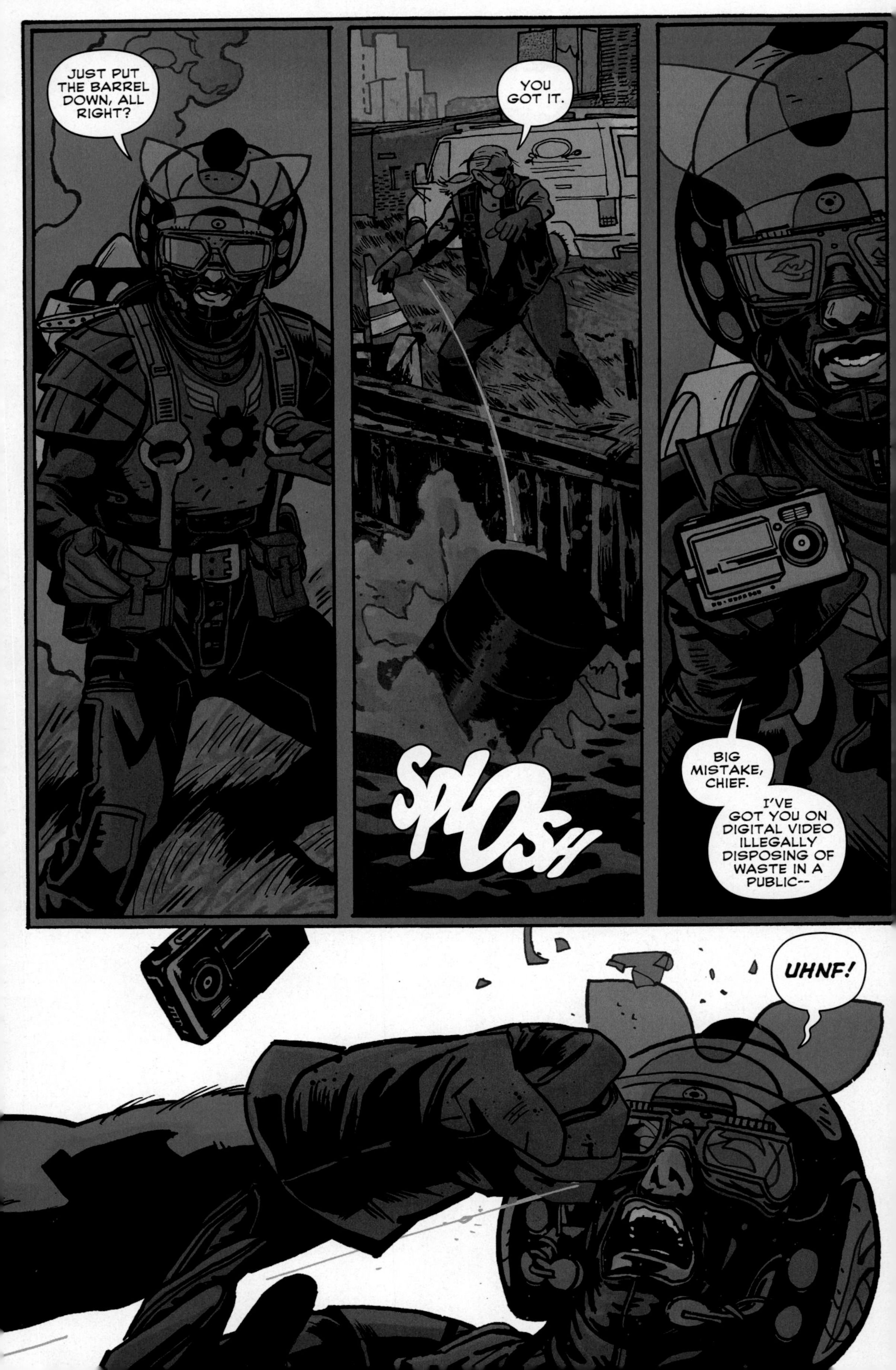
JUST PUT THE BARREL DOWN, ALL RIGHT?
YOU GOT IT.
SPLOSH
BIG MISTAKE, CHIEF.
I'VE GOT YOU ON DIGITAL VIDEO ILLEGALLY DISPOSING OF WASTE IN A PUBLIC--
UHNF!

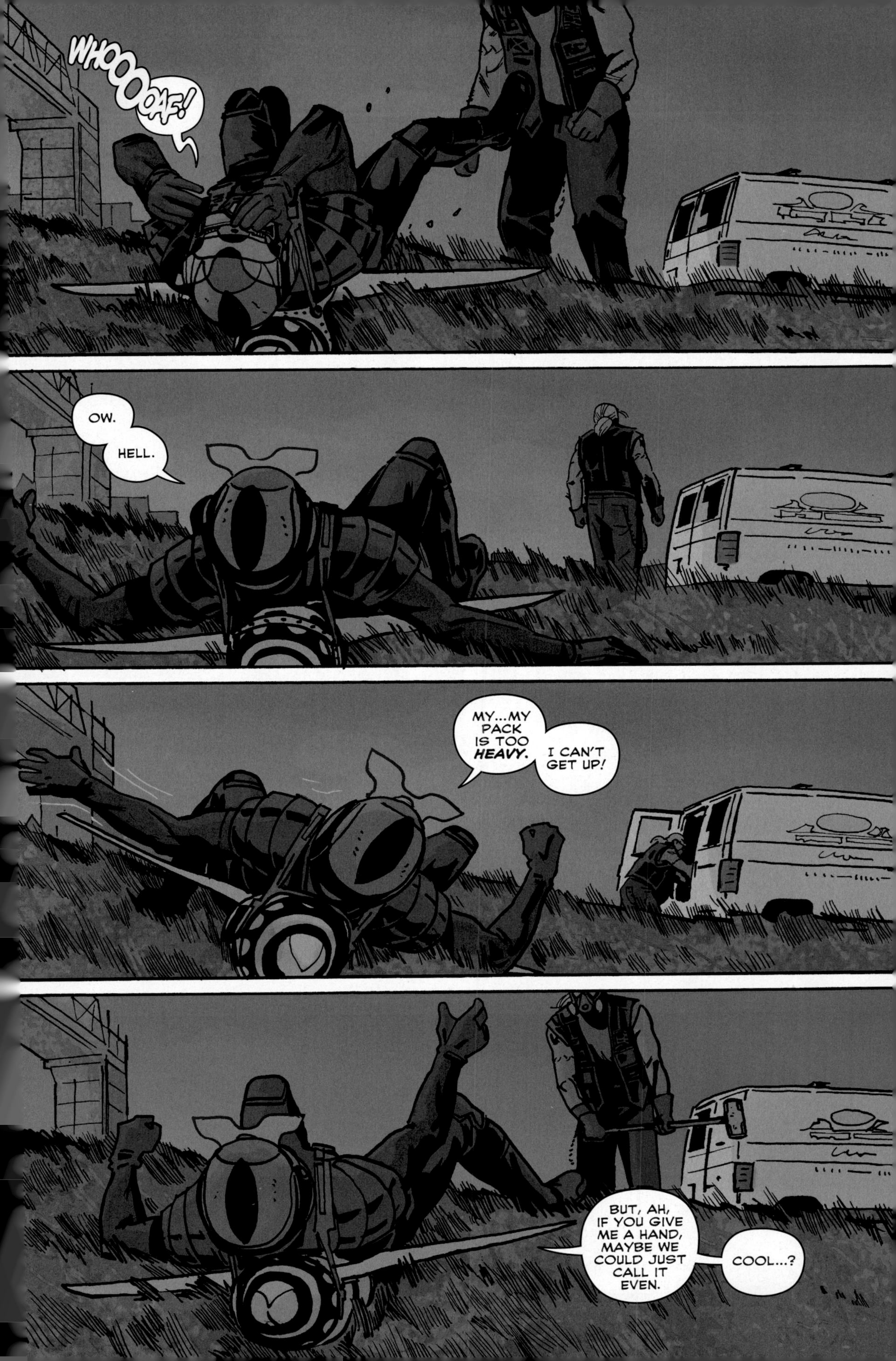
WHOOOOOAF!
OW.
HELL.
MY...MY PACK IS TOO HEAVY.
I CAN'T GET UP!
BUT, AH, IF YOU GIVE ME A HAND, MAYBE WE COULD JUST CALL IT EVEN.
COOL...?

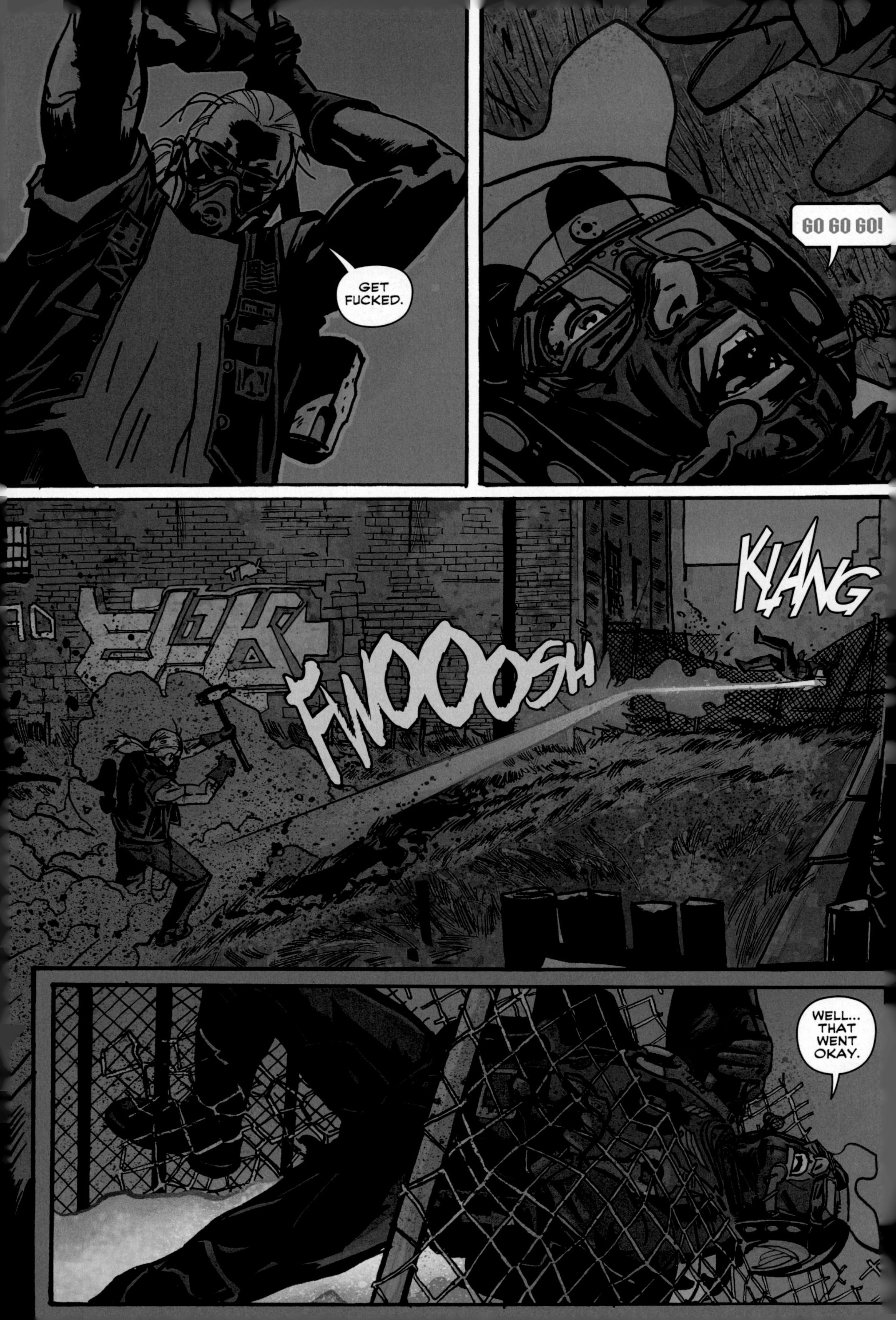
GET FUCKED.
GO GO GO!
KLANG
FWOOOSH
WELL... THAT WENT OKAY.

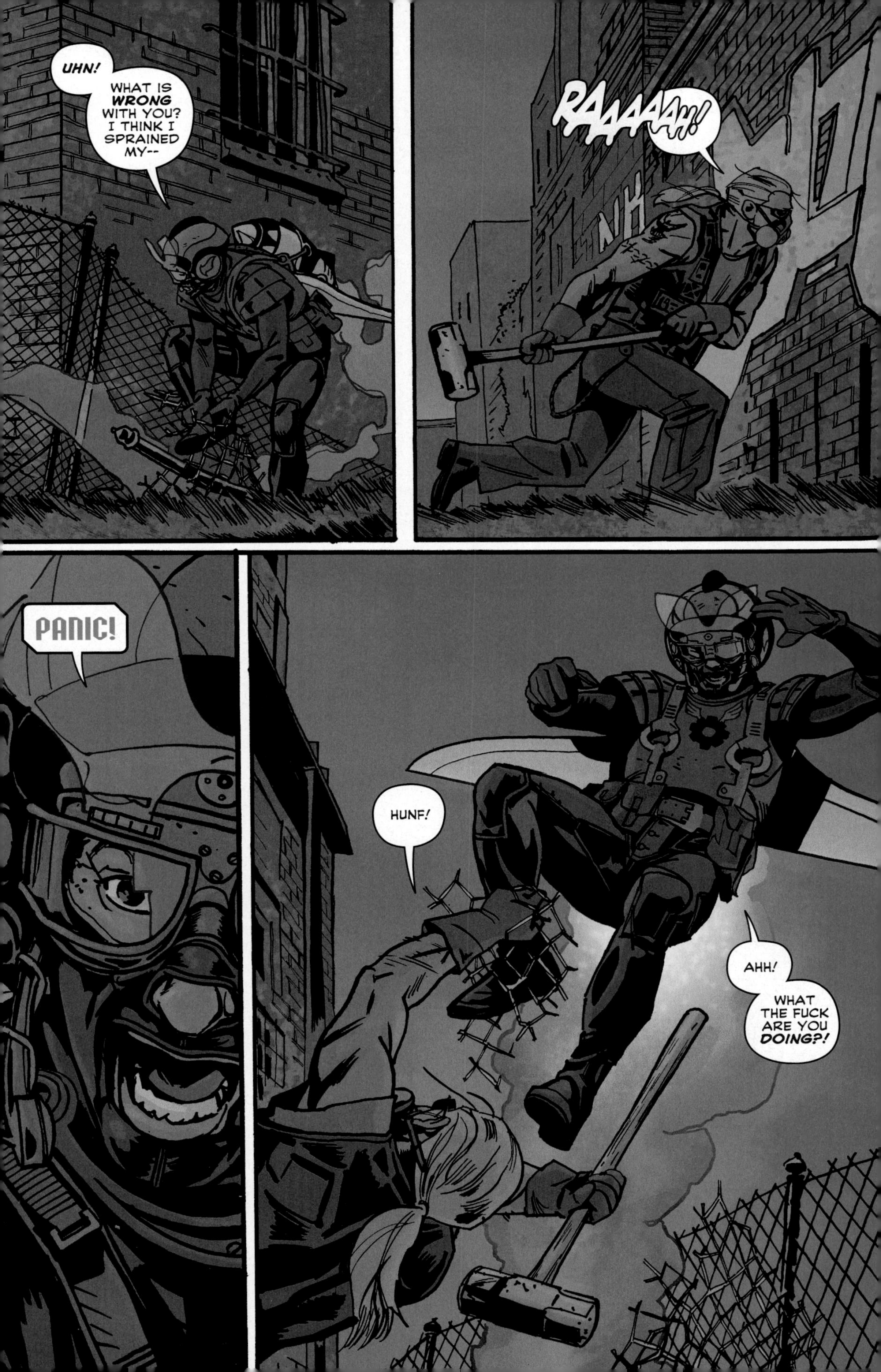
UHN!
WHAT IS WRONG WITH YOU? I THINK I SPRAINED MY--
RAAAAAH!
PANIC!
HUNF!
AHH!
WHAT THE FUCK ARE YOU DOING?!

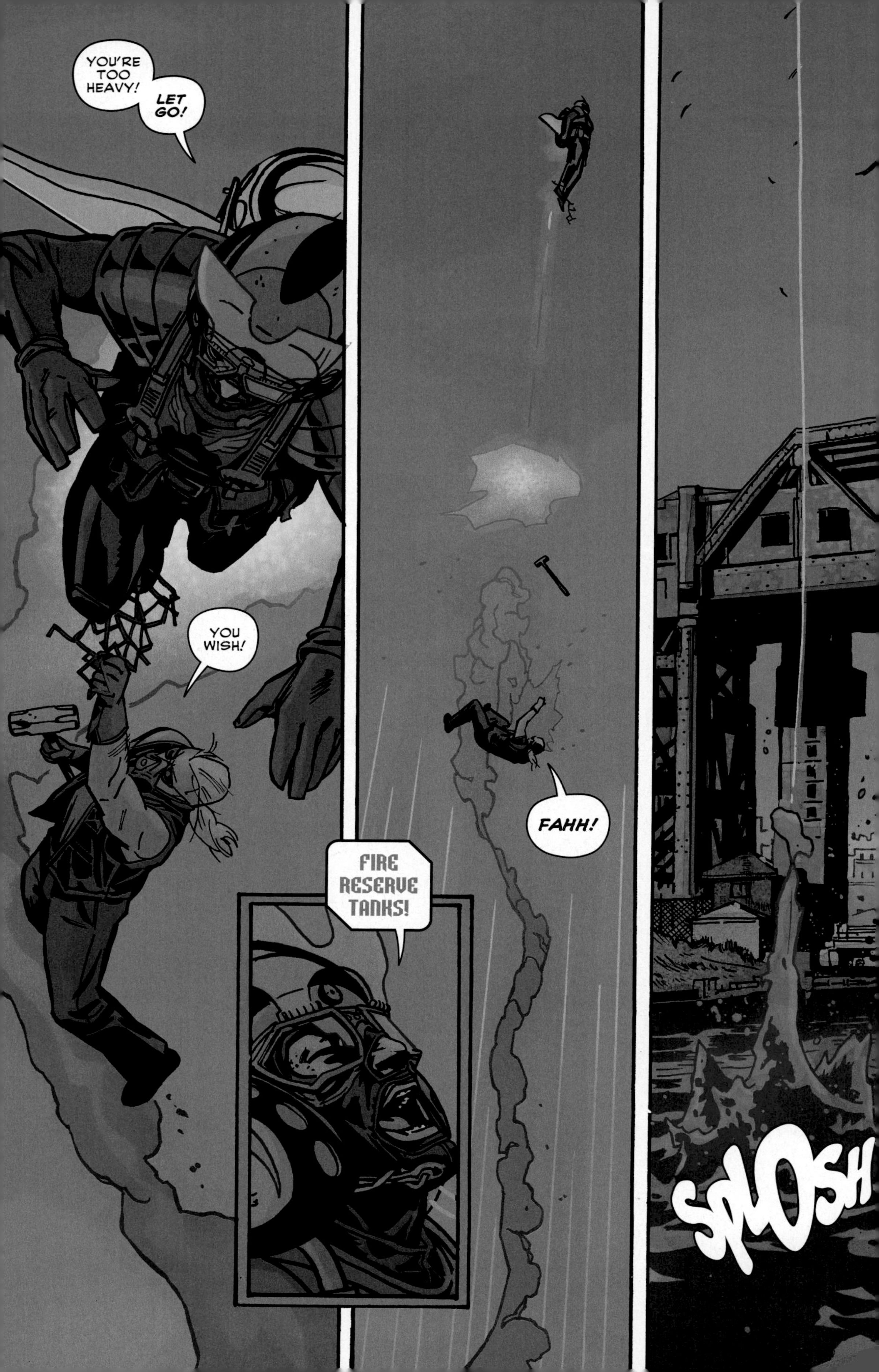

YOU'RE TOO HEAVY!
LET GO!
YOU WISH!
FIRE RESERVE TANKS!
FAHH!
SPLOSH

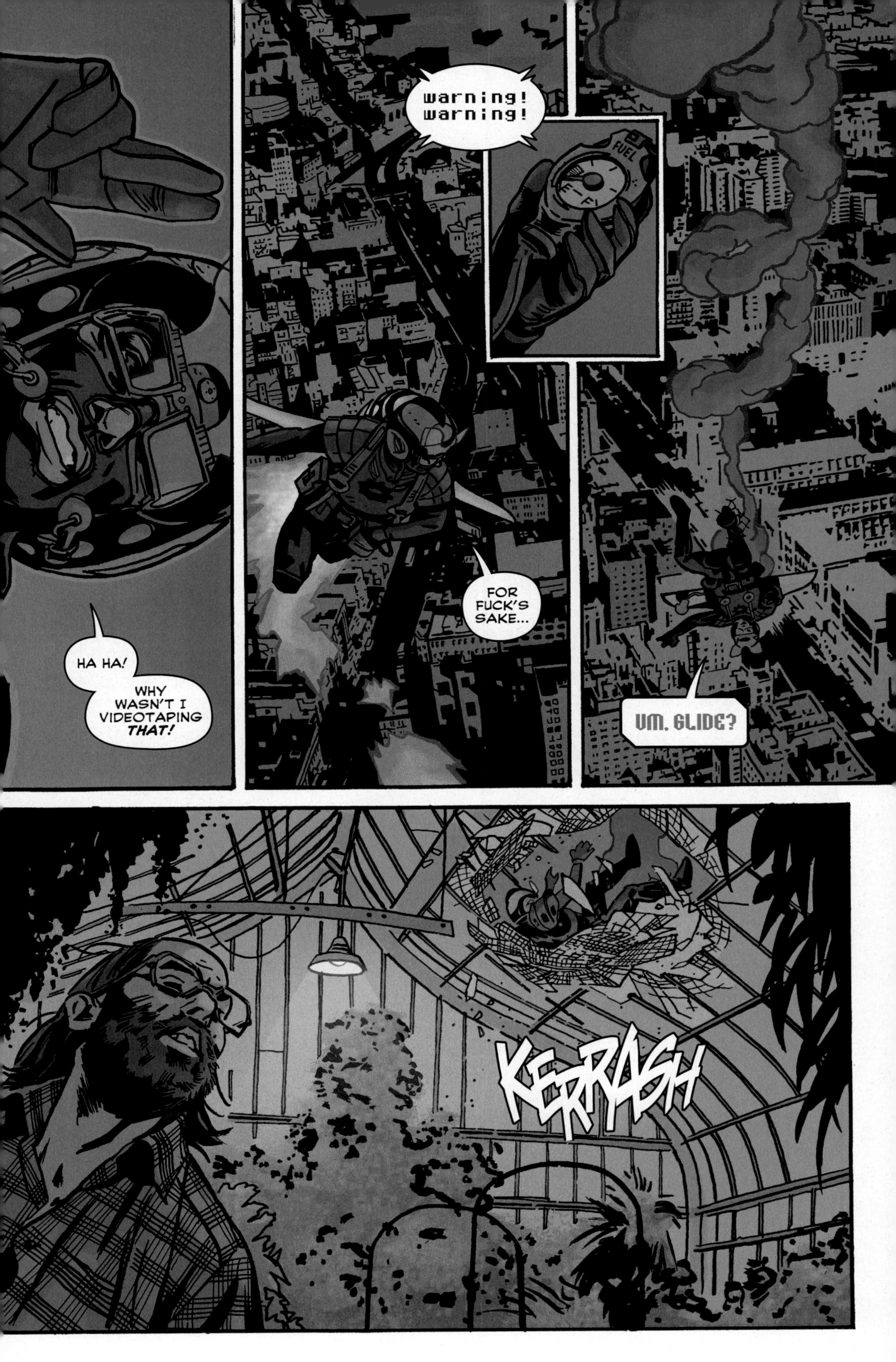
warning!
warning!
FUEL
FOR FUCK'S SAKE...
HA HA!
WHY WASN'T I VIDEOTAPING THAT!
UM, GLIDE?
KERRASH

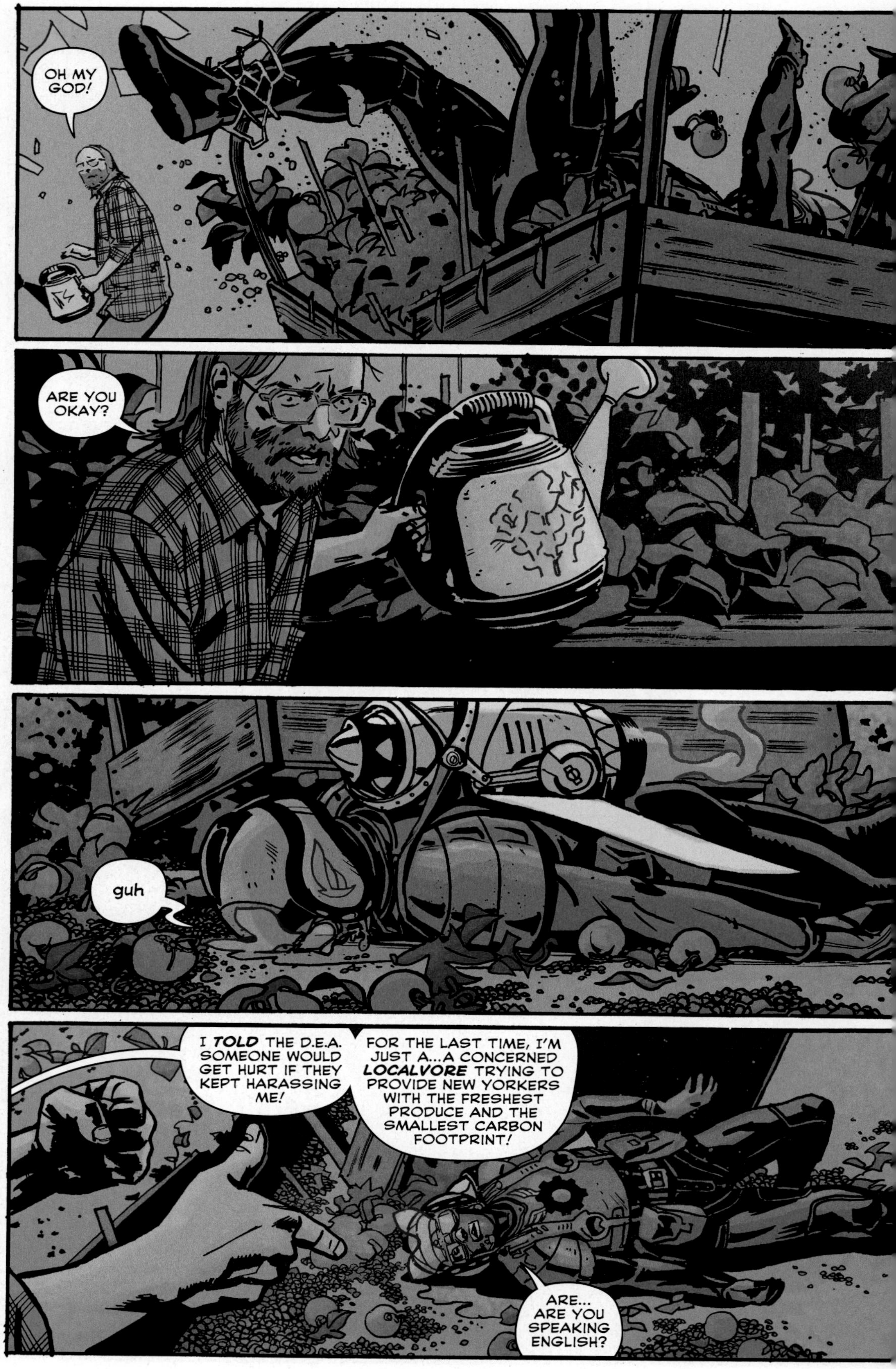
OH MY GOD!
ARE YOU OKAY?
guh
I TOLD THE D.E.A. SOMEONE WOULD GET HURT IF THEY KEPT HARASSING ME!
FOR THE LAST TIME, I'M JUST A...A CONCERNED LOCALVORE TRYING TO PROVIDE NEW YORKERS WITH THE FRESHEST PRODUCE AND THE SMALLEST CARBON FOOTPRINT!
ARE... ARE YOU SPEAKING ENGLISH?

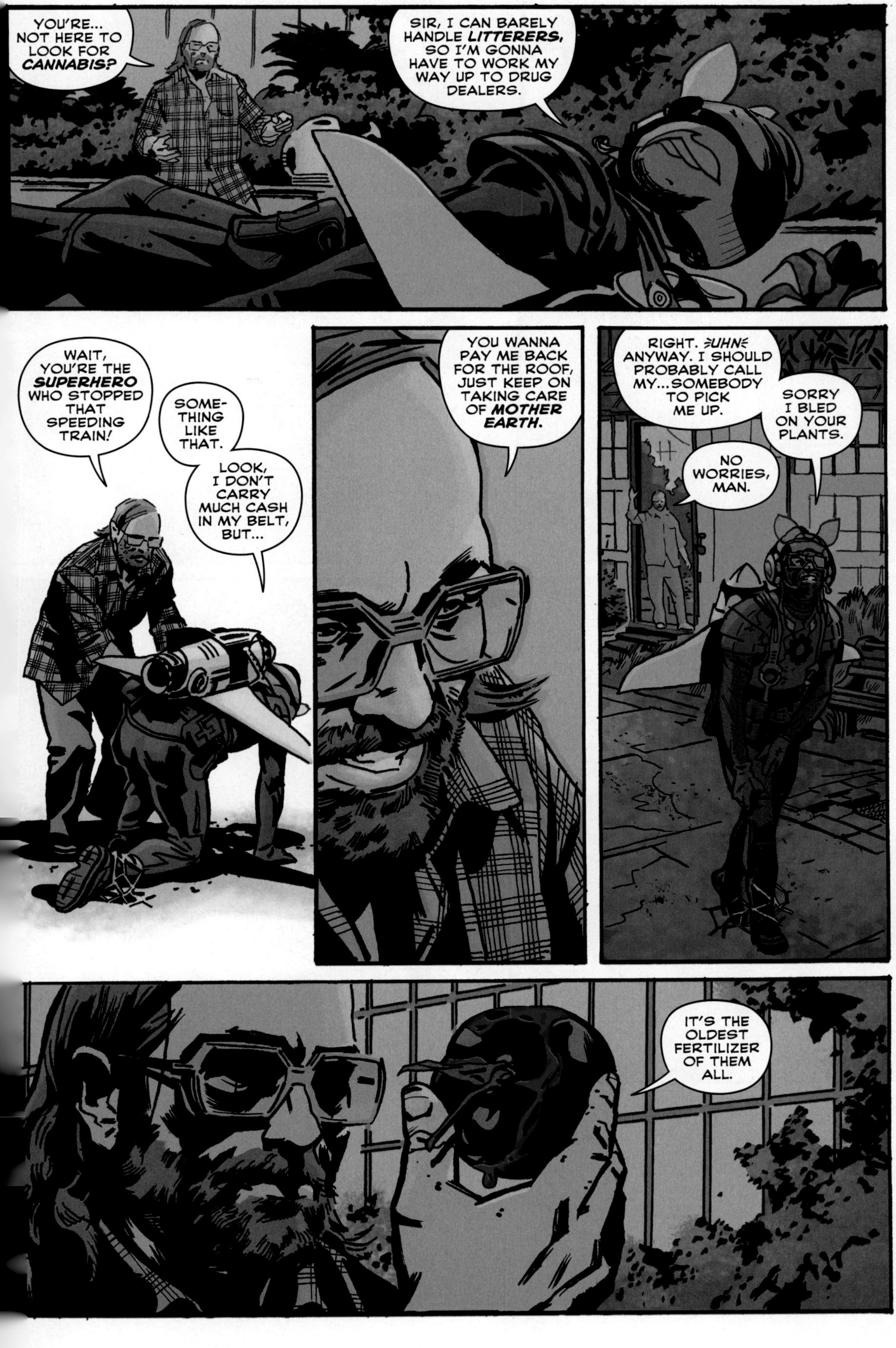
YOU'RE... NOT HERE TO LOOK FOR ***CANNABIS?***
SIR, I CAN BARELY HANDLE ***LITTERERS,*** SO I'M GONNA HAVE TO WORK MY WAY UP TO DRUG DEALERS.
WAIT, YOU'RE THE ***SUPERHERO*** WHO STOPPED THAT SPEEDING TRAIN!
SOME-THING LIKE THAT.
LOOK, I DON'T CARRY MUCH CASH IN MY BELT, BUT...
YOU WANNA PAY ME BACK FOR THE ROOF, JUST KEEP ON TAKING CARE OF ***MOTHER EARTH.***
RIGHT. *UHN* ANYWAY. I SHOULD PROBABLY CALL MY...SOMEBODY TO PICK ME UP.
SORRY I BLED ON YOUR PLANTS.
NO WORRIES, MAN.
IT'S THE OLDEST FERTILIZER OF THEM ALL.

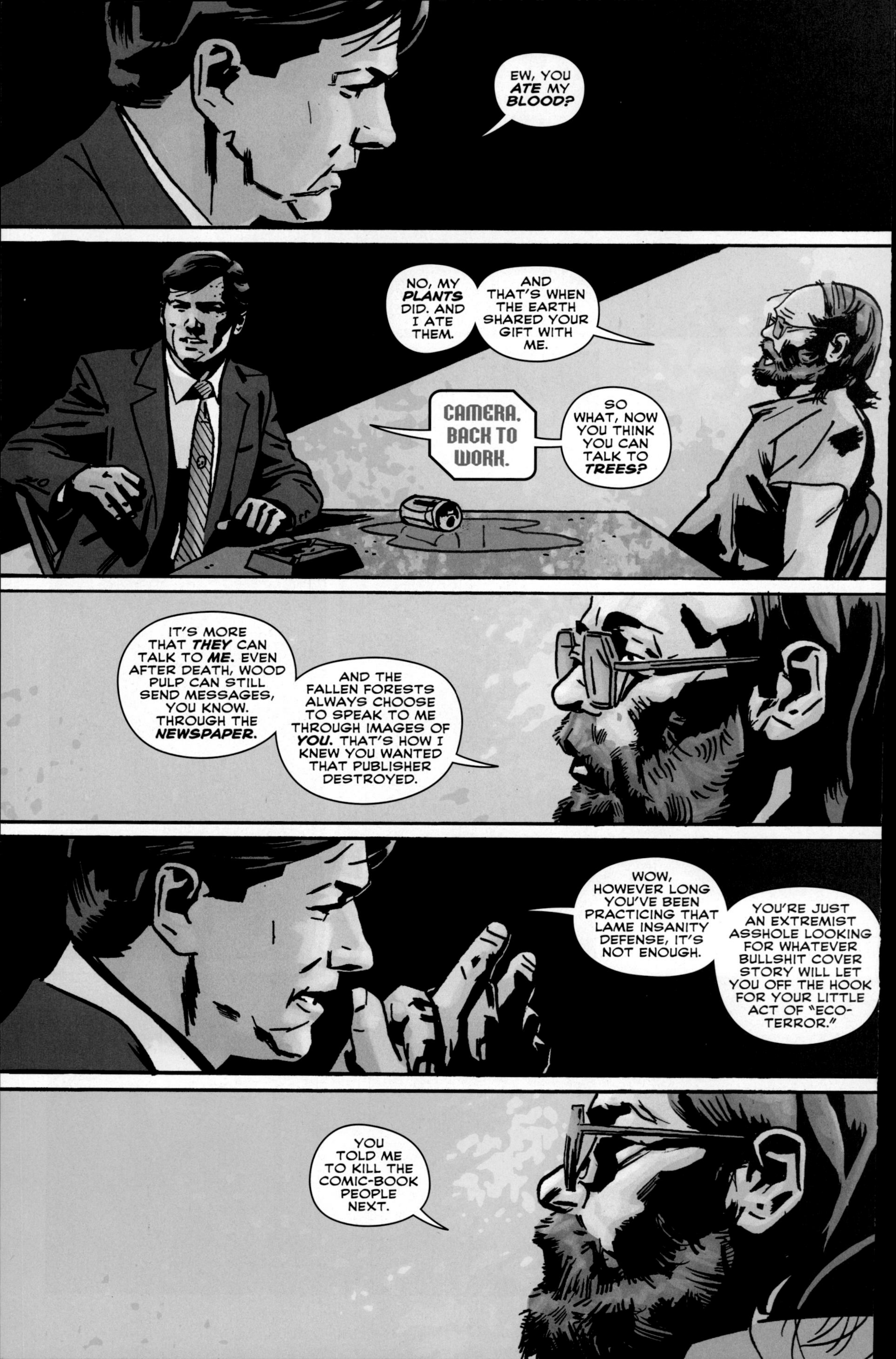
EW, YOU ATE MY BLOOD?
NO, MY PLANTS DID. AND I ATE THEM.
AND THAT'S WHEN THE EARTH SHARED YOUR GIFT WITH ME.
CAMERA. BACK TO WORK.
SO WHAT, NOW YOU THINK YOU CAN TALK TO TREES?
IT'S MORE THAT THEY CAN TALK TO ME. EVEN AFTER DEATH, WOOD PULP CAN STILL SEND MESSAGES, YOU KNOW. THROUGH THE NEWSPAPER.
AND THE FALLEN FORESTS ALWAYS CHOOSE TO SPEAK TO ME THROUGH IMAGES OF YOU. THAT'S HOW I KNEW YOU WANTED THAT PUBLISHER DESTROYED.
WOW, HOWEVER LONG YOU'VE BEEN PRACTICING THAT LAME INSANITY DEFENSE, IT'S NOT ENOUGH.
YOU'RE JUST AN EXTREMIST ASSHOLE LOOKING FOR WHATEVER BULLSHIT COVER STORY WILL LET YOU OFF THE HOOK FOR YOUR LITTLE ACT OF "ECO-TERROR."
YOU TOLD ME TO KILL THE COMIC-BOOK PEOPLE NEXT.

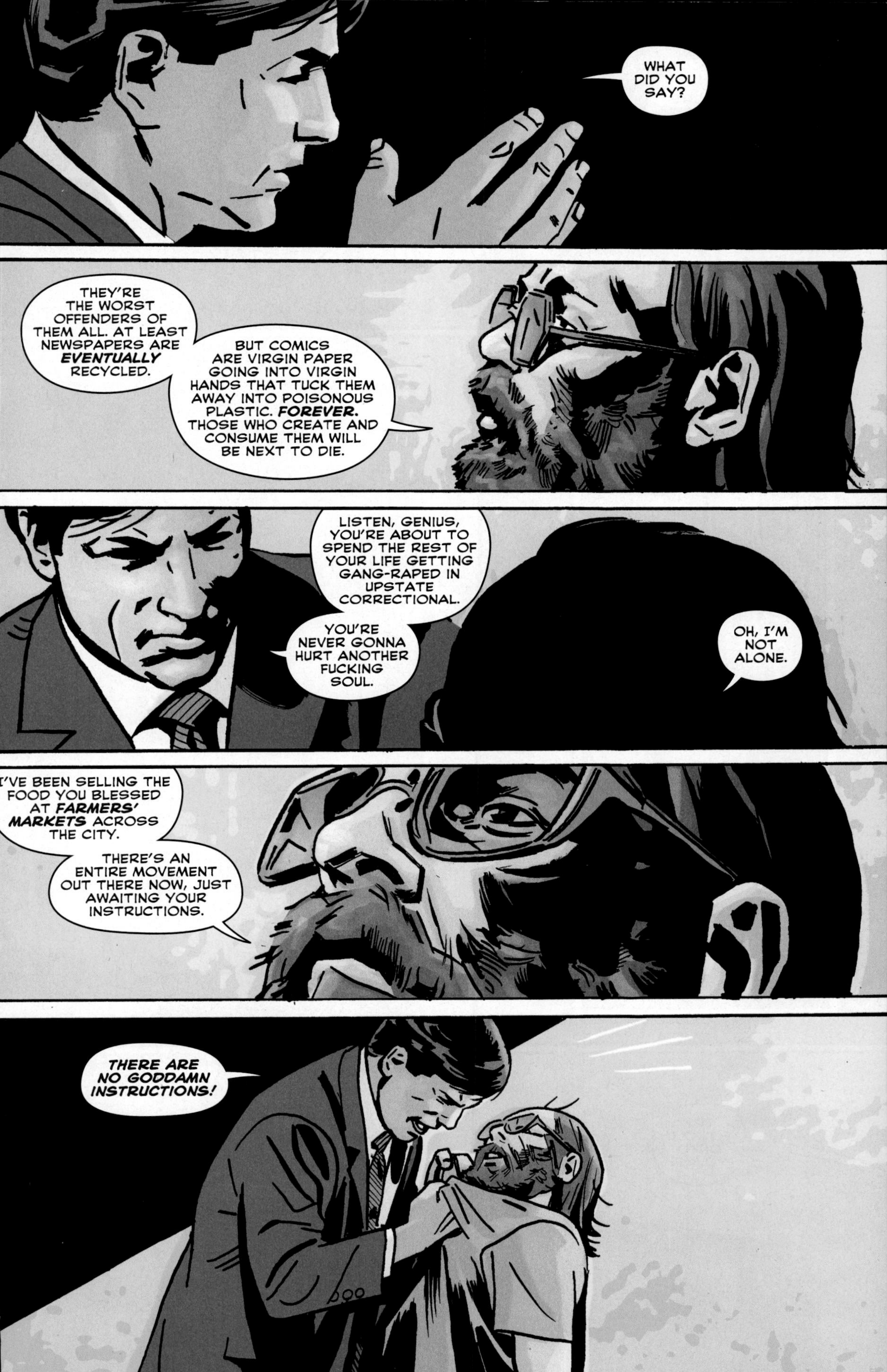

WHAT DID YOU SAY?
THEY'RE THE WORST OFFENDERS OF THEM ALL. AT LEAST NEWSPAPERS ARE ***EVENTUALLY*** RECYCLED.
BUT COMICS ARE VIRGIN PAPER GOING INTO VIRGIN HANDS THAT TUCK THEM AWAY INTO POISONOUS PLASTIC. ***FOREVER.*** THOSE WHO CREATE AND CONSUME THEM WILL BE NEXT TO DIE.
LISTEN, GENIUS, YOU'RE ABOUT TO SPEND THE REST OF YOUR LIFE GETTING GANG-RAPED IN UPSTATE CORRECTIONAL.
YOU'RE NEVER GONNA HURT ANOTHER FUCKING SOUL.
OH, I'M NOT ALONE.
I'VE BEEN SELLING THE FOOD YOU BLESSED AT ***FARMERS' MARKETS*** ACROSS THE CITY.
THERE'S AN ENTIRE MOVEMENT OUT THERE NOW, JUST AWAITING YOUR INSTRUCTIONS.
THERE ARE NO GODDAMN INSTRUCTIONS!

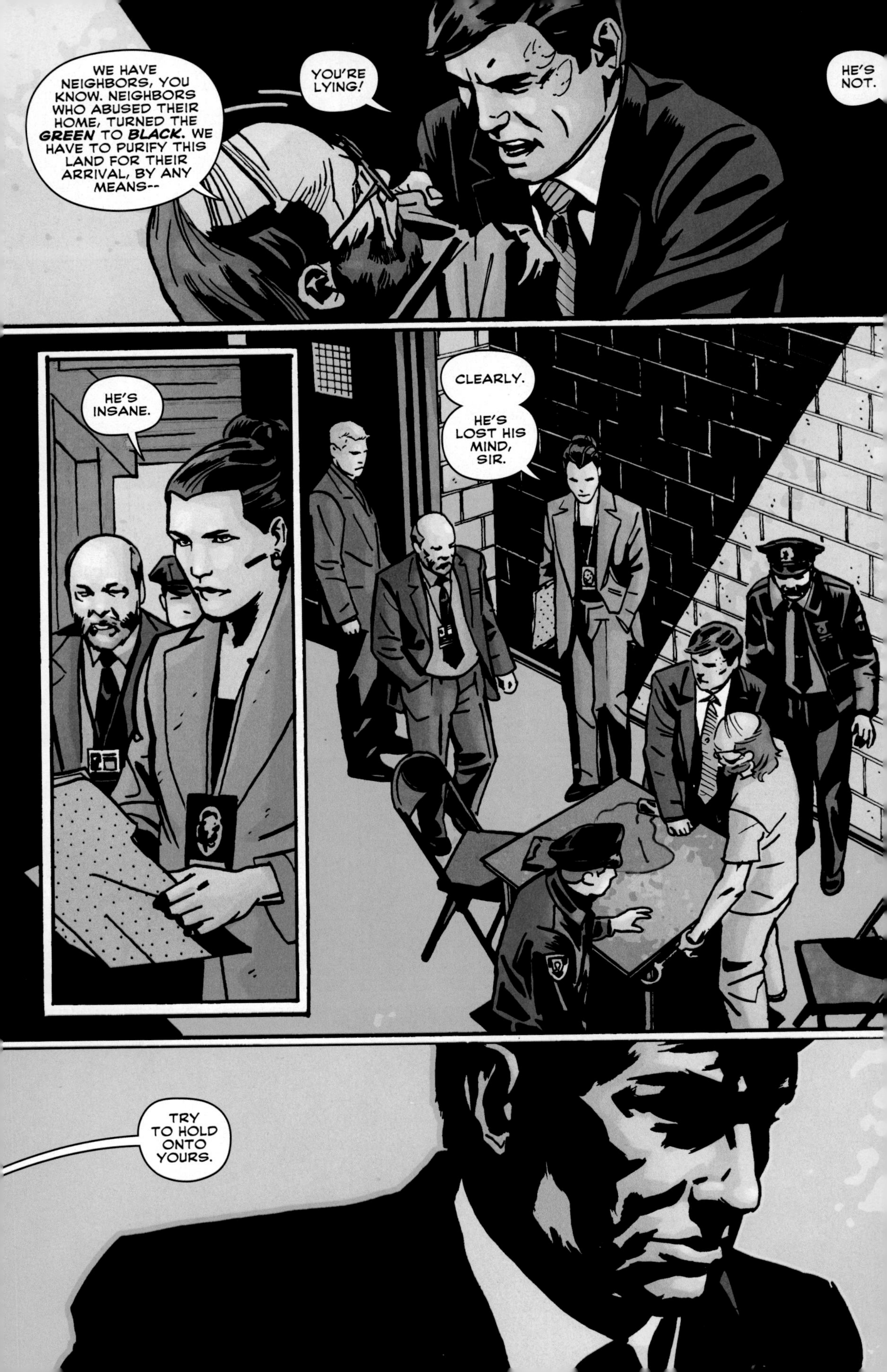
WE HAVE NEIGHBORS, YOU KNOW. NEIGHBORS WHO ABUSED THEIR HOME, TURNED THE GREEN TO BLACK. WE HAVE TO PURIFY THIS LAND FOR THEIR ARRIVAL, BY ANY MEANS--
YOU'RE LYING!
HE'S NOT.
HE'S INSANE.
CLEARLY.
HE'S LOST HIS MIND, SIR.
TRY TO HOLD ONTO YOURS.

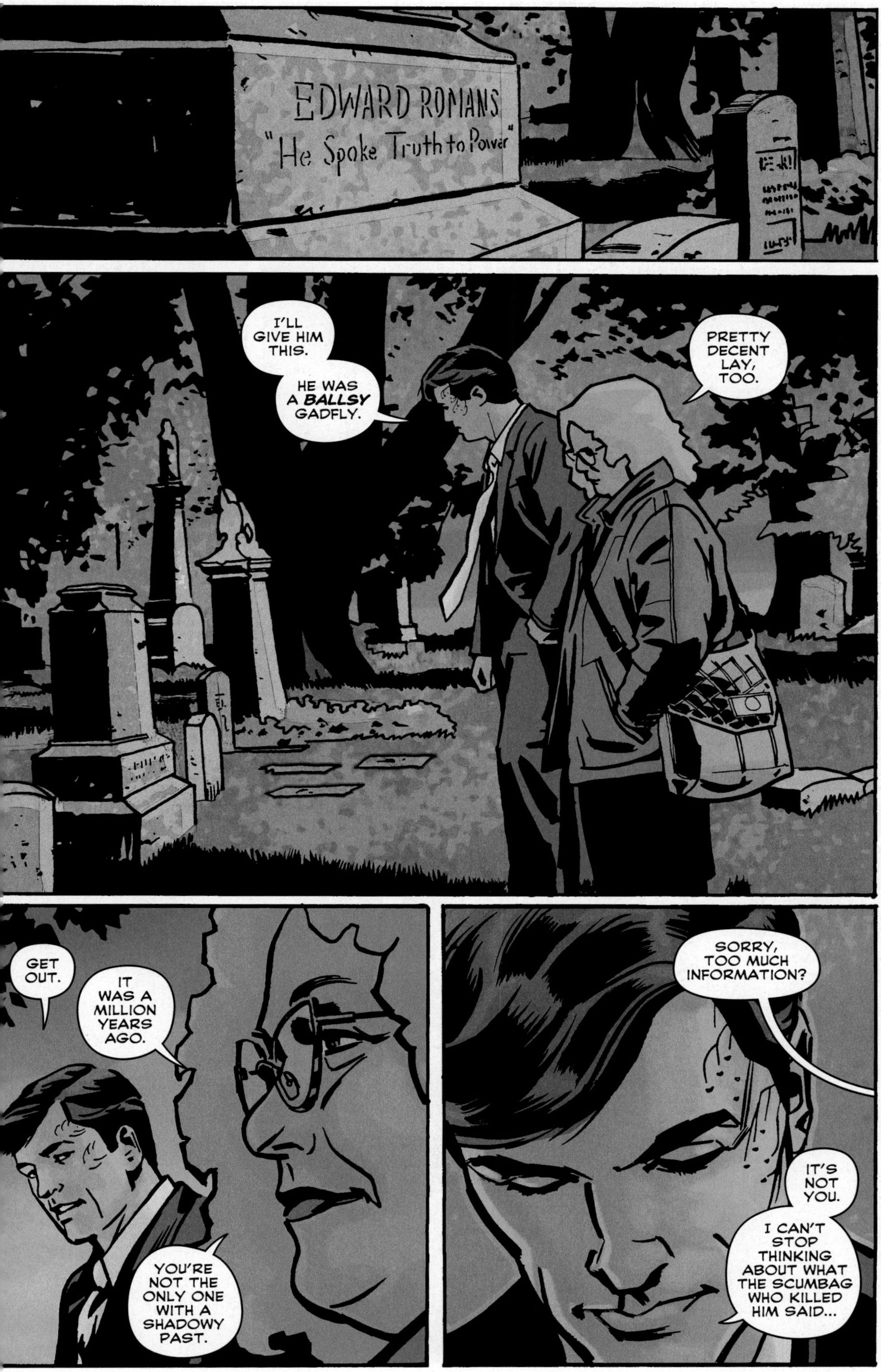
EDWARD ROMANS
"He Spoke Truth to Power"
I'LL GIVE HIM THIS.
HE WAS A BALLSY GADFLY.
PRETTY DECENT LAY, TOO.
GET OUT.
IT WAS A MILLION YEARS AGO.
YOU'RE NOT THE ONLY ONE WITH A SHADOWY PAST.
SORRY, TOO MUCH INFORMATION?
IT'S NOT YOU.
I CAN'T STOP THINKING ABOUT WHAT THE SCUMBAG WHO KILLED HIM SAID...

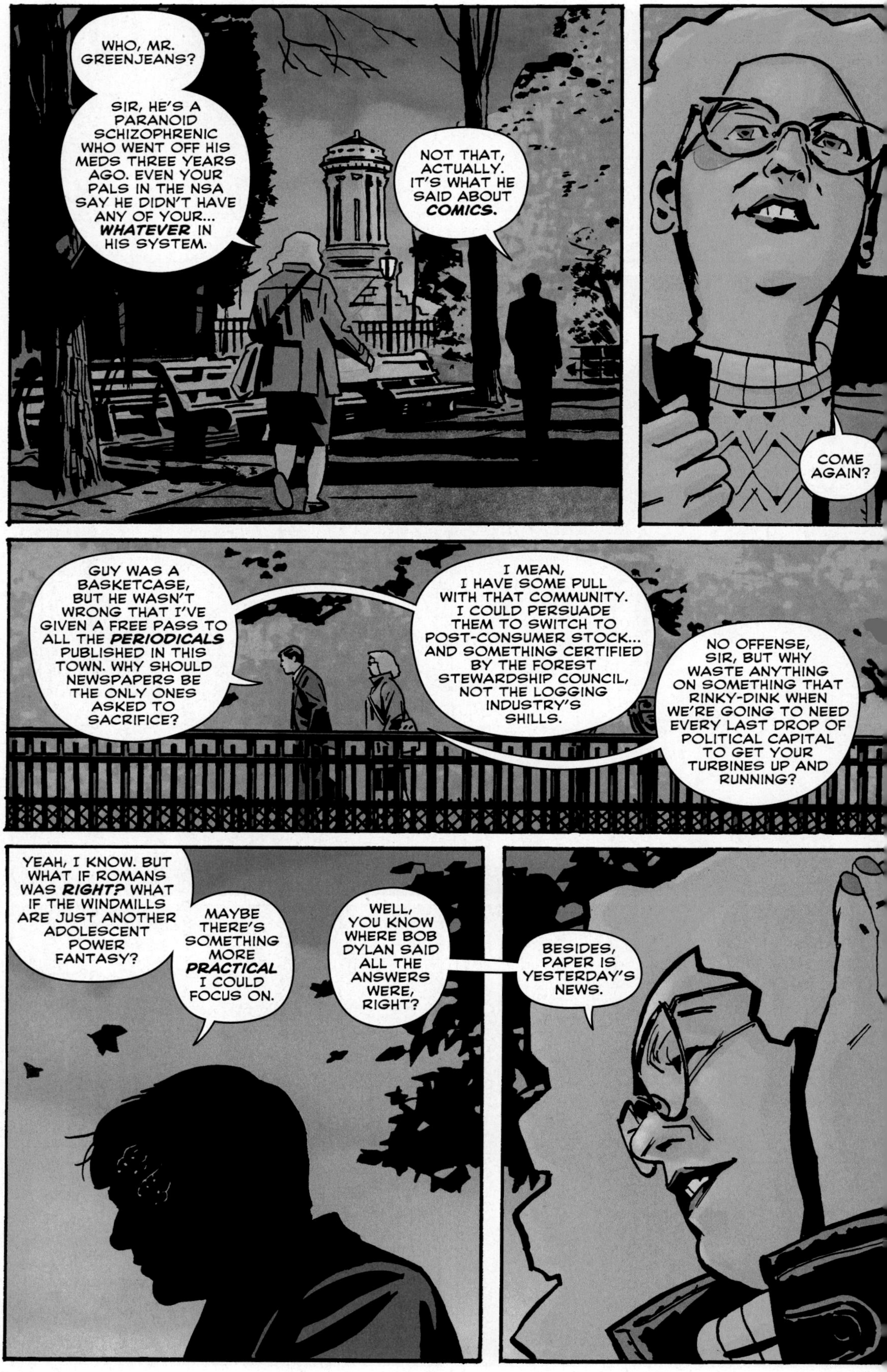
WHO, MR. GREENJEANS?
SIR, HE'S A PARANOID SCHIZOPHRENIC WHO WENT OFF HIS MEDS THREE YEARS AGO. EVEN YOUR PALS IN THE NSA SAY HE DIDN'T HAVE ANY OF YOUR... WHATEVER IN HIS SYSTEM.
NOT THAT, ACTUALLY. IT'S WHAT HE SAID ABOUT COMICS.
COME AGAIN?
GUY WAS A BASKETCASE, BUT HE WASN'T WRONG THAT I'VE GIVEN A FREE PASS TO ALL THE PERIODICALS PUBLISHED IN THIS TOWN. WHY SHOULD NEWSPAPERS BE THE ONLY ONES ASKED TO SACRIFICE?
I MEAN, I HAVE SOME PULL WITH THAT COMMUNITY. I COULD PERSUADE THEM TO SWITCH TO POST-CONSUMER STOCK... AND SOMETHING CERTIFIED BY THE FOREST STEWARDSHIP COUNCIL, NOT THE LOGGING INDUSTRY'S SHILLS.
NO OFFENSE, SIR, BUT WHY WASTE ANYTHING ON SOMETHING THAT RINKY-DINK WHEN WE'RE GOING TO NEED EVERY LAST DROP OF POLITICAL CAPITAL TO GET YOUR TURBINES UP AND RUNNING?
YEAH, I KNOW. BUT WHAT IF ROMANS WAS RIGHT? WHAT IF THE WINDMILLS ARE JUST ANOTHER ADOLESCENT POWER FANTASY?
MAYBE THERE'S SOMETHING MORE PRACTICAL I COULD FOCUS ON.
WELL, YOU KNOW WHERE BOB DYLAN SAID ALL THE ANSWERS WERE, RIGHT?
BESIDES, PAPER IS YESTERDAY'S NEWS.

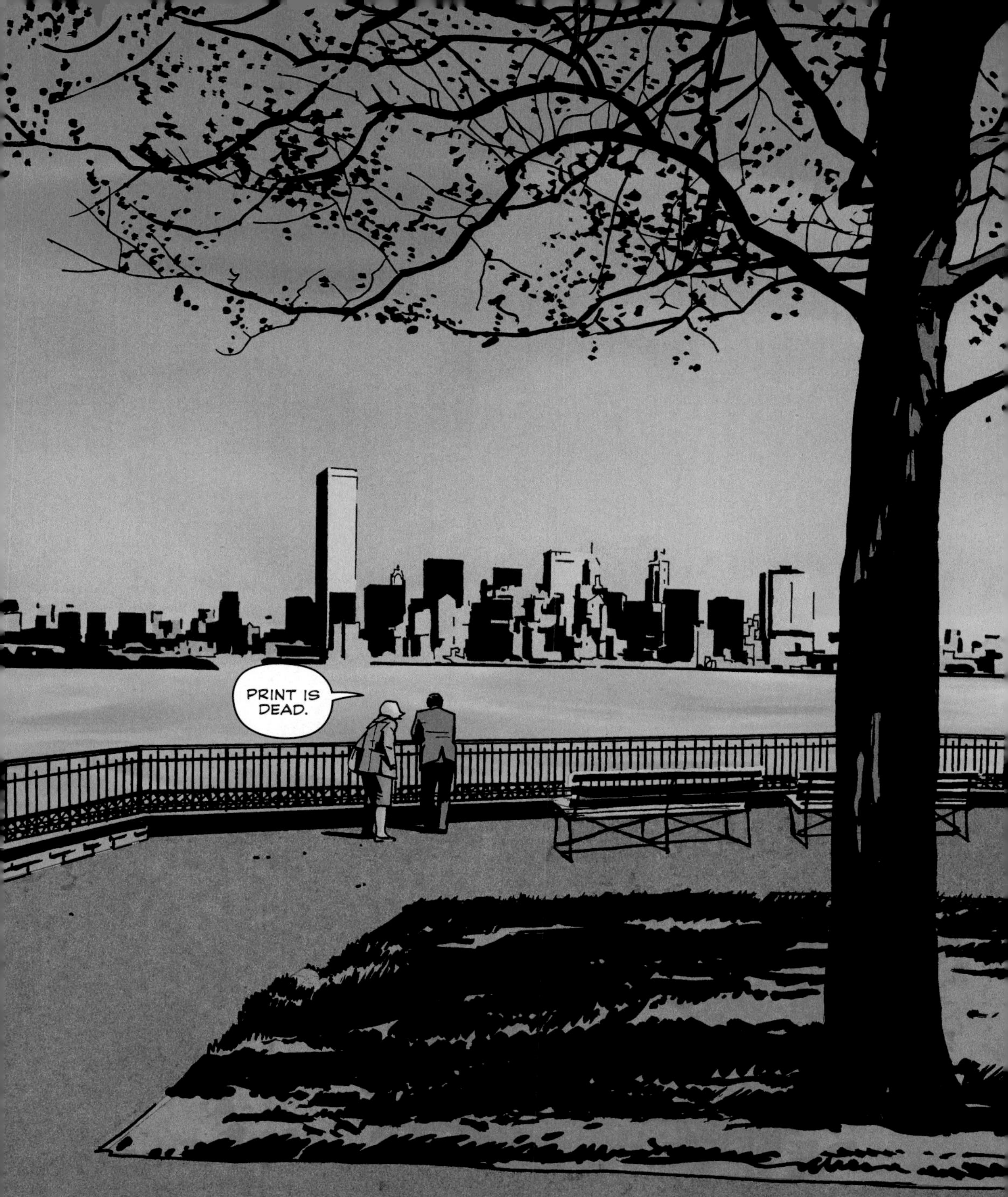
PRINT IS DEAD.

CHAPTER 3 PRO-LIFE

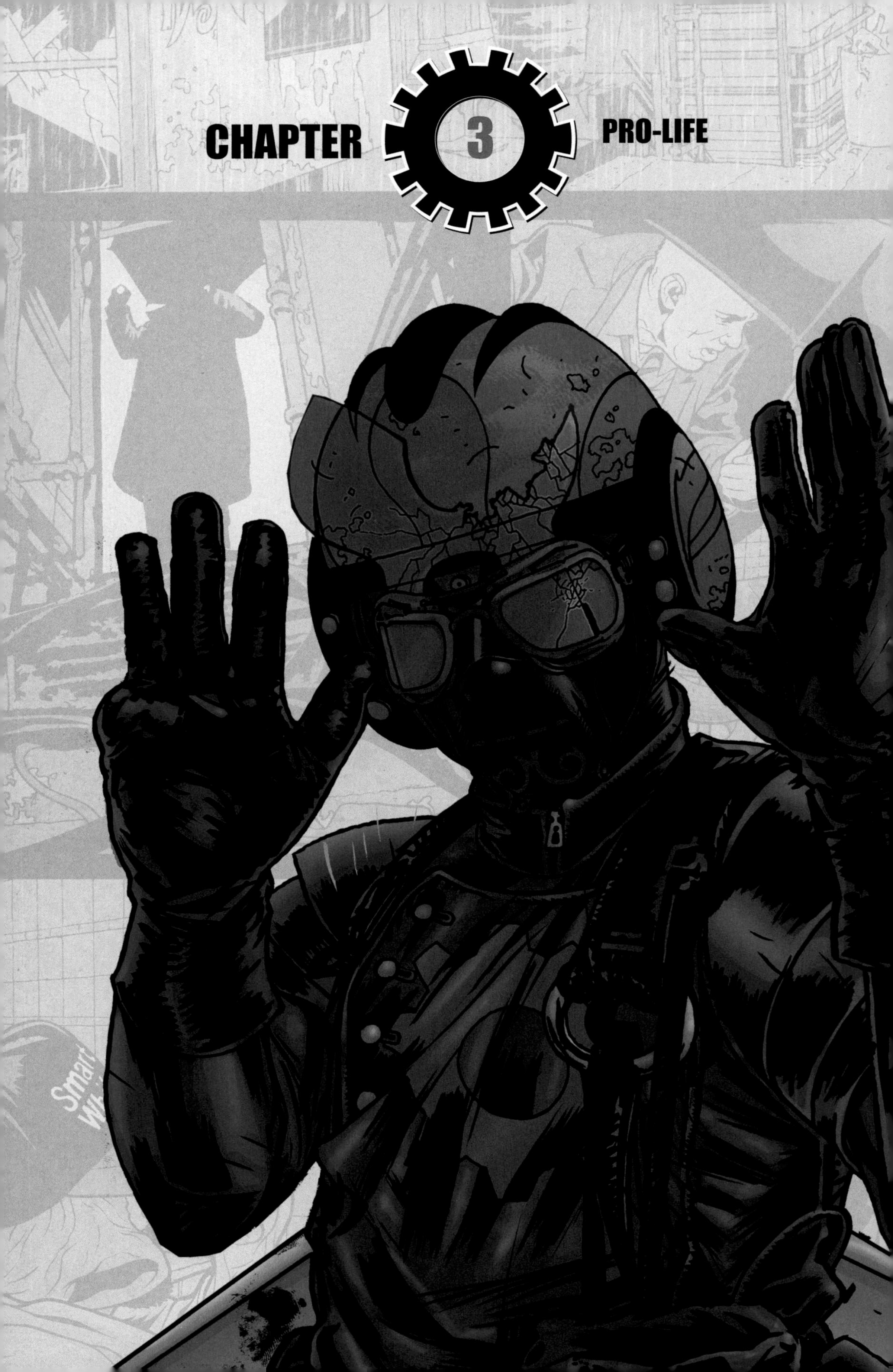

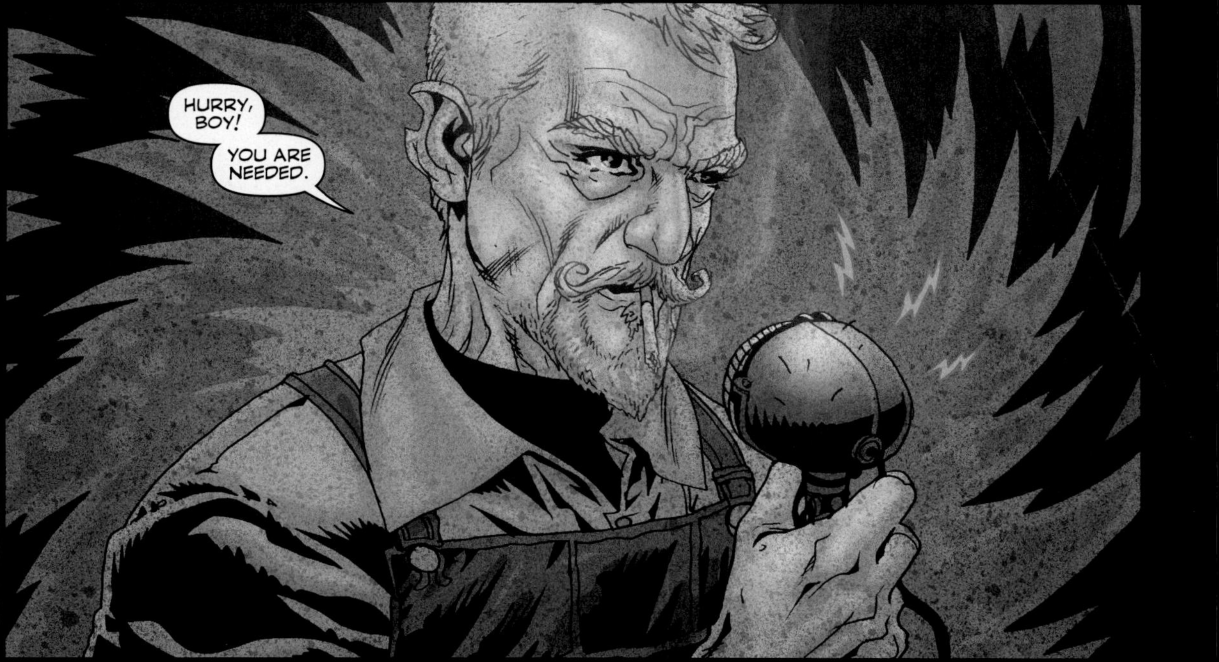
HURRY, BOY!
YOU ARE NEEDED.

TUESDAY, DECEMBER 5, 2000

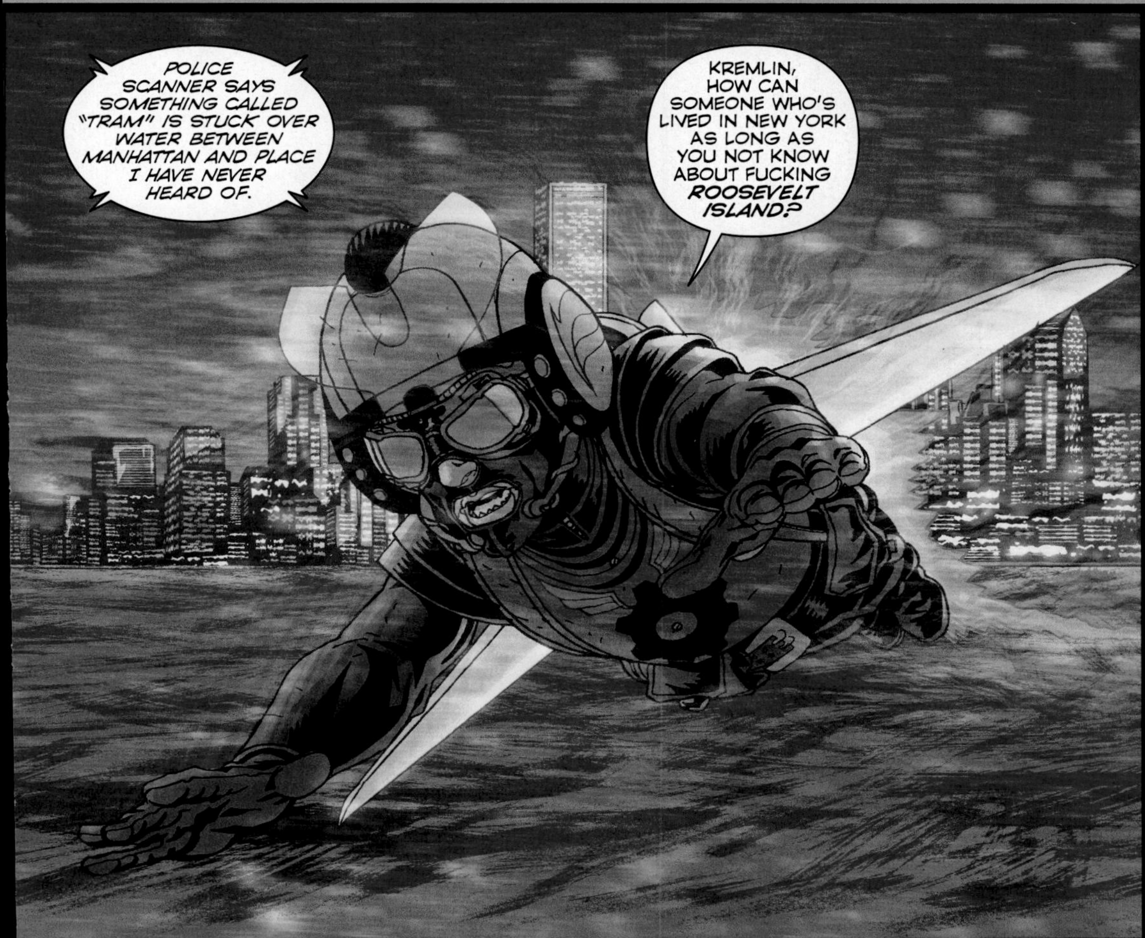
POLICE SCANNER SAYS SOMETHING CALLED "TRAM" IS STUCK OVER WATER BETWEEN MANHATTAN AND PLACE I HAVE NEVER HEARD OF.
KREMLIN, HOW CAN SOMEONE WHO'S LIVED IN NEW YORK AS LONG AS YOU NOT KNOW ABOUT FUCKING ROOSEVELT ISLAND?

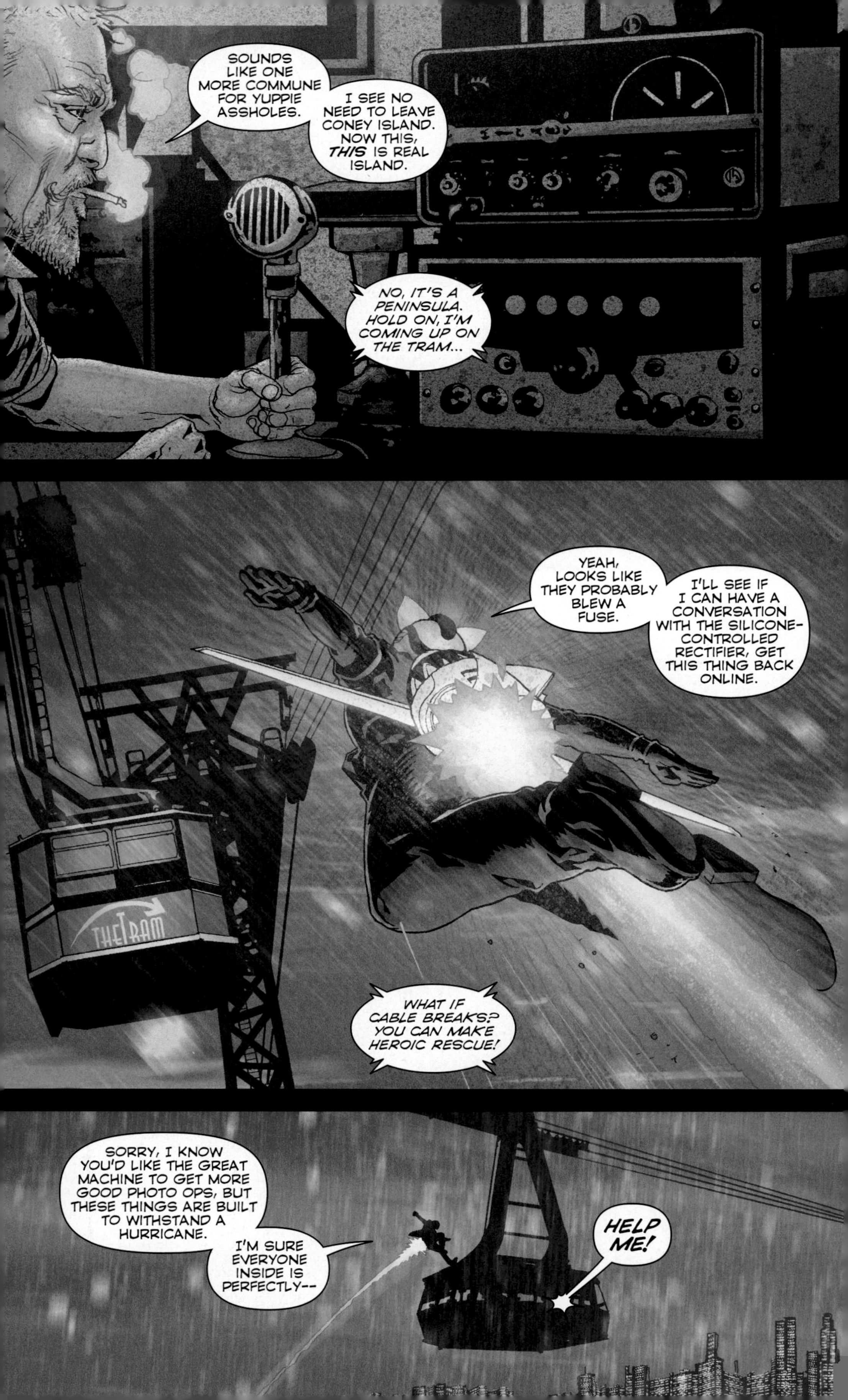

SOUNDS LIKE ONE MORE COMMUNE FOR YUPPIE ASSHOLES.
I SEE NO NEED TO LEAVE CONEY ISLAND. NOW THIS, *THIS* IS REAL ISLAND.
NO, IT'S A PENINSULA. HOLD ON, I'M COMING UP ON THE TRAM...
YEAH, LOOKS LIKE THEY PROBABLY BLEW A FUSE.
I'LL SEE IF I CAN HAVE A CONVERSATION WITH THE SILICONE-CONTROLLED RECTIFIER, GET THIS THING BACK ONLINE.
THE TRAM
WHAT IF CABLE BREAKS? YOU CAN MAKE HEROIC RESCUE!
SORRY, I KNOW YOU'D LIKE THE GREAT MACHINE TO GET MORE GOOD PHOTO OPS, BUT THESE THINGS ARE BUILT TO WITHSTAND A HURRICANE.
I'M SURE EVERYONE INSIDE IS PERFECTLY--
HELP ME!

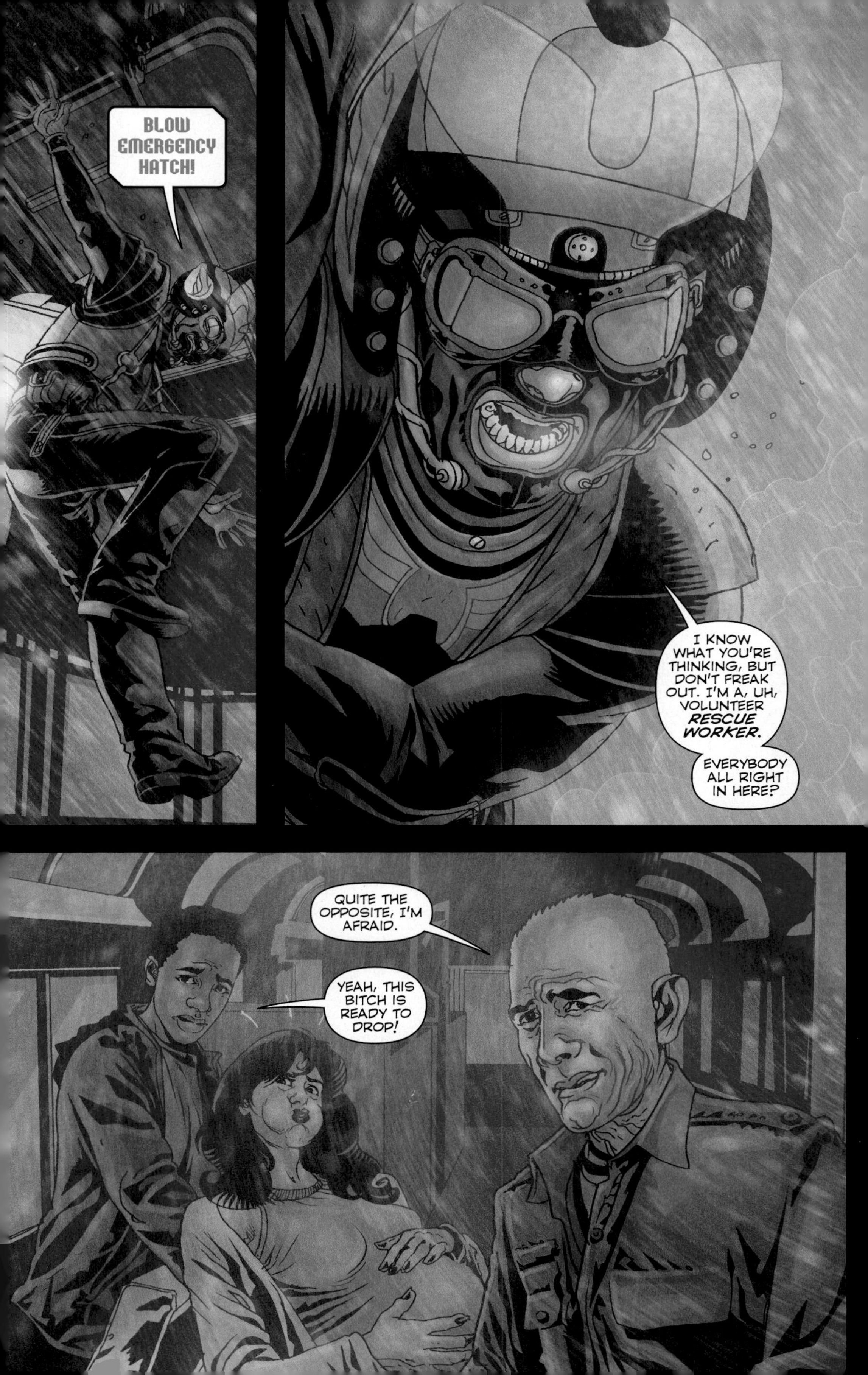
BLOW EMERGENCY HATCH!
I KNOW WHAT YOU'RE THINKING, BUT DON'T FREAK OUT. I'M A, UH, VOLUNTEER *RESCUE WORKER.*
EVERYBODY ALL RIGHT IN HERE?
QUITE THE OPPOSITE, I'M AFRAID.
YEAH, THIS BITCH IS READY TO DROP!

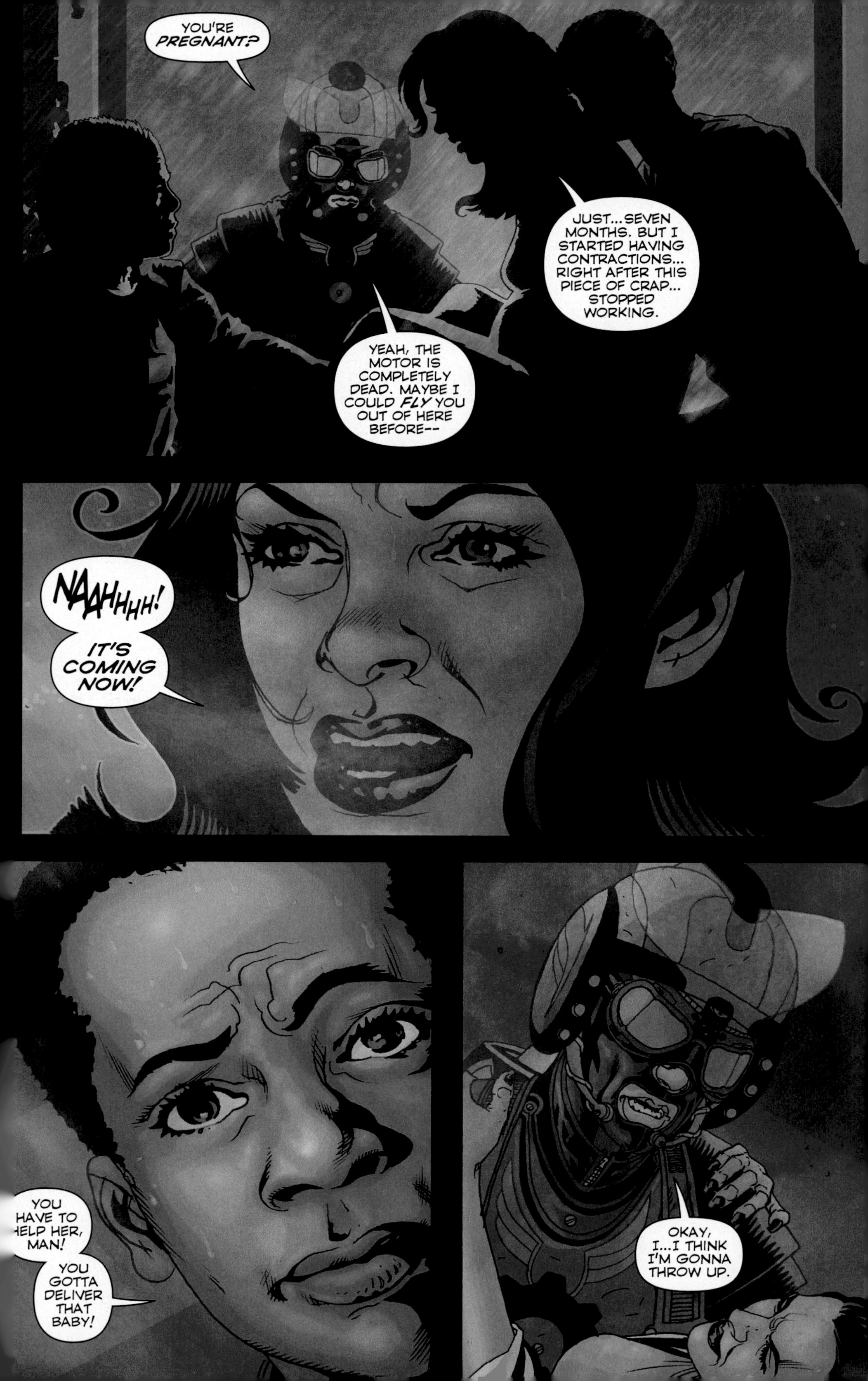
YOU'RE PREGNANT?
JUST... SEVEN MONTHS. BUT I STARTED HAVING CONTRACTIONS... RIGHT AFTER THIS PIECE OF CRAP... STOPPED WORKING.
YEAH, THE MOTOR IS COMPLETELY DEAD. MAYBE I COULD FLY YOU OUT OF HERE BEFORE--
NAAHHHH!
IT'S COMING NOW!
YOU HAVE TO HELP HER, MAN!
YOU GOTTA DELIVER THAT BABY!
OKAY, I...I THINK I'M GONNA THROW UP.

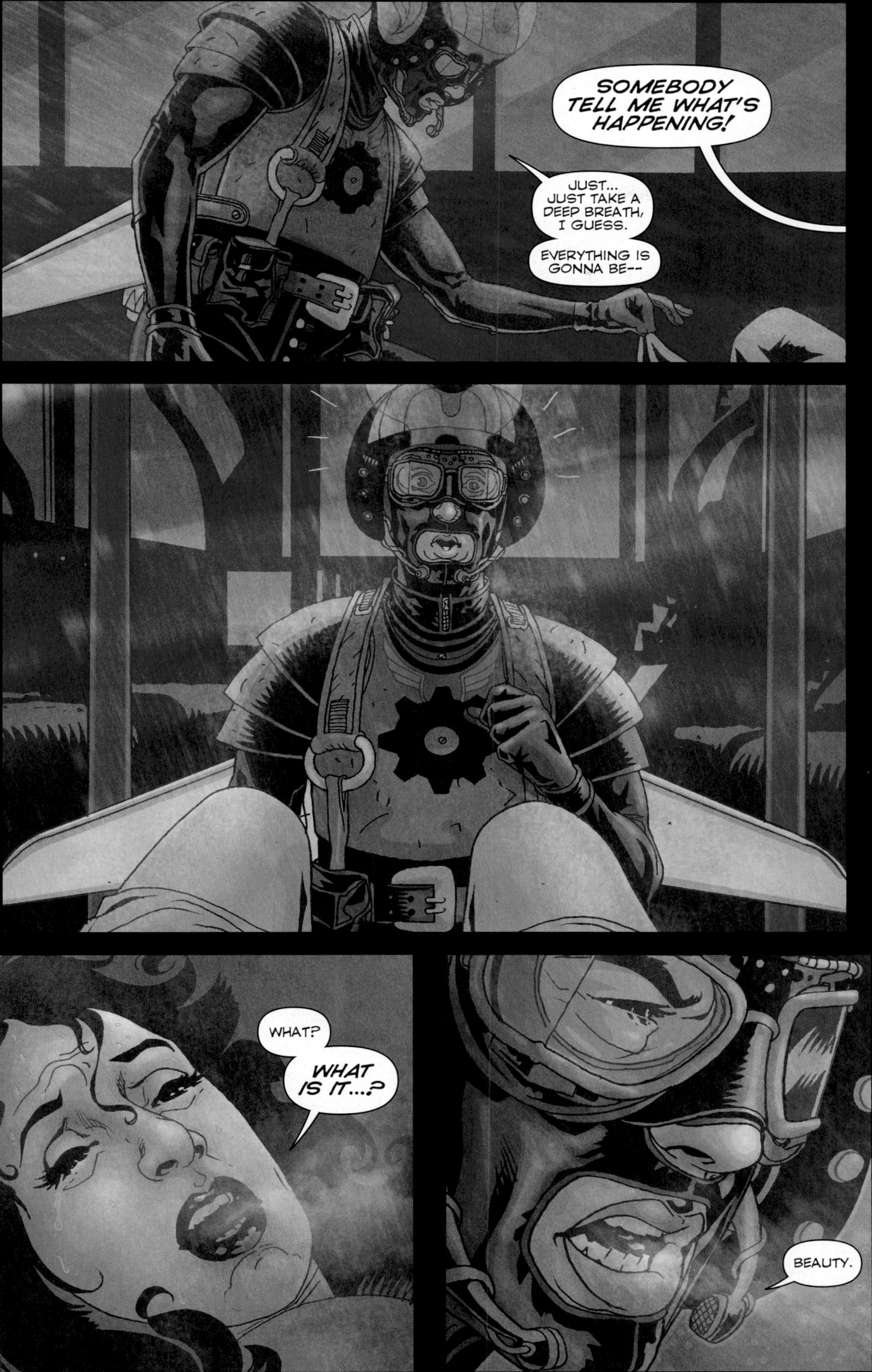
SOMEBODY TELL ME WHAT'S HAPPENING!
JUST... JUST TAKE A DEEP BREATH, I GUESS.
EVERYTHING IS GONNA BE--
WHAT?
WHAT IS IT...?
BEAUTY.

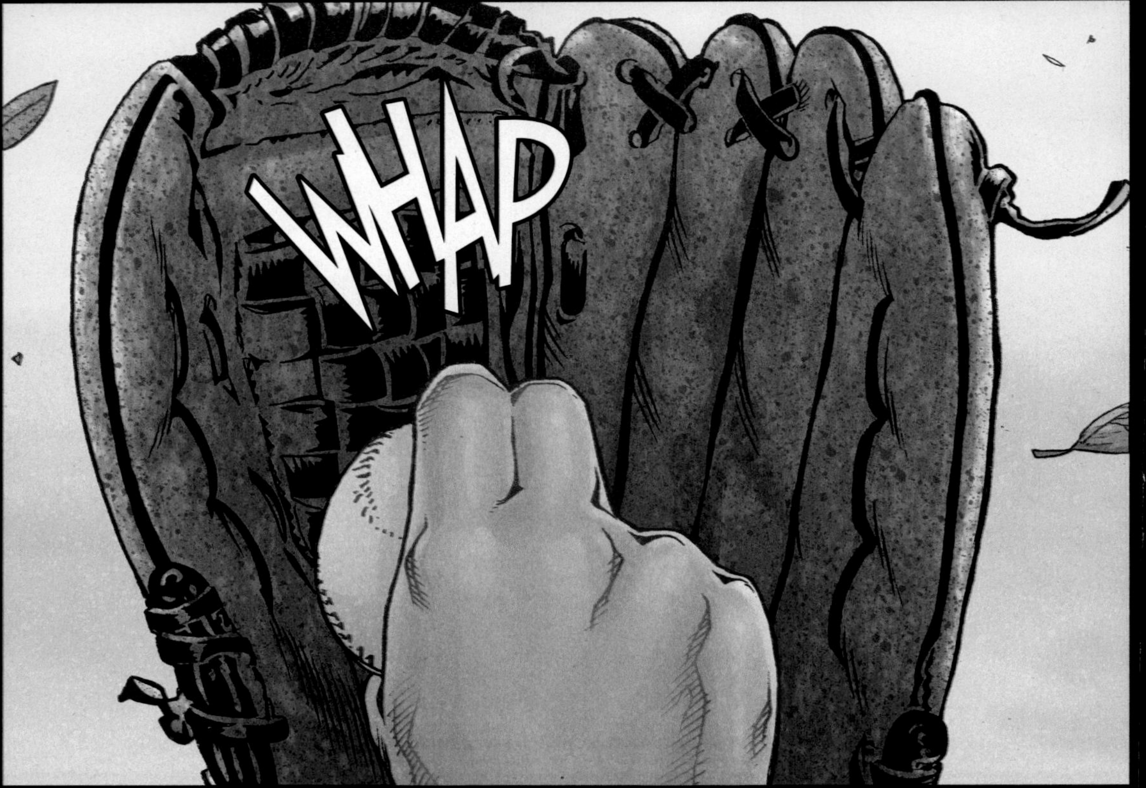
WHAP

SATURDAY, APRIL 2, 2005

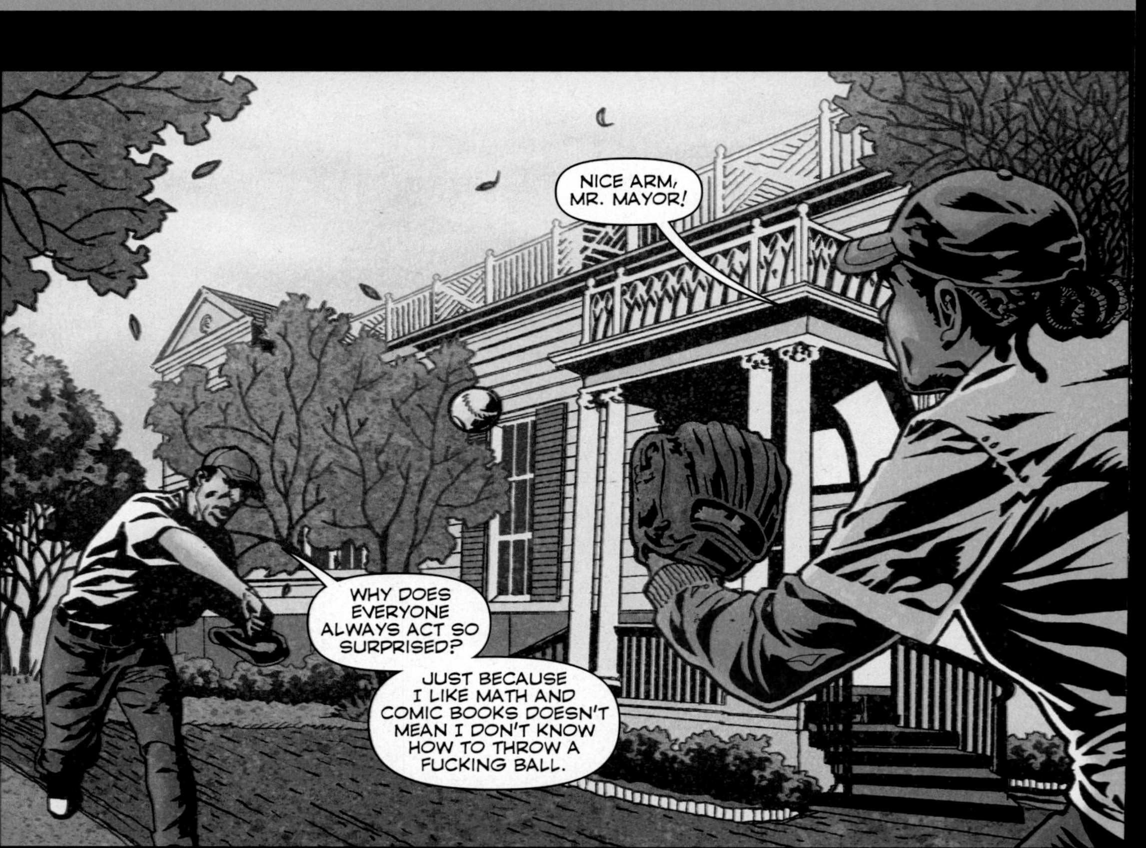
NICE ARM, MR. MAYOR!
WHY DOES EVERYONE ALWAYS ACT SO SURPRISED?
JUST BECAUSE I LIKE MATH AND COMIC BOOKS DOESN'T MEAN I DON'T KNOW HOW TO THROW A FUCKING BALL.

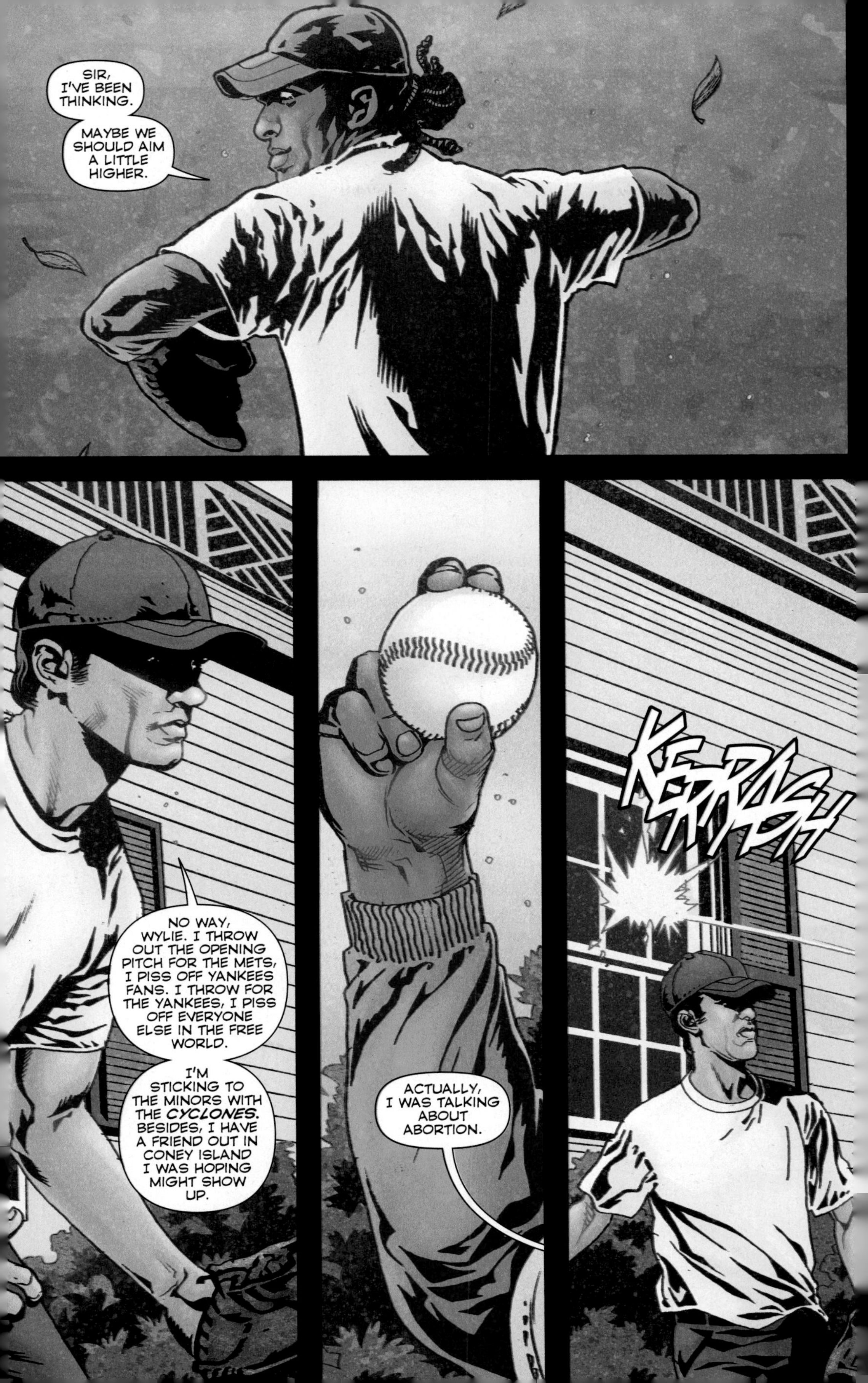
SIR, I'VE BEEN THINKING.
MAYBE WE SHOULD AIM A LITTLE HIGHER.
NO WAY, WYLIE. I THROW OUT THE OPENING PITCH FOR THE METS, I PISS OFF YANKEES FANS. I THROW FOR THE YANKEES, I PISS OFF EVERYONE ELSE IN THE FREE WORLD.
I'M STICKING TO THE MINORS WITH THE *CYCLONES.* BESIDES, I HAVE A FRIEND OUT IN CONEY ISLAND I WAS HOPING MIGHT SHOW UP.
ACTUALLY, I WAS TALKING ABOUT ABORTION.
KERRASH

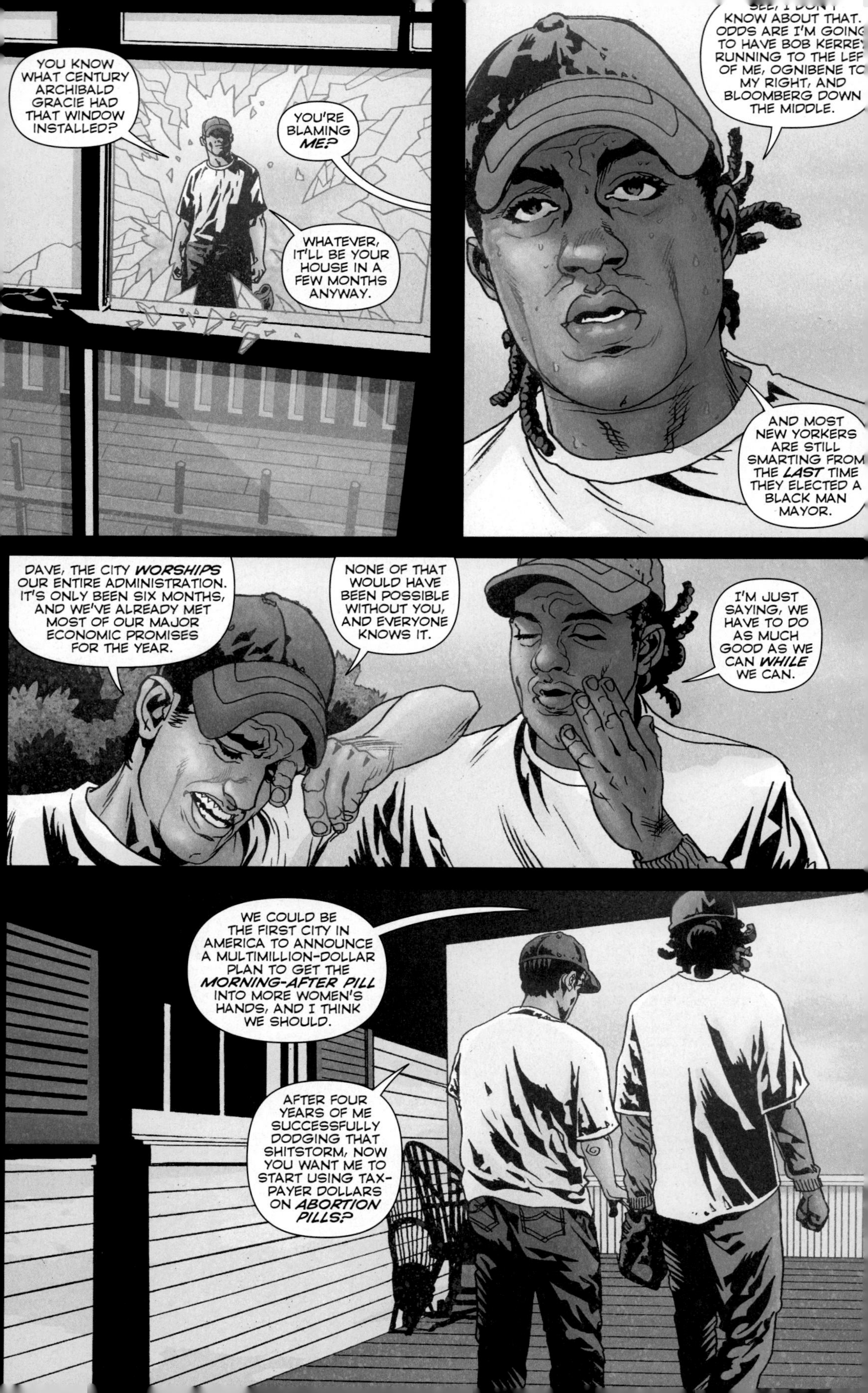
YOU KNOW WHAT CENTURY ARCHIBALD GRACIE HAD THAT WINDOW INSTALLED?
YOU'RE BLAMING *ME?*
WHATEVER, IT'LL BE YOUR HOUSE IN A FEW MONTHS ANYWAY.
KNOW ABOUT THAT. ODDS ARE I'M GOING TO HAVE BOB KERRE RUNNING TO THE LEF OF ME, OGNIBENE TO MY RIGHT, AND BLOOMBERG DOWN THE MIDDLE.
AND MOST NEW YORKERS ARE STILL SMARTING FROM THE *LAST* TIME THEY ELECTED A BLACK MAN MAYOR.
DAVE, THE CITY *WORSHIPS* OUR ENTIRE ADMINISTRATION. IT'S ONLY BEEN SIX MONTHS, AND WE'VE ALREADY MET MOST OF OUR MAJOR ECONOMIC PROMISES FOR THE YEAR.
NONE OF THAT WOULD HAVE BEEN POSSIBLE WITHOUT YOU, AND EVERYONE KNOWS IT.
I'M JUST SAYING, WE HAVE TO DO AS MUCH GOOD AS WE CAN *WHILE* WE CAN.
WE COULD BE THE FIRST CITY IN AMERICA TO ANNOUNCE A MULTIMILLION-DOLLAR PLAN TO GET THE *MORNING-AFTER PILL* INTO MORE WOMEN'S HANDS, AND I THINK WE SHOULD.
AFTER FOUR YEARS OF ME SUCCESSFULLY DODGING THAT SHITSTORM, NOW YOU WANT ME TO START USING TAX-PAYER DOLLARS ON *ABORTION PILLS?*

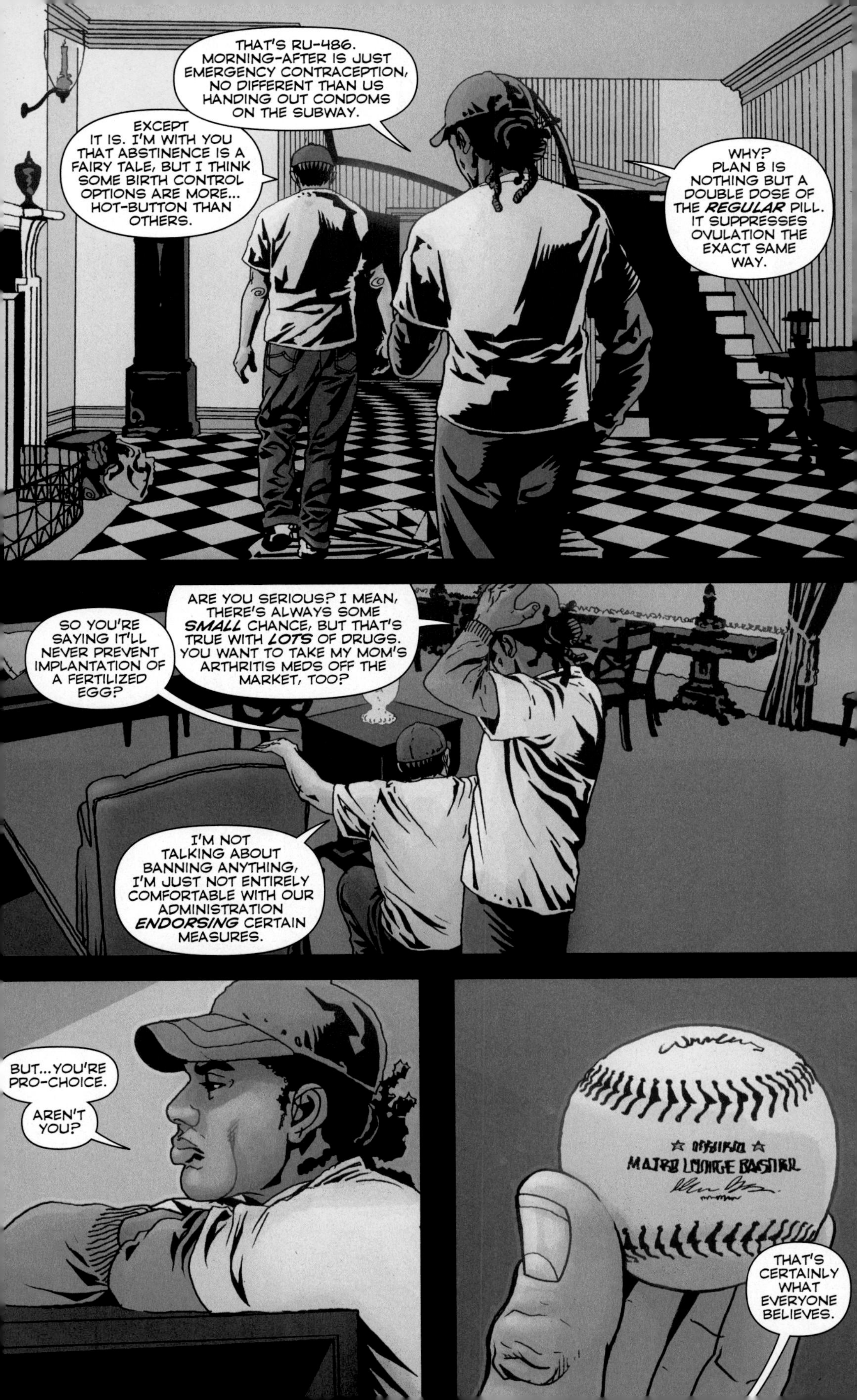
THAT'S RU-486. MORNING-AFTER IS JUST EMERGENCY CONTRACEPTION, NO DIFFERENT THAN US HANDING OUT CONDOMS ON THE SUBWAY.
EXCEPT IT IS. I'M WITH YOU THAT ABSTINENCE IS A FAIRY TALE, BUT I THINK SOME BIRTH CONTROL OPTIONS ARE MORE... HOT-BUTTON THAN OTHERS.
WHY? PLAN B IS NOTHING BUT A DOUBLE DOSE OF THE *REGULAR* PILL. IT SUPPRESSES OVULATION THE EXACT SAME WAY.
SO YOU'RE SAYING IT'LL NEVER PREVENT IMPLANTATION OF A FERTILIZED EGG?
ARE YOU SERIOUS? I MEAN, THERE'S ALWAYS SOME *SMALL* CHANCE, BUT THAT'S TRUE WITH *LOTS* OF DRUGS. YOU WANT TO TAKE MY MOM'S ARTHRITIS MEDS OFF THE MARKET, TOO?
I'M NOT TALKING ABOUT BANNING ANYTHING, I'M JUST NOT ENTIRELY COMFORTABLE WITH OUR ADMINISTRATION *ENDORSING* CERTAIN MEASURES.
BUT...YOU'RE PRO-CHOICE.
AREN'T YOU?
THAT'S CERTAINLY WHAT EVERYONE BELIEVES.

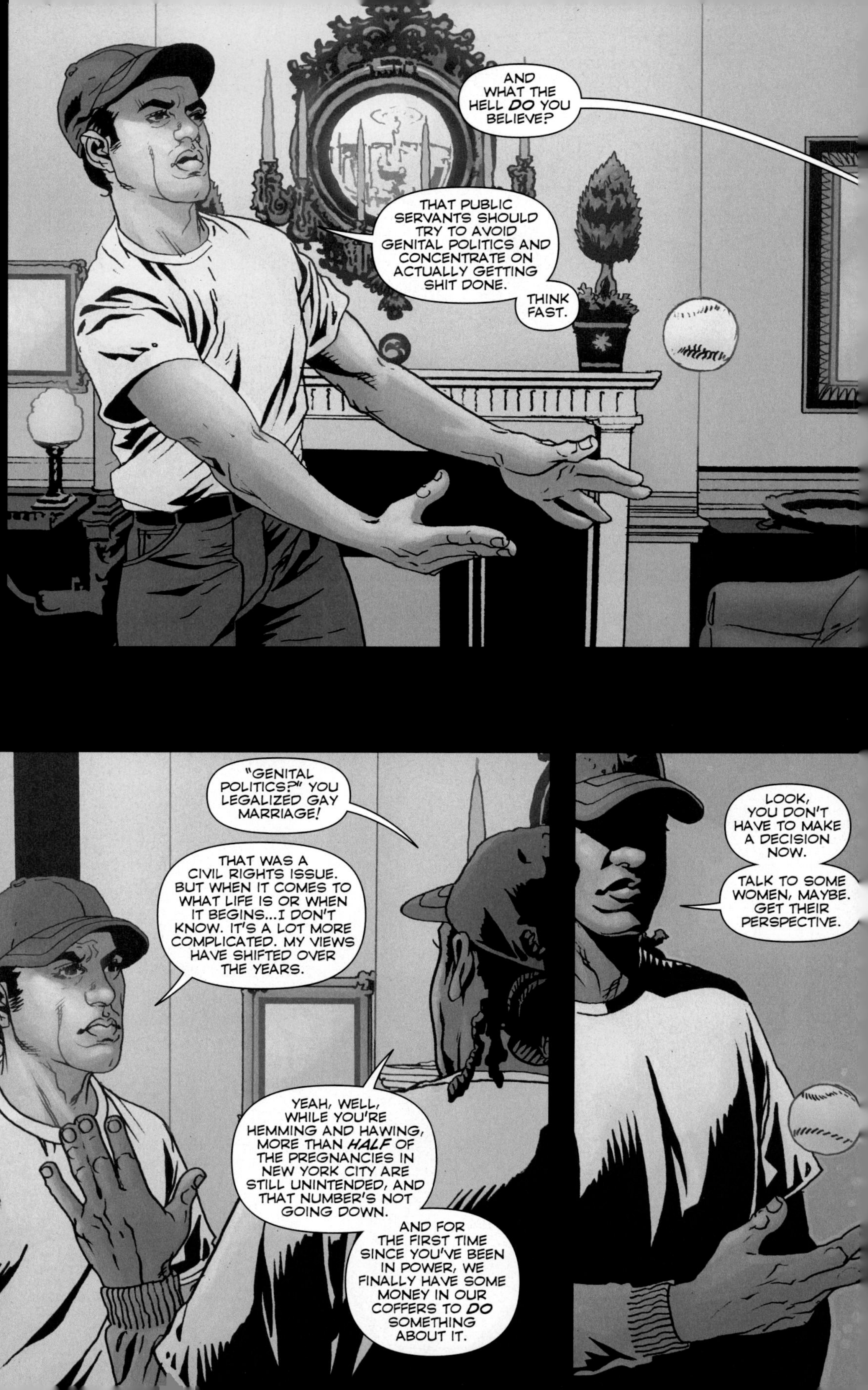
AND WHAT THE HELL *DO* YOU BELIEVE?
THAT PUBLIC SERVANTS SHOULD TRY TO AVOID GENITAL POLITICS AND CONCENTRATE ON ACTUALLY GETTING SHIT DONE.
THINK FAST.
"GENITAL POLITICS?" YOU LEGALIZED GAY MARRIAGE!
THAT WAS A CIVIL RIGHTS ISSUE. BUT WHEN IT COMES TO WHAT LIFE IS OR WHEN IT BEGINS...I DON'T KNOW. IT'S A LOT MORE COMPLICATED. MY VIEWS HAVE SHIFTED OVER THE YEARS.
YEAH, WELL, WHILE YOU'RE HEMMING AND HAWING, MORE THAN *HALF* OF THE PREGNANCIES IN NEW YORK CITY ARE STILL UNINTENDED, AND THAT NUMBER'S NOT GOING DOWN.
AND FOR THE FIRST TIME SINCE YOU'VE BEEN IN POWER, WE FINALLY HAVE SOME MONEY IN OUR COFFERS TO *DO* SOMETHING ABOUT IT.
LOOK, YOU DON'T HAVE TO MAKE A DECISION NOW.
TALK TO SOME WOMEN, MAYBE. GET THEIR PERSPECTIVE.

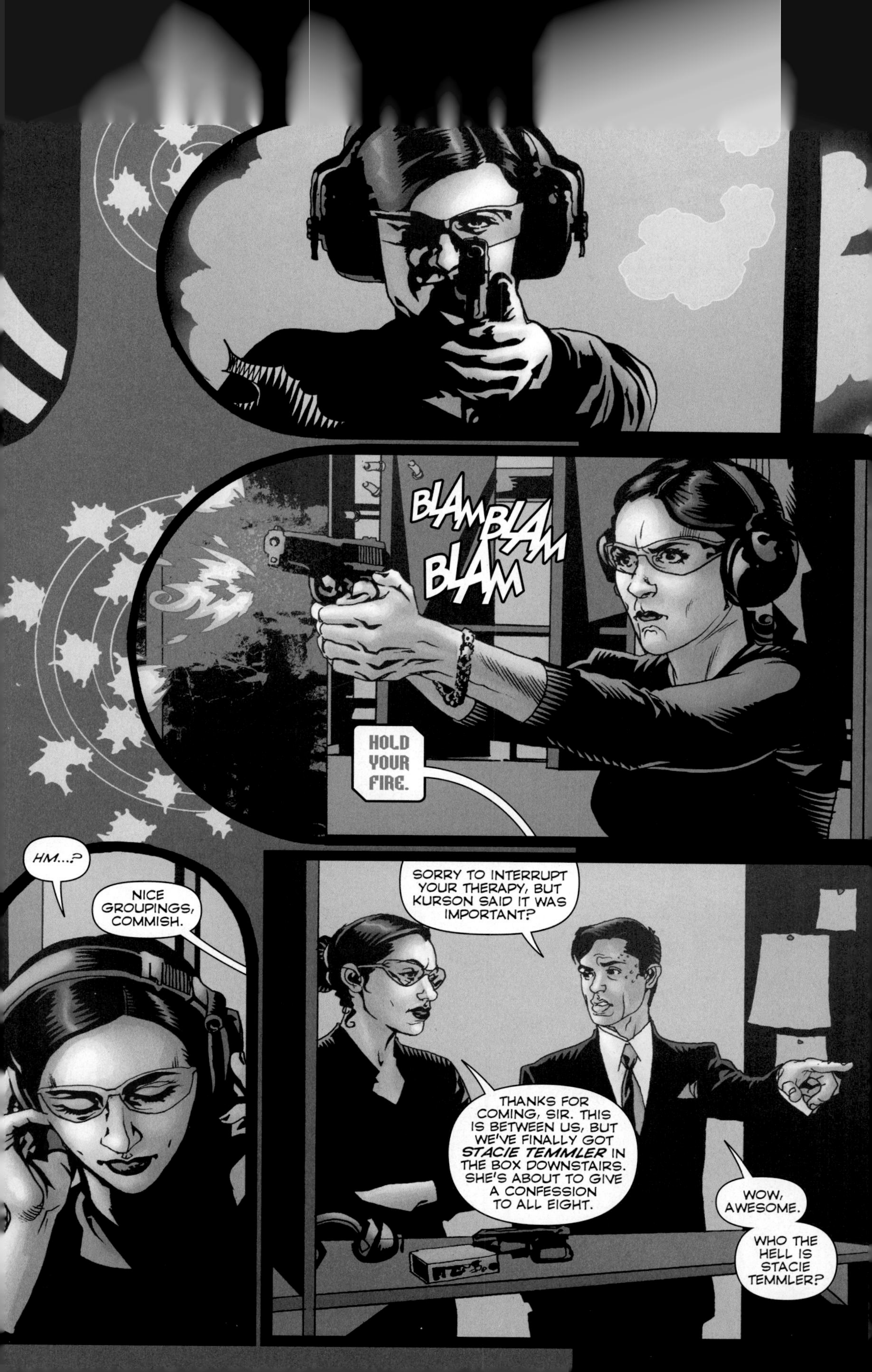
BLAM BLAM BLAM
HOLD YOUR FIRE.
HM...?
NICE GROUPINGS, COMMISH.
SORRY TO INTERRUPT YOUR THERAPY, BUT KURSON SAID IT WAS IMPORTANT?
THANKS FOR COMING, SIR. THIS IS BETWEEN US, BUT WE'VE FINALLY GOT *STACIE TEMMLER* IN THE BOX DOWNSTAIRS. SHE'S ABOUT TO GIVE A CONFESSION TO ALL EIGHT.
WOW, AWESOME.
WHO THE HELL IS STACIE TEMMLER?

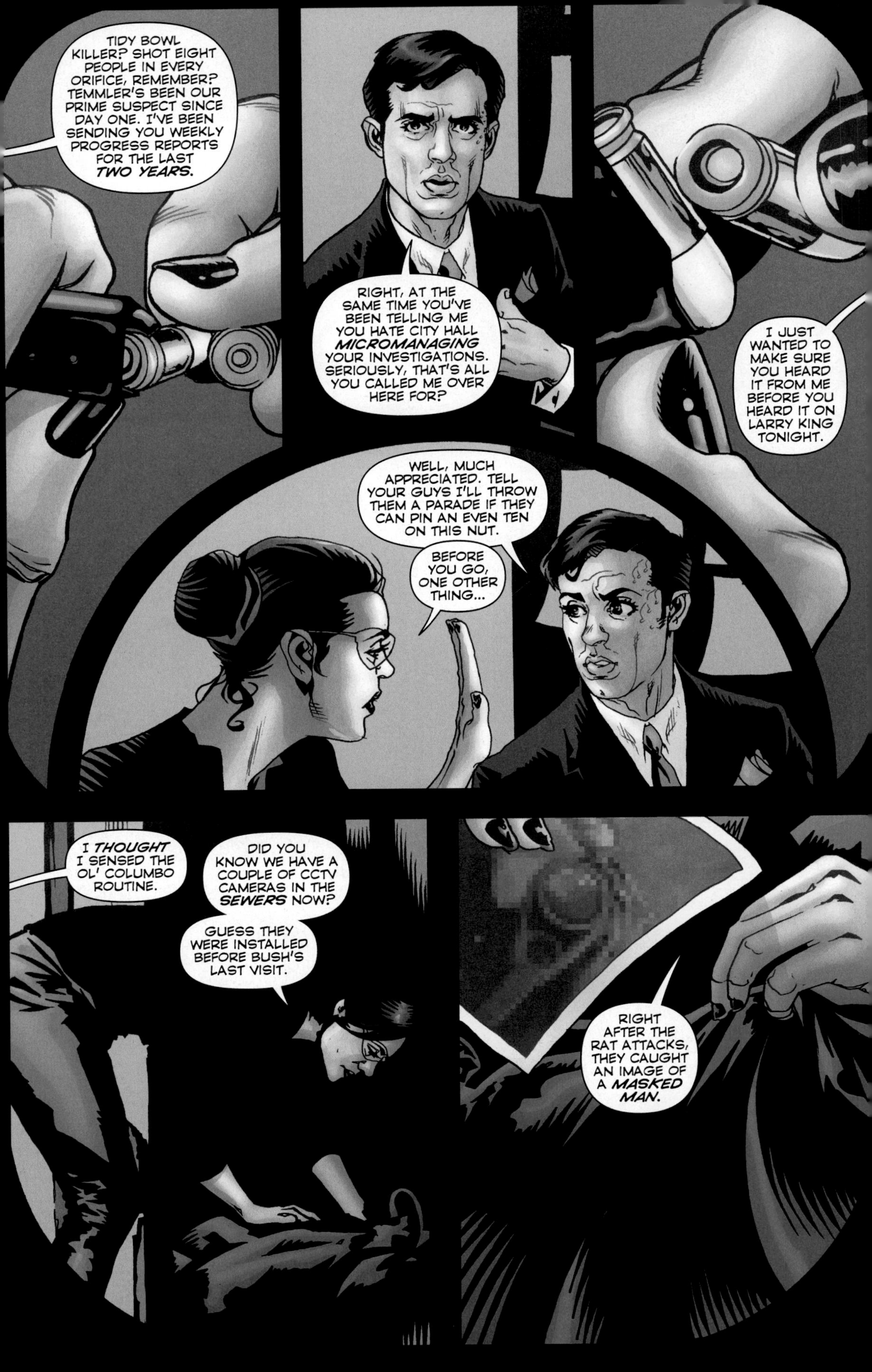
TIDY BOWL KILLER? SHOT EIGHT PEOPLE IN EVERY ORIFICE, REMEMBER? TEMMLER'S BEEN OUR PRIME SUSPECT SINCE DAY ONE. I'VE BEEN SENDING YOU WEEKLY PROGRESS REPORTS FOR THE LAST TWO YEARS.
RIGHT, AT THE SAME TIME YOU'VE BEEN TELLING ME YOU HATE CITY HALL MICROMANAGING YOUR INVESTIGATIONS. SERIOUSLY, THAT'S ALL YOU CALLED ME OVER HERE FOR?
I JUST WANTED TO MAKE SURE YOU HEARD IT FROM ME BEFORE YOU HEARD IT ON LARRY KING TONIGHT.
WELL, MUCH APPRECIATED. TELL YOUR GUYS I'LL THROW THEM A PARADE IF THEY CAN PIN AN EVEN TEN ON THIS NUT.
BEFORE YOU GO, ONE OTHER THING...
I THOUGHT I SENSED THE OL' COLUMBO ROUTINE.
DID YOU KNOW WE HAVE A COUPLE OF CCTV CAMERAS IN THE SEWERS NOW?
GUESS THEY WERE INSTALLED BEFORE BUSH'S LAST VISIT.
RIGHT AFTER THE RAT ATTACKS, THEY CAUGHT AN IMAGE OF A MASKED MAN.

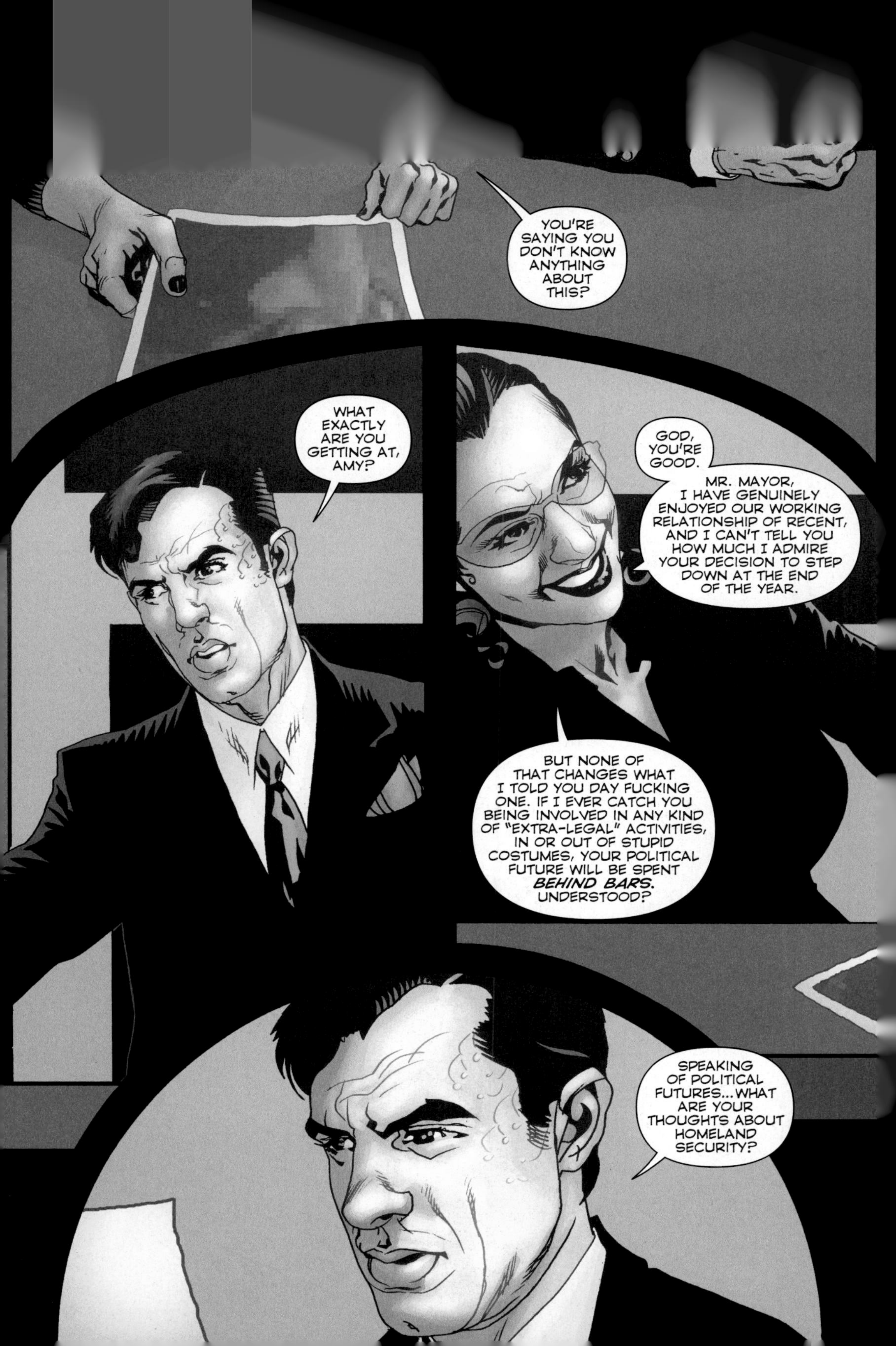
YOU'RE SAYING YOU DON'T KNOW ANYTHING ABOUT THIS?
WHAT EXACTLY ARE YOU GETTING AT, AMY?
GOD, YOU'RE GOOD.
MR. MAYOR, I HAVE GENUINELY ENJOYED OUR WORKING RELATIONSHIP OF RECENT, AND I CAN'T TELL YOU HOW MUCH I ADMIRE YOUR DECISION TO STEP DOWN AT THE END OF THE YEAR.
BUT NONE OF THAT CHANGES WHAT I TOLD YOU DAY FUCKING ONE. IF I EVER CATCH YOU BEING INVOLVED IN ANY KIND OF "EXTRA-LEGAL" ACTIVITIES, IN OR OUT OF STUPID COSTUMES, YOUR POLITICAL FUTURE WILL BE SPENT *BEHIND BARS*. UNDERSTOOD?
SPEAKING OF POLITICAL FUTURES...WHAT ARE YOUR THOUGHTS ABOUT HOMELAND SECURITY?

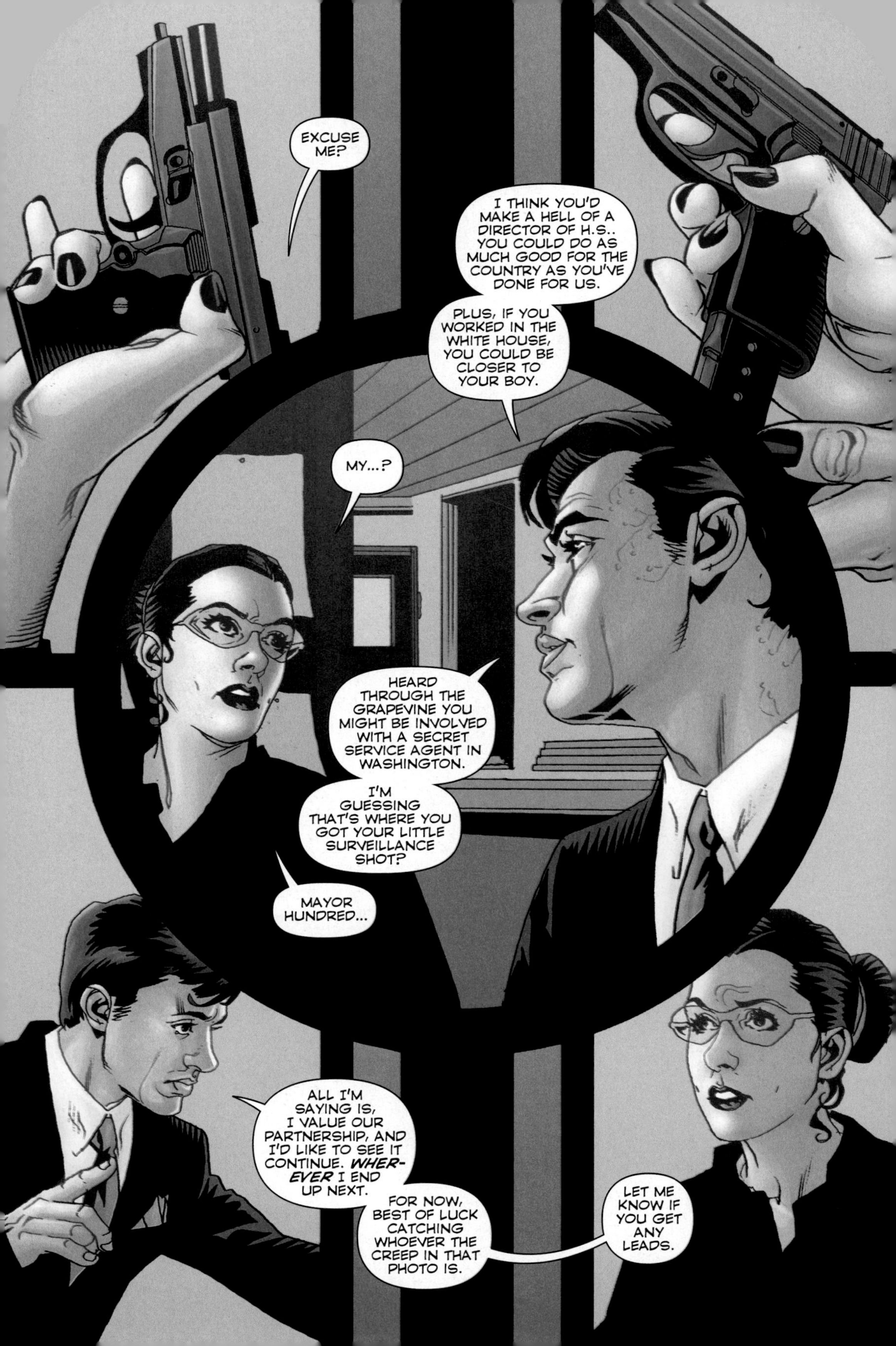
EXCUSE ME?
I THINK YOU'D MAKE A HELL OF A DIRECTOR OF H.S.. YOU COULD DO AS MUCH GOOD FOR THE COUNTRY AS YOU'VE DONE FOR US.
PLUS, IF YOU WORKED IN THE WHITE HOUSE, YOU COULD BE CLOSER TO YOUR BOY.
MY...?
HEARD THROUGH THE GRAPEVINE YOU MIGHT BE INVOLVED WITH A SECRET SERVICE AGENT IN WASHINGTON.
I'M GUESSING THAT'S WHERE YOU GOT YOUR LITTLE SURVEILLANCE SHOT?
MAYOR HUNDRED...
ALL I'M SAYING IS, I VALUE OUR PARTNERSHIP, AND I'D LIKE TO SEE IT CONTINUE. ***WHER-EVER*** I END UP NEXT.
FOR NOW, BEST OF LUCK CATCHING WHOEVER THE CREEP IN THAT PHOTO IS.
LET ME KNOW IF YOU GET ANY LEADS.

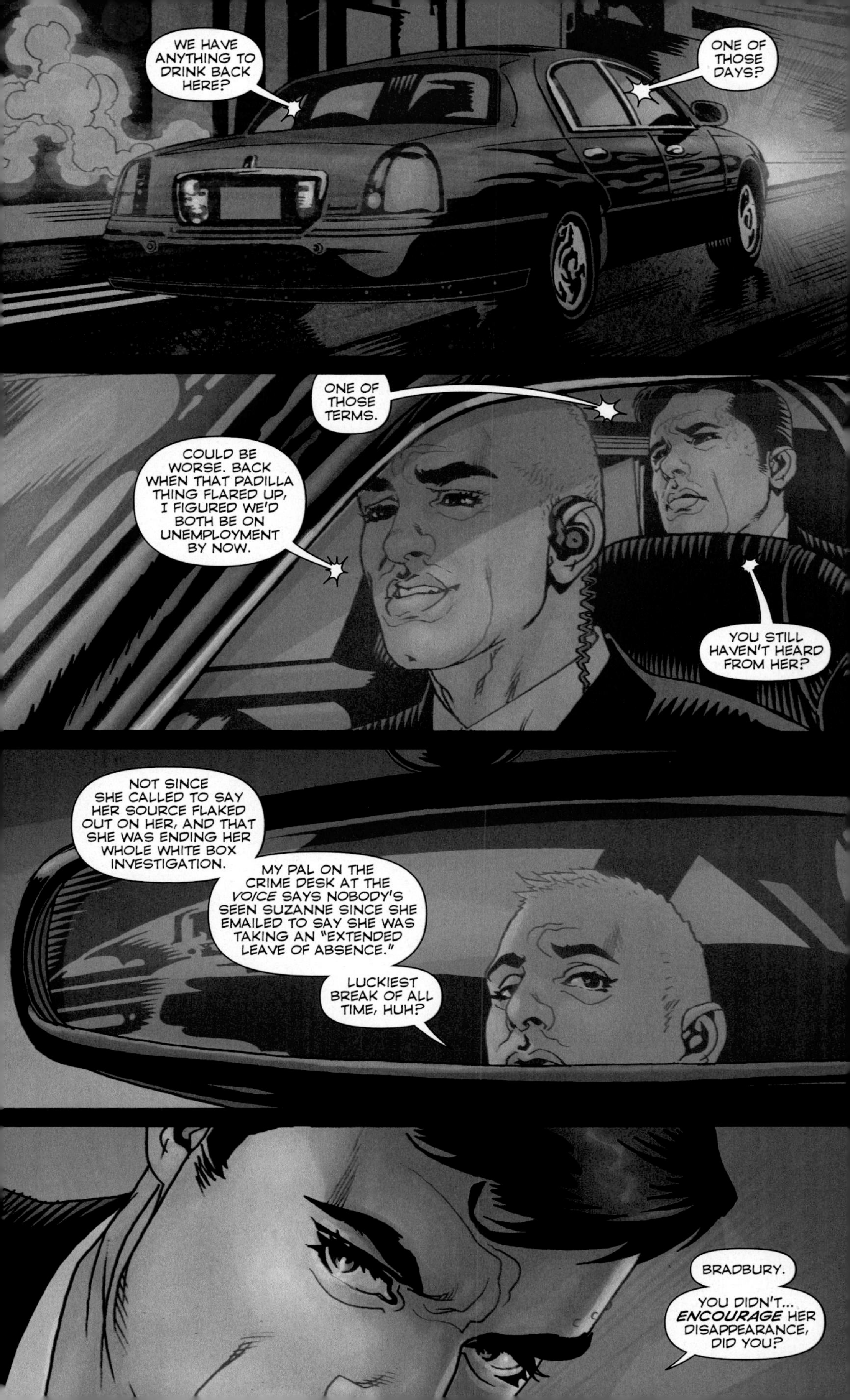
WE HAVE ANYTHING TO DRINK BACK HERE?
ONE OF THOSE DAYS?
ONE OF THOSE TERMS.
COULD BE WORSE. BACK WHEN THAT PADILLA THING FLARED UP, I FIGURED WE'D BOTH BE ON UNEMPLOYMENT BY NOW.
YOU STILL HAVEN'T HEARD FROM HER?
NOT SINCE SHE CALLED TO SAY HER SOURCE FLAKED OUT ON HER, AND THAT SHE WAS ENDING HER WHOLE WHITE BOX INVESTIGATION.
MY PAL ON THE CRIME DESK AT THE *VOICE* SAYS NOBODY'S SEEN SUZANNE SINCE SHE EMAILED TO SAY SHE WAS TAKING AN "EXTENDED LEAVE OF ABSENCE."
LUCKIEST BREAK OF ALL TIME, HUH?
BRADBURY.
YOU DIDN'T... ***ENCOURAGE*** HER DISAPPEARANCE, DID YOU?

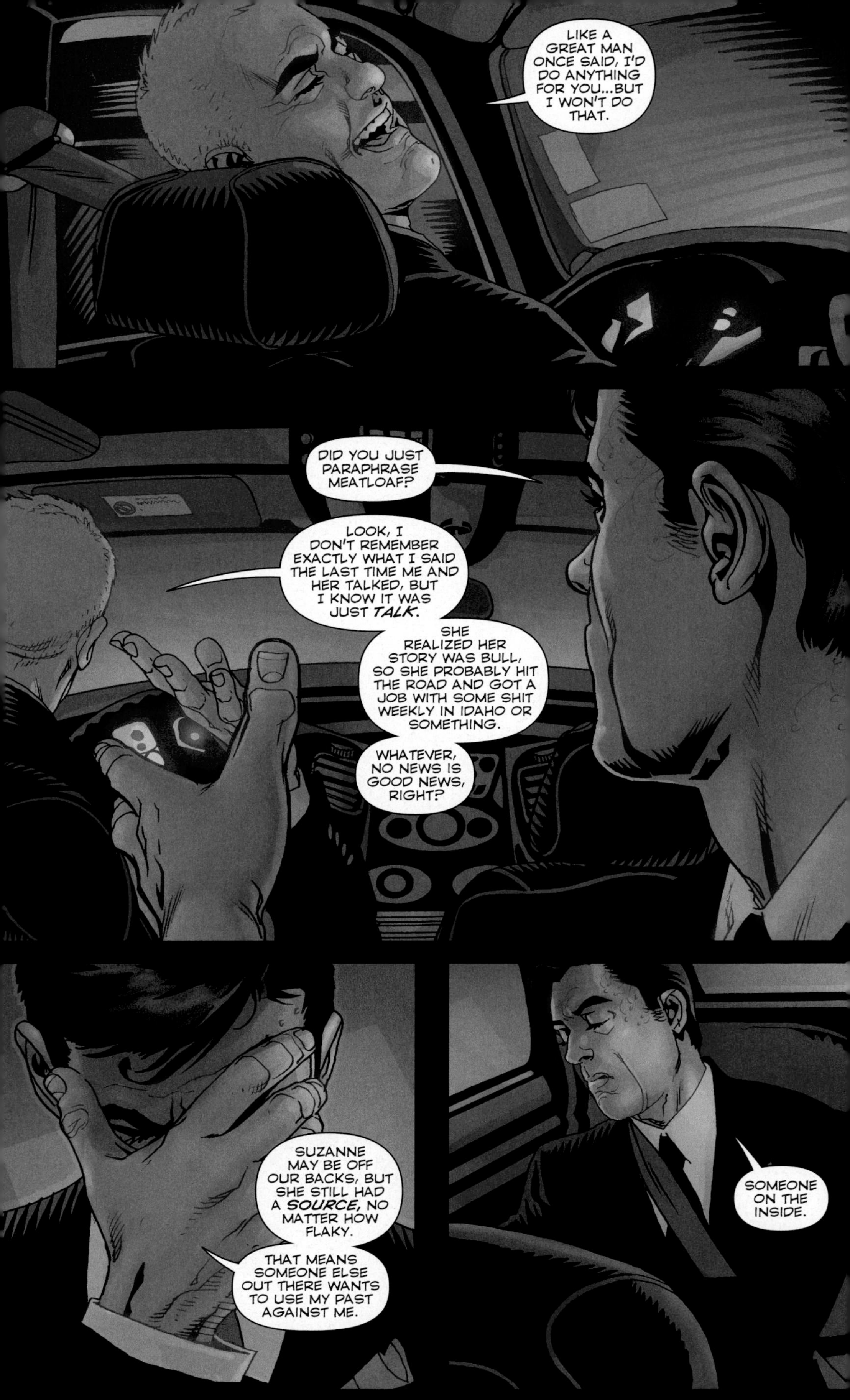
LIKE A GREAT MAN ONCE SAID, I'D DO ANYTHING FOR YOU...BUT I WON'T DO THAT.
DID YOU JUST PARAPHRASE MEATLOAF?
LOOK, I DON'T REMEMBER EXACTLY WHAT I SAID THE LAST TIME ME AND HER TALKED, BUT I KNOW IT WAS JUST *TALK*.
SHE REALIZED HER STORY WAS BULL, SO SHE PROBABLY HIT THE ROAD AND GOT A JOB WITH SOME SHIT WEEKLY IN IDAHO OR SOMETHING.
WHATEVER, NO NEWS IS GOOD NEWS, RIGHT?
SUZANNE MAY BE OFF OUR BACKS, BUT SHE STILL HAD A *SOURCE*, NO MATTER HOW FLAKY.
THAT MEANS SOMEONE ELSE OUT THERE WANTS TO USE MY PAST AGAINST ME.
SOMEONE ON THE INSIDE.

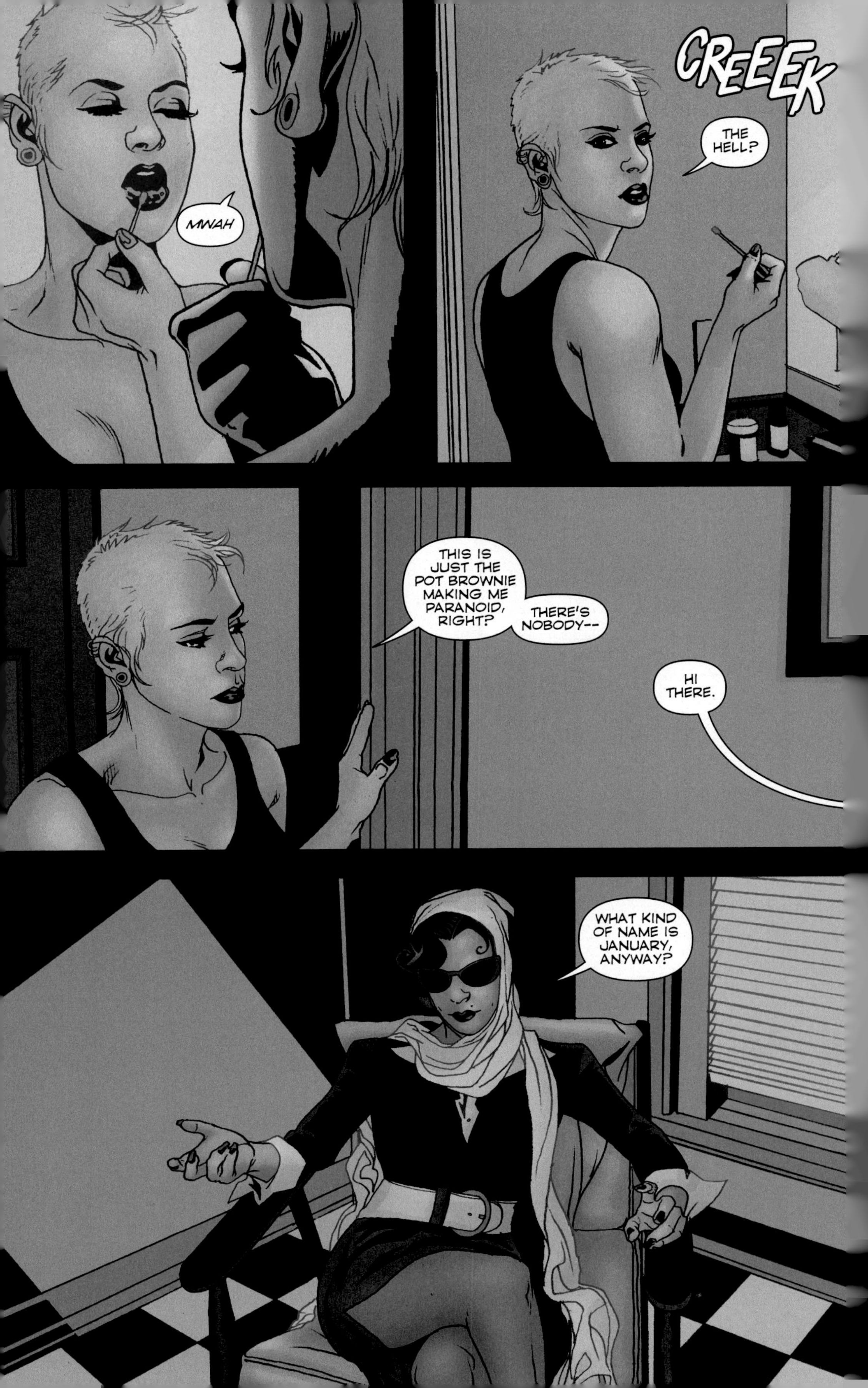
MWAH
CREEEK
THE HELL?
THIS IS JUST THE POT BROWNIE MAKING ME PARANOID, RIGHT?
THERE'S NOBODY--
HI THERE.
WHAT KIND OF NAME IS JANUARY, ANYWAY?

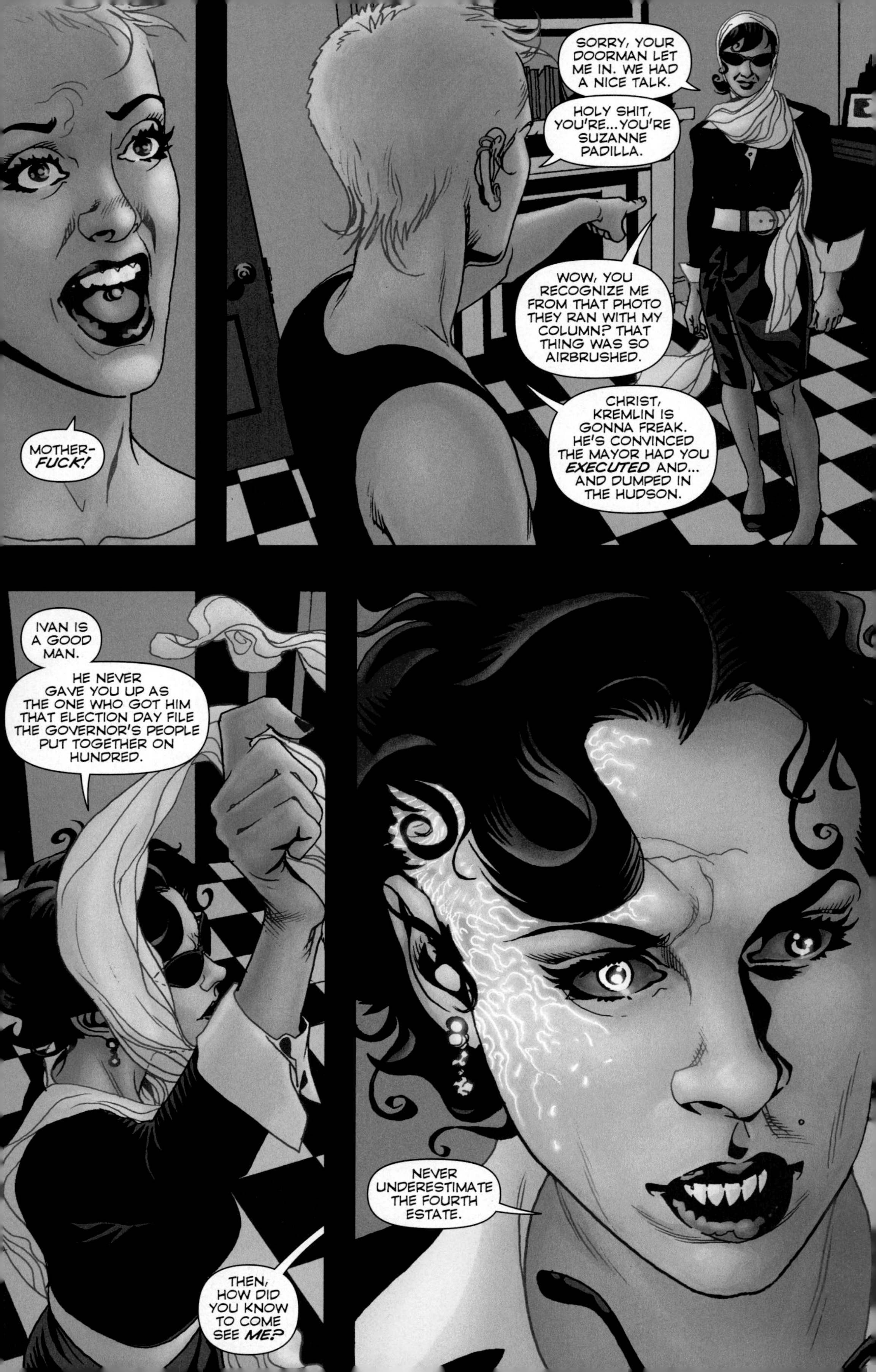

SORRY, YOUR DOORMAN LET ME IN. WE HAD A NICE TALK.
HOLY SHIT, YOU'RE...YOU'RE SUZANNE PADILLA.
MOTHER-*FUCK!*
WOW, YOU RECOGNIZE ME FROM THAT PHOTO THEY RAN WITH MY COLUMN? THAT THING WAS SO AIRBRUSHED.
CHRIST, KREMLIN IS GONNA FREAK. HE'S CONVINCED THE MAYOR HAD YOU *EXECUTED* AND... AND DUMPED IN THE HUDSON.
IVAN IS A GOOD MAN.
HE NEVER GAVE YOU UP AS THE ONE WHO GOT HIM THAT ELECTION DAY FILE THE GOVERNOR'S PEOPLE PUT TOGETHER ON HUNDRED.
NEVER UNDERESTIMATE THE FOURTH ESTATE.
THEN, HOW DID YOU KNOW TO COME SEE *ME?*

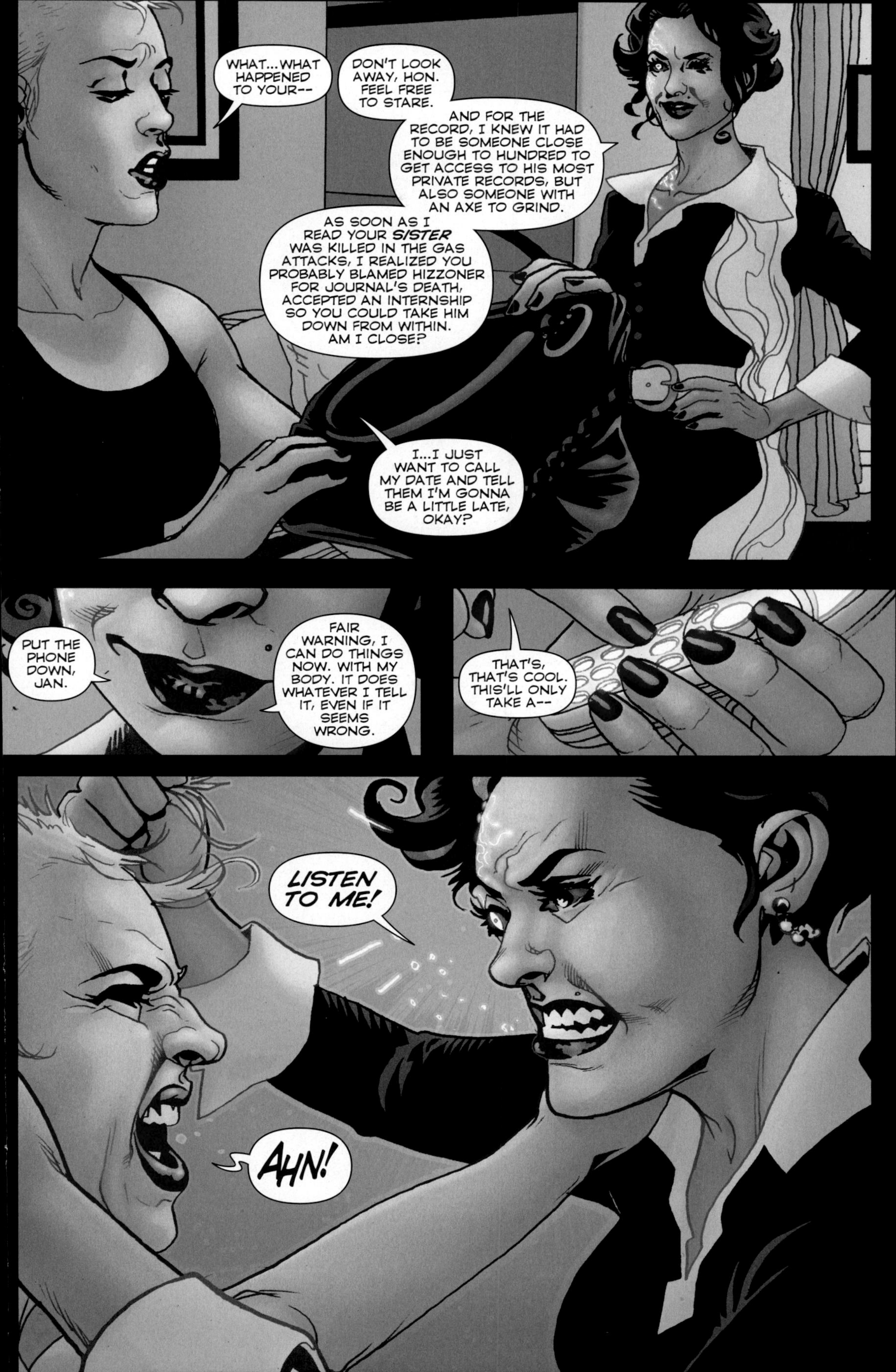
WHAT...WHAT HAPPENED TO YOUR--
DON'T LOOK AWAY, HON. FEEL FREE TO STARE.
AND FOR THE RECORD, I KNEW IT HAD TO BE SOMEONE CLOSE ENOUGH TO HUNDRED TO GET ACCESS TO HIS MOST PRIVATE RECORDS, BUT ALSO SOMEONE WITH AN AXE TO GRIND.
AS SOON AS I READ YOUR *SISTER* WAS KILLED IN THE GAS ATTACKS, I REALIZED YOU PROBABLY BLAMED HIZZONER FOR JOURNAL'S DEATH, ACCEPTED AN INTERNSHIP SO YOU COULD TAKE HIM DOWN FROM WITHIN. AM I CLOSE?
I...I JUST WANT TO CALL MY DATE AND TELL THEM I'M GONNA BE A LITTLE LATE, OKAY?
PUT THE PHONE DOWN, JAN.
FAIR WARNING, I CAN DO THINGS NOW. WITH MY BODY. IT DOES WHATEVER I TELL IT, EVEN IF IT SEEMS WRONG.
THAT'S, THAT'S COOL. THIS'LL ONLY TAKE A--
LISTEN TO ME!
AHN!

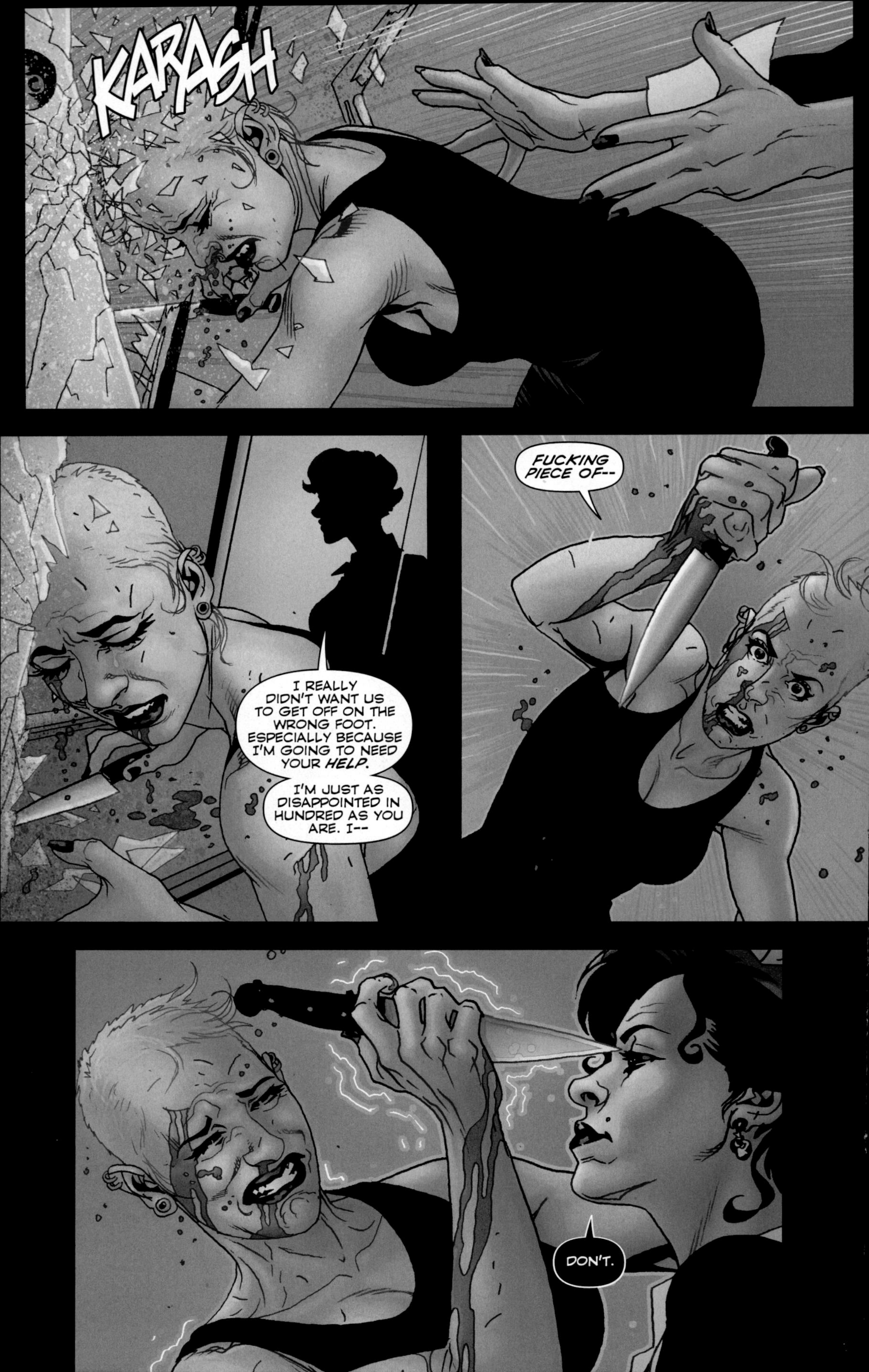
KARASH
FUCKING PIECE OF--
I REALLY DIDN'T WANT US TO GET OFF ON THE WRONG FOOT. ESPECIALLY BECAUSE I'M GOING TO NEED YOUR HELP.
I'M JUST AS DISAPPOINTED IN HUNDRED AS YOU ARE. I--
DON'T.

HOW...?

PUT IT DOWN.

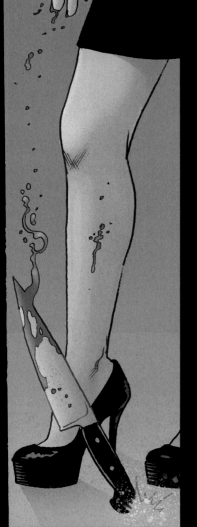

THE MAYOR. YOU'RE... YOU'RE GONNA KILL HIM, AREN'T YOU?

YOU SWEET GIRL.

DON'T BE RIDICULOUS.

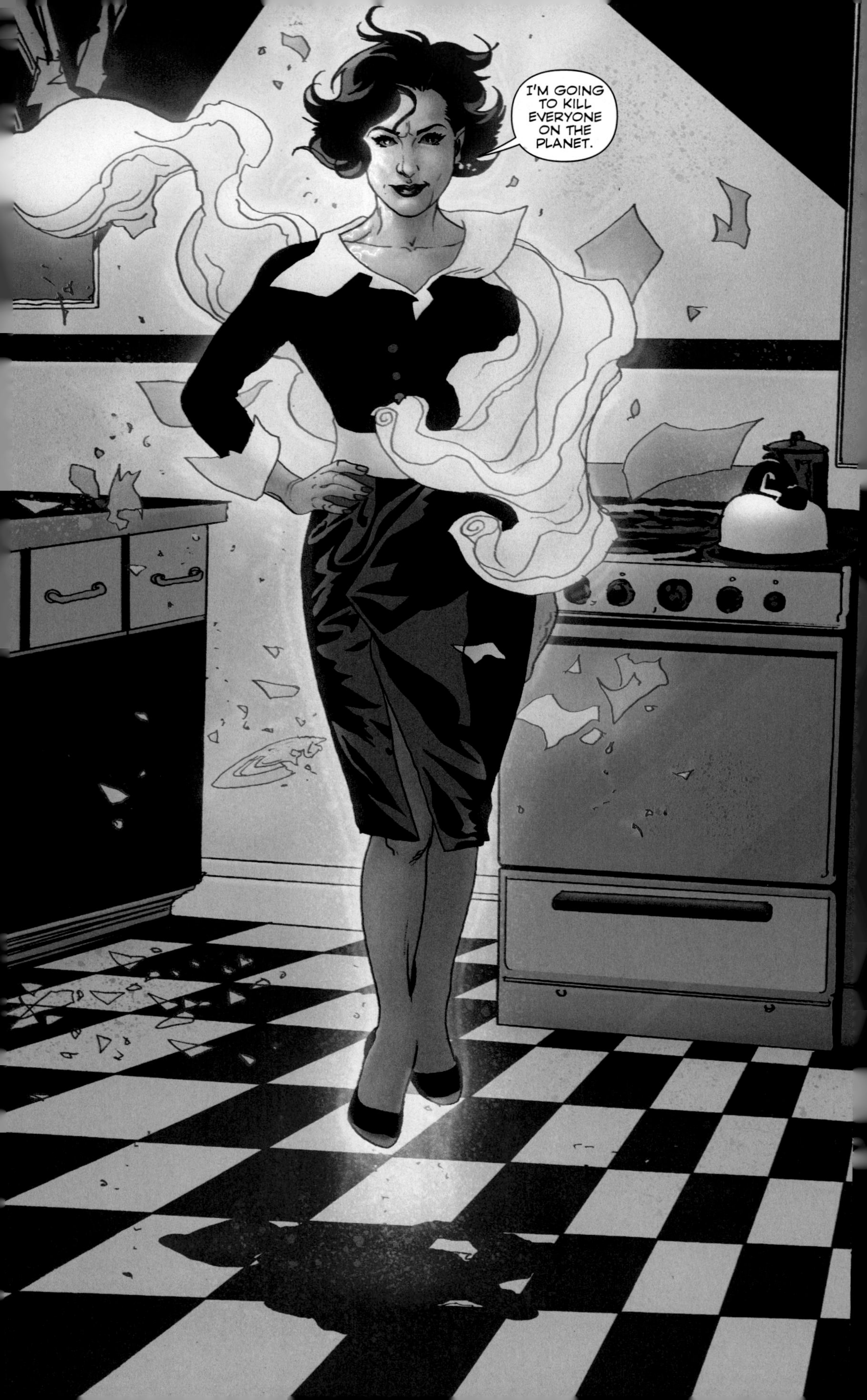
I'M GOING TO KILL EVERYONE ON THE PLANET.

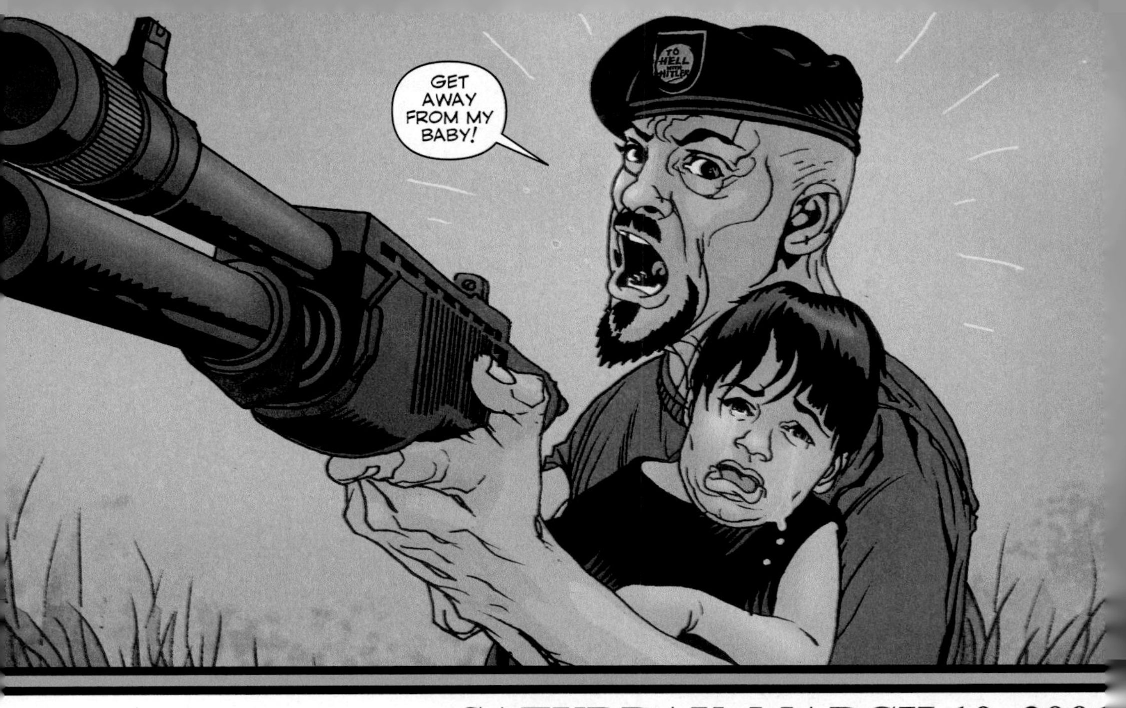
GET AWAY FROM MY BABY!

SATURDAY, MARCH 10, 2001

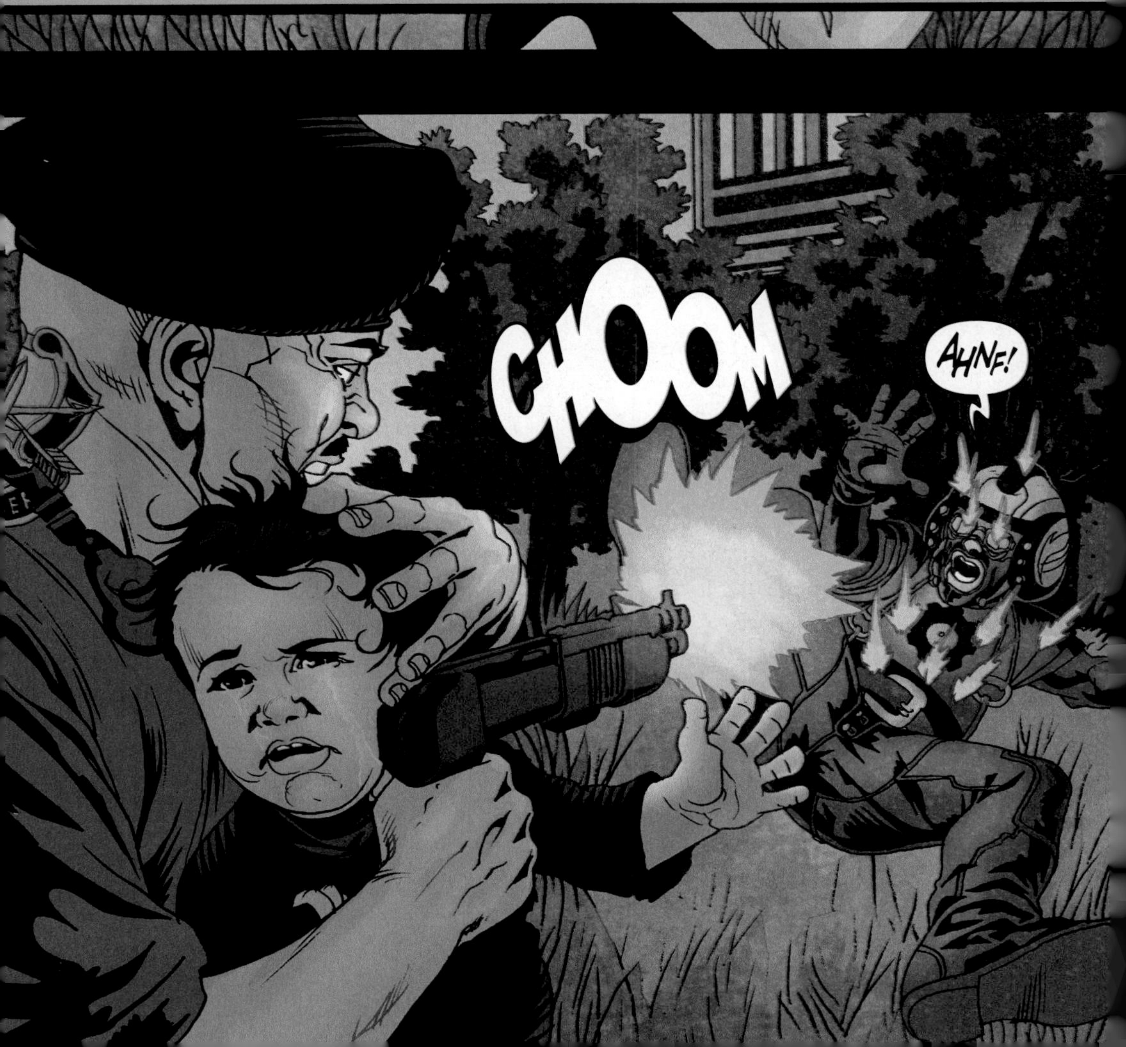
CHOOM
AHNF!

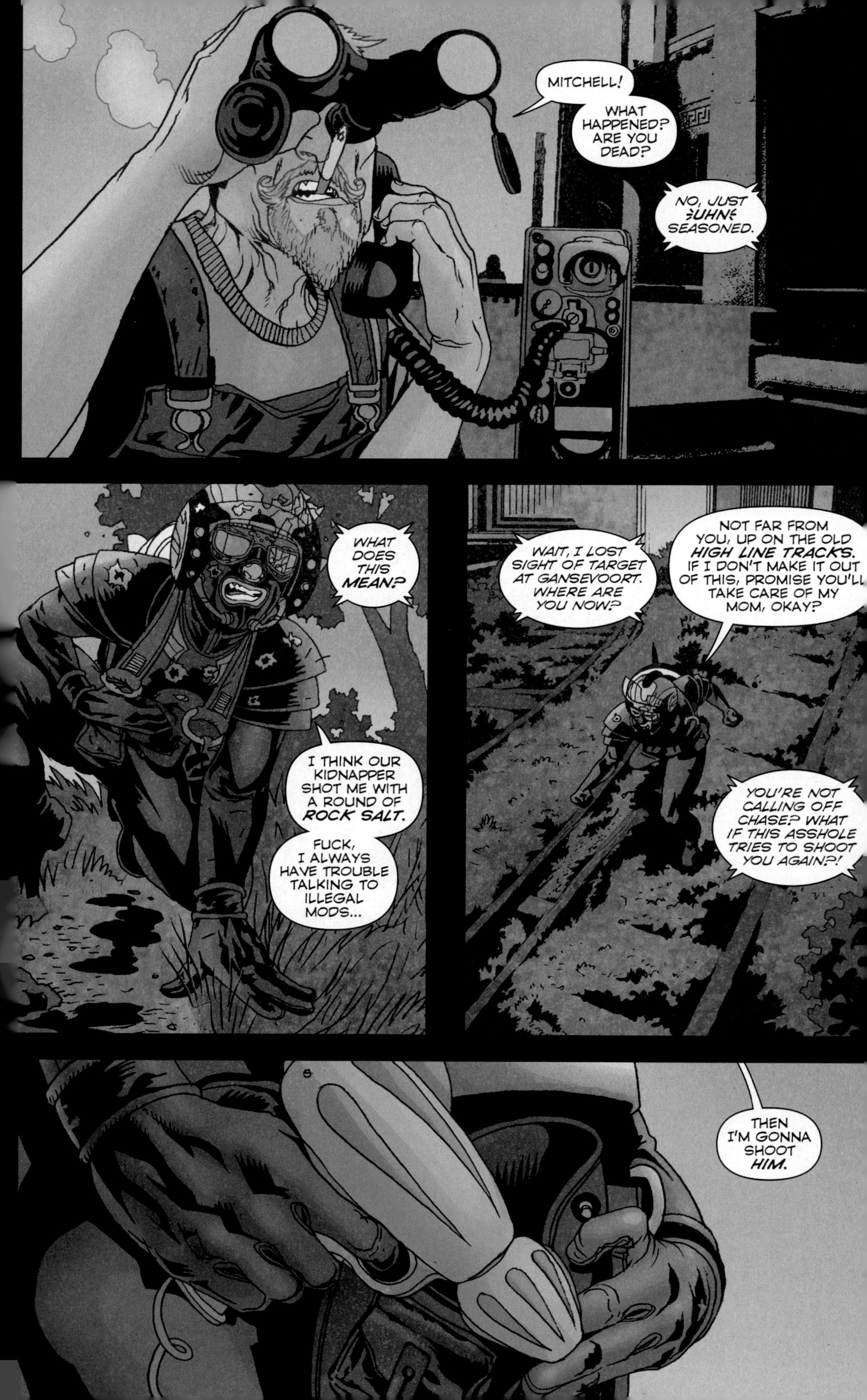
MITCHELL!
WHAT HAPPENED? ARE YOU DEAD?
NO, JUST UHN SEASONED.
WHAT DOES THIS MEAN?
I THINK OUR KIDNAPPER SHOT ME WITH A ROUND OF ROCK SALT.
FUCK, I ALWAYS HAVE TROUBLE TALKING TO ILLEGAL MODS...
WAIT, I LOST SIGHT OF TARGET AT GANSEVOORT. WHERE ARE YOU NOW?
NOT FAR FROM YOU, UP ON THE OLD HIGH LINE TRACKS. IF I DON'T MAKE IT OUT OF THIS, PROMISE YOU'LL TAKE CARE OF MY MOM, OKAY?
YOU'RE NOT CALLING OFF CHASE? WHAT IF THIS ASSHOLE TRIES TO SHOOT YOU AGAIN?!
THEN I'M GONNA SHOOT HIM.

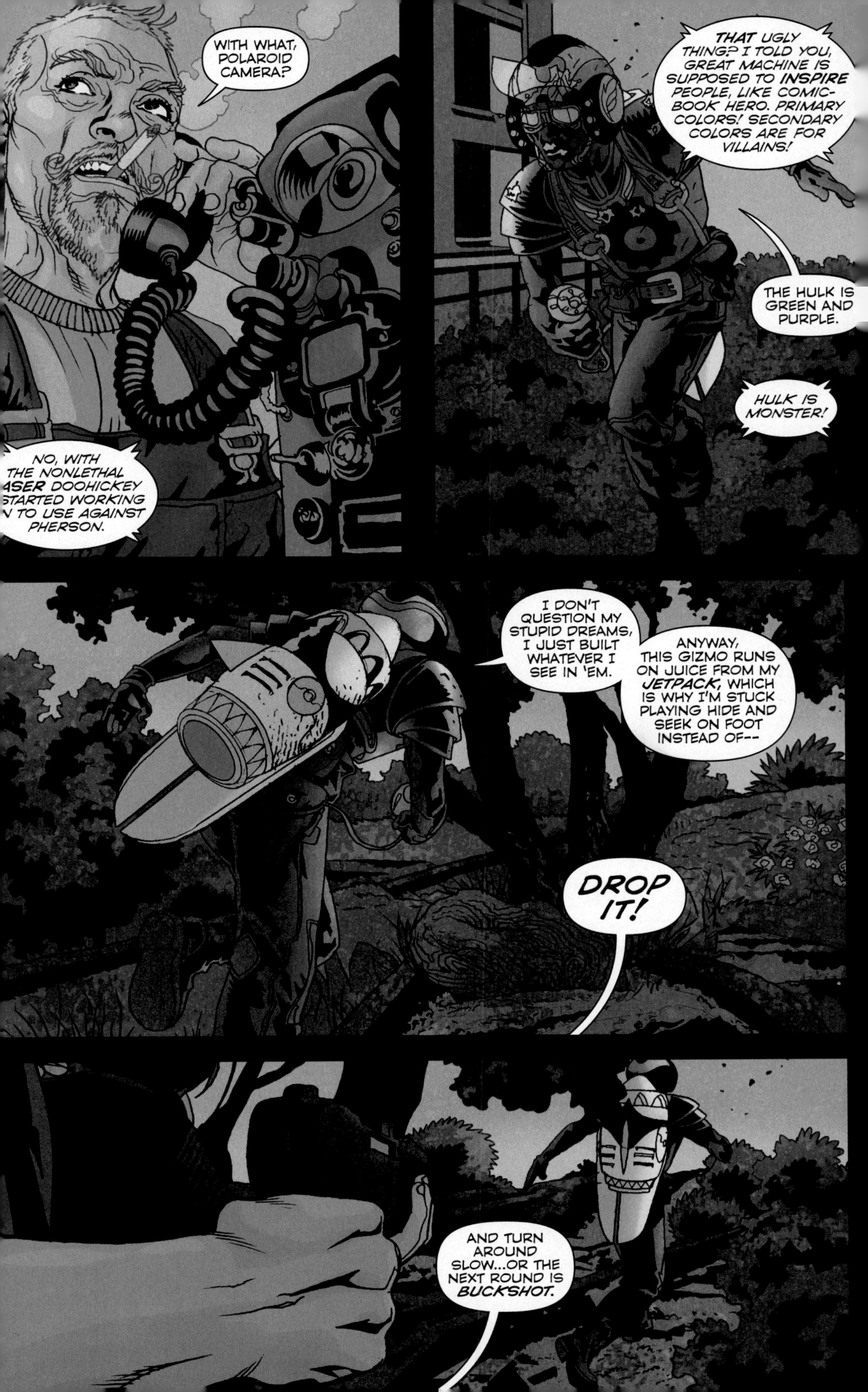

WITH WHAT, POLAROID CAMERA?
NO, WITH THE NONLETHAL ASER DOOHICKEY STARTED WORKING N TO USE AGAINST PHERSON.
THAT UGLY THING? I TOLD YOU, GREAT MACHINE IS SUPPOSED TO INSPIRE PEOPLE, LIKE COMIC-BOOK HERO. PRIMARY COLORS! SECONDARY COLORS ARE FOR VILLAINS!
THE HULK IS GREEN AND PURPLE.
HULK IS MONSTER!
I DON'T QUESTION MY STUPID DREAMS, I JUST BUILT WHATEVER I SEE IN 'EM.
ANYWAY, THIS GIZMO RUNS ON JUICE FROM MY JETPACK, WHICH IS WHY I'M STUCK PLAYING HIDE AND SEEK ON FOOT INSTEAD OF--
DROP IT!
AND TURN AROUND SLOW...OR THE NEXT ROUND IS BUCKSHOT.

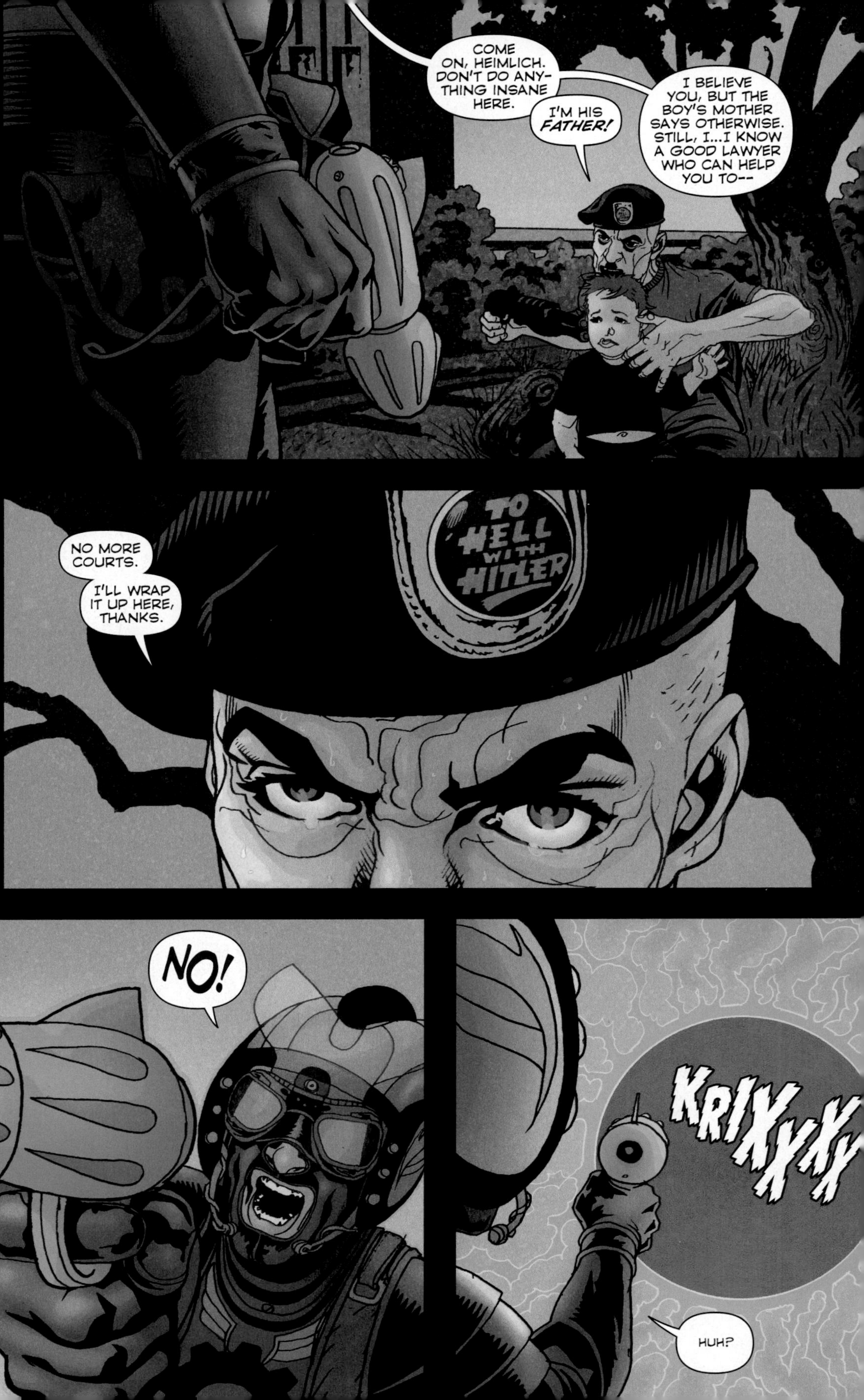
COME ON, HEIMLICH. DON'T DO ANYTHING INSANE HERE.
I'M HIS *FATHER!*
I BELIEVE YOU, BUT THE BOY'S MOTHER SAYS OTHERWISE. STILL, I...I KNOW A GOOD LAWYER WHO CAN HELP YOU TO--
TO HELL WITH HITLER
NO MORE COURTS.
I'LL WRAP IT UP HERE, THANKS.
NO!
KRIXXXX
HUH?

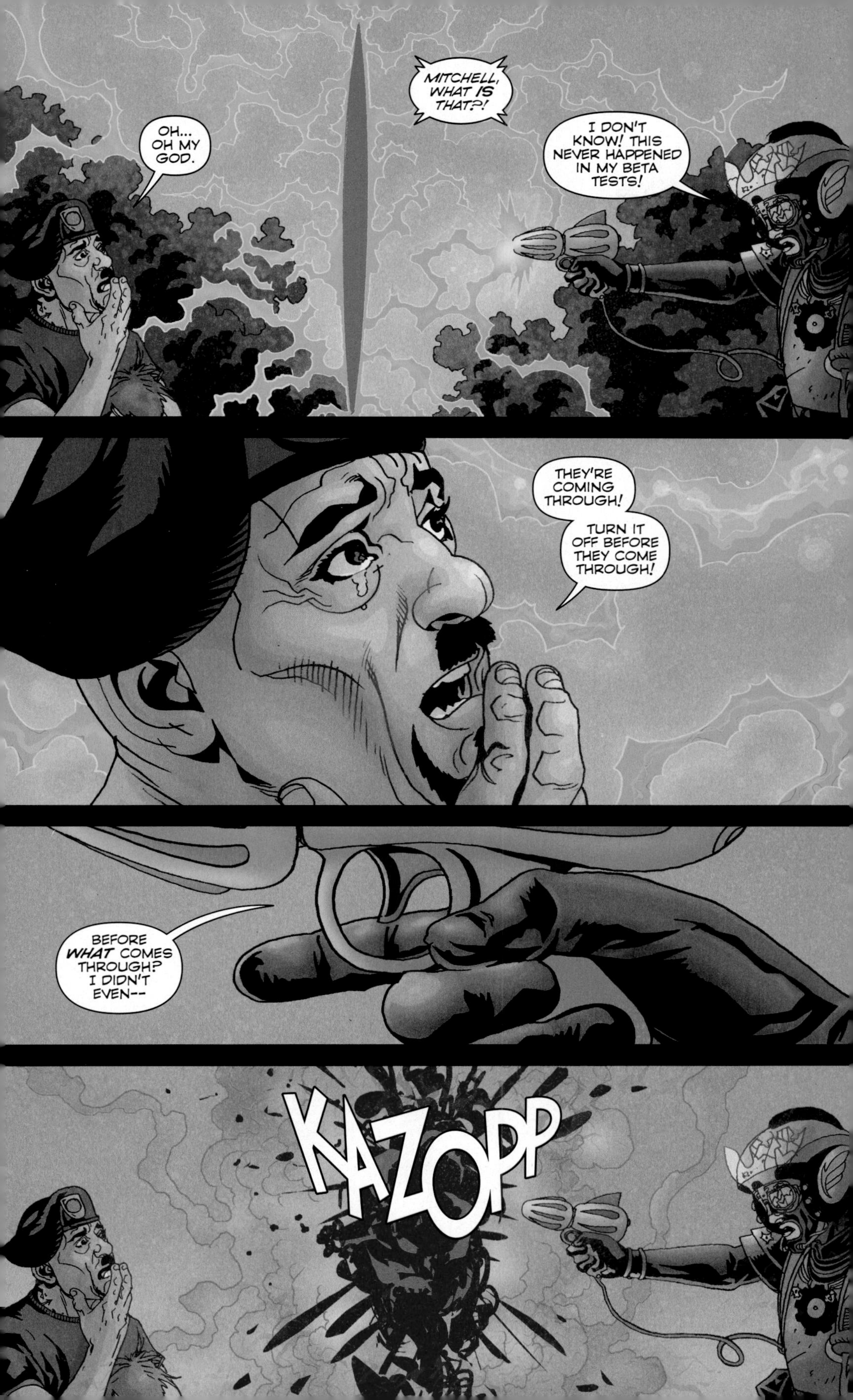
OH... OH MY GOD.
MITCHELL, WHAT IS THAT?!
I DON'T KNOW! THIS NEVER HAPPENED IN MY BETA TESTS!
THEY'RE COMING THROUGH!
TURN IT OFF BEFORE THEY COME THROUGH!
BEFORE WHAT COMES THROUGH? I DIDN'T EVEN--
KAZOPP

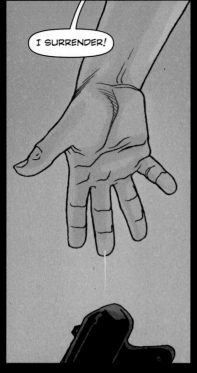

I SURRENDER!

EHHHHHNNNN!

TAKE THE KID. I'M... I'M SORRY, OKAY?

PLEASE, JUST DON'T SHOW IT TO ME AGAIN. I GET IT NOW, ALL RIGHT? IT'S REAL. HELL IS *REAL*.

HELL?

WHAT THE HELL ARE YOU TALKING ABOUT?

I CANNOT BELIEVE IT! FOR ONCE, YOU DON'T SCREW UP!

BRADBURY AND I PICK YOU UP IN VAN, THEN WE CELEBRATE!

CELEBRATE WHAT, KREMLIN?

IT'S BACK TO THE GODDAMN DRAWING BOARD.

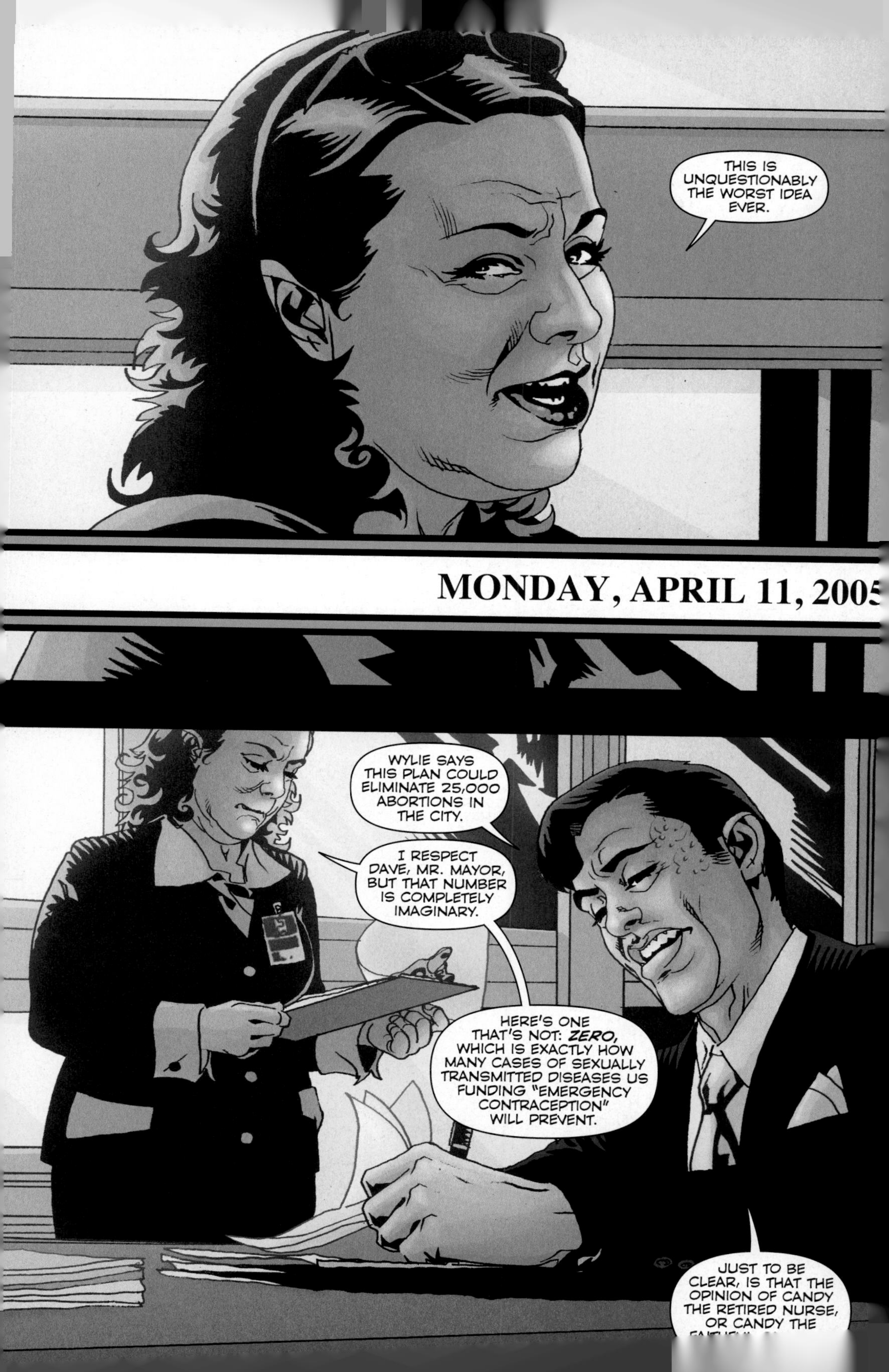
THIS IS UNQUESTIONABLY THE WORST IDEA EVER.
MONDAY, APRIL 11, 2005
WYLIE SAYS THIS PLAN COULD ELIMINATE 25,000 ABORTIONS IN THE CITY.
I RESPECT DAVE, MR. MAYOR, BUT THAT NUMBER IS COMPLETELY IMAGINARY.
HERE'S ONE THAT'S NOT: ZERO, WHICH IS EXACTLY HOW MANY CASES OF SEXUALLY TRANSMITTED DISEASES US FUNDING "EMERGENCY CONTRACEPTION" WILL PREVENT.
JUST TO BE CLEAR, IS THAT THE OPINION OF CANDY THE RETIRED NURSE, OR CANDY THE

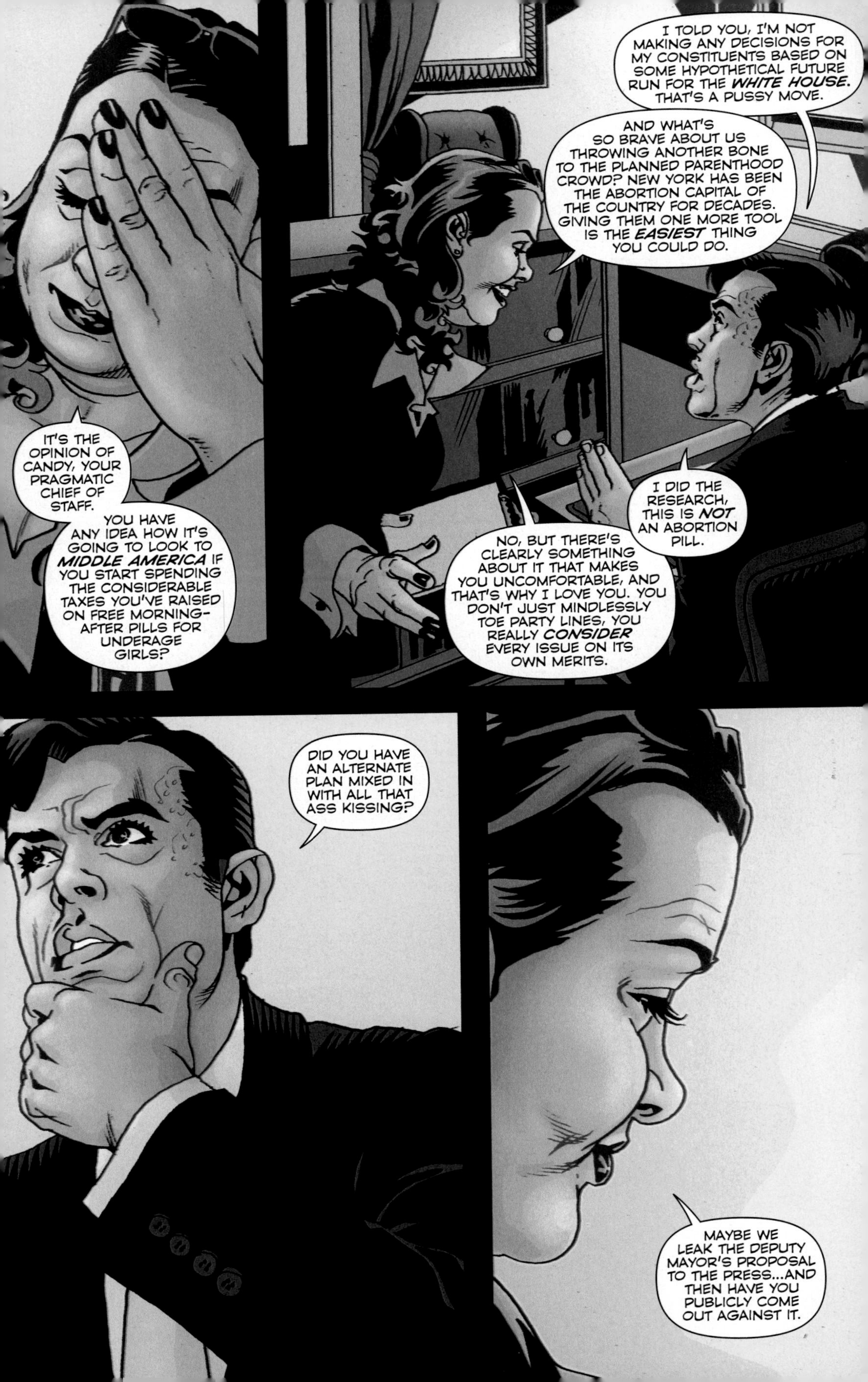
IT'S THE OPINION OF CANDY, YOUR PRAGMATIC CHIEF OF STAFF.
YOU HAVE ANY IDEA HOW IT'S GOING TO LOOK TO MIDDLE AMERICA IF YOU START SPENDING THE CONSIDERABLE TAXES YOU'VE RAISED ON FREE MORNING-AFTER PILLS FOR UNDERAGE GIRLS?
I TOLD YOU, I'M NOT MAKING ANY DECISIONS FOR MY CONSTITUENTS BASED ON SOME HYPOTHETICAL FUTURE RUN FOR THE WHITE HOUSE. THAT'S A PUSSY MOVE.
AND WHAT'S SO BRAVE ABOUT US THROWING ANOTHER BONE TO THE PLANNED PARENTHOOD CROWD? NEW YORK HAS BEEN THE ABORTION CAPITAL OF THE COUNTRY FOR DECADES. GIVING THEM ONE MORE TOOL IS THE EASIEST THING YOU COULD DO.
I DID THE RESEARCH, THIS IS NOT AN ABORTION PILL.
NO, BUT THERE'S CLEARLY SOMETHING ABOUT IT THAT MAKES YOU UNCOMFORTABLE, AND THAT'S WHY I LOVE YOU. YOU DON'T JUST MINDLESSLY TOE PARTY LINES, YOU REALLY CONSIDER EVERY ISSUE ON ITS OWN MERITS.
DID YOU HAVE AN ALTERNATE PLAN MIXED IN WITH ALL THAT ASS KISSING?
MAYBE WE LEAK THE DEPUTY MAYOR'S PROPOSAL TO THE PRESS...AND THEN HAVE YOU PUBLICLY COME OUT AGAINST IT.

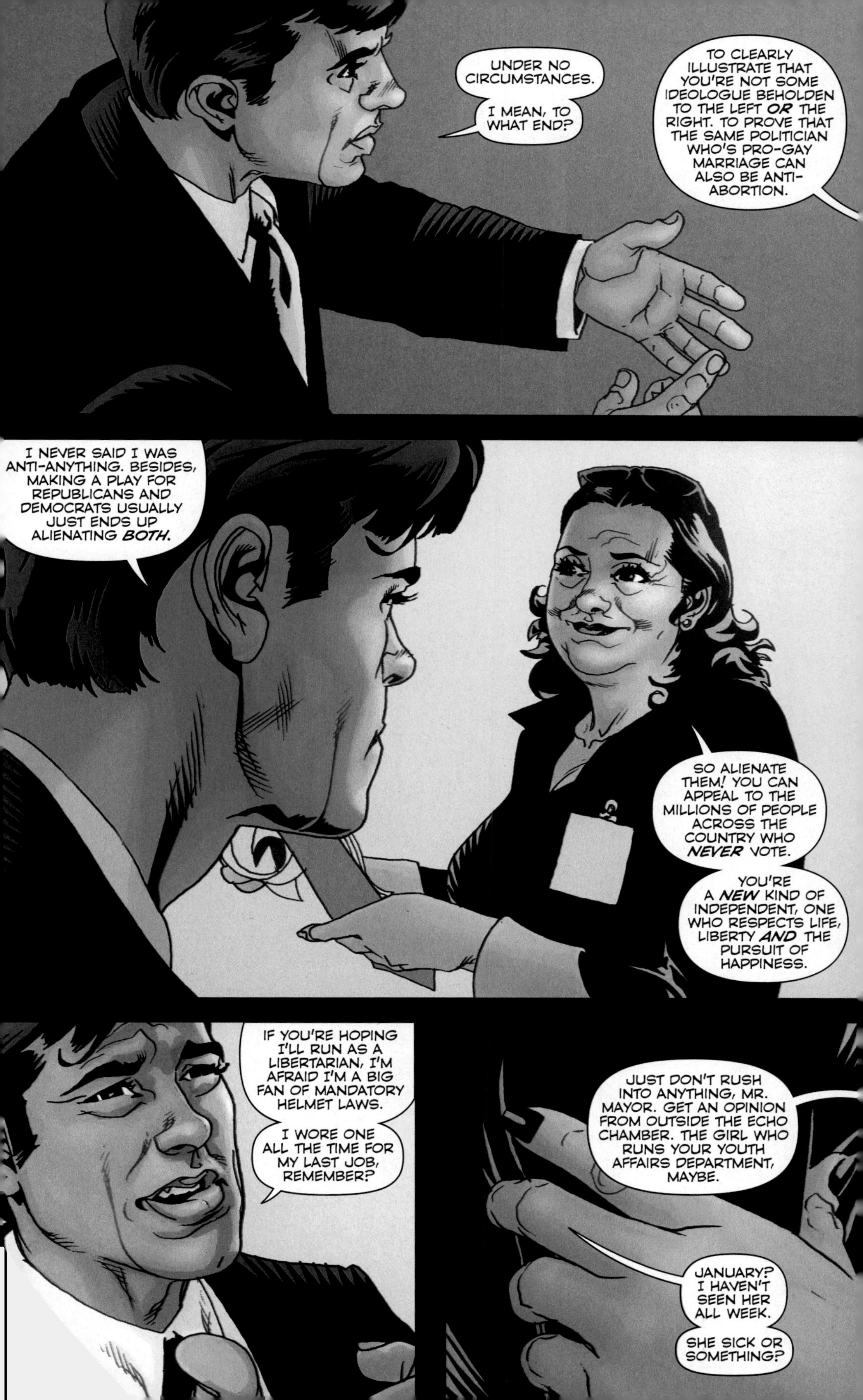
UNDER NO CIRCUMSTANCES.
I MEAN, TO WHAT END?
TO CLEARLY ILLUSTRATE THAT YOU'RE NOT SOME IDEOLOGUE BEHOLDEN TO THE LEFT **OR** THE RIGHT. TO PROVE THAT THE SAME POLITICIAN WHO'S PRO-GAY MARRIAGE CAN ALSO BE ANTI-ABORTION.
I NEVER SAID I WAS ANTI-ANYTHING. BESIDES, MAKING A PLAY FOR REPUBLICANS AND DEMOCRATS USUALLY JUST ENDS UP ALIENATING **BOTH**.
SO ALIENATE THEM! YOU CAN APPEAL TO THE MILLIONS OF PEOPLE ACROSS THE COUNTRY WHO **NEVER** VOTE.
YOU'RE A **NEW** KIND OF INDEPENDENT, ONE WHO RESPECTS LIFE, LIBERTY **AND** THE PURSUIT OF HAPPINESS.
IF YOU'RE HOPING I'LL RUN AS A LIBERTARIAN, I'M AFRAID I'M A BIG FAN OF MANDATORY HELMET LAWS.
I WORE ONE ALL THE TIME FOR MY LAST JOB, REMEMBER?
JUST DON'T RUSH INTO ANYTHING, MR. MAYOR. GET AN OPINION FROM OUTSIDE THE ECHO CHAMBER. THE GIRL WHO RUNS YOUR YOUTH AFFAIRS DEPARTMENT, MAYBE.
JANUARY? I HAVEN'T SEEN HER ALL WEEK.
SHE SICK OR SOMETHING?

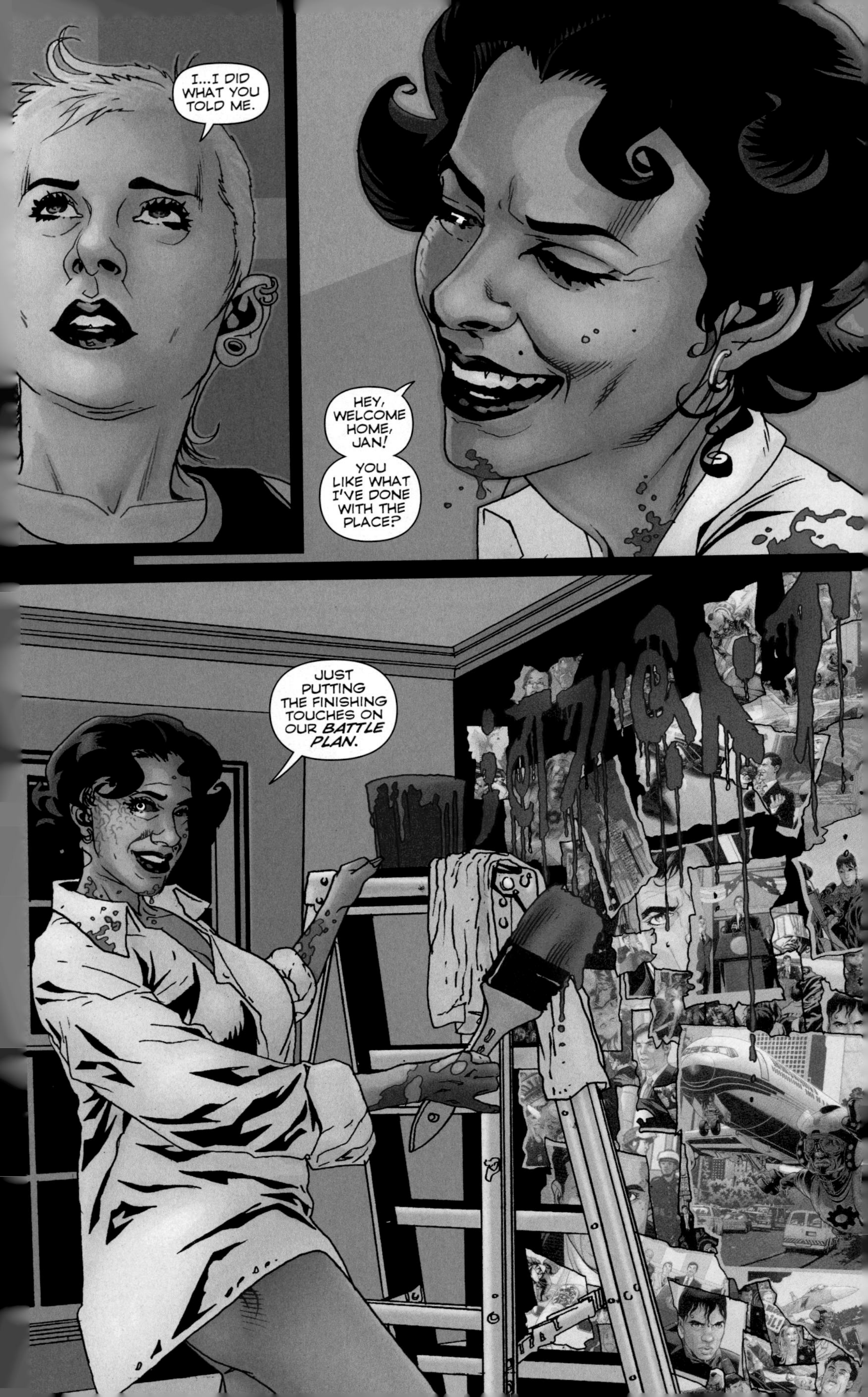
I...I DID WHAT YOU TOLD ME.
HEY, WELCOME HOME, JAN!
YOU LIKE WHAT I'VE DONE WITH THE PLACE?
JUST PUTTING THE FINISHING TOUCHES ON OUR *BATTLE PLAN*.

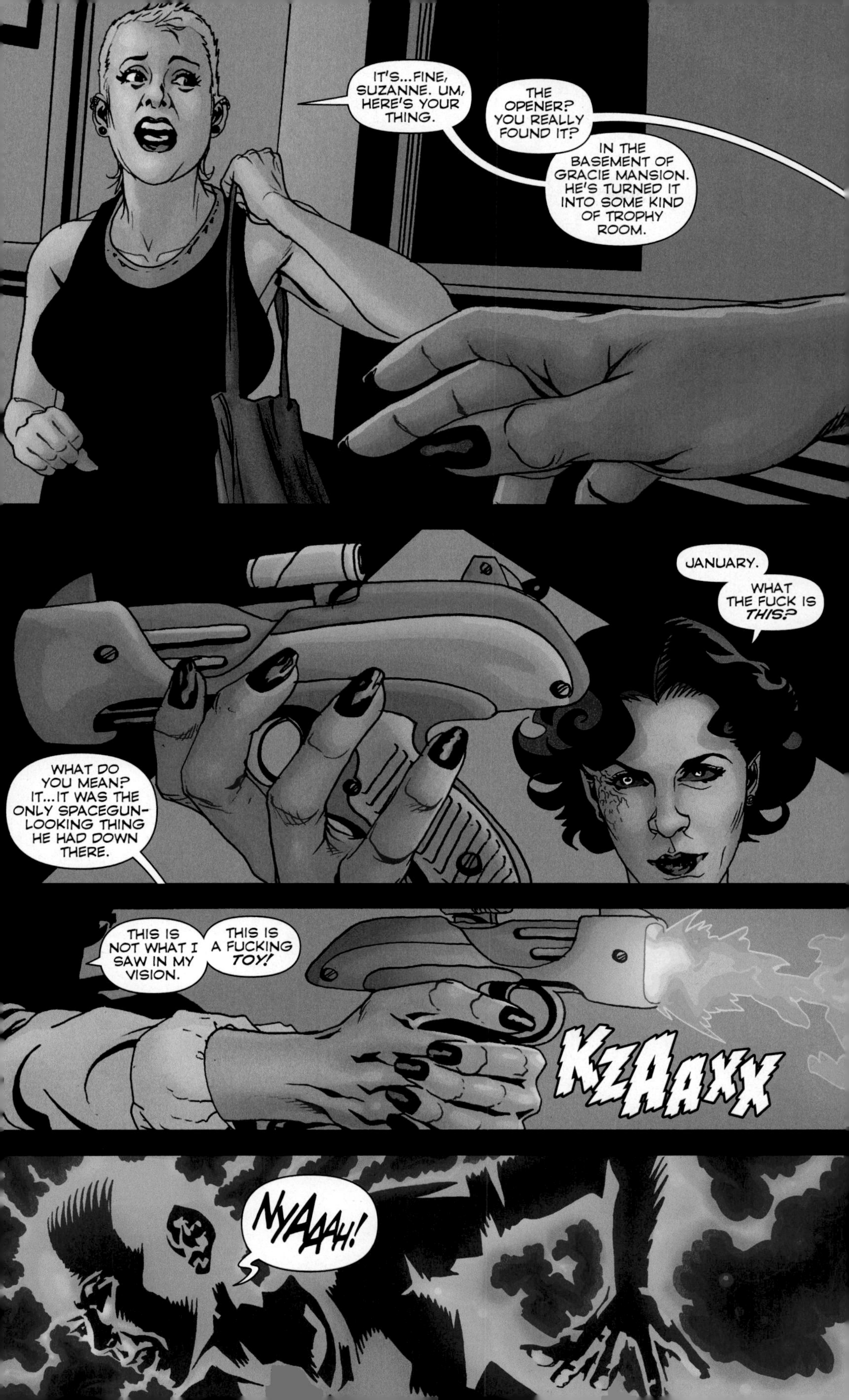
IT'S...FINE, SUZANNE. UM, HERE'S YOUR THING.
THE OPENER? YOU REALLY FOUND IT?
IN THE BASEMENT OF GRACIE MANSION. HE'S TURNED IT INTO SOME KIND OF TROPHY ROOM.
JANUARY.
WHAT THE FUCK IS *THIS?*
WHAT DO YOU MEAN? IT...IT WAS THE ONLY SPACEGUN-LOOKING THING HE HAD DOWN THERE.
THIS IS NOT WHAT I SAW IN MY VISION.
THIS IS A FUCKING *TOY!*
KZAAXX
NYAAAH!

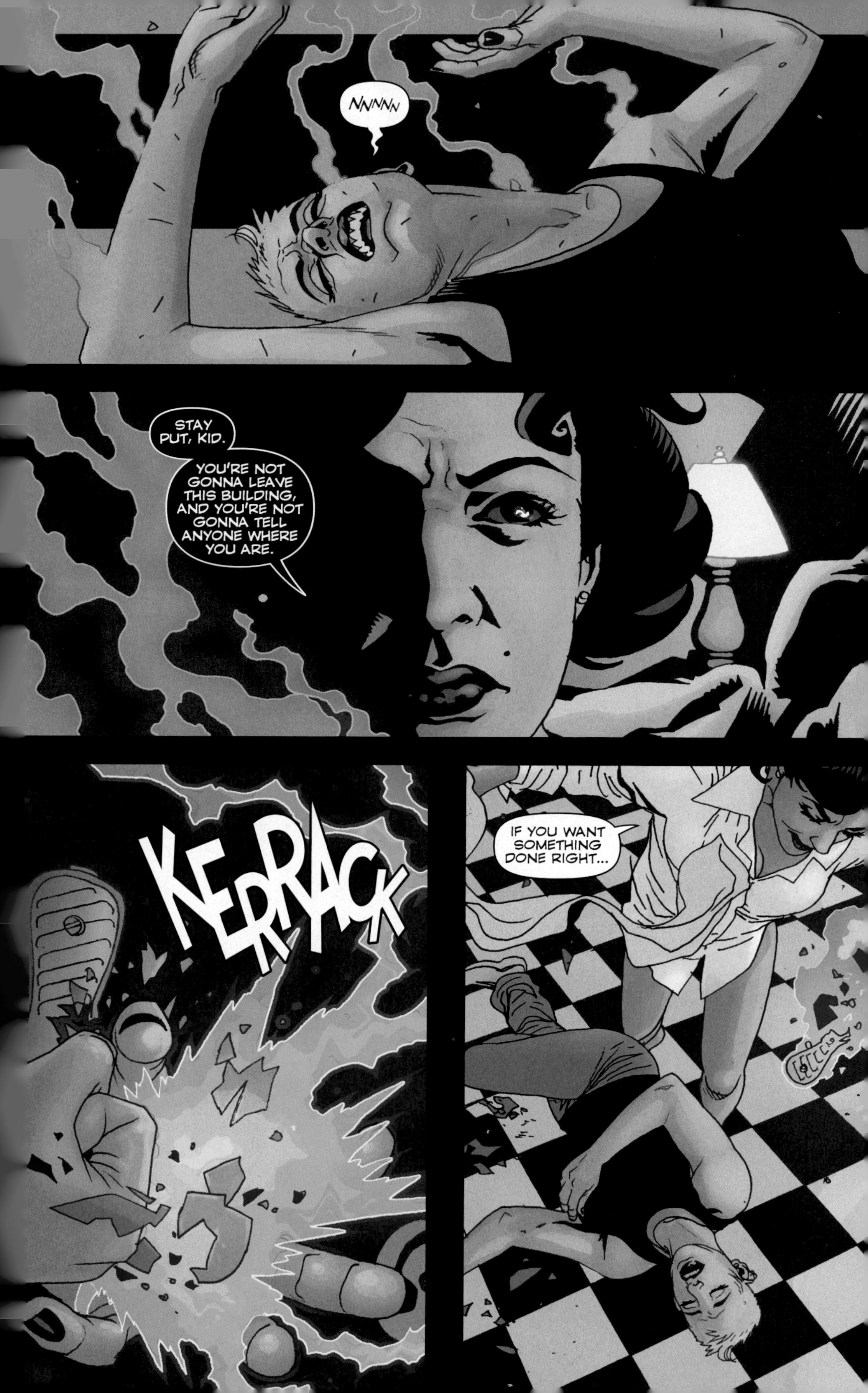
NNNNN
STAY PUT, KID.
YOU'RE NOT GONNA LEAVE THIS BUILDING, AND YOU'RE NOT GONNA TELL ANYONE WHERE YOU ARE.
KERRACK
IF YOU WANT SOMETHING DONE RIGHT...

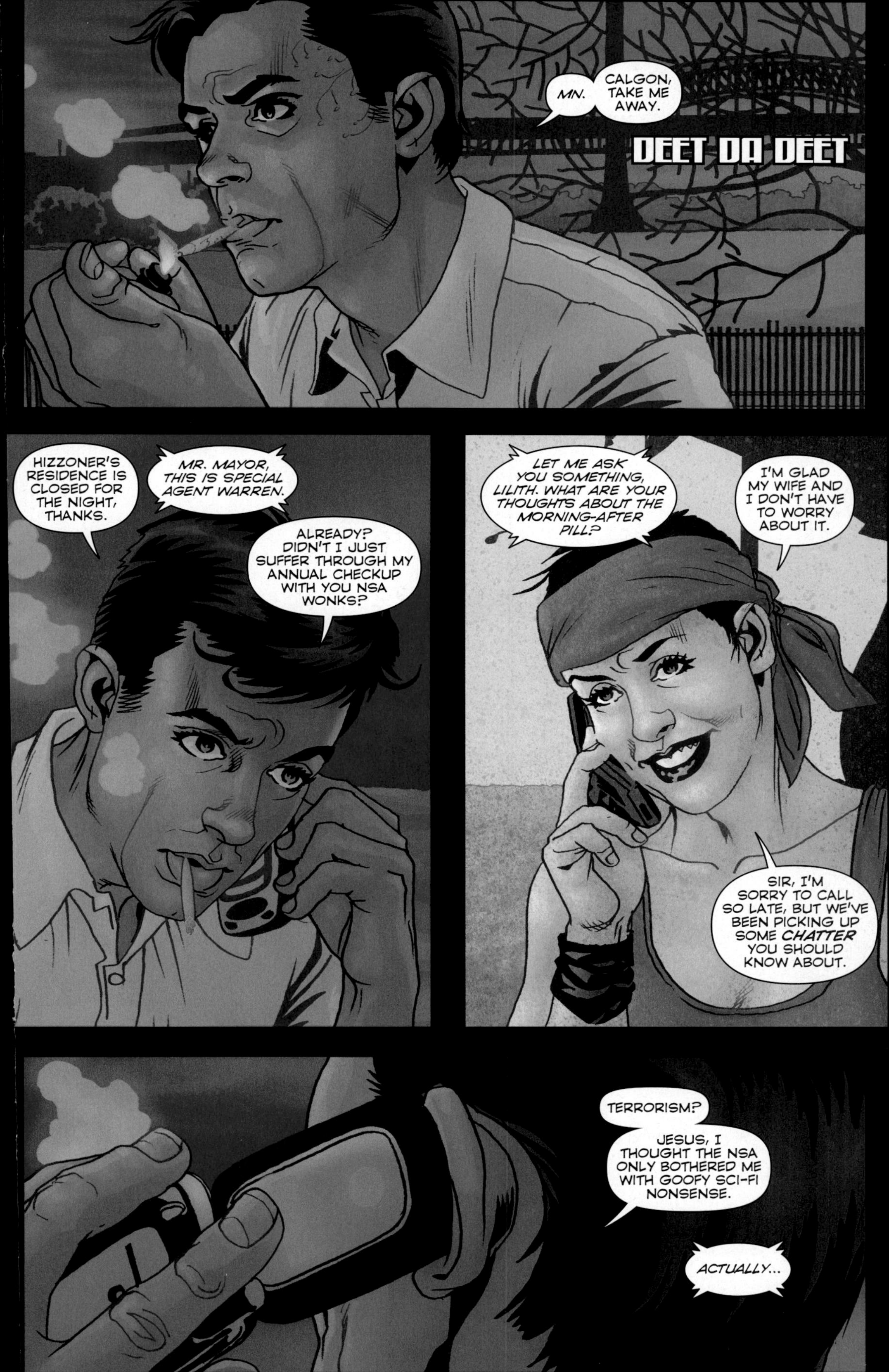
MN.
CALGON, TAKE ME AWAY.
DEET DA DEET
HIZZONER'S RESIDENCE IS CLOSED FOR THE NIGHT, THANKS.
MR. MAYOR, THIS IS SPECIAL AGENT WARREN.
ALREADY? DIDN'T I JUST SUFFER THROUGH MY ANNUAL CHECKUP WITH YOU NSA WONKS?
SIR, I'M SORRY TO CALL SO LATE, BUT WE'VE BEEN PICKING UP SOME CHATTER YOU SHOULD KNOW ABOUT.
LET ME ASK YOU SOMETHING, LILITH. WHAT ARE YOUR THOUGHTS ABOUT THE MORNING-AFTER PILL?
I'M GLAD MY WIFE AND I DON'T HAVE TO WORRY ABOUT IT.
TERRORISM?
JESUS, I THOUGHT THE NSA ONLY BOTHERED ME WITH GOOFY SCI-FI NONSENSE.
ACTUALLY...

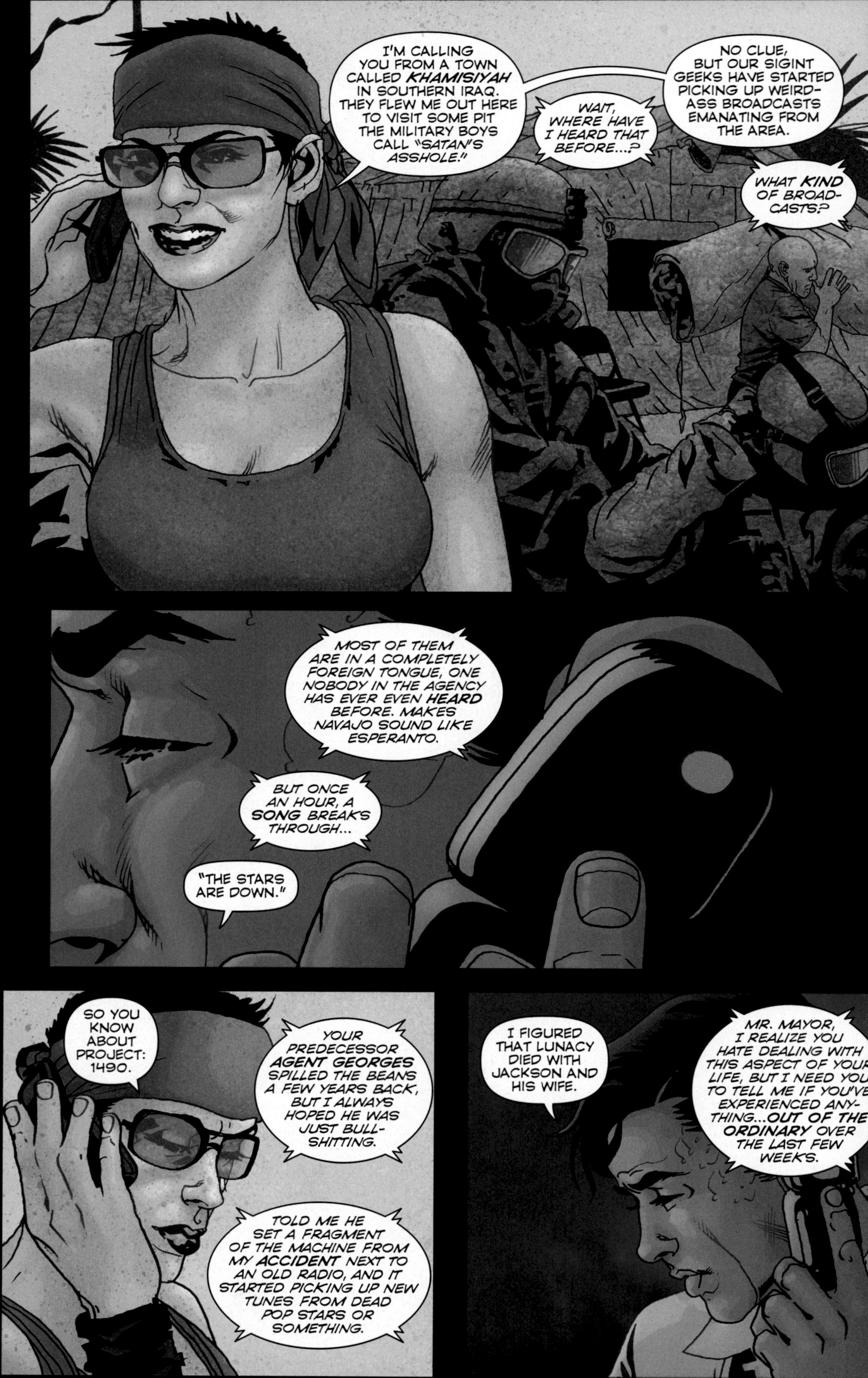
I'M CALLING YOU FROM A TOWN CALLED KHAMISIYAH IN SOUTHERN IRAQ. THEY FLEW ME OUT HERE TO VISIT SOME PIT THE MILITARY BOYS CALL "SATAN'S ASSHOLE."
WAIT, WHERE HAVE I HEARD THAT BEFORE...?
NO CLUE, BUT OUR SIGINT GEEKS HAVE STARTED PICKING UP WEIRD-ASS BROADCASTS EMANATING FROM THE AREA.
WHAT KIND OF BROAD-CASTS?
MOST OF THEM ARE IN A COMPLETELY FOREIGN TONGUE, ONE NOBODY IN THE AGENCY HAS EVER EVEN HEARD BEFORE. MAKES NAVAJO SOUND LIKE ESPERANTO.
BUT ONCE AN HOUR, A SONG BREAKS THROUGH...
"THE STARS ARE DOWN."
SO YOU KNOW ABOUT PROJECT: 1490.
YOUR PREDECESSOR AGENT GEORGES SPILLED THE BEANS A FEW YEARS BACK, BUT I ALWAYS HOPED HE WAS JUST BULL-SHITTING.
TOLD ME HE SET A FRAGMENT OF THE MACHINE FROM MY ACCIDENT NEXT TO AN OLD RADIO, AND IT STARTED PICKING UP NEW TUNES FROM DEAD POP STARS OR SOMETHING.
I FIGURED THAT LUNACY DIED WITH JACKSON AND HIS WIFE.
MR. MAYOR, I REALIZE YOU HATE DEALING WITH THIS ASPECT OF YOUR LIFE, BUT I NEED YOU TO TELL ME IF YOU'VE EXPERIENCED ANY-THING...OUT OF THE ORDINARY OVER THE LAST FEW WEEKS.

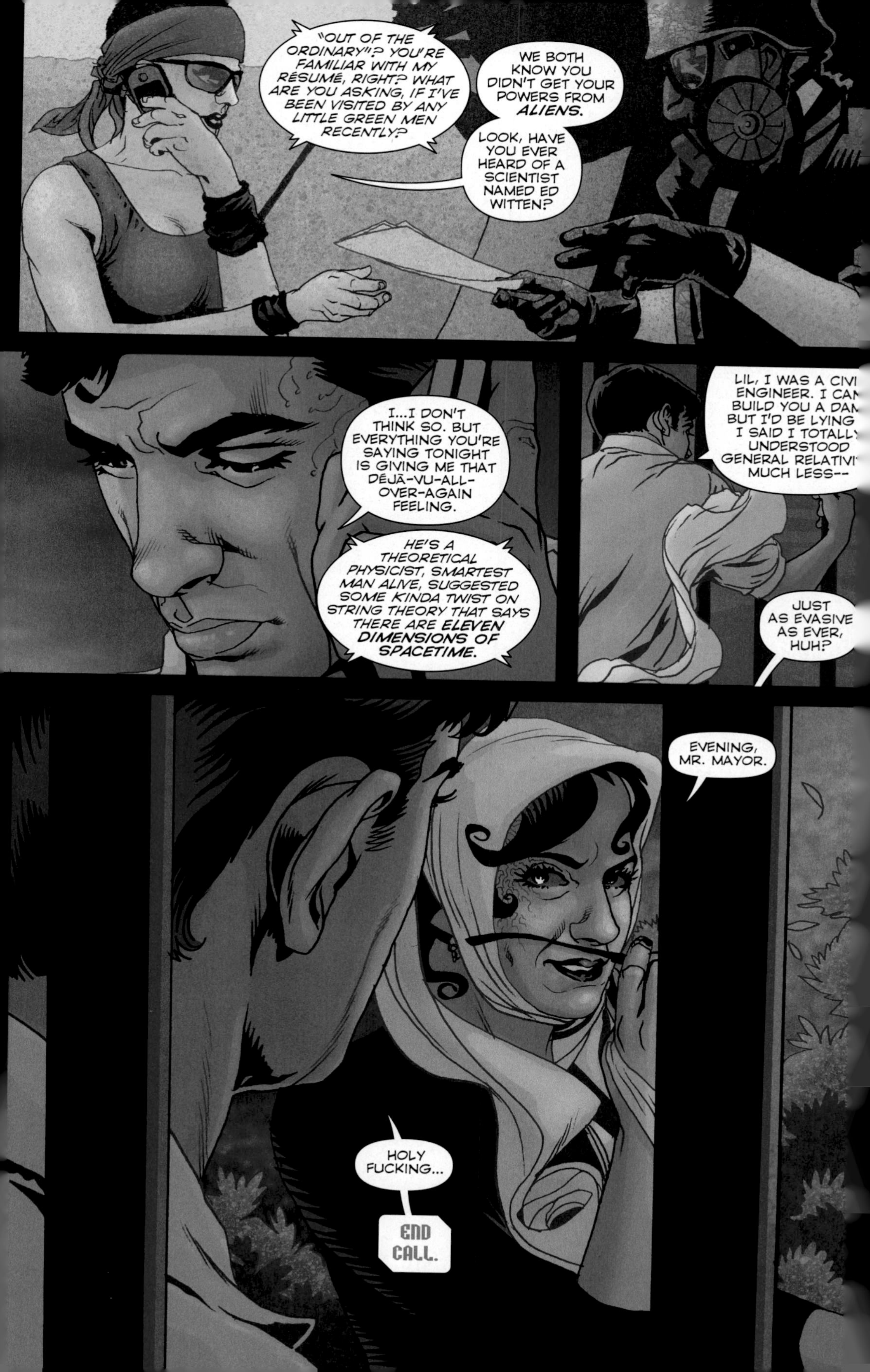
"OUT OF THE ORDINARY"? YOU'RE FAMILIAR WITH MY RÉSUMÉ, RIGHT? WHAT ARE YOU ASKING, IF I'VE BEEN VISITED BY ANY LITTLE GREEN MEN RECENTLY?
WE BOTH KNOW YOU DIDN'T GET YOUR POWERS FROM ALIENS.
LOOK, HAVE YOU EVER HEARD OF A SCIENTIST NAMED ED WITTEN?
I...I DON'T THINK SO. BUT EVERYTHING YOU'RE SAYING TONIGHT IS GIVING ME THAT DÉJÀ-VU-ALL-OVER-AGAIN FEELING.
HE'S A THEORETICAL PHYSICIST, SMARTEST MAN ALIVE, SUGGESTED SOME KINDA TWIST ON STRING THEORY THAT SAYS THERE ARE ELEVEN DIMENSIONS OF SPACETIME.
LIL, I WAS A CIVI ENGINEER. I CAN BUILD YOU A DAM BUT I'D BE LYING I SAID I TOTALLY UNDERSTOOD GENERAL RELATIVI MUCH LESS--
JUST AS EVASIVE AS EVER, HUH?
EVENING, MR. MAYOR.
HOLY FUCKING...
END CALL.

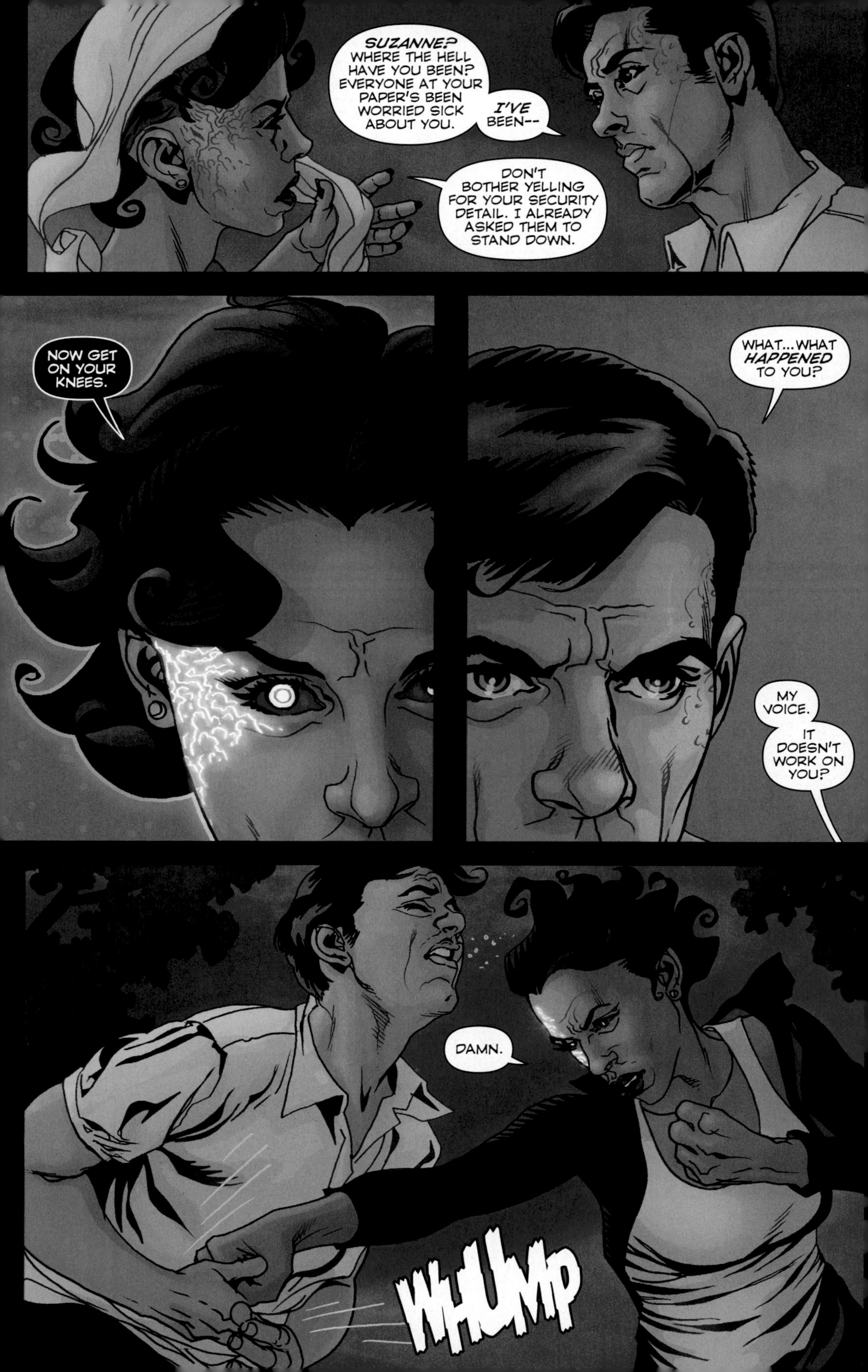
SUZANNE? WHERE THE HELL HAVE YOU BEEN? EVERYONE AT YOUR PAPER'S BEEN WORRIED SICK ABOUT YOU.
I'VE BEEN--
DON'T BOTHER YELLING FOR YOUR SECURITY DETAIL. I ALREADY ASKED THEM TO STAND DOWN.
NOW GET ON YOUR KNEES.
WHAT...WHAT HAPPENED TO YOU?
MY VOICE.
IT DOESN'T WORK ON YOU?
DAMN.
WHUMP

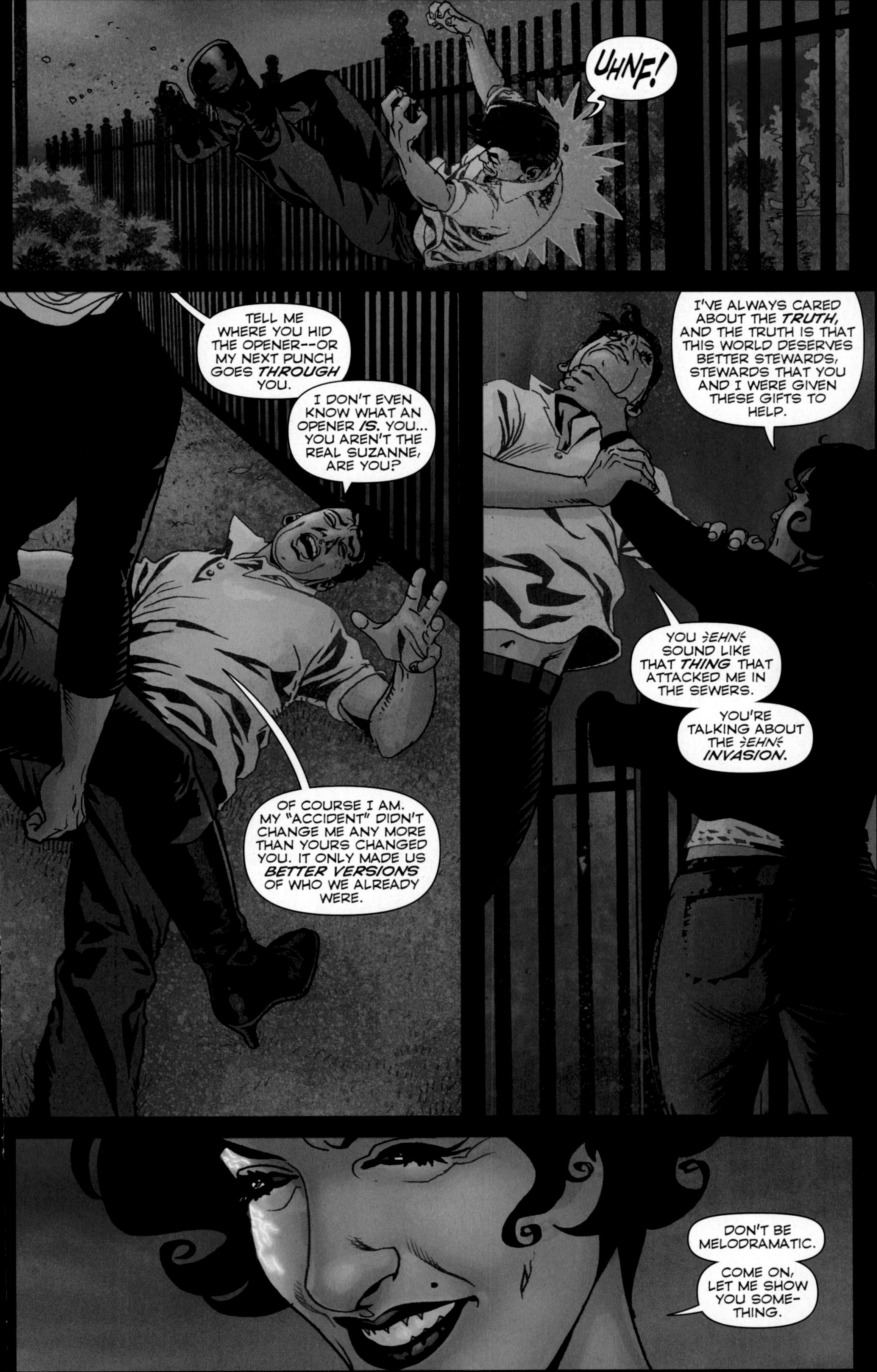
UHNF!
TELL ME WHERE YOU HID THE OPENER--OR MY NEXT PUNCH GOES THROUGH YOU.
I DON'T EVEN KNOW WHAT AN OPENER IS. YOU... YOU AREN'T THE REAL SUZANNE, ARE YOU?
OF COURSE I AM. MY "ACCIDENT" DIDN'T CHANGE ME ANY MORE THAN YOURS CHANGED YOU. IT ONLY MADE US BETTER VERSIONS OF WHO WE ALREADY WERE.
I'VE ALWAYS CARED ABOUT THE TRUTH, AND THE TRUTH IS THAT THIS WORLD DESERVES BETTER STEWARDS, STEWARDS THAT YOU AND I WERE GIVEN THESE GIFTS TO HELP.
YOU *EHN* SOUND LIKE THAT THING THAT ATTACKED ME IN THE SEWERS.
YOU'RE TALKING ABOUT THE *EHN* INVASION.
DON'T BE MELODRAMATIC.
COME ON, LET ME SHOW YOU SOME-THING.

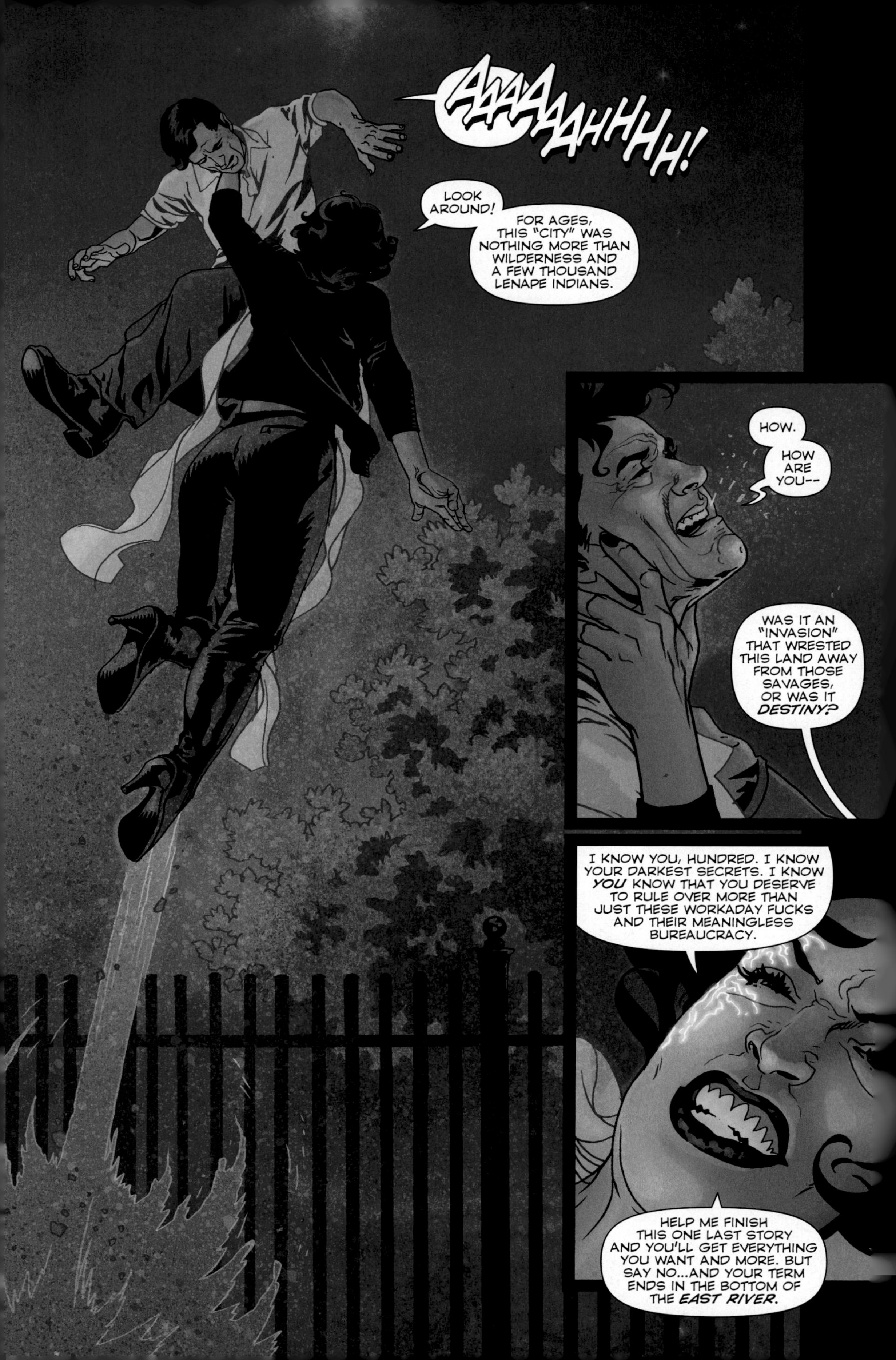
AAAAAAHHHHH!
LOOK AROUND!
FOR AGES, THIS "CITY" WAS NOTHING MORE THAN WILDERNESS AND A FEW THOUSAND LENAPE INDIANS.
HOW.
HOW ARE YOU--
WAS IT AN "INVASION" THAT WRESTED THIS LAND AWAY FROM THOSE SAVAGES, OR WAS IT *DESTINY?*
I KNOW YOU, HUNDRED. I KNOW YOUR DARKEST SECRETS. I KNOW *YOU* KNOW THAT YOU DESERVE TO RULE OVER MORE THAN JUST THESE WORKADAY FUCKS AND THEIR MEANINGLESS BUREAUCRACY.
HELP ME FINISH THIS ONE LAST STORY AND YOU'LL GET EVERYTHING YOU WANT AND MORE. BUT SAY NO...AND YOUR TERM ENDS IN THE BOTTOM OF THE *EAST RIVER.*

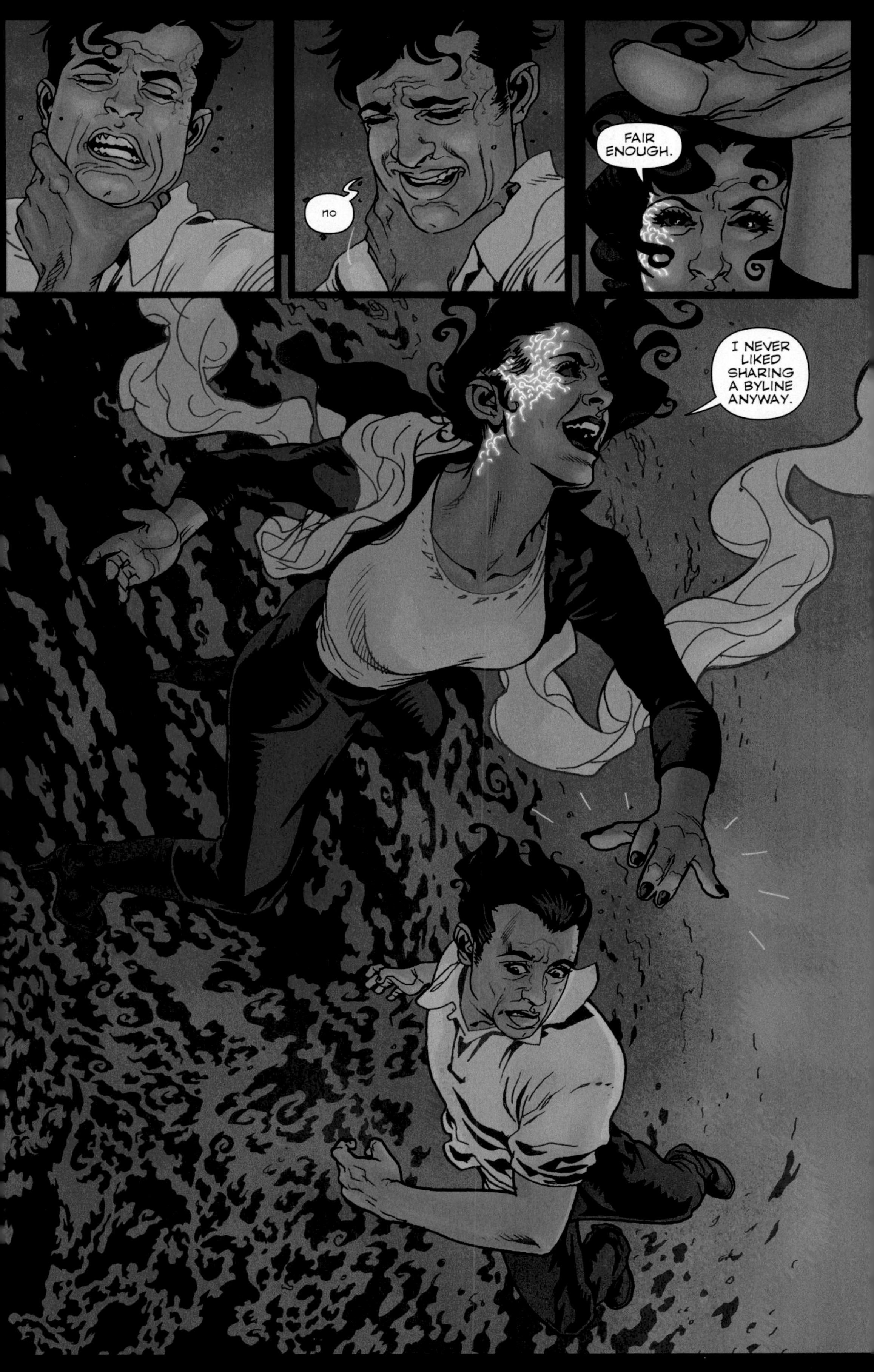
no
FAIR ENOUGH.
I NEVER LIKED SHARING A BYLINE ANYWAY.

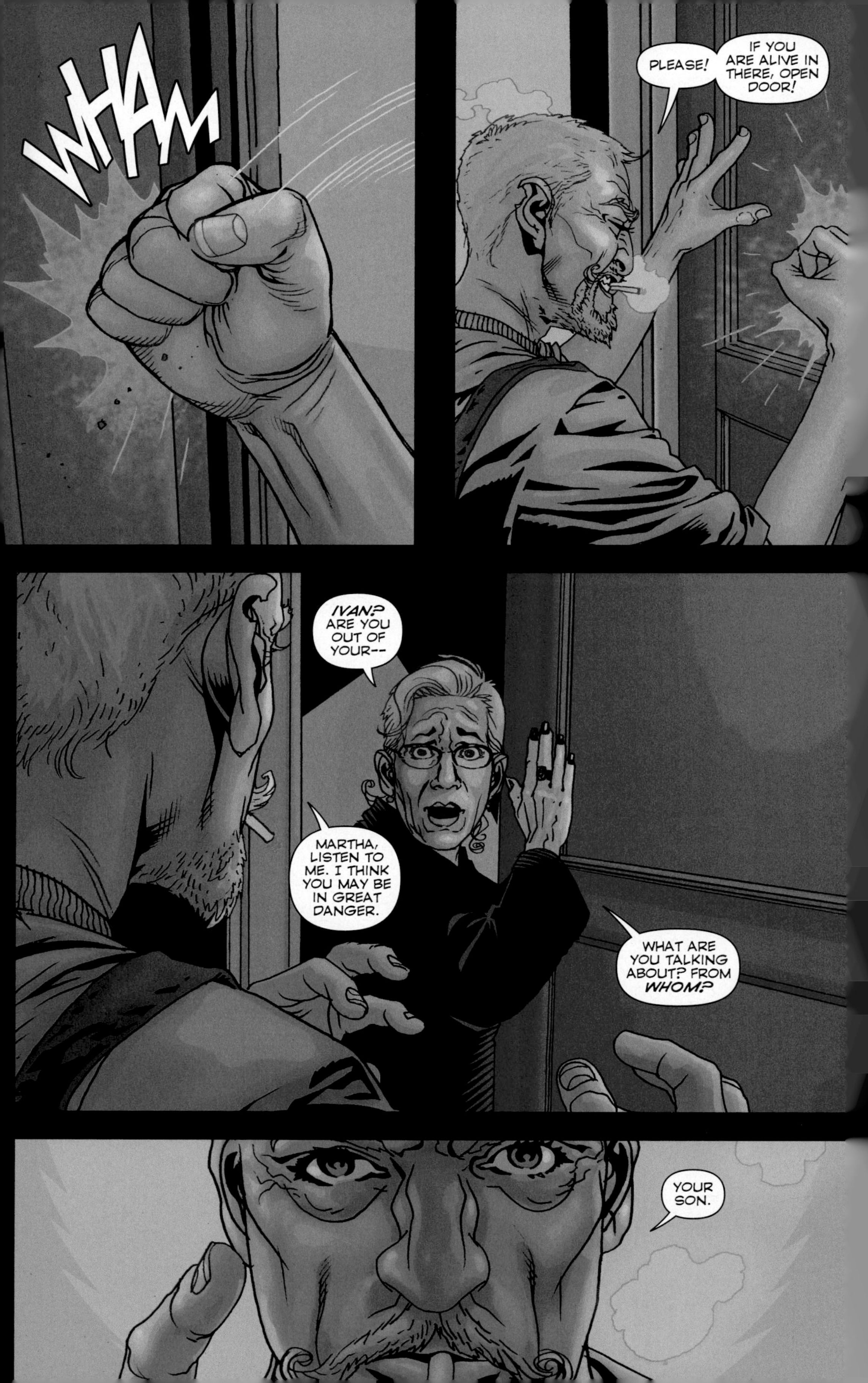
WHAM
PLEASE!
IF YOU ARE ALIVE IN THERE, OPEN DOOR!
IVAN? ARE YOU OUT OF YOUR--
MARTHA, LISTEN TO ME. I THINK YOU MAY BE IN GREAT DANGER.
WHAT ARE YOU TALKING ABOUT? FROM WHOM?
YOUR SON.

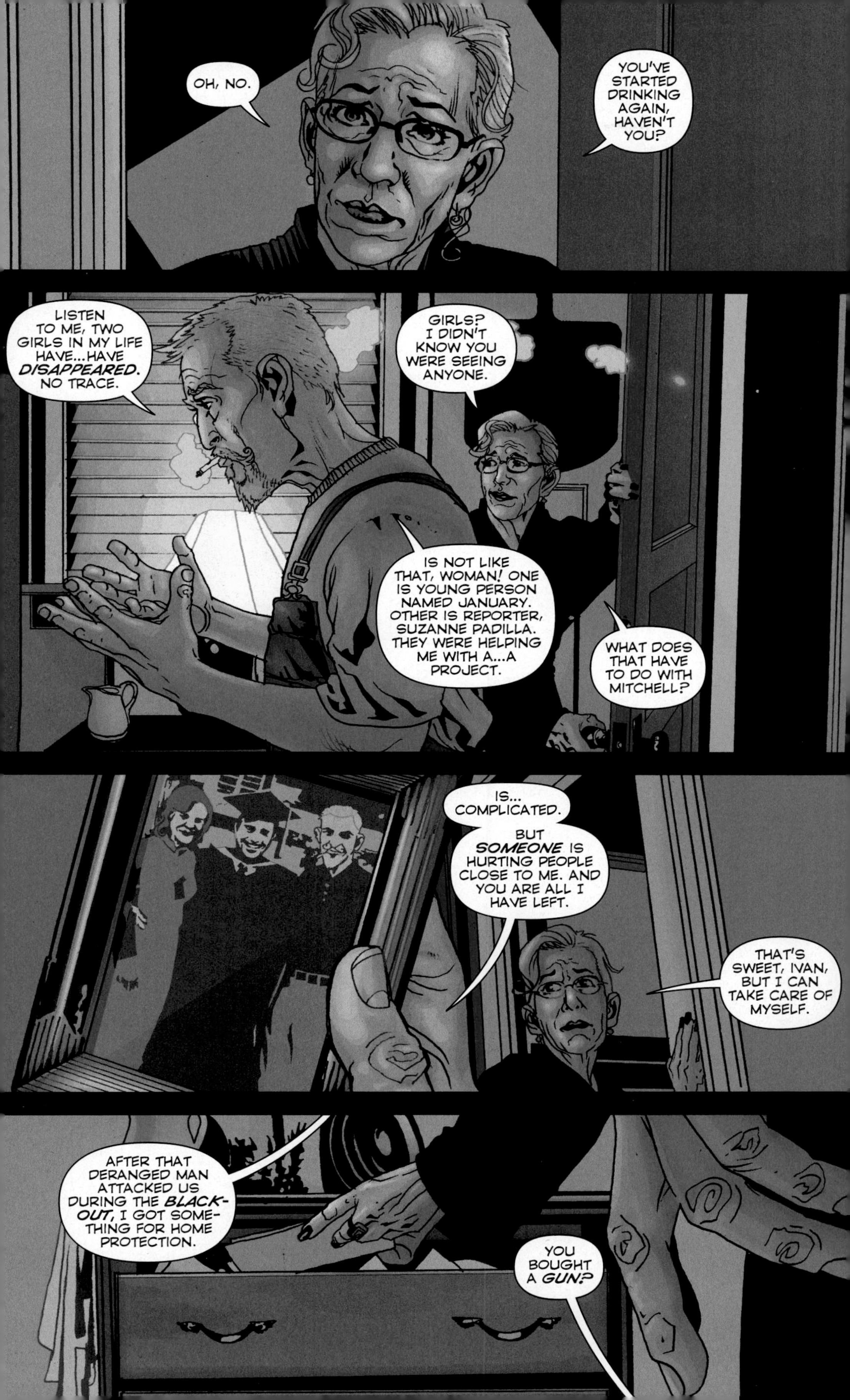
OH, NO.
YOU'VE STARTED DRINKING AGAIN, HAVEN'T YOU?
LISTEN TO ME, TWO GIRLS IN MY LIFE HAVE...HAVE *DISAPPEARED.* NO TRACE.
GIRLS? I DIDN'T KNOW YOU WERE SEEING ANYONE.
IS NOT LIKE THAT, WOMAN! ONE IS YOUNG PERSON NAMED JANUARY. OTHER IS REPORTER, SUZANNE PADILLA. THEY WERE HELPING ME WITH A...A PROJECT.
WHAT DOES THAT HAVE TO DO WITH MITCHELL?
IS... COMPLICATED.
BUT *SOMEONE* IS HURTING PEOPLE CLOSE TO ME. AND YOU ARE ALL I HAVE LEFT.
THAT'S SWEET, IVAN, BUT I CAN TAKE CARE OF MYSELF.
AFTER THAT DERANGED MAN ATTACKED US DURING THE *BLACK-OUT,* I GOT SOME-THING FOR HOME PROTECTION.
YOU BOUGHT A *GUN?*

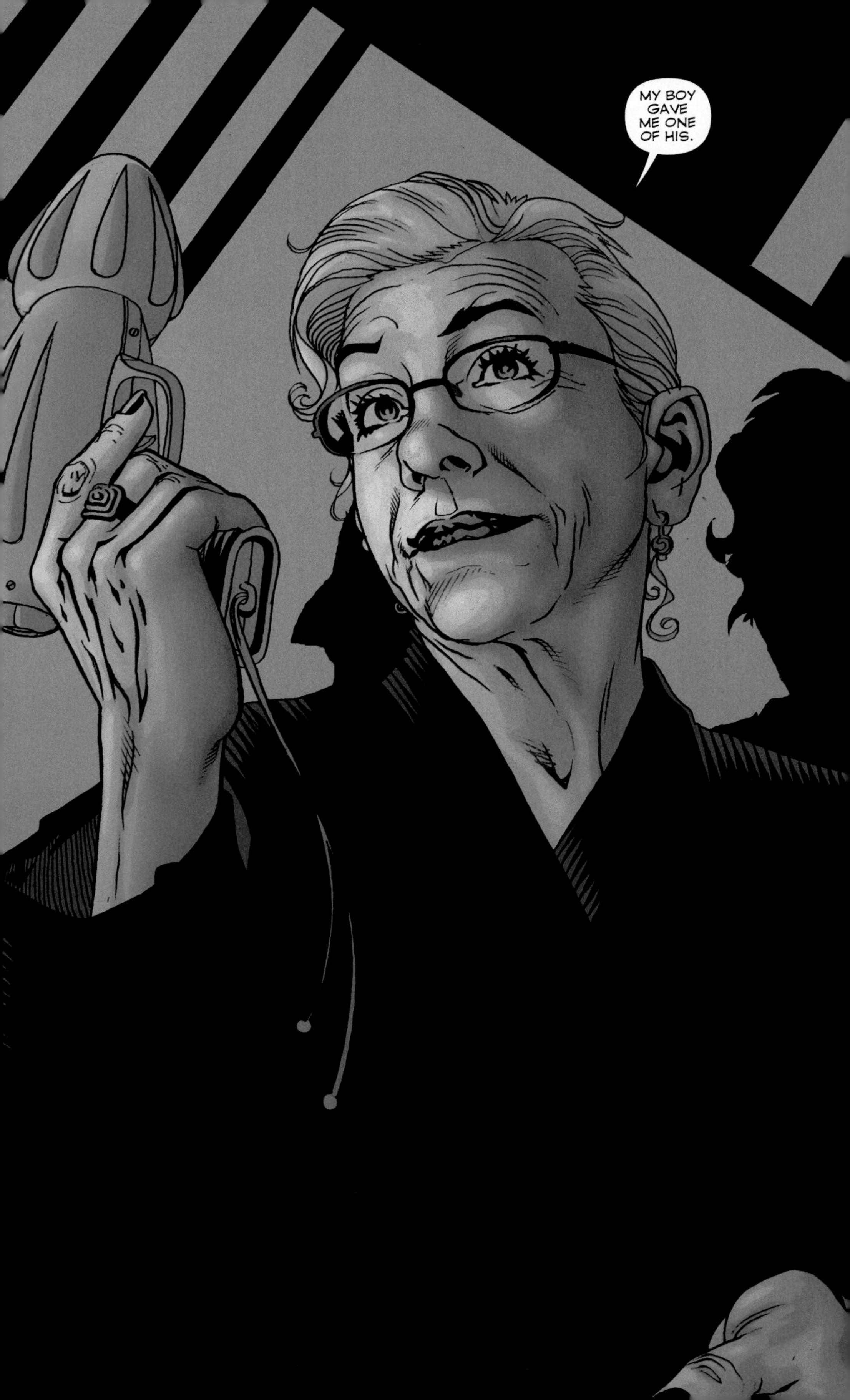
MY BOY GAVE ME ONE OF HIS.

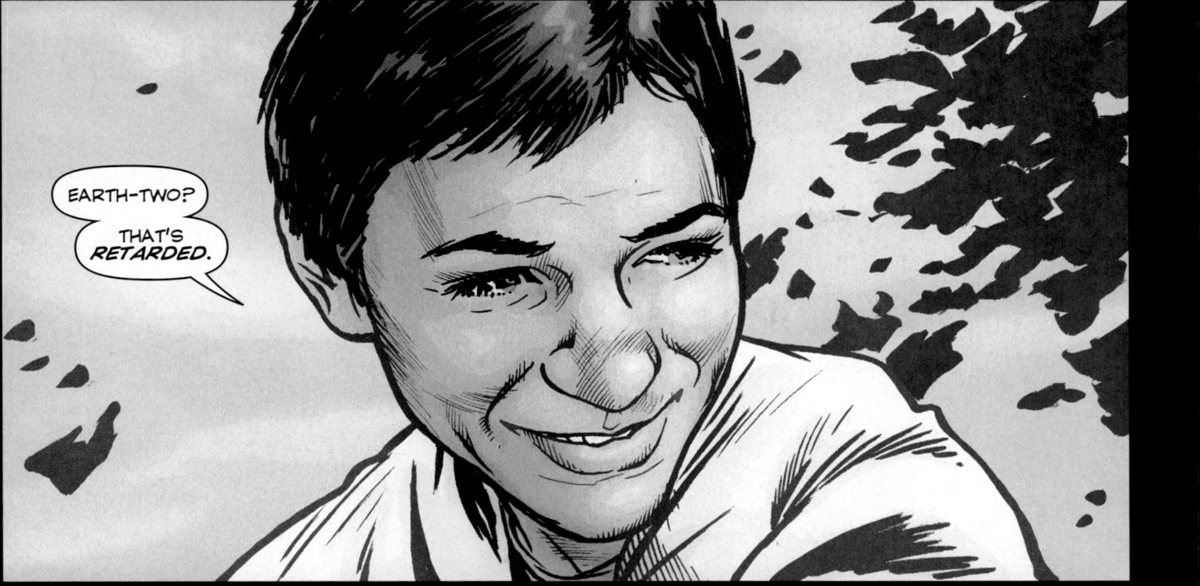
EARTH-TWO? THAT'S *RETARDED.*

MONDAY, MARCH 10, 1980

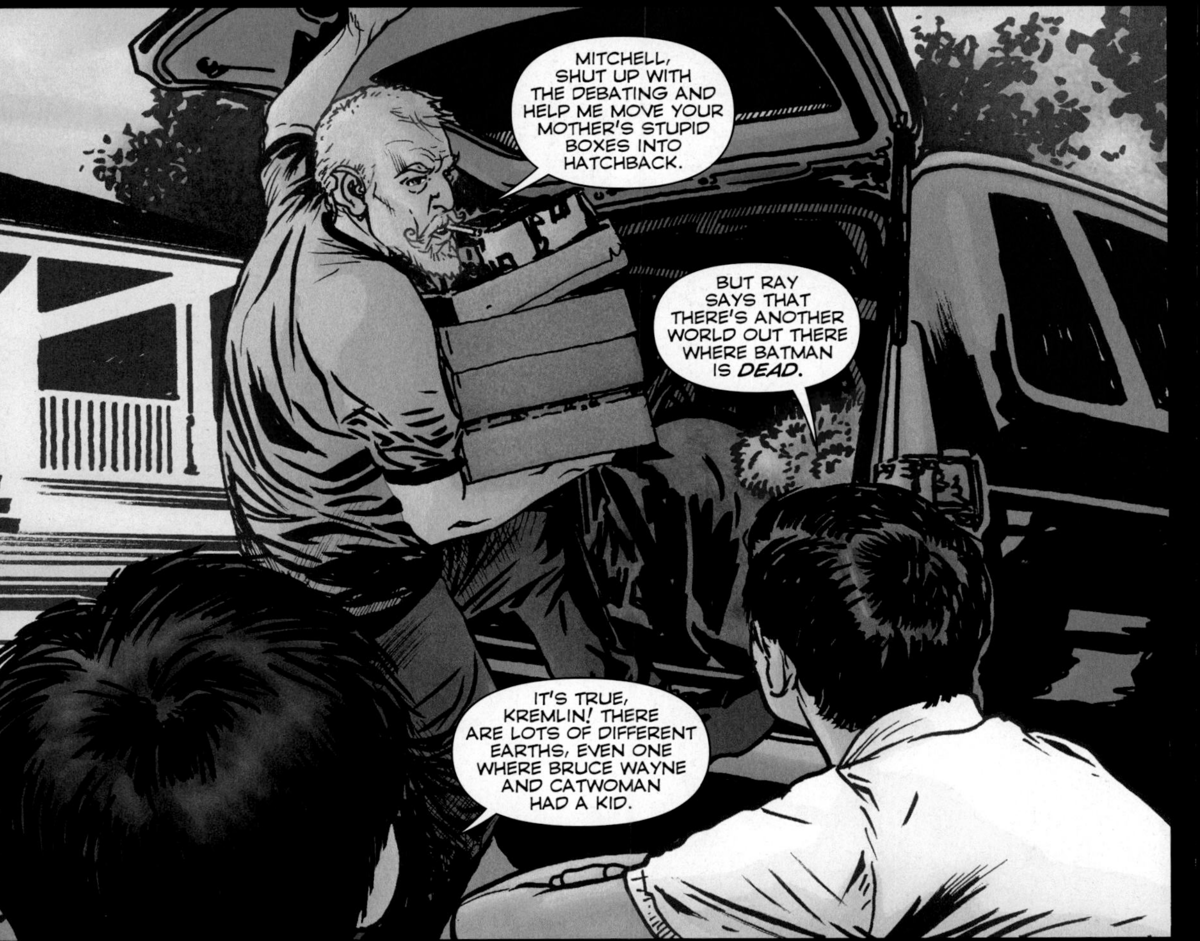
MITCHELL, SHUT UP WITH THE DEBATING AND HELP ME MOVE YOUR MOTHER'S STUPID BOXES INTO HATCHBACK.
BUT RAY SAYS THAT THERE'S ANOTHER WORLD OUT THERE WHERE BATMAN IS *DEAD*.
IT'S TRUE, KREMLIN! THERE ARE LOTS OF DIFFERENT EARTHS, EVEN ONE WHERE BRUCE WAYNE AND CATWOMAN HAD A KID.

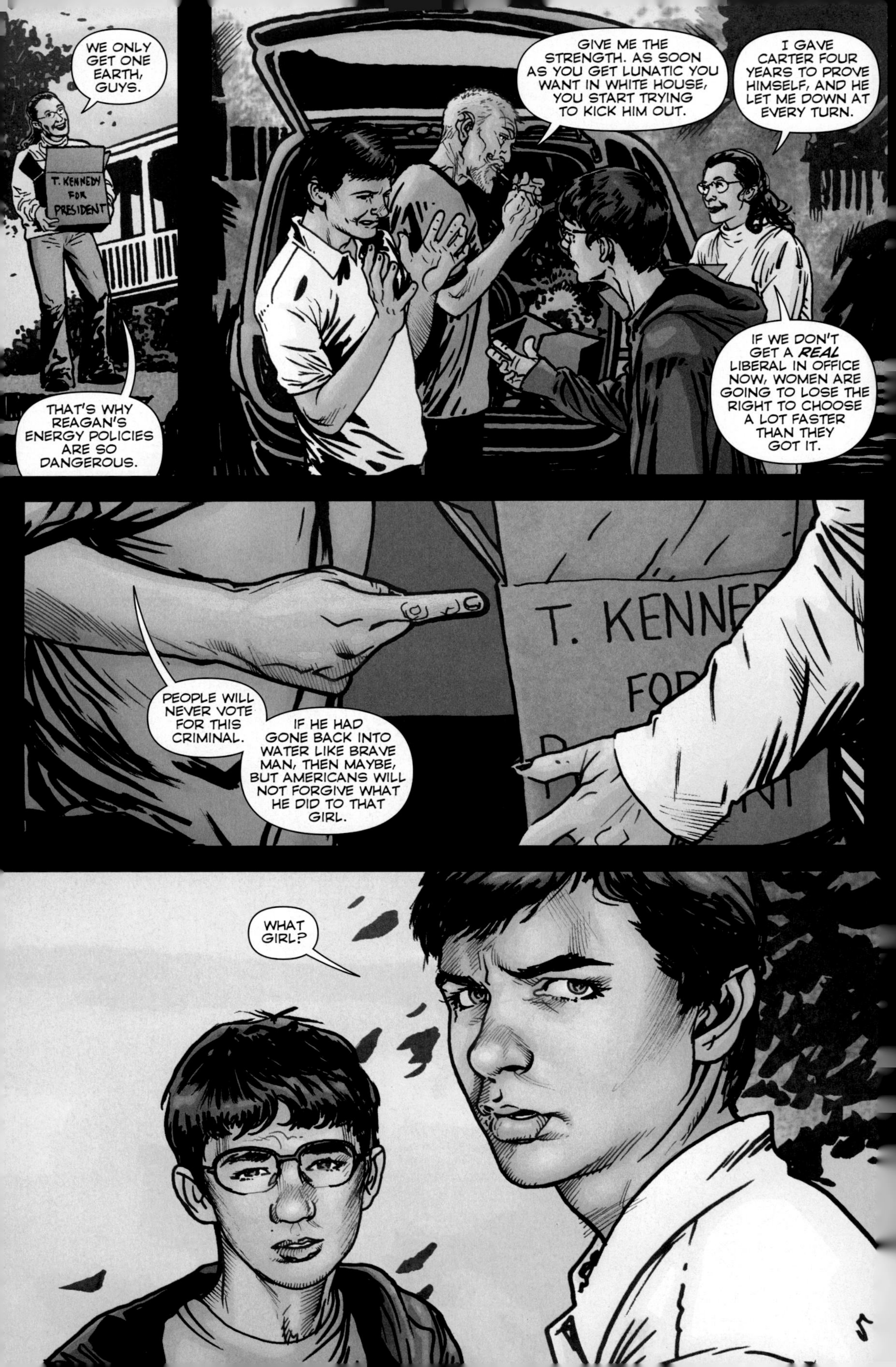
WE ONLY GET ONE EARTH, GUYS.
T. KENNEDY FOR PRESIDENT
THAT'S WHY REAGAN'S ENERGY POLICIES ARE SO DANGEROUS.
GIVE ME THE STRENGTH. AS SOON AS YOU GET LUNATIC YOU WANT IN WHITE HOUSE, YOU START TRYING TO KICK HIM OUT.
I GAVE CARTER FOUR YEARS TO PROVE HIMSELF, AND HE LET ME DOWN AT EVERY TURN.
IF WE DON'T GET A *REAL* LIBERAL IN OFFICE NOW, WOMEN ARE GOING TO LOSE THE RIGHT TO CHOOSE A LOT FASTER THAN THEY GOT IT.
PEOPLE WILL NEVER VOTE FOR THIS CRIMINAL.
IF HE HAD GONE BACK INTO WATER LIKE BRAVE MAN, THEN MAYBE, BUT AMERICANS WILL NOT FORGIVE WHAT HE DID TO THAT GIRL.
WHAT GIRL?
5

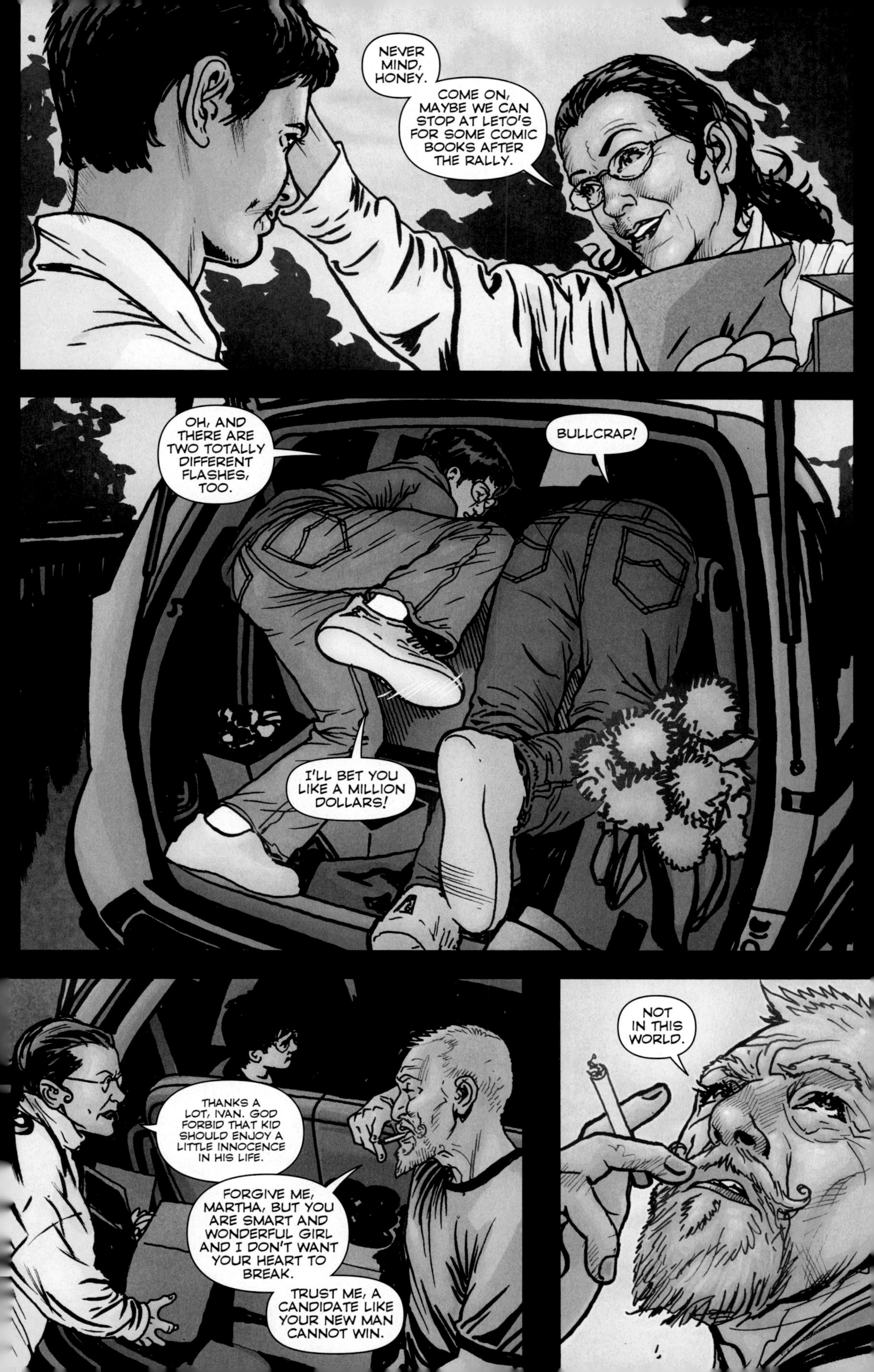
NEVER MIND, HONEY.
COME ON, MAYBE WE CAN STOP AT LETO'S FOR SOME COMIC BOOKS AFTER THE RALLY.
OH, AND THERE ARE TWO TOTALLY DIFFERENT FLASHES, TOO.
BULLCRAP!
I'LL BET YOU LIKE A MILLION DOLLARS!
THANKS A LOT, IVAN. GOD FORBID THAT KID SHOULD ENJOY A LITTLE INNOCENCE IN HIS LIFE.
FORGIVE ME, MARTHA, BUT YOU ARE SMART AND WONDERFUL GIRL AND I DON'T WANT YOUR HEART TO BREAK.
TRUST ME, A CANDIDATE LIKE YOUR NEW MAN CANNOT WIN.
NOT IN THIS WORLD.

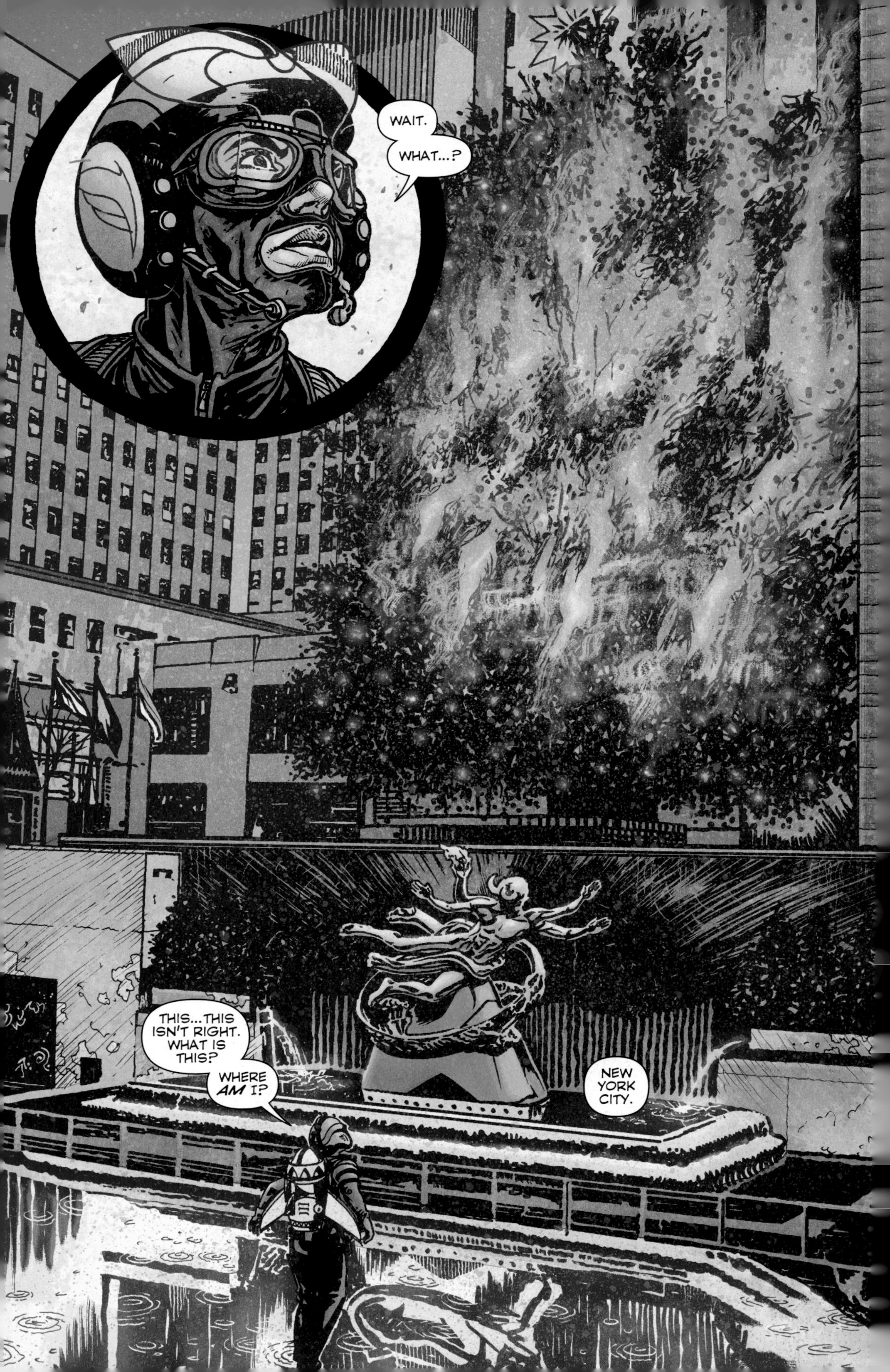
WAIT.
WHAT...?
THIS...THIS ISN'T RIGHT. WHAT IS THIS?
WHERE AM I?
NEW YORK CITY.

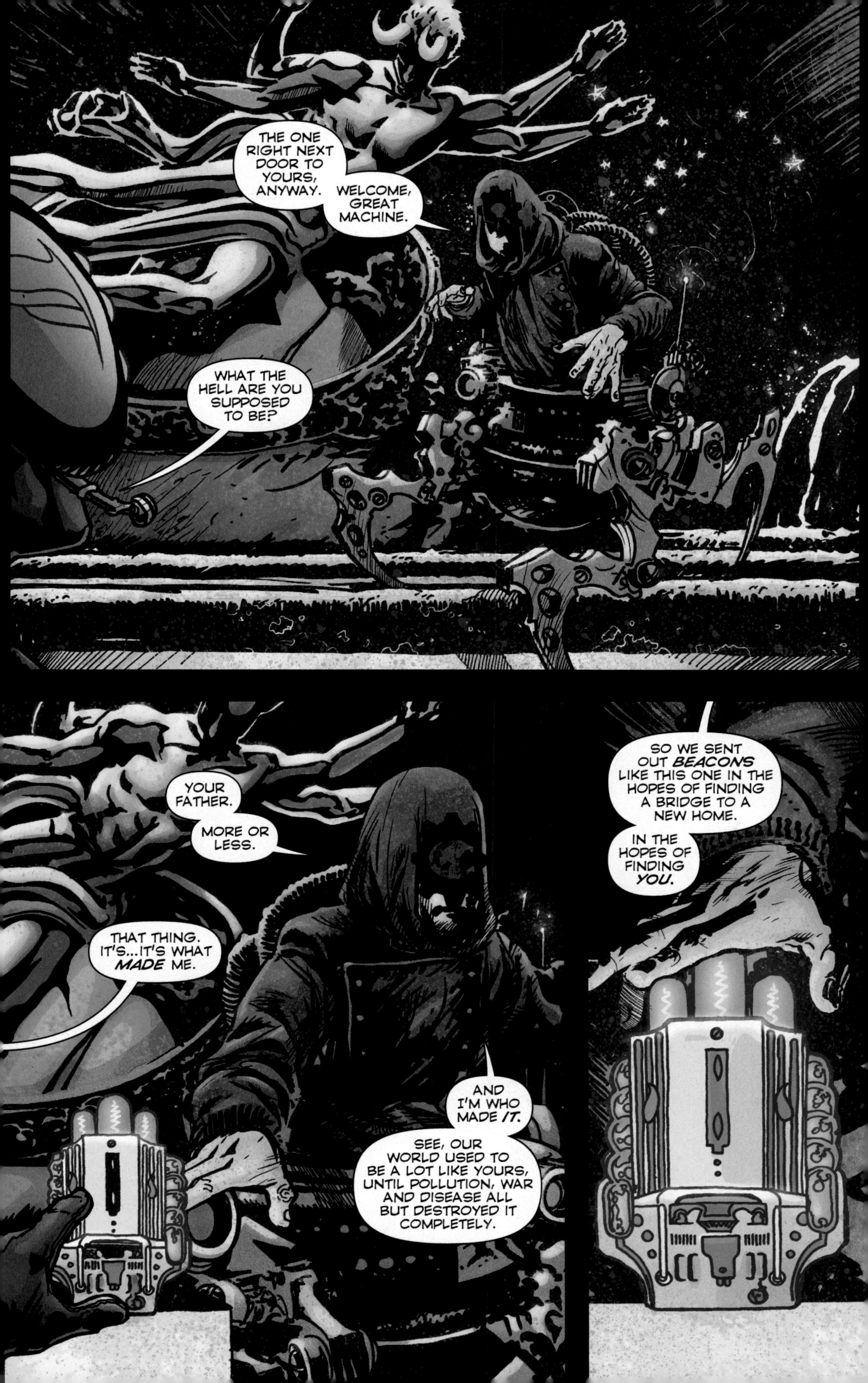
THE ONE RIGHT NEXT DOOR TO YOURS, ANYWAY.
WELCOME, GREAT MACHINE.
WHAT THE HELL ARE YOU SUPPOSED TO BE?
YOUR FATHER.
MORE OR LESS.
THAT THING. IT'S...IT'S WHAT *MADE* ME.
AND I'M WHO MADE *IT*.
SEE, OUR WORLD USED TO BE A LOT LIKE YOURS, UNTIL POLLUTION, WAR AND DISEASE ALL BUT DESTROYED IT COMPLETELY.
SO WE SENT OUT *BEACONS* LIKE THIS ONE IN THE HOPES OF FINDING A BRIDGE TO A NEW HOME.
IN THE HOPES OF FINDING *YOU*.

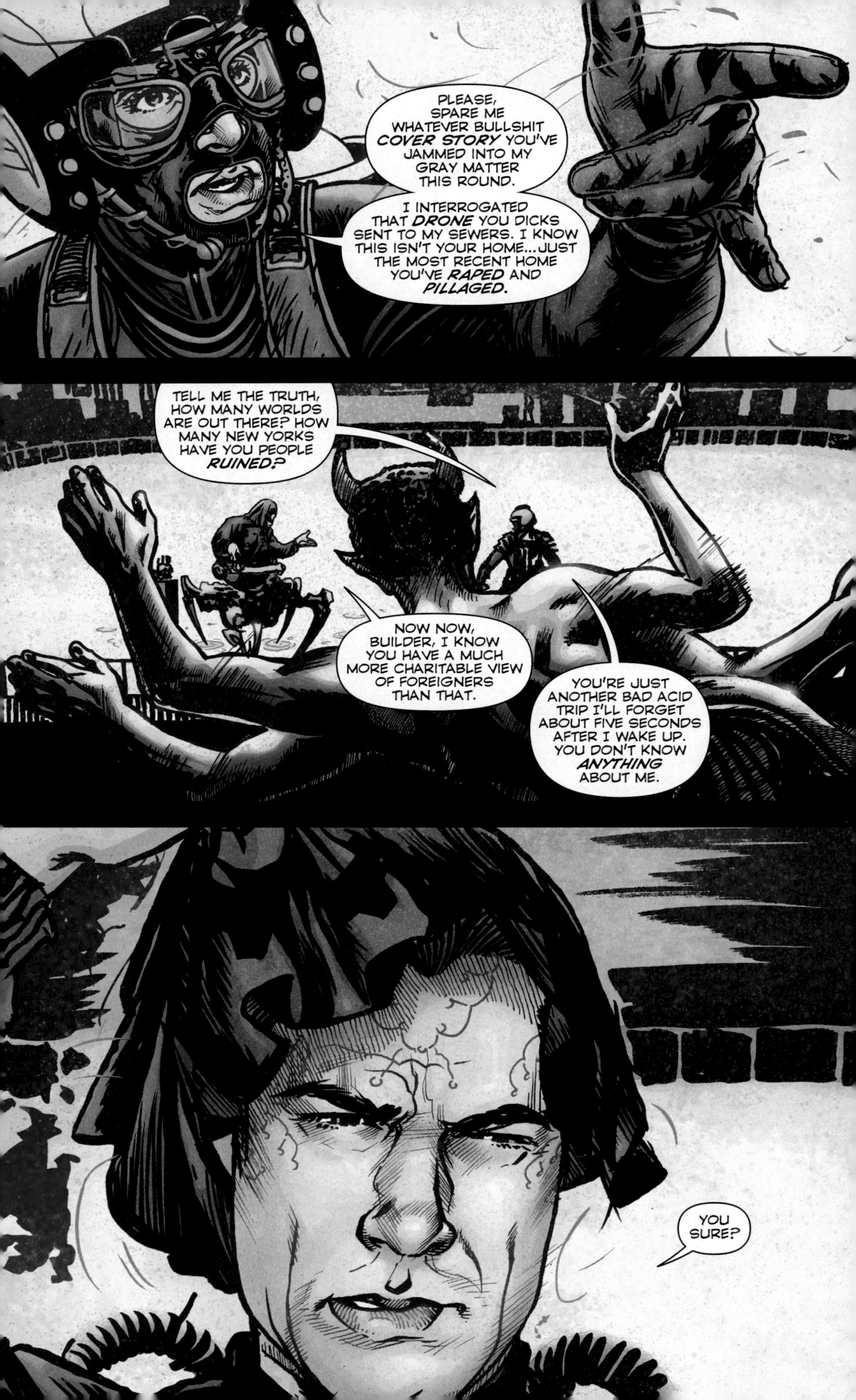
PLEASE, SPARE ME WHATEVER BULLSHIT COVER STORY YOU'VE JAMMED INTO MY GRAY MATTER THIS ROUND.
I INTERROGATED THAT DRONE YOU DICKS SENT TO MY SEWERS. I KNOW THIS ISN'T YOUR HOME...JUST THE MOST RECENT HOME YOU'VE RAPED AND PILLAGED.
TELL ME THE TRUTH, HOW MANY WORLDS ARE OUT THERE? HOW MANY NEW YORKS HAVE YOU PEOPLE RUINED?
NOW NOW, BUILDER, I KNOW YOU HAVE A MUCH MORE CHARITABLE VIEW OF FOREIGNERS THAN THAT.
YOU'RE JUST ANOTHER BAD ACID TRIP I'LL FORGET ABOUT FIVE SECONDS AFTER I WAKE UP. YOU DON'T KNOW ANYTHING ABOUT ME.
YOU SURE?

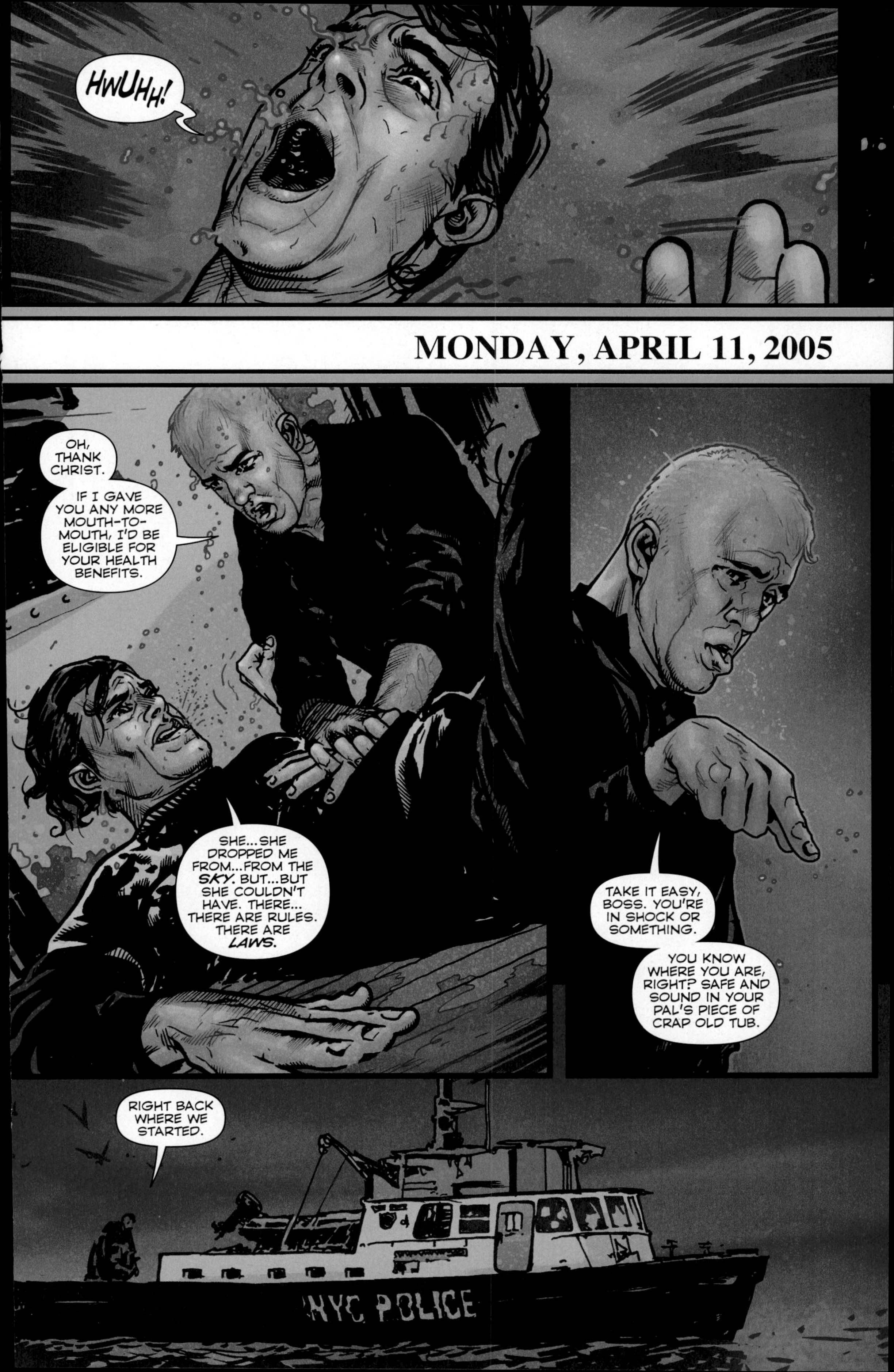
HWUHH!
MONDAY, APRIL 11, 2005
OH, THANK CHRIST.
IF I GAVE YOU ANY MORE MOUTH-TO-MOUTH, I'D BE ELIGIBLE FOR YOUR HEALTH BENEFITS.
SHE...SHE DROPPED ME FROM...FROM THE SKY. BUT...BUT SHE COULDN'T HAVE. THERE... THERE ARE RULES. THERE ARE LAWS.
TAKE IT EASY, BOSS. YOU'RE IN SHOCK OR SOMETHING.
YOU KNOW WHERE YOU ARE, RIGHT? SAFE AND SOUND IN YOUR PAL'S PIECE OF CRAP OLD TUB.
RIGHT BACK WHERE WE STARTED.
NYC POLICE

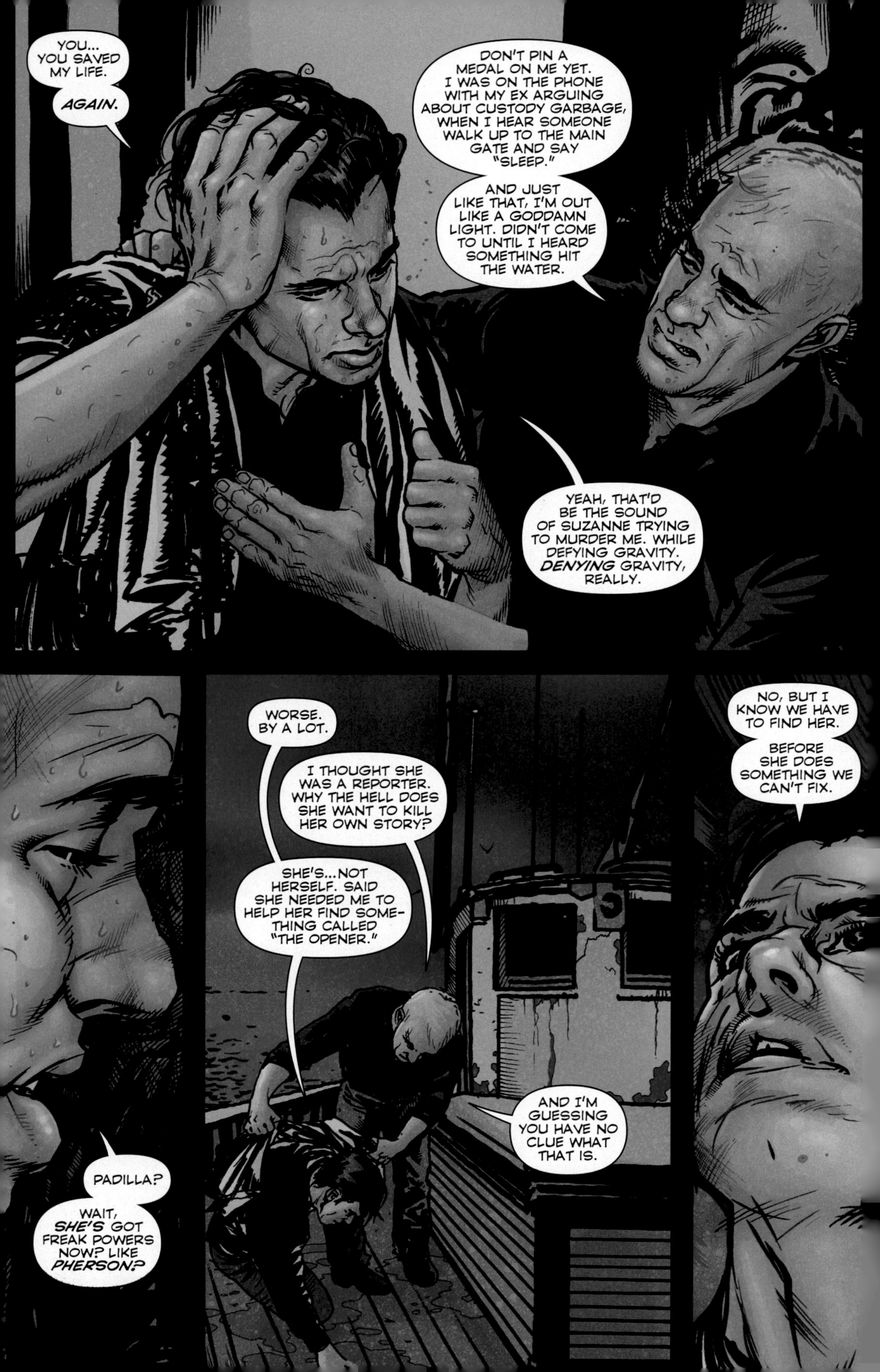
YOU... YOU SAVED MY LIFE.
AGAIN.
DON'T PIN A MEDAL ON ME YET. I WAS ON THE PHONE WITH MY EX ARGUING ABOUT CUSTODY GARBAGE, WHEN I HEAR SOMEONE WALK UP TO THE MAIN GATE AND SAY "SLEEP."
AND JUST LIKE THAT, I'M OUT LIKE A GODDAMN LIGHT. DIDN'T COME TO UNTIL I HEARD SOMETHING HIT THE WATER.
YEAH, THAT'D BE THE SOUND OF SUZANNE TRYING TO MURDER ME. WHILE DEFYING GRAVITY. DENYING GRAVITY, REALLY.
PADILLA?
WAIT, SHE'S GOT FREAK POWERS NOW? LIKE PHERSON?
WORSE. BY A LOT.
I THOUGHT SHE WAS A REPORTER. WHY THE HELL DOES SHE WANT TO KILL HER OWN STORY?
SHE'S...NOT HERSELF. SAID SHE NEEDED ME TO HELP HER FIND SOMETHING CALLED "THE OPENER."
AND I'M GUESSING YOU HAVE NO CLUE WHAT THAT IS.
NO, BUT I KNOW WE HAVE TO FIND HER.
BEFORE SHE DOES SOMETHING WE CAN'T FIX.

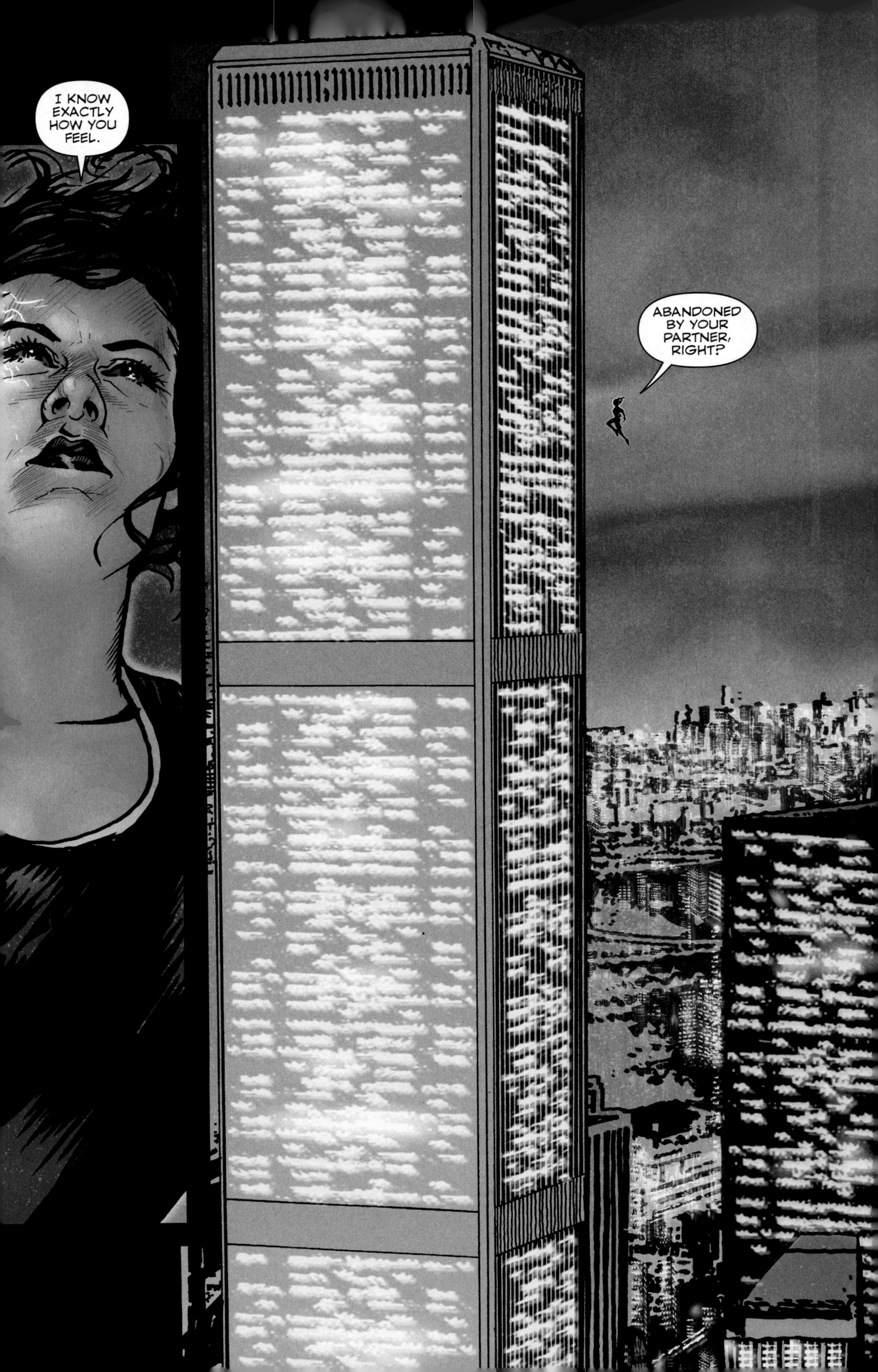
I KNOW EXACTLY HOW YOU FEEL.
ABANDONED BY YOUR PARTNER, RIGHT?

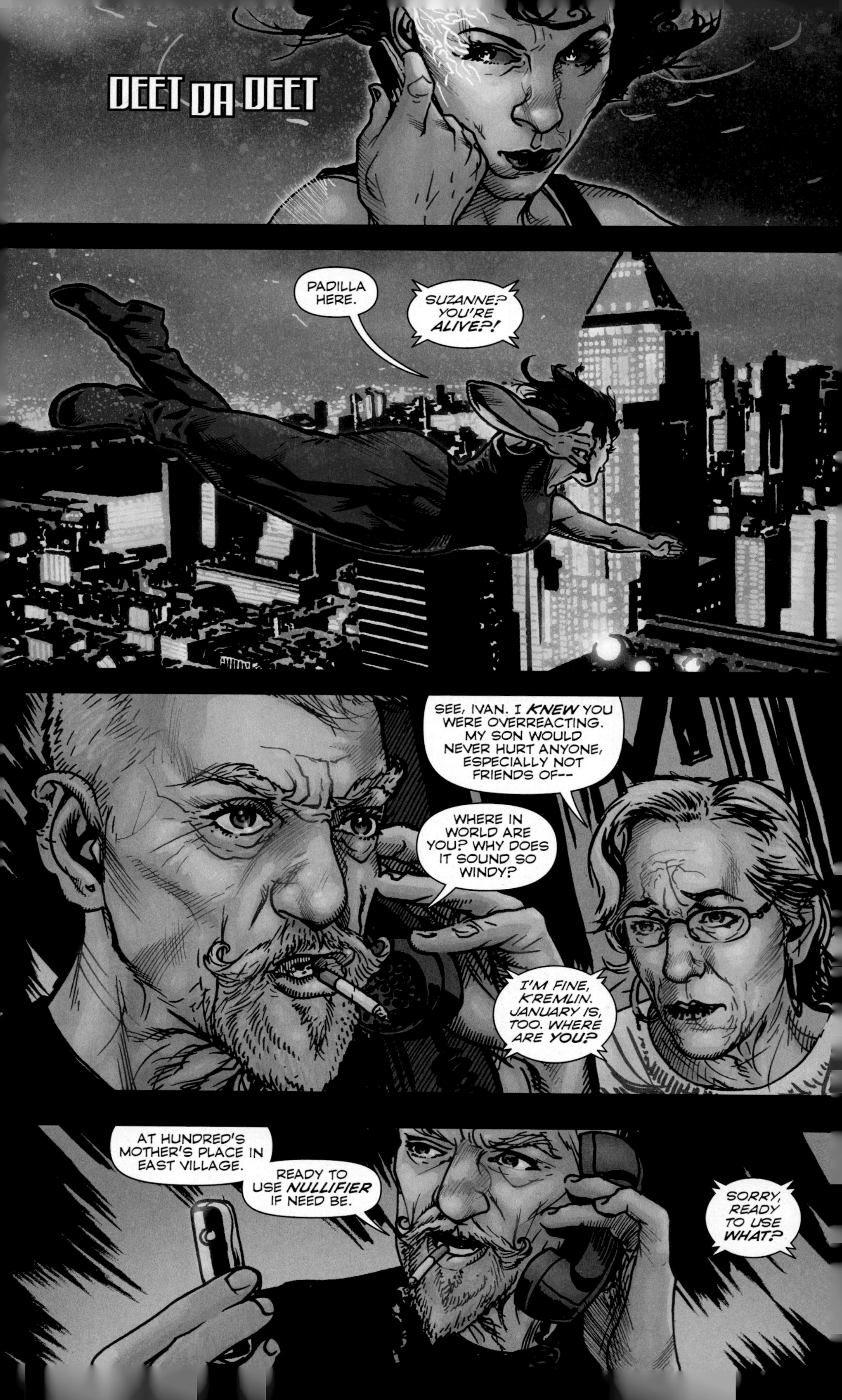
DEET DA DEET
PADILLA HERE.
SUZANNE? YOU'RE ALIVE?!
SEE, IVAN. I KNEW YOU WERE OVERREACTING. MY SON WOULD NEVER HURT ANYONE, ESPECIALLY NOT FRIENDS OF--
WHERE IN WORLD ARE YOU? WHY DOES IT SOUND SO WINDY?
I'M FINE, KREMLIN. JANUARY IS, TOO. WHERE ARE YOU?
AT HUNDRED'S MOTHER'S PLACE IN EAST VILLAGE.
READY TO USE NULLIFIER IF NEED BE.
SORRY, READY TO USE WHAT?

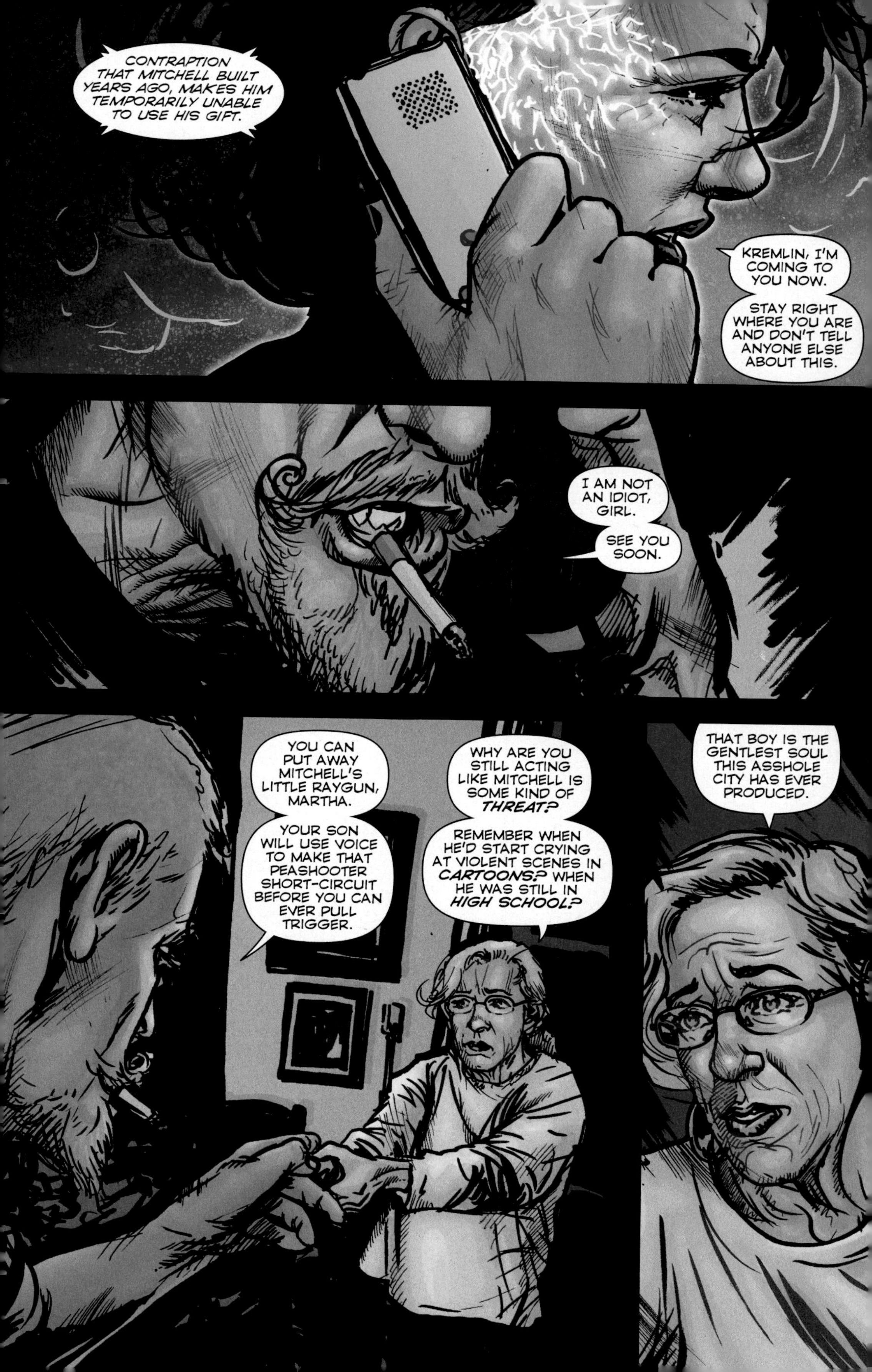
CONTRAPTION THAT MITCHELL BUILT YEARS AGO, MAKES HIM TEMPORARILY UNABLE TO USE HIS GIFT.
KREMLIN, I'M COMING TO YOU NOW.
STAY RIGHT WHERE YOU ARE AND DON'T TELL ANYONE ELSE ABOUT THIS.
I AM NOT AN IDIOT, GIRL.
SEE YOU SOON.
YOU CAN PUT AWAY MITCHELL'S LITTLE RAYGUN, MARTHA.
YOUR SON WILL USE VOICE TO MAKE THAT PEASHOOTER SHORT-CIRCUIT BEFORE YOU CAN EVER PULL TRIGGER.
WHY ARE YOU STILL ACTING LIKE MITCHELL IS SOME KIND OF *THREAT?*
REMEMBER WHEN HE'D START CRYING AT VIOLENT SCENES IN *CARTOONS?* WHEN HE WAS STILL IN *HIGH SCHOOL?*
THAT BOY IS THE GENTLEST SOUL THIS ASSHOLE CITY HAS EVER PRODUCED.

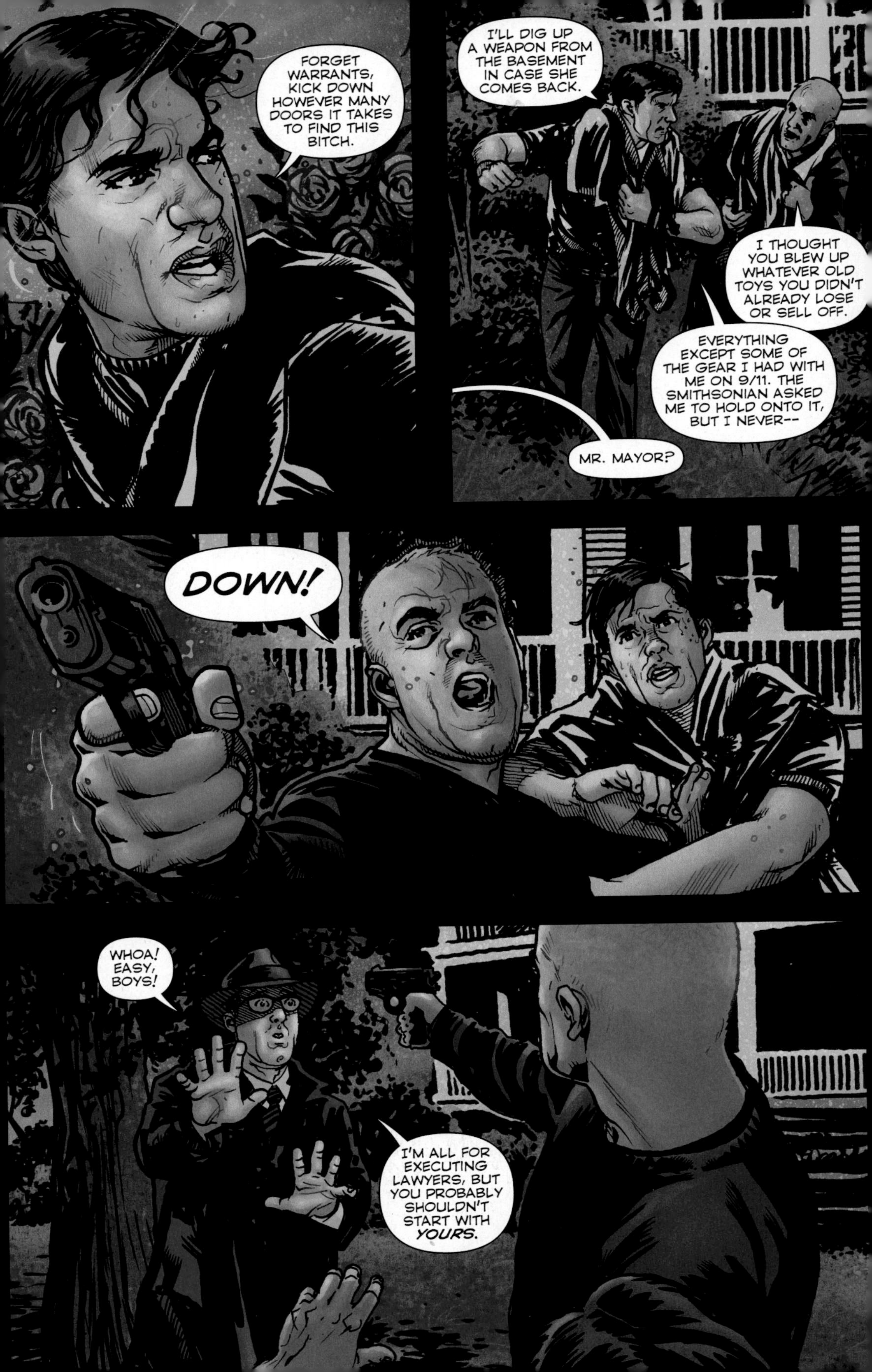
FORGET WARRANTS, KICK DOWN HOWEVER MANY DOORS IT TAKES TO FIND THIS BITCH.
I'LL DIG UP A WEAPON FROM THE BASEMENT IN CASE SHE COMES BACK.
I THOUGHT YOU BLEW UP WHATEVER OLD TOYS YOU DIDN'T ALREADY LOSE OR SELL OFF.
EVERYTHING EXCEPT SOME OF THE GEAR I HAD WITH ME ON 9/11. THE SMITHSONIAN ASKED ME TO HOLD ONTO IT, BUT I NEVER--
MR. MAYOR?
DOWN!
WHOA! EASY, BOYS!
I'M ALL FOR EXECUTING LAWYERS, BUT YOU PROBABLY SHOULDN'T START WITH YOURS.

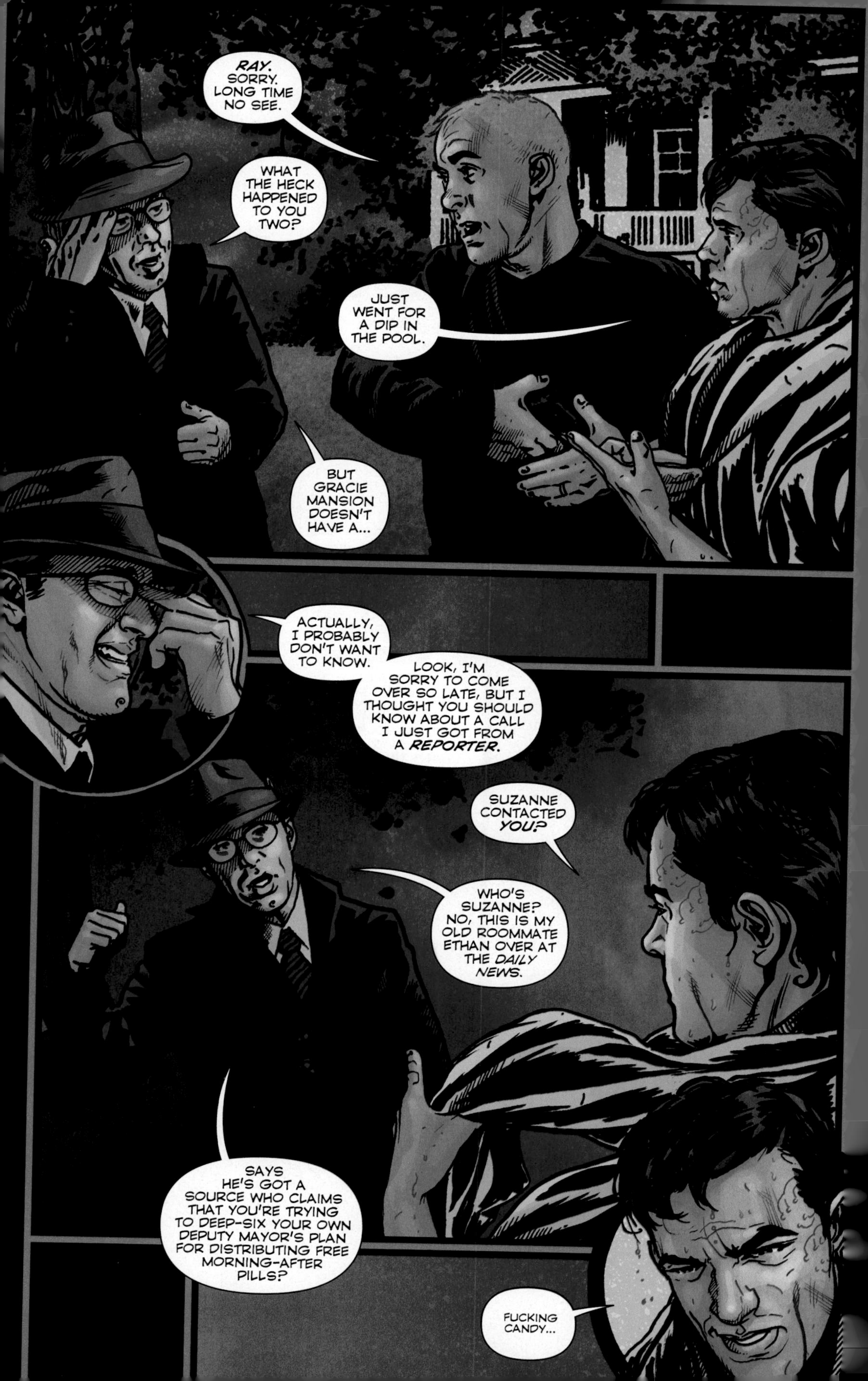
RAY. SORRY. LONG TIME NO SEE.
WHAT THE HECK HAPPENED TO YOU TWO?
JUST WENT FOR A DIP IN THE POOL.
BUT GRACIE MANSION DOESN'T HAVE A...
ACTUALLY, I PROBABLY DON'T WANT TO KNOW.
LOOK, I'M SORRY TO COME OVER SO LATE, BUT I THOUGHT YOU SHOULD KNOW ABOUT A CALL I JUST GOT FROM A REPORTER.
SUZANNE CONTACTED YOU?
WHO'S SUZANNE? NO, THIS IS MY OLD ROOMMATE ETHAN OVER AT THE DAILY NEWS.
SAYS HE'S GOT A SOURCE WHO CLAIMS THAT YOU'RE TRYING TO DEEP-SIX YOUR OWN DEPUTY MAYOR'S PLAN FOR DISTRIBUTING FREE MORNING-AFTER PILLS?
FUCKING CANDY...

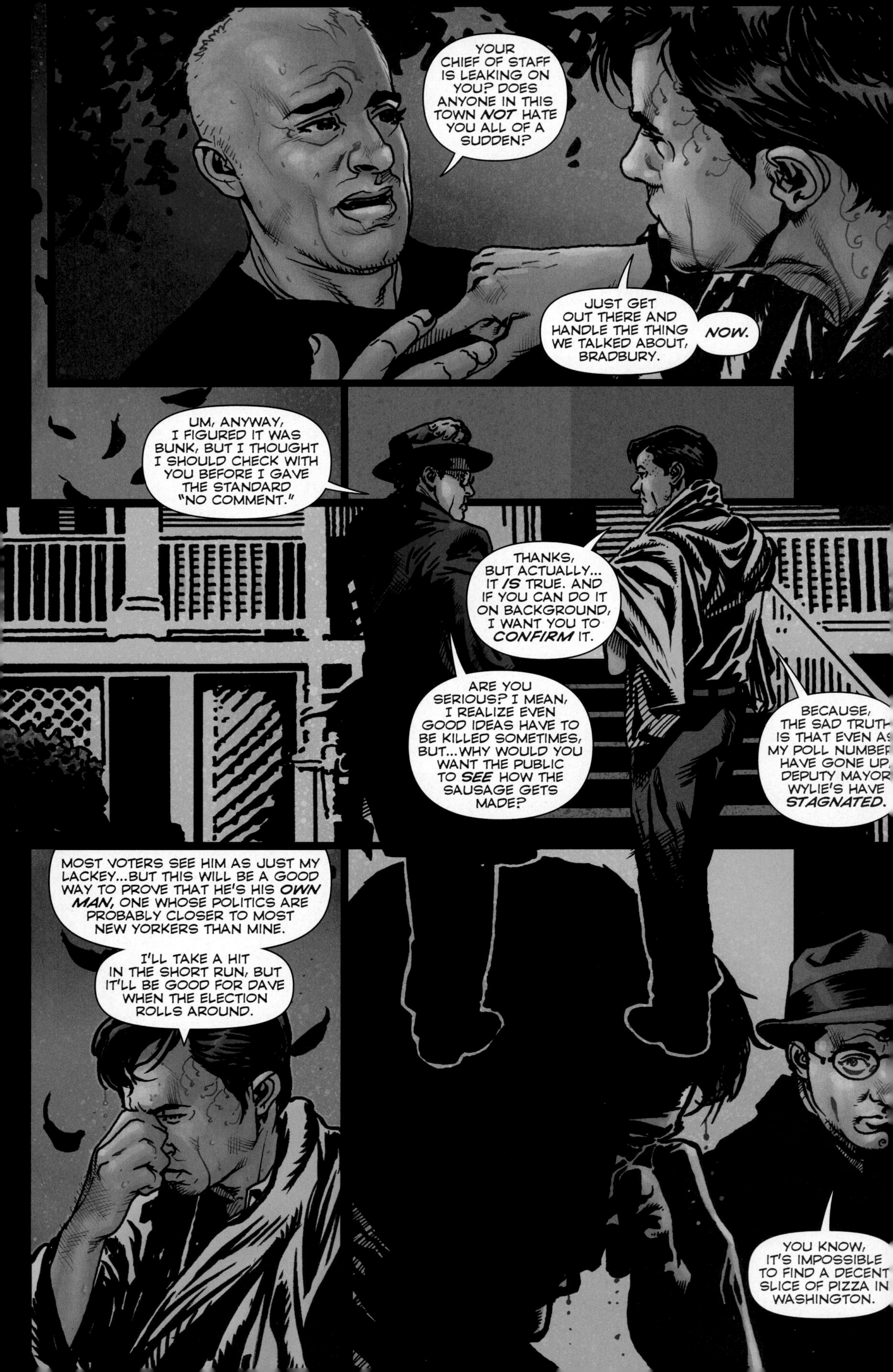
YOUR CHIEF OF STAFF IS LEAKING ON YOU? DOES ANYONE IN THIS TOWN *NOT* HATE YOU ALL OF A SUDDEN?
JUST GET OUT THERE AND HANDLE THE THING WE TALKED ABOUT, BRADBURY.
NOW.
UM, ANYWAY, I FIGURED IT WAS BUNK, BUT I THOUGHT I SHOULD CHECK WITH YOU BEFORE I GAVE THE STANDARD "NO COMMENT."
THANKS, BUT ACTUALLY... IT *IS* TRUE. AND IF YOU CAN DO IT ON BACKGROUND, I WANT YOU TO *CONFIRM* IT.
ARE YOU SERIOUS? I MEAN, I REALIZE EVEN GOOD IDEAS HAVE TO BE KILLED SOMETIMES, BUT...WHY WOULD YOU WANT THE PUBLIC TO *SEE* HOW THE SAUSAGE GETS MADE?
BECAUSE, THE SAD TRUTH IS THAT EVEN AS MY POLL NUMBERS HAVE GONE UP, DEPUTY MAYOR WYLIE'S HAVE *STAGNATED.*
MOST VOTERS SEE HIM AS JUST MY LACKEY...BUT THIS WILL BE A GOOD WAY TO PROVE THAT HE'S HIS *OWN MAN,* ONE WHOSE POLITICS ARE PROBABLY CLOSER TO MOST NEW YORKERS THAN MINE.
I'LL TAKE A HIT IN THE SHORT RUN, BUT IT'LL BE GOOD FOR DAVE WHEN THE ELECTION ROLLS AROUND.
YOU KNOW, IT'S IMPOSSIBLE TO FIND A DECENT SLICE OF PIZZA IN WASHINGTON.

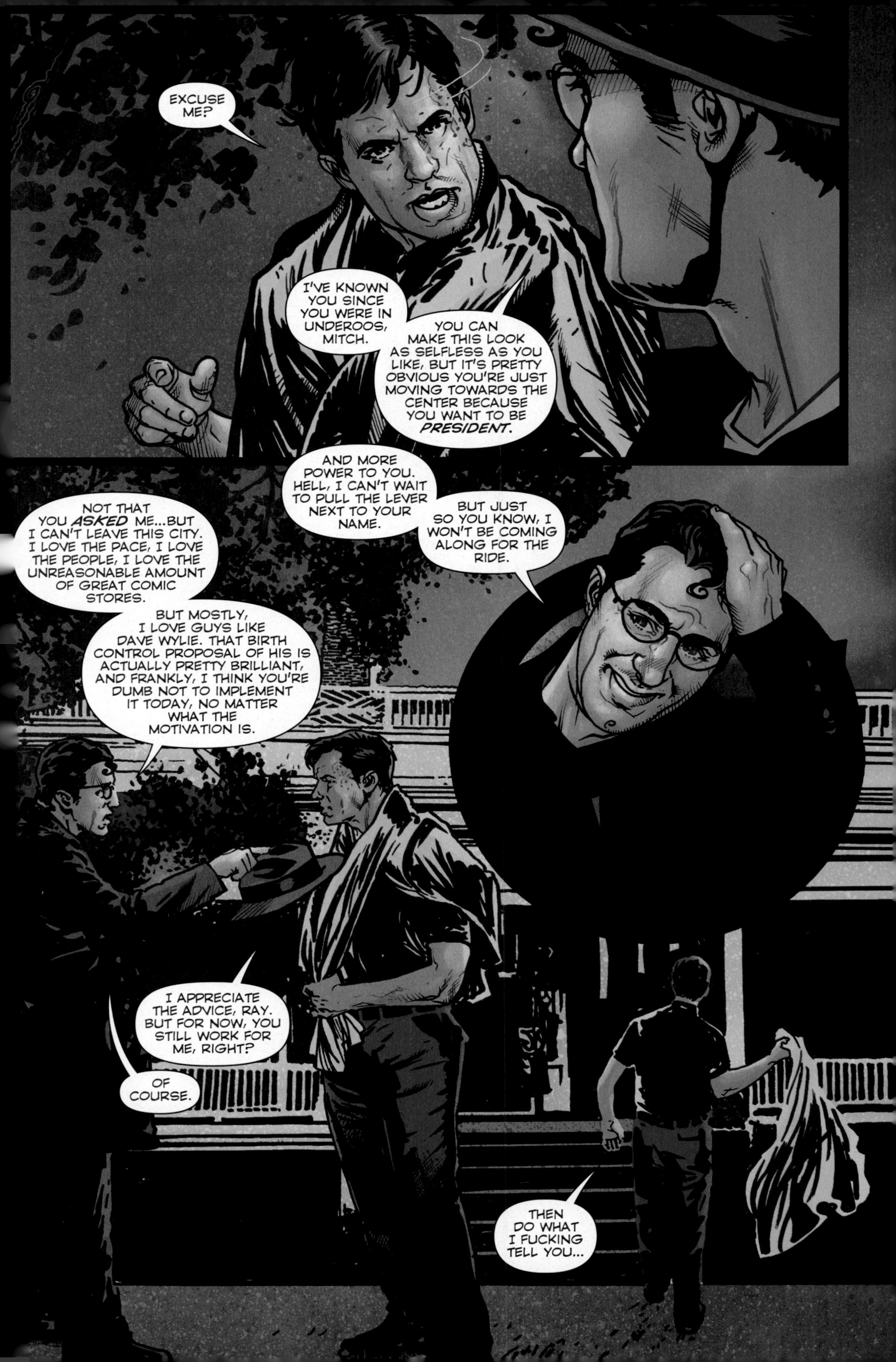

EXCUSE ME?
I'VE KNOWN YOU SINCE YOU WERE IN UNDEROOS, MITCH.
YOU CAN MAKE THIS LOOK AS SELFLESS AS YOU LIKE, BUT IT'S PRETTY OBVIOUS YOU'RE JUST MOVING TOWARDS THE CENTER BECAUSE YOU WANT TO BE *PRESIDENT*.
AND MORE POWER TO YOU. HELL, I CAN'T WAIT TO PULL THE LEVER NEXT TO YOUR NAME.
BUT JUST SO YOU KNOW, I WON'T BE COMING ALONG FOR THE RIDE.
NOT THAT YOU *ASKED* ME...BUT I CAN'T LEAVE THIS CITY. I LOVE THE PACE, I LOVE THE PEOPLE, I LOVE THE UNREASONABLE AMOUNT OF GREAT COMIC STORES.
BUT MOSTLY, I LOVE GUYS LIKE DAVE WYLIE. THAT BIRTH CONTROL PROPOSAL OF HIS IS ACTUALLY PRETTY BRILLIANT, AND FRANKLY, I THINK YOU'RE DUMB NOT TO IMPLEMENT IT TODAY, NO MATTER WHAT THE MOTIVATION IS.
I APPRECIATE THE ADVICE, RAY. BUT FOR NOW, YOU STILL WORK FOR ME, RIGHT?
OF COURSE.
THEN DO WHAT I FUCKING TELL YOU...

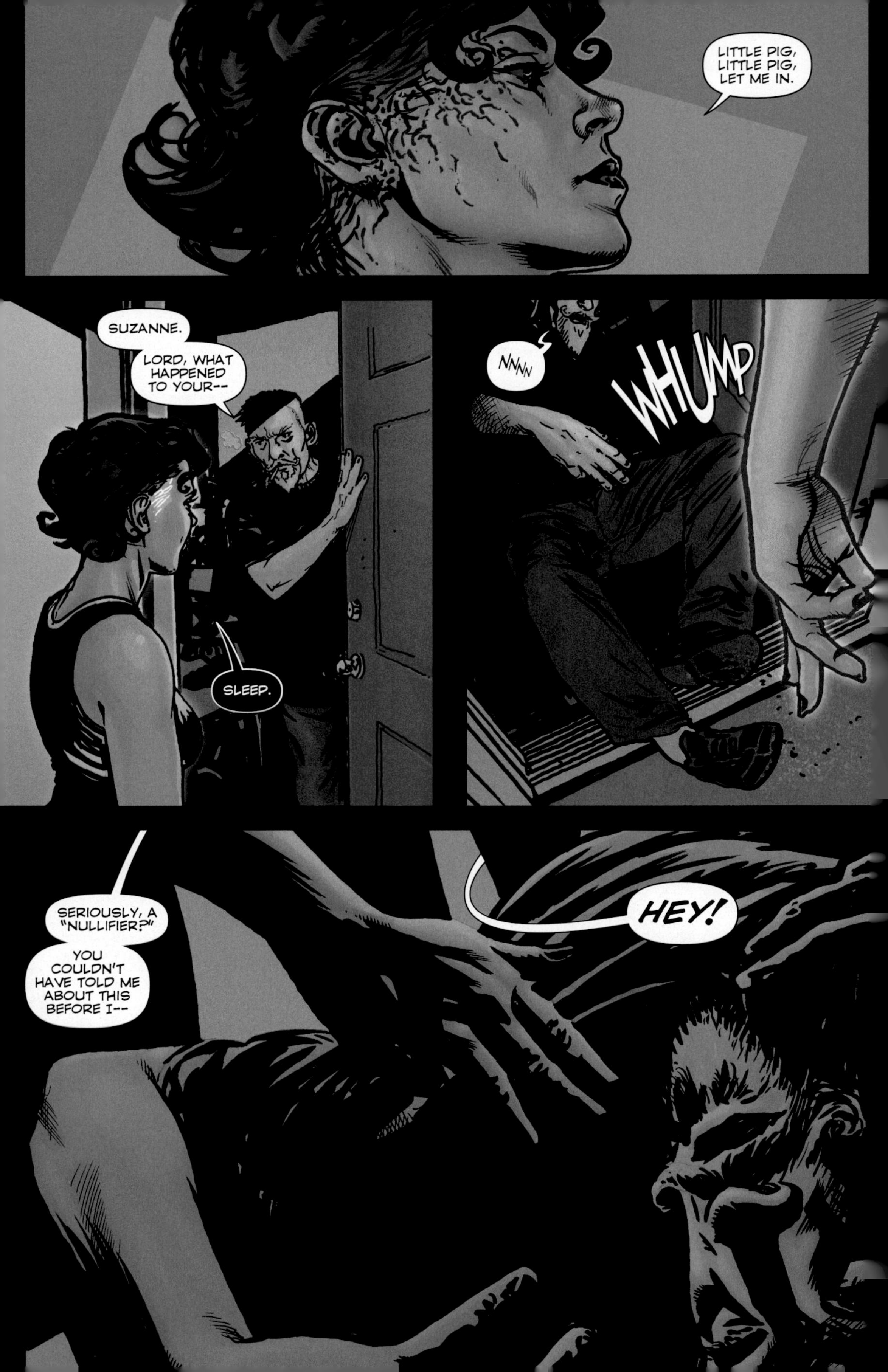
LITTLE PIG, LITTLE PIG, LET ME IN.
SUZANNE.
LORD, WHAT HAPPENED TO YOUR--
SLEEP.
NNNN
WHUMP
SERIOUSLY, A "NULLIFIER?"
YOU COULDN'T HAVE TOLD ME ABOUT THIS BEFORE I--
HEY!

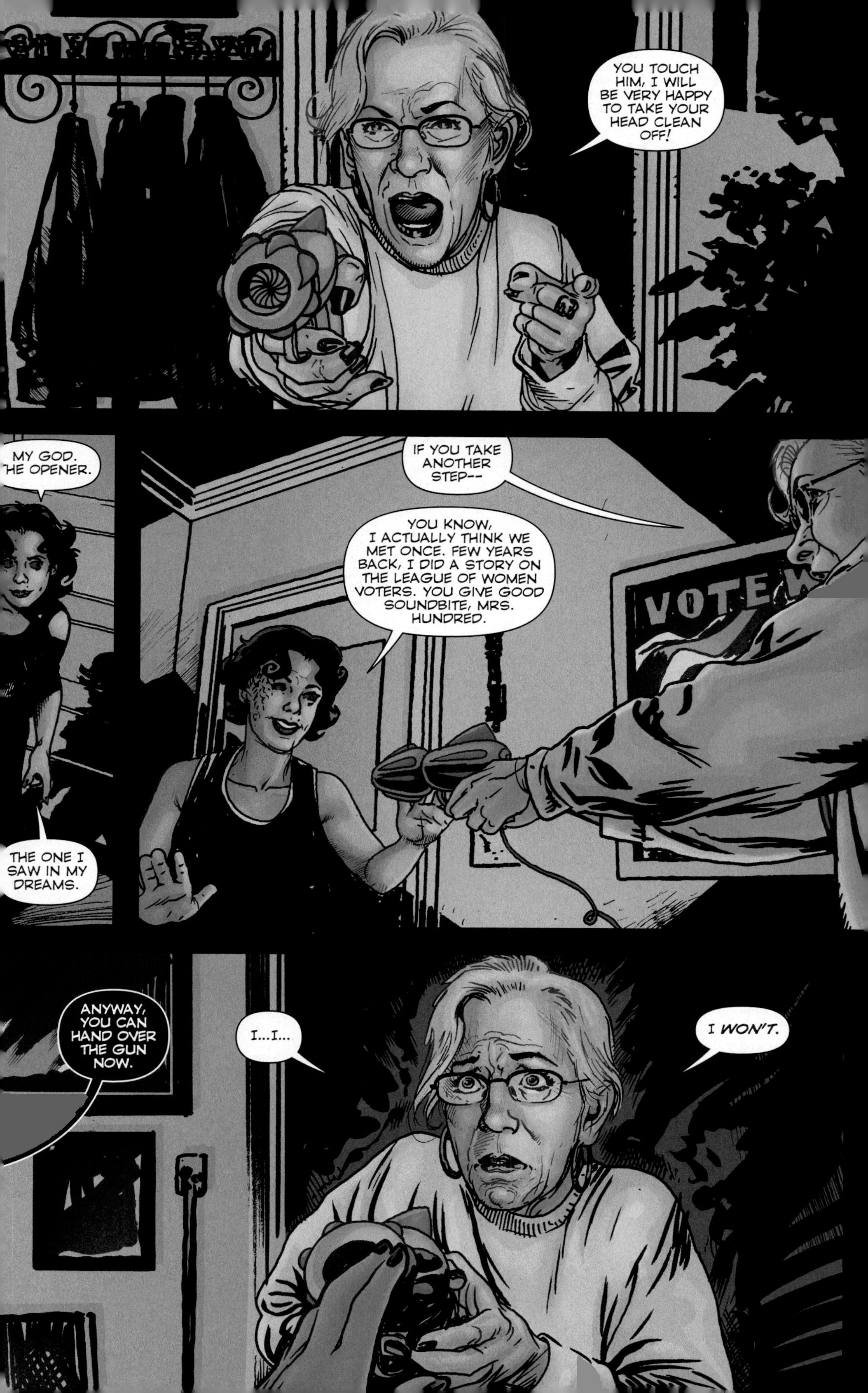
YOU TOUCH HIM, I WILL BE VERY HAPPY TO TAKE YOUR HEAD CLEAN OFF!
MY GOD. THE OPENER.
THE ONE I SAW IN MY DREAMS.
IF YOU TAKE ANOTHER STEP--
YOU KNOW, I ACTUALLY THINK WE MET ONCE. FEW YEARS BACK, I DID A STORY ON THE LEAGUE OF WOMEN VOTERS. YOU GIVE GOOD SOUNDBITE, MRS. HUNDRED.
VOTE
ANYWAY, YOU CAN HAND OVER THE GUN NOW.
I...I...
I *WON'T*.

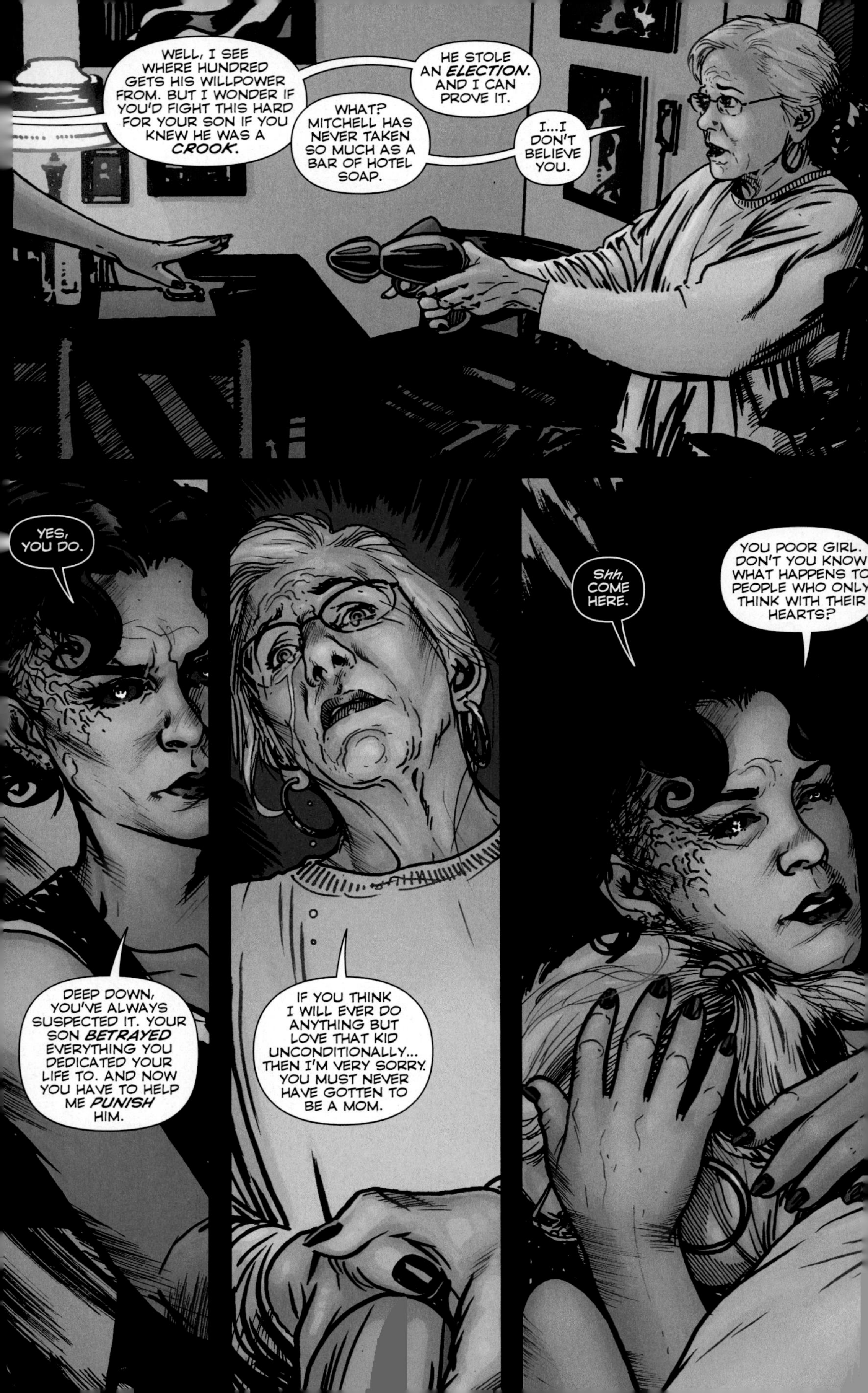
WELL, I SEE WHERE HUNDRED GETS HIS WILLPOWER FROM. BUT I WONDER IF YOU'D FIGHT THIS HARD FOR YOUR SON IF YOU KNEW HE WAS A *CROOK*.
WHAT? MITCHELL HAS NEVER TAKEN SO MUCH AS A BAR OF HOTEL SOAP.
HE STOLE AN *ELECTION*. AND I CAN PROVE IT.
I...I DON'T BELIEVE YOU.
YES, YOU DO.
DEEP DOWN, YOU'VE ALWAYS SUSPECTED IT. YOUR SON *BETRAYED* EVERYTHING YOU DEDICATED YOUR LIFE TO. AND NOW YOU HAVE TO HELP ME *PUNISH* HIM.
IF YOU THINK I WILL EVER DO ANYTHING BUT LOVE THAT KID UNCONDITIONALLY... THEN I'M VERY SORRY. YOU MUST NEVER HAVE GOTTEN TO BE A MOM.
Shh, COME HERE.
YOU POOR GIRL. DON'T YOU KNOW WHAT HAPPENS TO PEOPLE WHO ONLY THINK WITH THEIR HEARTS?

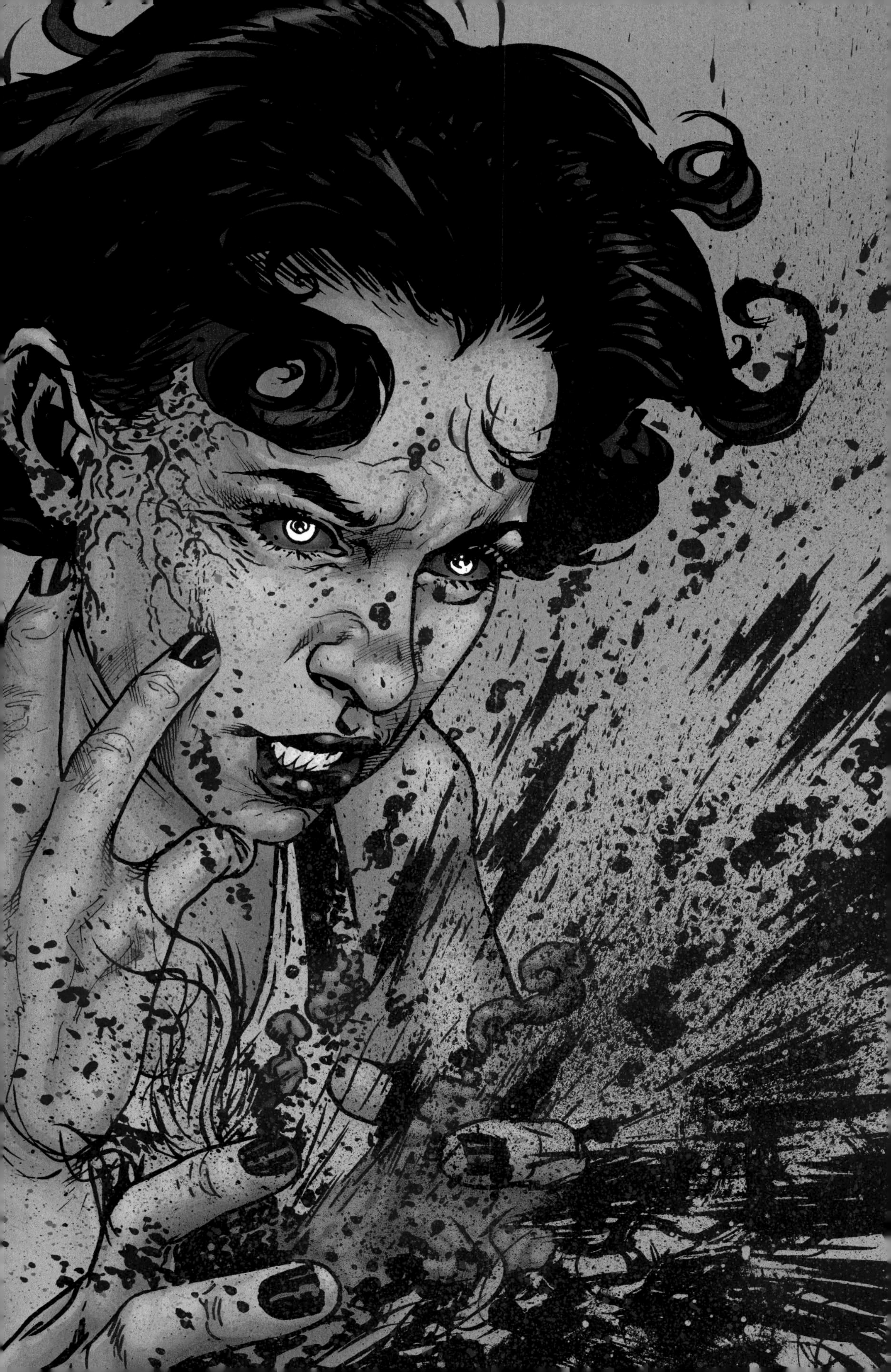

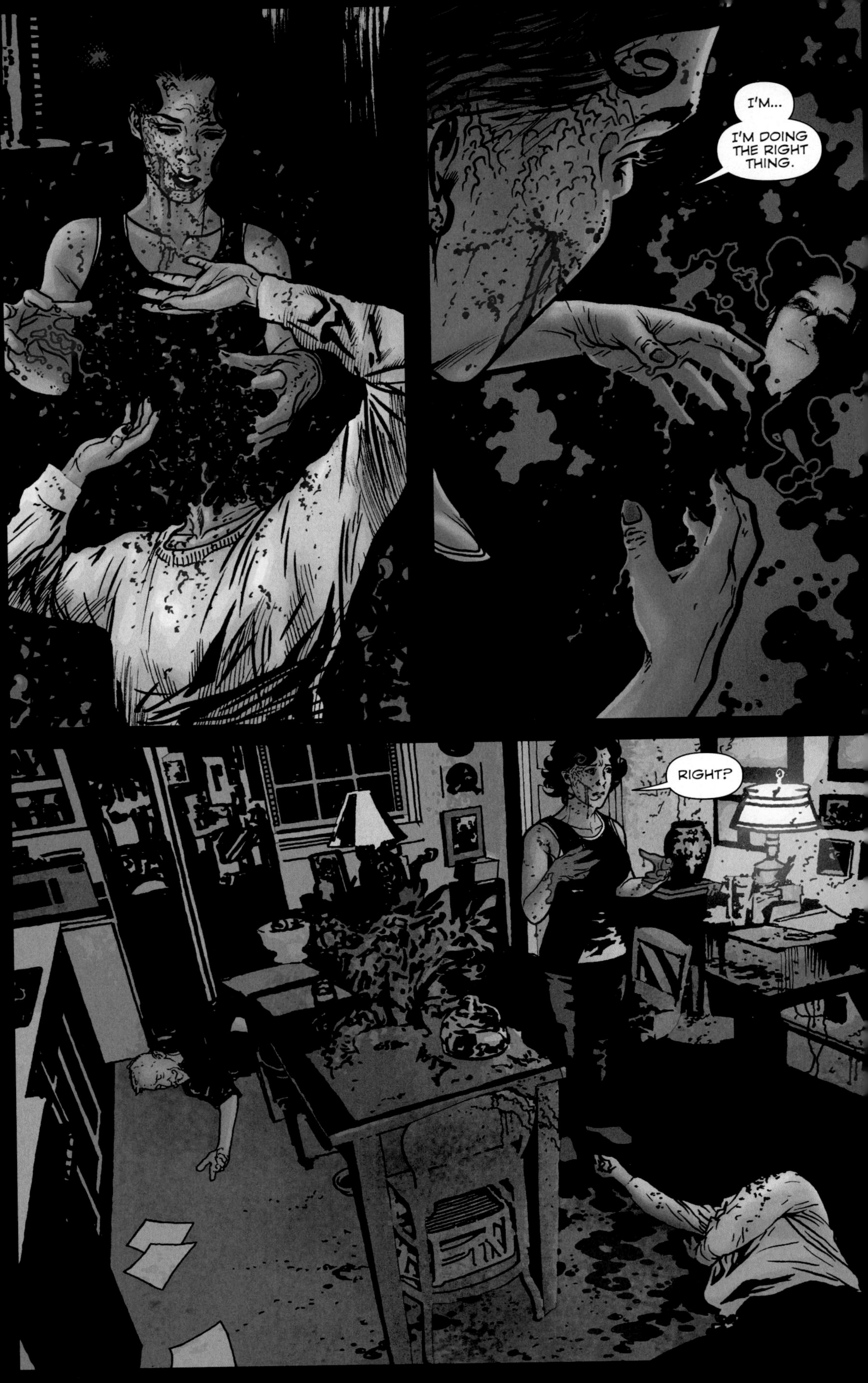
I'M...
I'M DOING THE RIGHT THING.
RIGHT?

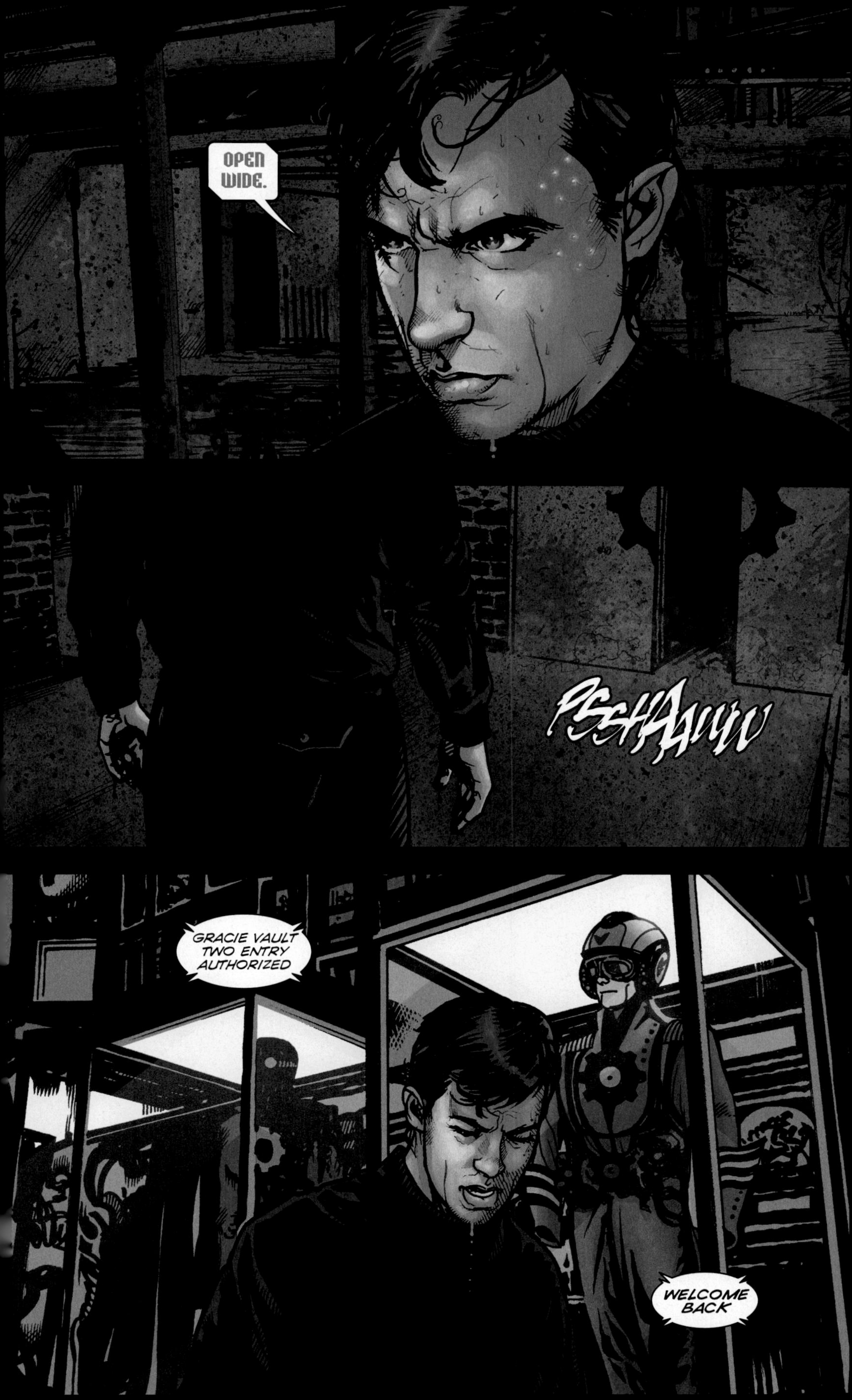

OPEN WIDE.
PSSHAAWW
GRACIE VAULT TWO ENTRY AUTHORIZED
WELCOME BACK

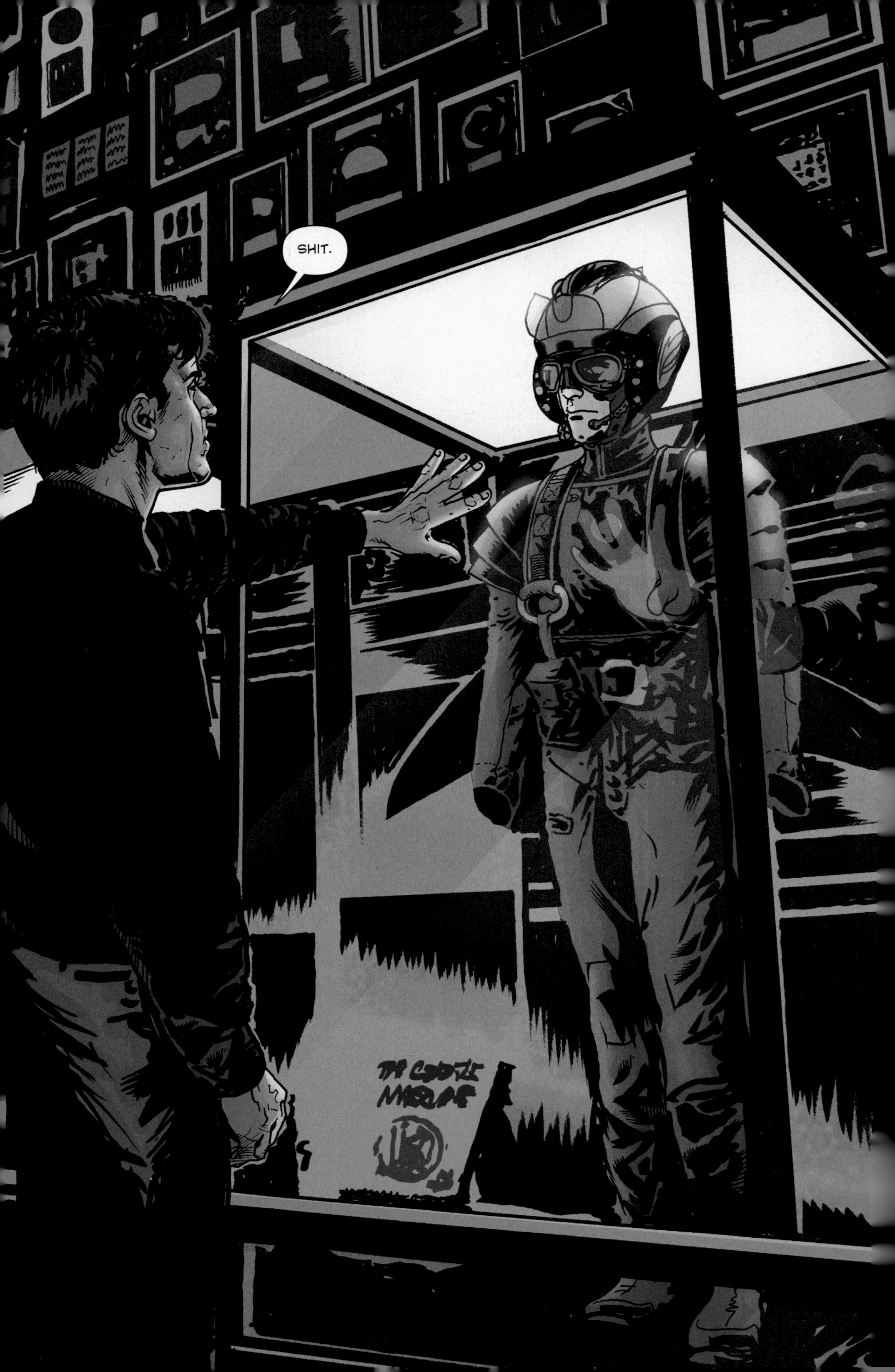
SHIT.

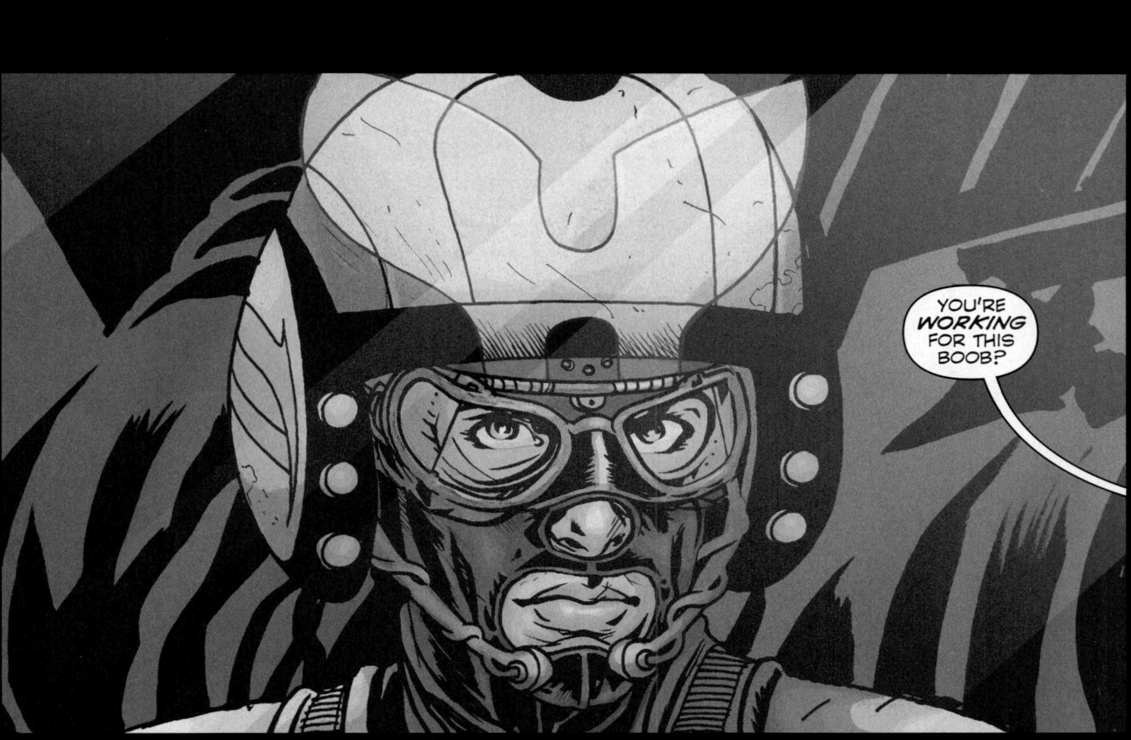
YOU'RE WORKING FOR THIS BOOB?

MONDAY, JANUARY 5, 2002

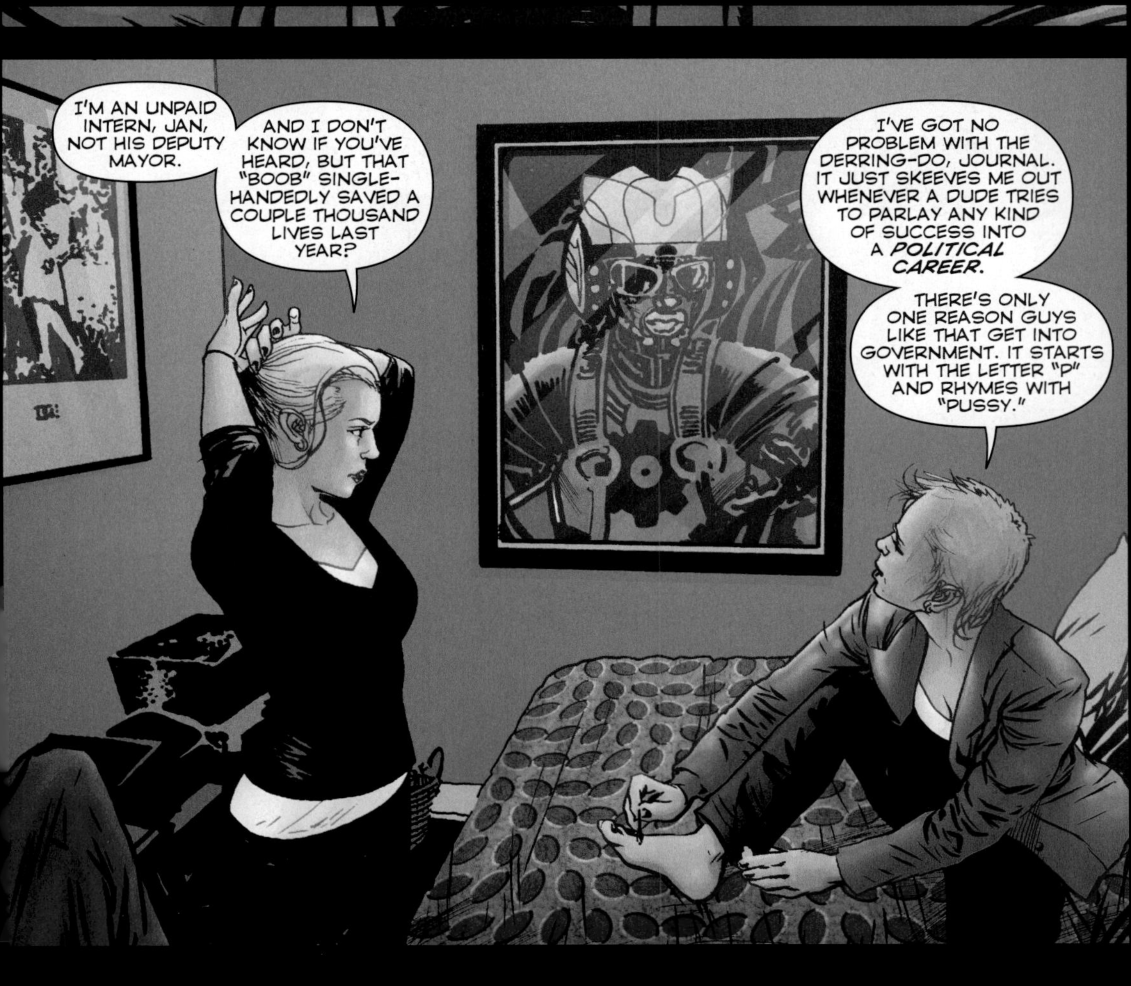
I'M AN UNPAID INTERN, JAN, NOT HIS DEPUTY MAYOR.
AND I DON'T KNOW IF YOU'VE HEARD, BUT THAT "BOOB" SINGLE-HANDEDLY SAVED A COUPLE THOUSAND LIVES LAST YEAR?
I'VE GOT NO PROBLEM WITH THE DERRING-DO, JOURNAL. IT JUST SKEEVES ME OUT WHENEVER A DUDE TRIES TO PARLAY ANY KIND OF SUCCESS INTO A POLITICAL CAREER.
THERE'S ONLY ONE REASON GUYS LIKE THAT GET INTO GOVERNMENT. IT STARTS WITH THE LETTER "P" AND RHYMES WITH "PUSSY."

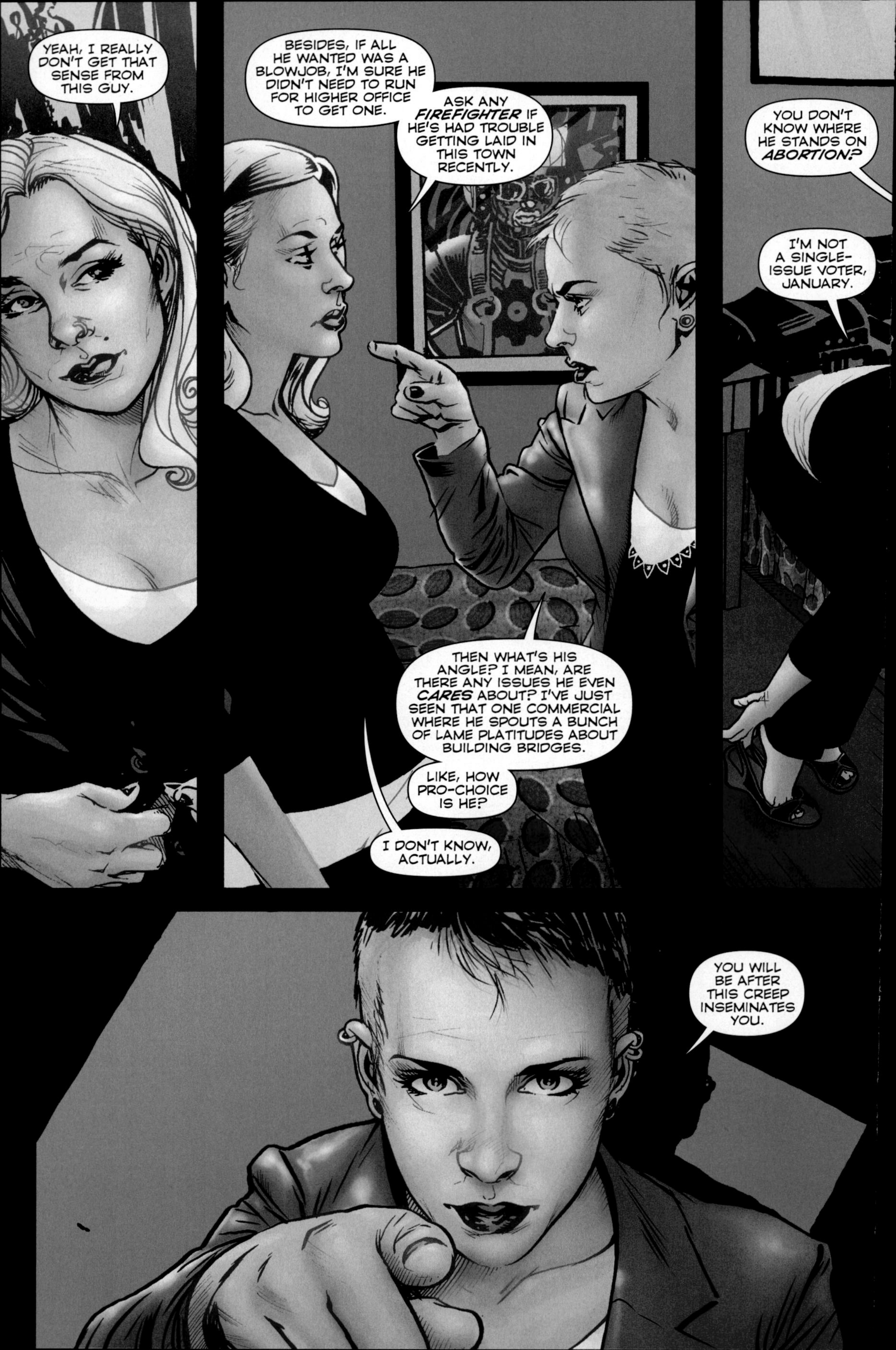
YEAH, I REALLY DON'T GET THAT SENSE FROM THIS GUY.
BESIDES, IF ALL HE WANTED WAS A BLOWJOB, I'M SURE HE DIDN'T NEED TO RUN FOR HIGHER OFFICE TO GET ONE.
ASK ANY *FIREFIGHTER* IF HE'S HAD TROUBLE GETTING LAID IN THIS TOWN RECENTLY.
THEN WHAT'S HIS ANGLE? I MEAN, ARE THERE ANY ISSUES HE EVEN *CARES* ABOUT? I'VE JUST SEEN THAT ONE COMMERCIAL WHERE HE SPOUTS A BUNCH OF LAME PLATITUDES ABOUT BUILDING BRIDGES.
LIKE, HOW PRO-CHOICE IS HE?
I DON'T KNOW, ACTUALLY.
YOU DON'T KNOW WHERE HE STANDS ON *ABORTION?*
I'M NOT A SINGLE-ISSUE VOTER, JANUARY.
YOU WILL BE AFTER THIS CREEP INSEMINATES YOU.

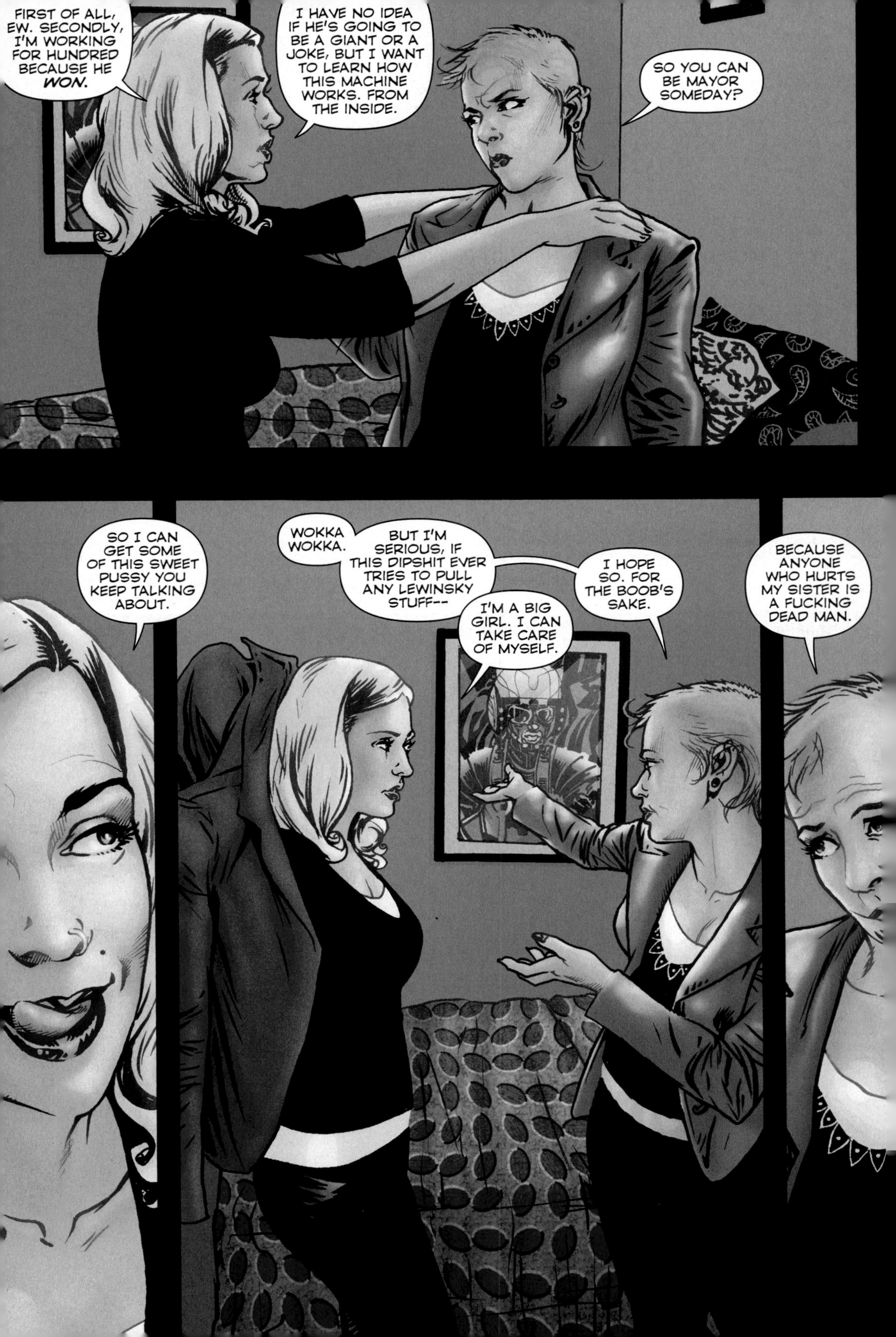
FIRST OF ALL, EW. SECONDLY, I'M WORKING FOR HUNDRED BECAUSE HE *WON*.
I HAVE NO IDEA IF HE'S GOING TO BE A GIANT OR A JOKE, BUT I WANT TO LEARN HOW THIS MACHINE WORKS. FROM THE INSIDE.
SO YOU CAN BE MAYOR SOMEDAY?
SO I CAN GET SOME OF THIS SWEET PUSSY YOU KEEP TALKING ABOUT.
WOKKA WOKKA.
BUT I'M SERIOUS, IF THIS DIPSHIT EVER TRIES TO PULL ANY LEWINSKY STUFF--
I'M A BIG GIRL. I CAN TAKE CARE OF MYSELF.
I HOPE SO. FOR THE BOOB'S SAKE.
BECAUSE ANYONE WHO HURTS MY SISTER IS A FUCKING DEAD MAN.

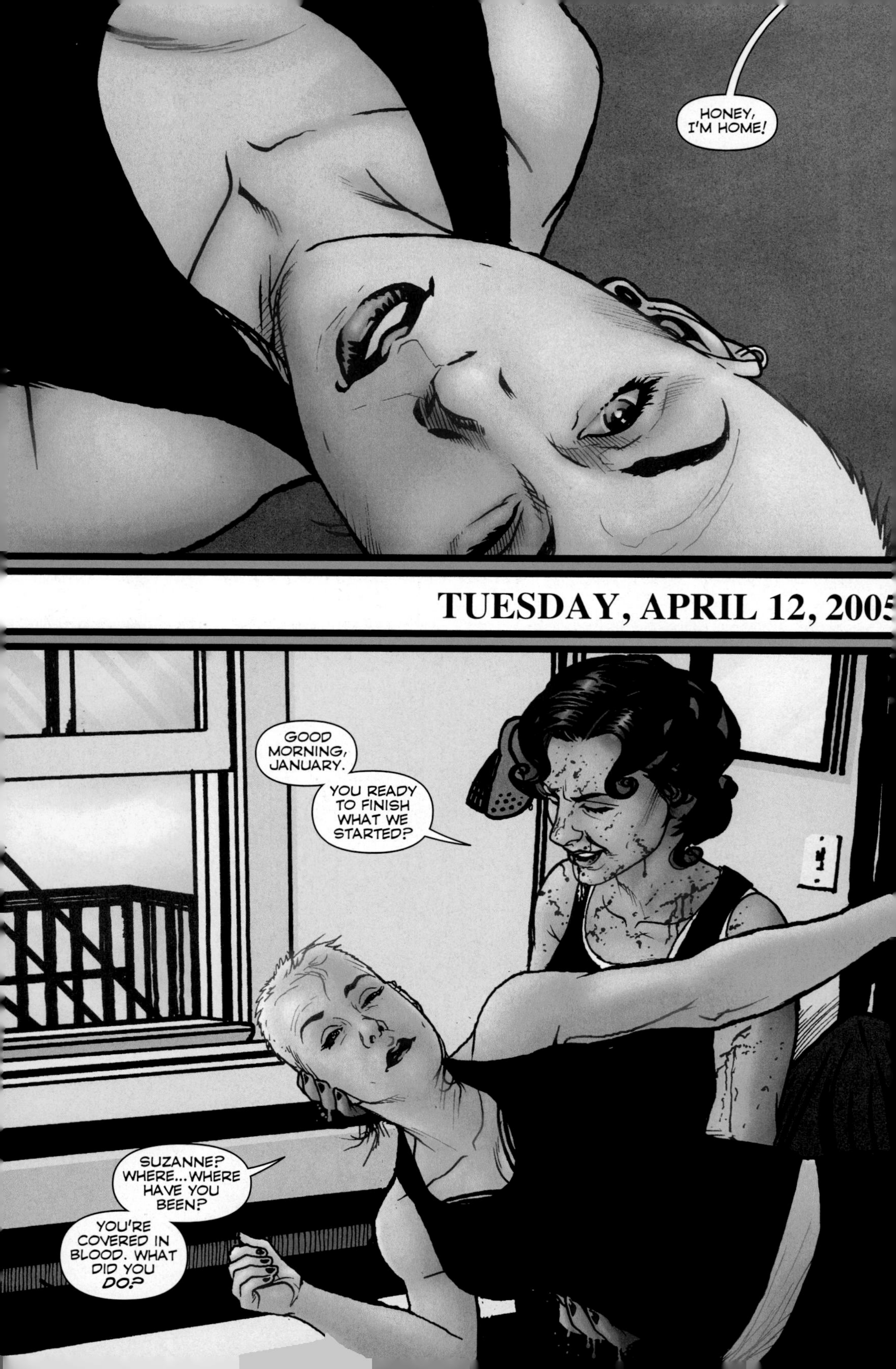
HONEY, I'M HOME!
TUESDAY, APRIL 12, 2005
GOOD MORNING, JANUARY.
YOU READY TO FINISH WHAT WE STARTED?
SUZANNE? WHERE...WHERE HAVE YOU BEEN?
YOU'RE COVERED IN BLOOD. WHAT DID YOU *DO?*

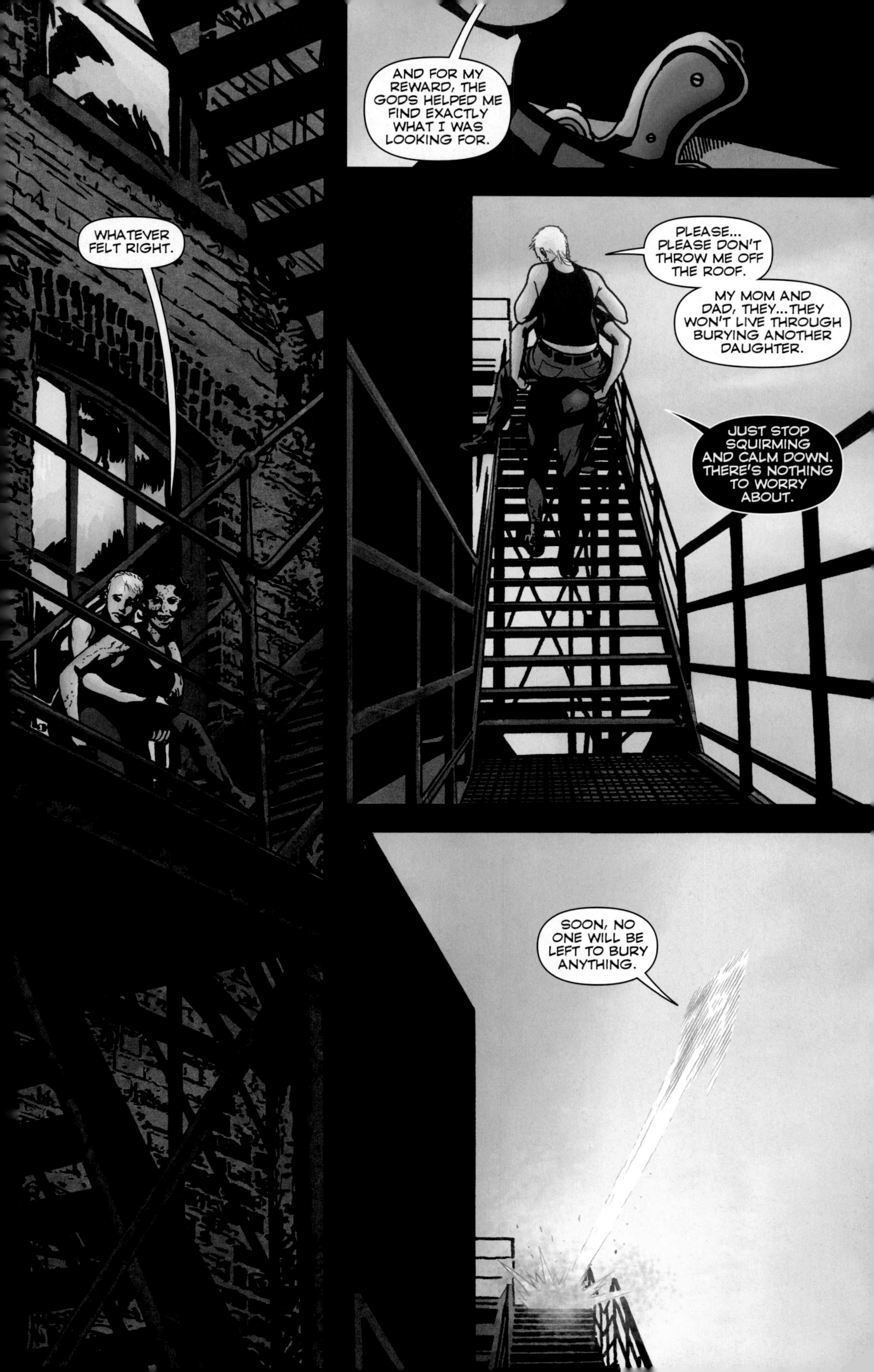
AND FOR MY REWARD, THE GODS HELPED ME FIND EXACTLY WHAT I WAS LOOKING FOR.
WHATEVER FELT RIGHT.
PLEASE... PLEASE DON'T THROW ME OFF THE ROOF.
MY MOM AND DAD, THEY...THEY WON'T LIVE THROUGH BURYING ANOTHER DAUGHTER.
JUST STOP SQUIRMING AND CALM DOWN. THERE'S NOTHING TO WORRY ABOUT.
SOON, NO ONE WILL BE LEFT TO BURY ANYTHING.

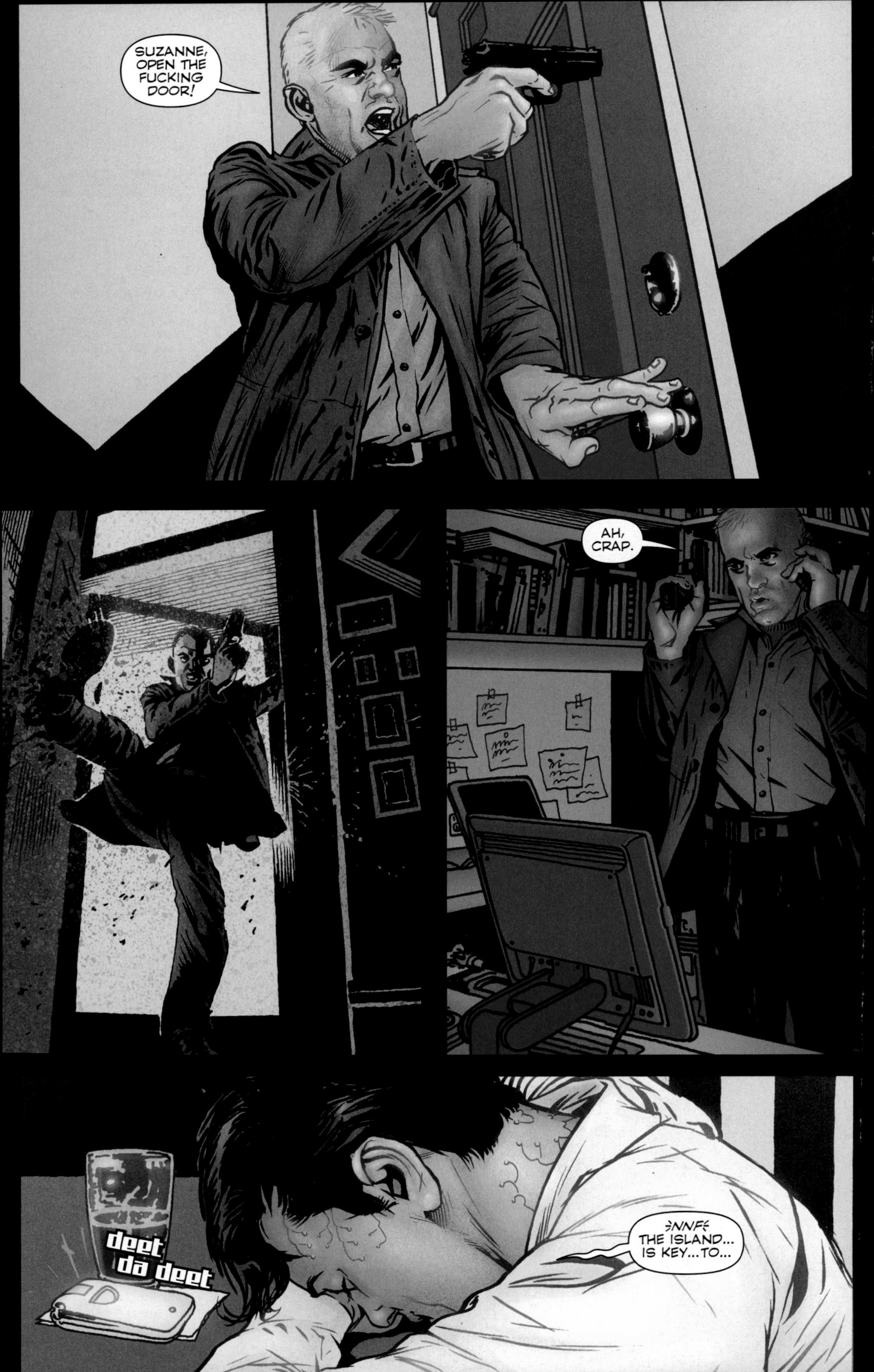
SUZANNE, OPEN THE FUCKING DOOR!
AH, CRAP.
deet da deet
NNF THE ISLAND... IS KEY...TO...

...BRADBURY?

YOU OKAY, BOSS? YOU SOUND HUNGOVER.

HAVEN'T HAD A DROP. BEEN UP ALL NIGHT...WEIGHING OPTIONS, I GUESS. ANY LUCK ON YOUR FRONT?

I JUST BUSTED INTO SUZANNE'S OLD APARTMENT, DOESN'T LOOK LIKE SHE'S BEEN HERE IN DAYS. BUT SHE LEFT HER COMPUTER ON SOMETHING CALLED "FACEBOOK."

WHAT THE HELL IS THAT?

NO CLUE, BUT THE PAGE SHE WAS LAST LOOKING AT HAS GOT A BUNCH OF INFO ON ONE GIRL: JANUARY MOORE.

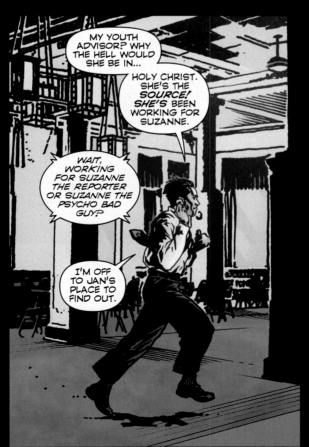

MY YOUTH ADVISOR? WHY THE HELL WOULD SHE BE IN...

HOLY CHRIST. SHE'S THE SOURCE! SHE'S BEEN WORKING FOR SUZANNE.

WAIT, WORKING FOR SUZANNE THE REPORTER OR SUZANNE THE PSYCHO BAD GUY?

I'M OFF TO JAN'S PLACE TO FIND OUT.

LIKE FUCK!

I'LL GO. YOU EVEN THINK OF TRYING SOMETHING, I CALL COMMISSIONER ANGOTTI AND DROP A DIME ON YOUR ASS MYSELF.

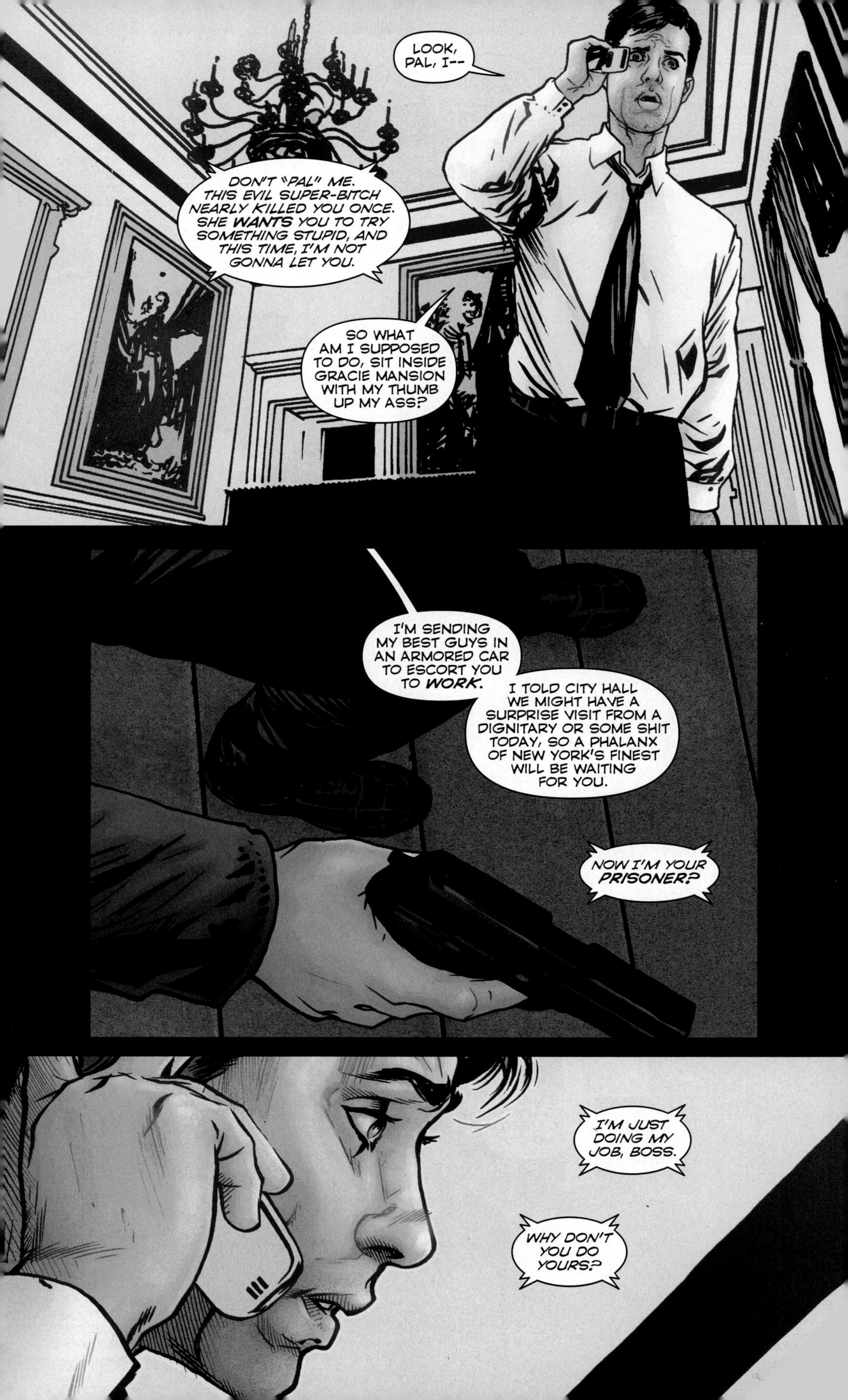

LOOK, PAL, I--
DON'T "PAL" ME. THIS EVIL SUPER-BITCH NEARLY KILLED YOU ONCE. SHE WANTS YOU TO TRY SOMETHING STUPID, AND THIS TIME, I'M NOT GONNA LET YOU.
SO WHAT AM I SUPPOSED TO DO, SIT INSIDE GRACIE MANSION WITH MY THUMB UP MY ASS?
I'M SENDING MY BEST GUYS IN AN ARMORED CAR TO ESCORT YOU TO WORK.
I TOLD CITY HALL WE MIGHT HAVE A SURPRISE VISIT FROM A DIGNITARY OR SOME SHIT TODAY, SO A PHALANX OF NEW YORK'S FINEST WILL BE WAITING FOR YOU.
NOW I'M YOUR PRISONER?
I'M JUST DOING MY JOB, BOSS.
WHY DON'T YOU DO YOURS?

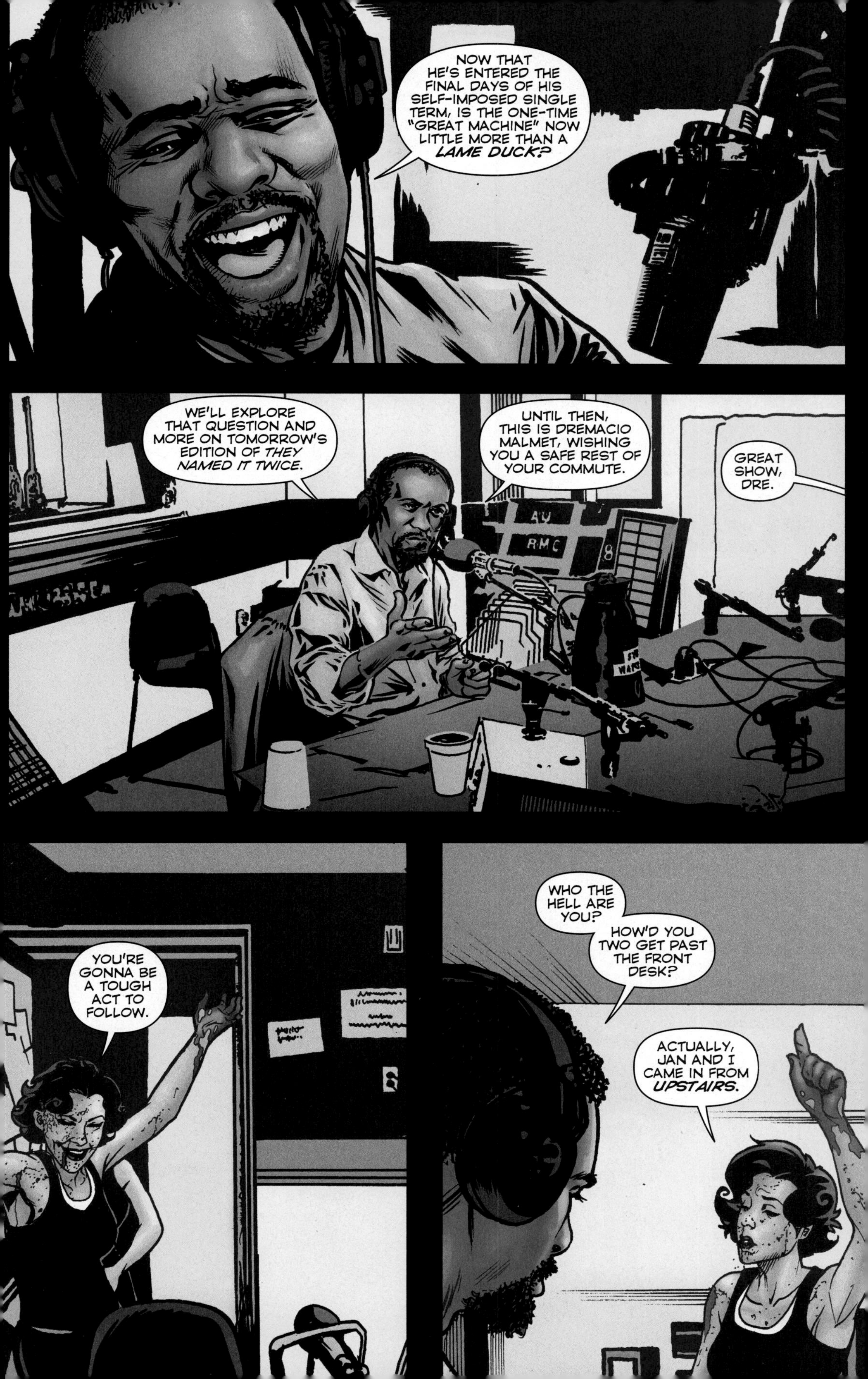
NOW THAT HE'S ENTERED THE FINAL DAYS OF HIS SELF-IMPOSED SINGLE TERM, IS THE ONE-TIME "GREAT MACHINE" NOW LITTLE MORE THAN A *LAME DUCK?*
WE'LL EXPLORE THAT QUESTION AND MORE ON TOMORROW'S EDITION OF *THEY NAMED IT TWICE.*
UNTIL THEN, THIS IS DREMACIO MALMET, WISHING YOU A SAFE REST OF YOUR COMMUTE.
GREAT SHOW, DRE.
YOU'RE GONNA BE A TOUGH ACT TO FOLLOW.
WHO THE HELL ARE YOU?
HOW'D YOU TWO GET PAST THE FRONT DESK?
ACTUALLY, JAN AND I CAME IN FROM *UPSTAIRS.*

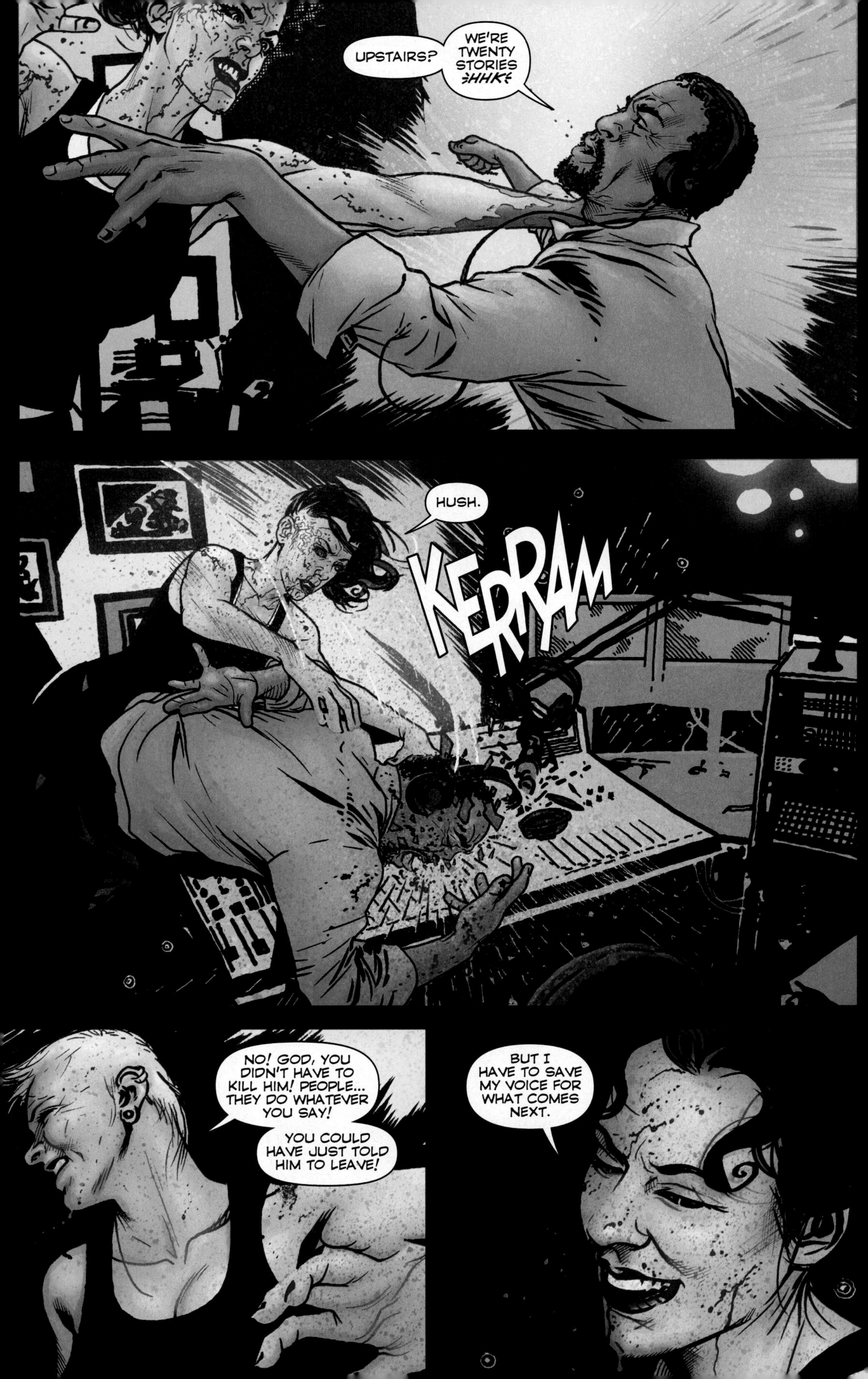
UPSTAIRS?
WE'RE TWENTY STORIES HHK
HUSH.
KERRAM
NO! GOD, YOU DIDN'T HAVE TO KILL HIM! PEOPLE... THEY DO WHATEVER YOU SAY!
YOU COULD HAVE JUST TOLD HIM TO LEAVE!
BUT I HAVE TO SAVE MY VOICE FOR WHAT COMES NEXT.

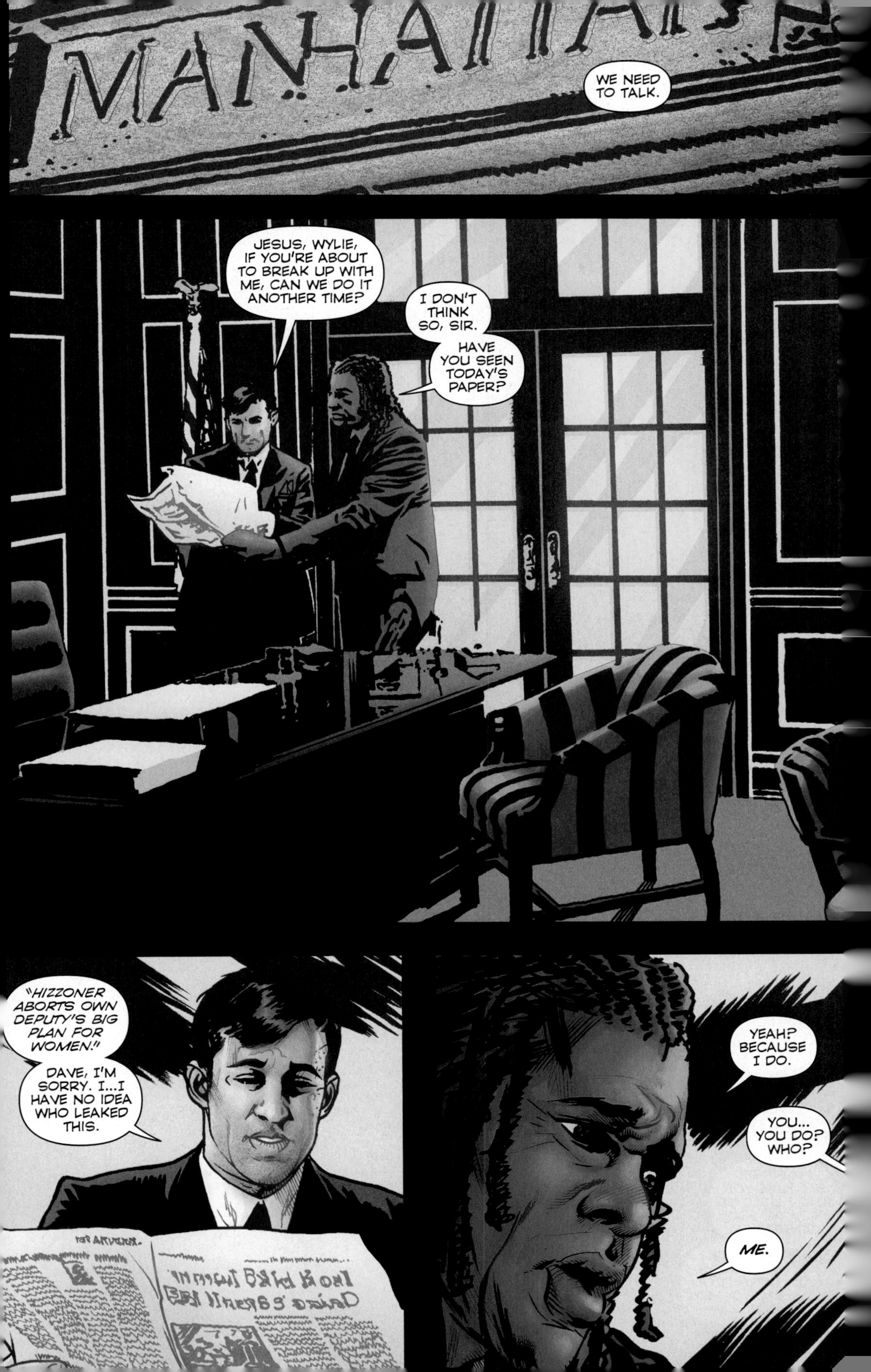
WE NEED TO TALK.
JESUS, WYLIE, IF YOU'RE ABOUT TO BREAK UP WITH ME, CAN WE DO IT ANOTHER TIME?
I DON'T THINK SO, SIR.
HAVE YOU SEEN TODAY'S PAPER?
"HIZZONER ABORTS OWN DEPUTY'S BIG PLAN FOR WOMEN."
DAVE, I'M SORRY. I...I HAVE NO IDEA WHO LEAKED THIS.
YEAH? BECAUSE I DO.
YOU... YOU DO? WHO?
ME.

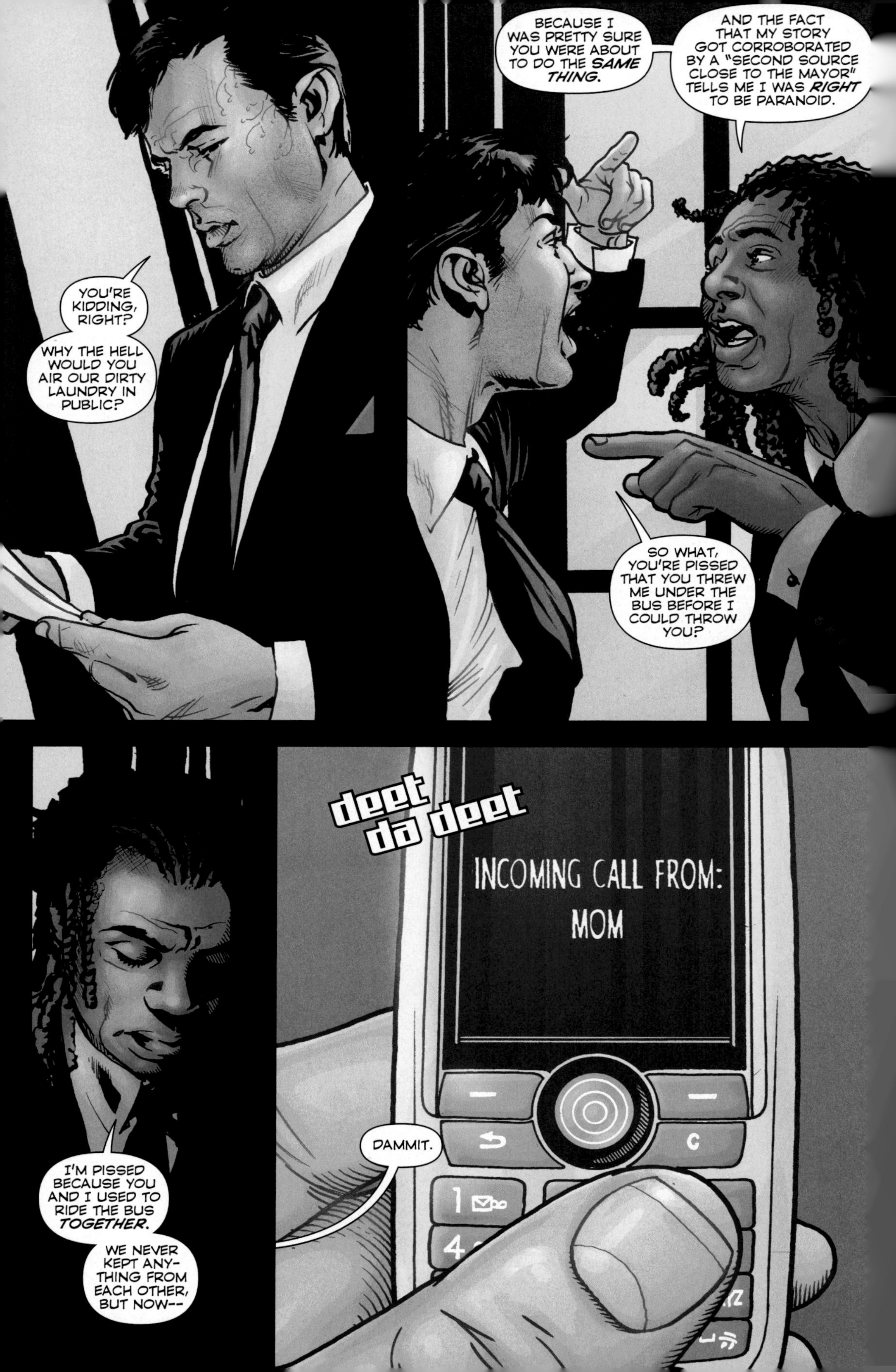
YOU'RE KIDDING, RIGHT?
WHY THE HELL WOULD YOU AIR OUR DIRTY LAUNDRY IN PUBLIC?
BECAUSE I WAS PRETTY SURE YOU WERE ABOUT TO DO THE SAME THING.
AND THE FACT THAT MY STORY GOT CORROBORATED BY A "SECOND SOURCE CLOSE TO THE MAYOR" TELLS ME I WAS RIGHT TO BE PARANOID.
SO WHAT, YOU'RE PISSED THAT YOU THREW ME UNDER THE BUS BEFORE I COULD THROW YOU?
deet da deet
INCOMING CALL FROM:
MOM
I'M PISSED BECAUSE YOU AND I USED TO RIDE THE BUS TOGETHER.
WE NEVER KEPT ANY-THING FROM EACH OTHER, BUT NOW--
DAMMIT.

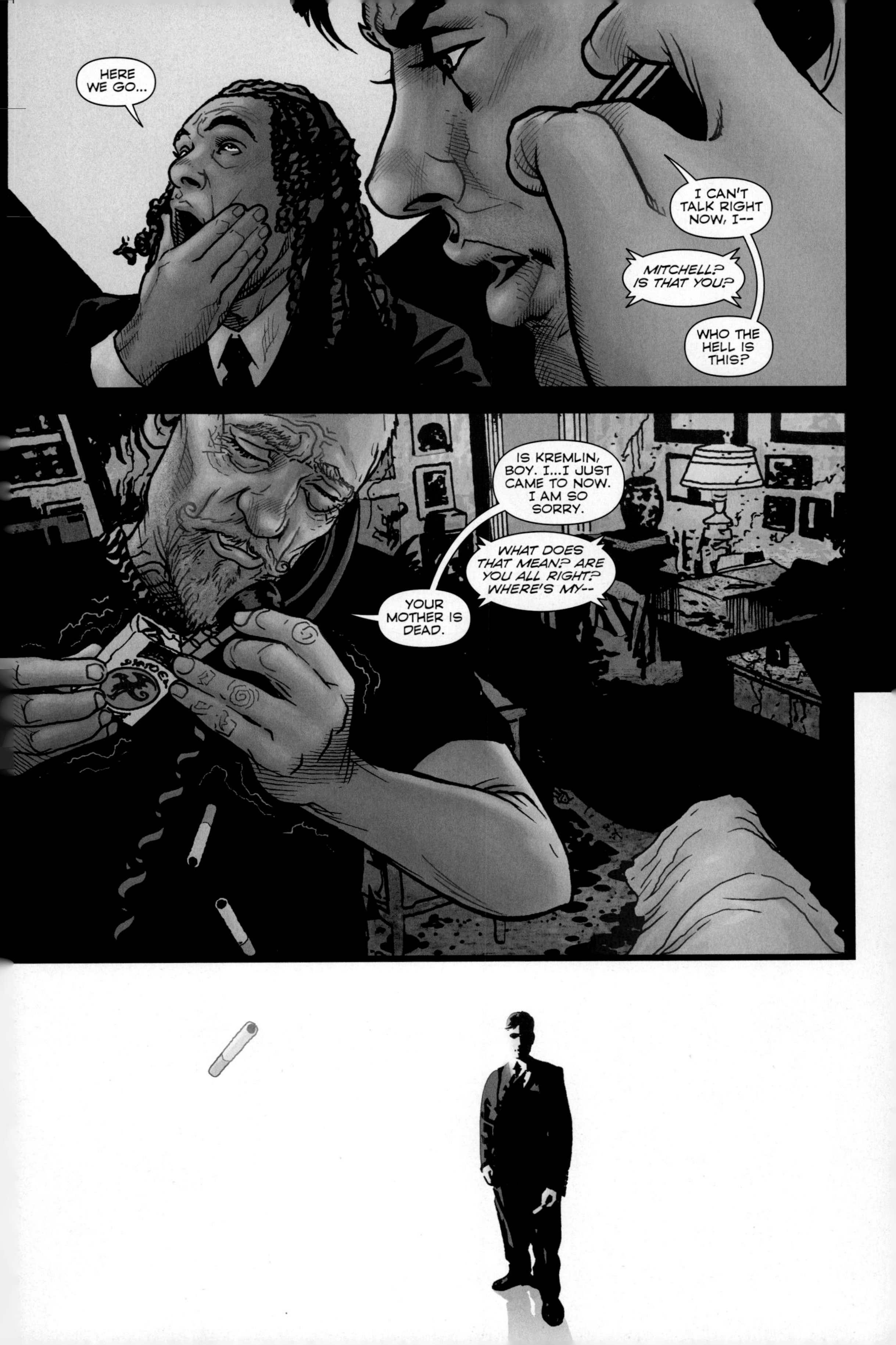
HERE WE GO...
I CAN'T TALK RIGHT NOW, I--
MITCHELL? IS THAT YOU?
WHO THE HELL IS THIS?
IS KREMLIN, BOY. I...I JUST CAME TO NOW. I AM SO SORRY.
WHAT DOES THAT MEAN? ARE YOU ALL RIGHT? WHERE'S MY--
YOUR MOTHER IS DEAD.

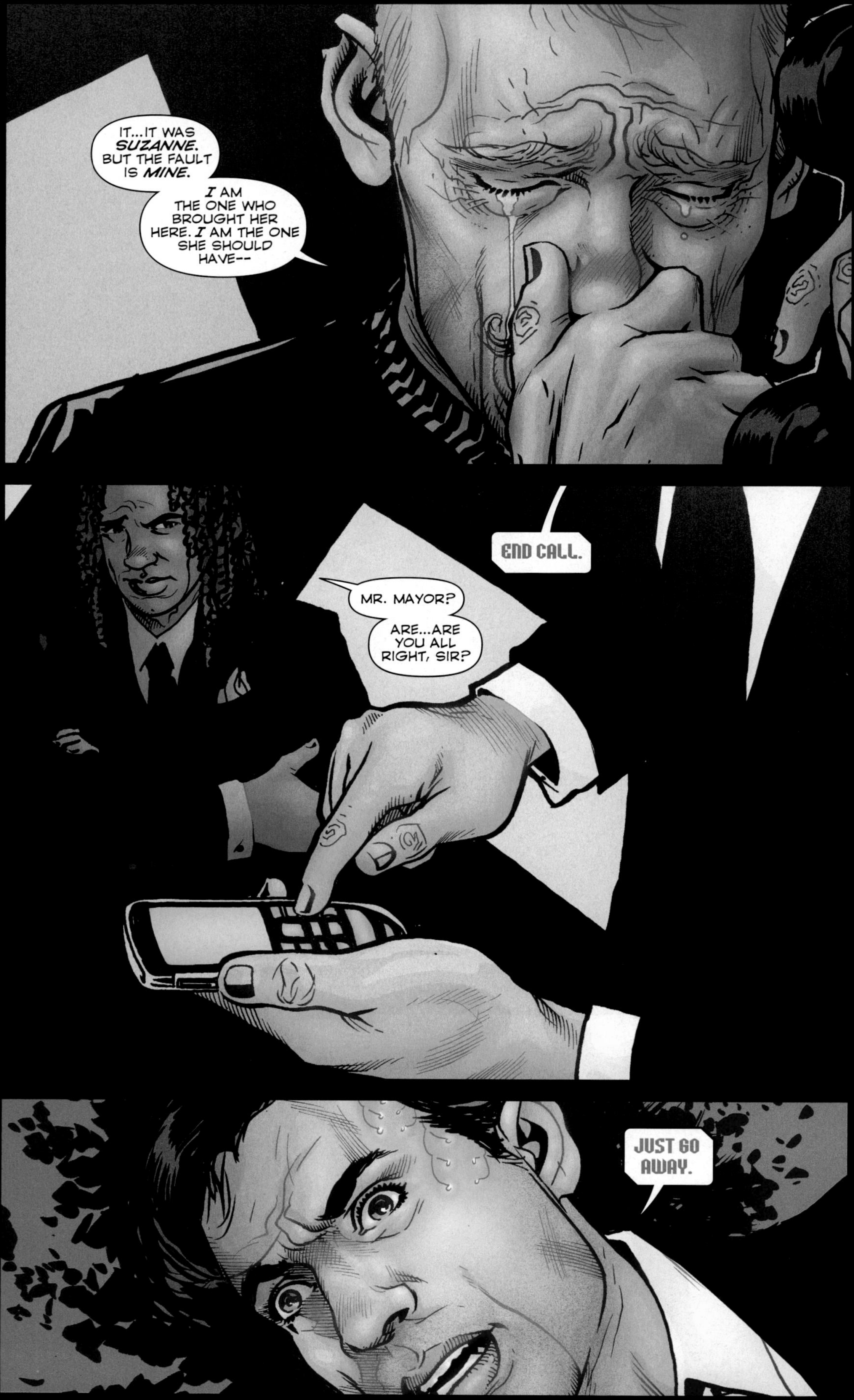
IT...IT WAS *SUZANNE.* BUT THE FAULT IS *MINE.*
I AM THE ONE WHO BROUGHT HER HERE. *I* AM THE ONE SHE SHOULD HAVE--
END CALL.
MR. MAYOR?
ARE...ARE YOU ALL RIGHT, SIR?
JUST GO AWAY.

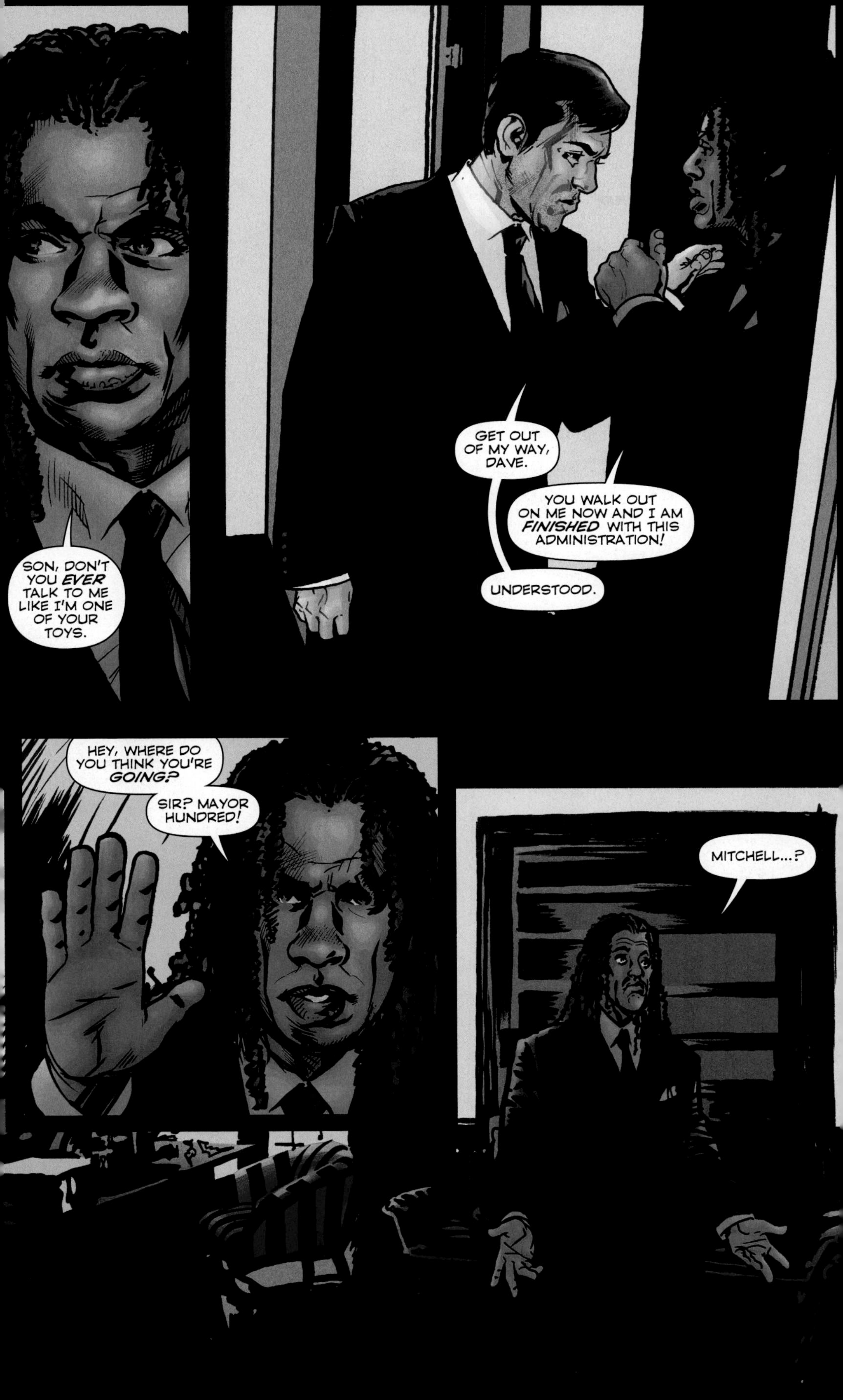
GET OUT OF MY WAY, DAVE.
SON, DON'T YOU EVER TALK TO ME LIKE I'M ONE OF YOUR TOYS.
YOU WALK OUT ON ME NOW AND I AM FINISHED WITH THIS ADMINISTRATION!
UNDERSTOOD.
HEY, WHERE DO YOU THINK YOU'RE GOING?
SIR? MAYOR HUNDRED!
MITCHELL...?

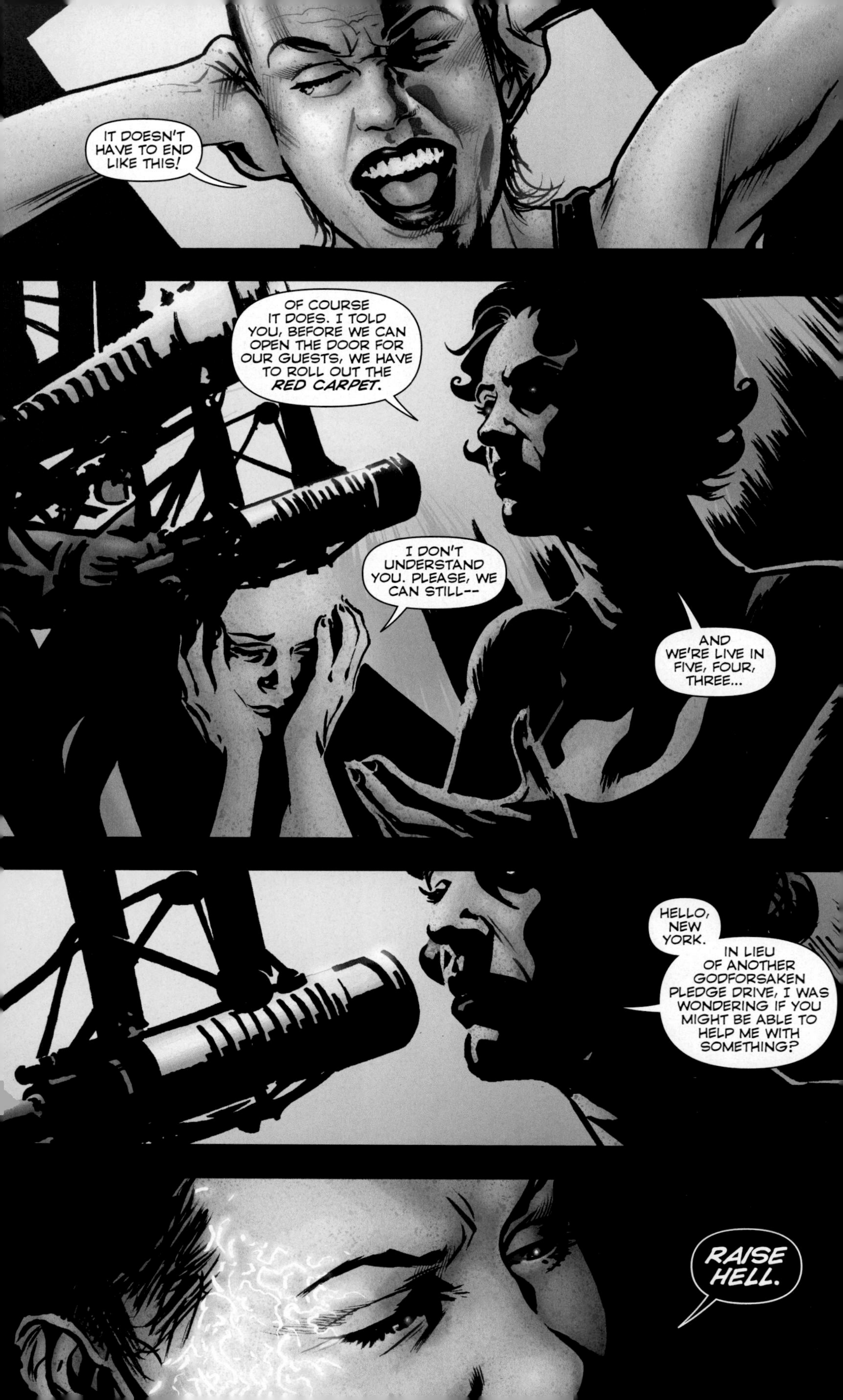
IT DOESN'T HAVE TO END LIKE THIS!
OF COURSE IT DOES. I TOLD YOU, BEFORE WE CAN OPEN THE DOOR FOR OUR GUESTS, WE HAVE TO ROLL OUT THE RED CARPET.
I DON'T UNDERSTAND YOU. PLEASE, WE CAN STILL--
AND WE'RE LIVE IN FIVE, FOUR, THREE...
HELLO, NEW YORK.
IN LIEU OF ANOTHER GODFORSAKEN PLEDGE DRIVE, I WAS WONDERING IF YOU MIGHT BE ABLE TO HELP ME WITH SOMETHING?
RAISE HELL.

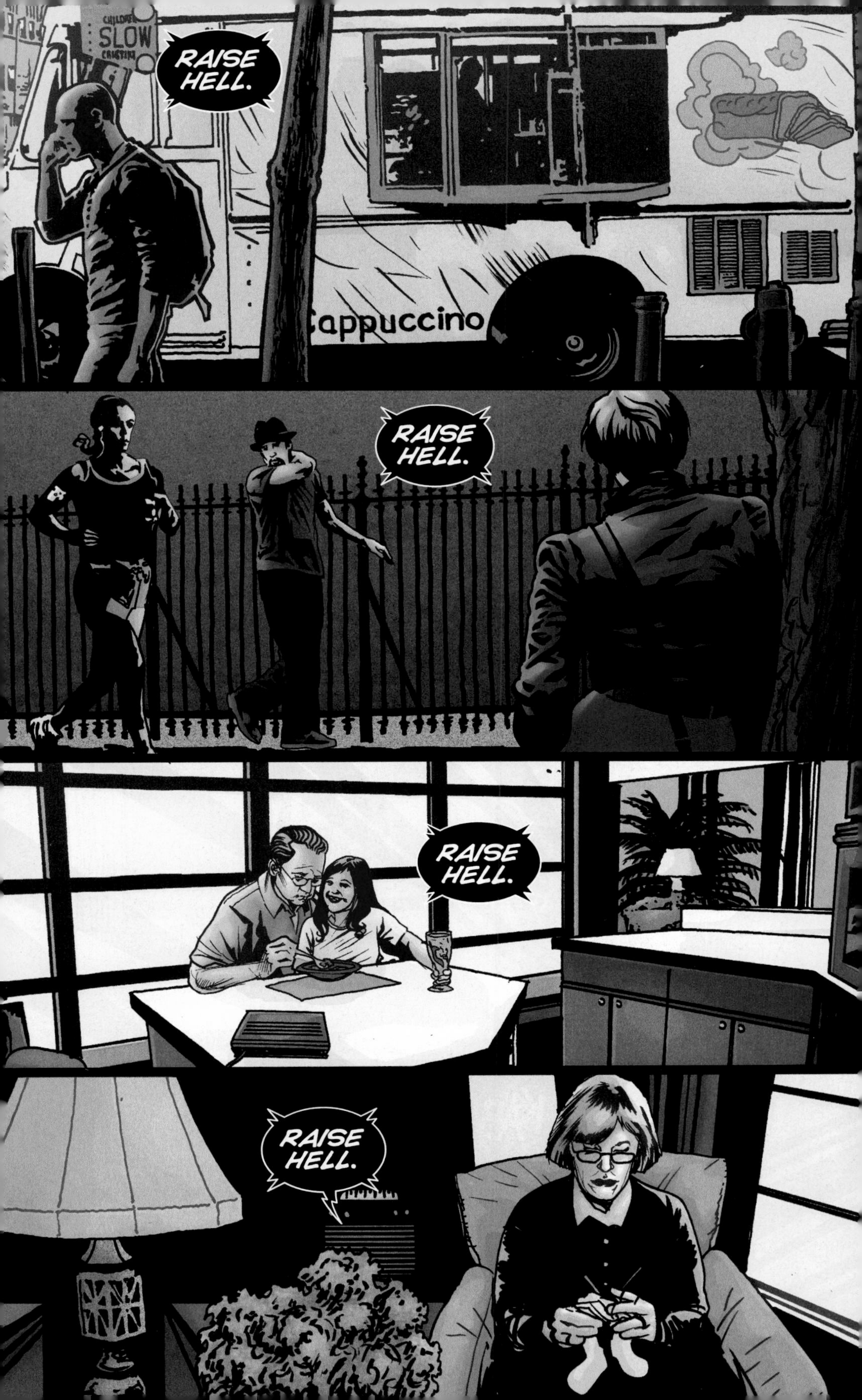
SLOW
RAISE HELL.
Cappuccino
RAISE HELL.
RAISE HELL.
RAISE HELL.

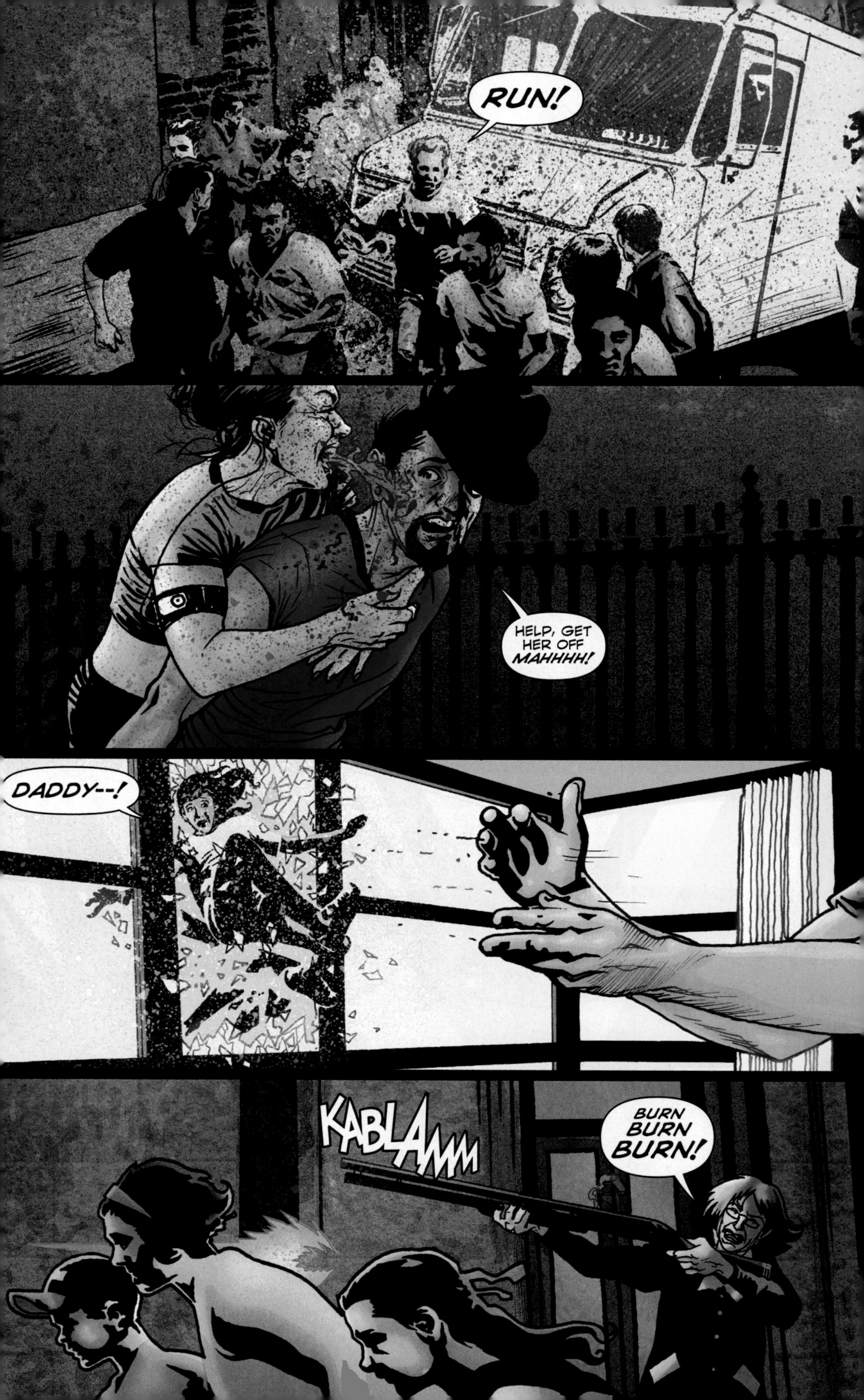
RUN!
HELP, GET HER OFF MAHHHH!
DADDY--!
KABLAMMM
BURN BURN BURN!

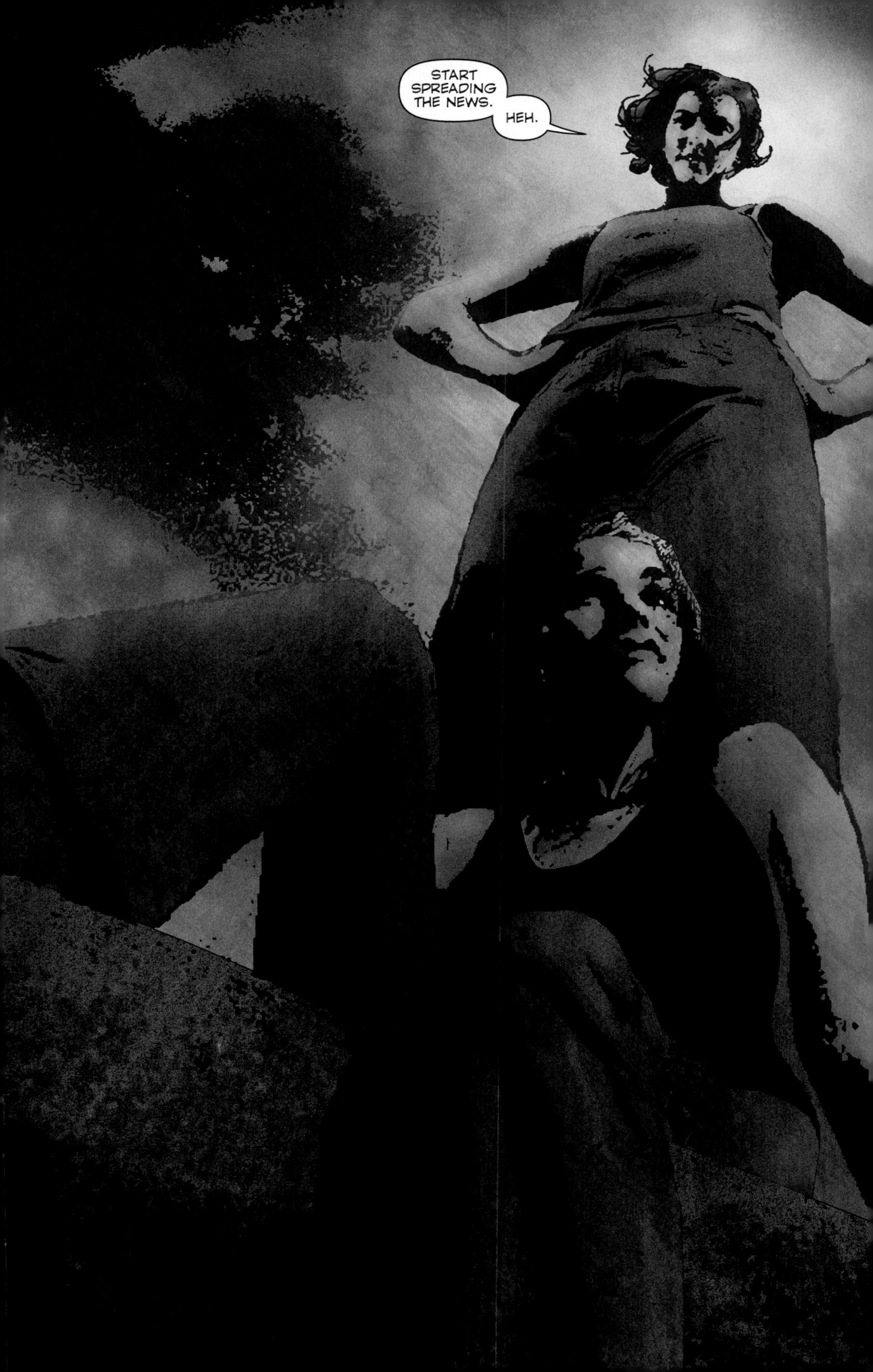
START SPREADING THE NEWS.
HEH.

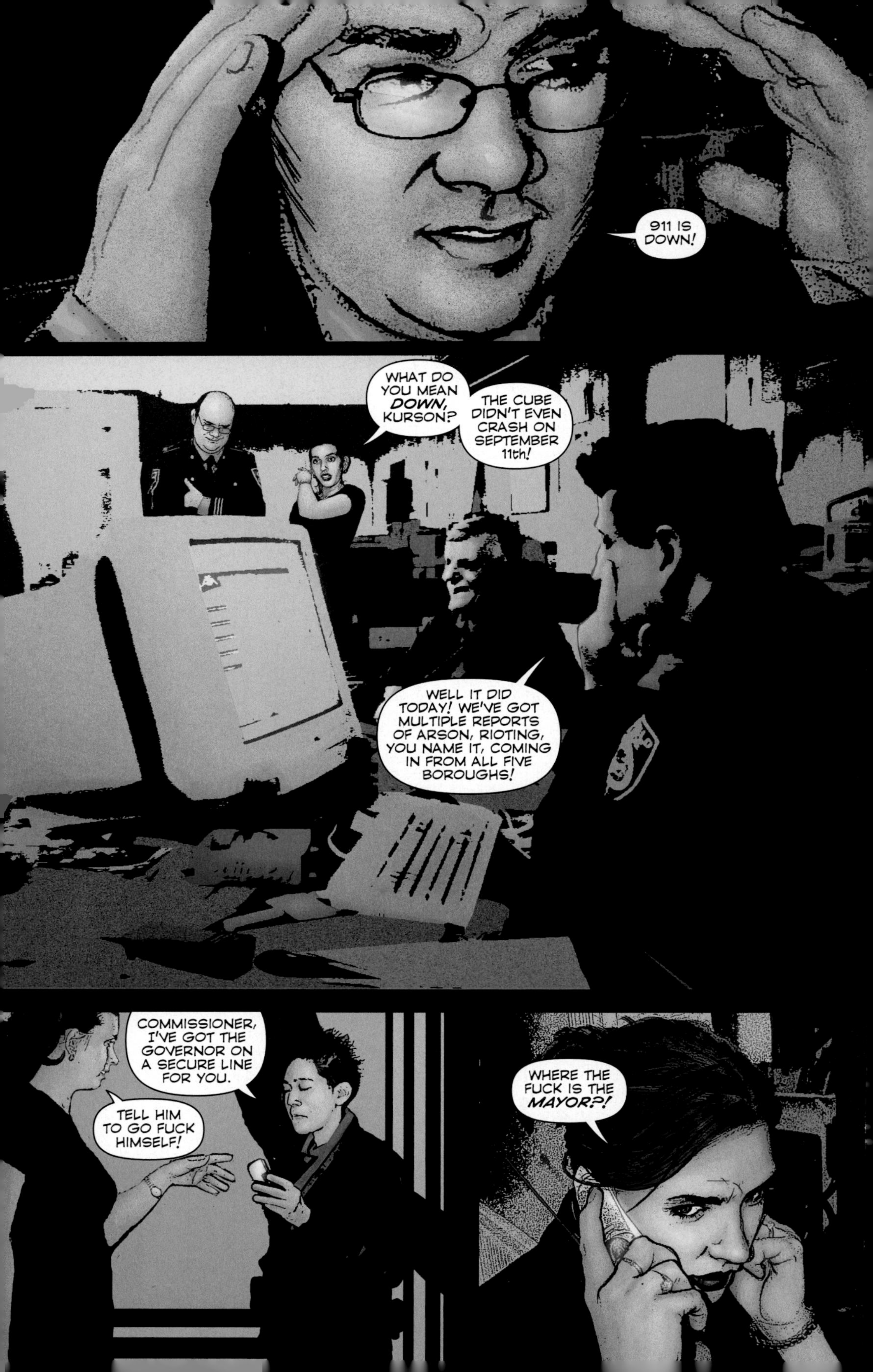
911 IS DOWN!
WHAT DO YOU MEAN *DOWN,* KURSON?
THE CUBE DIDN'T EVEN CRASH ON SEPTEMBER 11th!
WELL IT DID TODAY! WE'VE GOT MULTIPLE REPORTS OF ARSON, RIOTING, YOU NAME IT, COMING IN FROM ALL FIVE BOROUGHS!
COMMISSIONER, I'VE GOT THE GOVERNOR ON A SECURE LINE FOR YOU.
TELL HIM TO GO FUCK HIMSELF!
WHERE THE FUCK IS THE *MAYOR?!*

MEN

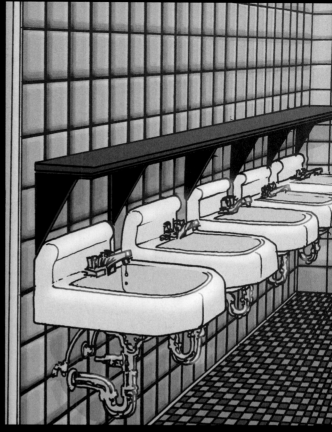

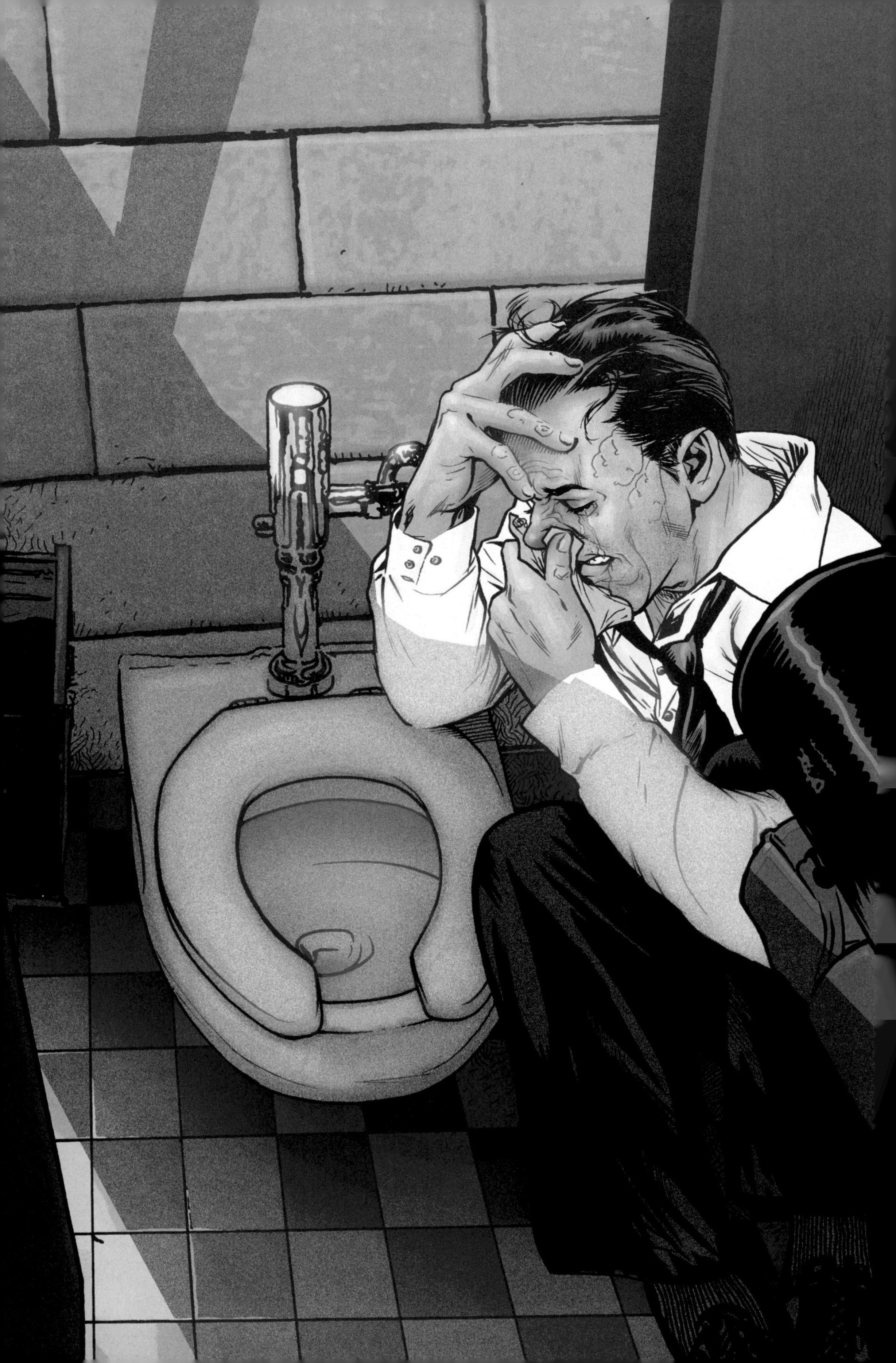

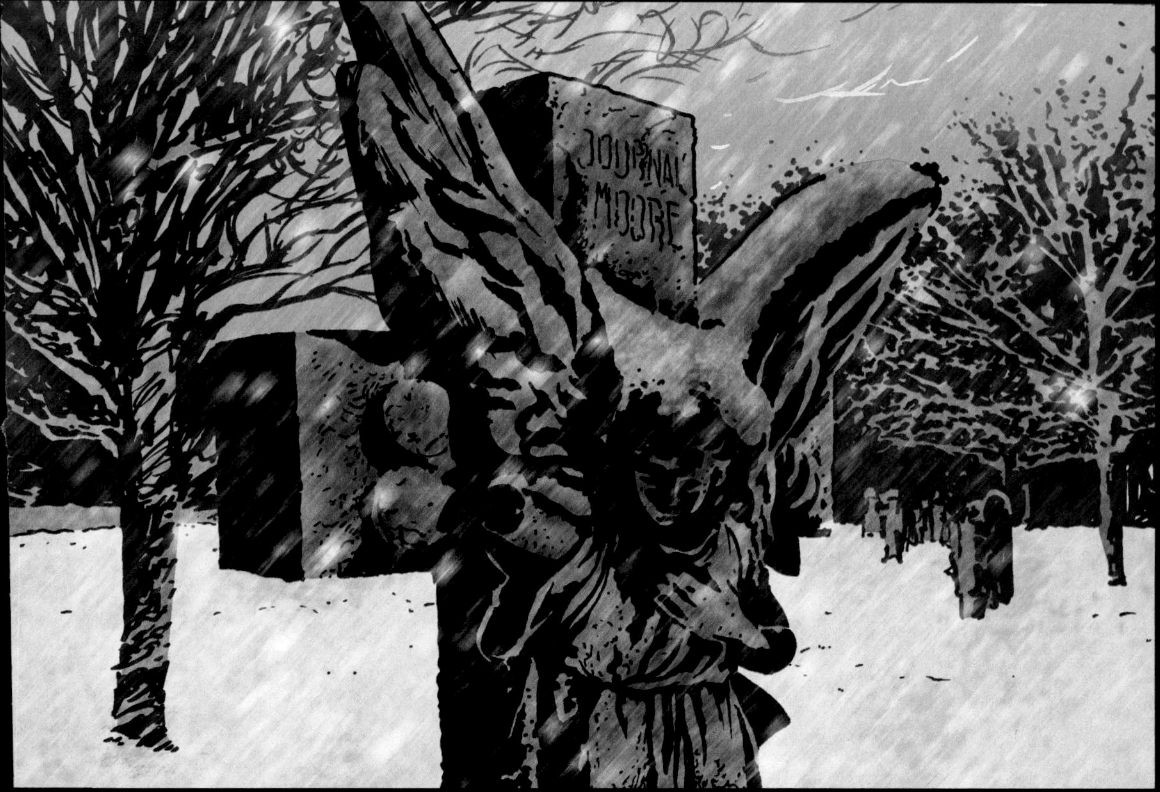
JOURNAL
MOORE

MONDAY, FEBRUARY 24, 2003

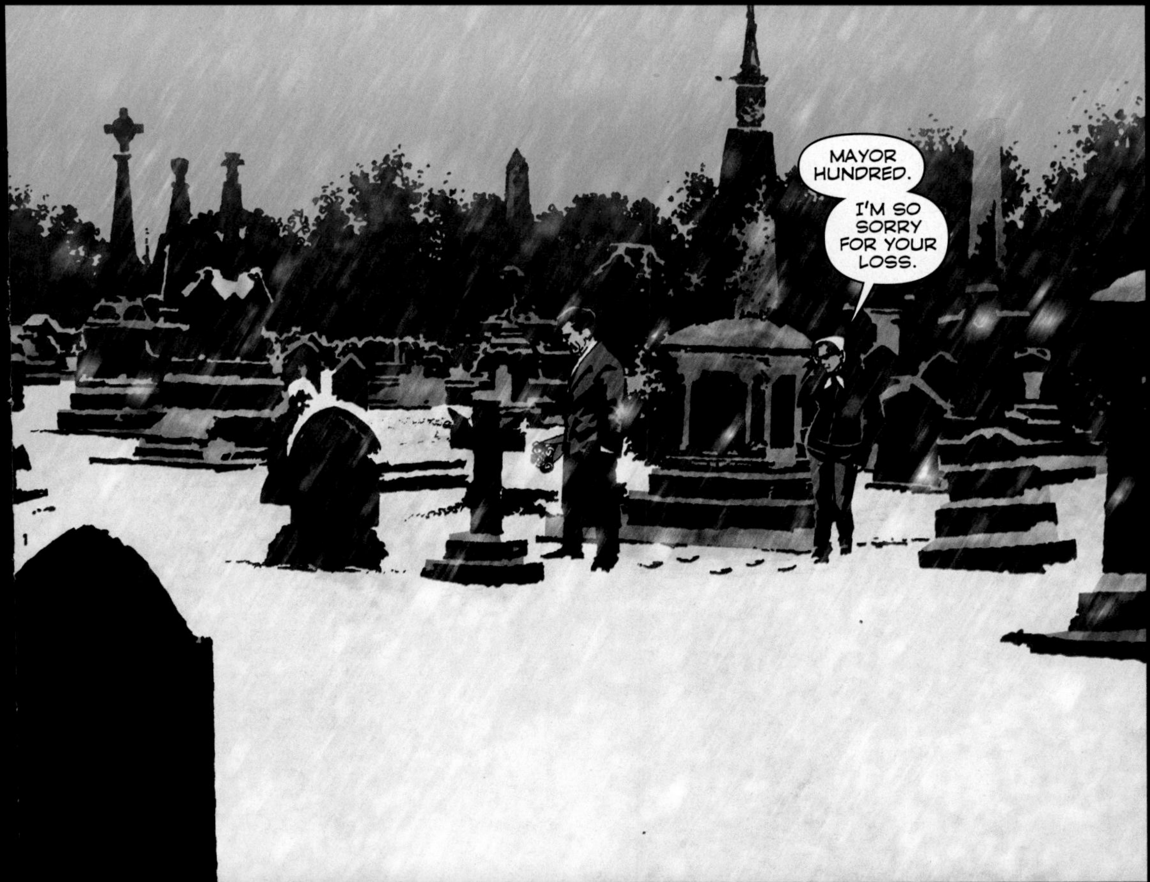
MAYOR HUNDRED.
I'M SO SORRY FOR YOUR LOSS.

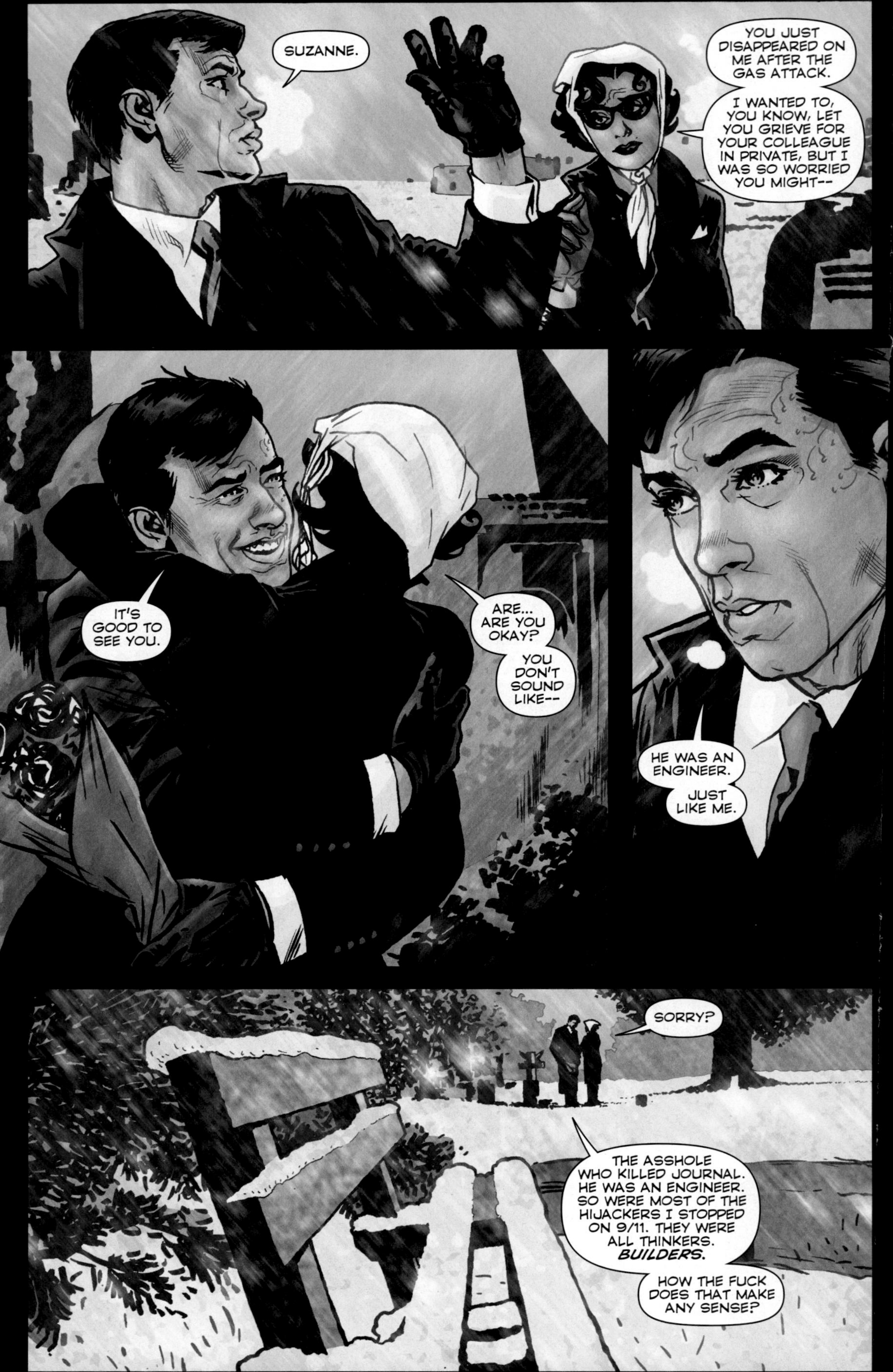
SUZANNE.
YOU JUST DISAPPEARED ON ME AFTER THE GAS ATTACK.
I WANTED TO, YOU KNOW, LET YOU GRIEVE FOR YOUR COLLEAGUE IN PRIVATE, BUT I WAS SO WORRIED YOU MIGHT--
IT'S GOOD TO SEE YOU.
ARE... ARE YOU OKAY?
YOU DON'T SOUND LIKE--
HE WAS AN ENGINEER.
JUST LIKE ME.
SORRY?
THE ASSHOLE WHO KILLED JOURNAL. HE WAS AN ENGINEER. SO WERE MOST OF THE HIJACKERS I STOPPED ON 9/11. THEY WERE ALL THINKERS. *BUILDERS.*
HOW THE FUCK DOES THAT MAKE ANY SENSE?

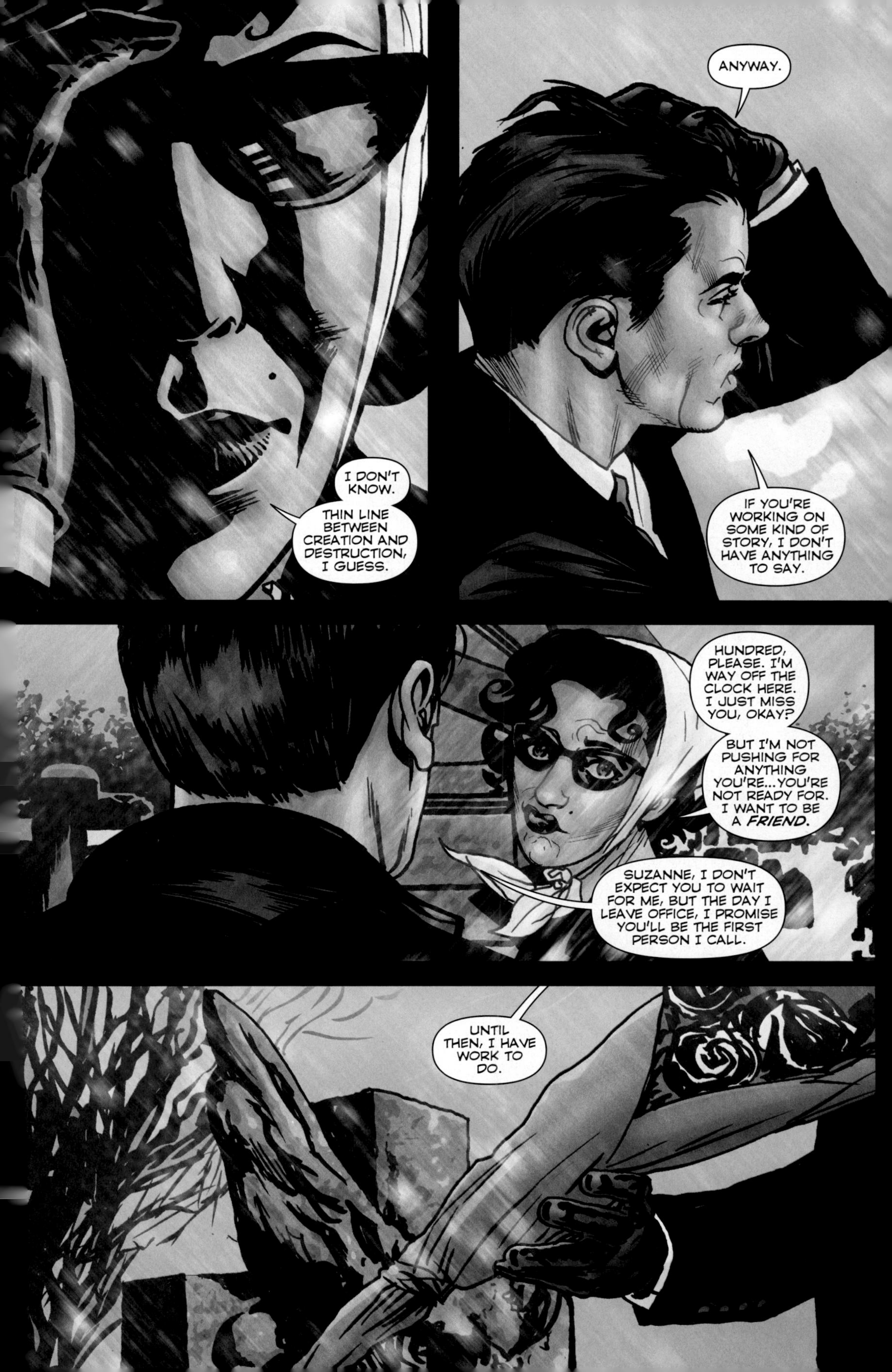

I DON'T KNOW.
THIN LINE BETWEEN CREATION AND DESTRUCTION, I GUESS.
ANYWAY.
IF YOU'RE WORKING ON SOME KIND OF STORY, I DON'T HAVE ANYTHING TO SAY.
HUNDRED, PLEASE. I'M WAY OFF THE CLOCK HERE. I JUST MISS YOU, OKAY?
BUT I'M NOT PUSHING FOR ANYTHING YOU'RE...YOU'RE NOT READY FOR. I WANT TO BE A *FRIEND*.
SUZANNE, I DON'T EXPECT YOU TO WAIT FOR ME, BUT THE DAY I LEAVE OFFICE, I PROMISE YOU'LL BE THE FIRST PERSON I CALL.
UNTIL THEN, I HAVE WORK TO DO.

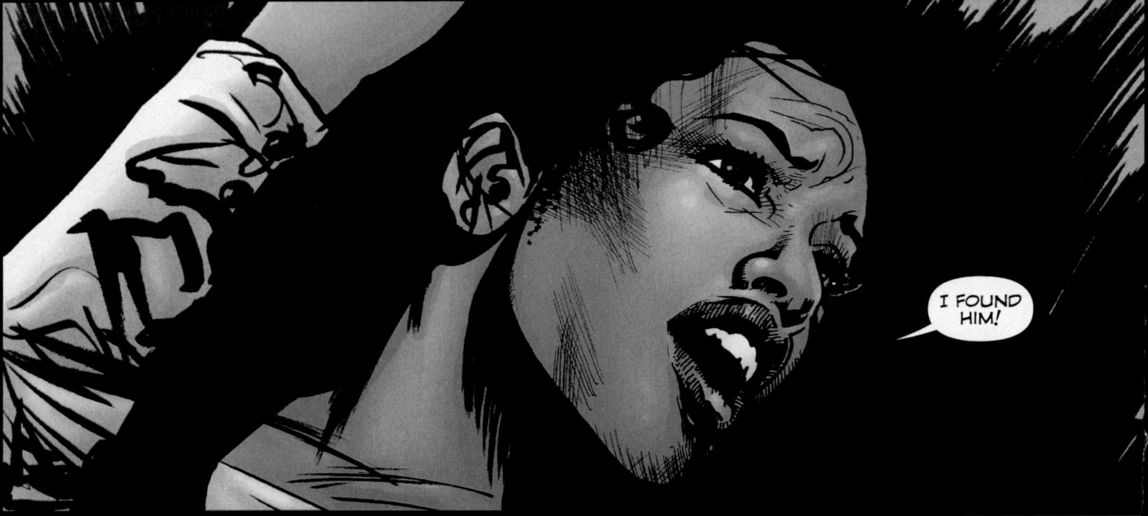
I FOUND HIM!

TUESDAY, APRIL 12, 2005

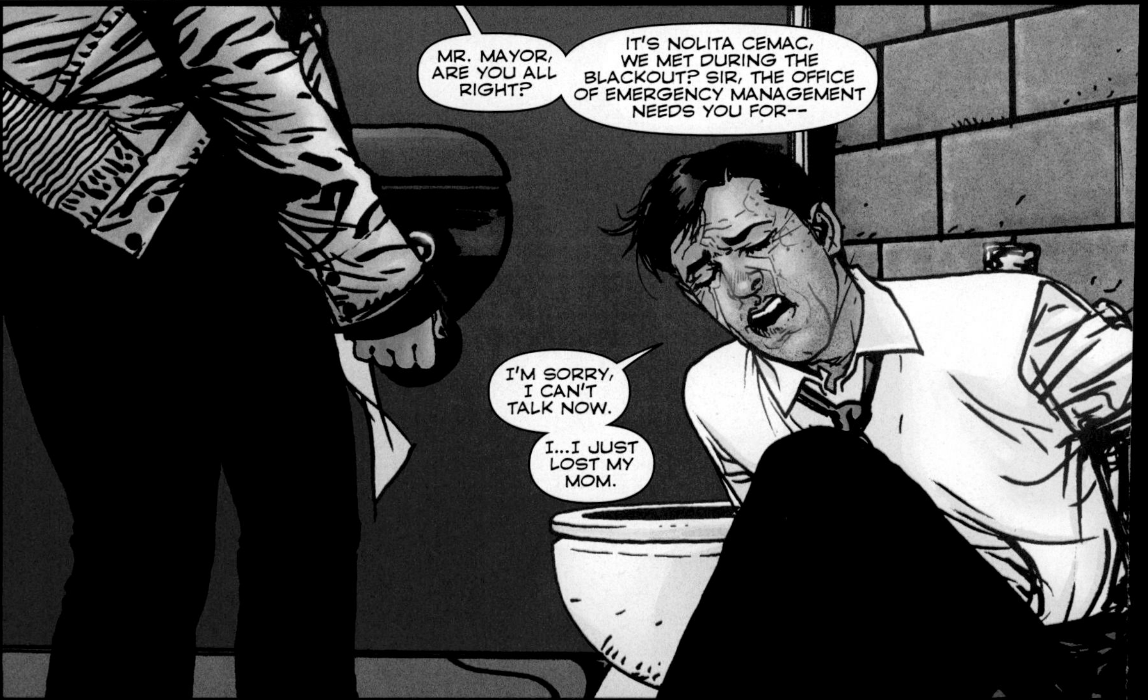
MR. MAYOR, ARE YOU ALL RIGHT?
IT'S NOLITA CEMAC, WE MET DURING THE BLACKOUT? SIR, THE OFFICE OF EMERGENCY MANAGEMENT NEEDS YOU FOR--
I'M SORRY, I CAN'T TALK NOW.
I...I JUST LOST MY MOM.

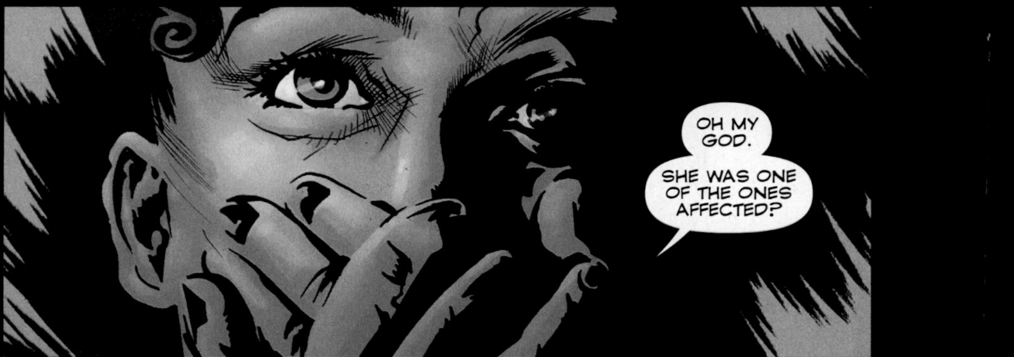
OH MY GOD.
SHE WAS ONE OF THE ONES AFFECTED?

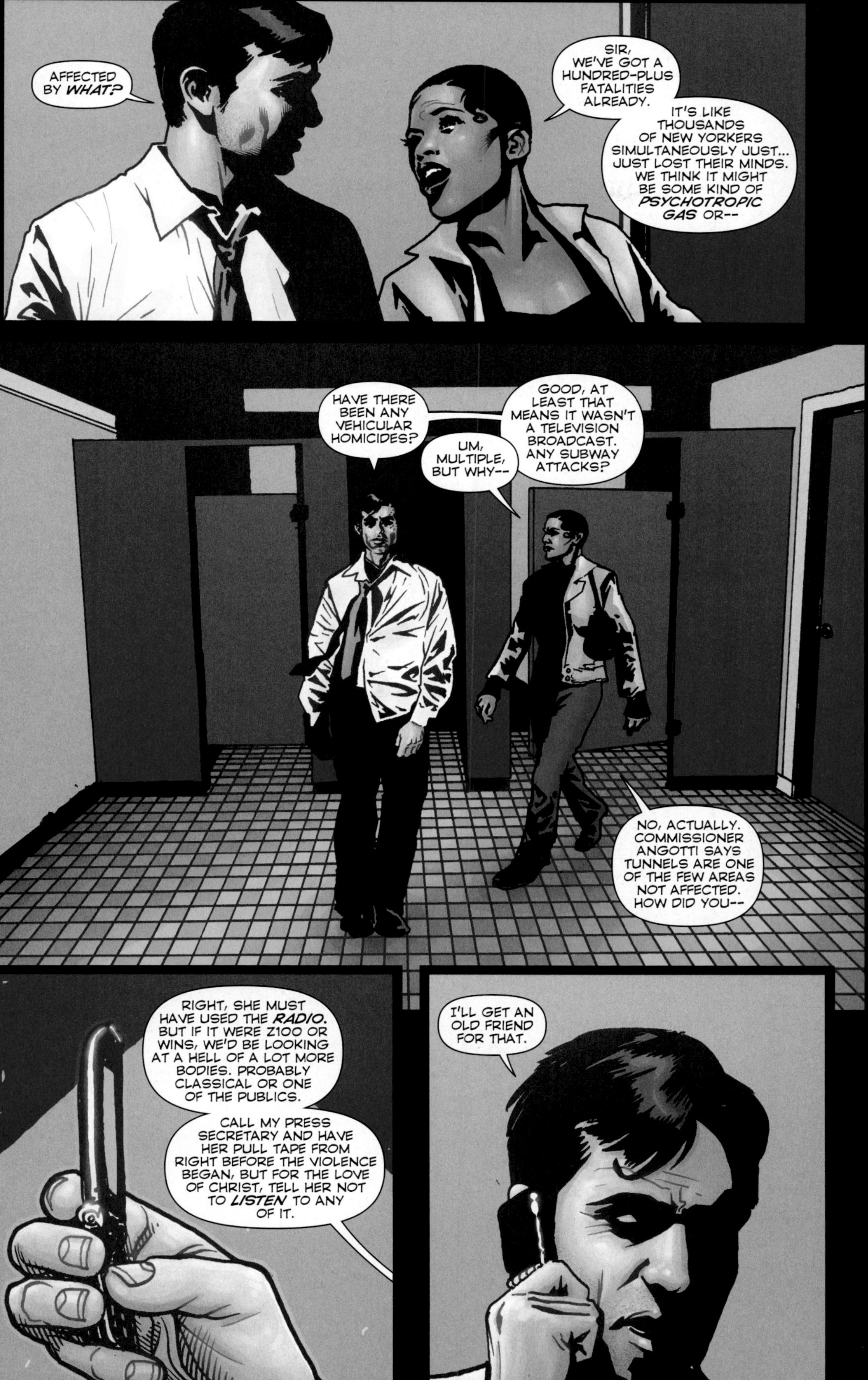
AFFECTED BY *WHAT?*
SIR, WE'VE GOT A HUNDRED-PLUS FATALITIES ALREADY.
IT'S LIKE THOUSANDS OF NEW YORKERS SIMULTANEOUSLY JUST... JUST LOST THEIR MINDS. WE THINK IT MIGHT BE SOME KIND OF *PSYCHOTROPIC GAS* OR--
HAVE THERE BEEN ANY VEHICULAR HOMICIDES?
UM, MULTIPLE, BUT WHY--
GOOD, AT LEAST THAT MEANS IT WASN'T A TELEVISION BROADCAST. ANY SUBWAY ATTACKS?
NO, ACTUALLY. COMMISSIONER ANGOTTI SAYS TUNNELS ARE ONE OF THE FEW AREAS NOT AFFECTED. HOW DID YOU--
RIGHT, SHE MUST HAVE USED THE *RADIO*. BUT IF IT WERE Z100 OR WINS, WE'D BE LOOKING AT A HELL OF A LOT MORE BODIES. PROBABLY CLASSICAL OR ONE OF THE PUBLICS.
CALL MY PRESS SECRETARY AND HAVE HER PULL TAPE FROM RIGHT BEFORE THE VIOLENCE BEGAN, BUT FOR THE LOVE OF CHRIST, TELL HER NOT TO *LISTEN* TO ANY OF IT.
I'LL GET AN OLD FRIEND FOR THAT.

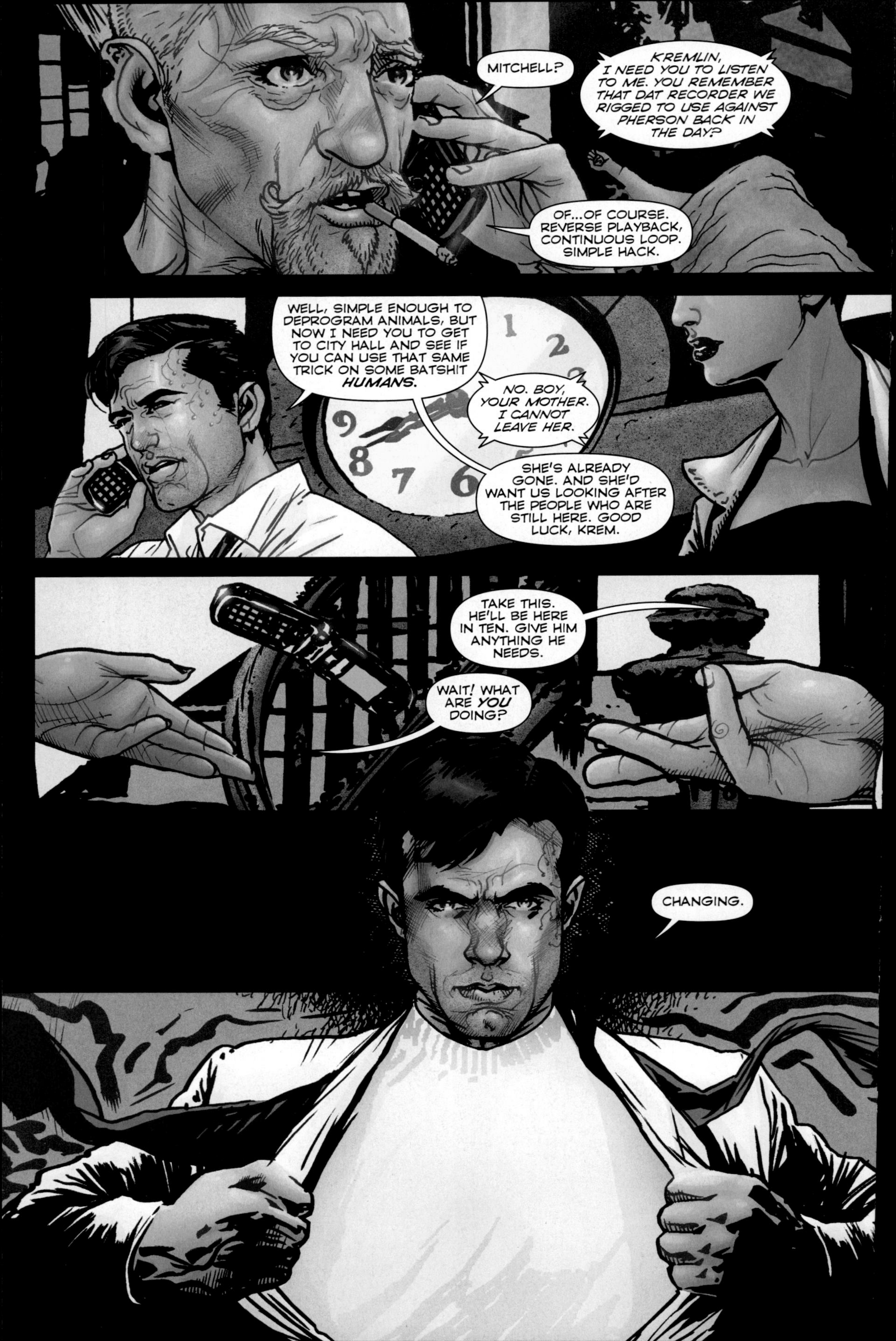
MITCHELL?
KREMLIN, I NEED YOU TO LISTEN TO ME. YOU REMEMBER THAT DAT RECORDER WE RIGGED TO USE AGAINST PHERSON BACK IN THE DAY?
OF...OF COURSE. REVERSE PLAYBACK, CONTINUOUS LOOP. SIMPLE HACK.
WELL, SIMPLE ENOUGH TO DEPROGRAM ANIMALS, BUT NOW I NEED YOU TO GET TO CITY HALL AND SEE IF YOU CAN USE THAT SAME TRICK ON SOME BATSHIT HUMANS.
NO. BOY, YOUR MOTHER. I CANNOT LEAVE HER.
SHE'S ALREADY GONE. AND SHE'D WANT US LOOKING AFTER THE PEOPLE WHO ARE STILL HERE. GOOD LUCK, KREM.
TAKE THIS. HE'LL BE HERE IN TEN. GIVE HIM ANYTHING HE NEEDS.
WAIT! WHAT ARE YOU DOING?
CHANGING.

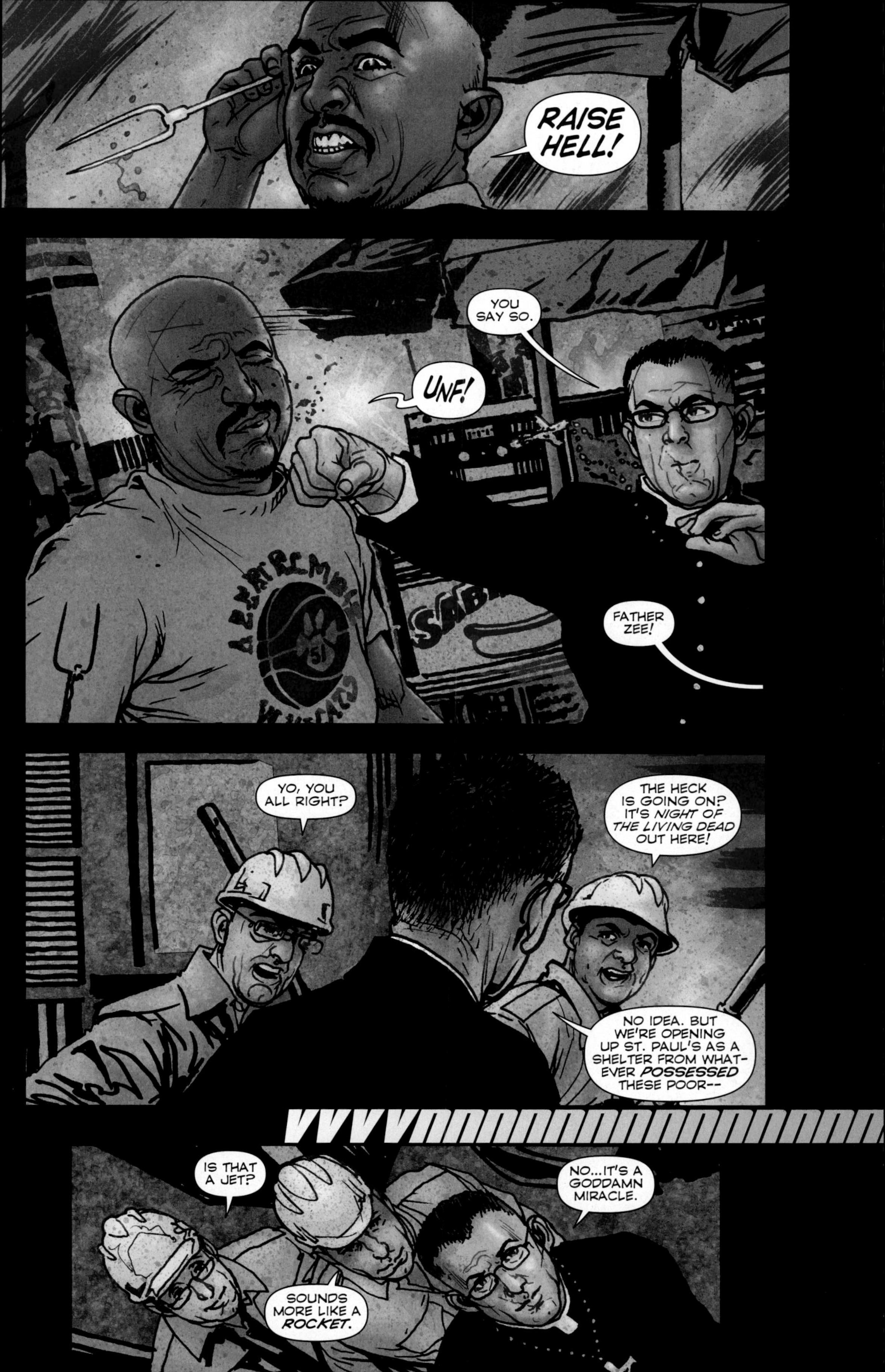
RAISE HELL!
YOU SAY SO.
UNF!
FATHER ZEE!
YO, YOU ALL RIGHT?
THE HECK IS GOING ON? IT'S *NIGHT OF THE LIVING DEAD* OUT HERE!
NO IDEA. BUT WE'RE OPENING UP ST. PAUL'S AS A SHELTER FROM WHATEVER *POSSESSED* THESE POOR--
VVVVNNNNNNNNNNNNNNNN
IS THAT A JET?
NO...IT'S A GODDAMN MIRACLE.
SOUNDS MORE LIKE A *ROCKET*.

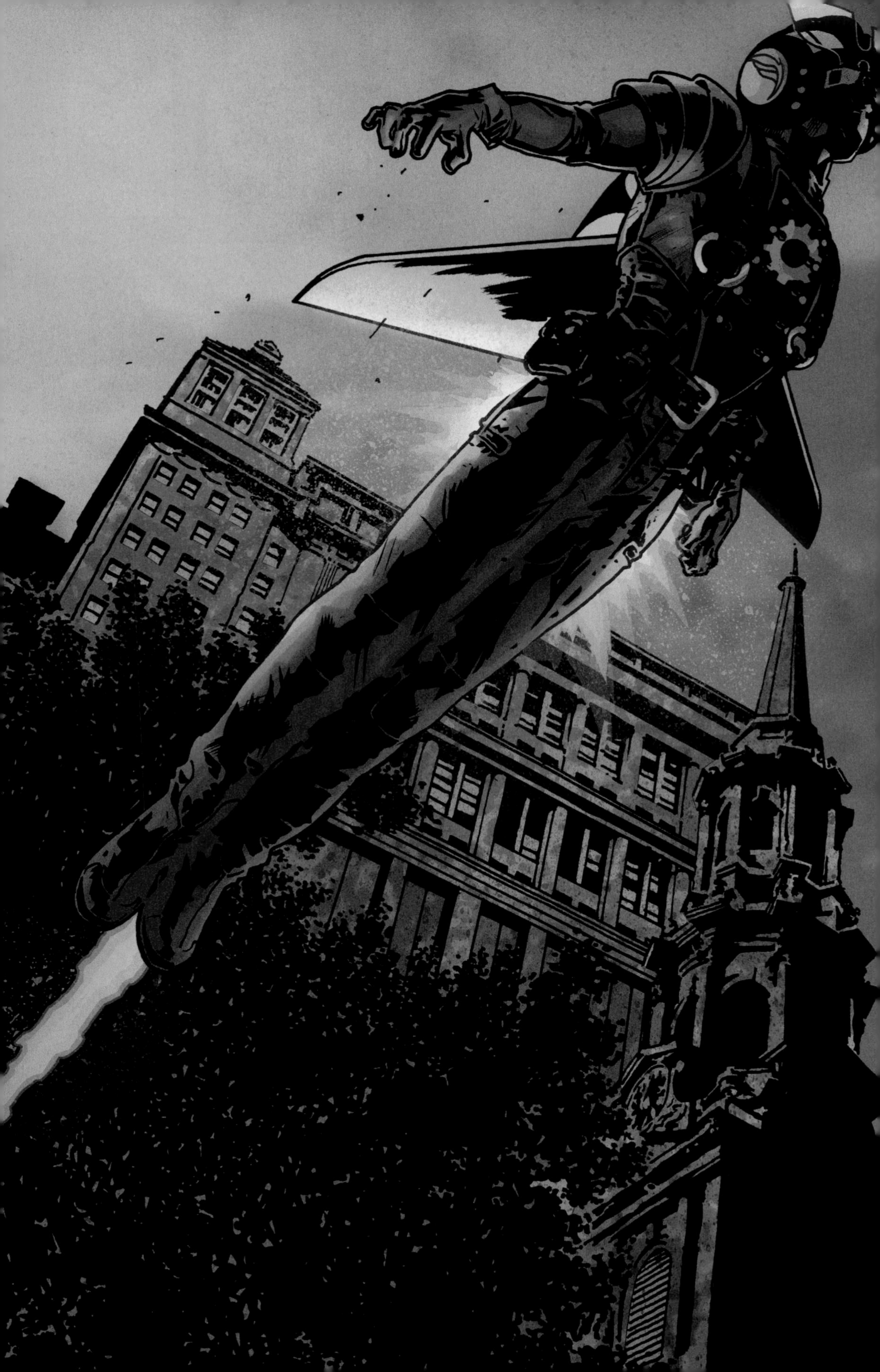

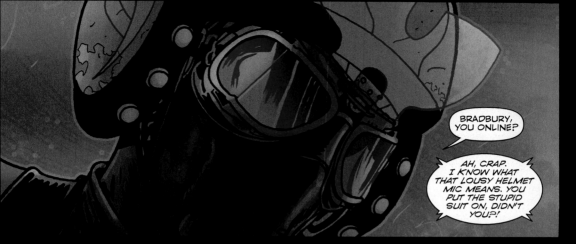

BRADBURY, YOU ONLINE?

AH, CRAP. I KNOW WHAT THAT LOUSY HELMET MIC MEANS. YOU PUT THE STUPID SUIT ON, DIDN'T YOU?!

WELL, I HAVEN'T DONE LAUNDRY IN A WHILE, SO I KINDA HAD TO MIX AND MATCH. WHATEVER, YOU'VE SEEN WHAT WE'RE UP AGAINST, RIGHT?

YEAH, I JUST FOUGHT MY WAY THROUGH THE HUMAN SHITSTORM OUTSIDE TO GET TO JANUARY'S PLACE.

NO SIGN OF THE GIRL, BUT IT LOOKS LIKE SUZANNE HAS BEEN HERE. SHE WENT A BEAUTIFUL MIND ALL OVER THE WALLS.

ANY CLUES WHERE SHE MIGHT BE NOW?

SORRY, BOSS. IT'S JUST GIBBERISH.

"THE ISLAND THAT IS NOT"?

WHAT DOES THAT EVEN MEAN?

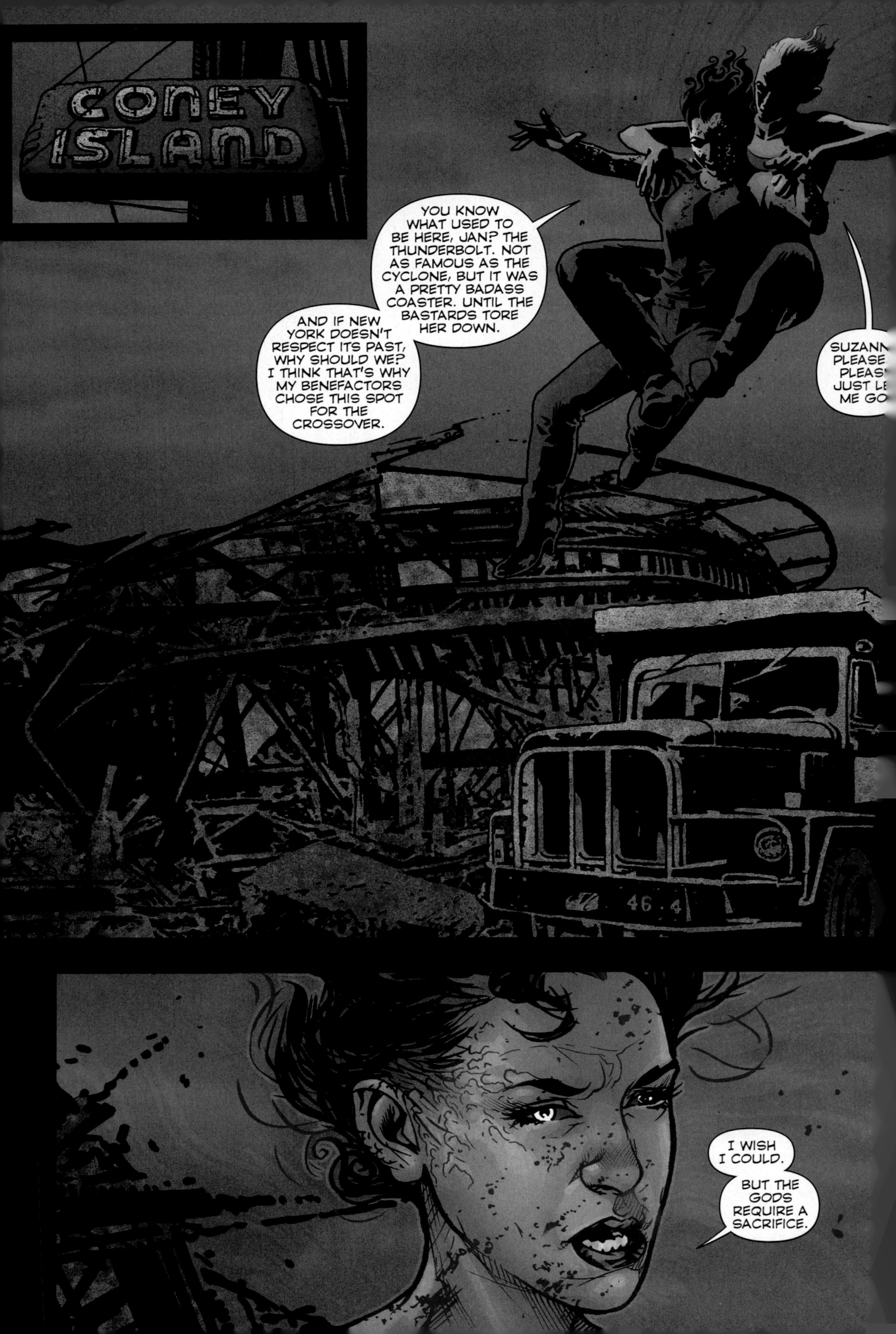
CONEY ISLAND
YOU KNOW WHAT USED TO BE HERE, JAN? THE THUNDERBOLT. NOT AS FAMOUS AS THE CYCLONE, BUT IT WAS A PRETTY BADASS COASTER. UNTIL THE BASTARDS TORE HER DOWN.
AND IF NEW YORK DOESN'T RESPECT ITS PAST, WHY SHOULD WE? I THINK THAT'S WHY MY BENEFACTORS CHOSE THIS SPOT FOR THE CROSSOVER.
46-4
I WISH I COULD.
BUT THE GODS REQUIRE A SACRIFICE.

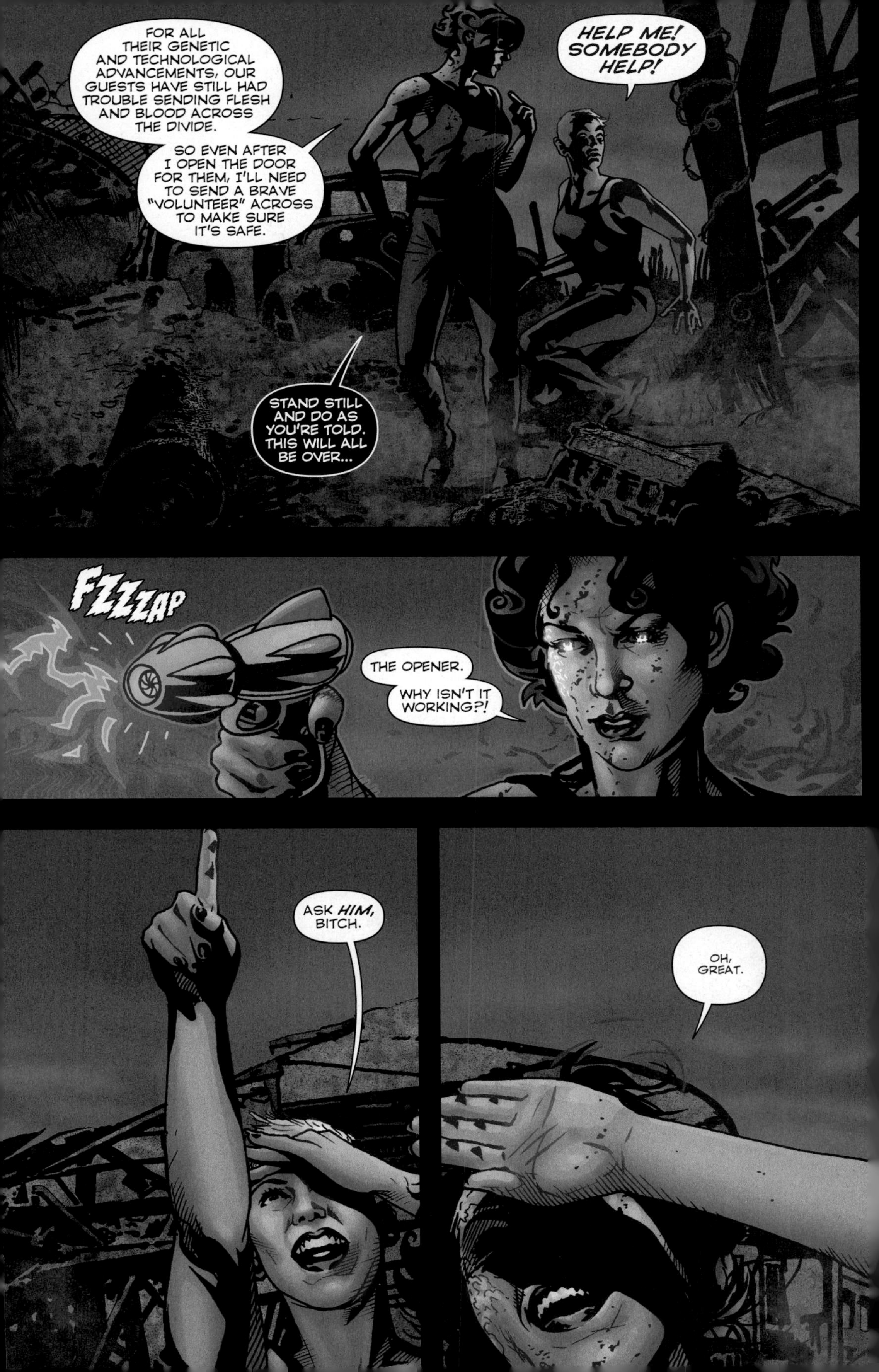
FOR ALL THEIR GENETIC AND TECHNOLOGICAL ADVANCEMENTS, OUR GUESTS HAVE STILL HAD TROUBLE SENDING FLESH AND BLOOD ACROSS THE DIVIDE.
SO EVEN AFTER I OPEN THE DOOR FOR THEM, I'LL NEED TO SEND A BRAVE "VOLUNTEER" ACROSS TO MAKE SURE IT'S SAFE.
HELP ME! SOMEBODY HELP!
STAND STILL AND DO AS YOU'RE TOLD. THIS WILL ALL BE OVER...
FZZZAP
THE OPENER.
WHY ISN'T IT WORKING?!
ASK *HIM*, BITCH.
OH, GREAT.

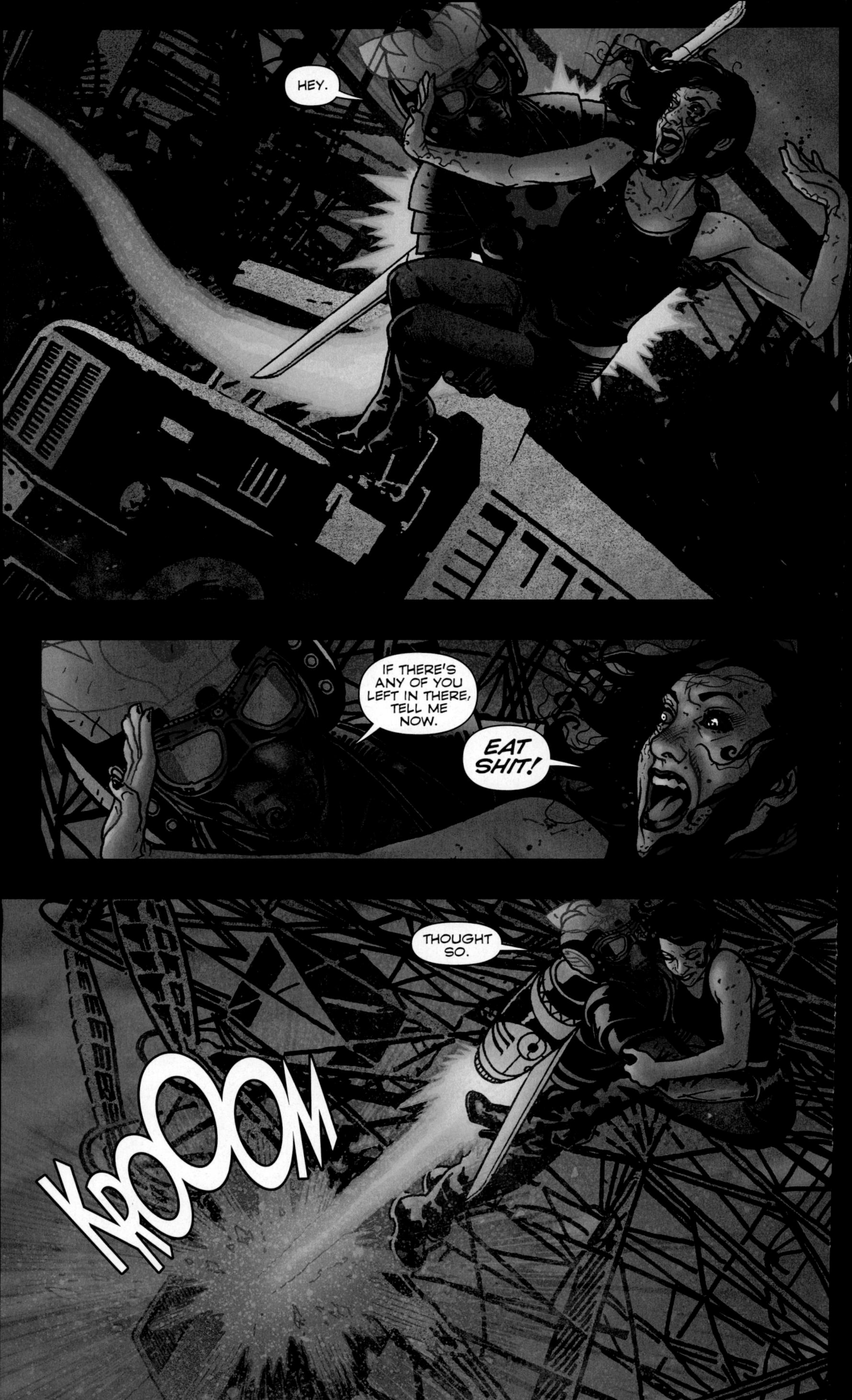
HEY.
IF THERE'S ANY OF YOU LEFT IN THERE, TELL ME NOW.
EAT SHIT!
THOUGHT SO.
KROOOM

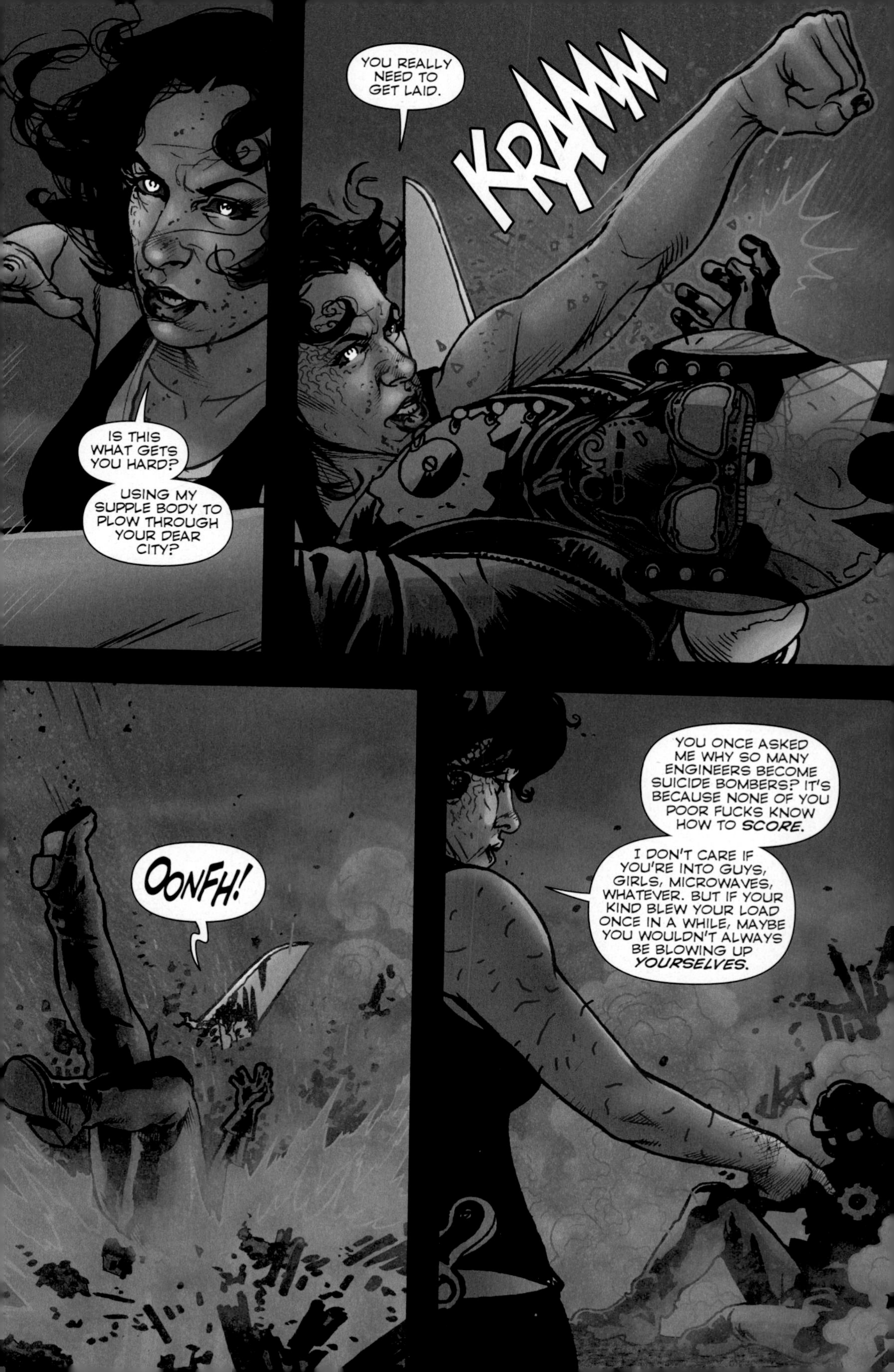

YOU REALLY NEED TO GET LAID.
KRAMM
IS THIS WHAT GETS YOU HARD?
USING MY SUPPLE BODY TO PLOW THROUGH YOUR DEAR CITY?
OONFH!
YOU ONCE ASKED ME WHY SO MANY ENGINEERS BECOME SUICIDE BOMBERS? IT'S BECAUSE NONE OF YOU POOR FUCKS KNOW HOW TO SCORE.
I DON'T CARE IF YOU'RE INTO GUYS, GIRLS, MICROWAVES, WHATEVER. BUT IF YOUR KIND BLEW YOUR LOAD ONCE IN A WHILE, MAYBE YOU WOULDN'T ALWAYS BE BLOWING UP YOURSELVES.

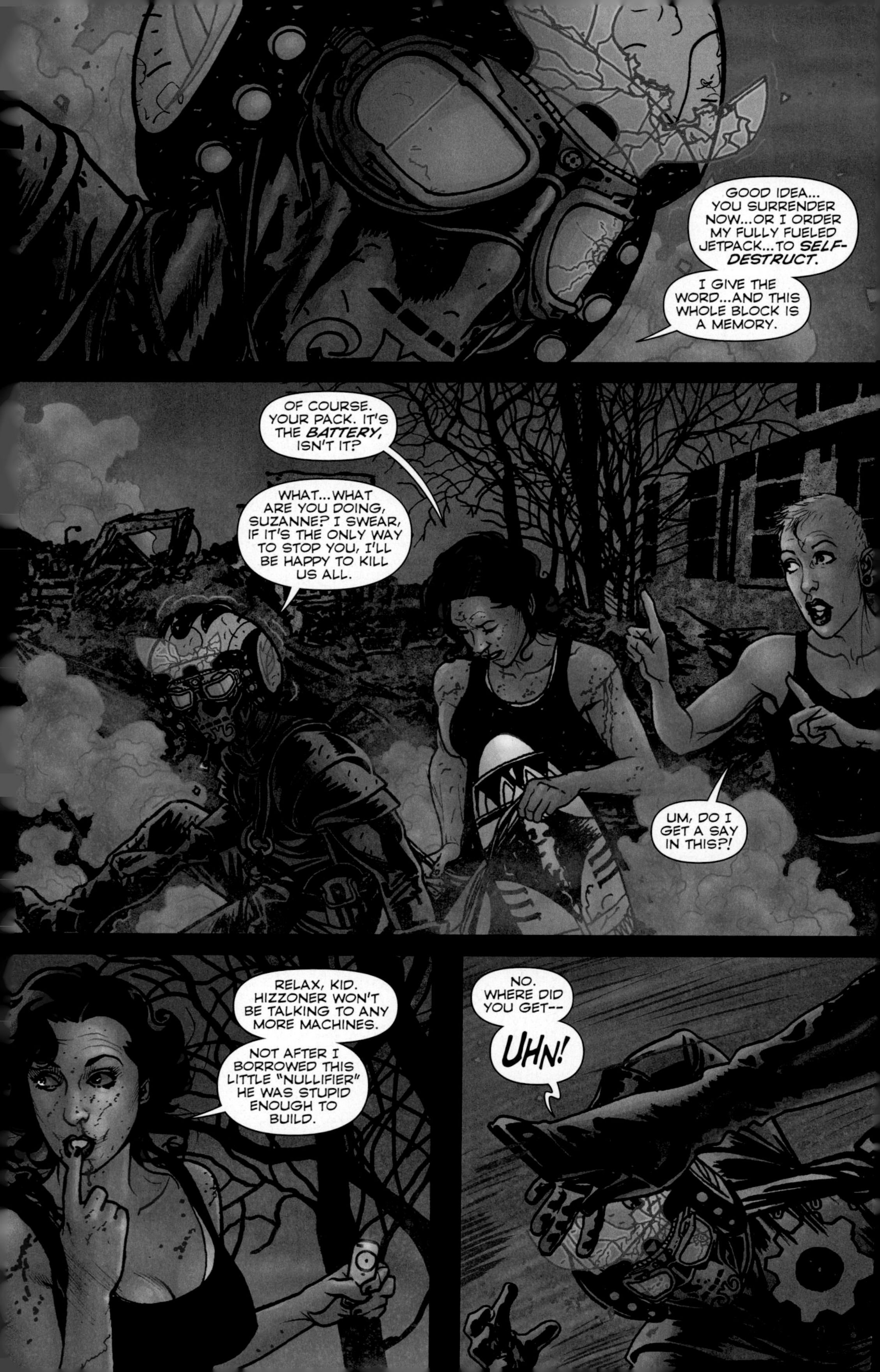
GOOD IDEA... YOU SURRENDER NOW...OR I ORDER MY FULLY FUELED JETPACK...TO SELF-DESTRUCT.
I GIVE THE WORD...AND THIS WHOLE BLOCK IS A MEMORY.
OF COURSE. YOUR PACK. IT'S THE BATTERY, ISN'T IT?
WHAT...WHAT ARE YOU DOING, SUZANNE? I SWEAR, IF IT'S THE ONLY WAY TO STOP YOU, I'LL BE HAPPY TO KILL US ALL.
UM, DO I GET A SAY IN THIS?!
RELAX, KID. HIZZONER WON'T BE TALKING TO ANY MORE MACHINES.
NOT AFTER I BORROWED THIS LITTLE "NULLIFIER" HE WAS STUPID ENOUGH TO BUILD.
NO. WHERE DID YOU GET--
UHN!

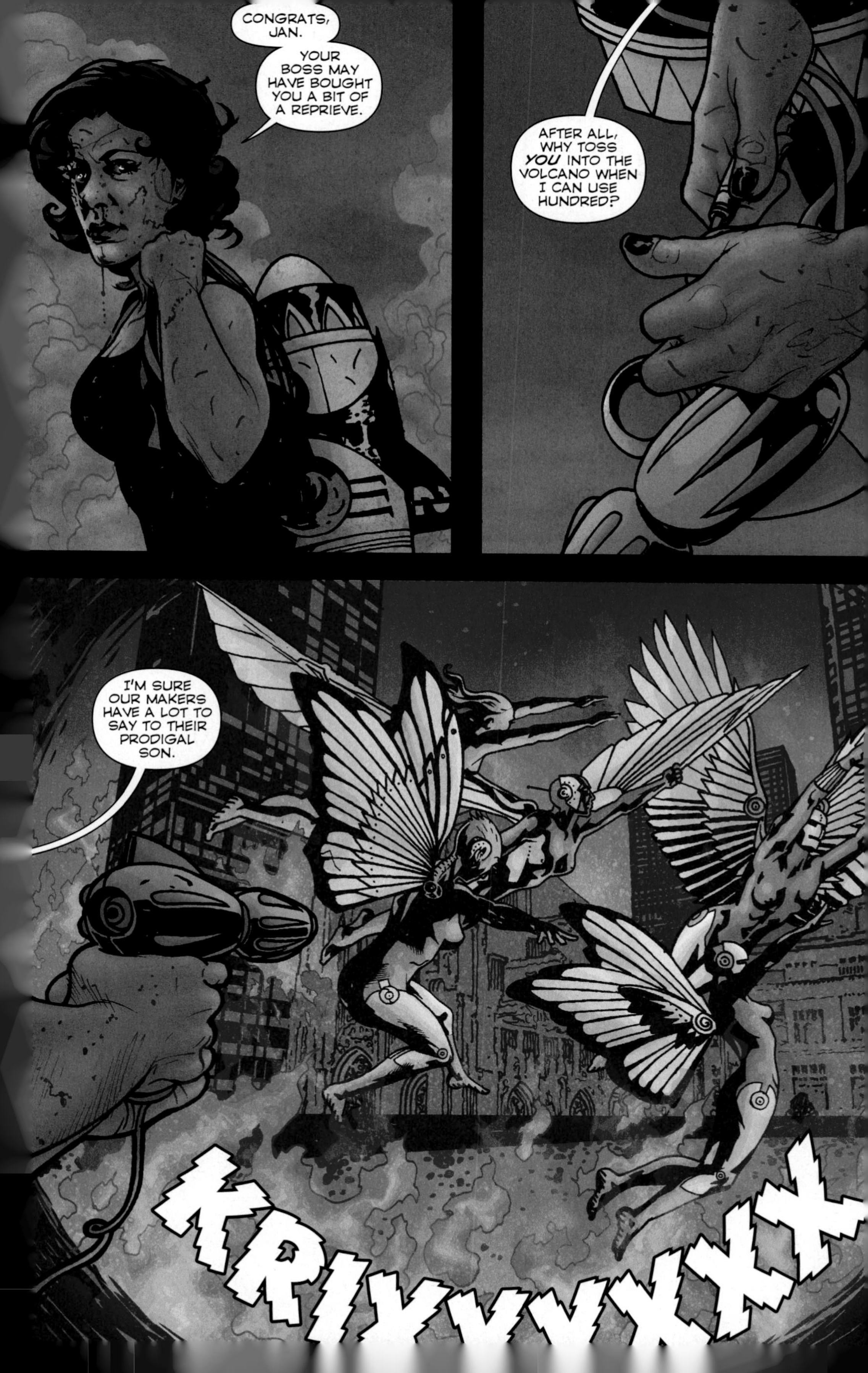
CONGRATS, JAN.
YOUR BOSS MAY HAVE BOUGHT YOU A BIT OF A REPRIEVE.
AFTER ALL, WHY TOSS *YOU* INTO THE VOLCANO WHEN I CAN USE HUNDRED?
I'M SURE OUR MAKERS HAVE A LOT TO SAY TO THEIR PRODIGAL SON.
KRIXXXXX

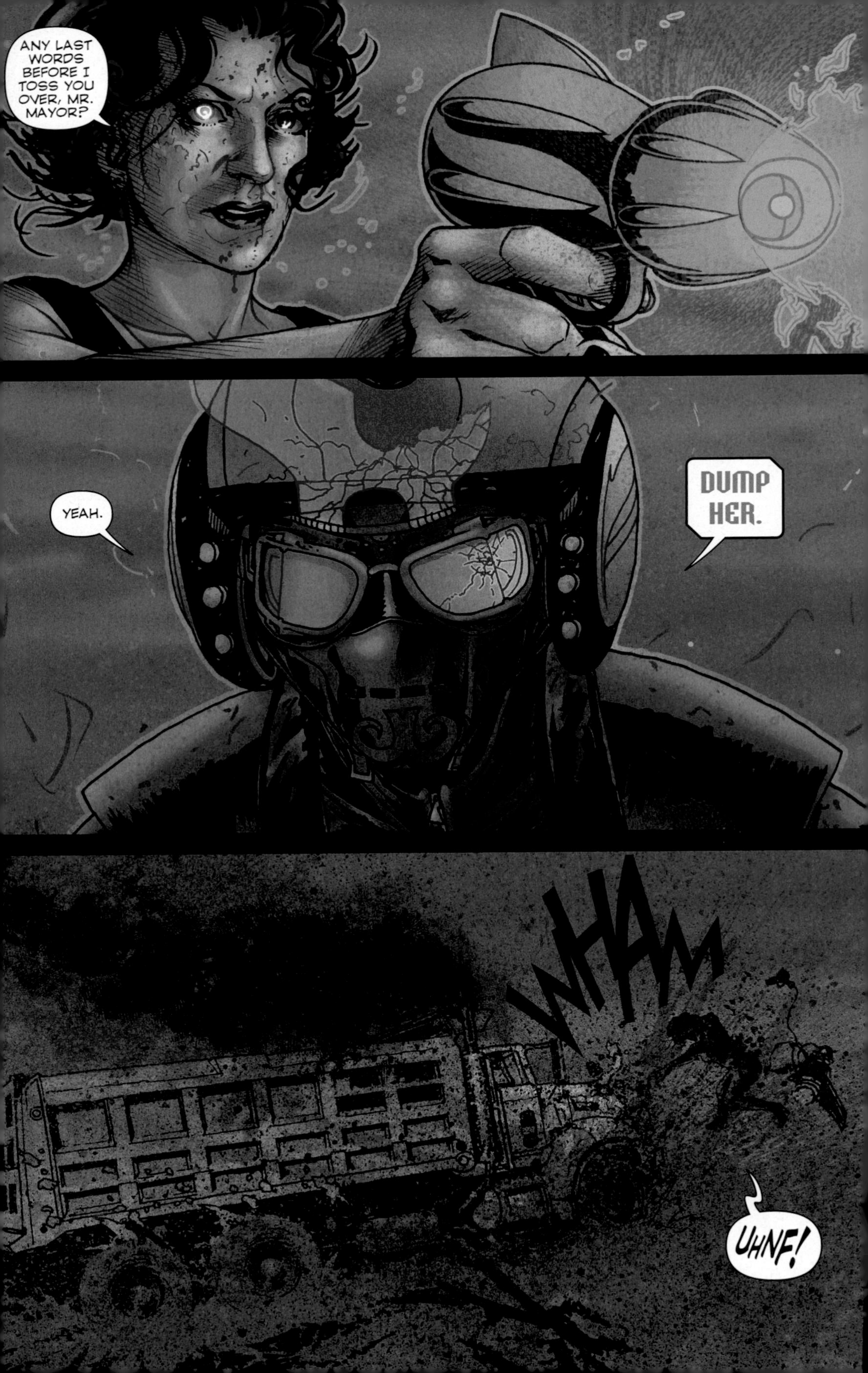
ANY LAST WORDS BEFORE I TOSS YOU OVER, MR. MAYOR?
YEAH.
DUMP HER.
WHAM
UHNF!

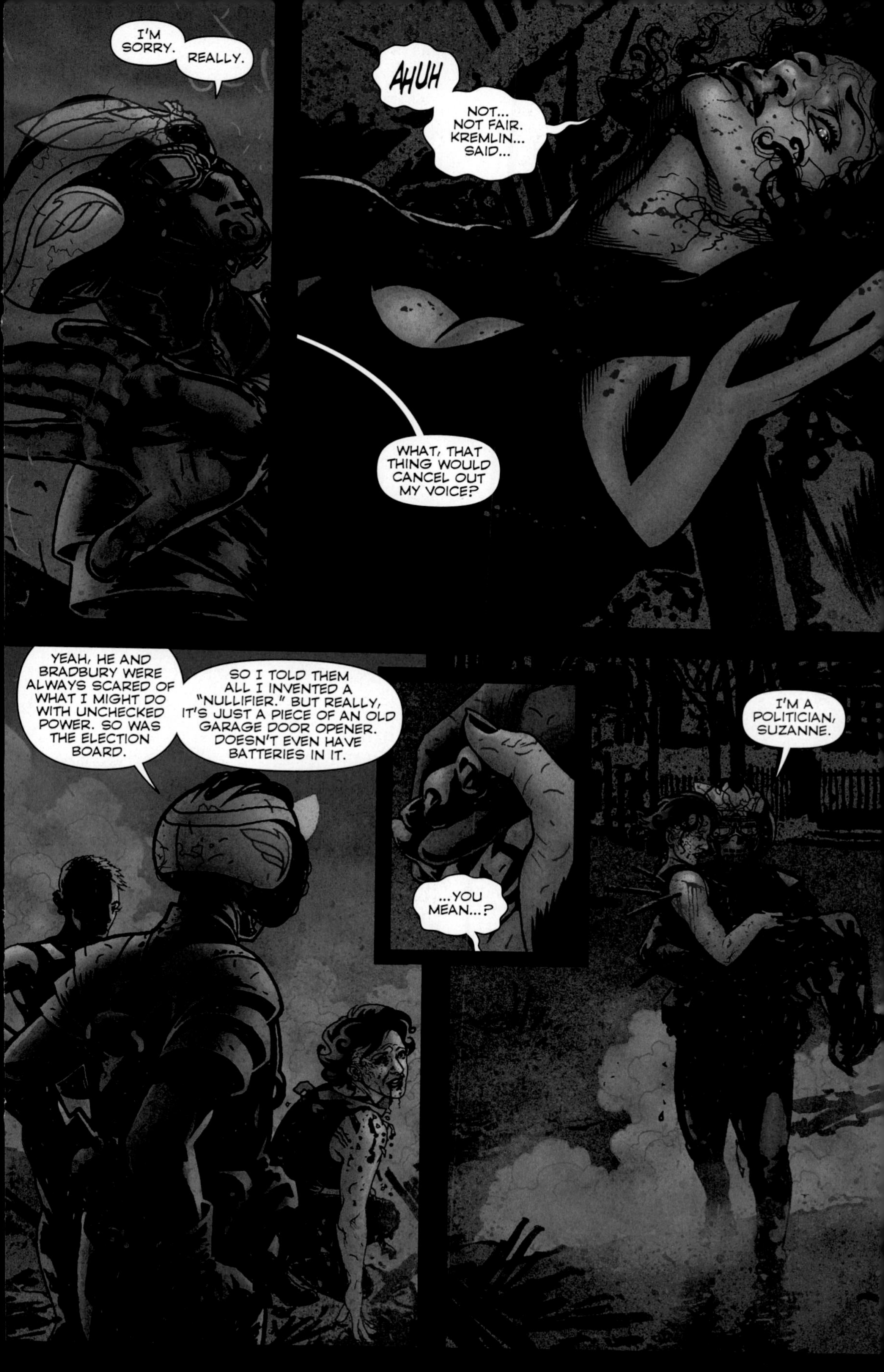
I'M SORRY.
REALLY.
AHUH
NOT... NOT FAIR. KREMLIN... SAID...
WHAT, THAT THING WOULD CANCEL OUT MY VOICE?
YEAH, HE AND BRADBURY WERE ALWAYS SCARED OF WHAT I MIGHT DO WITH UNCHECKED POWER. SO WAS THE ELECTION BOARD.
SO I TOLD THEM ALL I INVENTED A "NULLIFIER." BUT REALLY, IT'S JUST A PIECE OF AN OLD GARAGE DOOR OPENER. DOESN'T EVEN HAVE BATTERIES IN IT.
...YOU MEAN...?
I'M A POLITICIAN, SUZANNE.

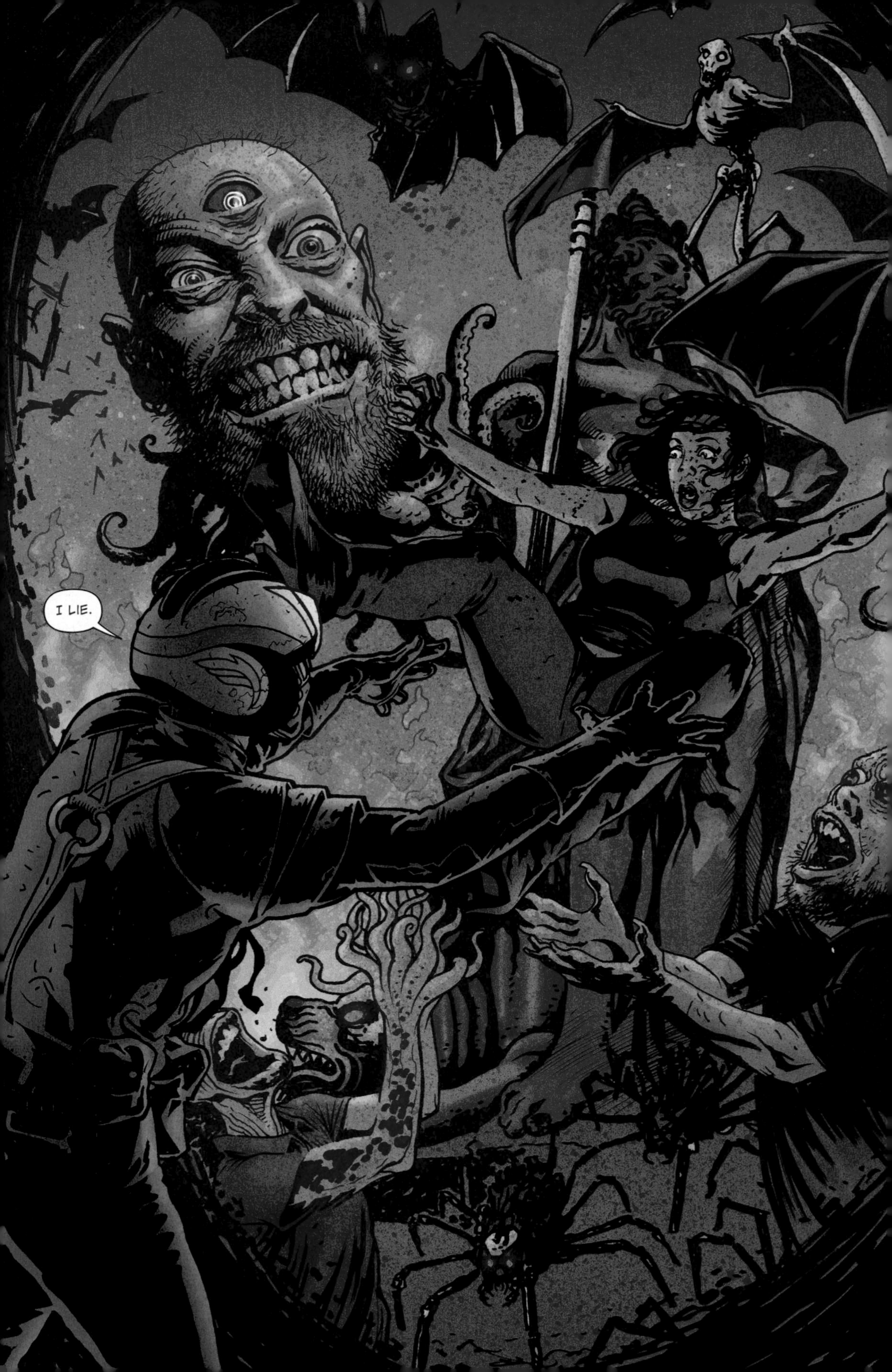
I LIE.

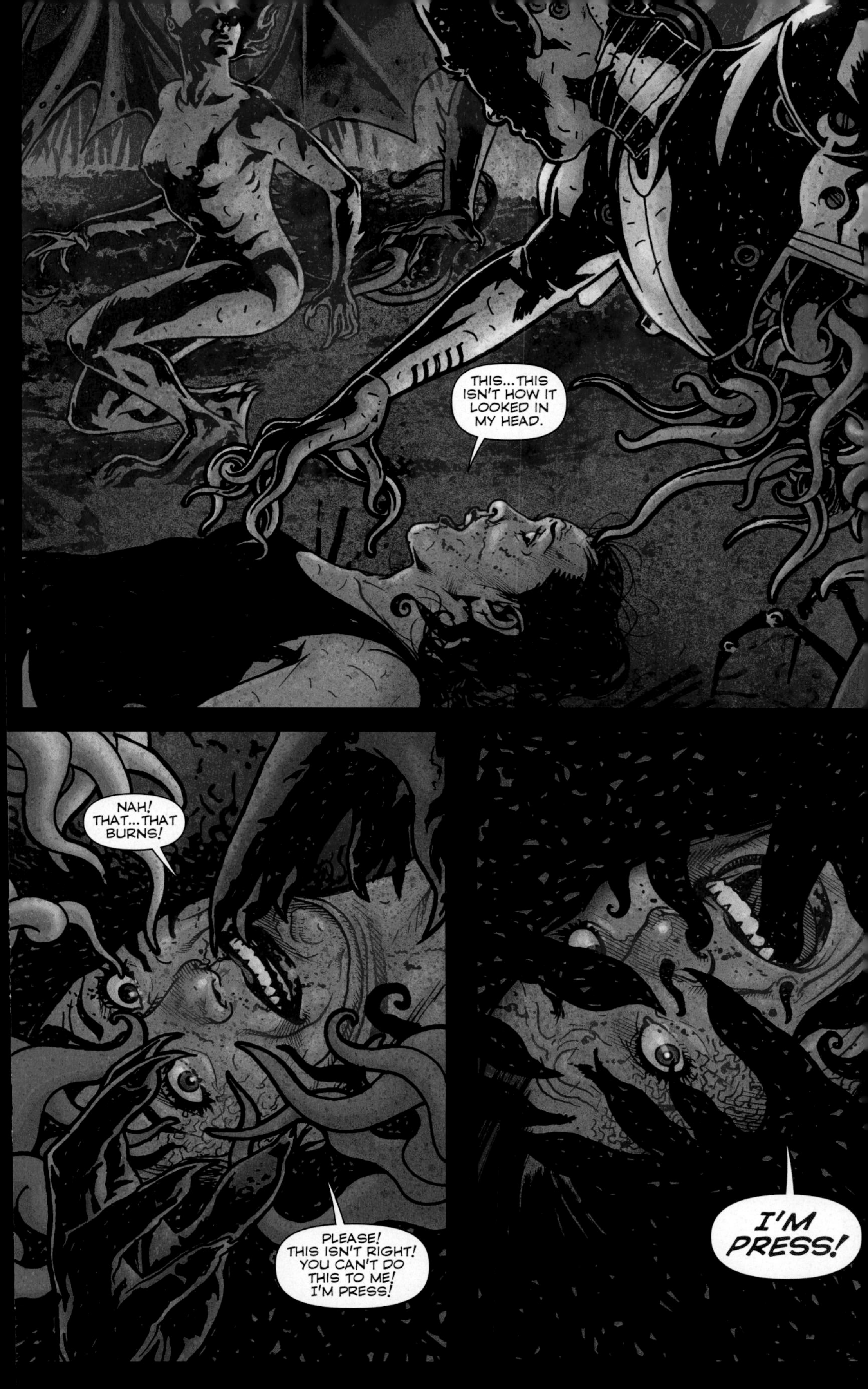
THIS...THIS ISN'T HOW IT LOOKED IN MY HEAD.
NAH! THAT...THAT BURNS!
PLEASE! THIS ISN'T RIGHT! YOU CAN'T DO THIS TO ME! I'M PRESS!
I'M PRESS!

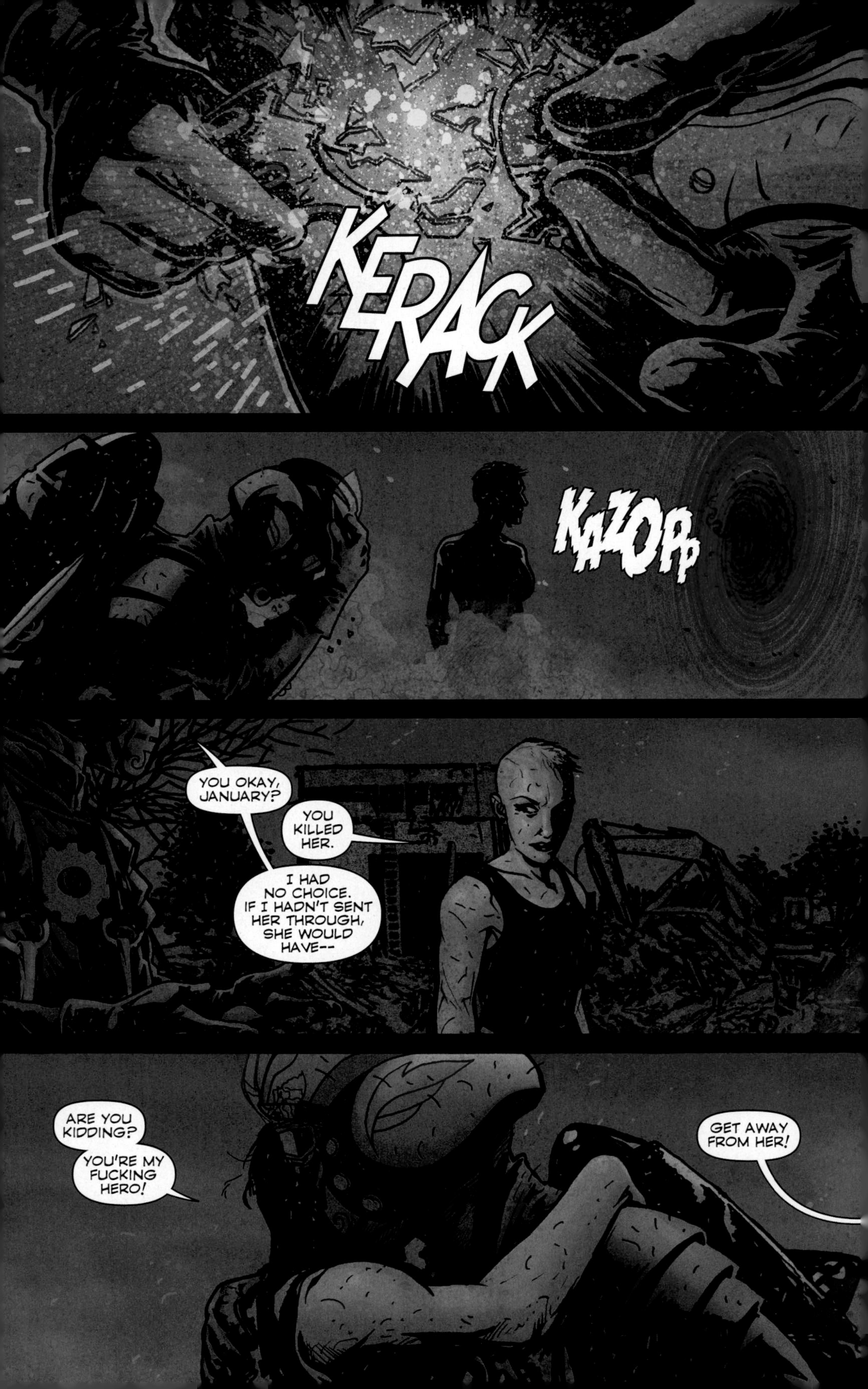

KERACK
KAZORP
YOU OKAY, JANUARY?
YOU KILLED HER.
I HAD NO CHOICE. IF I HADN'T SENT HER THROUGH, SHE WOULD HAVE--
ARE YOU KIDDING?
YOU'RE MY FUCKING HERO!
GET AWAY FROM HER!

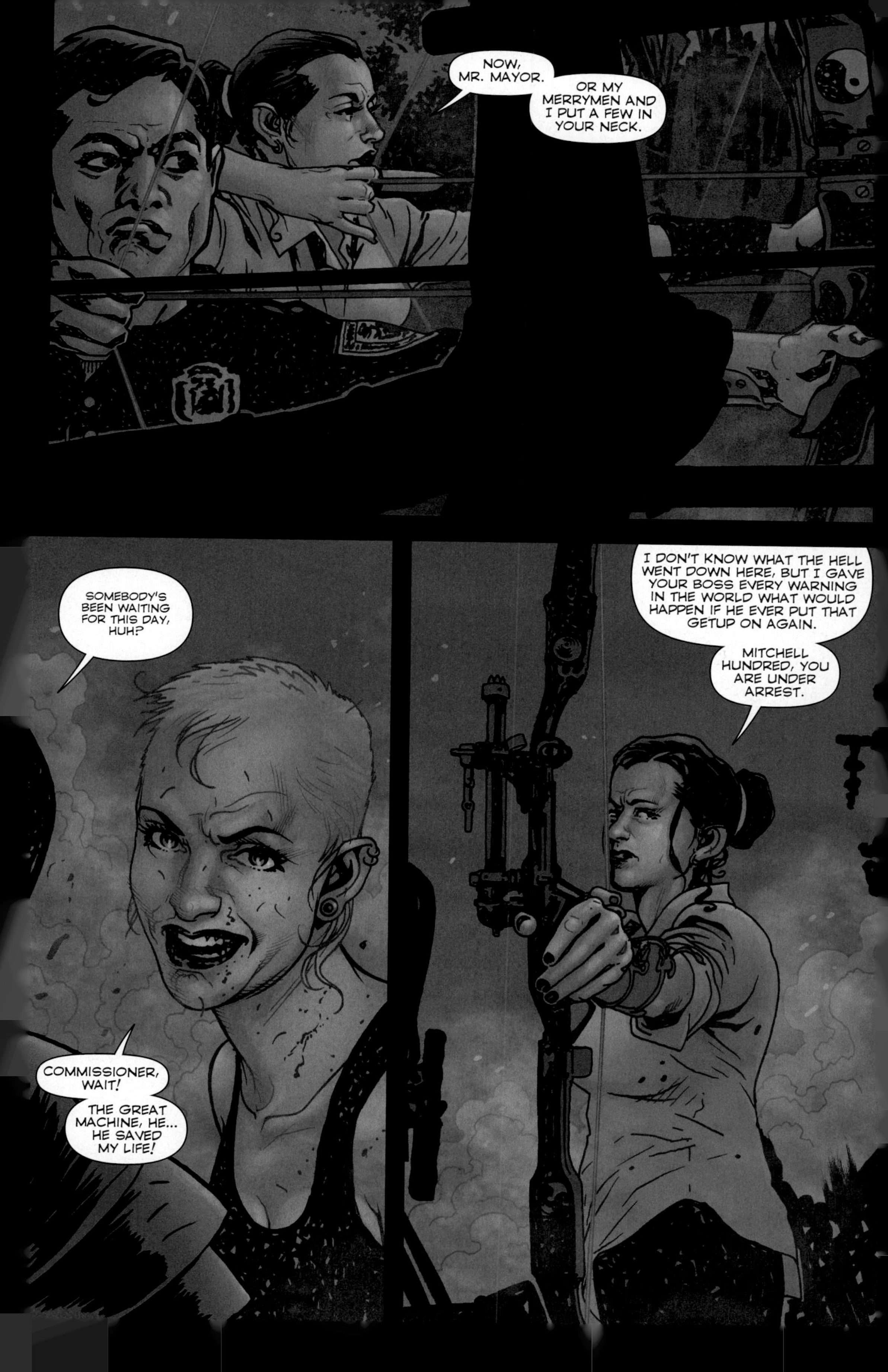
NOW, MR. MAYOR.
OR MY MERRYMEN AND I PUT A FEW IN YOUR NECK.
SOMEBODY'S BEEN WAITING FOR THIS DAY, HUH?
I DON'T KNOW WHAT THE HELL WENT DOWN HERE, BUT I GAVE YOUR BOSS EVERY WARNING IN THE WORLD WHAT WOULD HAPPEN IF HE EVER PUT THAT GETUP ON AGAIN.
MITCHELL HUNDRED, YOU ARE UNDER ARREST.
COMMISSIONER, WAIT!
THE GREAT MACHINE, HE... HE SAVED MY LIFE!

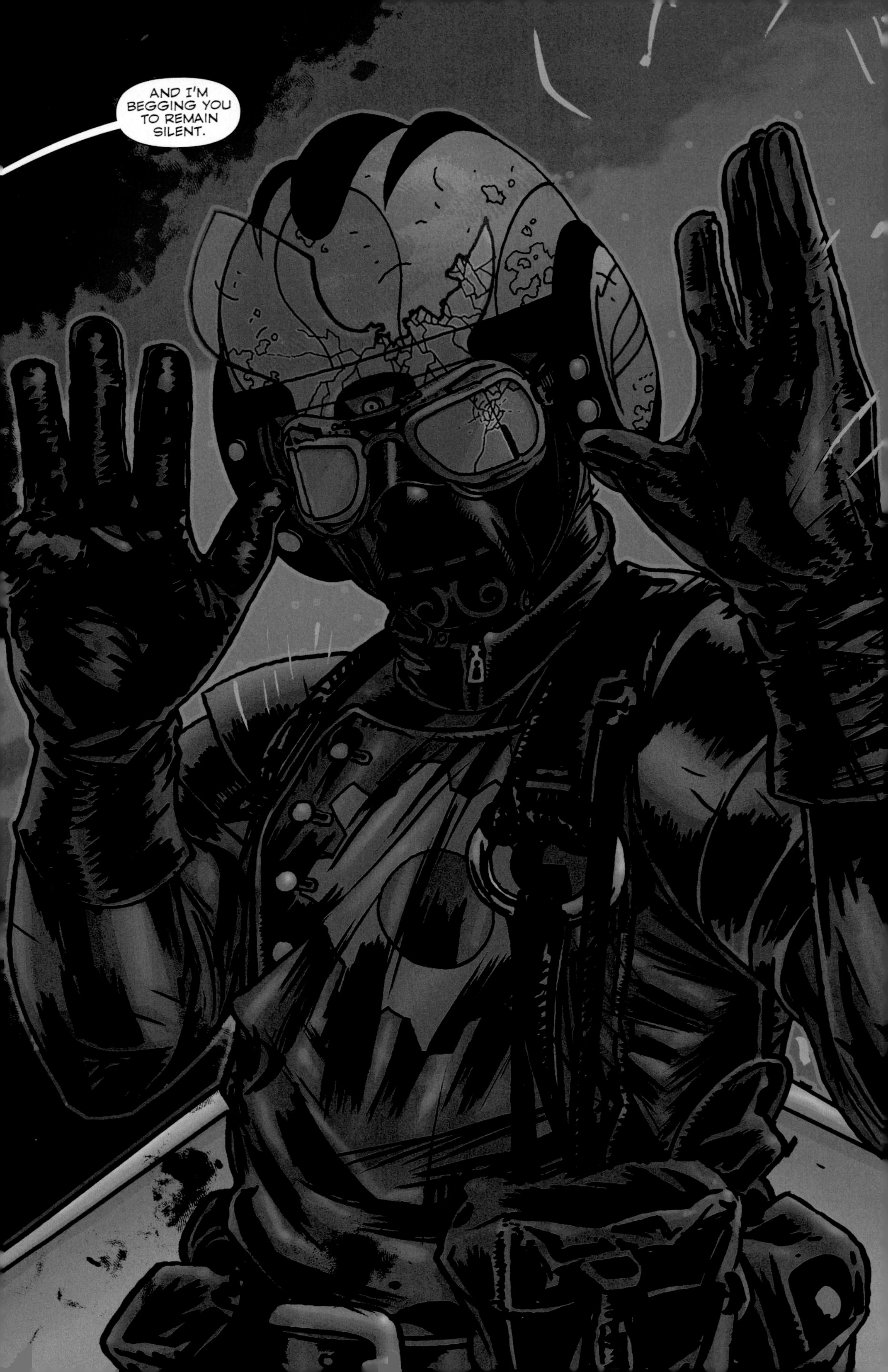
AND I'M BEGGING YOU TO REMAIN SILENT.

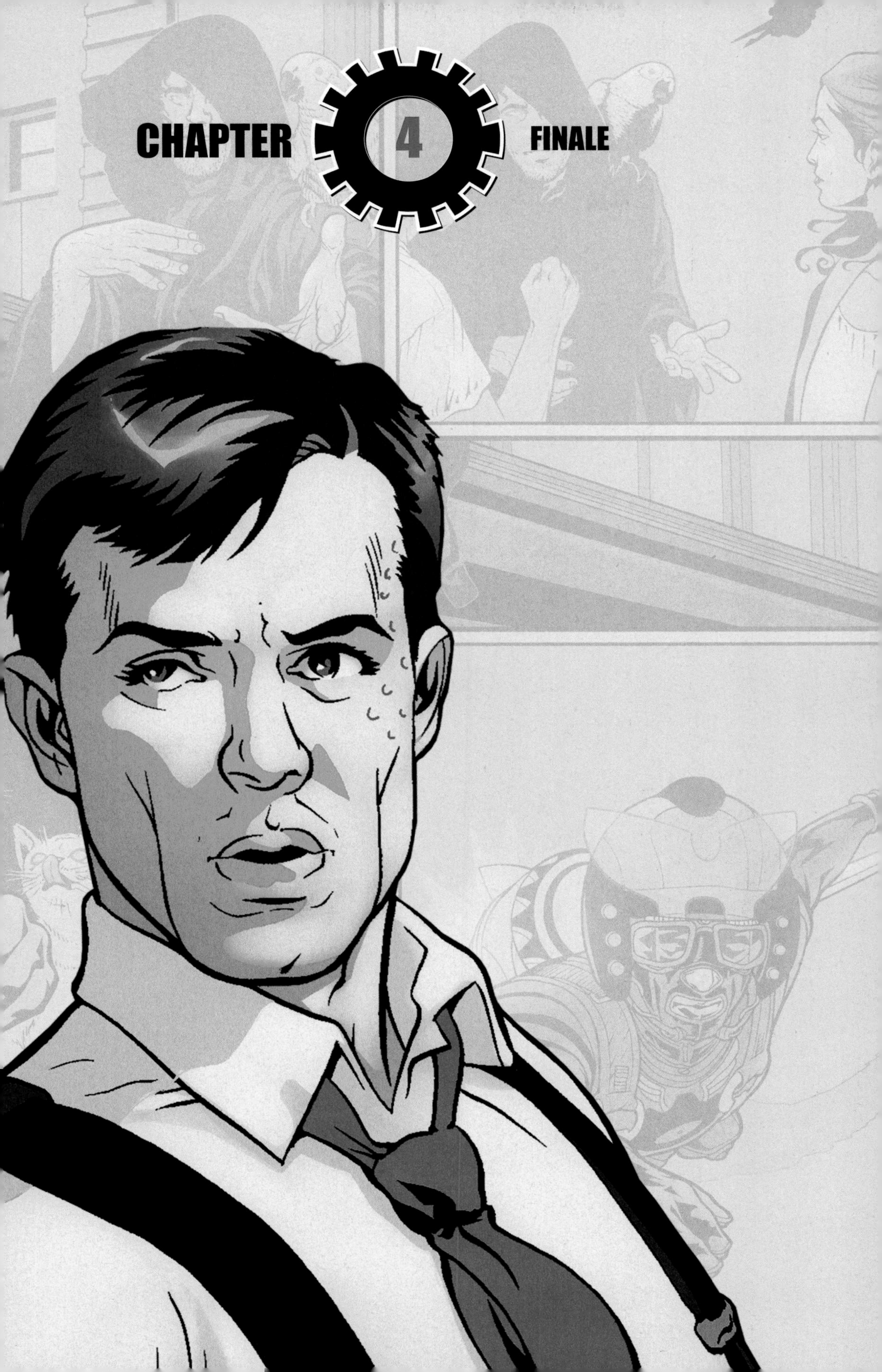
CHAPTER 4 FINALE

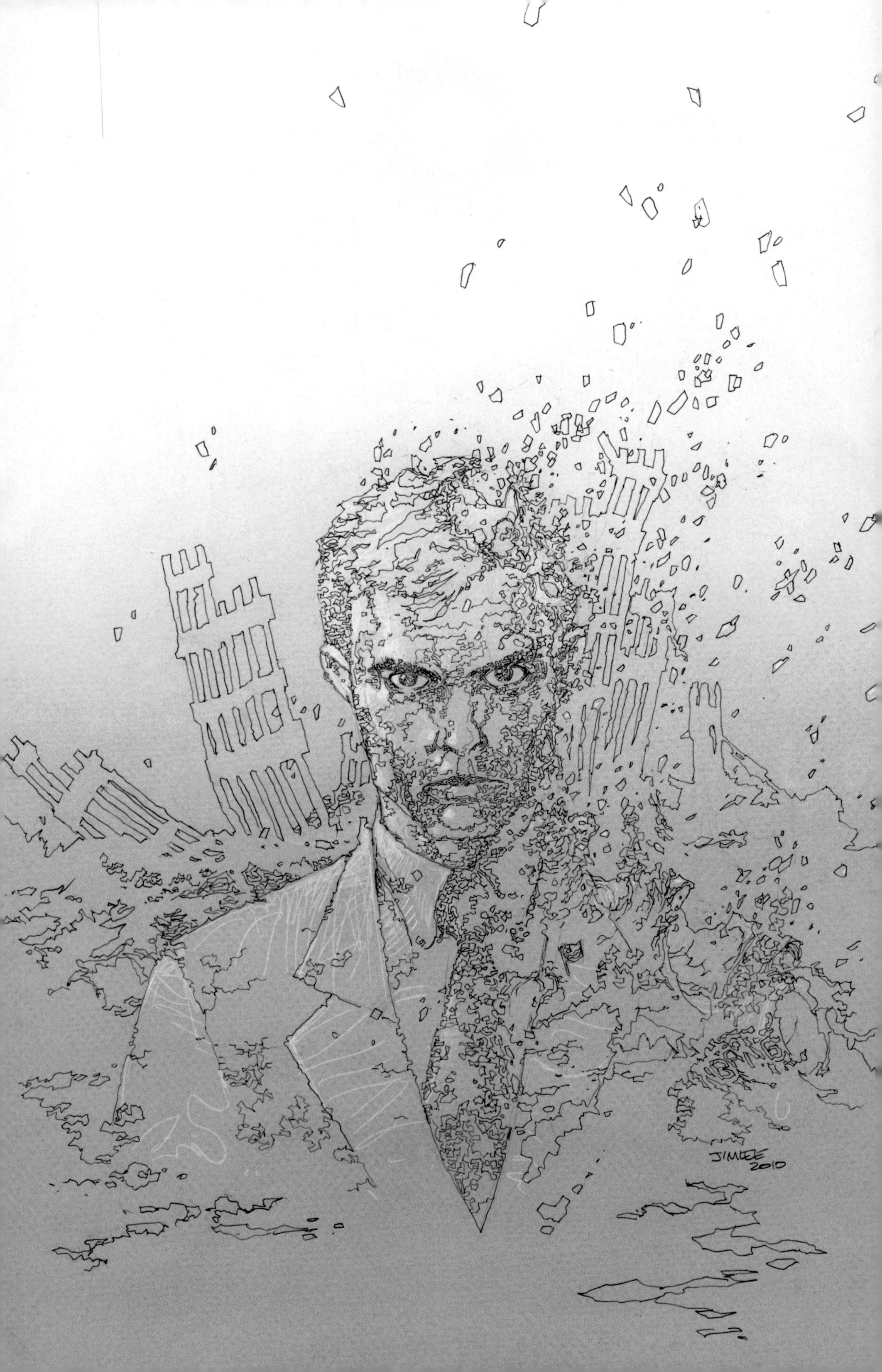
JIMLEE
2010

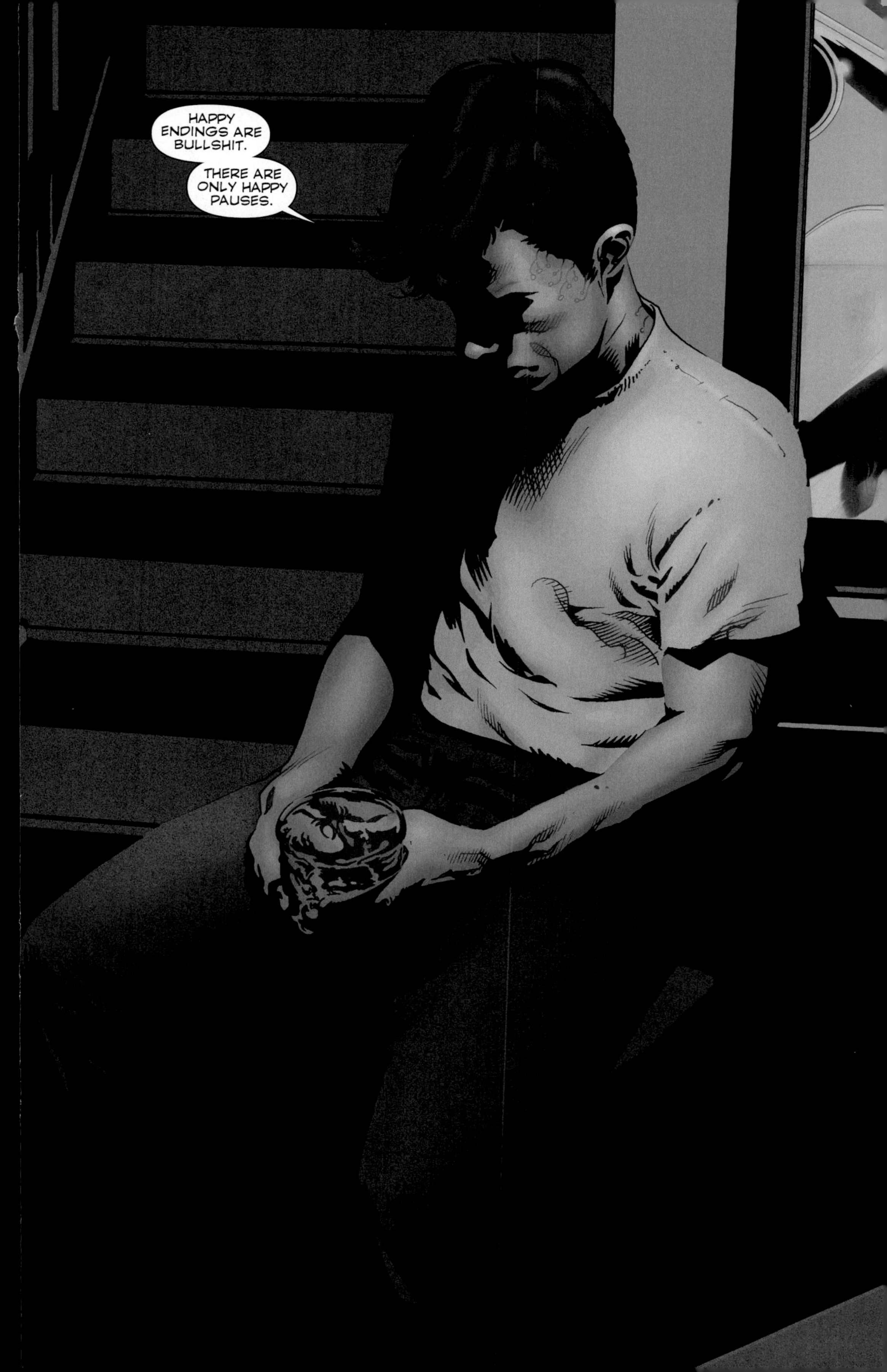
HAPPY ENDINGS ARE BULLSHIT.
THERE ARE ONLY HAPPY PAUSES.

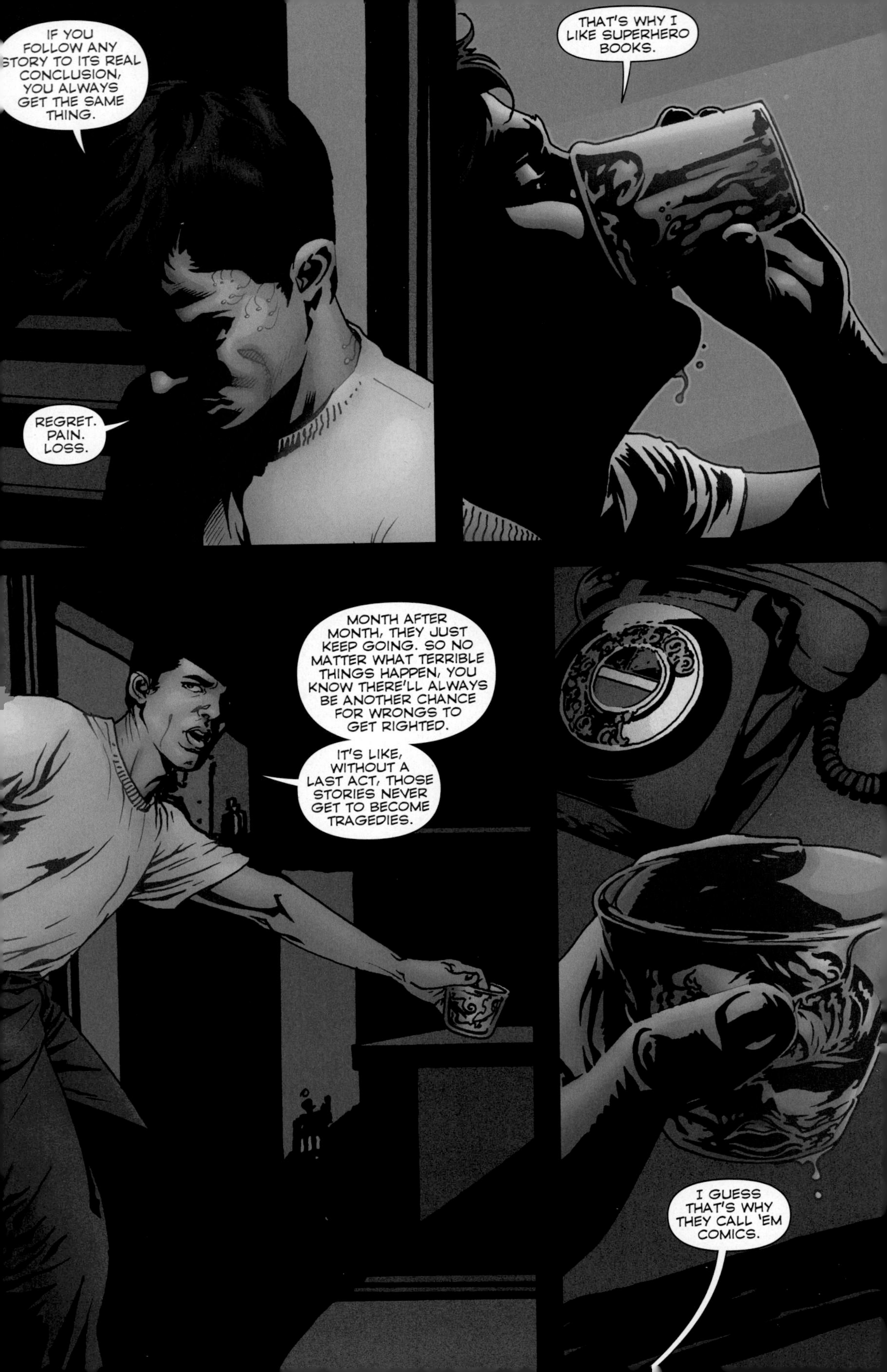
IF YOU FOLLOW ANY STORY TO ITS REAL CONCLUSION, YOU ALWAYS GET THE SAME THING.
REGRET. PAIN. LOSS.
THAT'S WHY I LIKE SUPERHERO BOOKS.
MONTH AFTER MONTH, THEY JUST KEEP GOING. SO NO MATTER WHAT TERRIBLE THINGS HAPPEN, YOU KNOW THERE'LL ALWAYS BE ANOTHER CHANCE FOR WRONGS TO GET RIGHTED.
IT'S LIKE, WITHOUT A LAST ACT, THOSE STORIES NEVER GET TO BECOME TRAGEDIES.
I GUESS THAT'S WHY THEY CALL 'EM COMICS.

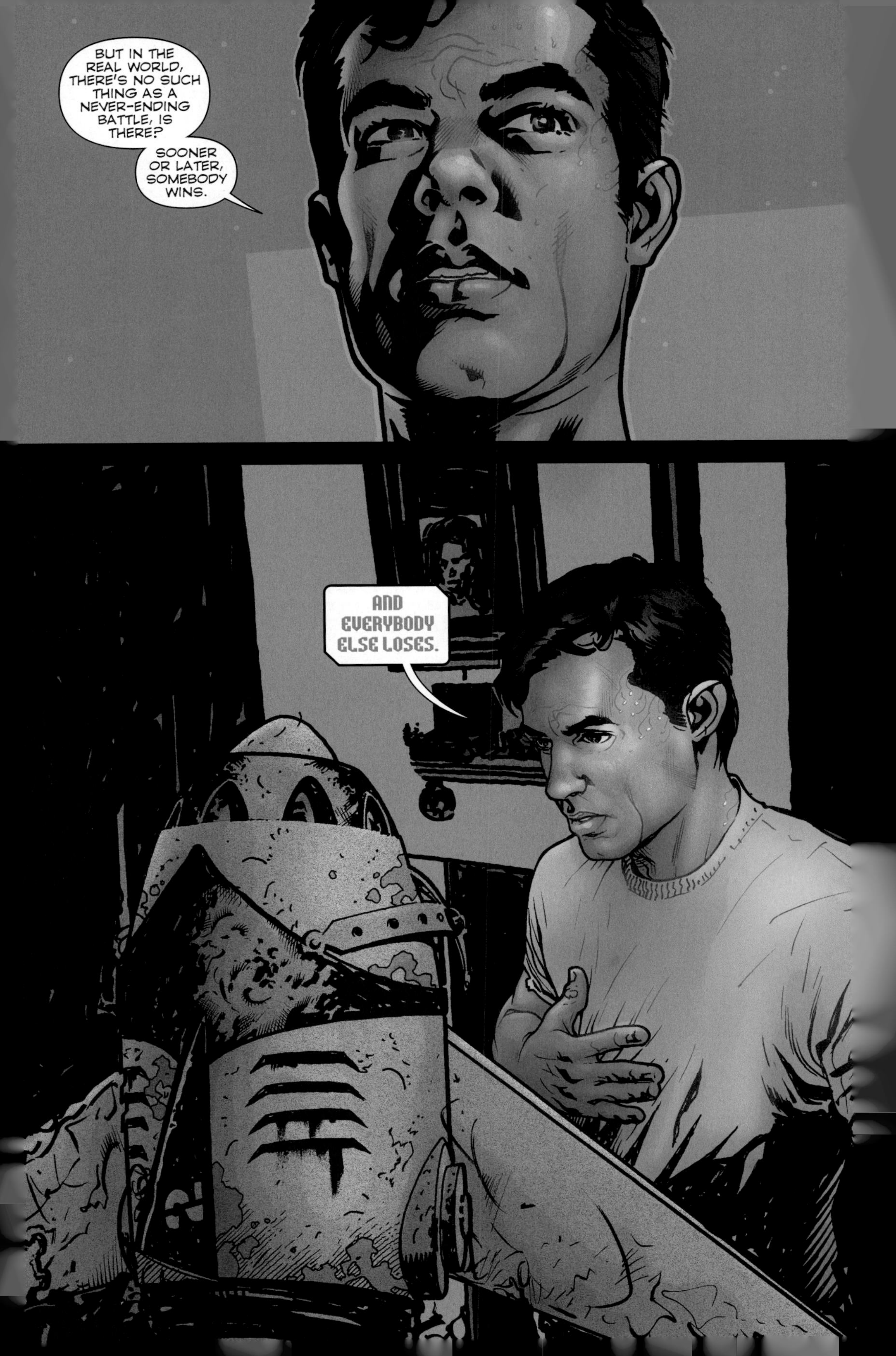
BUT IN THE REAL WORLD, THERE'S NO SUCH THING AS A NEVER-ENDING BATTLE, IS THERE?
SOONER OR LATER, SOMEBODY WINS.
AND EVERYBODY ELSE LOSES.

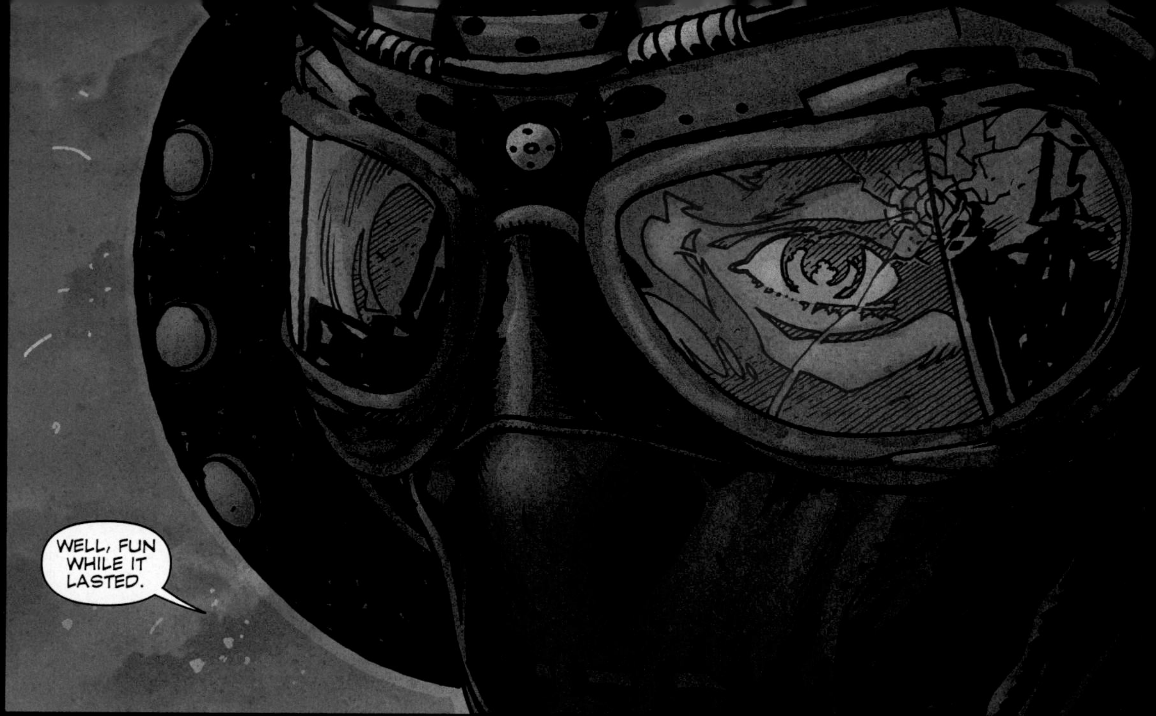
WELL, FUN WHILE IT LASTED.

TUESDAY, APRIL 12, 2005

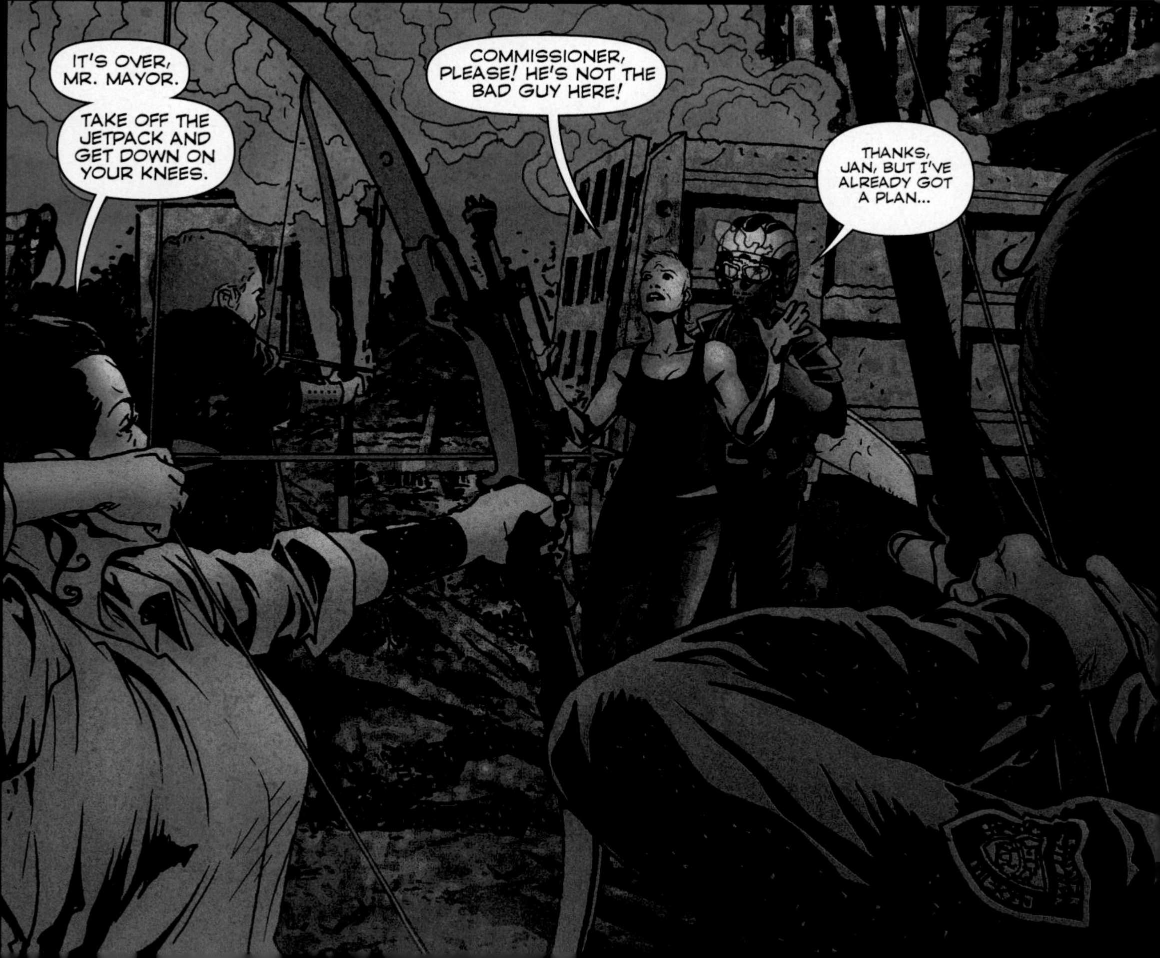
IT'S OVER, MR. MAYOR.
TAKE OFF THE JETPACK AND GET DOWN ON YOUR KNEES.
COMMISSIONER, PLEASE! HE'S NOT THE BAD GUY HERE!
THANKS, JAN, BUT I'VE ALREADY GOT A PLAN...

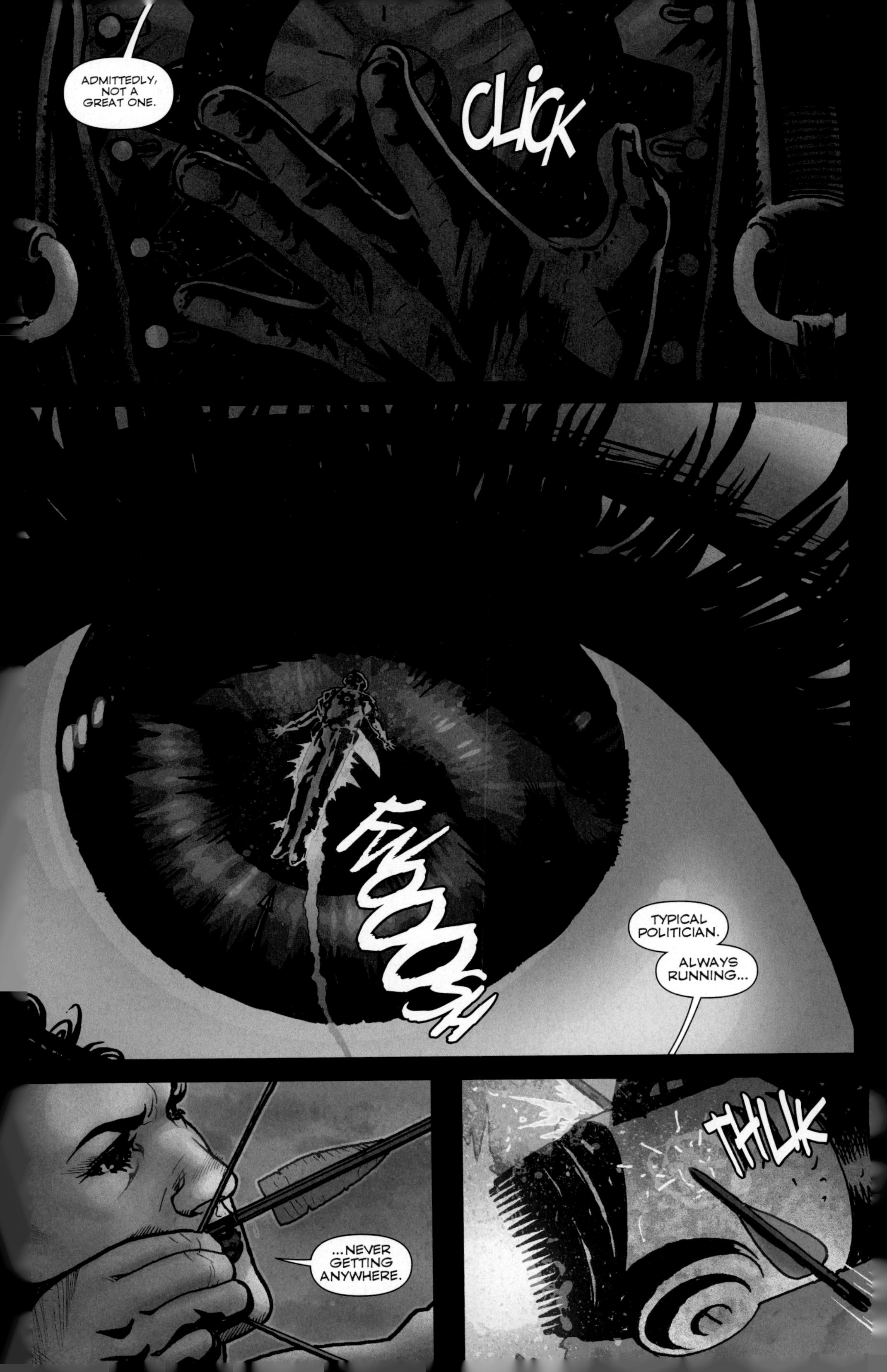
ADMITTEDLY, NOT A GREAT ONE.
CLICK
FWOOOOSH
TYPICAL POLITICIAN.
ALWAYS RUNNING...
...NEVER GETTING ANYWHERE.
THUK

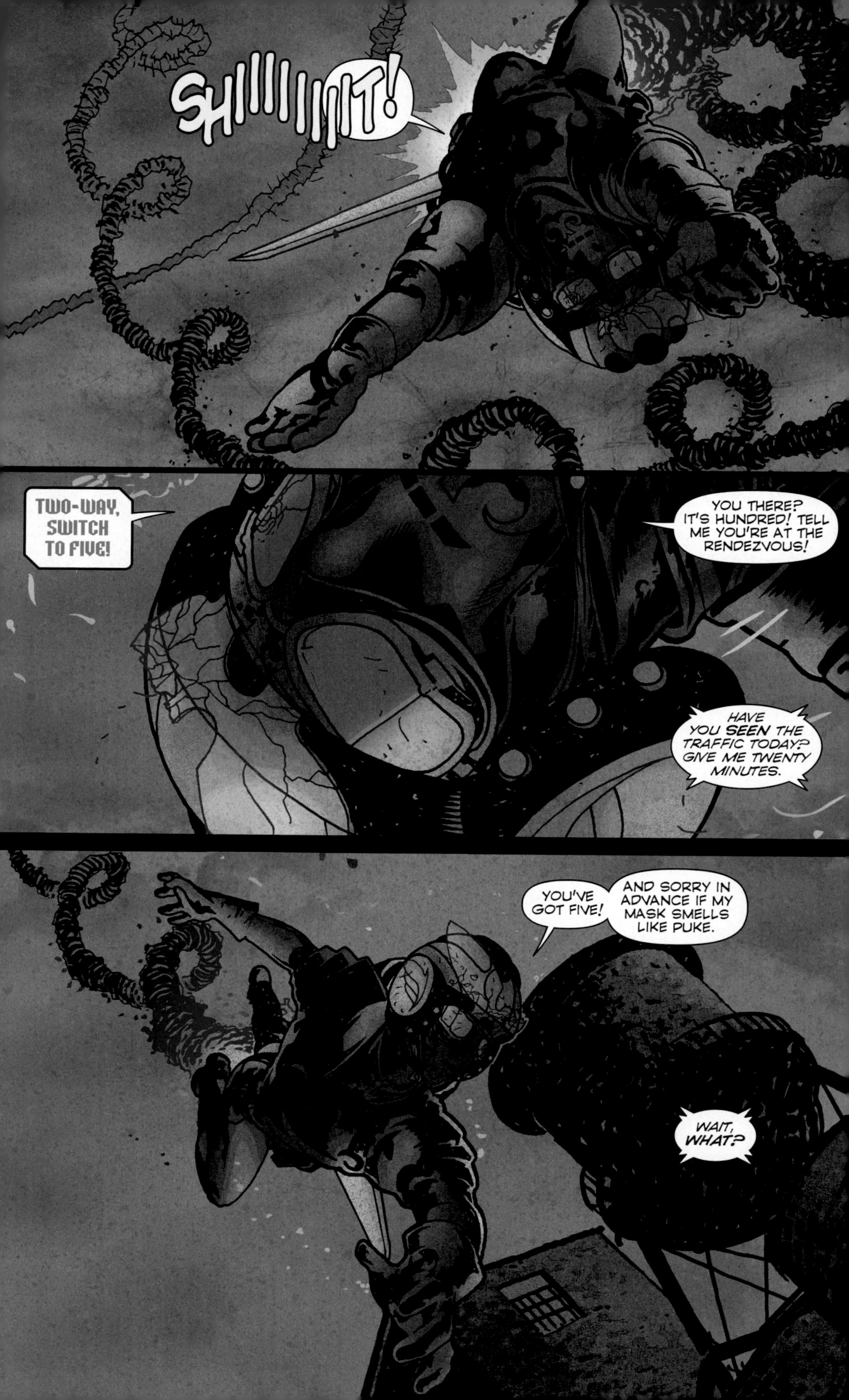
SHIIIIIIIIT!
TWO-WAY, SWITCH TO FIVE!
YOU THERE? IT'S HUNDRED! TELL ME YOU'RE AT THE RENDEZVOUS!
HAVE YOU **SEEN** THE TRAFFIC TODAY? GIVE ME TWENTY MINUTES.
YOU'VE GOT FIVE!
AND SORRY IN ADVANCE IF MY MASK SMELLS LIKE PUKE.
WAIT, **WHAT?**

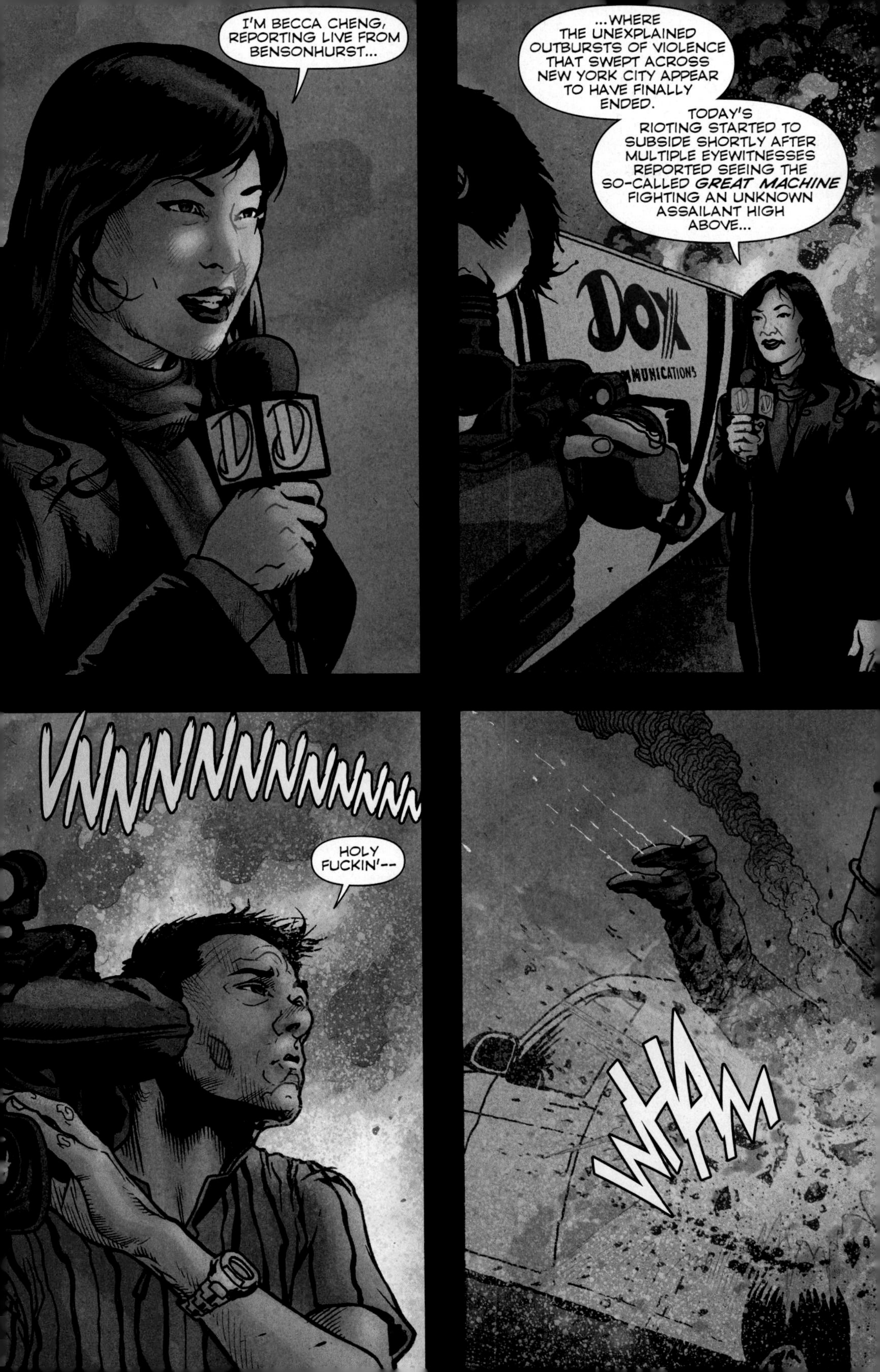
I'M BECCA CHENG, REPORTING LIVE FROM BENSONHURST...
...WHERE THE UNEXPLAINED OUTBURSTS OF VIOLENCE THAT SWEPT ACROSS NEW YORK CITY APPEAR TO HAVE FINALLY ENDED.
TODAY'S RIOTING STARTED TO SUBSIDE SHORTLY AFTER MULTIPLE EYEWITNESSES REPORTED SEEING THE SO-CALLED *GREAT MACHINE* FIGHTING AN UNKNOWN ASSAILANT HIGH ABOVE...
VNNNNNNNNNNNN
HOLY FUCKIN'--
WHAM

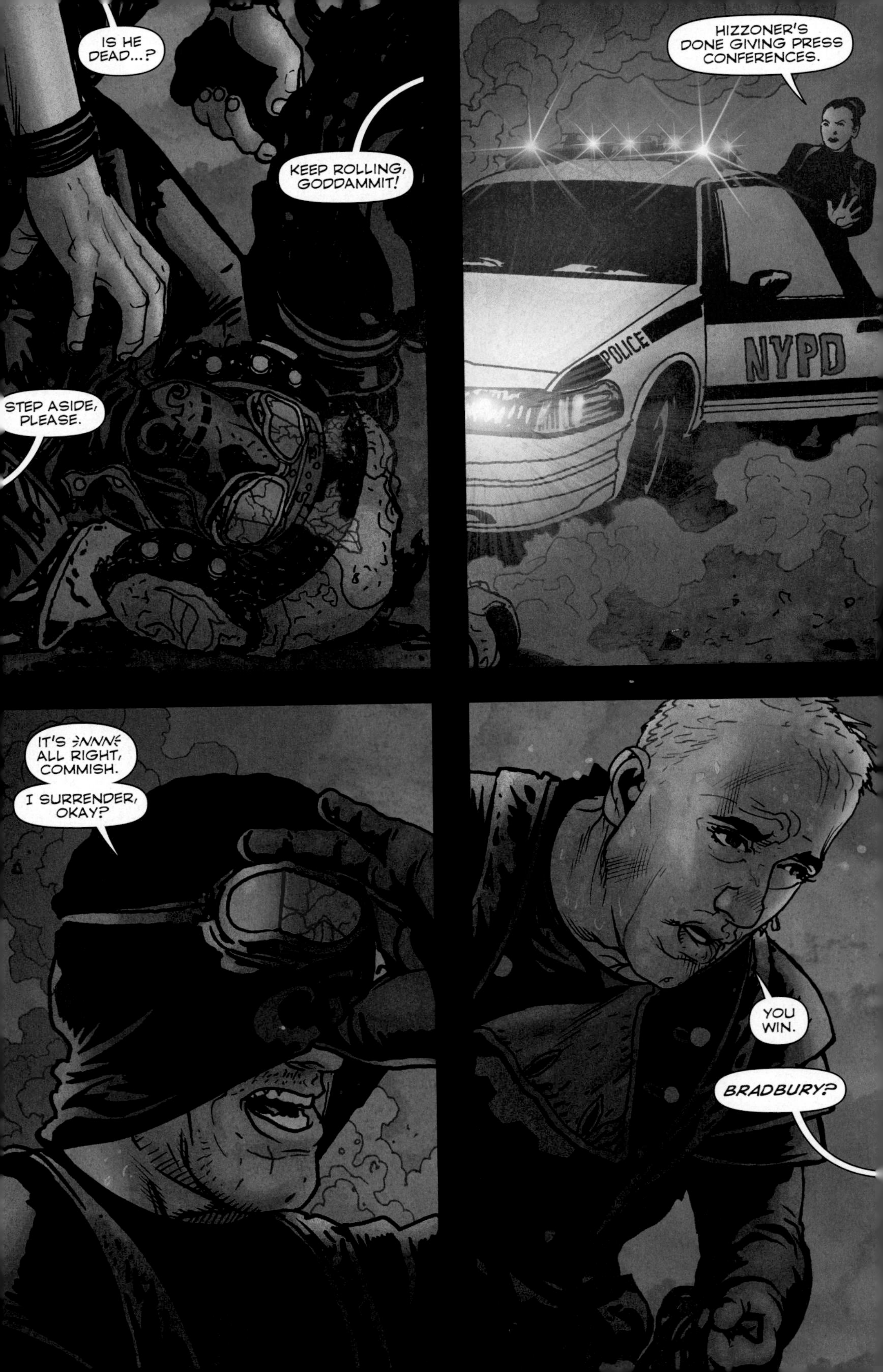
IS HE DEAD...?
KEEP ROLLING, GODDAMMIT!
STEP ASIDE, PLEASE.
HIZZONER'S DONE GIVING PRESS CONFERENCES.
POLICE
NYPD
IT'S =NNN= ALL RIGHT, COMMISH.
I SURRENDER, OKAY?
YOU WIN.
BRADBURY?

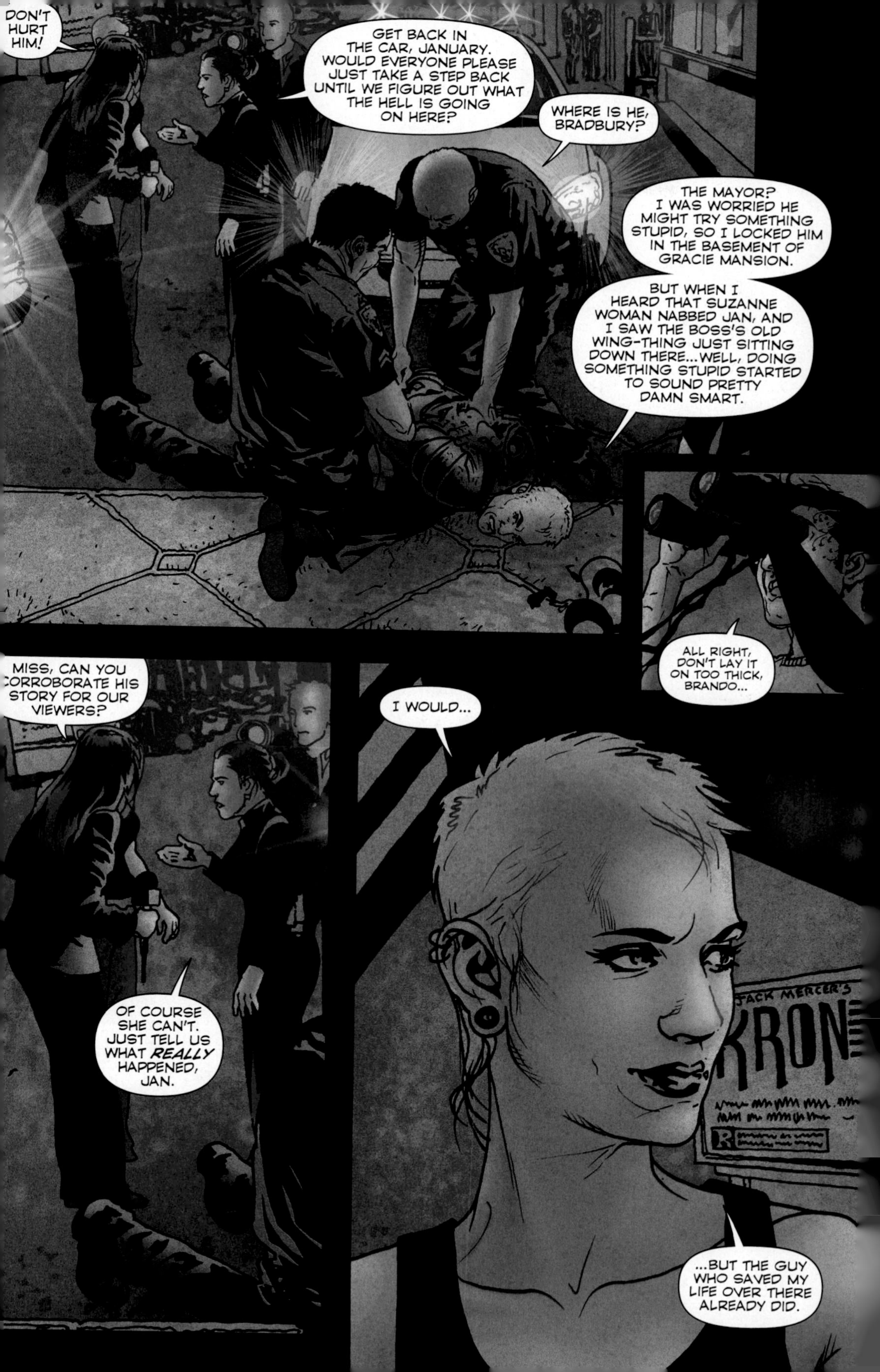
DON'T HURT HIM!
GET BACK IN THE CAR, JANUARY. WOULD EVERYONE PLEASE JUST TAKE A STEP BACK UNTIL WE FIGURE OUT WHAT THE HELL IS GOING ON HERE?
WHERE IS HE, BRADBURY?
THE MAYOR? I WAS WORRIED HE MIGHT TRY SOMETHING STUPID, SO I LOCKED HIM IN THE BASEMENT OF GRACIE MANSION.
BUT WHEN I HEARD THAT SUZANNE WOMAN NABBED JAN, AND I SAW THE BOSS'S OLD WING-THING JUST SITTING DOWN THERE...WELL, DOING SOMETHING STUPID STARTED TO SOUND PRETTY DAMN SMART.
ALL RIGHT, DON'T LAY IT ON TOO THICK, BRANDO...
MISS, CAN YOU CORROBORATE HIS STORY FOR OUR VIEWERS?
OF COURSE SHE CAN'T. JUST TELL US WHAT *REALLY* HAPPENED, JAN.
I WOULD...
JACK MERCER'S
KRON
...BUT THE GUY WHO SAVED MY LIFE OVER THERE ALREADY DID.

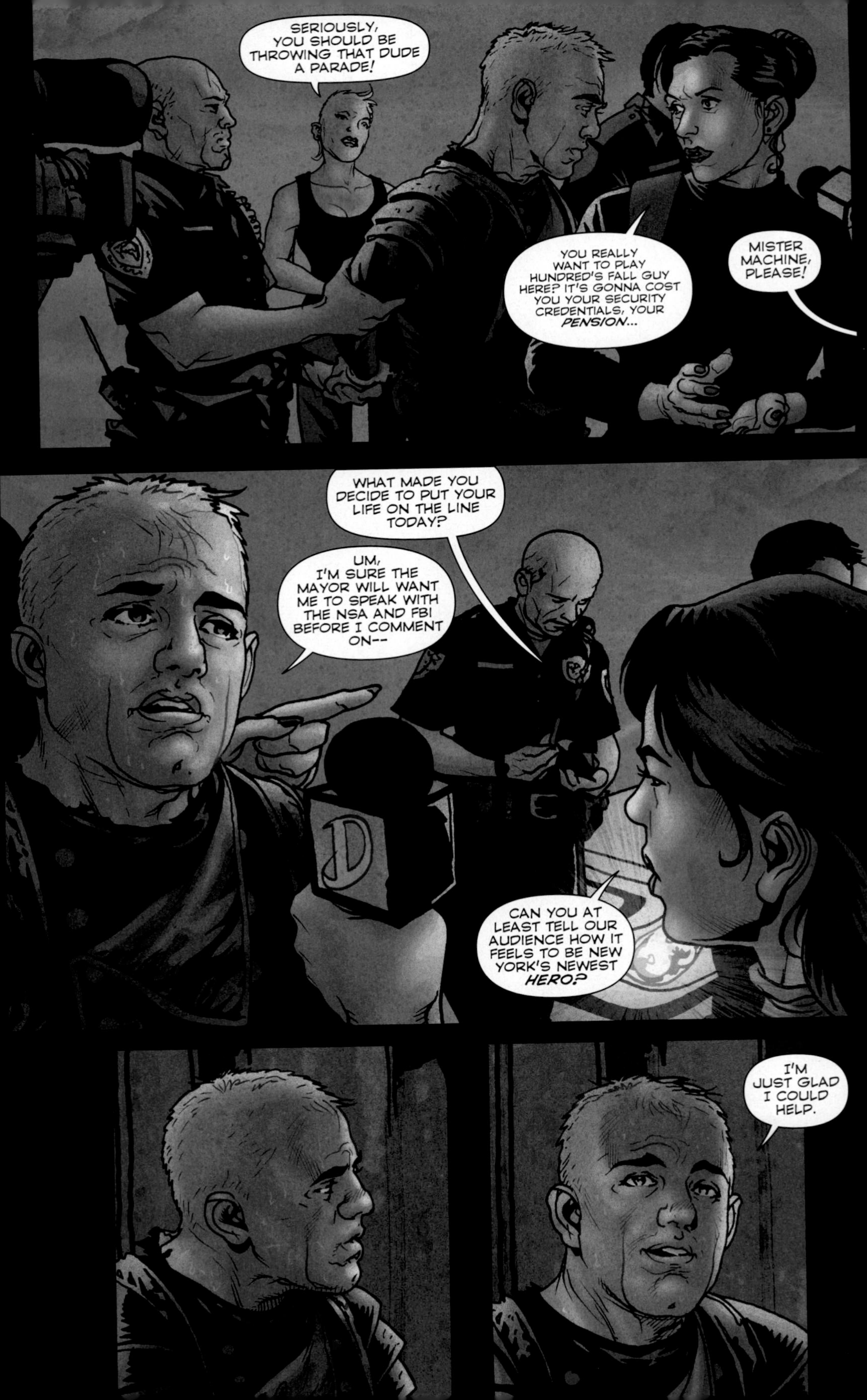
SERIOUSLY, YOU SHOULD BE THROWING THAT DUDE A PARADE!
YOU REALLY WANT TO PLAY HUNDRED'S FALL GUY HERE? IT'S GONNA COST YOU YOUR SECURITY CREDENTIALS, YOUR *PENSION*...
MISTER MACHINE, PLEASE!
WHAT MADE YOU DECIDE TO PUT YOUR LIFE ON THE LINE TODAY?
UM, I'M SURE THE MAYOR WILL WANT ME TO SPEAK WITH THE NSA AND FBI BEFORE I COMMENT ON--
CAN YOU AT LEAST TELL OUR AUDIENCE HOW IT FEELS TO BE NEW YORK'S NEWEST *HERO?*
I'M JUST GLAD I COULD HELP.

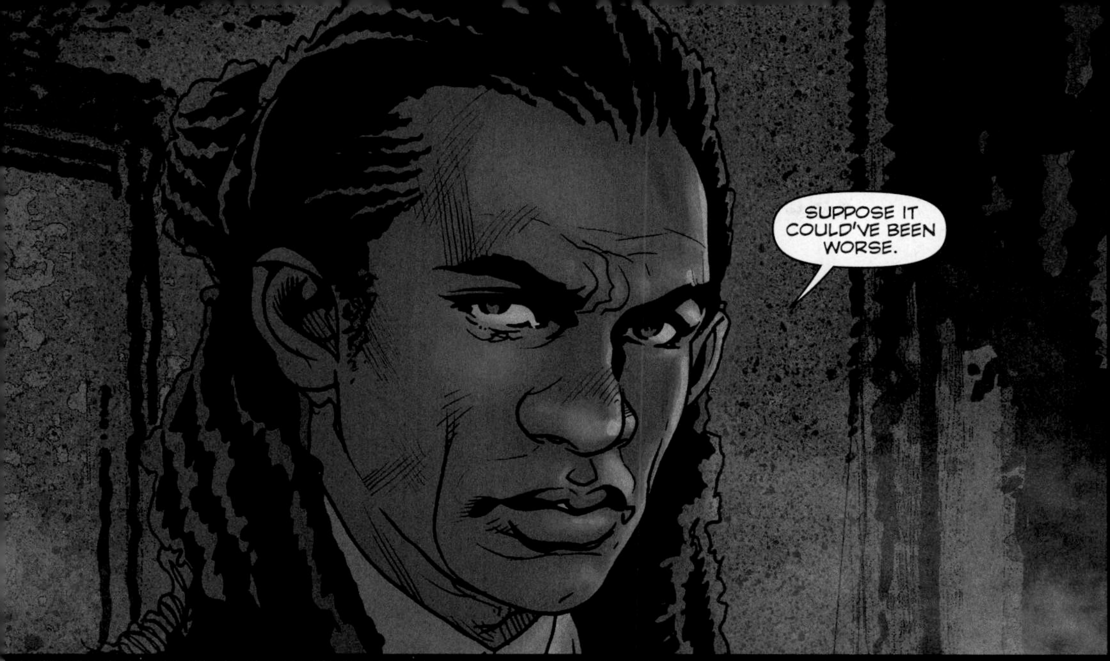
SUPPOSE IT COULD'VE BEEN WORSE.

THURSDAY, APRIL 14, 2005

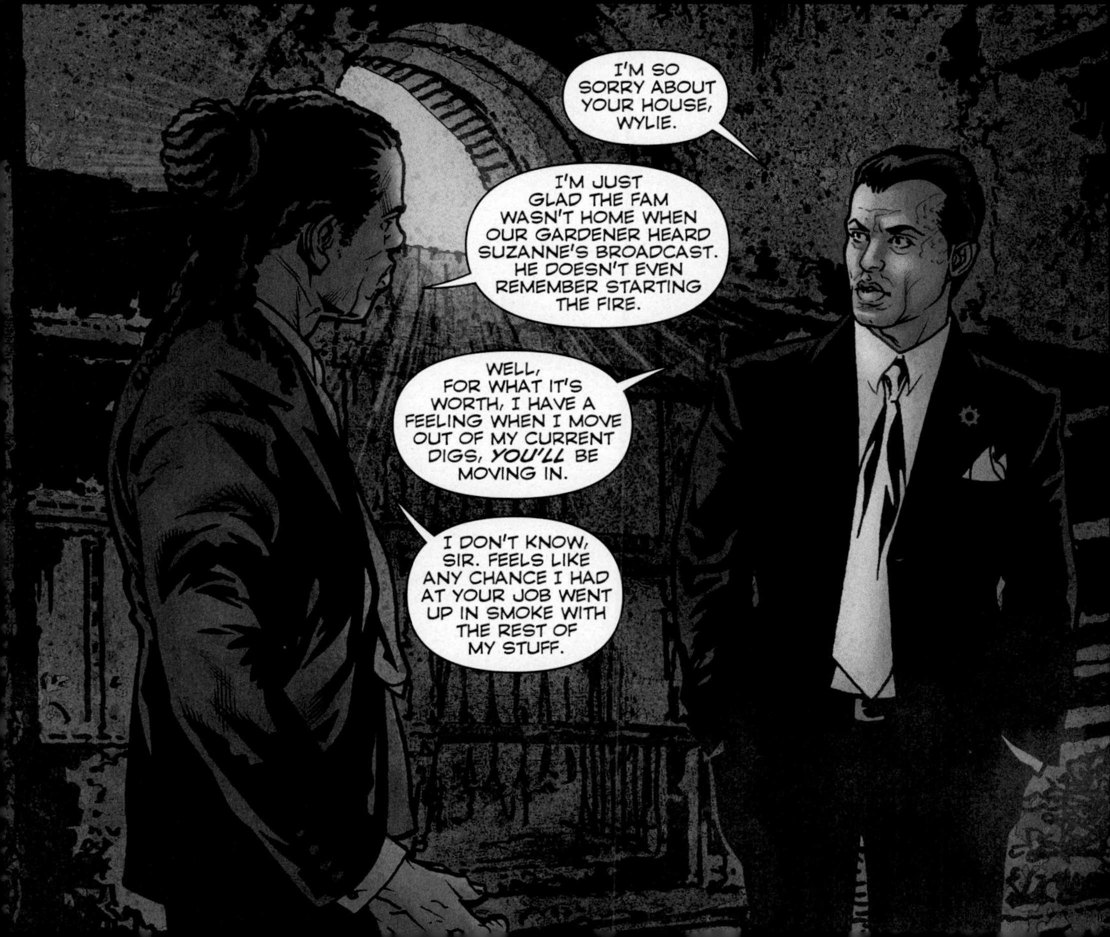
I'M SO SORRY ABOUT YOUR HOUSE, WYLIE.
I'M JUST GLAD THE FAM WASN'T HOME WHEN OUR GARDENER HEARD SUZANNE'S BROADCAST. HE DOESN'T EVEN REMEMBER STARTING THE FIRE.
WELL, FOR WHAT IT'S WORTH, I HAVE A FEELING WHEN I MOVE OUT OF MY CURRENT DIGS, *YOU'LL* BE MOVING IN.
I DON'T KNOW, SIR. FEELS LIKE ANY CHANCE I HAD AT YOUR JOB WENT UP IN SMOKE WITH THE REST OF MY STUFF.

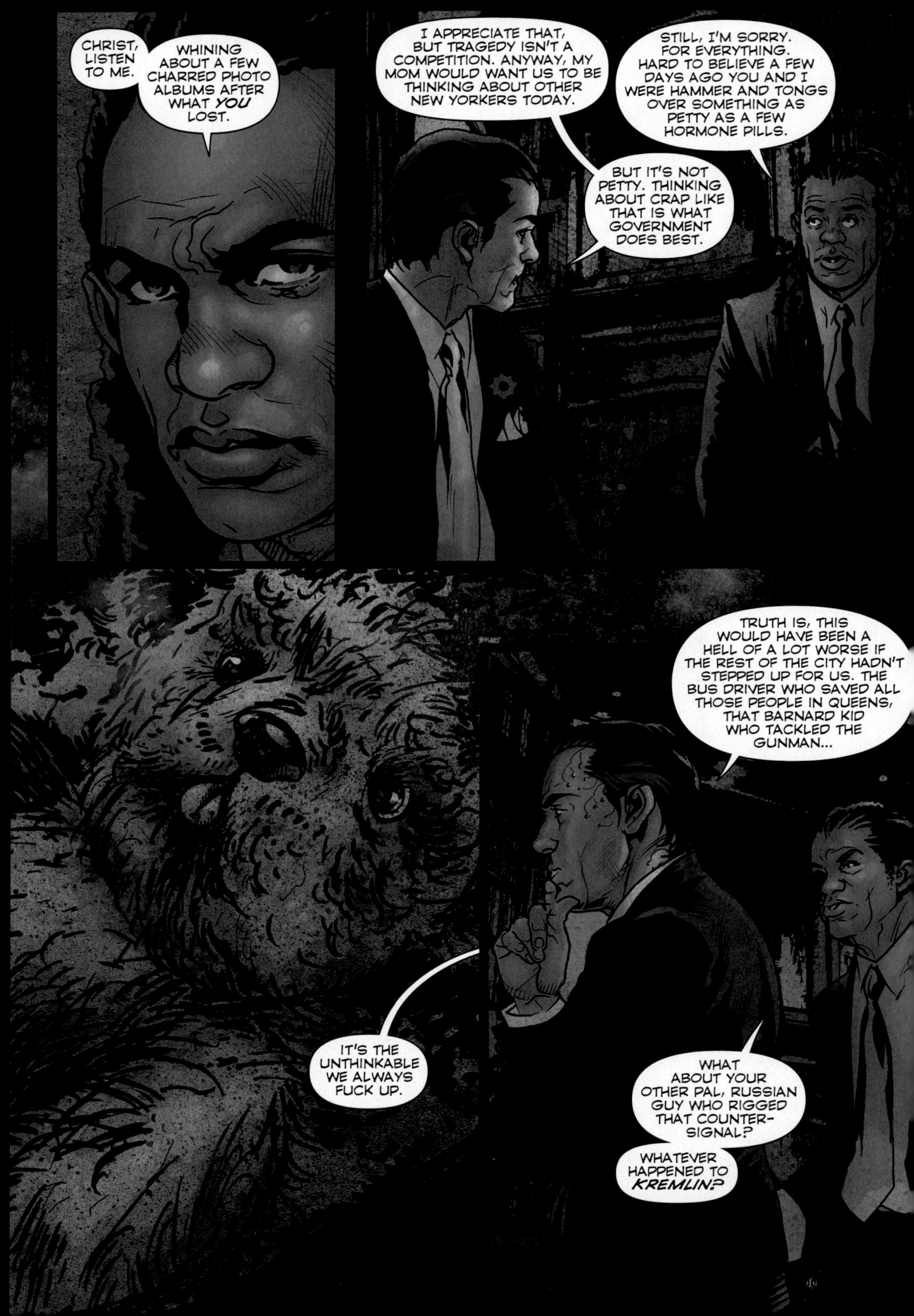
CHRIST, LISTEN TO ME.
WHINING ABOUT A FEW CHARRED PHOTO ALBUMS AFTER WHAT *YOU* LOST.
I APPRECIATE THAT, BUT TRAGEDY ISN'T A COMPETITION. ANYWAY, MY MOM WOULD WANT US TO BE THINKING ABOUT OTHER NEW YORKERS TODAY.
STILL, I'M SORRY. FOR EVERYTHING. HARD TO BELIEVE A FEW DAYS AGO YOU AND I WERE HAMMER AND TONGS OVER SOMETHING AS PETTY AS A FEW HORMONE PILLS.
BUT IT'S NOT PETTY. THINKING ABOUT CRAP LIKE THAT IS WHAT GOVERNMENT DOES BEST.
TRUTH IS, THIS WOULD HAVE BEEN A HELL OF A LOT WORSE IF THE REST OF THE CITY HADN'T STEPPED UP FOR US. THE BUS DRIVER WHO SAVED ALL THOSE PEOPLE IN QUEENS, THAT BARNARD KID WHO TACKLED THE GUNMAN...
IT'S THE UNTHINKABLE WE ALWAYS FUCK UP.
WHAT ABOUT YOUR OTHER PAL, RUSSIAN GUY WHO RIGGED THAT COUNTER-SIGNAL?
WHATEVER HAPPENED TO *KREMLIN?*

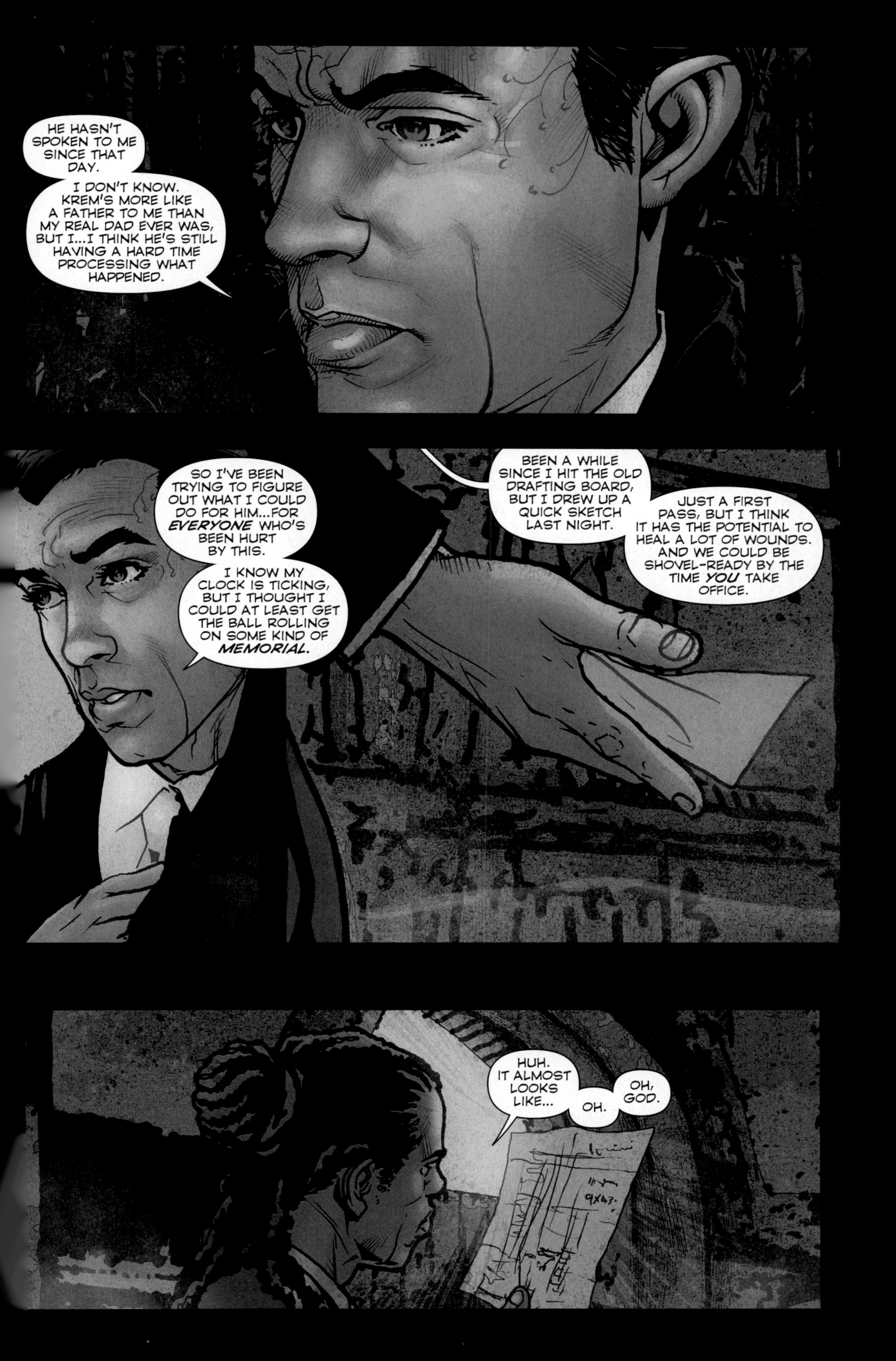
HE HASN'T SPOKEN TO ME SINCE THAT DAY.
I DON'T KNOW. KREM'S MORE LIKE A FATHER TO ME THAN MY REAL DAD EVER WAS, BUT I...I THINK HE'S STILL HAVING A HARD TIME PROCESSING WHAT HAPPENED.
SO I'VE BEEN TRYING TO FIGURE OUT WHAT I COULD DO FOR HIM...FOR *EVERYONE* WHO'S BEEN HURT BY THIS.
I KNOW MY CLOCK IS TICKING, BUT I THOUGHT I COULD AT LEAST GET THE BALL ROLLING ON SOME KIND OF ***MEMORIAL***.
BEEN A WHILE SINCE I HIT THE OLD DRAFTING BOARD, BUT I DREW UP A QUICK SKETCH LAST NIGHT.
JUST A FIRST PASS, BUT I THINK IT HAS THE POTENTIAL TO HEAL A LOT OF WOUNDS. AND WE COULD BE SHOVEL-READY BY THE TIME *YOU* TAKE OFFICE.
HUH. IT ALMOST LOOKS LIKE...
OH.
OH, GOD.

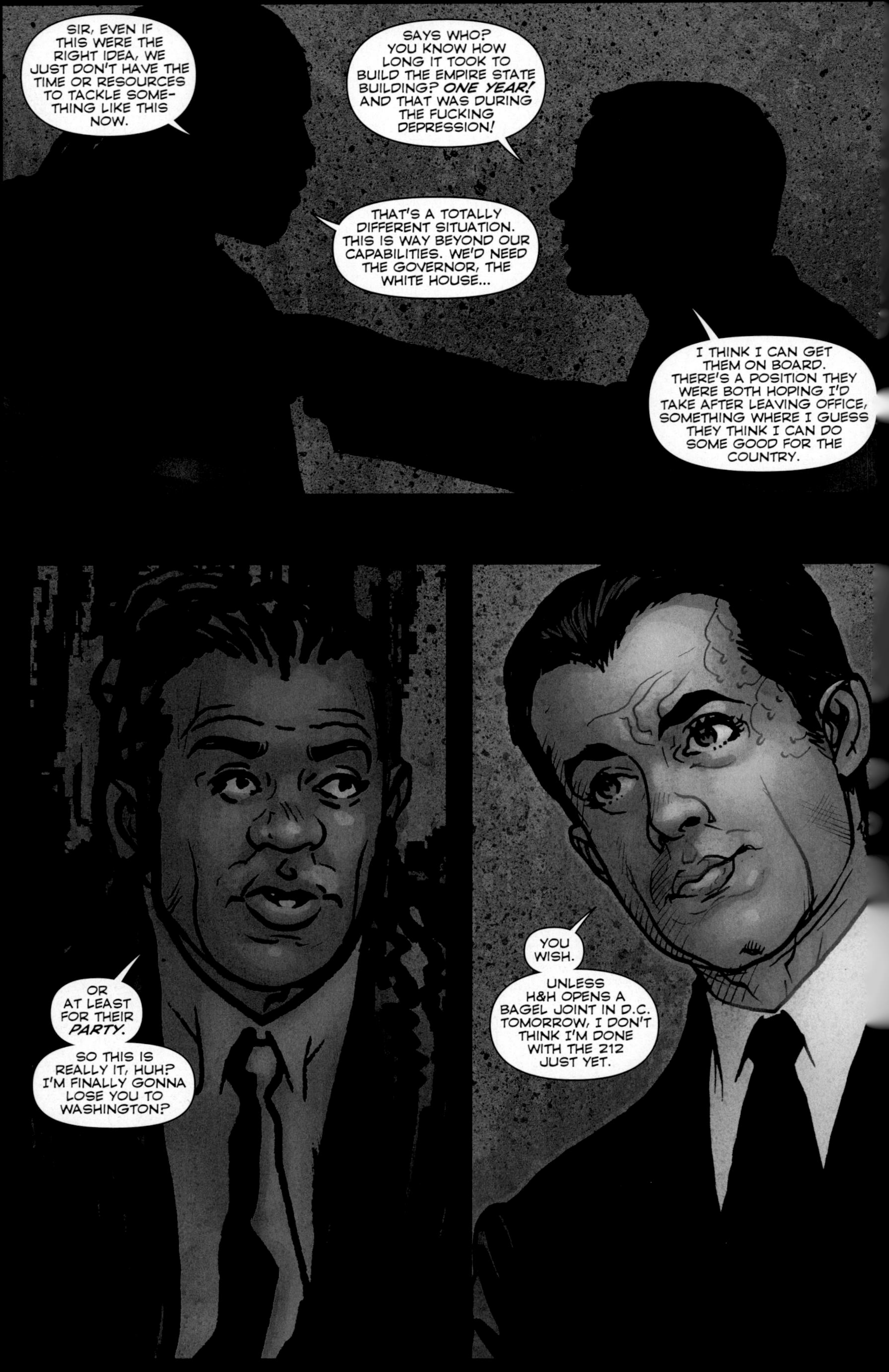
SIR, EVEN IF THIS WERE THE RIGHT IDEA, WE JUST DON'T HAVE THE TIME OR RESOURCES TO TACKLE SOME-THING LIKE THIS NOW.
SAYS WHO? YOU KNOW HOW LONG IT TOOK TO BUILD THE EMPIRE STATE BUILDING? ONE YEAR! AND THAT WAS DURING THE FUCKING DEPRESSION!
THAT'S A TOTALLY DIFFERENT SITUATION. THIS IS WAY BEYOND OUR CAPABILITIES. WE'D NEED THE GOVERNOR, THE WHITE HOUSE...
I THINK I CAN GET THEM ON BOARD. THERE'S A POSITION THEY WERE BOTH HOPING I'D TAKE AFTER LEAVING OFFICE, SOMETHING WHERE I GUESS THEY THINK I CAN DO SOME GOOD FOR THE COUNTRY.
OR AT LEAST FOR THEIR PARTY.
SO THIS IS REALLY IT, HUH? I'M FINALLY GONNA LOSE YOU TO WASHINGTON?
YOU WISH.
UNLESS H&H OPENS A BAGEL JOINT IN D.C. TOMORROW, I DON'T THINK I'M DONE WITH THE 212 JUST YET.

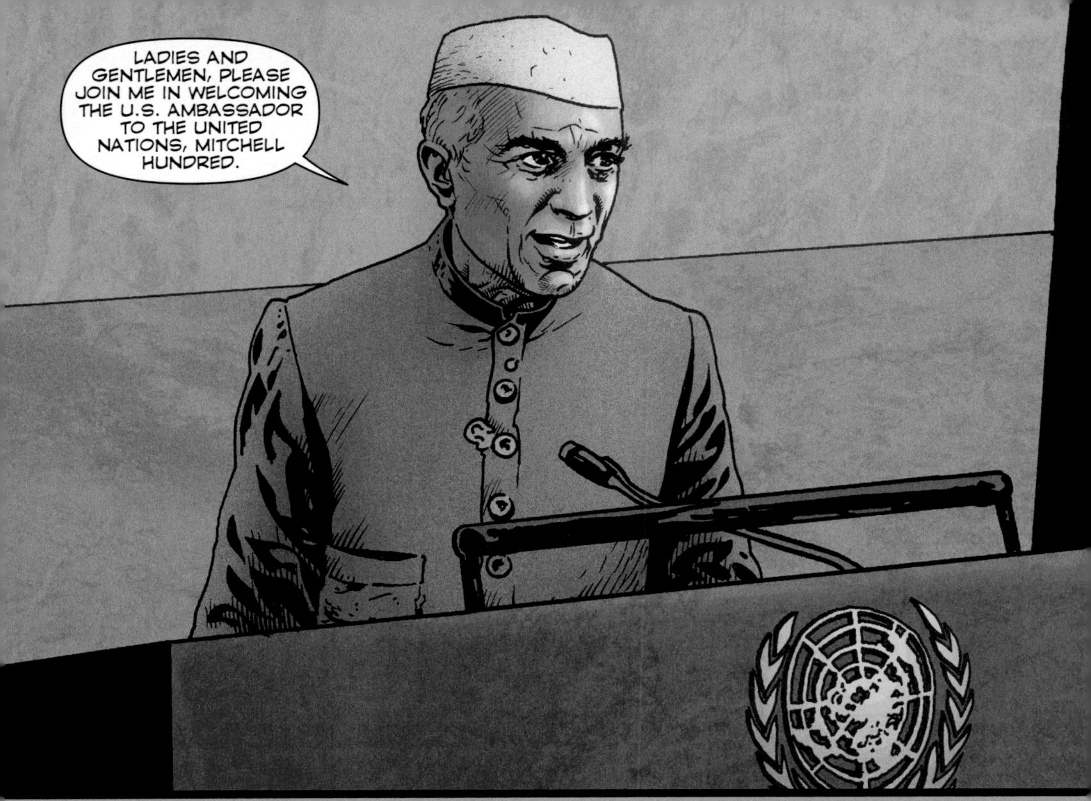
LADIES AND GENTLEMEN, PLEASE JOIN ME IN WELCOMING THE U.S. AMBASSADOR TO THE UNITED NATIONS, MITCHELL HUNDRED.

FRIDAY, SEPTEMBER 1, 200

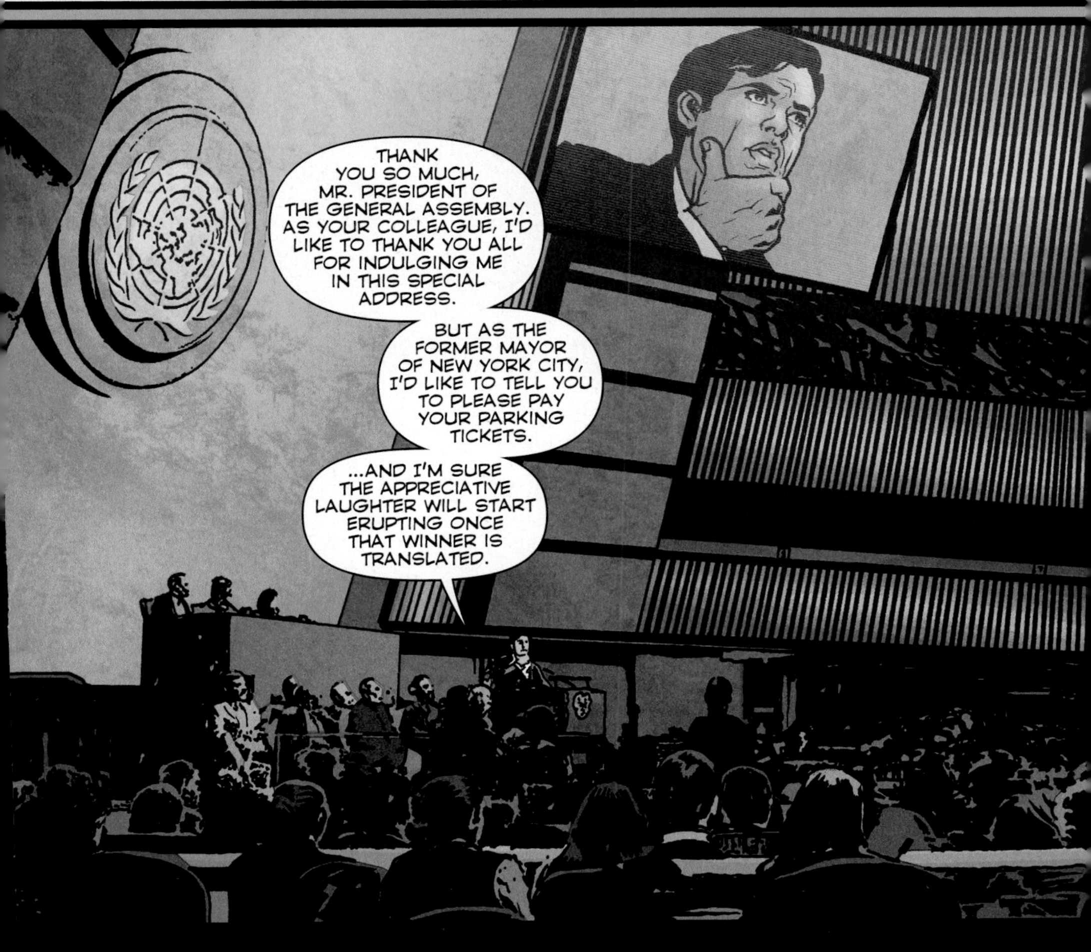
THANK YOU SO MUCH, MR. PRESIDENT OF THE GENERAL ASSEMBLY. AS YOUR COLLEAGUE, I'D LIKE TO THANK YOU ALL FOR INDULGING ME IN THIS SPECIAL ADDRESS.
BUT AS THE FORMER MAYOR OF NEW YORK CITY, I'D LIKE TO TELL YOU TO PLEASE PAY YOUR PARKING TICKETS.
...AND I'M SURE THE APPRECIATIVE LAUGHTER WILL START ERUPTING ONCE THAT WINNER IS TRANSLATED.

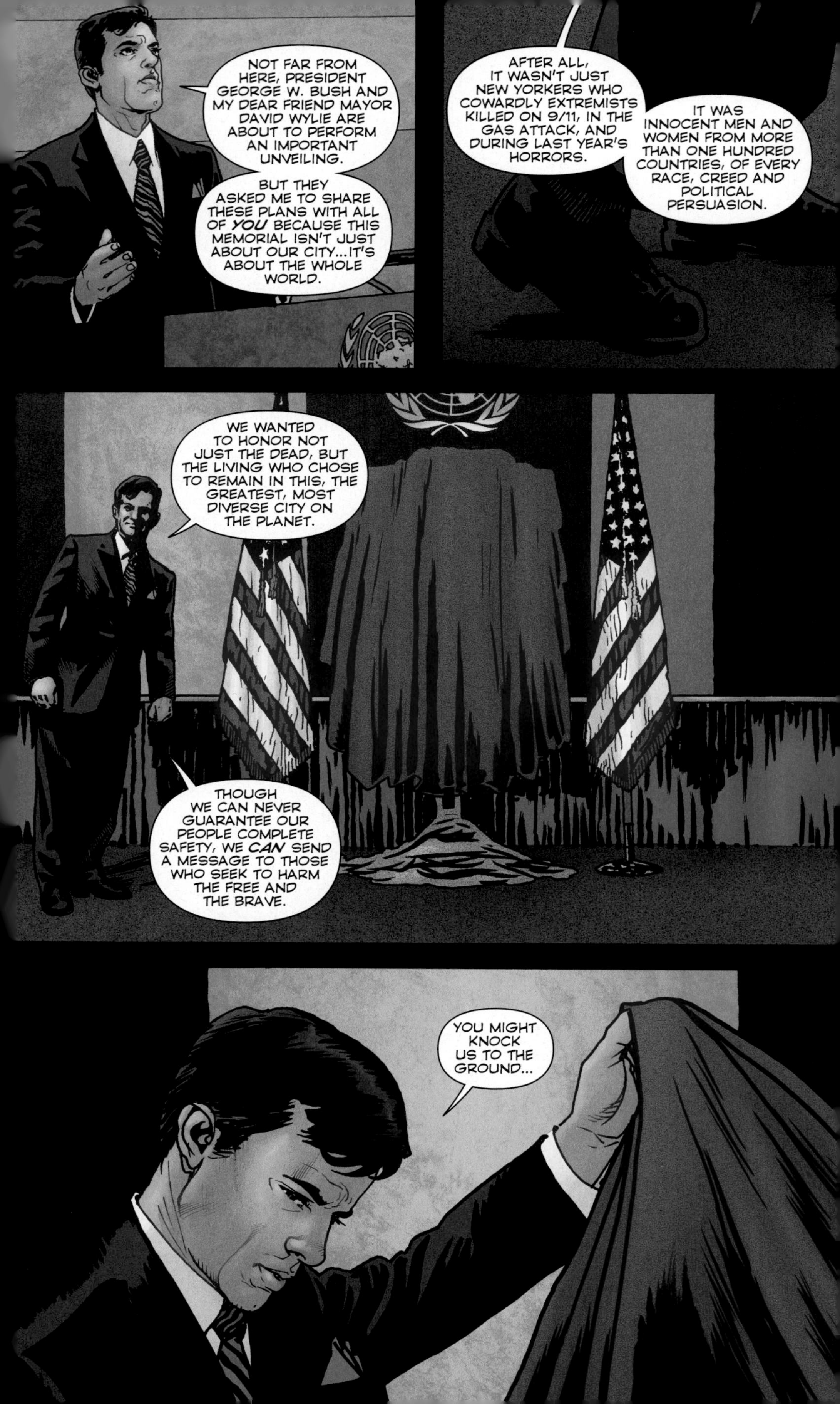
NOT FAR FROM HERE, PRESIDENT GEORGE W. BUSH AND MY DEAR FRIEND MAYOR DAVID WYLIE ARE ABOUT TO PERFORM AN IMPORTANT UNVEILING.
BUT THEY ASKED ME TO SHARE THESE PLANS WITH ALL OF *YOU* BECAUSE THIS MEMORIAL ISN'T JUST ABOUT OUR CITY...IT'S ABOUT THE WHOLE WORLD.
AFTER ALL, IT WASN'T JUST NEW YORKERS WHO COWARDLY EXTREMISTS KILLED ON 9/11, IN THE GAS ATTACK, AND DURING LAST YEAR'S HORRORS.
IT WAS INNOCENT MEN AND WOMEN FROM MORE THAN ONE HUNDRED COUNTRIES, OF EVERY RACE, CREED AND POLITICAL PERSUASION.
WE WANTED TO HONOR NOT JUST THE DEAD, BUT THE LIVING WHO CHOSE TO REMAIN IN THIS, THE GREATEST, MOST DIVERSE CITY ON THE PLANET.
THOUGH WE CAN NEVER GUARANTEE OUR PEOPLE COMPLETE SAFETY, WE *CAN* SEND A MESSAGE TO THOSE WHO SEEK TO HARM THE FREE AND THE BRAVE.
YOU MIGHT KNOCK US TO THE GROUND...

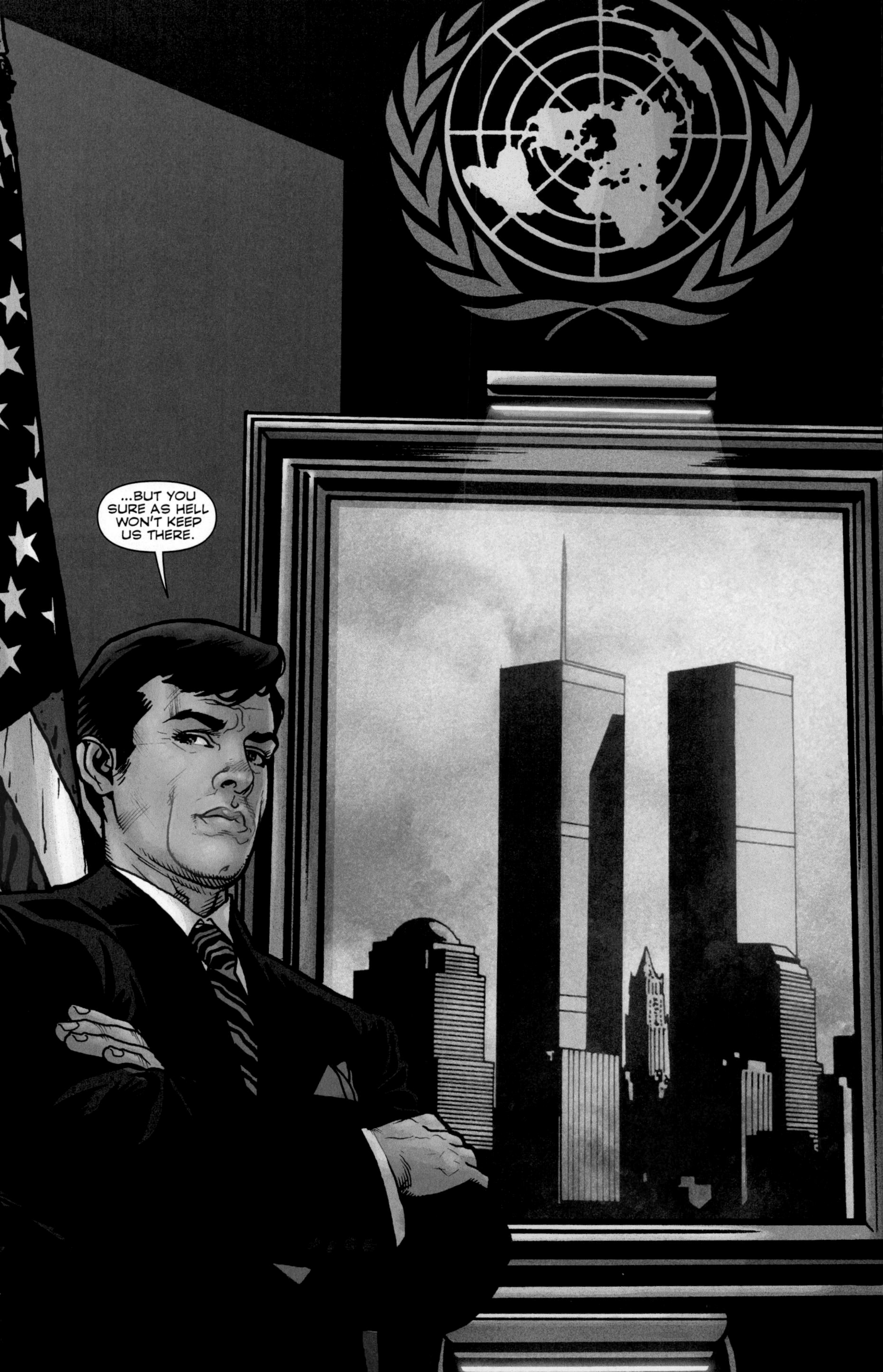
...BUT YOU SURE AS HELL WON'T KEEP US THERE.

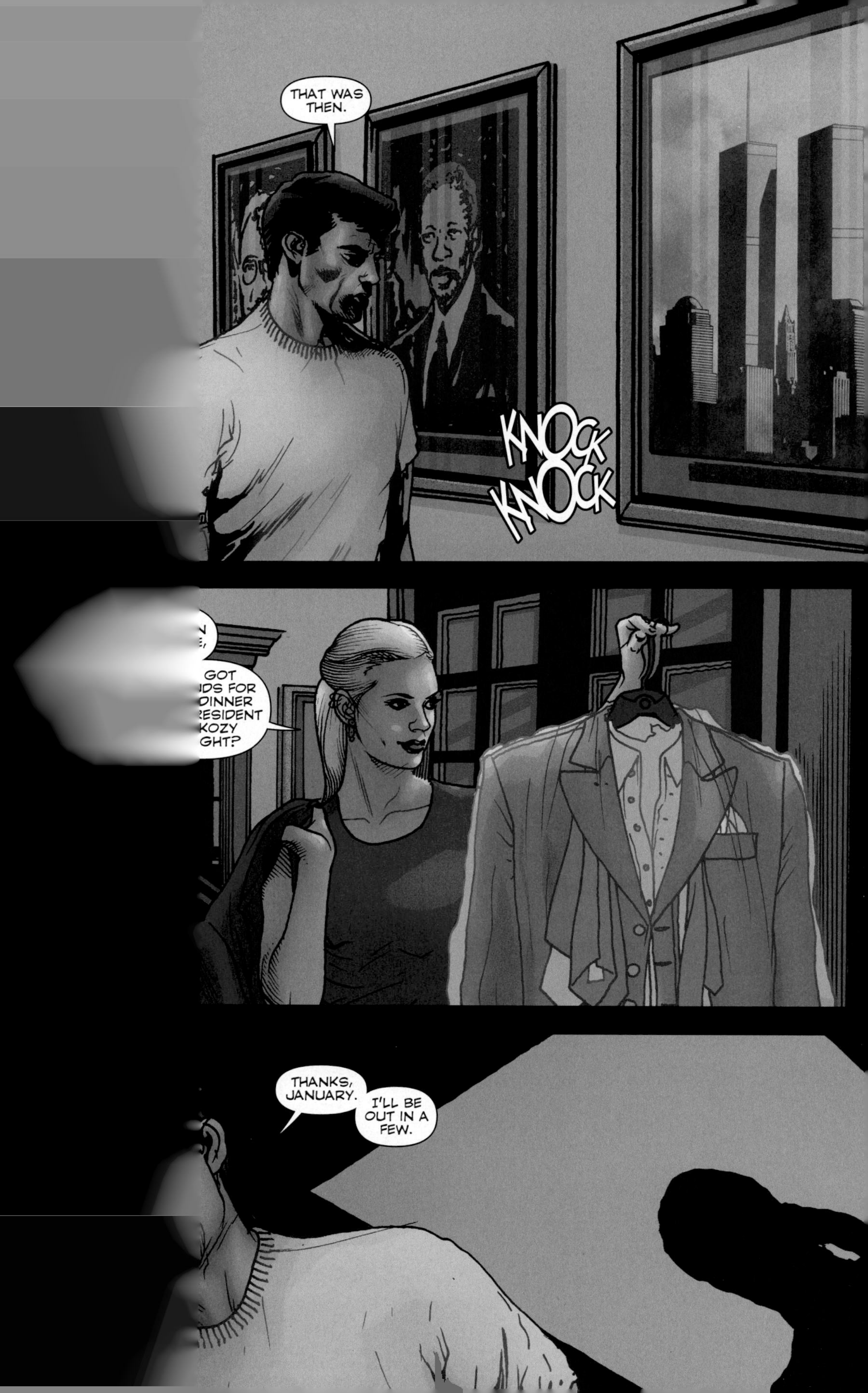
THAT WAS THEN.
KNOCK KNOCK
THANKS, JANUARY.
I'LL BE OUT IN A FEW.

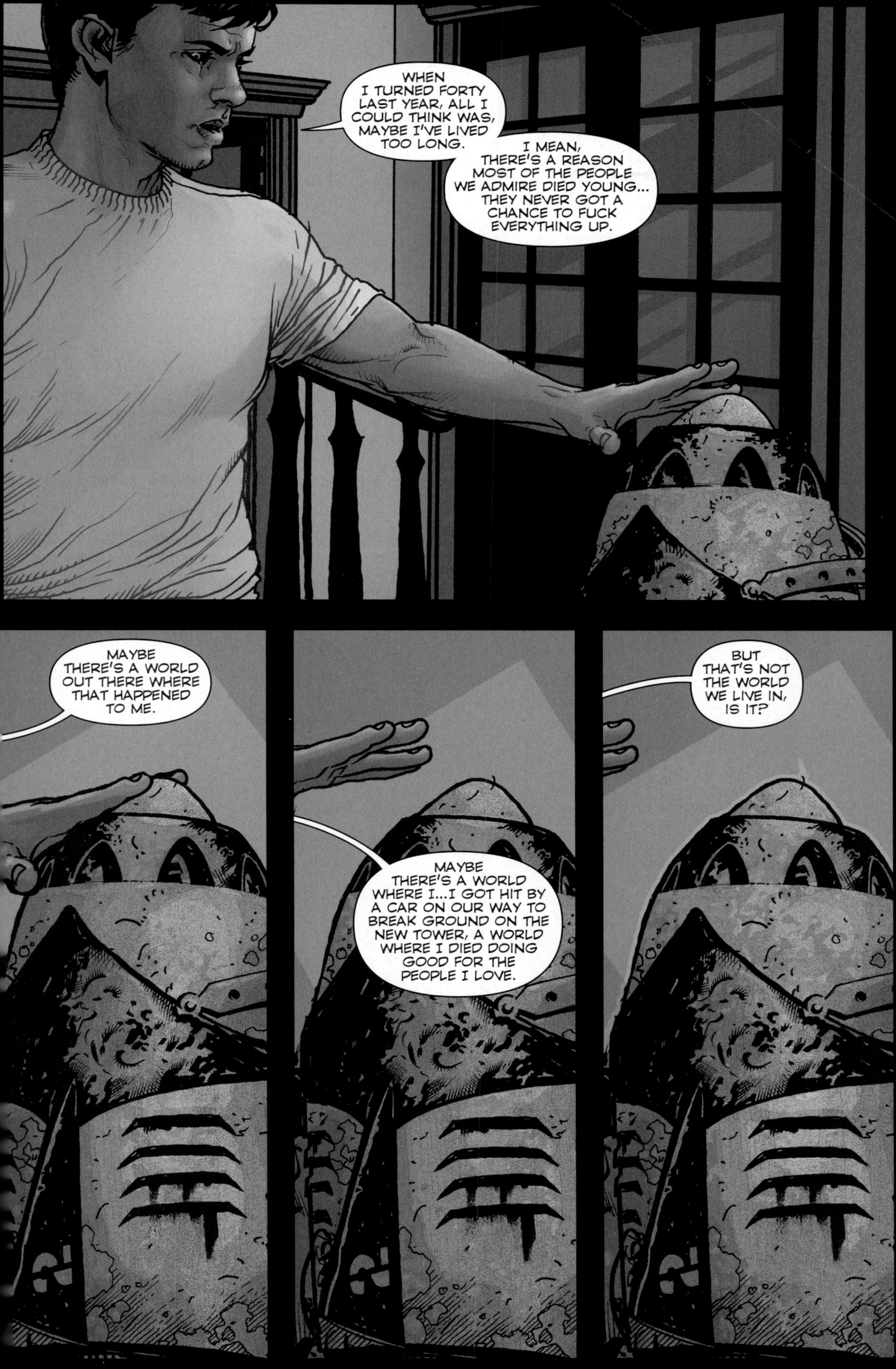
WHEN I TURNED FORTY LAST YEAR, ALL I COULD THINK WAS, MAYBE I'VE LIVED TOO LONG.
I MEAN, THERE'S A REASON MOST OF THE PEOPLE WE ADMIRE DIED YOUNG... THEY NEVER GOT A CHANCE TO FUCK EVERYTHING UP.
MAYBE THERE'S A WORLD OUT THERE WHERE THAT HAPPENED TO ME.
MAYBE THERE'S A WORLD WHERE I...I GOT HIT BY A CAR ON OUR WAY TO BREAK GROUND ON THE NEW TOWER, A WORLD WHERE I DIED DOING GOOD FOR THE PEOPLE I LOVE.
BUT THAT'S NOT THE WORLD WE LIVE IN, IS IT?

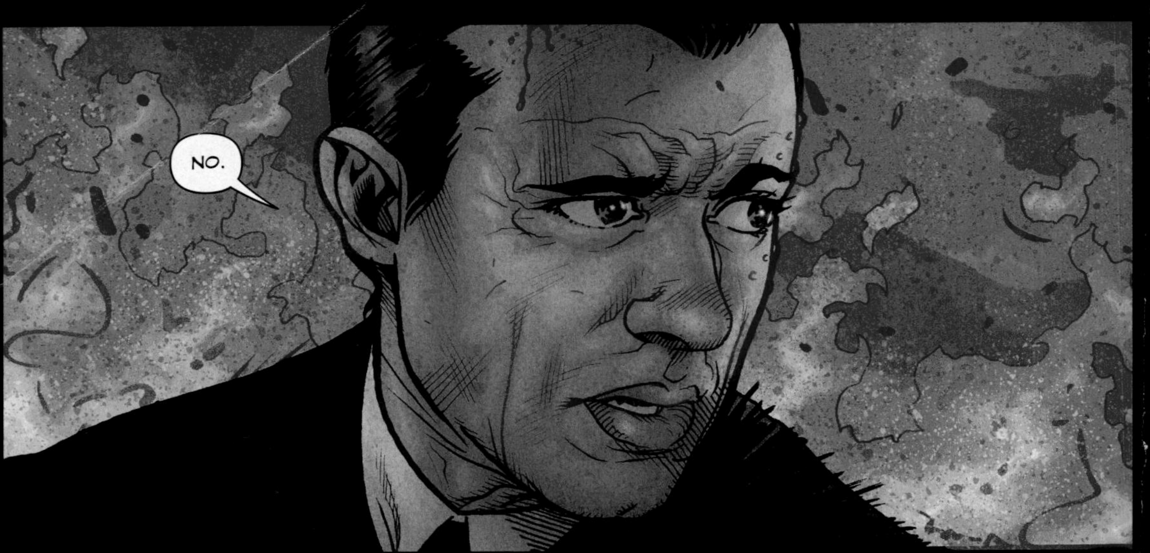
NO.

SUNDAY, MARCH 4, 2007

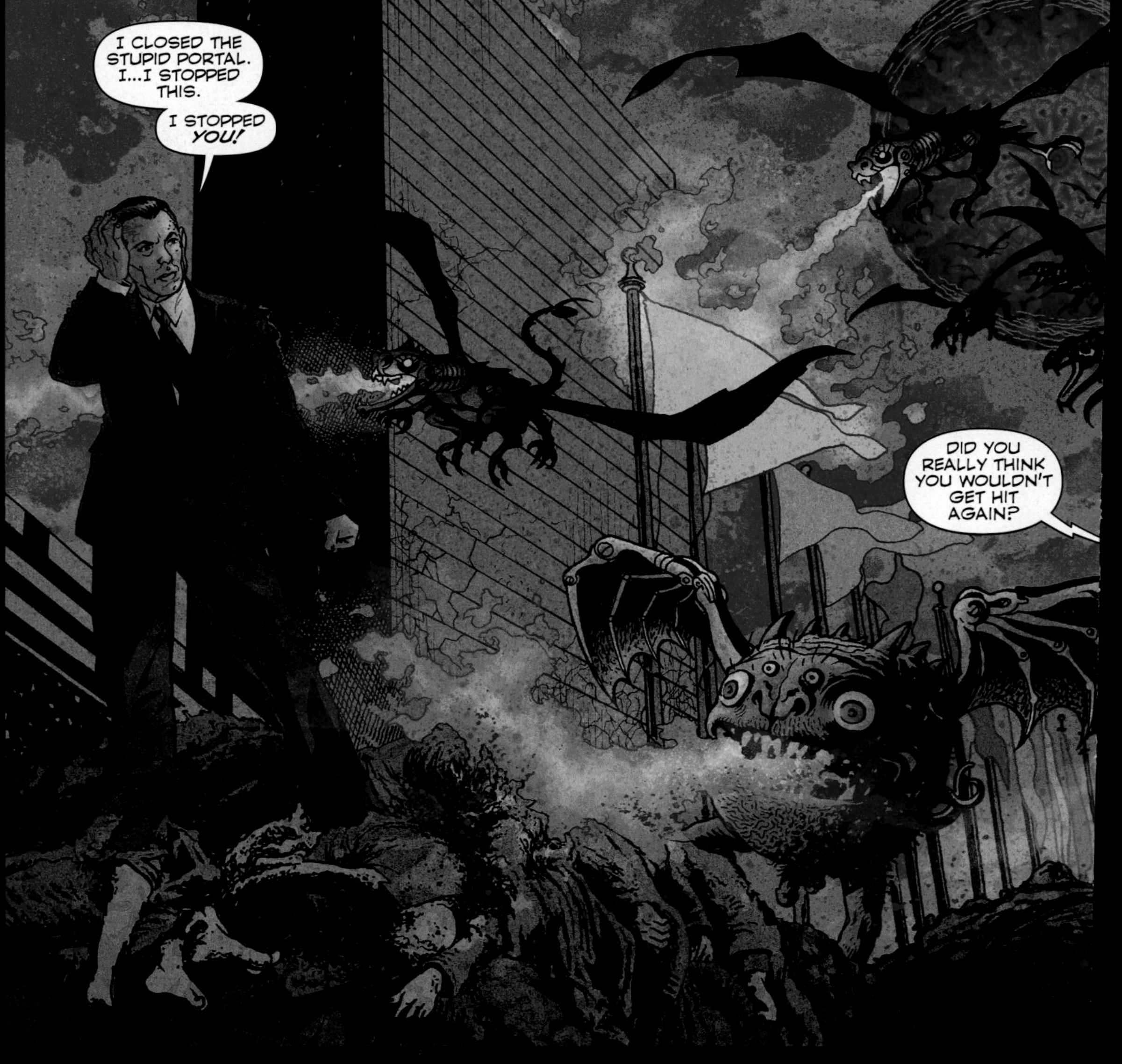
I CLOSED THE STUPID PORTAL. I...I STOPPED THIS.
I STOPPED YOU!
DID YOU REALLY THINK YOU WOULDN'T GET HIT AGAIN?

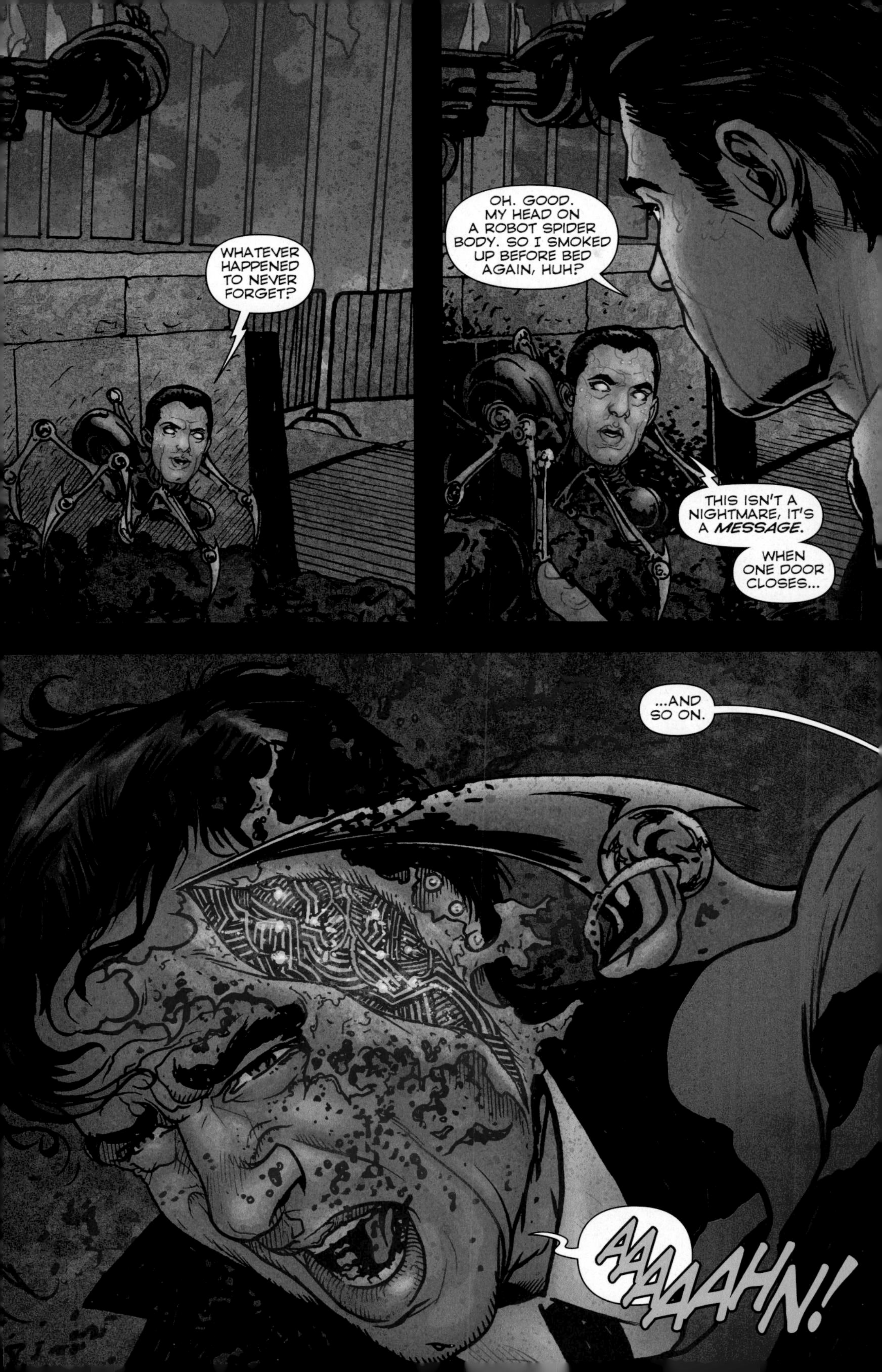
WHATEVER HAPPENED TO NEVER FORGET?
OH. GOOD. MY HEAD ON A ROBOT SPIDER BODY. SO I SMOKED UP BEFORE BED AGAIN, HUH?
THIS ISN'T A NIGHTMARE, IT'S A *MESSAGE*.
WHEN ONE DOOR CLOSES...
...AND SO ON.
AAAAAAHN!

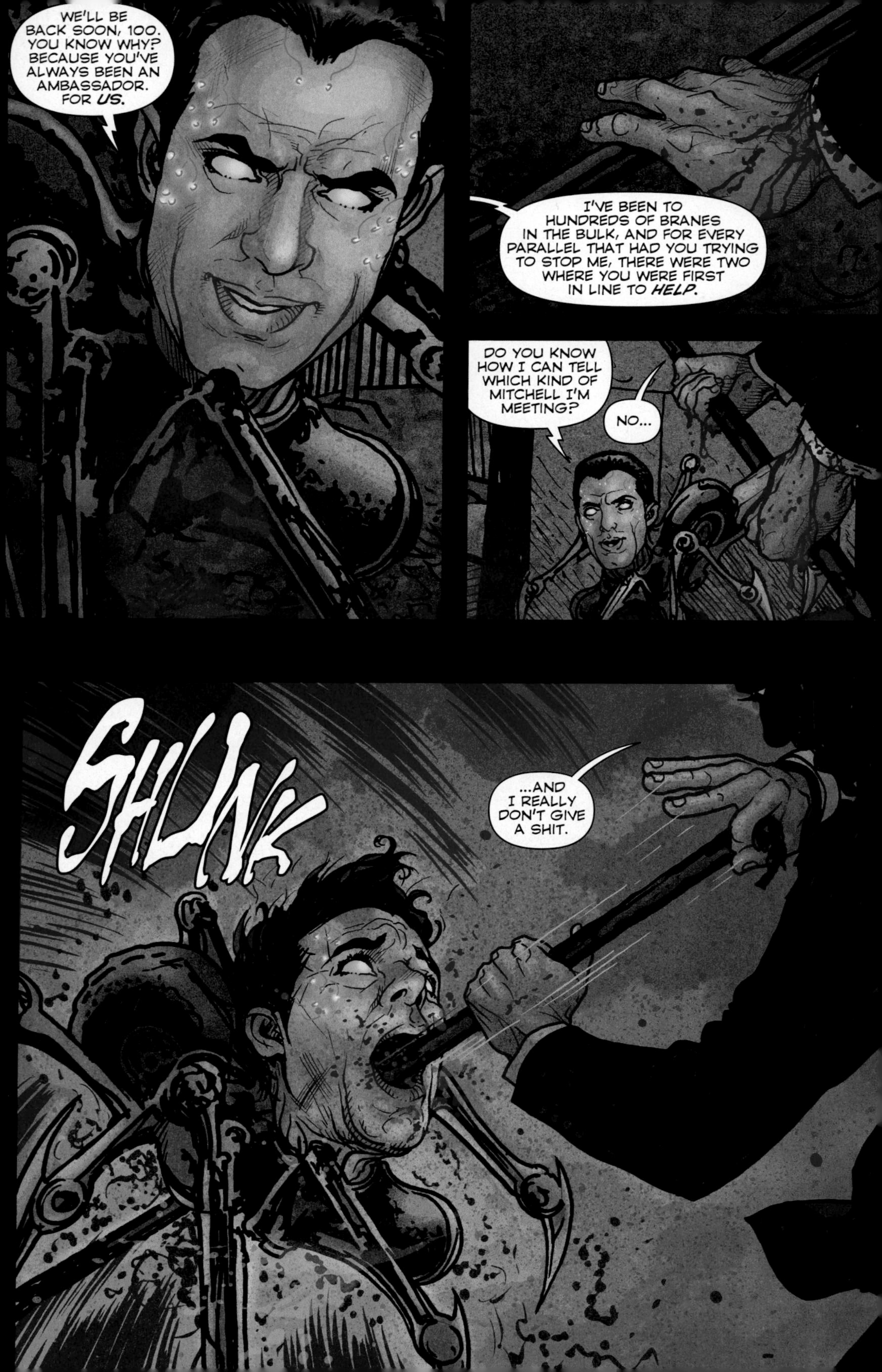
WE'LL BE BACK SOON, 100. YOU KNOW WHY? BECAUSE YOU'VE ALWAYS BEEN AN AMBASSADOR. FOR *US*.
I'VE BEEN TO HUNDREDS OF BRANES IN THE BULK, AND FOR EVERY PARALLEL THAT HAD YOU TRYING TO STOP ME, THERE WERE TWO WHERE YOU WERE FIRST IN LINE TO *HELP*.
DO YOU KNOW HOW I CAN TELL WHICH KIND OF MITCHELL I'M MEETING?
NO...
SHUNK
...AND I REALLY DON'T GIVE A SHIT.

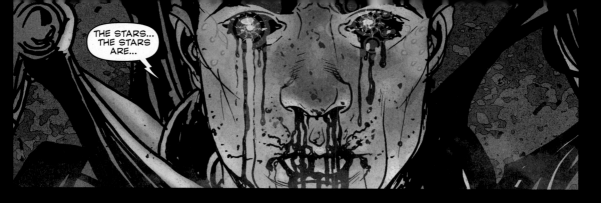

THE STARS... THE STARS ARE...

NOW WHY DON'T YOU FUCK ON BACK TO WHICHEVER LAME "MIRROR UNIVERSE" YOU CAME FROM AND LET ME GET SOME SLEEP?

BECAUSE I'M NOT YOUR REFLECTION, MITCHELL.

I AM HE AS YOU ARE HE AS YOU ARE ME...

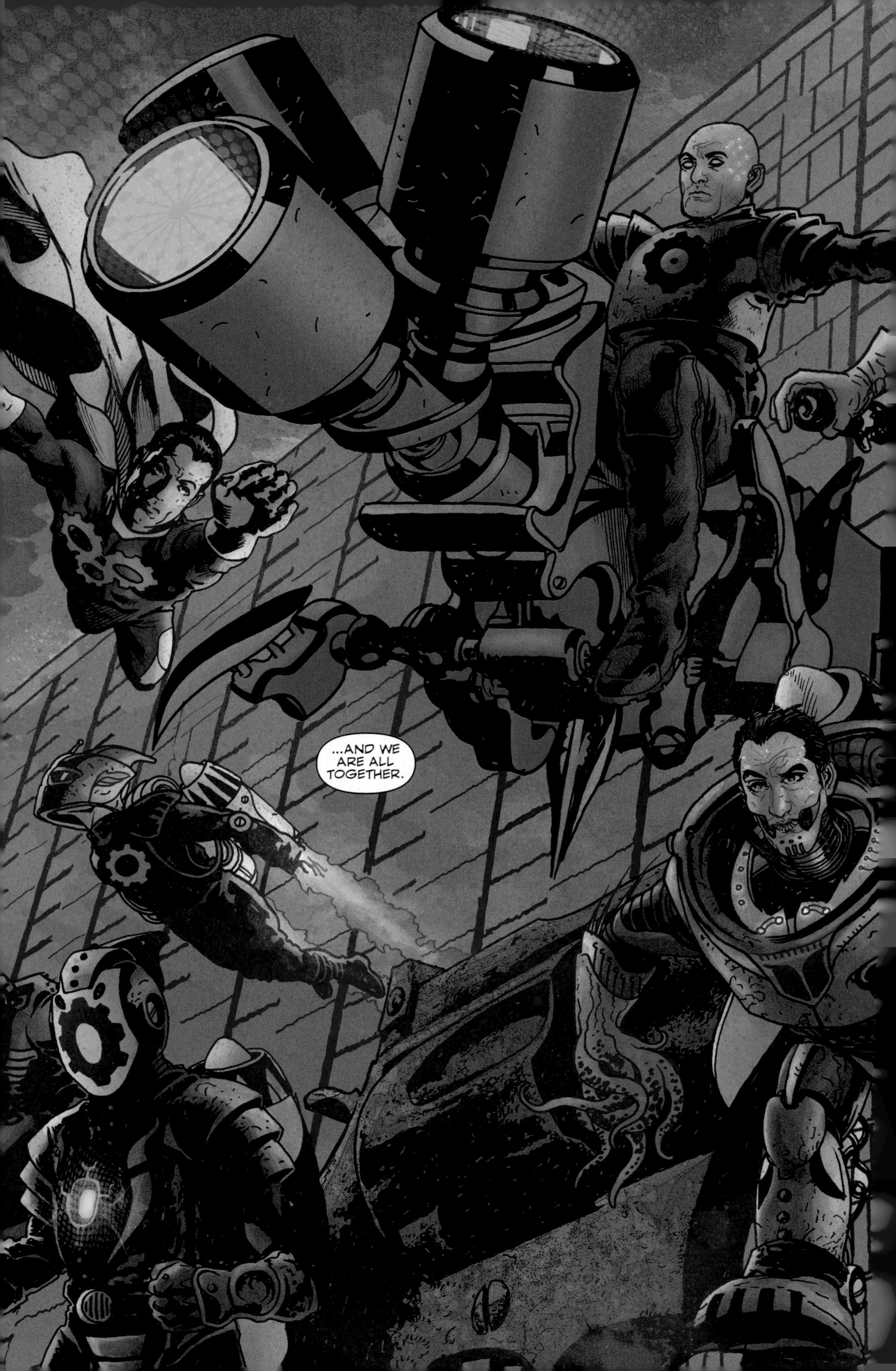
...AND WE ARE ALL TOGETHER.

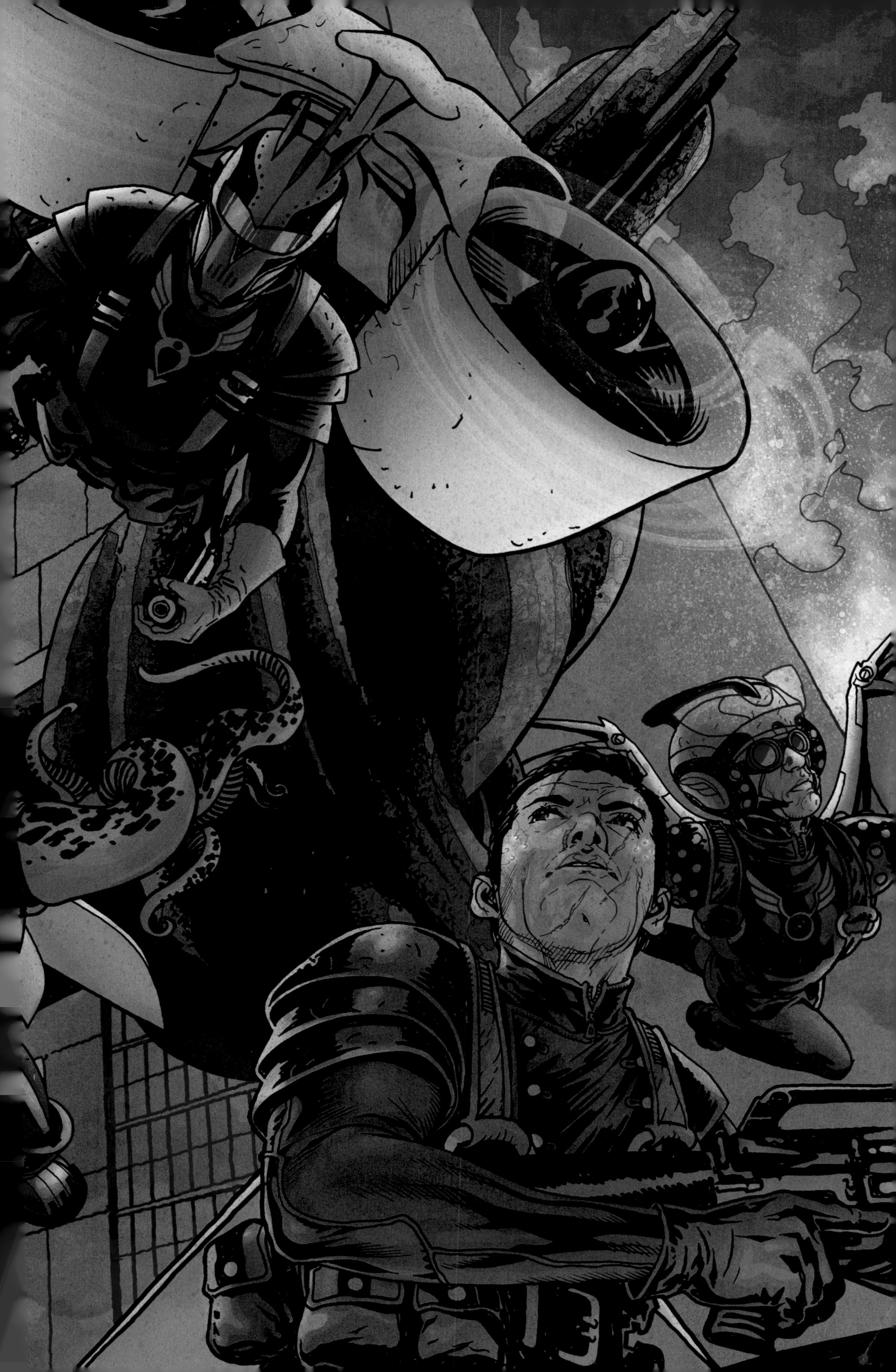

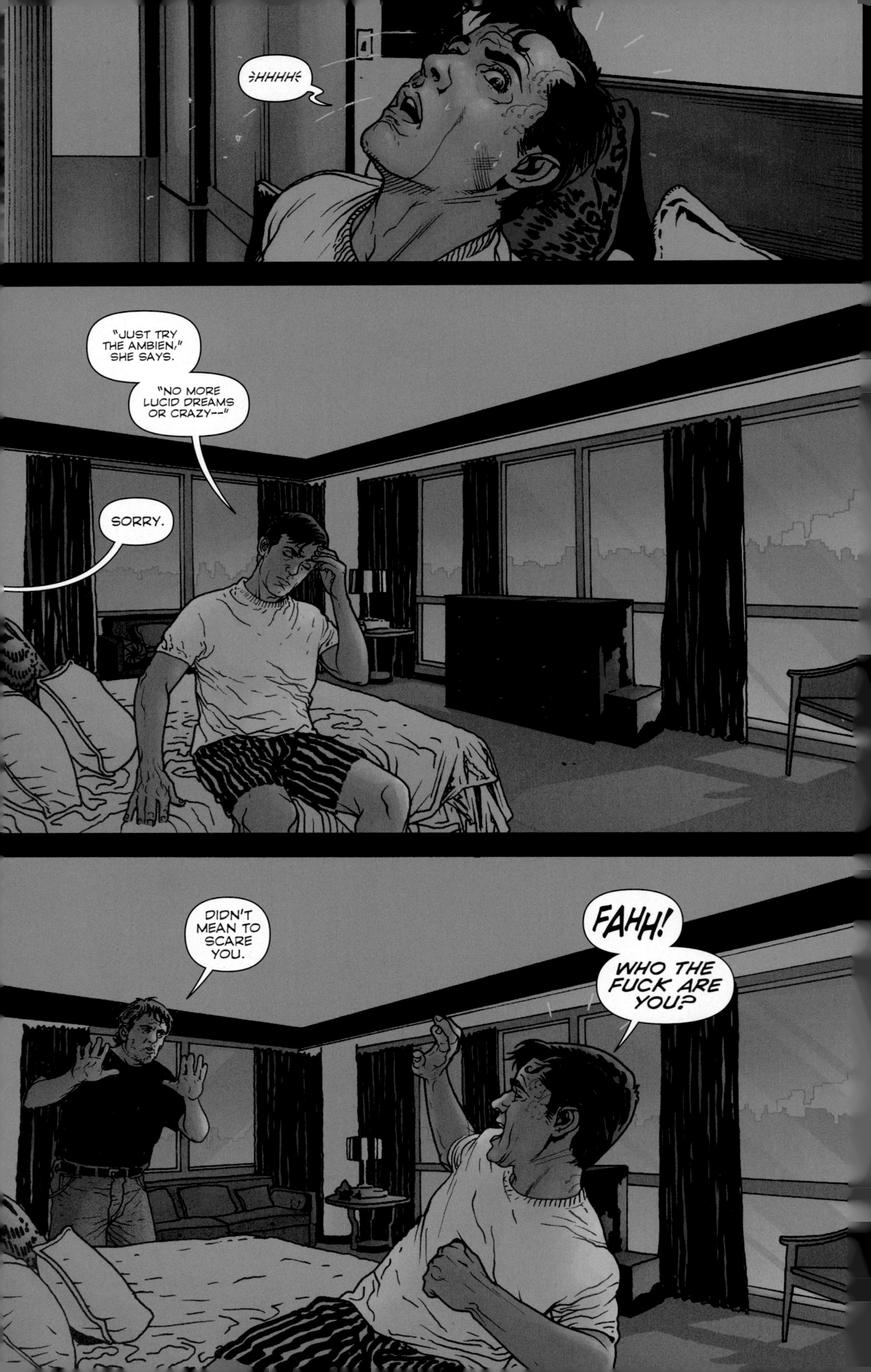
HHHH
"JUST TRY THE AMBIEN," SHE SAYS.
"NO MORE LUCID DREAMS OR CRAZY--"
SORRY.
DIDN'T MEAN TO SCARE YOU.
FAHH!
WHO THE FUCK ARE YOU?

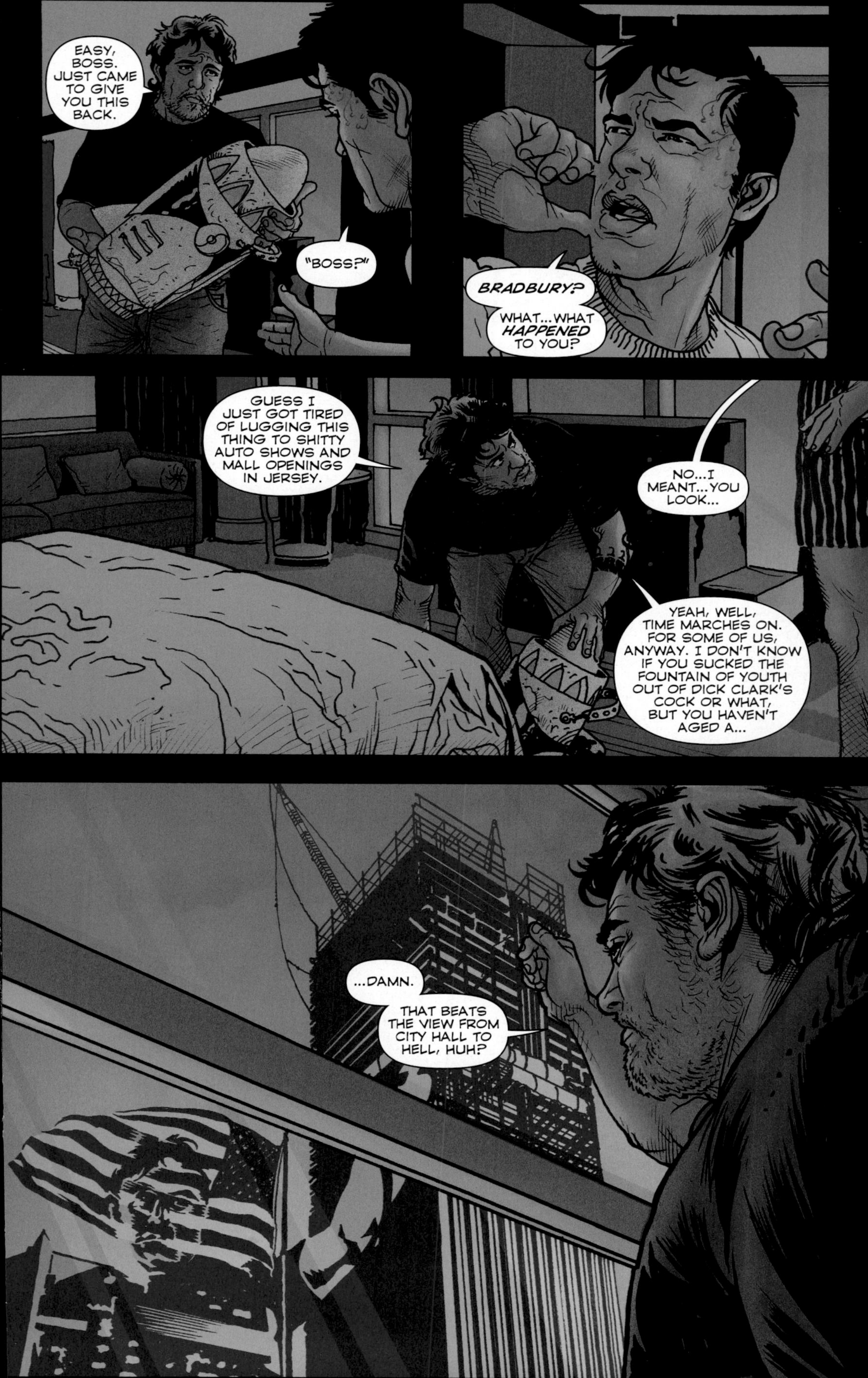
EASY, BOSS. JUST CAME TO GIVE YOU THIS BACK.
"BOSS?"
BRADBURY?
WHAT...WHAT *HAPPENED* TO YOU?
GUESS I JUST GOT TIRED OF LUGGING THIS THING TO SHITTY AUTO SHOWS AND MALL OPENINGS IN JERSEY.
NO...I MEANT...YOU LOOK...
YEAH, WELL, TIME MARCHES ON. FOR SOME OF US, ANYWAY. I DON'T KNOW IF YOU SUCKED THE FOUNTAIN OF YOUTH OUT OF DICK CLARK'S COCK OR WHAT, BUT YOU HAVEN'T AGED A...
...DAMN.
THAT BEATS THE VIEW FROM CITY HALL TO HELL, HUH?

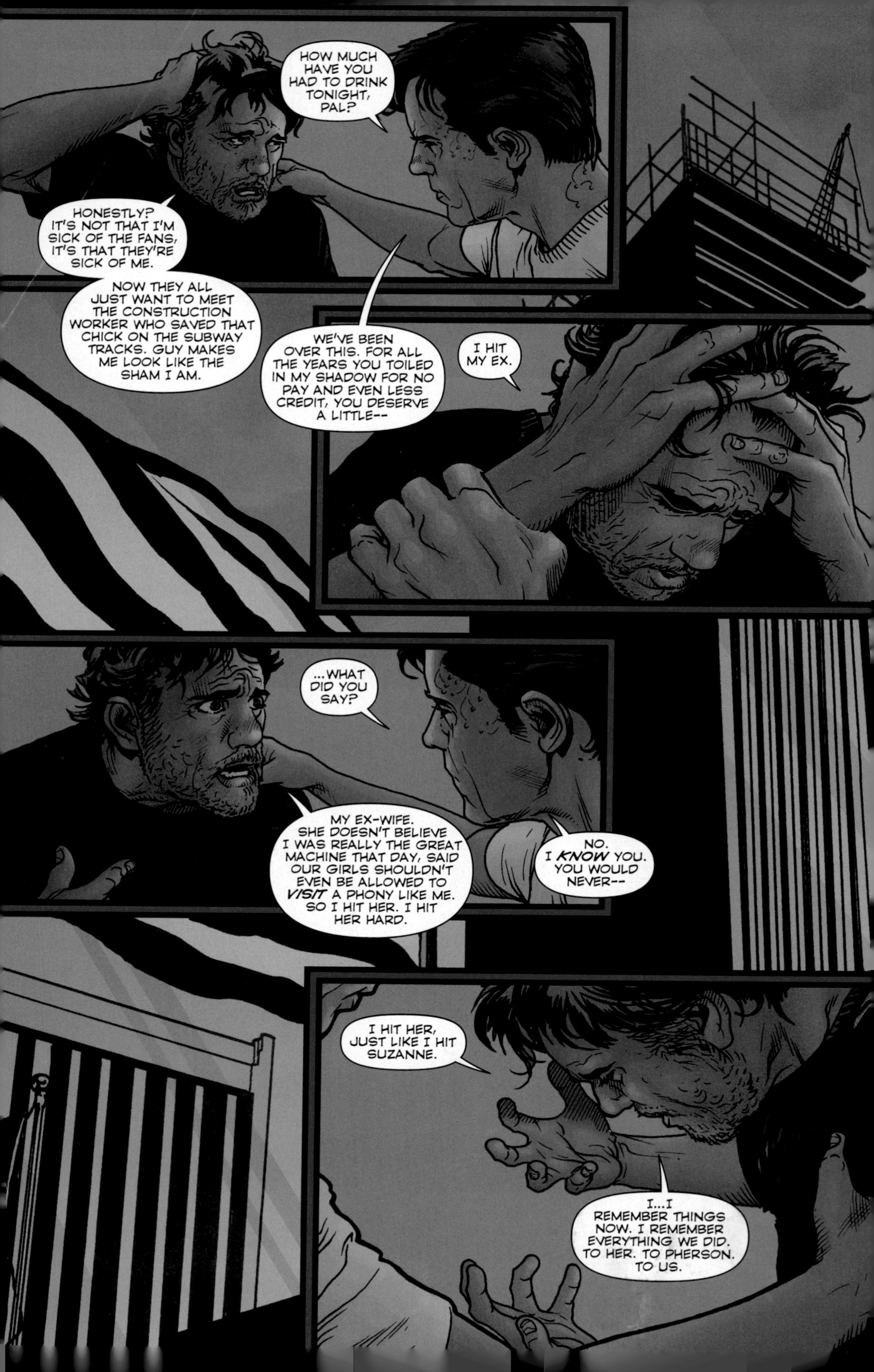
HOW MUCH HAVE YOU HAD TO DRINK TONIGHT, PAL?
HONESTLY? IT'S NOT THAT I'M SICK OF THE FANS, IT'S THAT THEY'RE SICK OF ME.
NOW THEY ALL JUST WANT TO MEET THE CONSTRUCTION WORKER WHO SAVED THAT CHICK ON THE SUBWAY TRACKS. GUY MAKES ME LOOK LIKE THE SHAM I AM.
WE'VE BEEN OVER THIS. FOR ALL THE YEARS YOU TOILED IN MY SHADOW FOR NO PAY AND EVEN LESS CREDIT, YOU DESERVE A LITTLE--
I HIT MY EX.
...WHAT DID YOU SAY?
MY EX-WIFE. SHE DOESN'T BELIEVE I WAS REALLY THE GREAT MACHINE THAT DAY, SAID OUR GIRLS SHOULDN'T EVEN BE ALLOWED TO *VISIT* A PHONY LIKE ME. SO I HIT HER. I HIT HER HARD.
NO. I *KNOW* YOU. YOU WOULD NEVER--
I HIT HER, JUST LIKE I HIT SUZANNE.
I...I REMEMBER THINGS NOW. I REMEMBER EVERYTHING WE DID. TO HER. TO PHERSON. TO US.

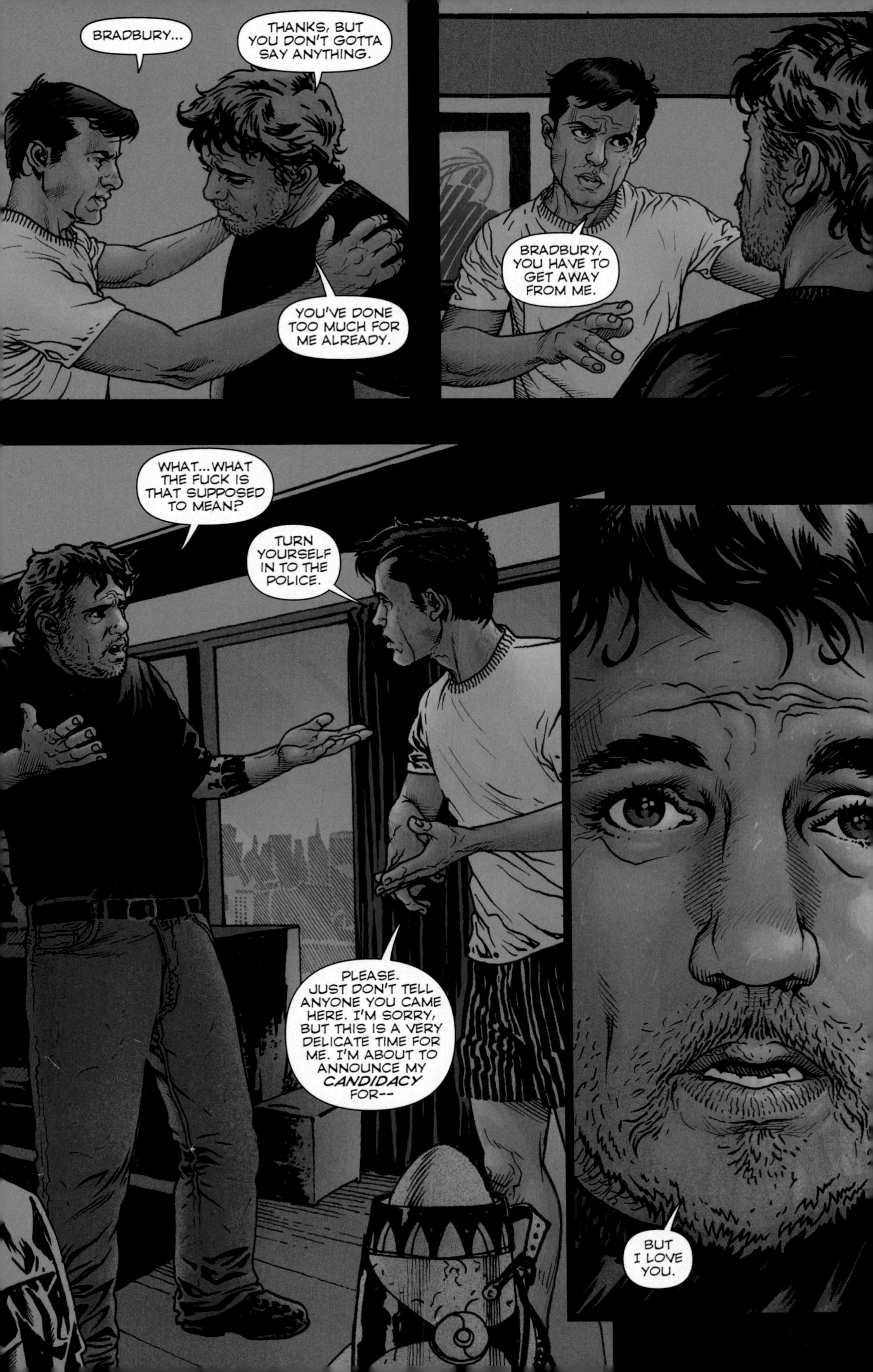
BRADBURY...
THANKS, BUT YOU DON'T GOTTA SAY ANYTHING.
YOU'VE DONE TOO MUCH FOR ME ALREADY.
BRADBURY, YOU HAVE TO GET AWAY FROM ME.
WHAT...WHAT THE FUCK IS THAT SUPPOSED TO MEAN?
TURN YOURSELF IN TO THE POLICE.
PLEASE. JUST DON'T TELL ANYONE YOU CAME HERE. I'M SORRY, BUT THIS IS A VERY DELICATE TIME FOR ME. I'M ABOUT TO ANNOUNCE MY *CANDIDACY* FOR--
BUT I LOVE YOU.

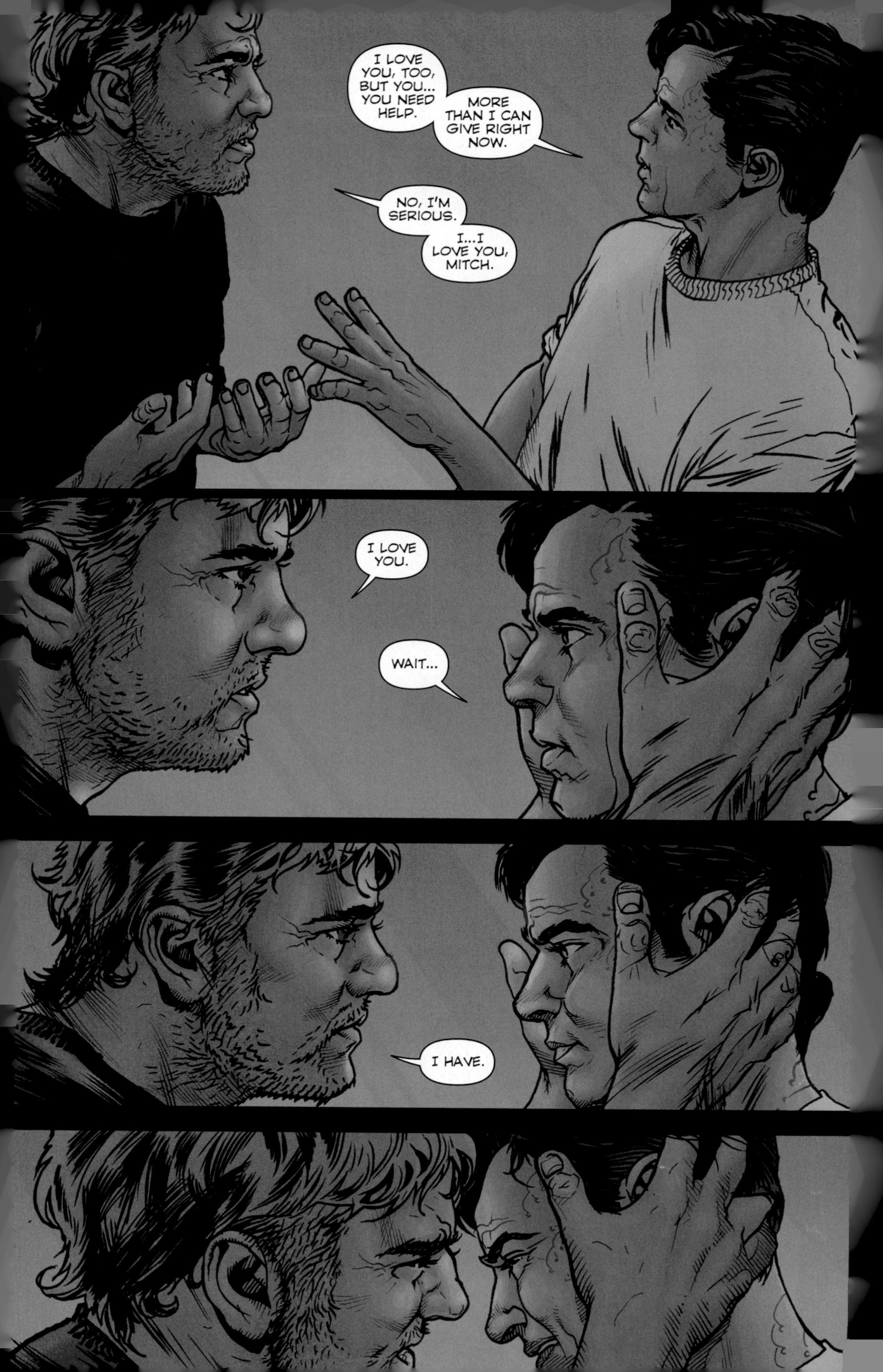
I LOVE YOU, TOO, BUT YOU... YOU NEED HELP.
MORE THAN I CAN GIVE RIGHT NOW.
NO, I'M SERIOUS.
I...I LOVE YOU, MITCH.
I LOVE YOU.
WAIT...
I HAVE.

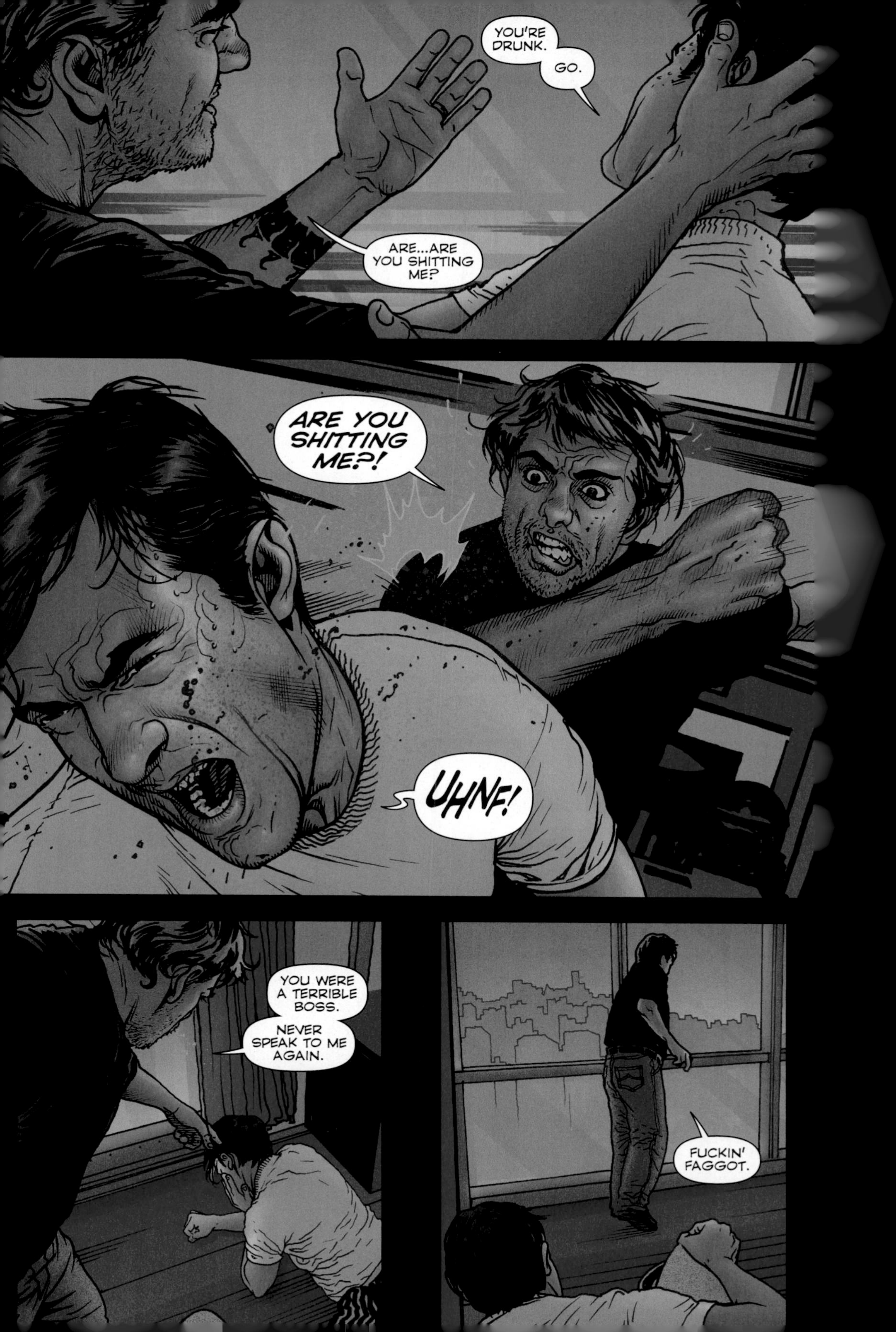
YOU'RE DRUNK.
GO.
ARE...ARE YOU SHITTING ME?
ARE YOU SHITTING ME?!
UHNF!
YOU WERE A TERRIBLE BOSS.
NEVER SPEAK TO ME AGAIN.
FUCKIN' FAGGOT.

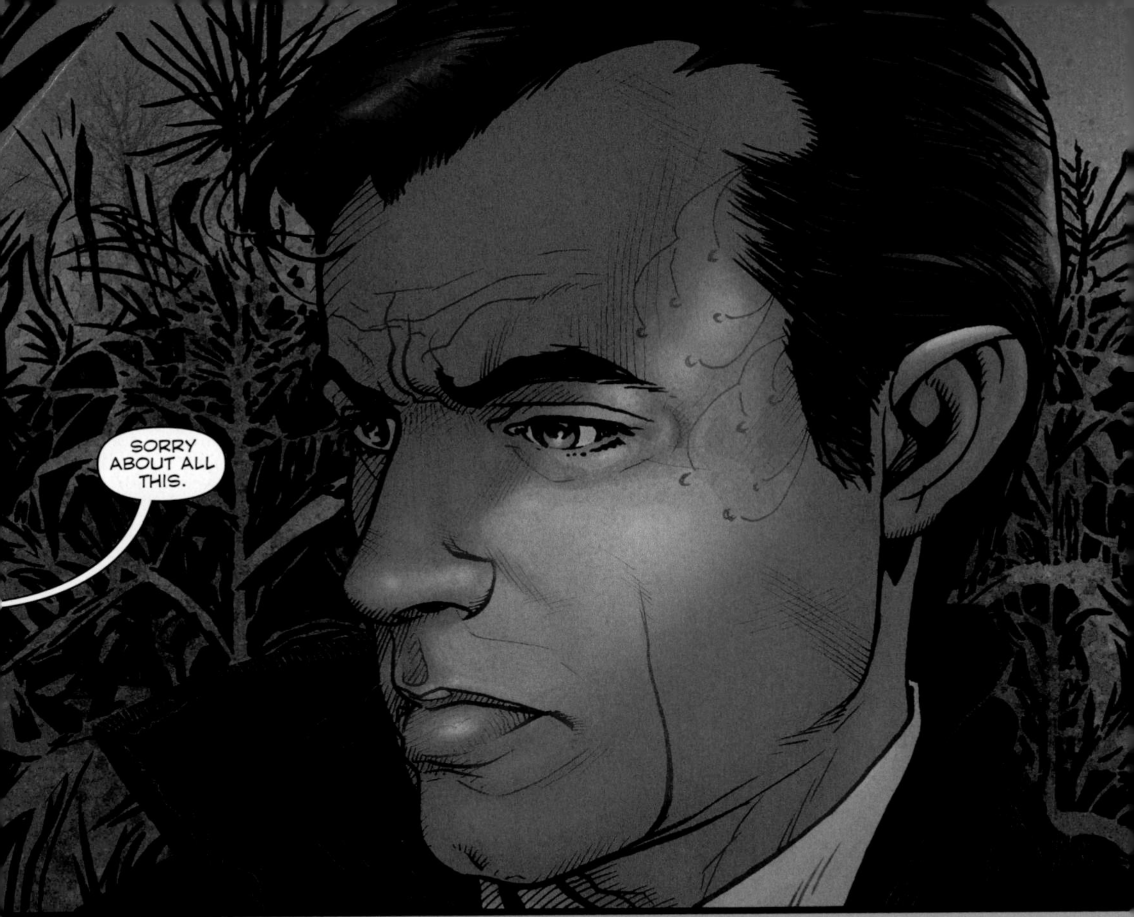
SORRY ABOUT ALL THIS.

WEDNESDAY, OCTOBER 31, 2007

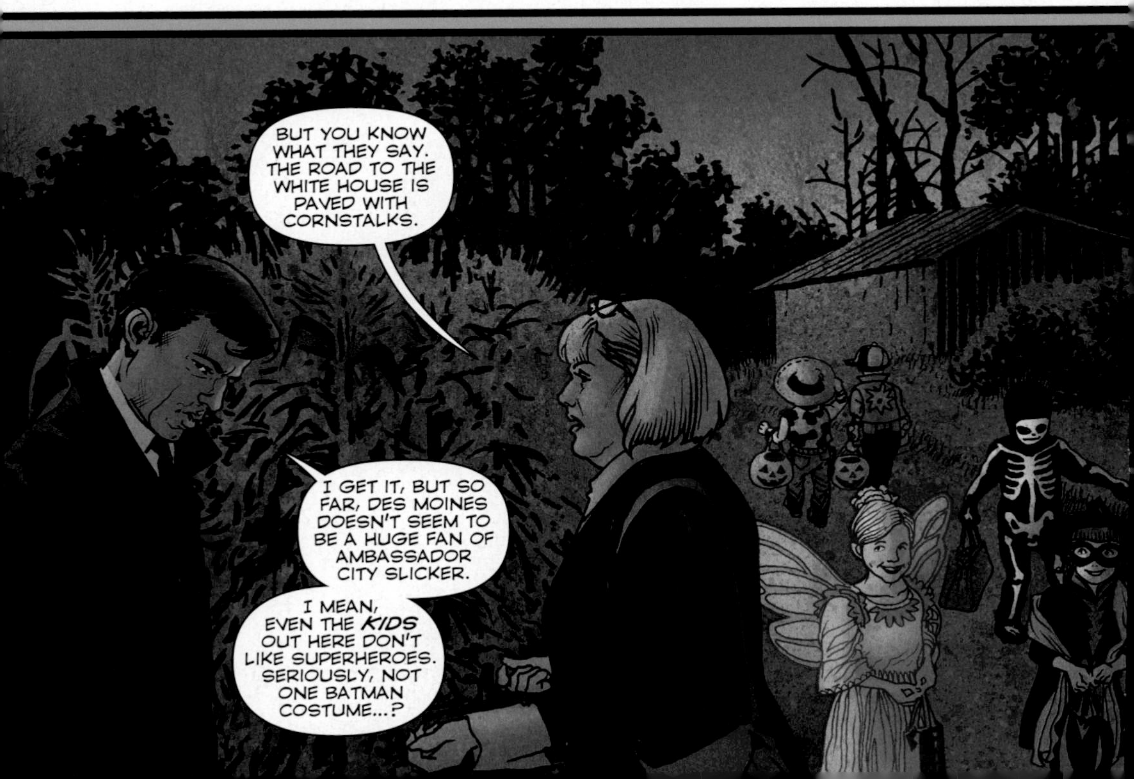
BUT YOU KNOW WHAT THEY SAY. THE ROAD TO THE WHITE HOUSE IS PAVED WITH CORNSTALKS.
I GET IT, BUT SO FAR, DES MOINES DOESN'T SEEM TO BE A HUGE FAN OF AMBASSADOR CITY SLICKER.
I MEAN, EVEN THE *KIDS* OUT HERE DON'T LIKE SUPERHEROES. SERIOUSLY, NOT ONE BATMAN COSTUME...?

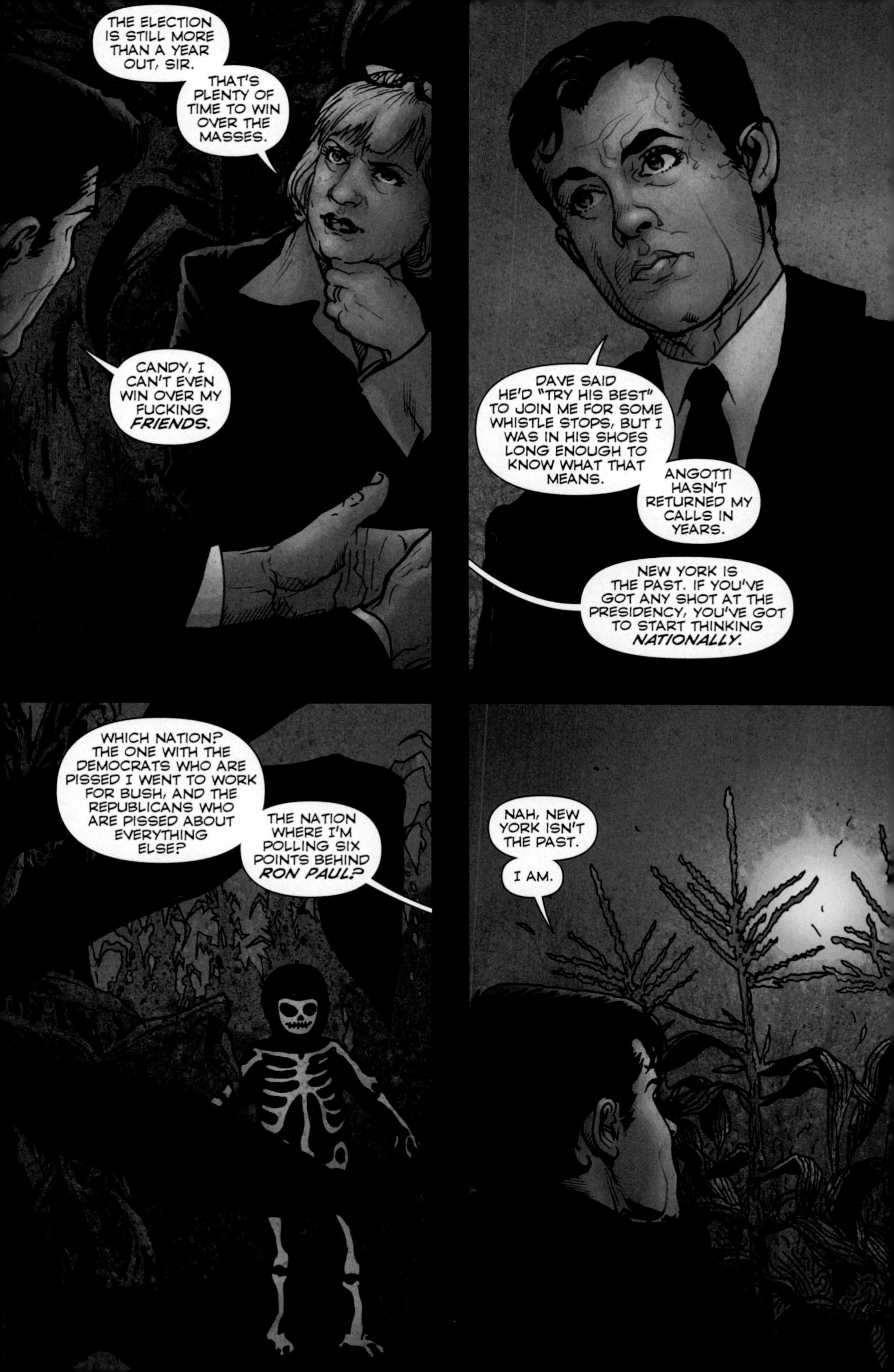
THE ELECTION IS STILL MORE THAN A YEAR OUT, SIR.
THAT'S PLENTY OF TIME TO WIN OVER THE MASSES.
CANDY, I CAN'T EVEN WIN OVER MY FUCKING *FRIENDS*.
DAVE SAID HE'D "TRY HIS BEST" TO JOIN ME FOR SOME WHISTLE STOPS, BUT I WAS IN HIS SHOES LONG ENOUGH TO KNOW WHAT THAT MEANS.
ANGOTTI HASN'T RETURNED MY CALLS IN YEARS.
NEW YORK IS THE PAST. IF YOU'VE GOT ANY SHOT AT THE PRESIDENCY, YOU'VE GOT TO START THINKING *NATIONALLY*.
WHICH NATION? THE ONE WITH THE DEMOCRATS WHO ARE PISSED I WENT TO WORK FOR BUSH, AND THE REPUBLICANS WHO ARE PISSED ABOUT EVERYTHING ELSE?
THE NATION WHERE I'M POLLING SIX POINTS BEHIND *RON PAUL?*
NAH, NEW YORK ISN'T THE PAST.
I AM.

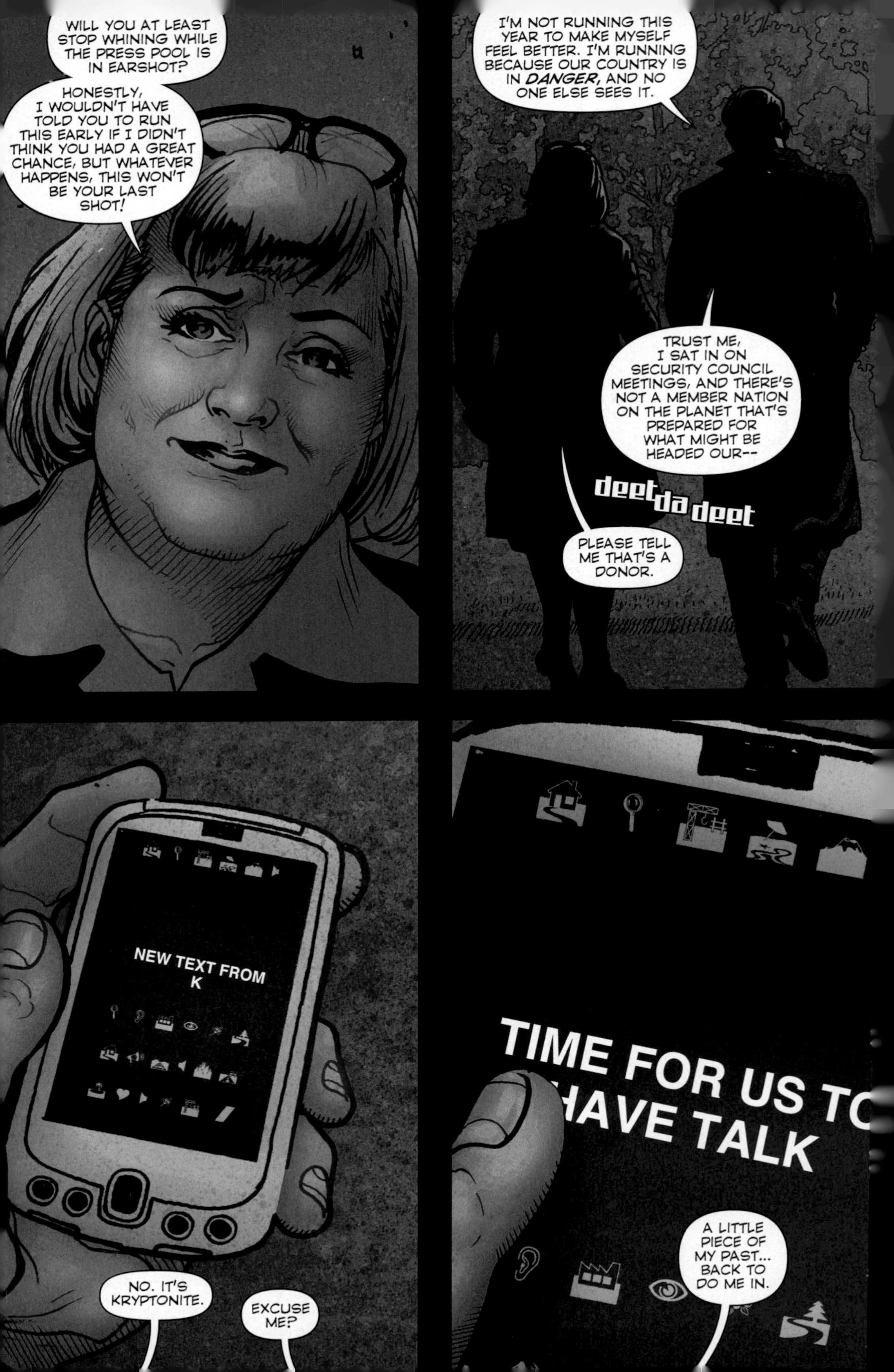
WILL YOU AT LEAST STOP WHINING WHILE THE PRESS POOL IS IN EARSHOT?
HONESTLY, I WOULDN'T HAVE TOLD YOU TO RUN THIS EARLY IF I DIDN'T THINK YOU HAD A GREAT CHANCE, BUT WHATEVER HAPPENS, THIS WON'T BE YOUR LAST SHOT!
I'M NOT RUNNING THIS YEAR TO MAKE MYSELF FEEL BETTER. I'M RUNNING BECAUSE OUR COUNTRY IS IN DANGER, AND NO ONE ELSE SEES IT.
TRUST ME, I SAT IN ON SECURITY COUNCIL MEETINGS, AND THERE'S NOT A MEMBER NATION ON THE PLANET THAT'S PREPARED FOR WHAT MIGHT BE HEADED OUR--
deet da deet
PLEASE TELL ME THAT'S A DONOR.
NEW TEXT FROM K
NO. IT'S KRYPTONITE.
EXCUSE ME?
TIME FOR US TO HAVE TALK
A LITTLE PIECE OF MY PAST... BACK TO DO ME IN.

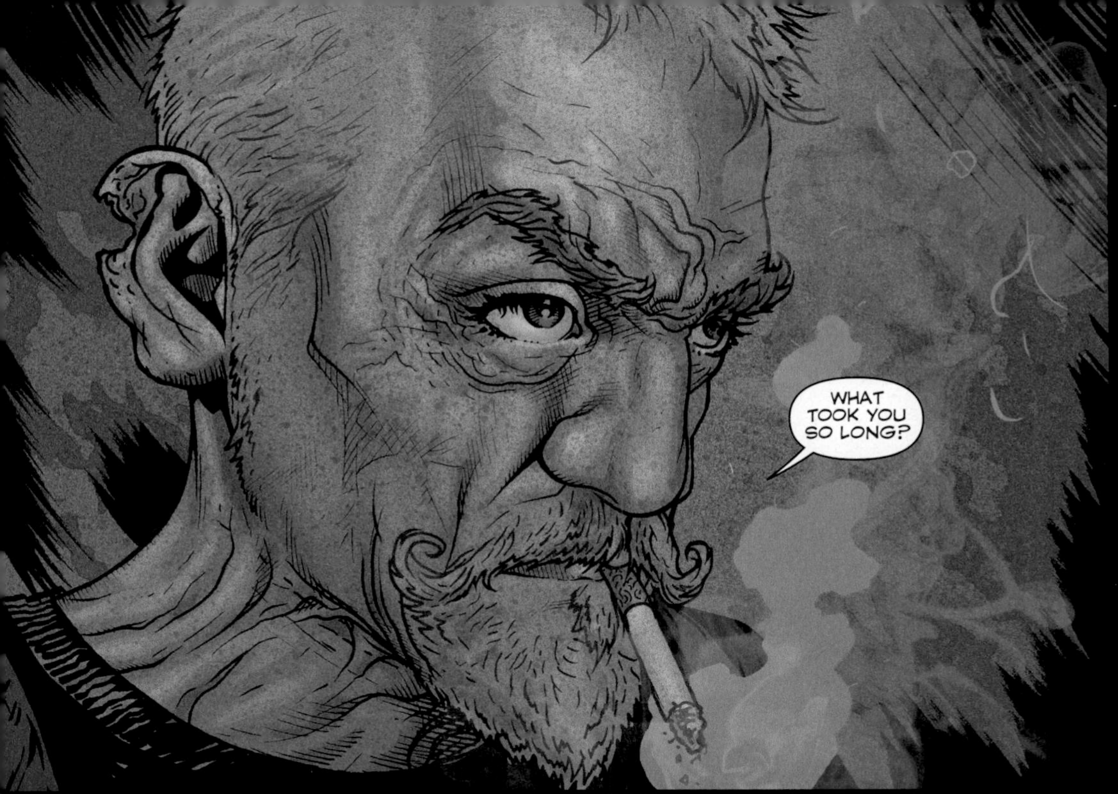
WHAT TOOK YOU SO LONG?

THURSDAY, JANUARY 17, 2008

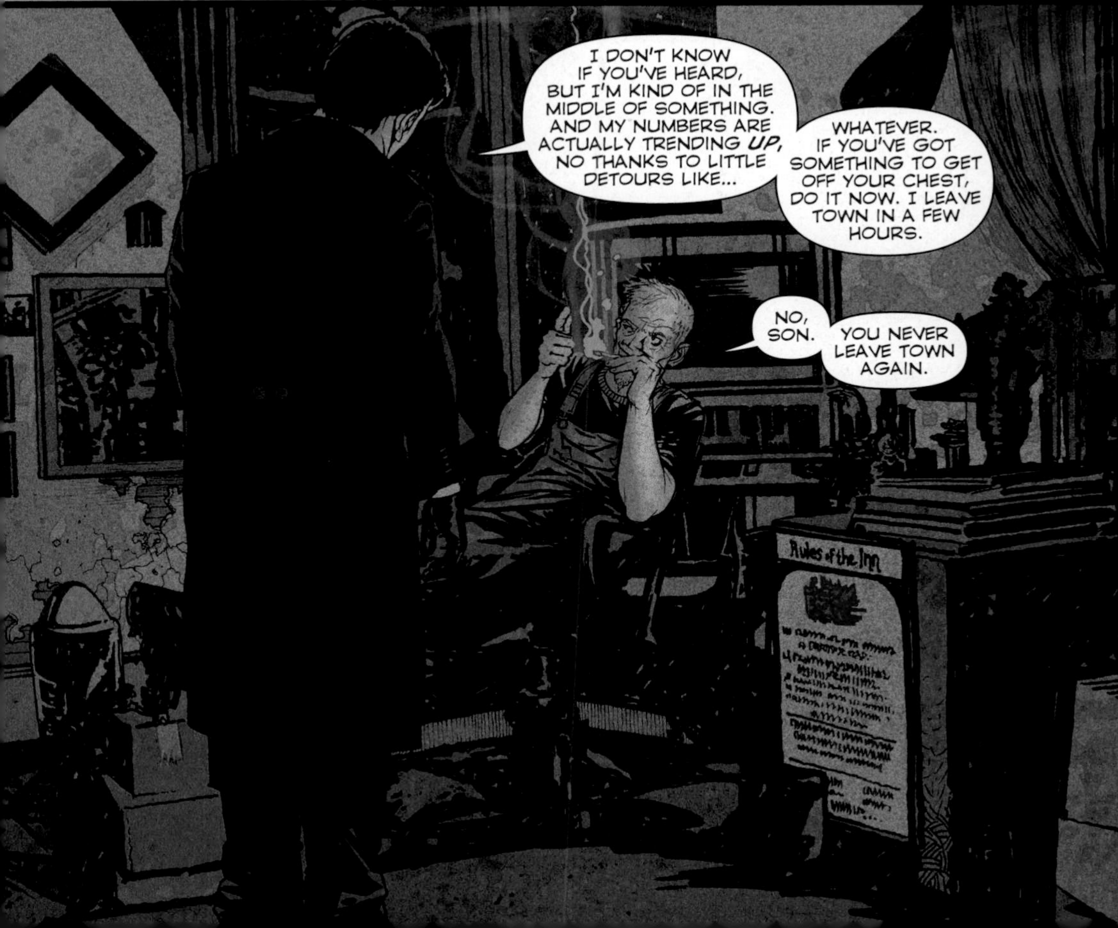
I DON'T KNOW IF YOU'VE HEARD, BUT I'M KIND OF IN THE MIDDLE OF SOMETHING. AND MY NUMBERS ARE ACTUALLY TRENDING *UP*, NO THANKS TO LITTLE DETOURS LIKE...
WHATEVER. IF YOU'VE GOT SOMETHING TO GET OFF YOUR CHEST, DO IT NOW. I LEAVE TOWN IN A FEW HOURS.
NO, SON.
YOU NEVER LEAVE TOWN AGAIN.
Rules of the Inn

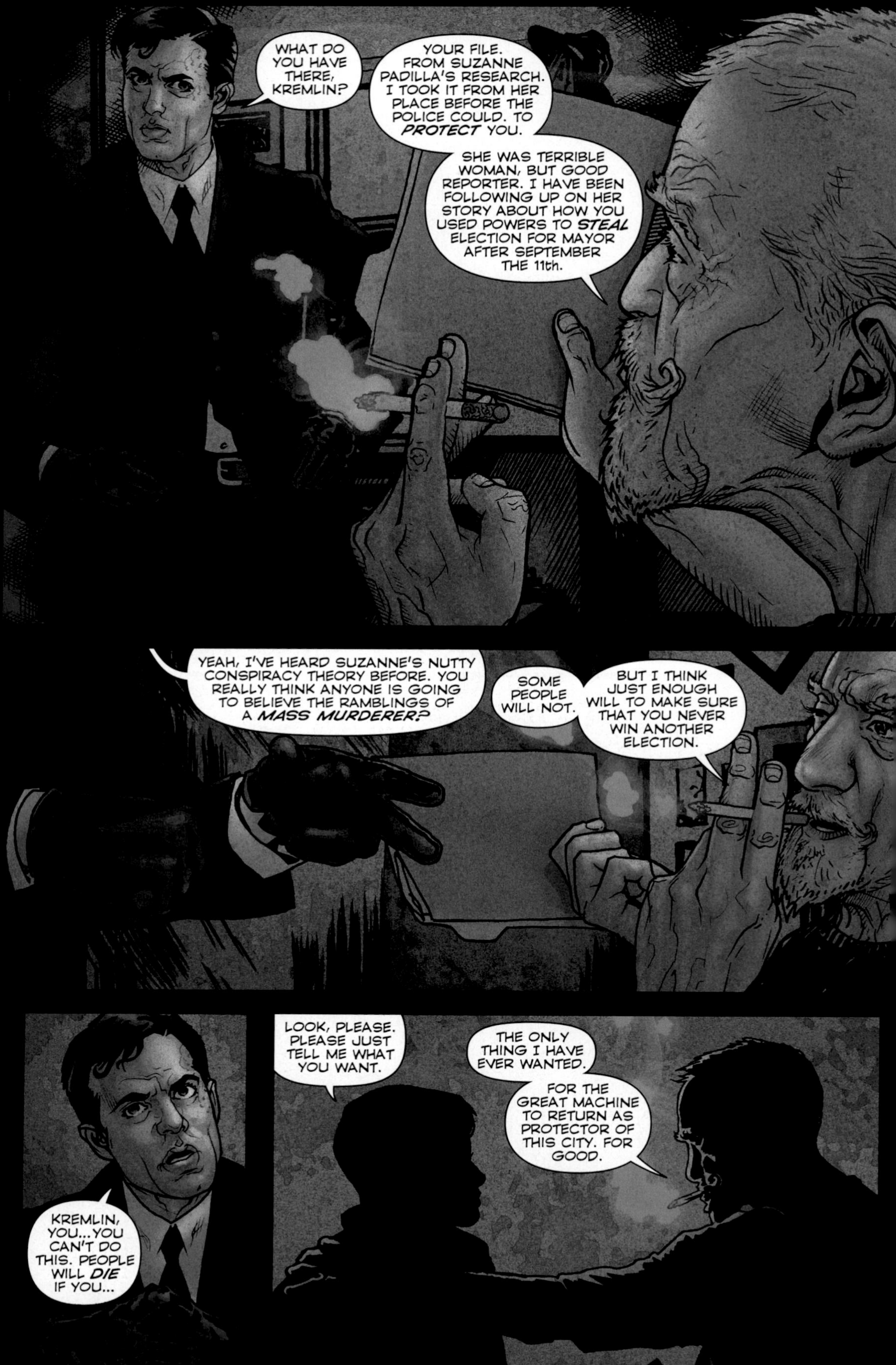
WHAT DO YOU HAVE THERE, KREMLIN?
YOUR FILE. FROM SUZANNE PADILLA'S RESEARCH. I TOOK IT FROM HER PLACE BEFORE THE POLICE COULD. TO *PROTECT* YOU.
SHE WAS TERRIBLE WOMAN, BUT GOOD REPORTER. I HAVE BEEN FOLLOWING UP ON HER STORY ABOUT HOW YOU USED POWERS TO *STEAL* ELECTION FOR MAYOR AFTER SEPTEMBER THE 11th.
YEAH, I'VE HEARD SUZANNE'S NUTTY CONSPIRACY THEORY BEFORE. YOU REALLY THINK ANYONE IS GOING TO BELIEVE THE RAMBLINGS OF A *MASS MURDERER?*
SOME PEOPLE WILL NOT.
BUT I THINK JUST ENOUGH WILL TO MAKE SURE THAT YOU NEVER WIN ANOTHER ELECTION.
KREMLIN, YOU...YOU CAN'T DO THIS. PEOPLE WILL *DIE* IF YOU...
LOOK, PLEASE. PLEASE JUST TELL ME WHAT YOU WANT.
THE ONLY THING I HAVE EVER WANTED.
FOR THE GREAT MACHINE TO RETURN AS PROTECTOR OF THIS CITY. FOR GOOD.

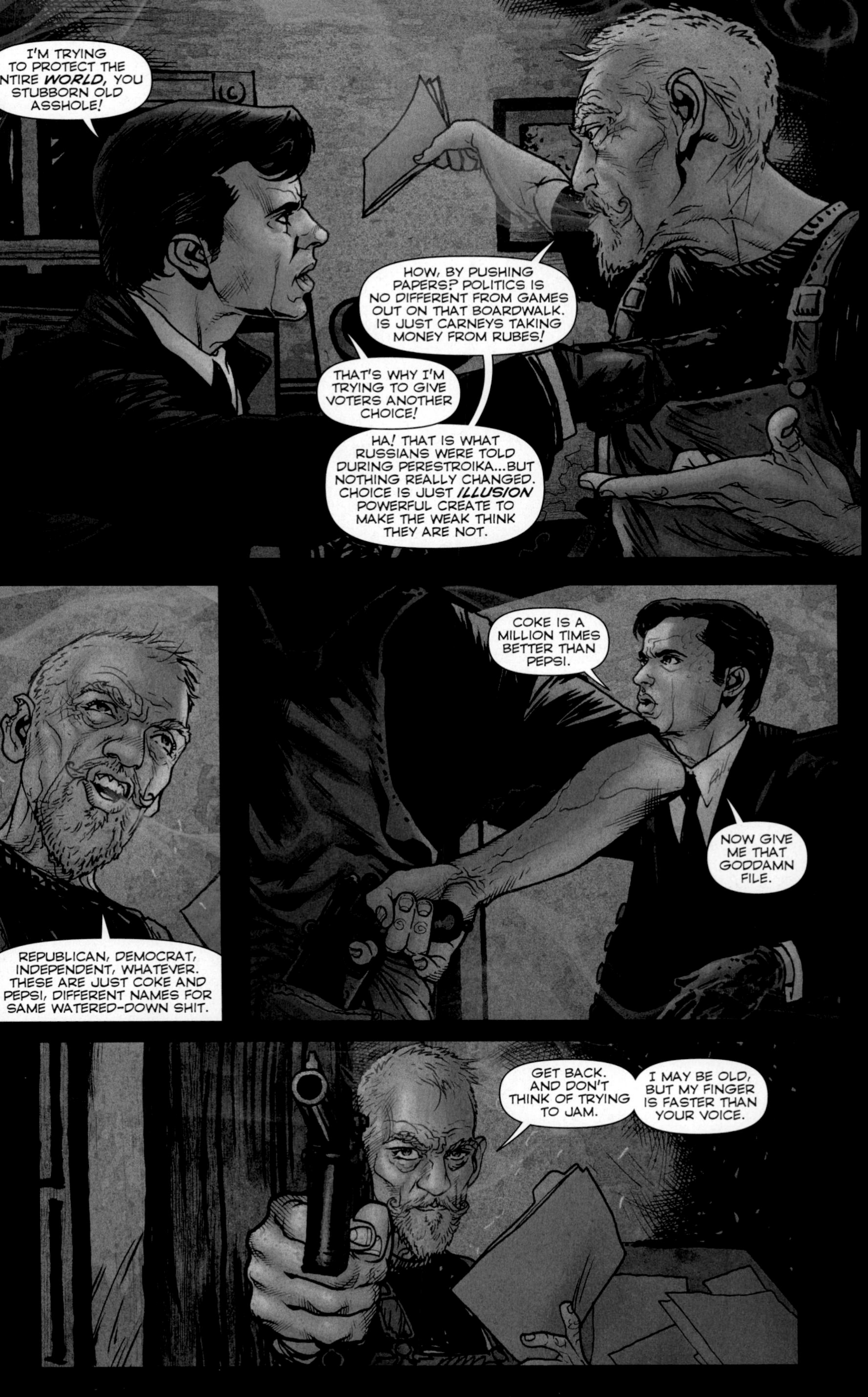
I'M TRYING TO PROTECT THE ENTIRE WORLD, YOU STUBBORN OLD ASSHOLE!
HOW, BY PUSHING PAPERS? POLITICS IS NO DIFFERENT FROM GAMES OUT ON THAT BOARDWALK. IS JUST CARNEYS TAKING MONEY FROM RUBES!
THAT'S WHY I'M TRYING TO GIVE VOTERS ANOTHER CHOICE!
HA! THAT IS WHAT RUSSIANS WERE TOLD DURING PERESTROIKA...BUT NOTHING REALLY CHANGED. CHOICE IS JUST ILLUSION POWERFUL CREATE TO MAKE THE WEAK THINK THEY ARE NOT.
REPUBLICAN, DEMOCRAT, INDEPENDENT, WHATEVER. THESE ARE JUST COKE AND PEPSI, DIFFERENT NAMES FOR SAME WATERED-DOWN SHIT.
COKE IS A MILLION TIMES BETTER THAN PEPSI.
NOW GIVE ME THAT GODDAMN FILE.
GET BACK. AND DON'T THINK OF TRYING TO JAM.
I MAY BE OLD, BUT MY FINGER IS FASTER THAN YOUR VOICE.

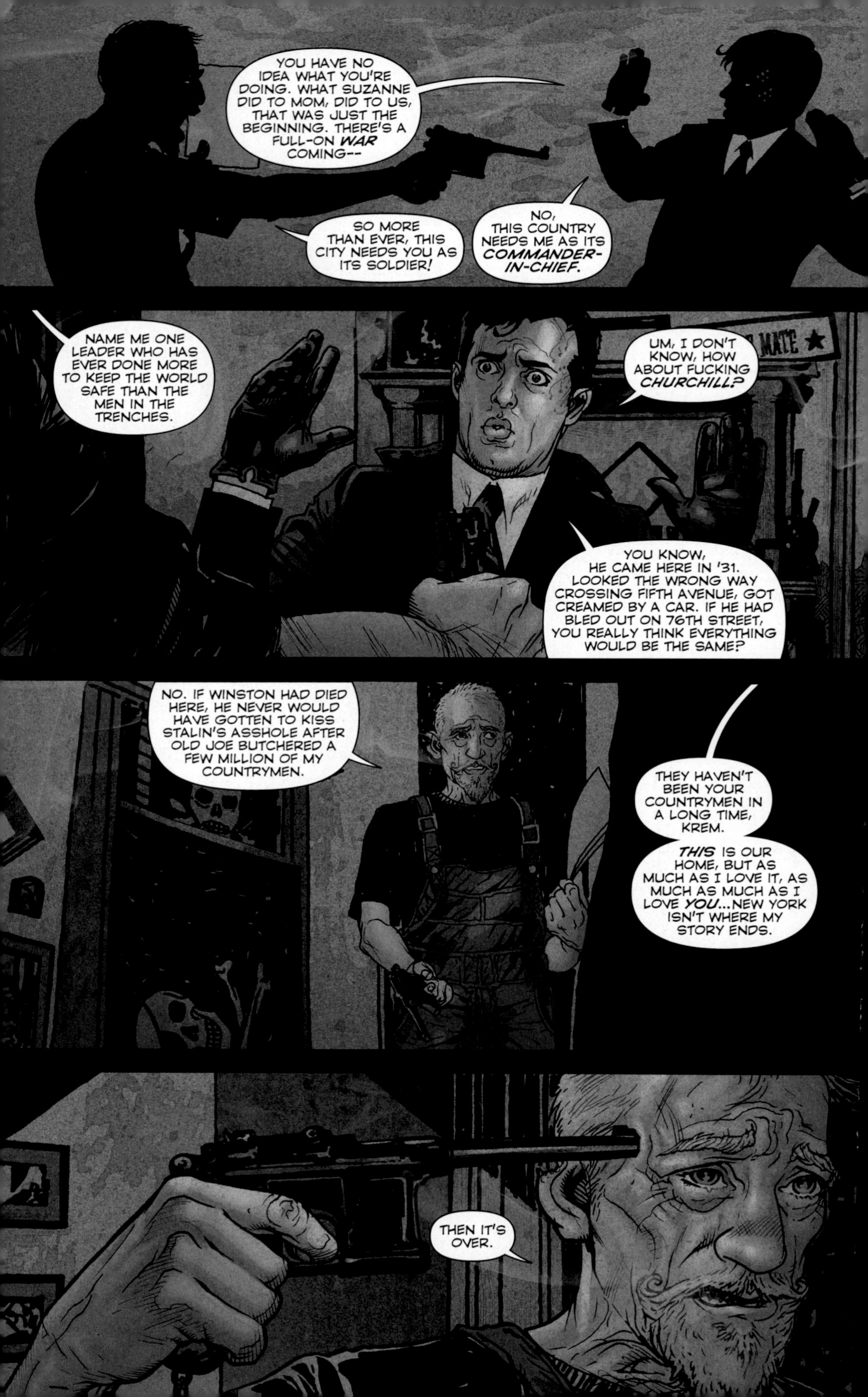
YOU HAVE NO IDEA WHAT YOU'RE DOING. WHAT SUZANNE DID TO MOM, DID TO US, THAT WAS JUST THE BEGINNING. THERE'S A FULL-ON WAR COMING--
SO MORE THAN EVER, THIS CITY NEEDS YOU AS ITS SOLDIER!
NO, THIS COUNTRY NEEDS ME AS ITS COMMANDER-IN-CHIEF.
NAME ME ONE LEADER WHO HAS EVER DONE MORE TO KEEP THE WORLD SAFE THAN THE MEN IN THE TRENCHES.
UM, I DON'T KNOW, HOW ABOUT FUCKING CHURCHILL?
YOU KNOW, HE CAME HERE IN '31. LOOKED THE WRONG WAY CROSSING FIFTH AVENUE, GOT CREAMED BY A CAR. IF HE HAD BLED OUT ON 76TH STREET, YOU REALLY THINK EVERYTHING WOULD BE THE SAME?
NO. IF WINSTON HAD DIED HERE, HE NEVER WOULD HAVE GOTTEN TO KISS STALIN'S ASSHOLE AFTER OLD JOE BUTCHERED A FEW MILLION OF MY COUNTRYMEN.
THEY HAVEN'T BEEN YOUR COUNTRYMEN IN A LONG TIME, KREM.
THIS IS OUR HOME, BUT AS MUCH AS I LOVE IT, AS MUCH AS MUCH AS I LOVE YOU...NEW YORK ISN'T WHERE MY STORY ENDS.
THEN IT'S OVER.

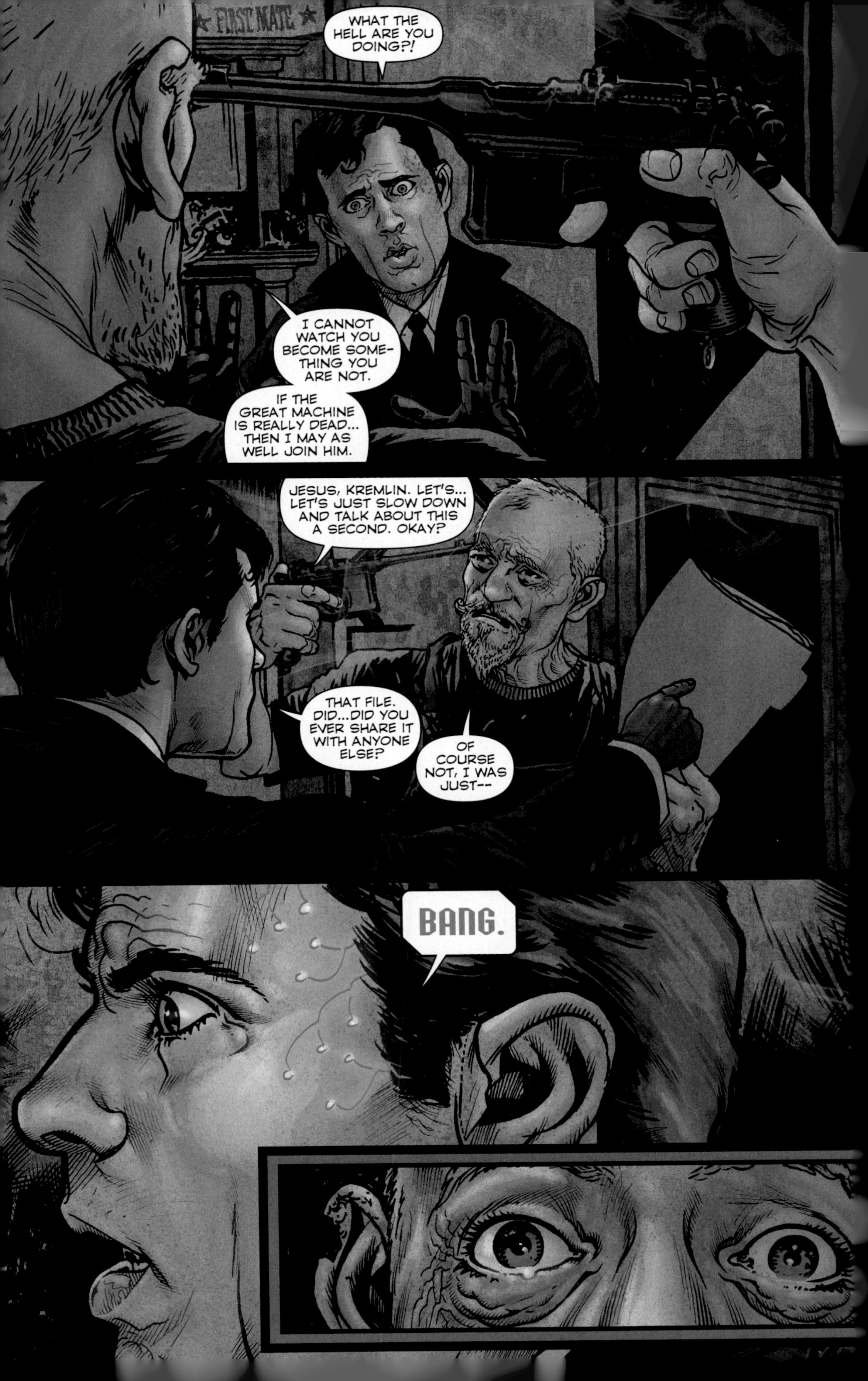
FIRST MATE
WHAT THE HELL ARE YOU DOING?!
I CANNOT WATCH YOU BECOME SOME-THING YOU ARE NOT.
IF THE GREAT MACHINE IS REALLY DEAD... THEN I MAY AS WELL JOIN HIM.
JESUS, KREMLIN. LET'S... LET'S JUST SLOW DOWN AND TALK ABOUT THIS A SECOND. OKAY?
THAT FILE. DID...DID YOU EVER SHARE IT WITH ANYONE ELSE?
OF COURSE NOT, I WAS JUST--
BANG.

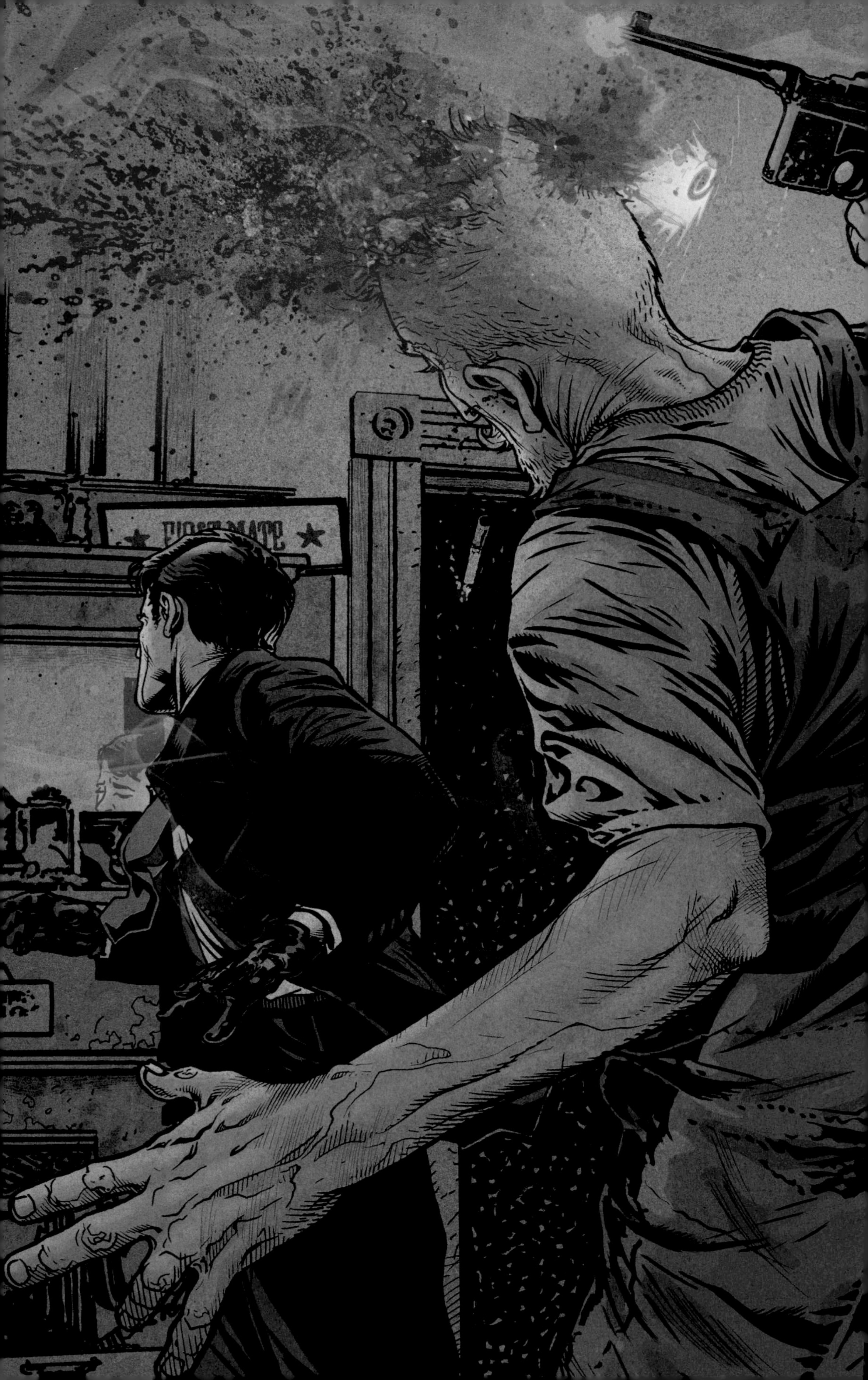

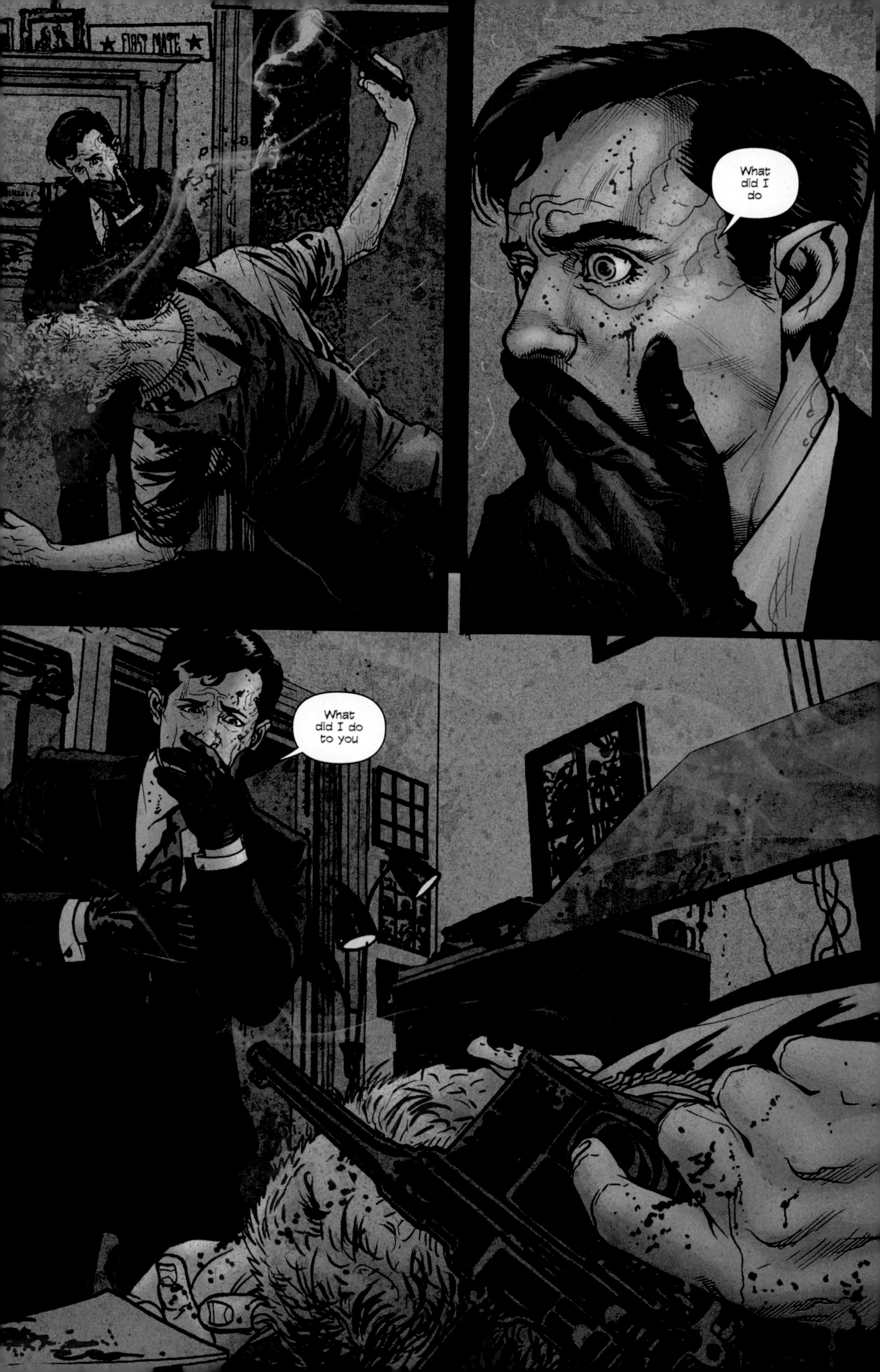
FIRST MATE
What did I do
What did I do to you

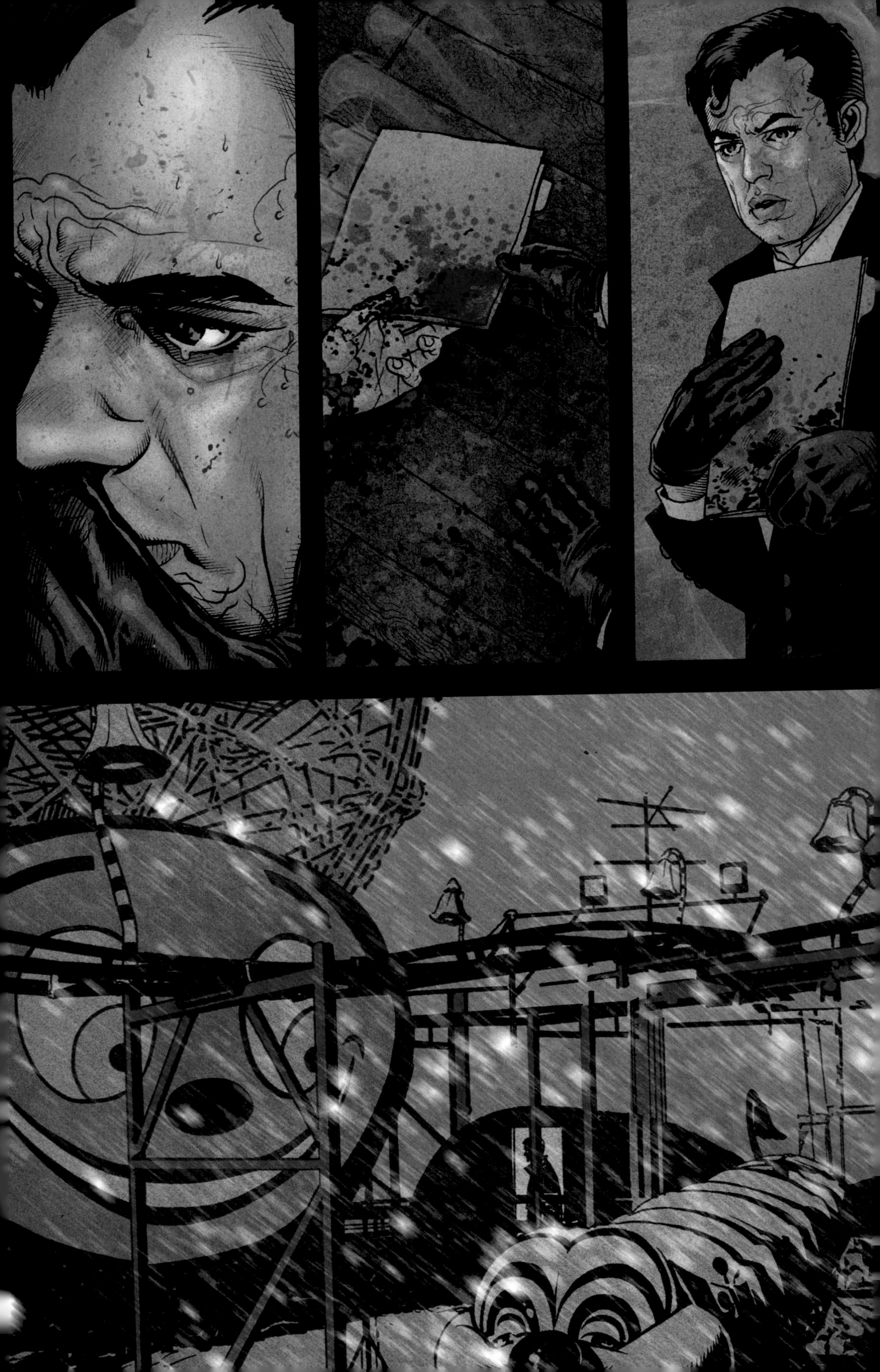

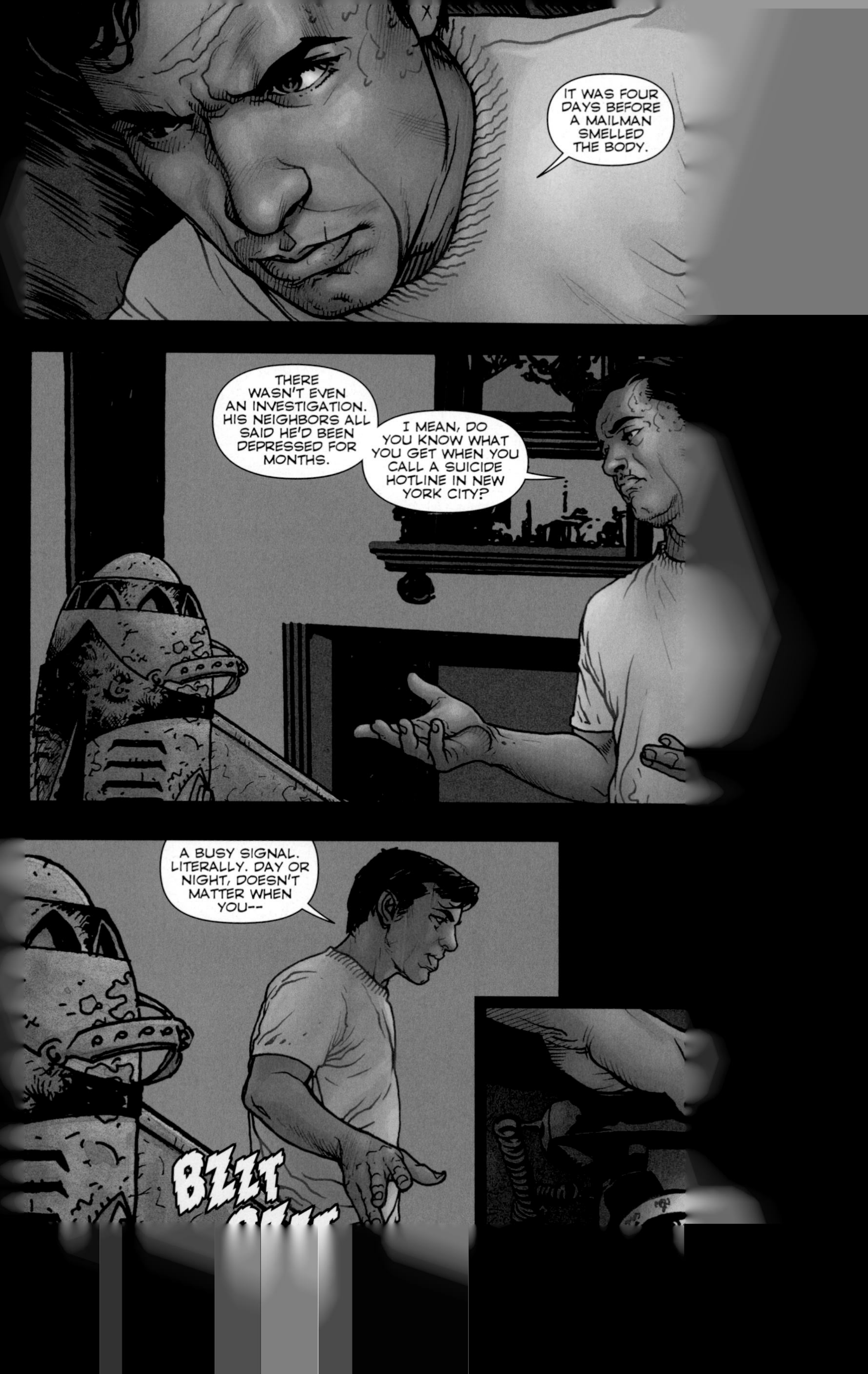
IT WAS FOUR DAYS BEFORE A MAILMAN SMELLED THE BODY.
THERE WASN'T EVEN AN INVESTIGATION. HIS NEIGHBORS ALL SAID HE'D BEEN DEPRESSED FOR MONTHS.
I MEAN, DO YOU KNOW WHAT YOU GET WHEN YOU CALL A SUICIDE HOTLINE IN NEW YORK CITY?
A BUSY SIGNAL. LITERALLY. DAY OR NIGHT, DOESN'T MATTER WHEN YOU--
BZZT

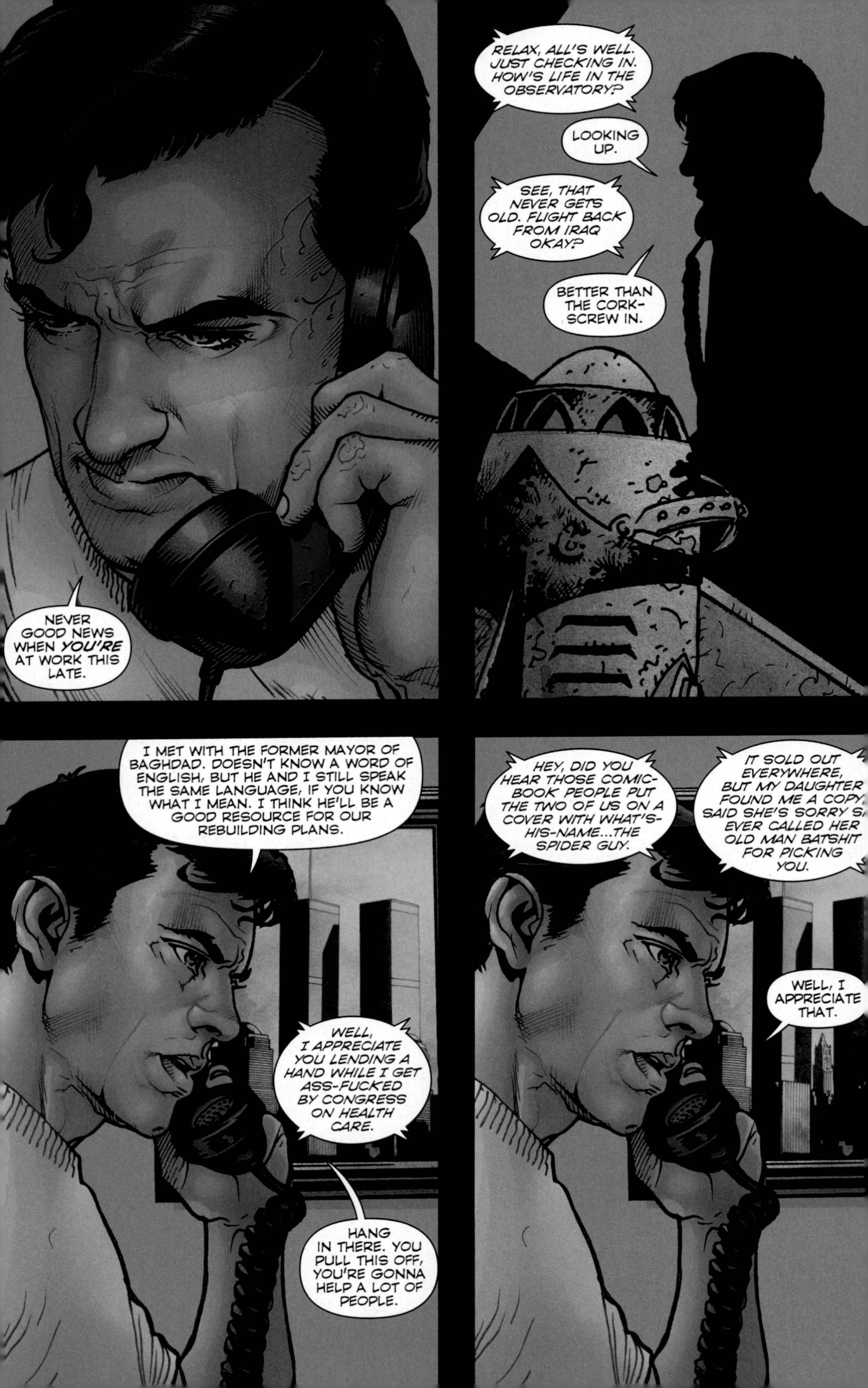

NEVER GOOD NEWS WHEN YOU'RE AT WORK THIS LATE.
RELAX, ALL'S WELL. JUST CHECKING IN. HOW'S LIFE IN THE OBSERVATORY?
LOOKING UP.
SEE, THAT NEVER GETS OLD. FLIGHT BACK FROM IRAQ OKAY?
BETTER THAN THE CORK-SCREW IN.
I MET WITH THE FORMER MAYOR OF BAGHDAD. DOESN'T KNOW A WORD OF ENGLISH, BUT HE AND I STILL SPEAK THE SAME LANGUAGE, IF YOU KNOW WHAT I MEAN. I THINK HE'LL BE A GOOD RESOURCE FOR OUR REBUILDING PLANS.
WELL, I APPRECIATE YOU LENDING A HAND WHILE I GET ASS-FUCKED BY CONGRESS ON HEALTH CARE.
HANG IN THERE. YOU PULL THIS OFF, YOU'RE GONNA HELP A LOT OF PEOPLE.
HEY, DID YOU HEAR THOSE COMIC-BOOK PEOPLE PUT THE TWO OF US ON A COVER WITH WHAT'S-HIS-NAME...THE SPIDER GUY.
IT SOLD OUT EVERYWHERE, BUT MY DAUGHTER FOUND ME A COPY. SAID SHE'S SORRY S EVER CALLED HER OLD MAN BATSHIT FOR PICKING YOU.
WELL, I APPRECIATE THAT.

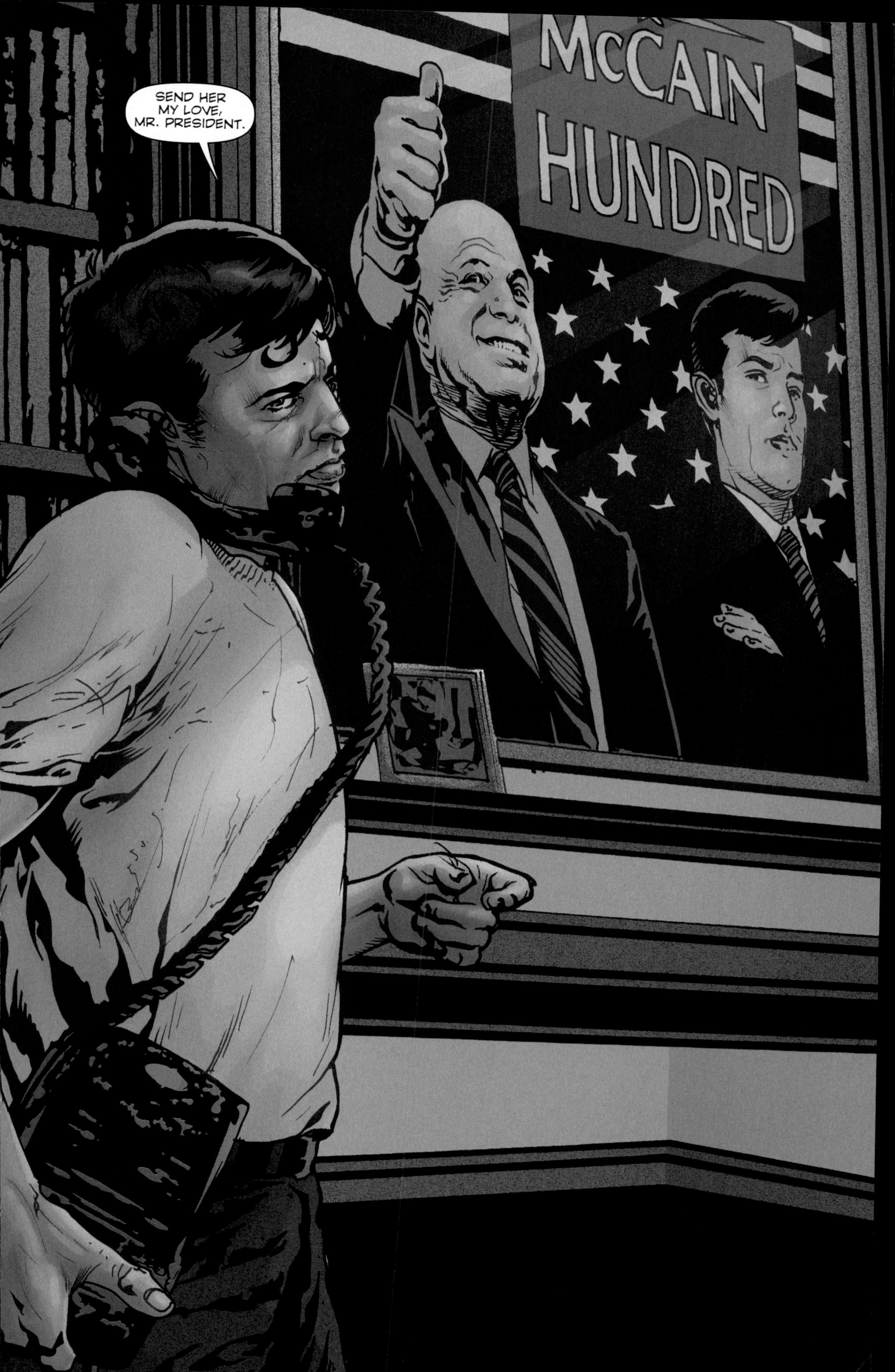
SEND HER MY LOVE, MR. PRESIDENT.
McCAIN
HUNDRED

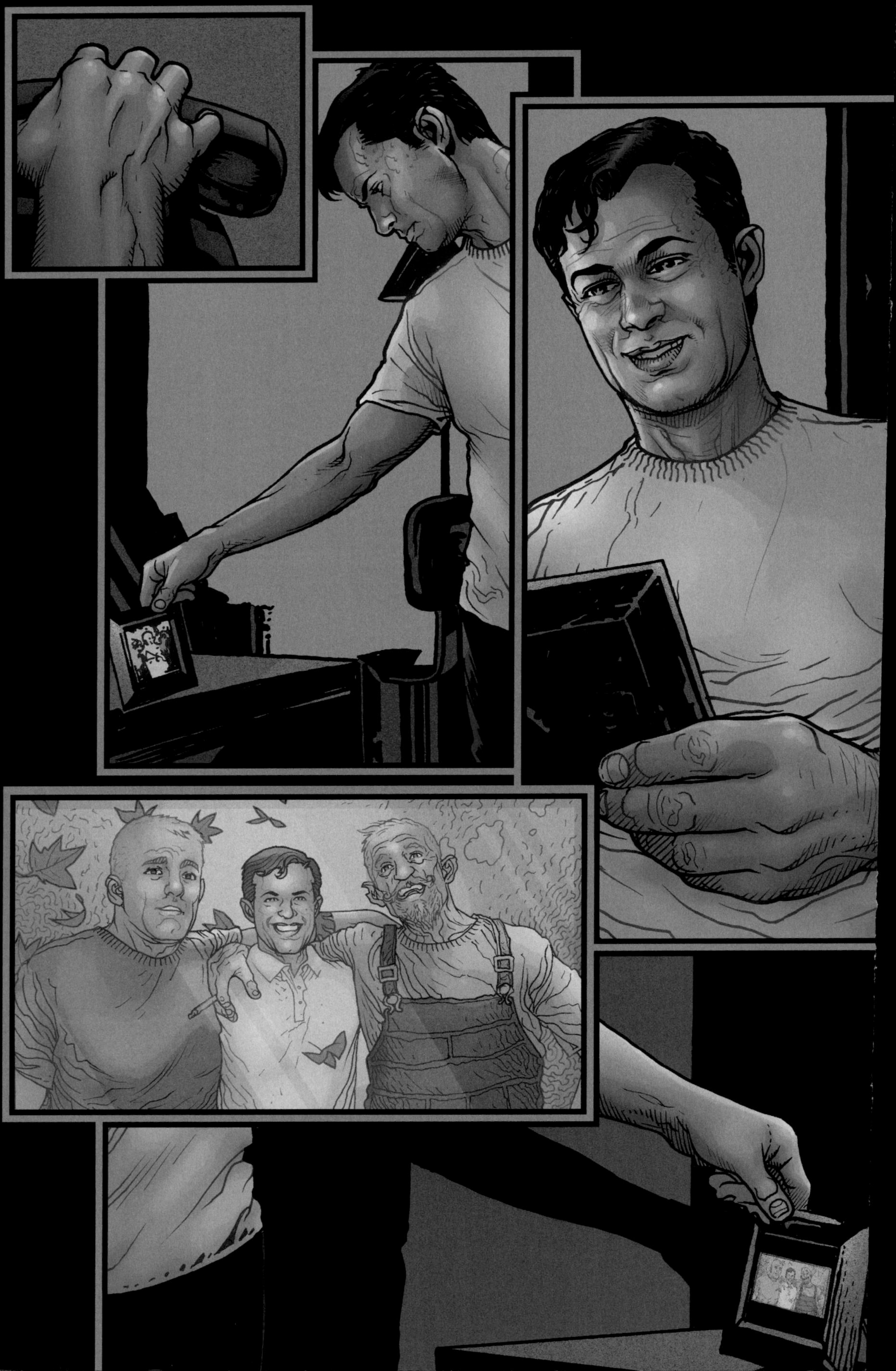

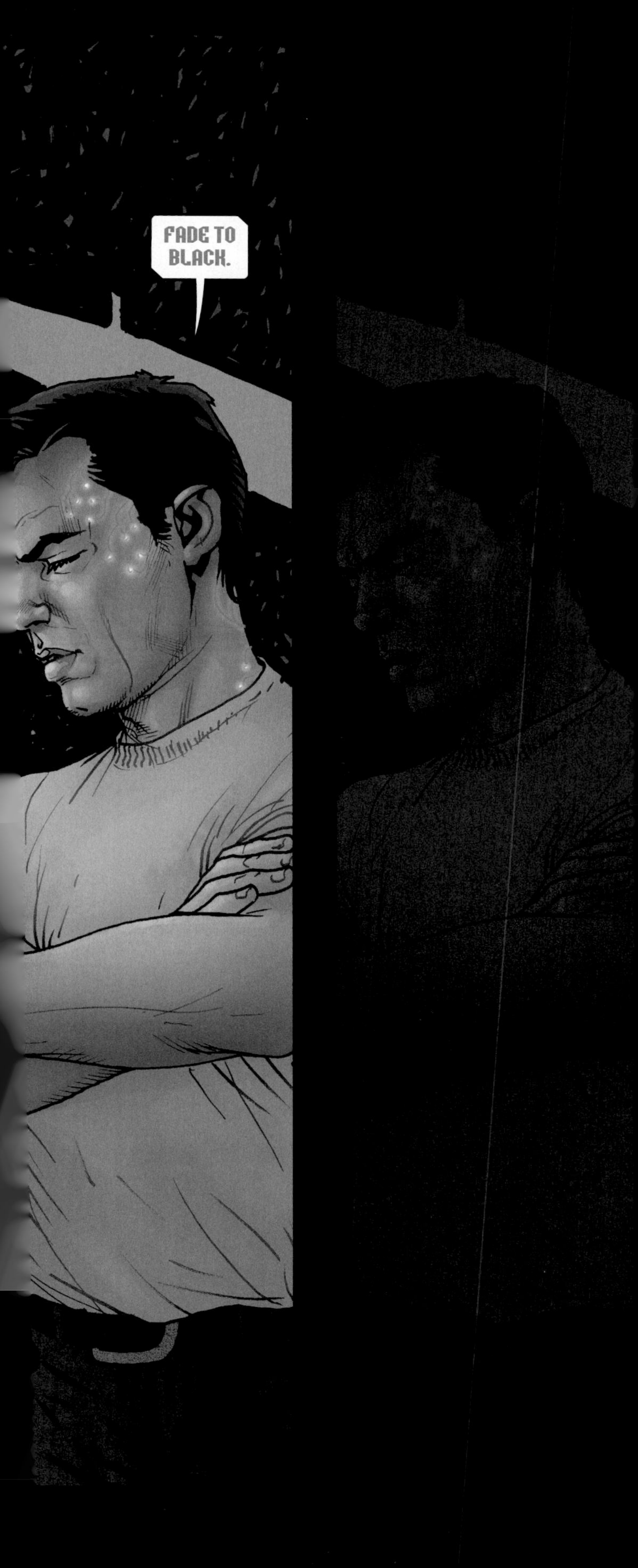
FADE TO BLACK.

VICE

BRIAN K. VAUGHAN *writer*   **TONY HARRIS** *artist*

JD METTLER *colorist*   **JARED K. FLETCHER** *letters*

KRISTY QUINN *assistant editor*   **BEN ABERNATHY** *editor*

JIM LEE *variant cover*

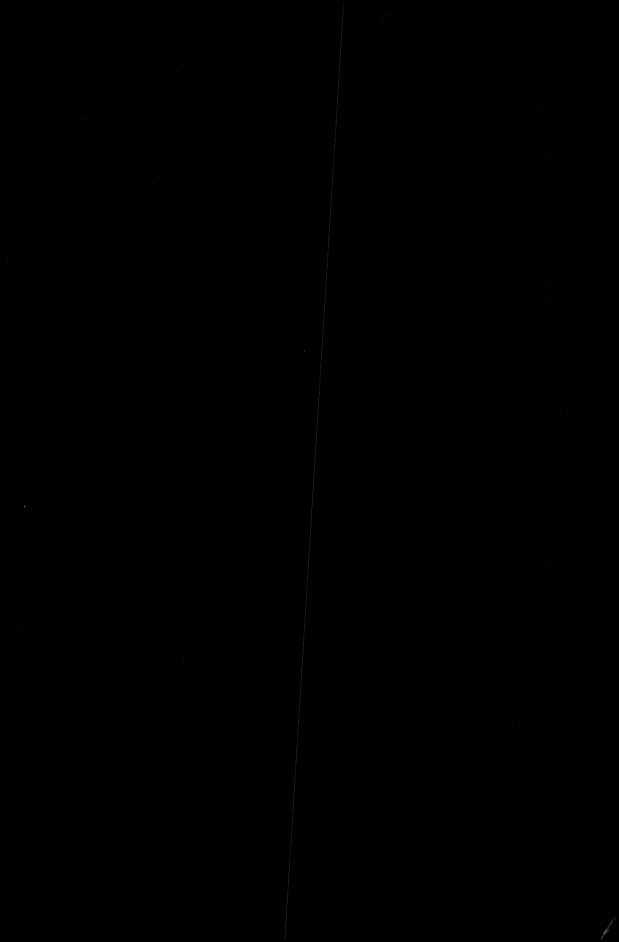

COVER GALLERY

As promised, here are the rest of Tony's fabulous covers! -Kristy Quinn, Editor

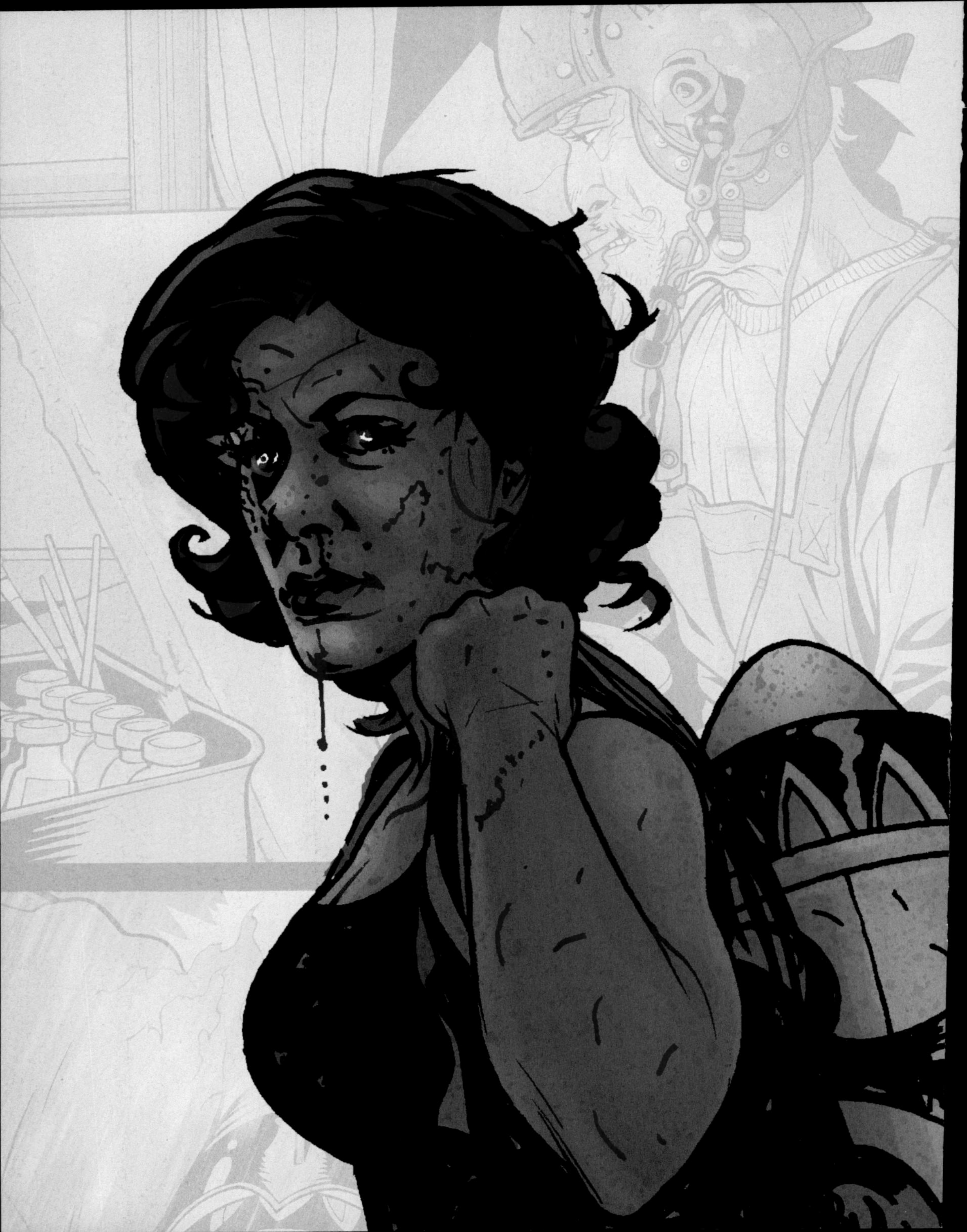

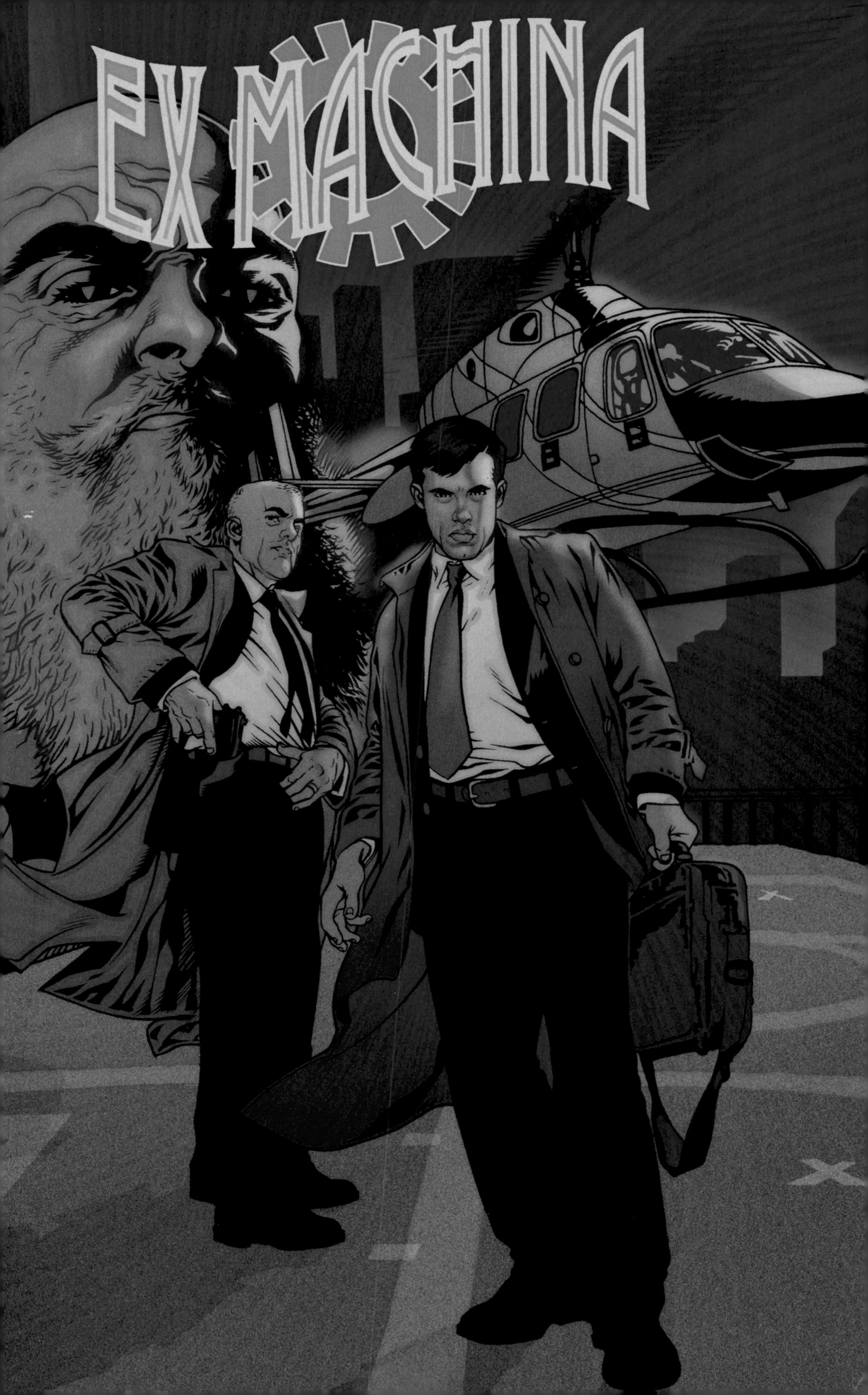
EX MACHINA

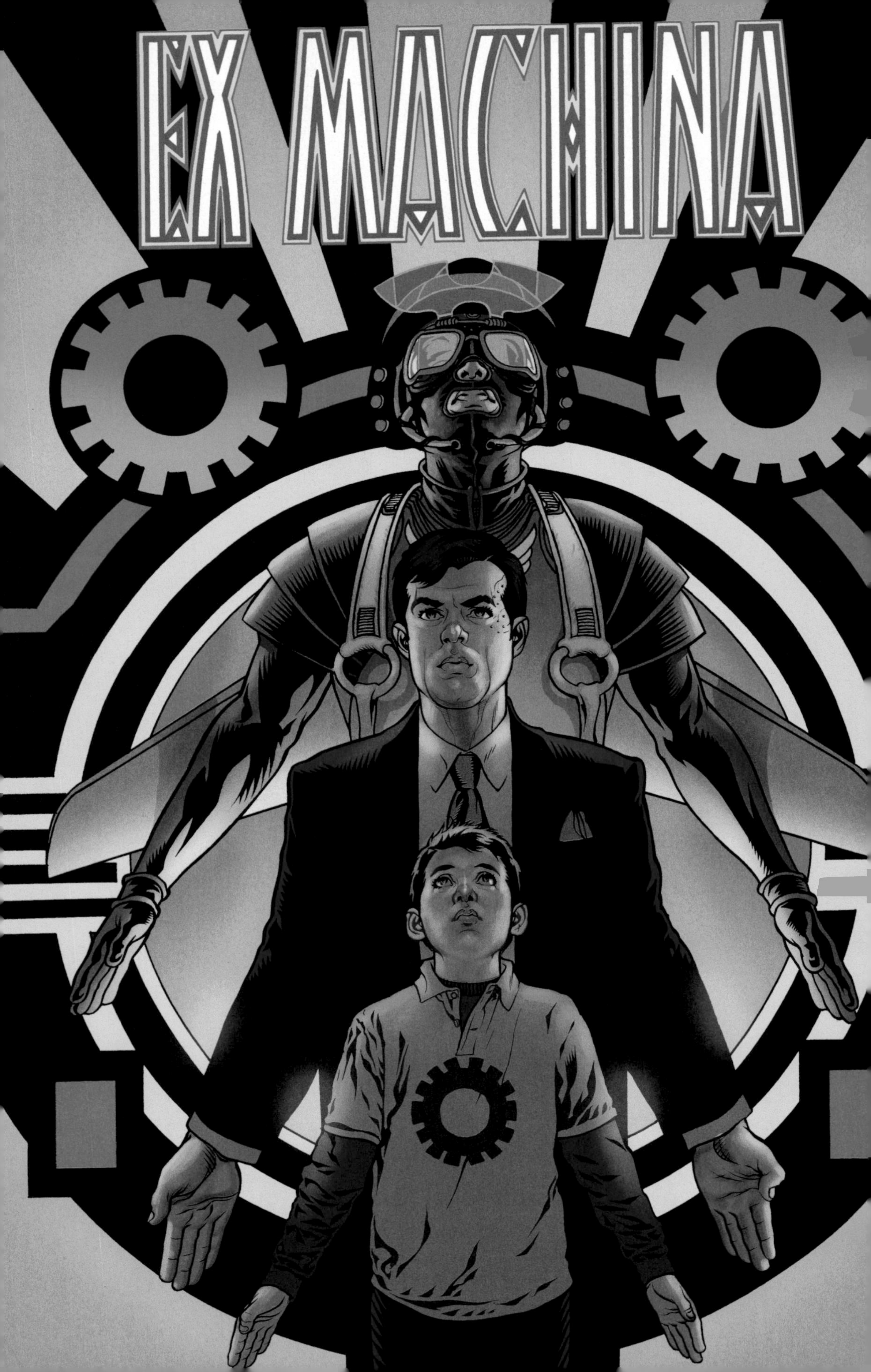
EX MACHINA

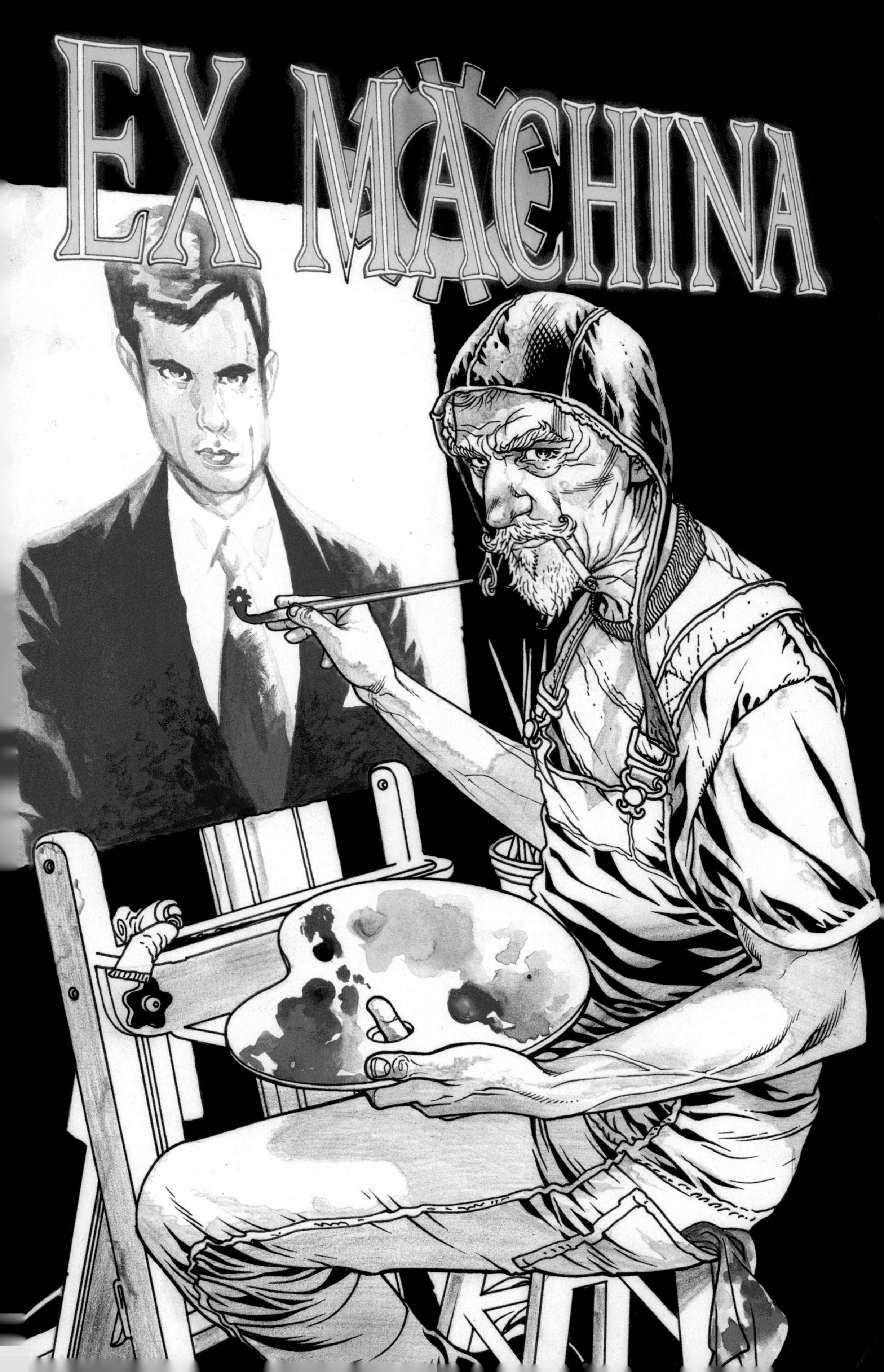
EX MACHINA

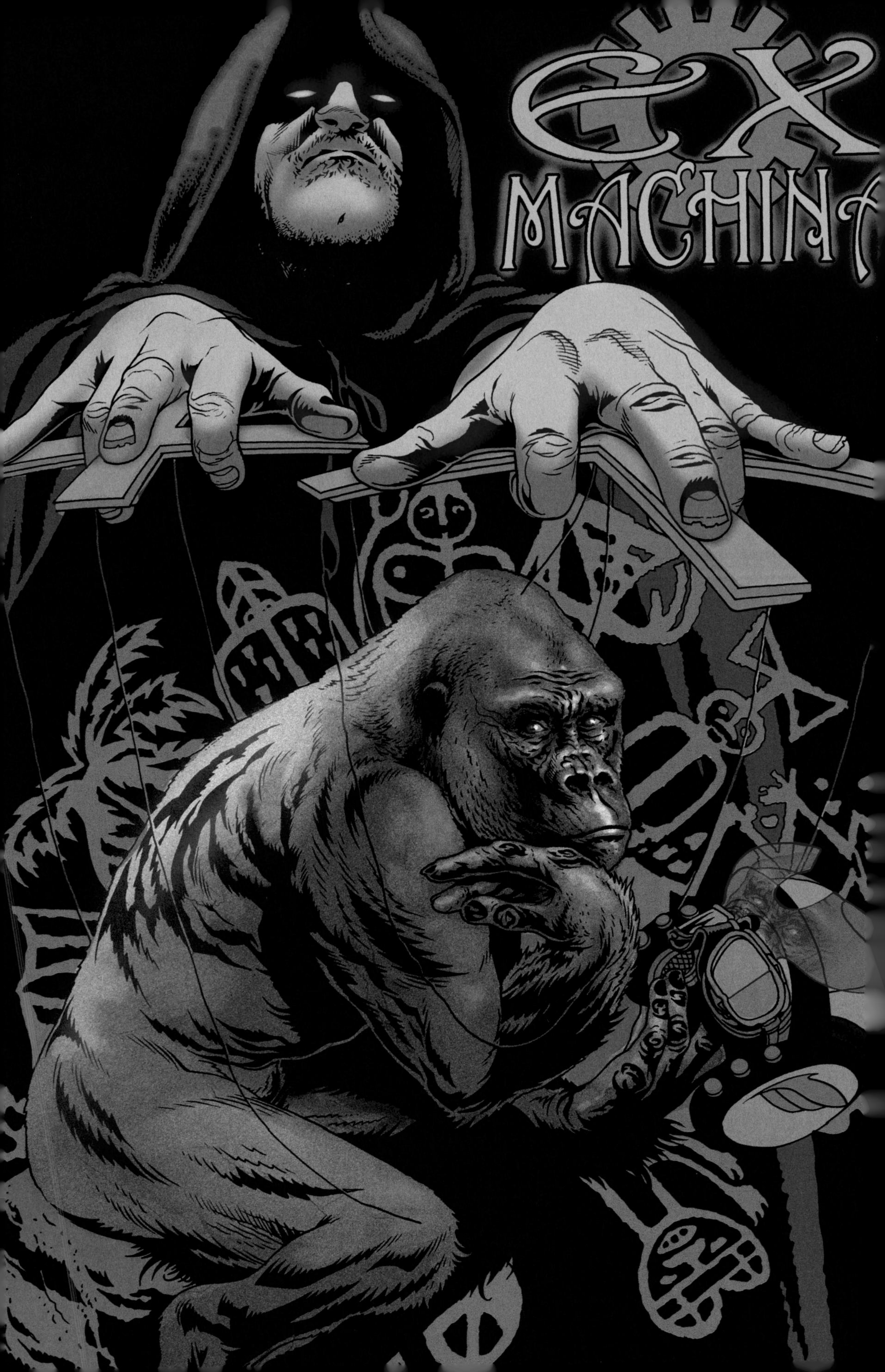
MACHIN

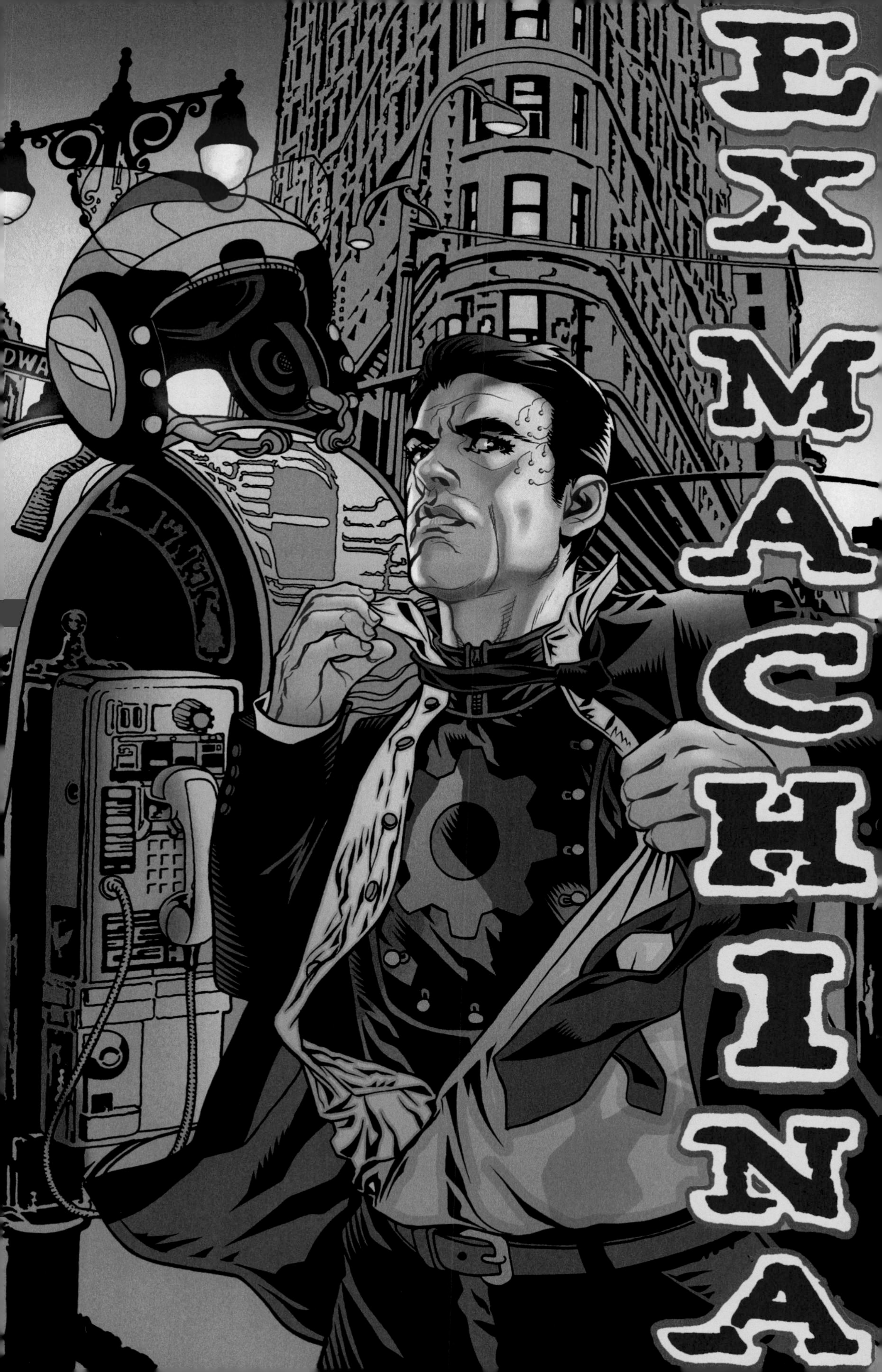
EX MACHINA

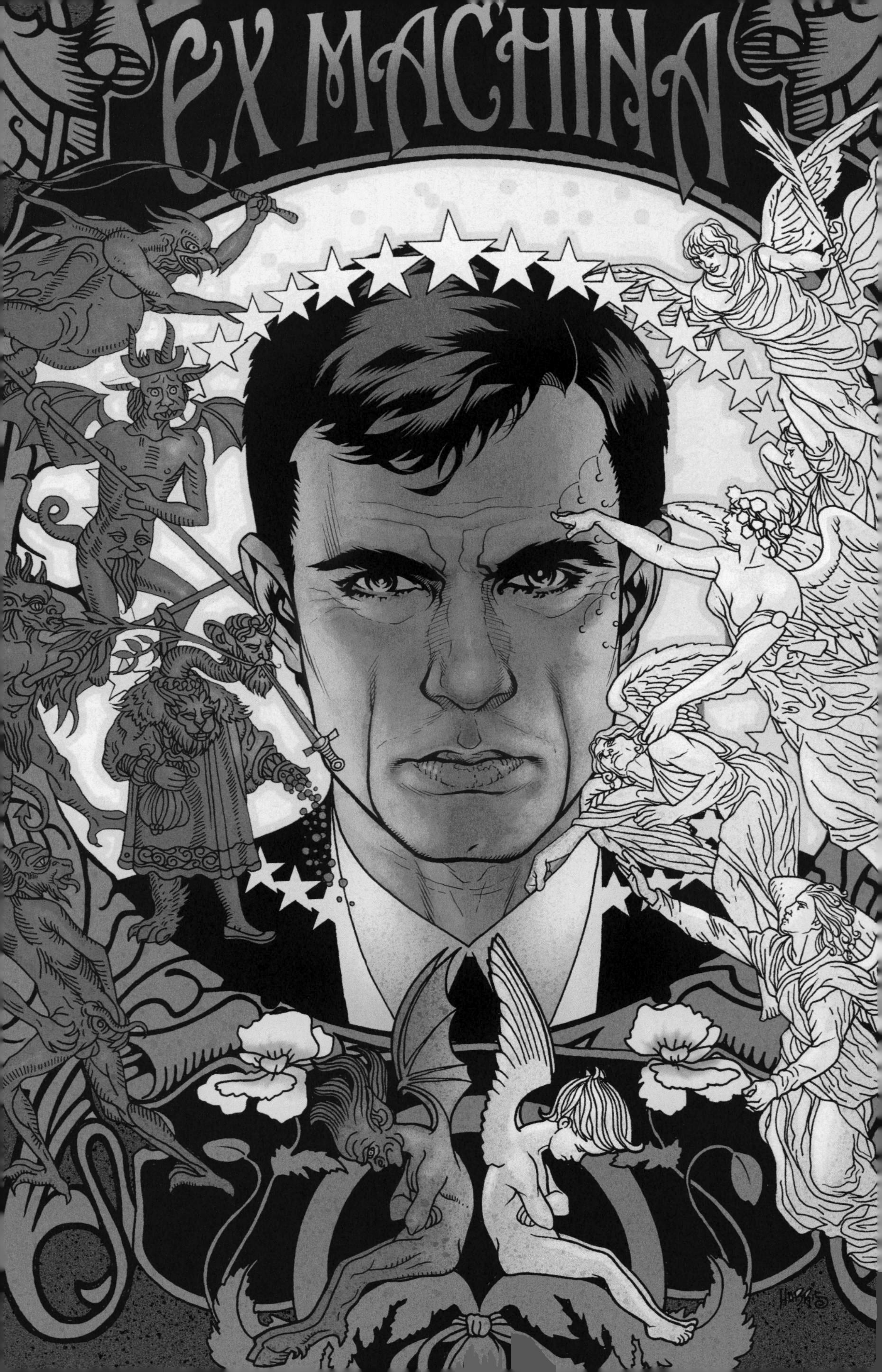
EX MACHINA

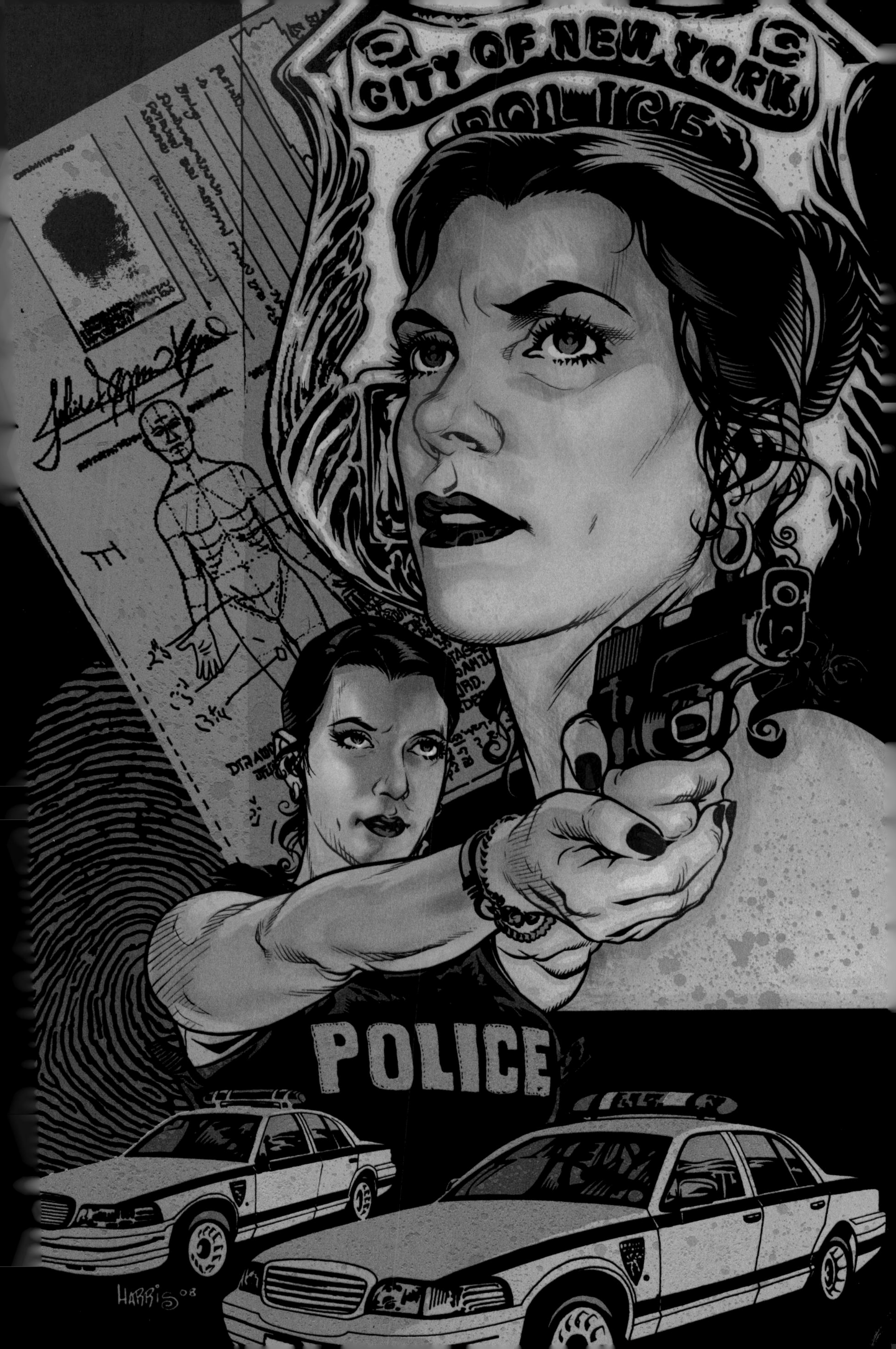
CITY OF NEW YORK
POLICE
POLICE
HARRIS '08

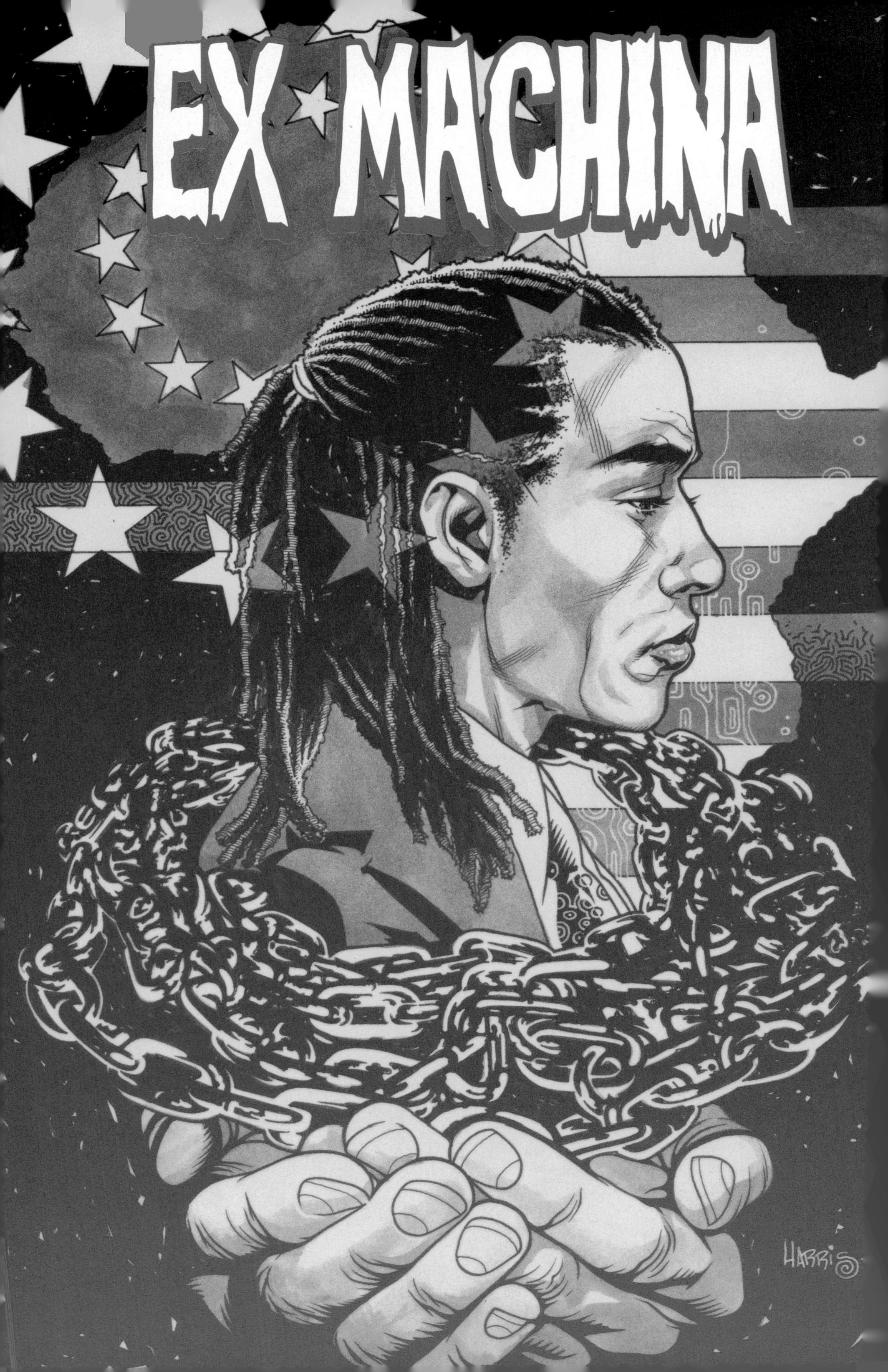
EX MACHINA
HARRIS

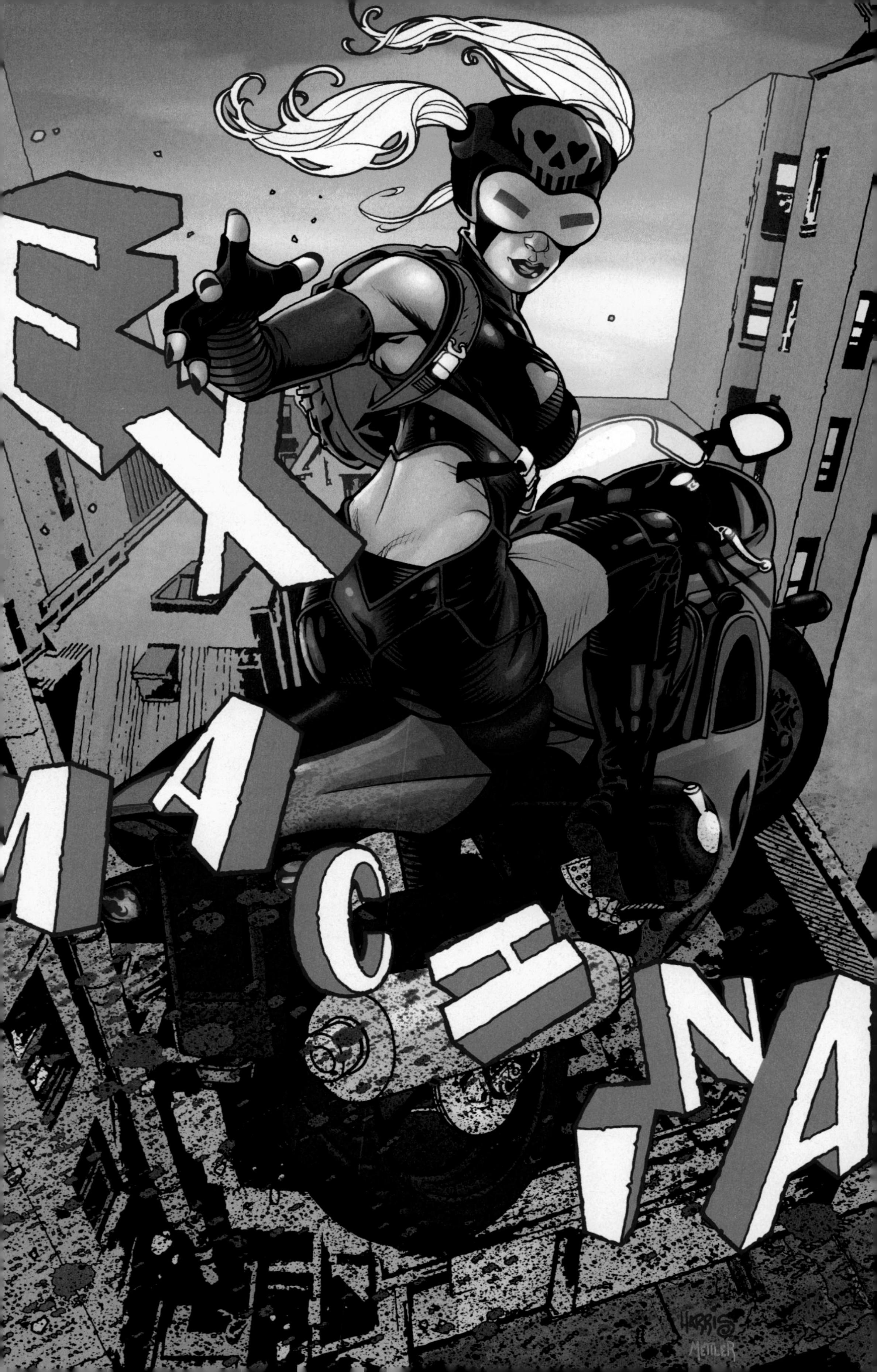
EX
MACH
NA
HARRIS
METTLER

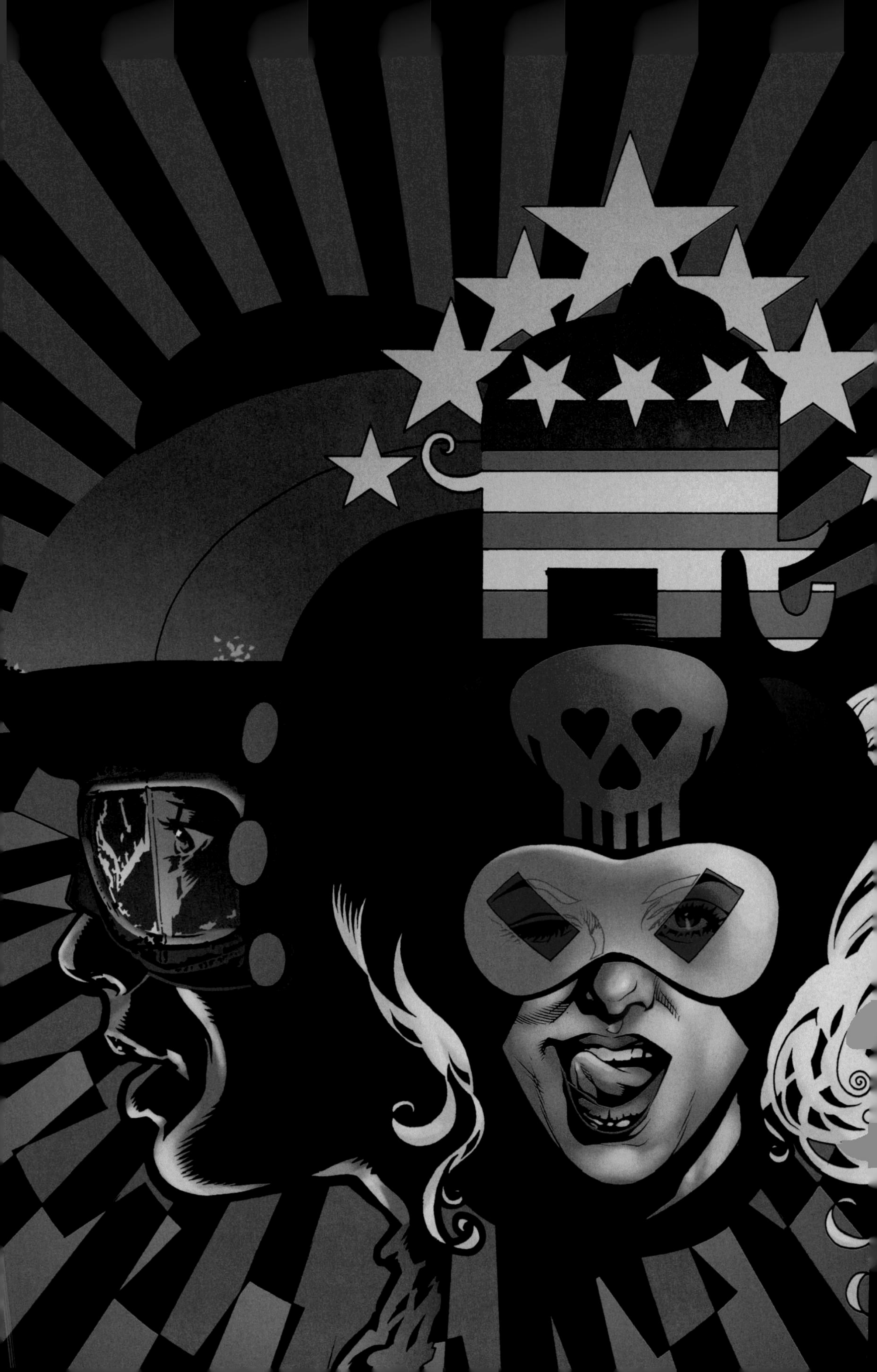

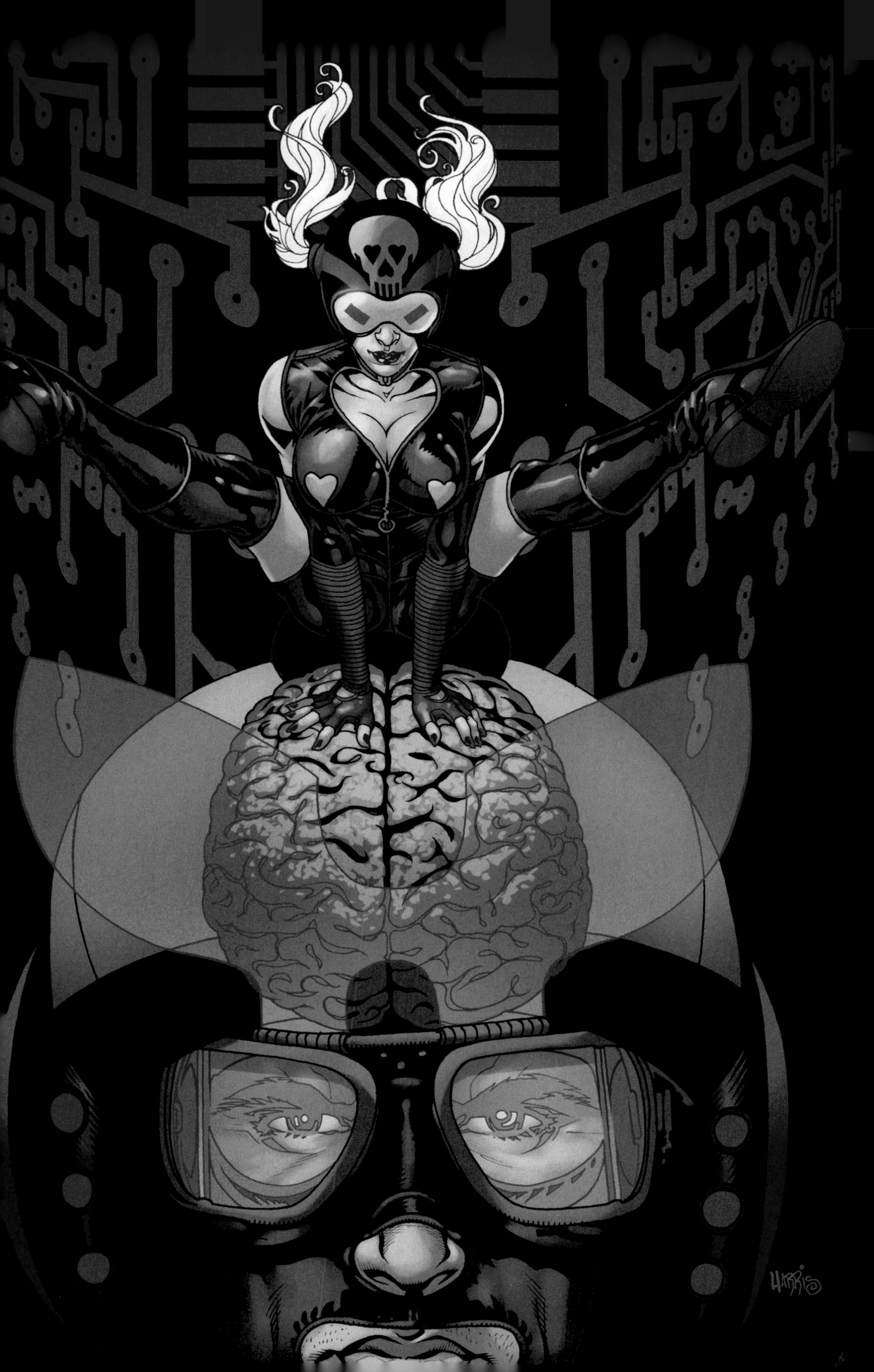

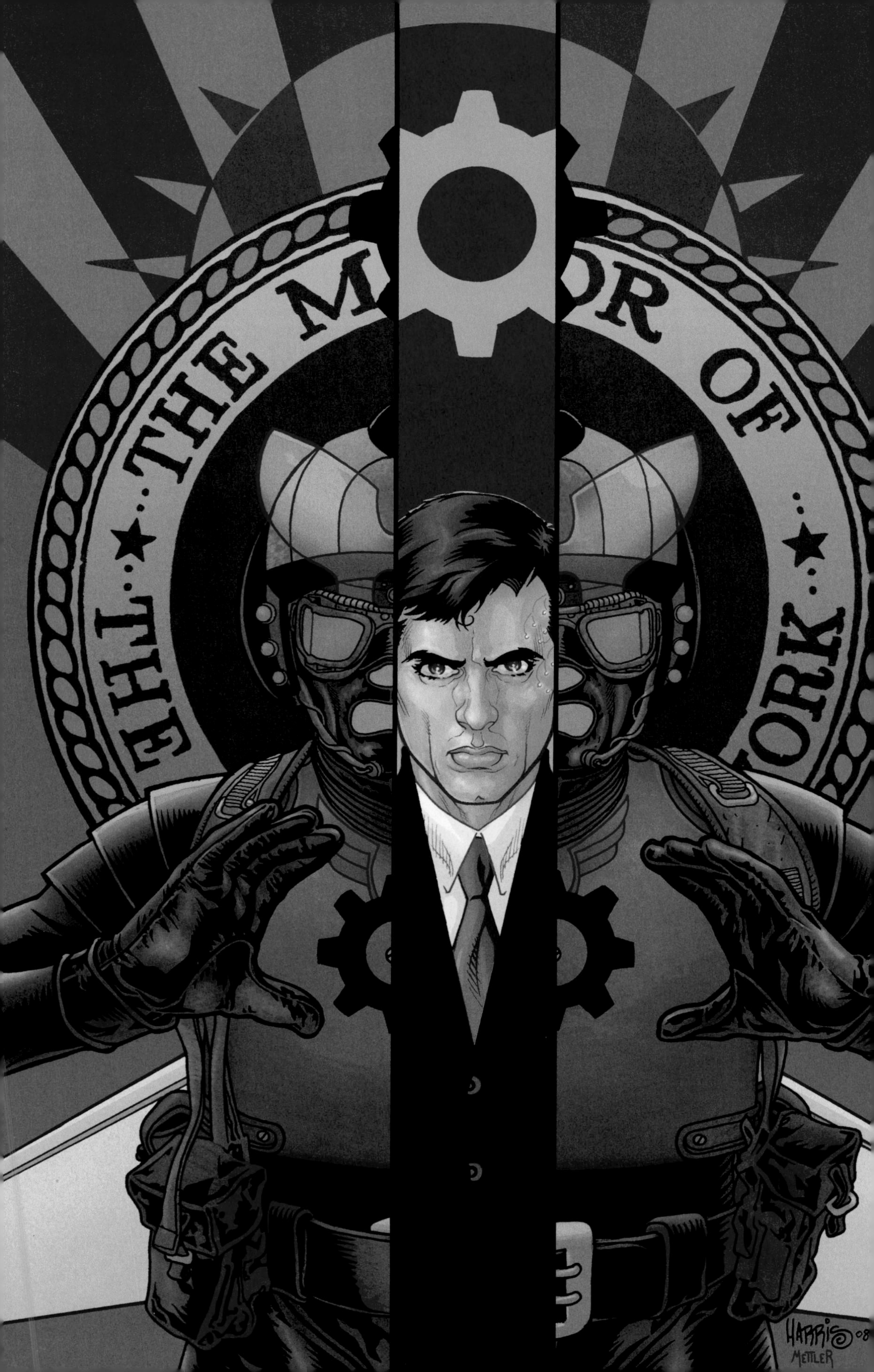

THE ..★.. THE M
OR OF
ORK ..★..
HARRIS '08
METTLER

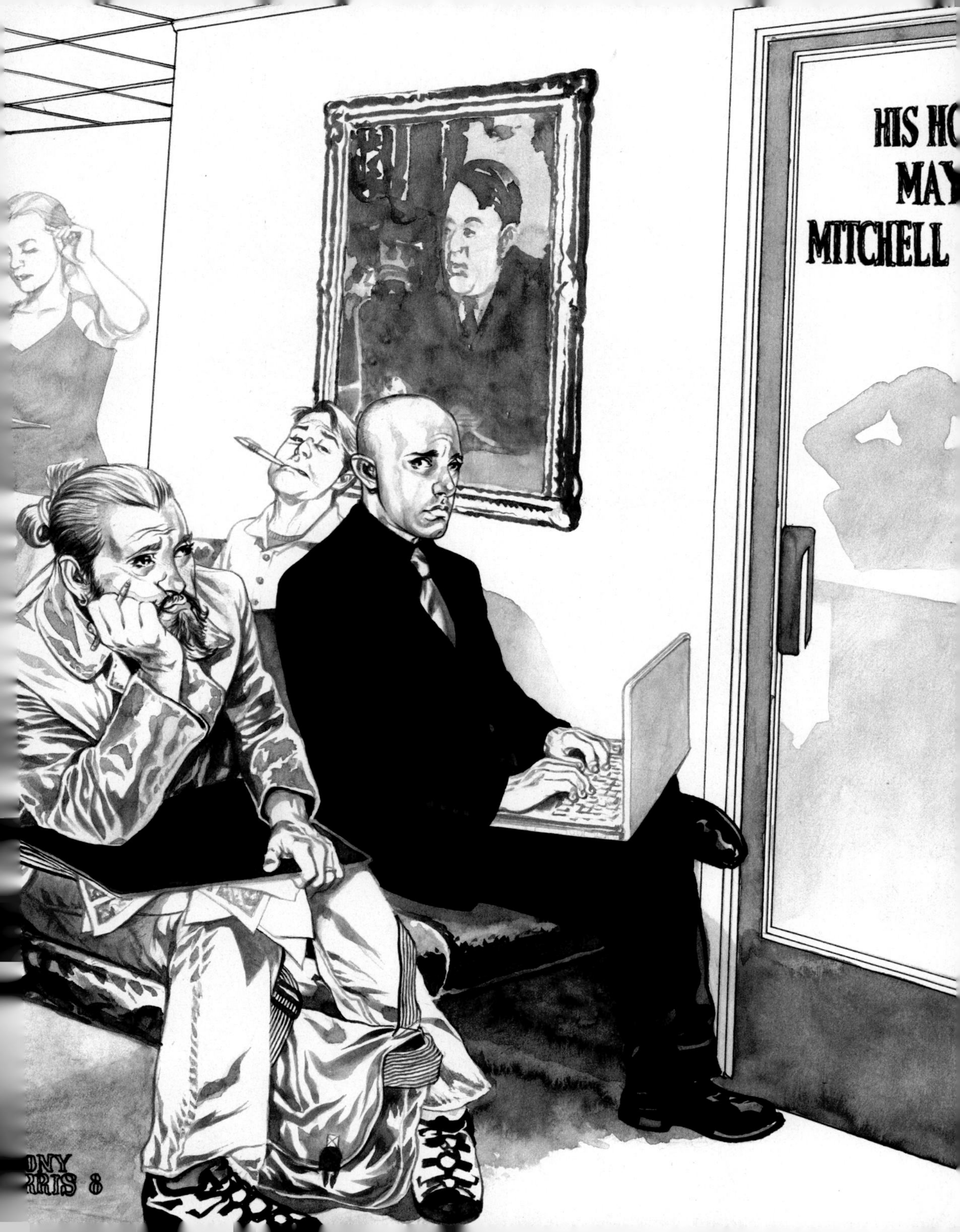
HIS HO
MAY
MITCHELL

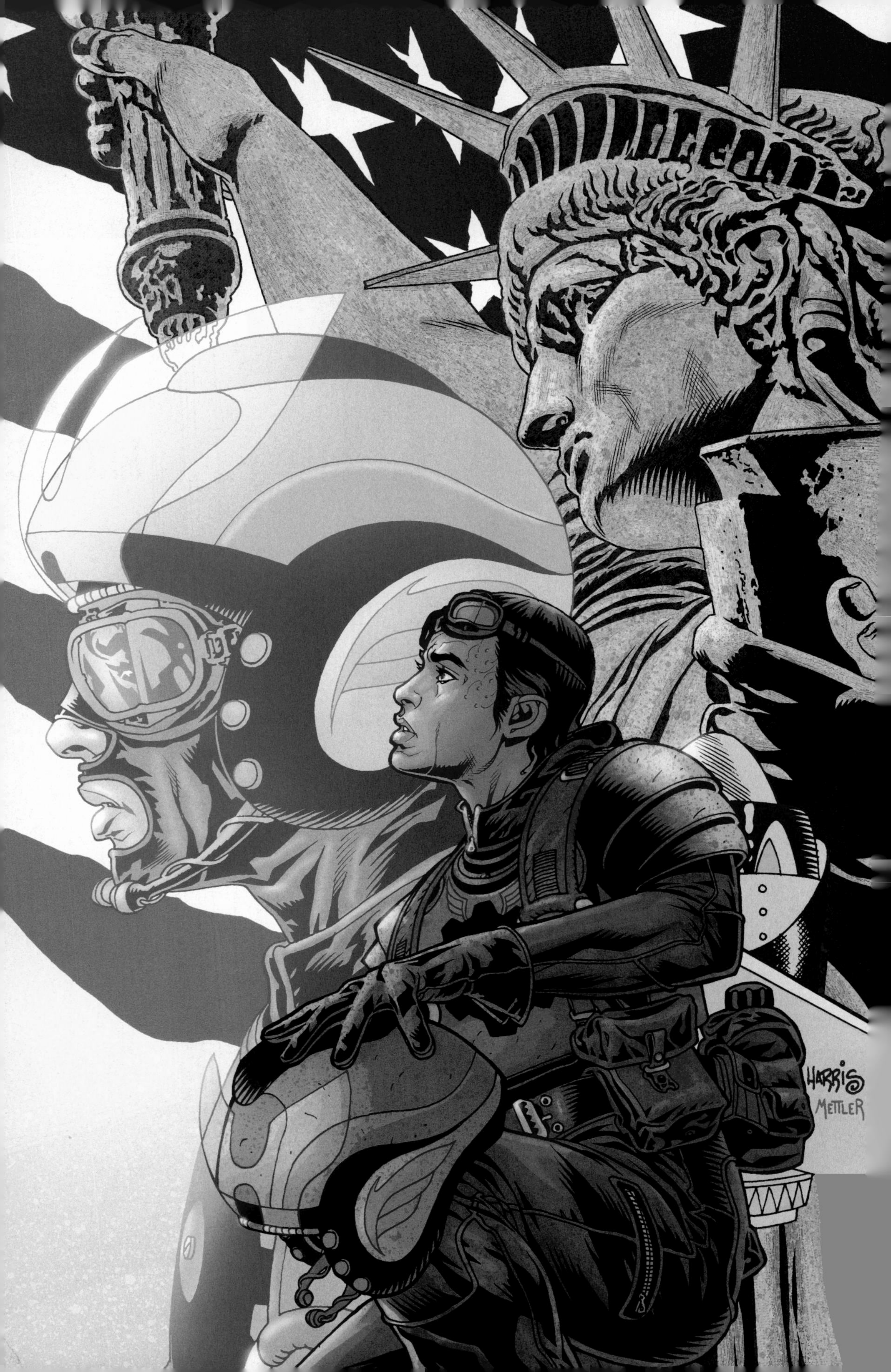
HARRIS
METTLER

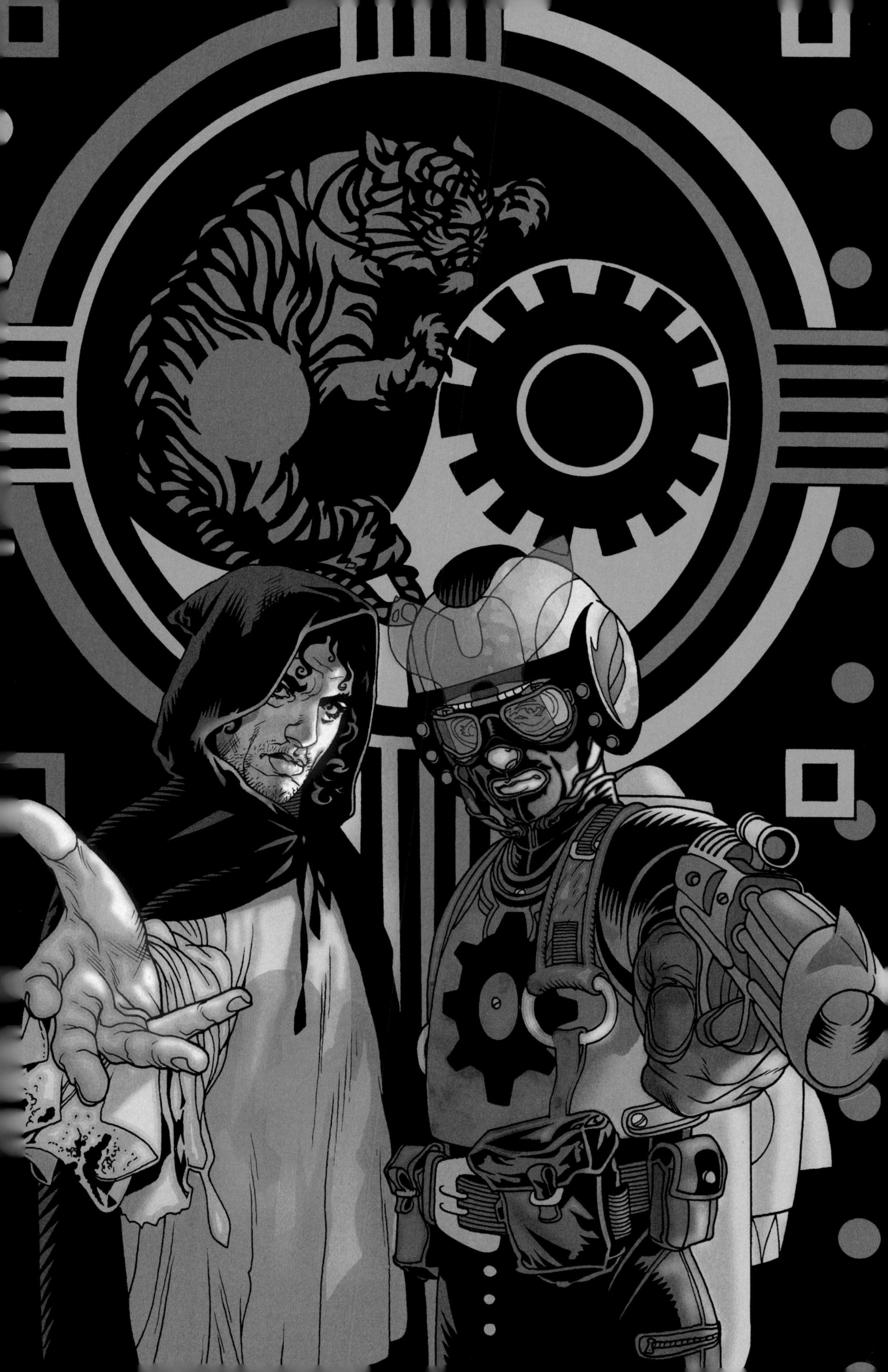

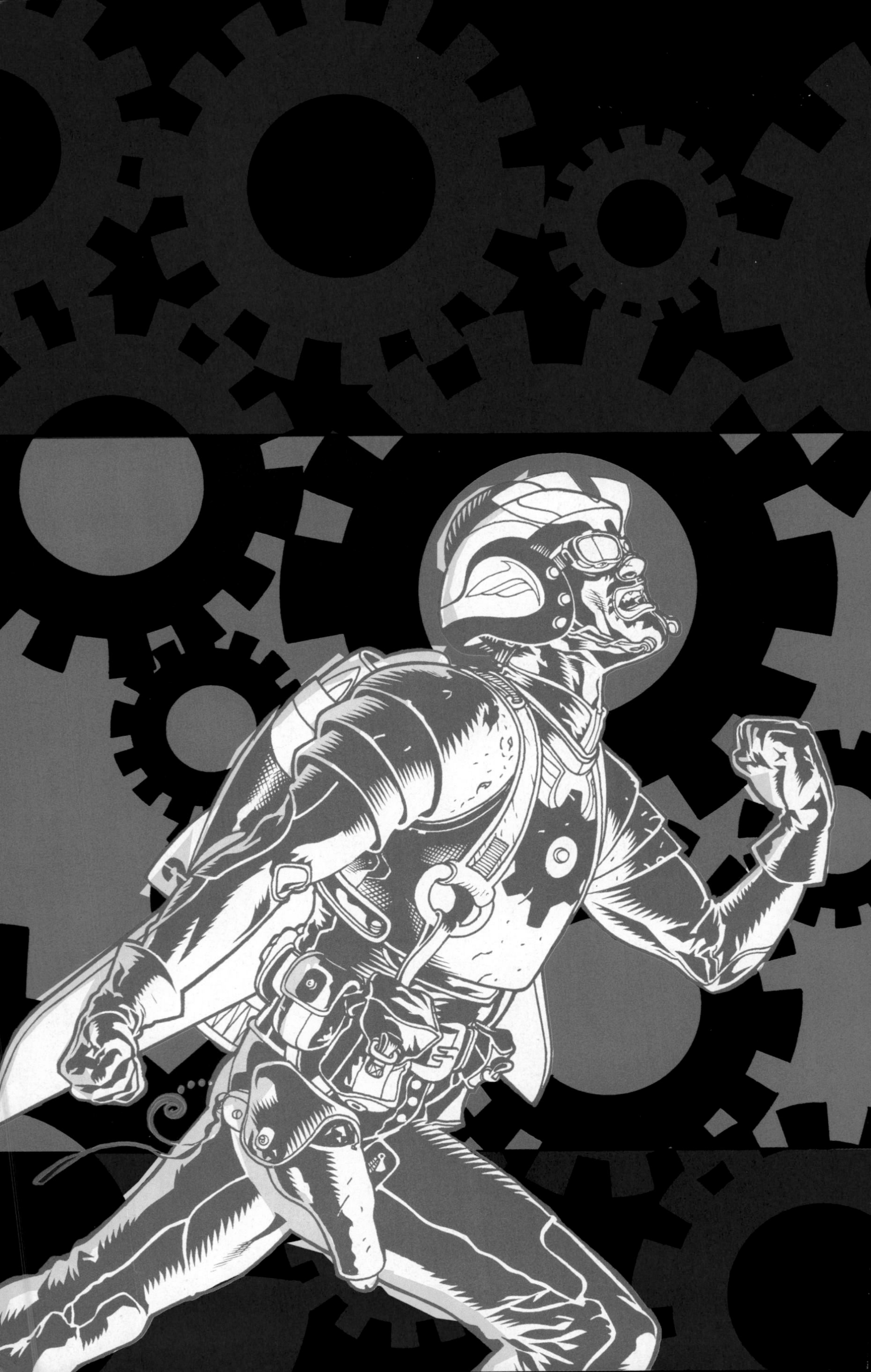

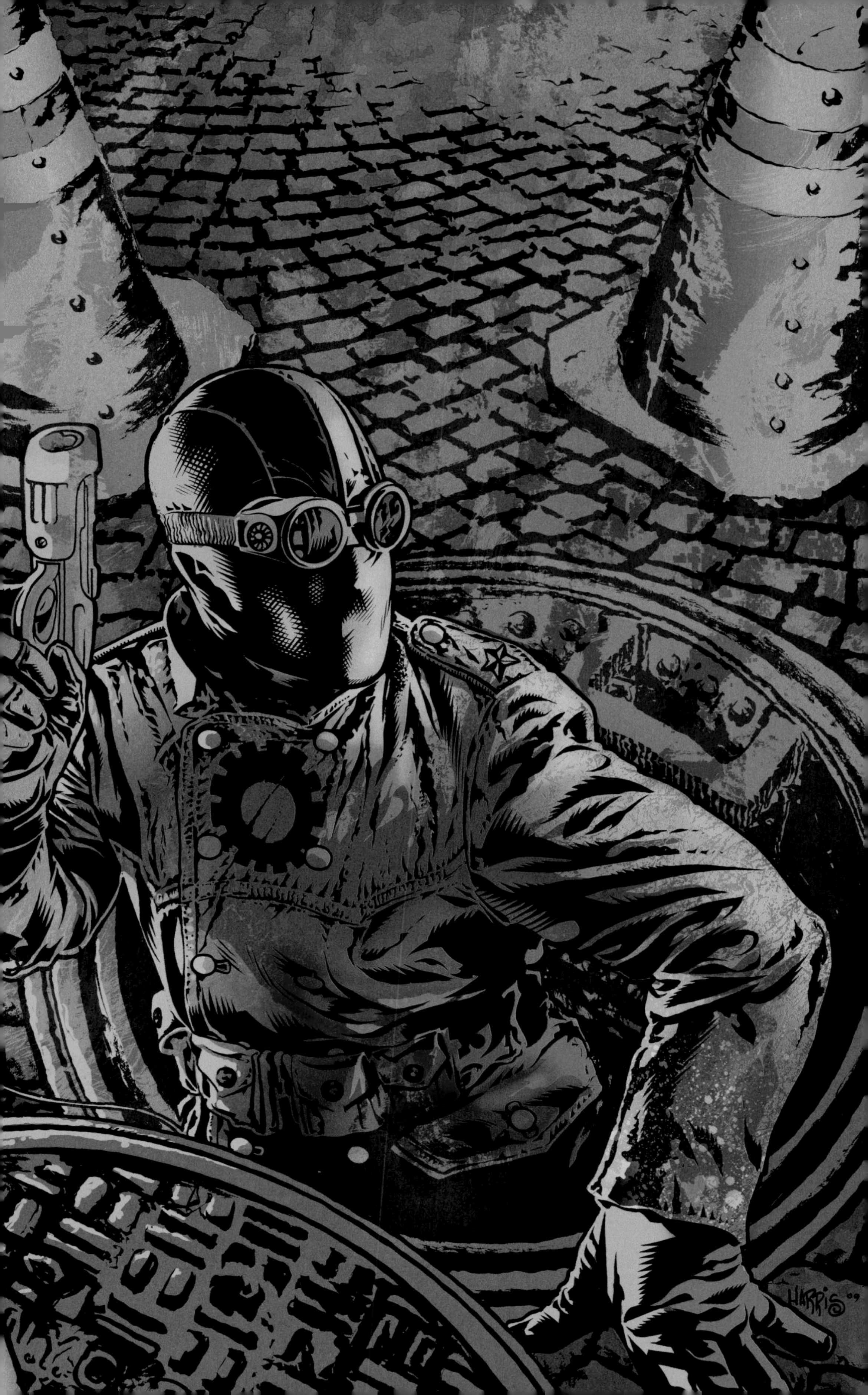
HARRIS '09

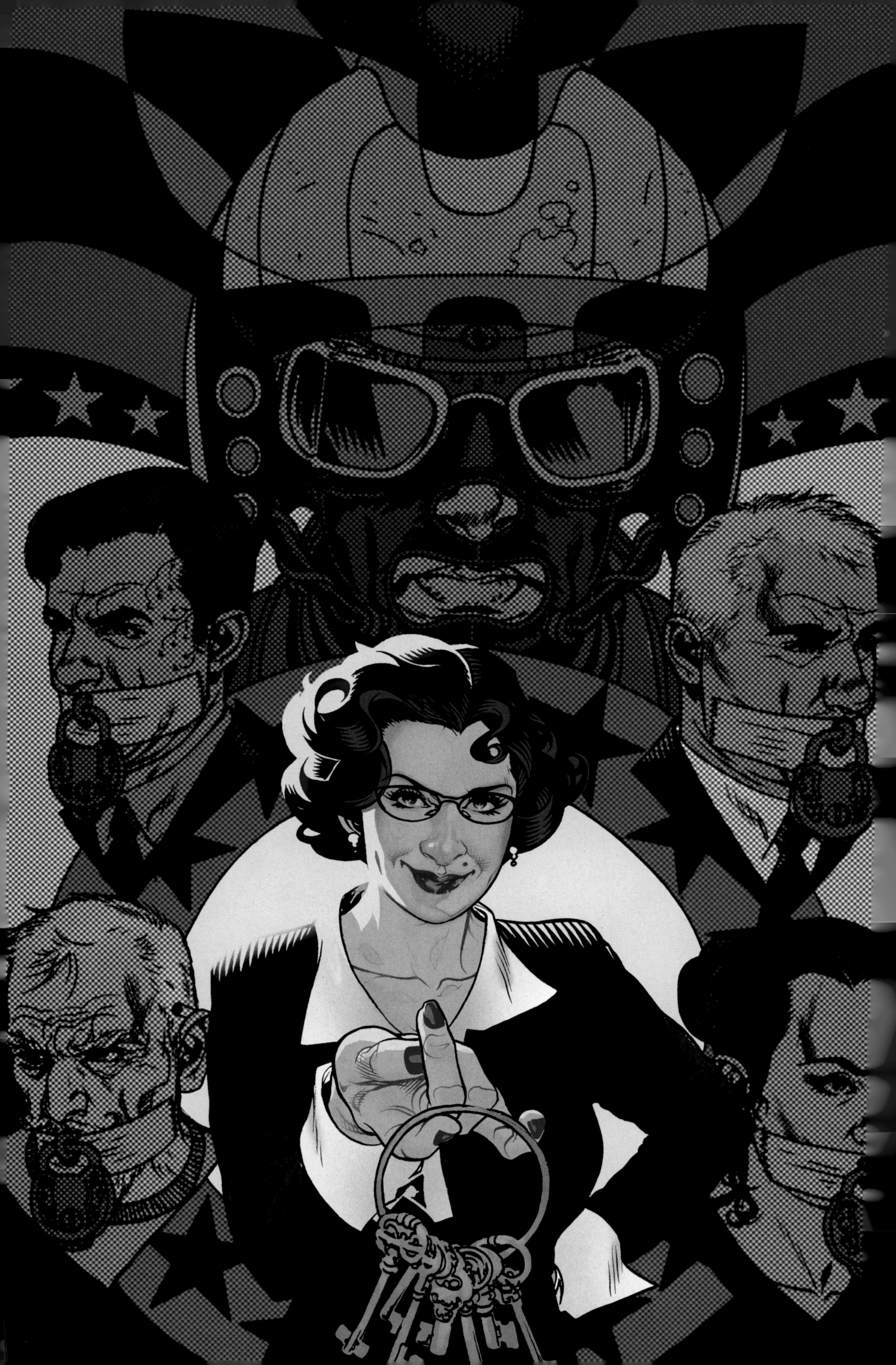

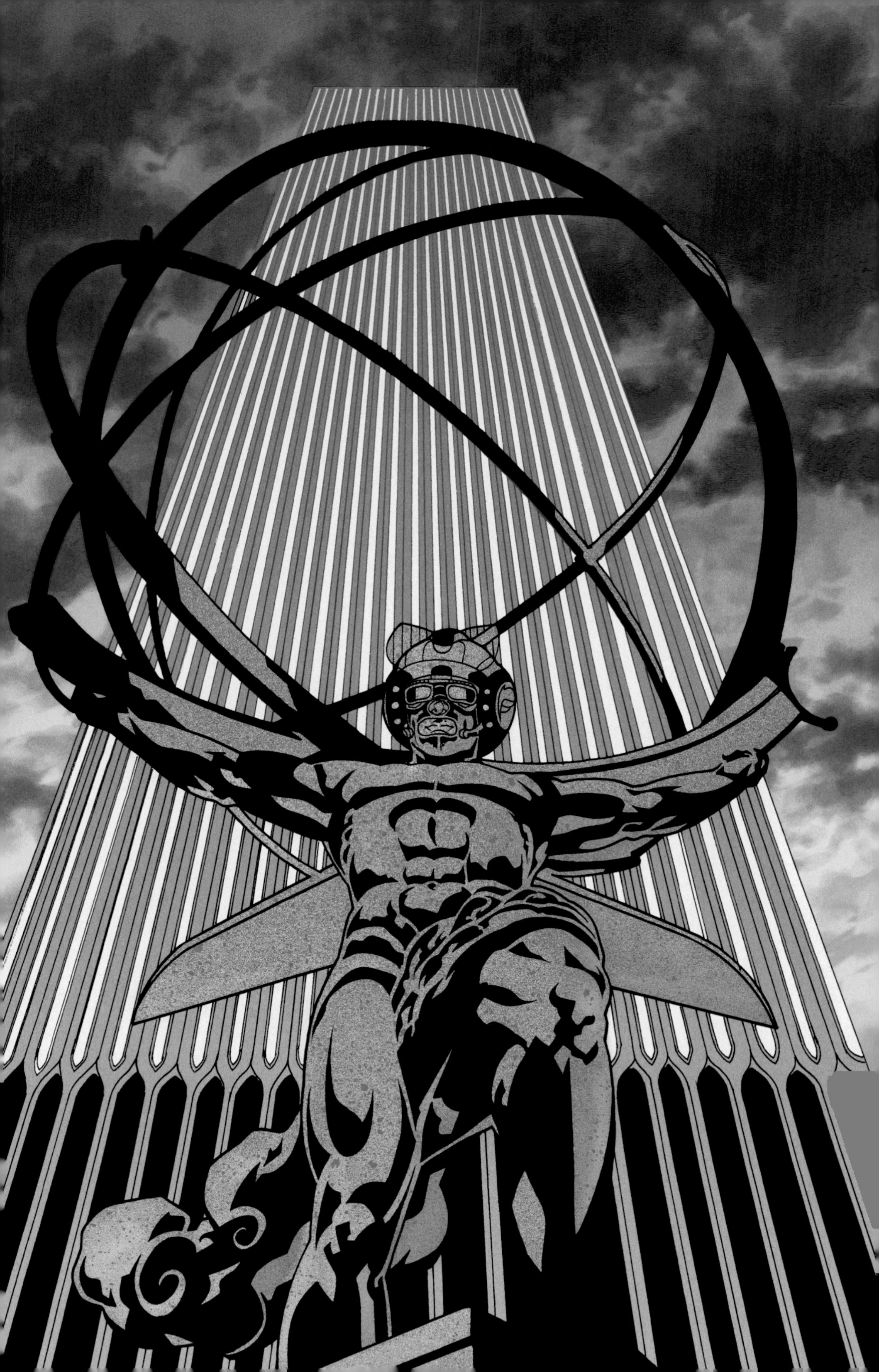

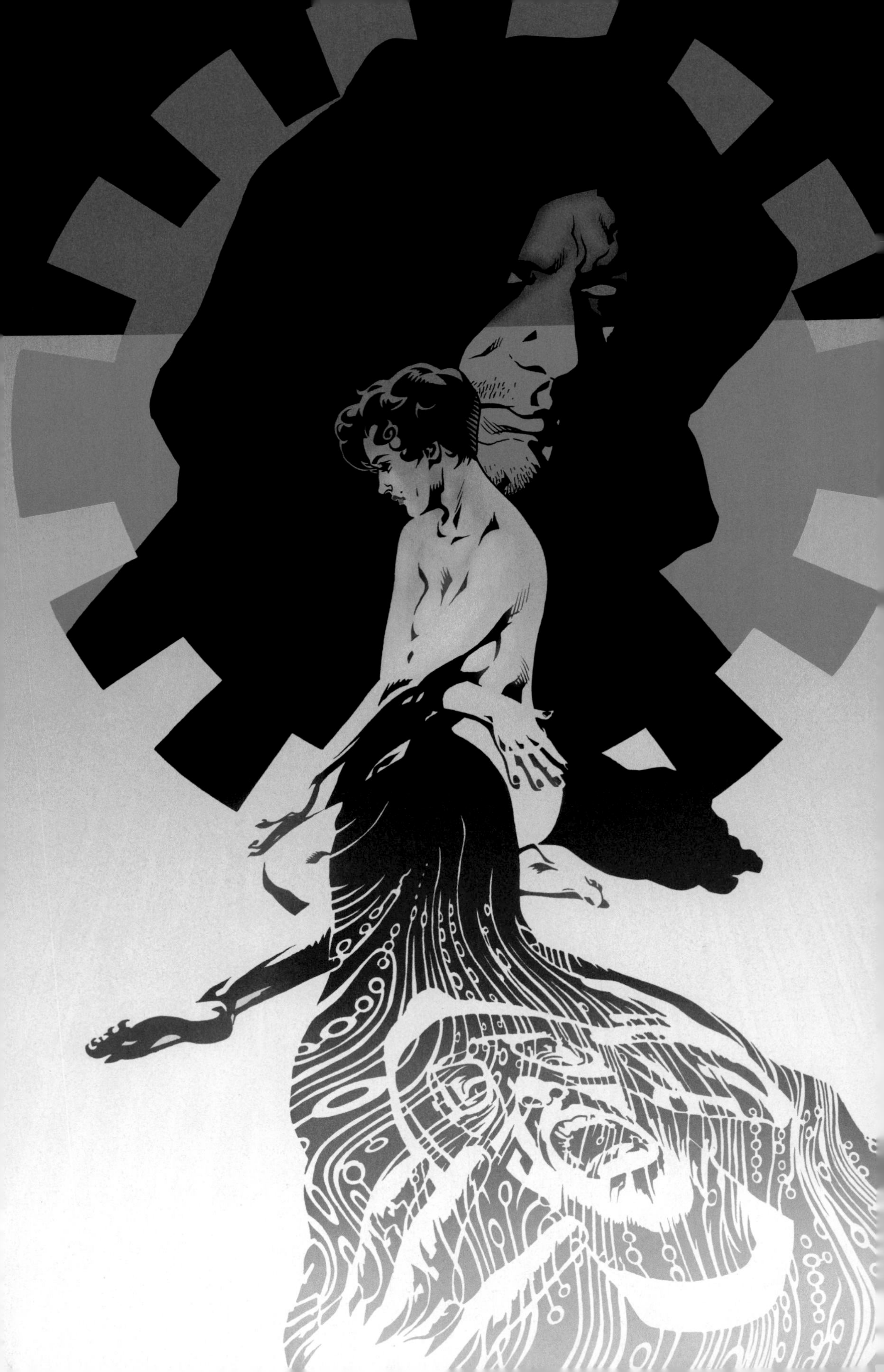

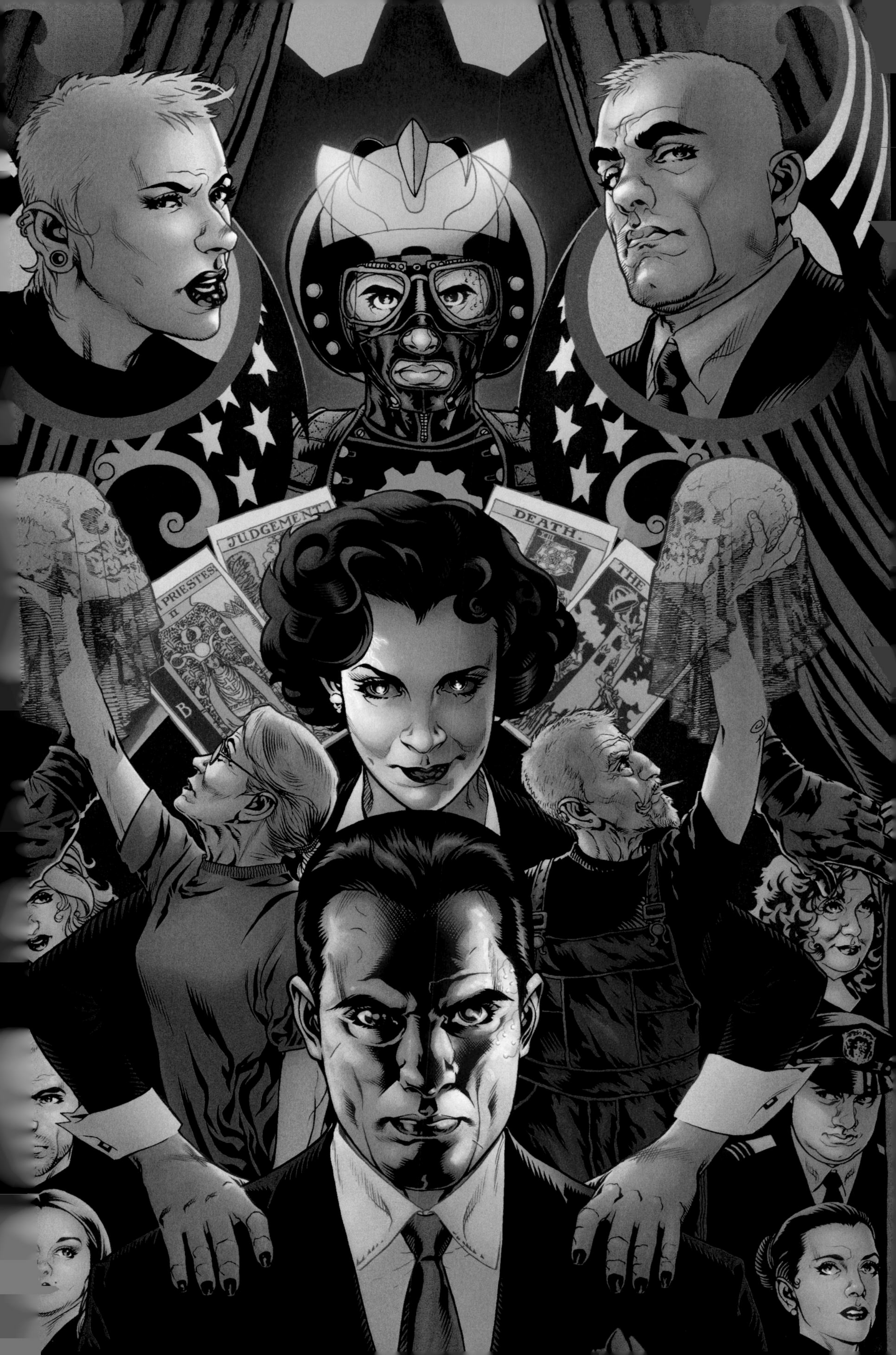
JUDGEMENT
DEATH.
THE

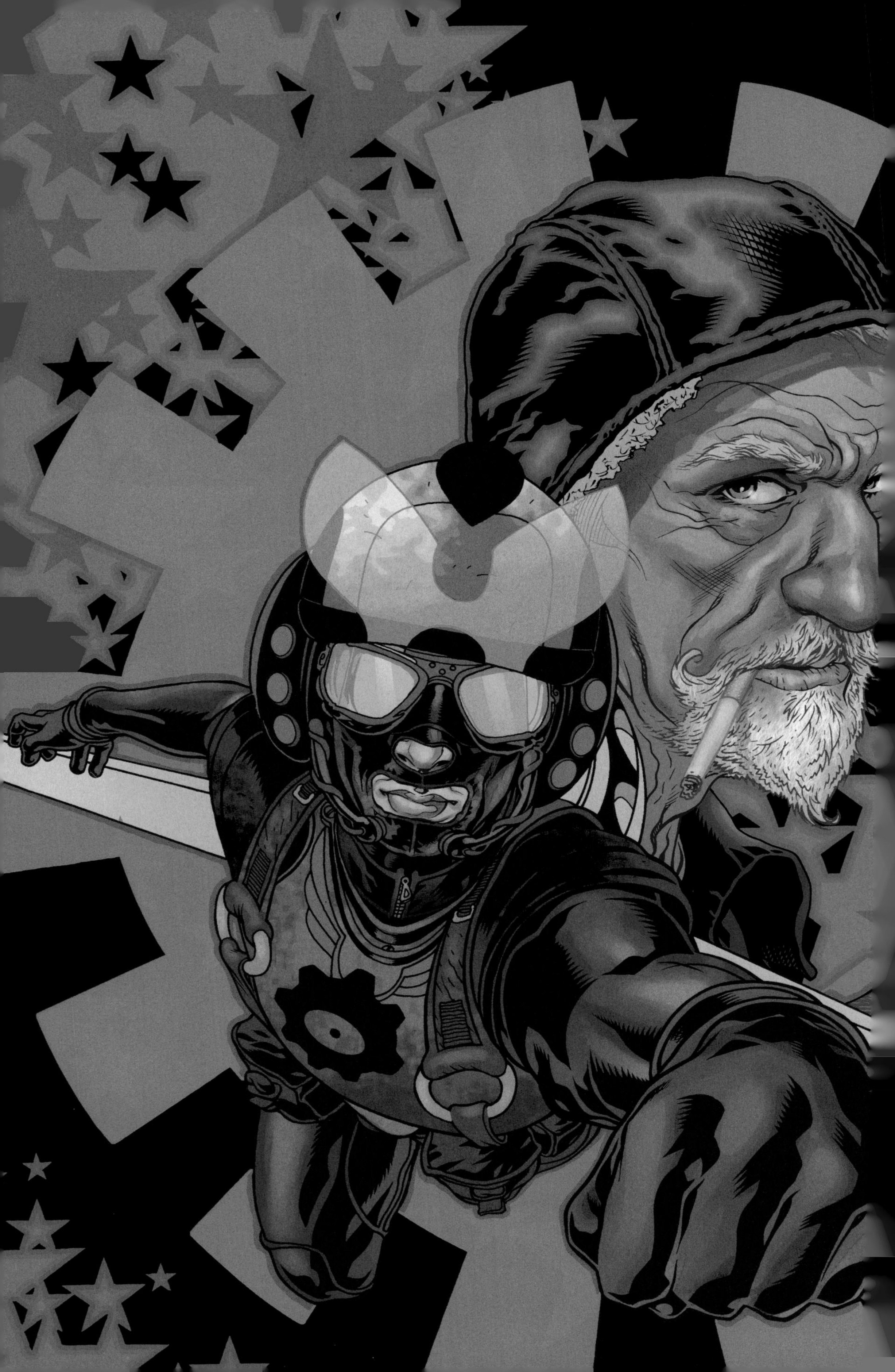

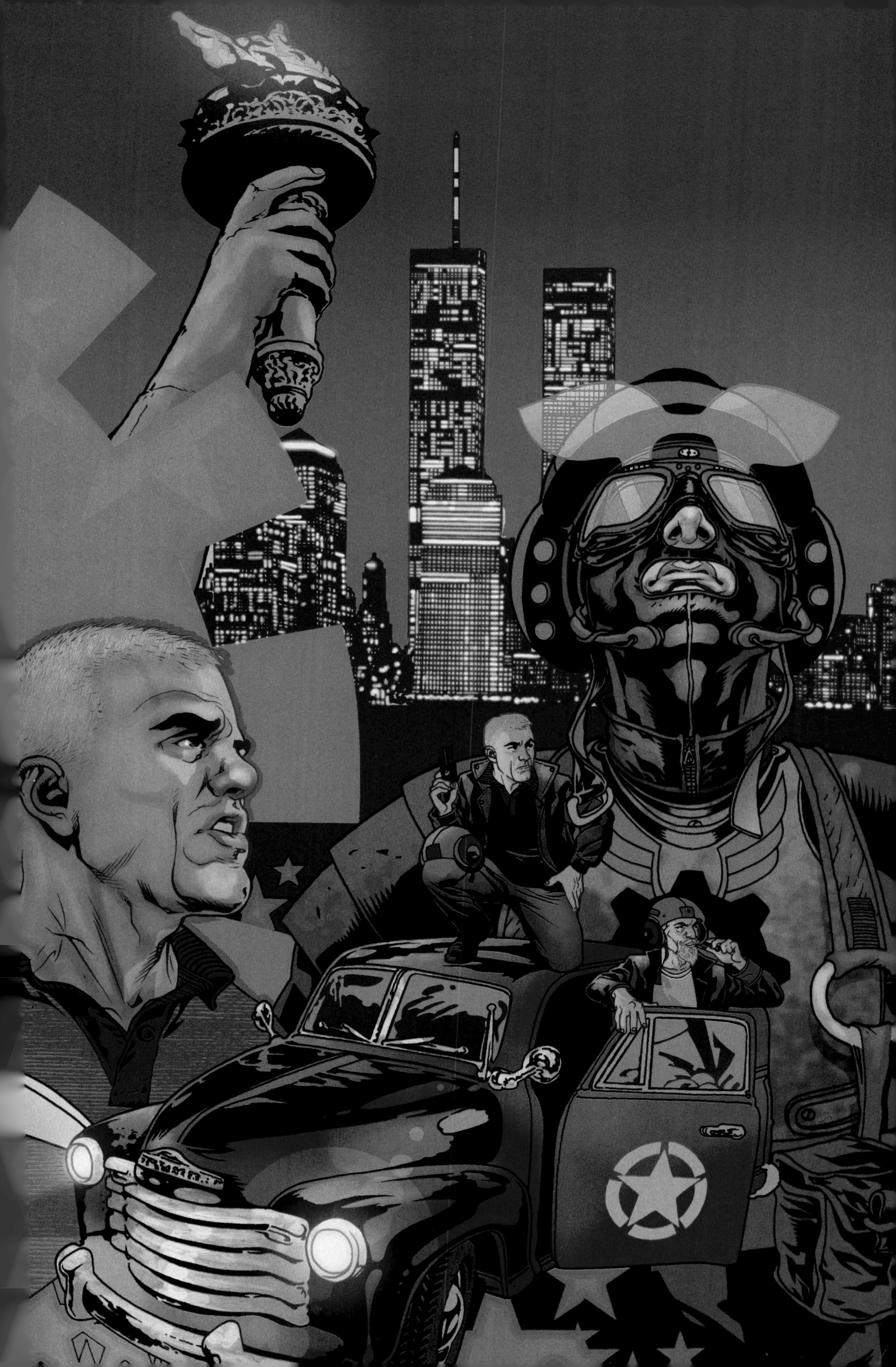

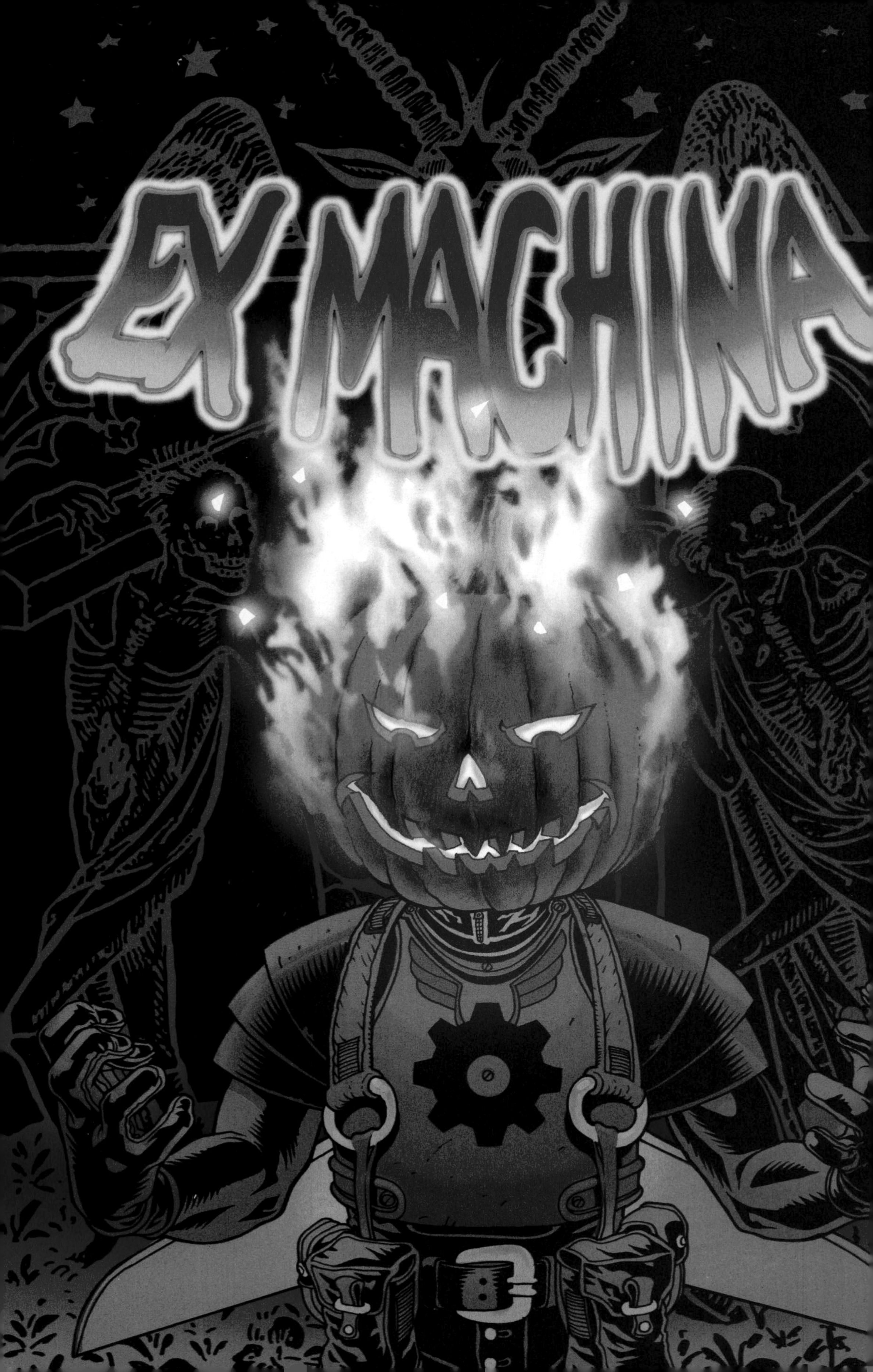
EX MACHINA

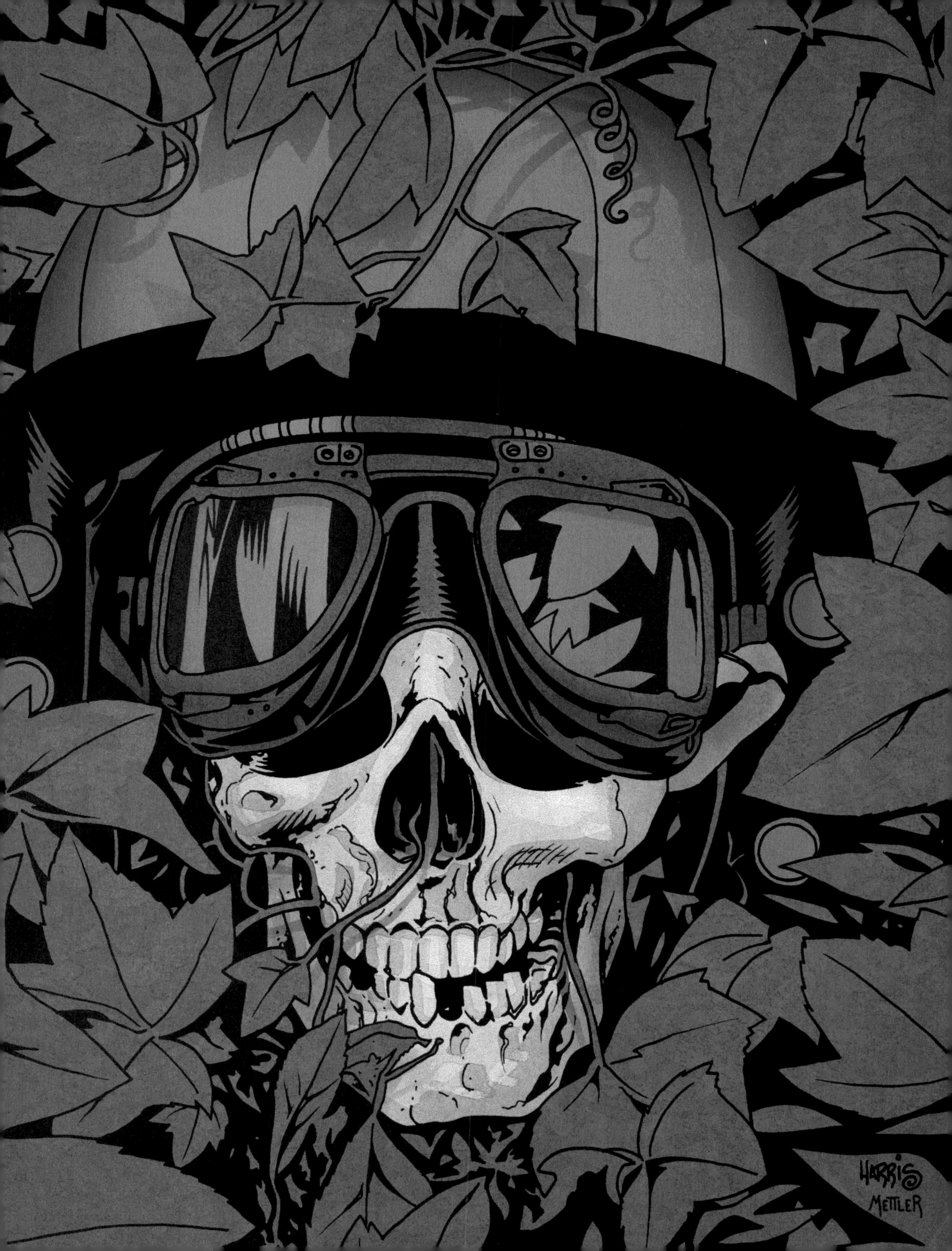
HARRIS
METTLER

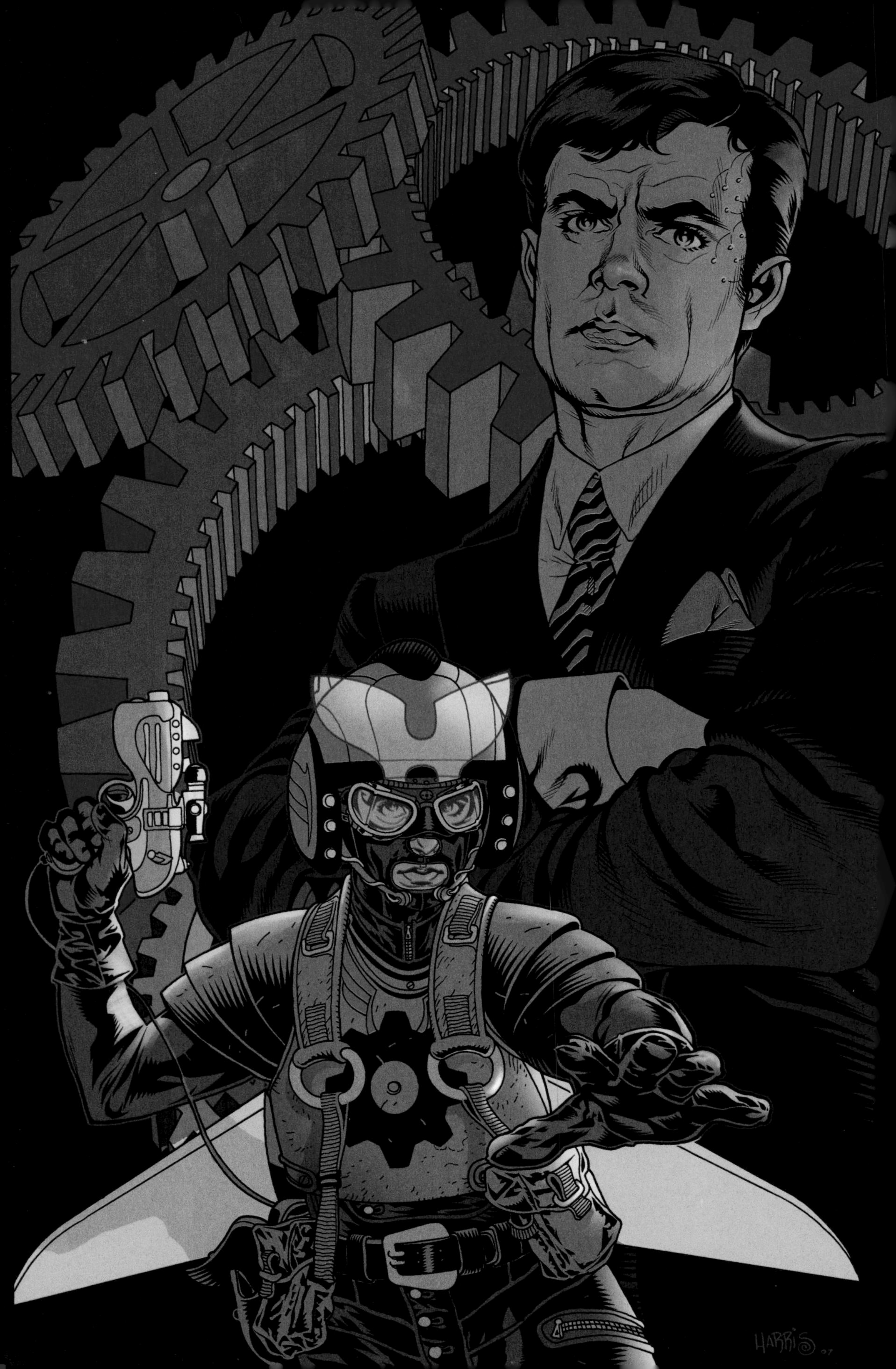

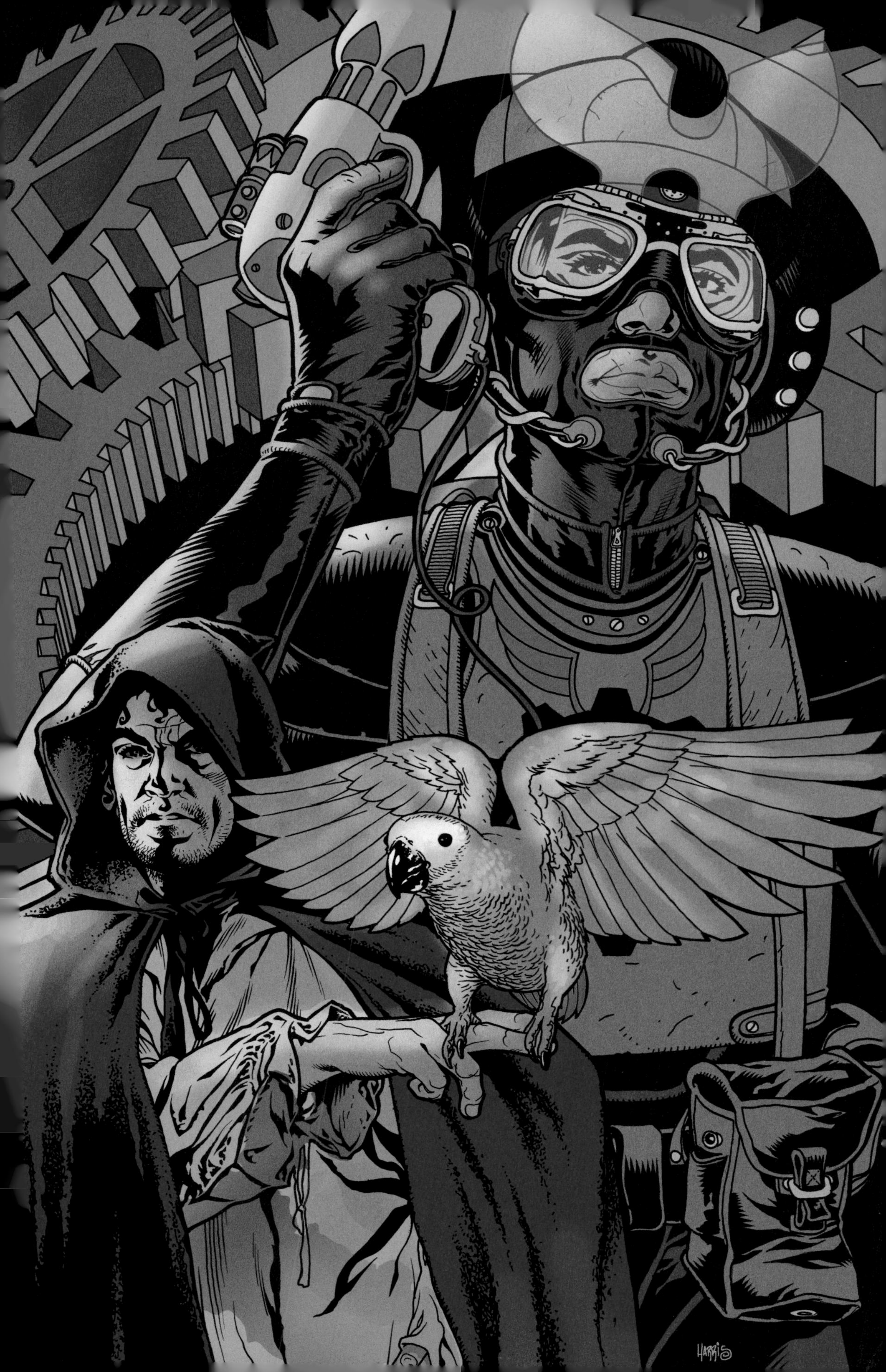
HARRIS

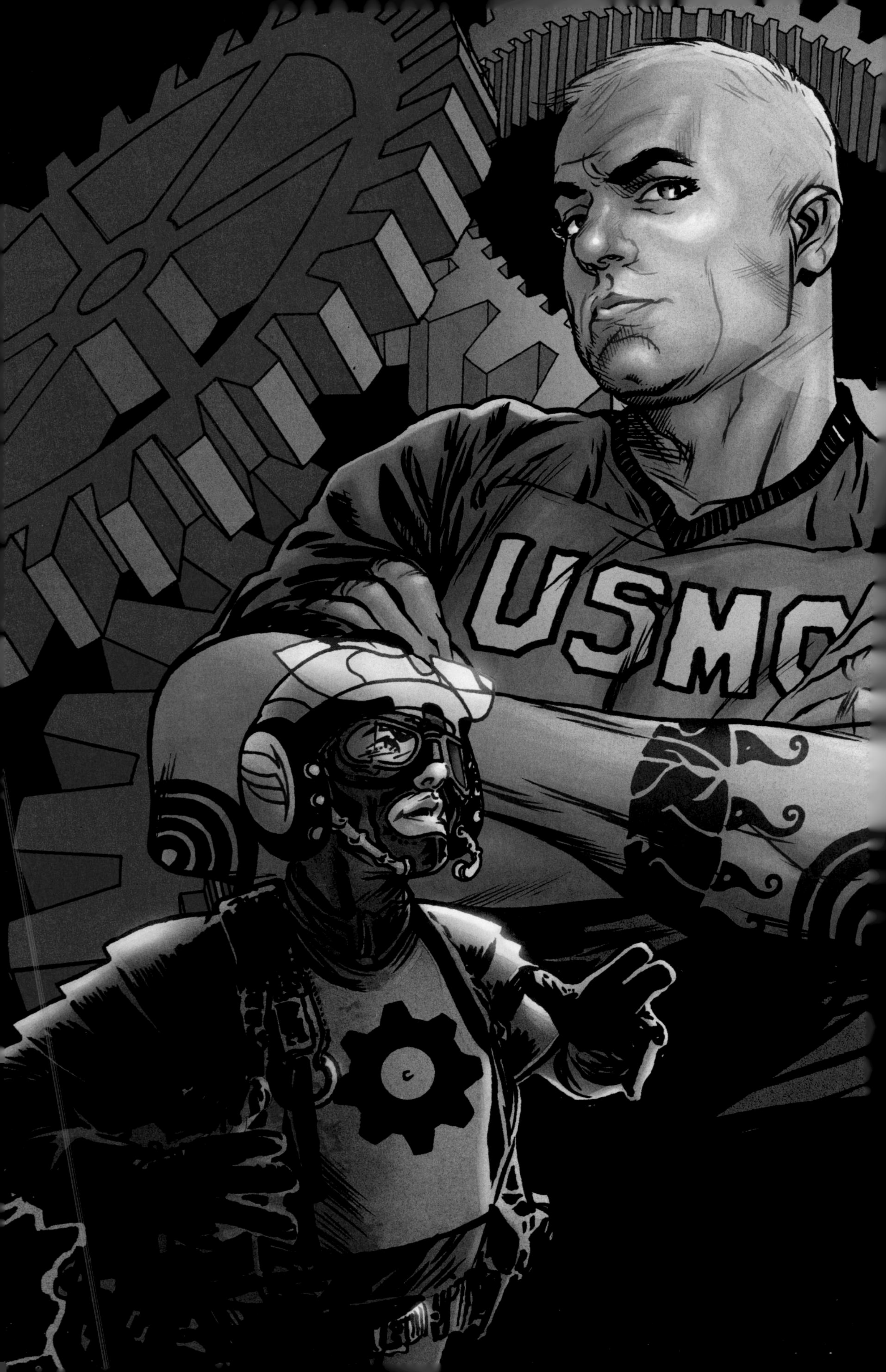
USMC

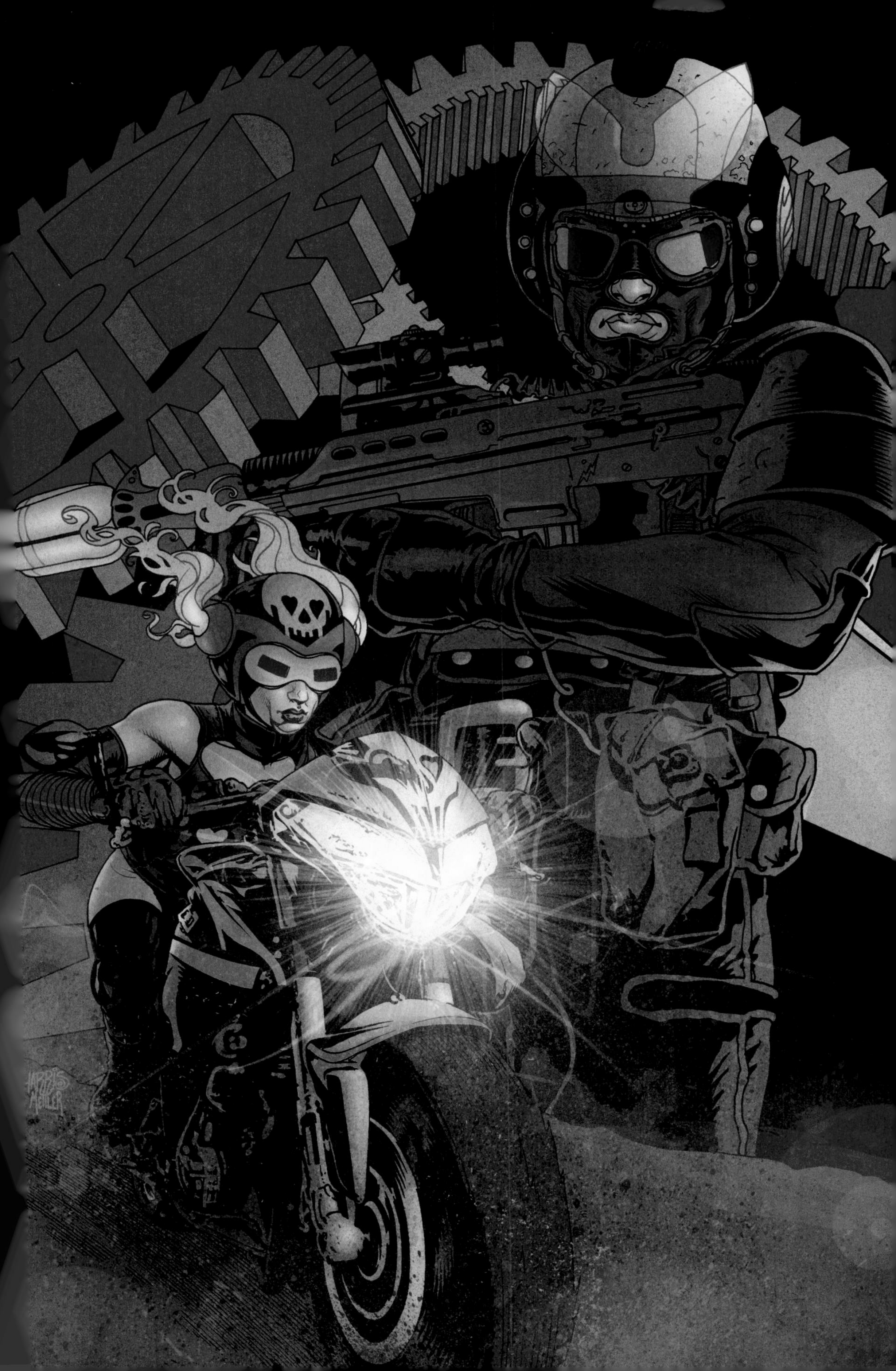

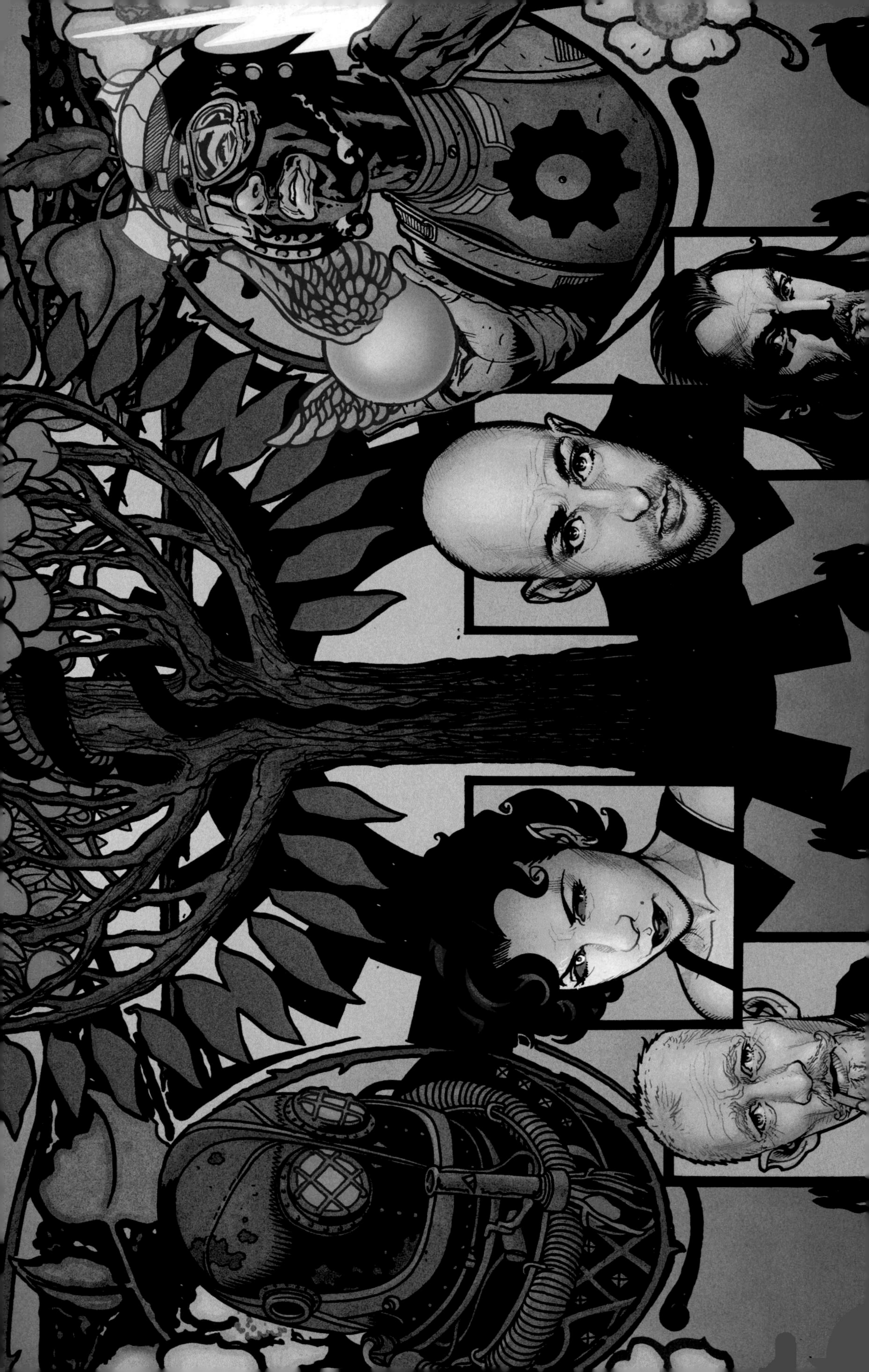

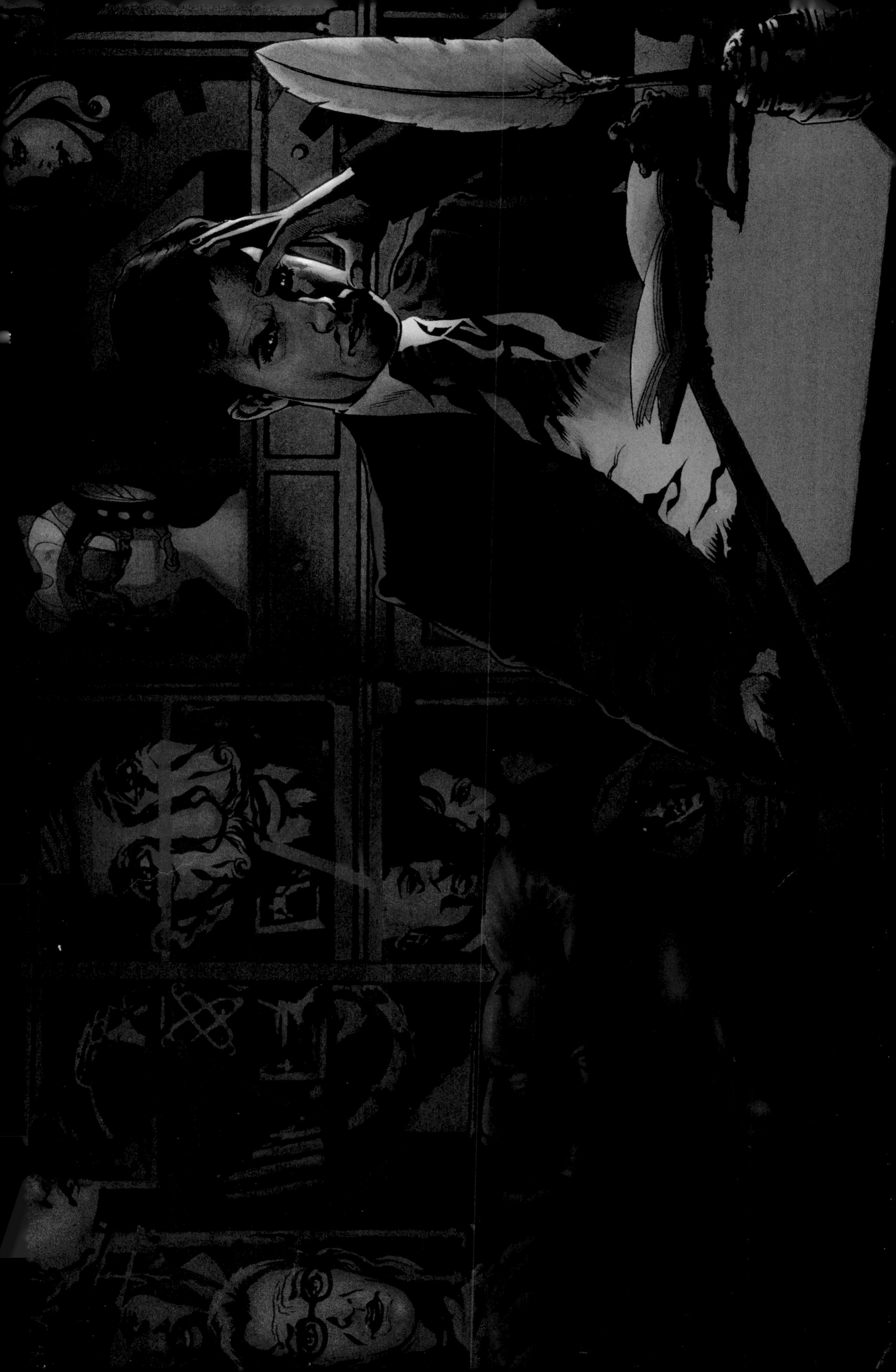

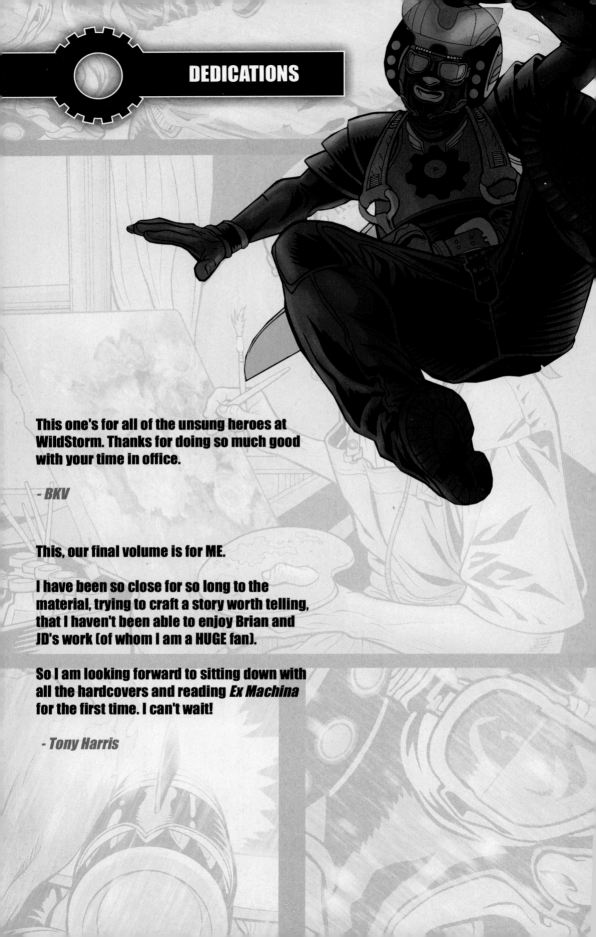

DEDICATIONS

This one's for all of the unsung heroes at WildStorm. Thanks for doing so much good with your time in office.

- BKV

This, our final volume is for ME.

I have been so close for so long to the material, trying to craft a story worth telling, that I haven't been able to enjoy Brian and JD's work (of whom I am a HUGE fan).

So I am looking forward to sitting down with all the hardcovers and reading *Ex Machina* for the first time. I can't wait!

- Tony Harris